myPerspectives™

ENGLISH LANGUAGE ARTS

SAVVAS
LEARNING COMPANY

ISBN-13: 978-0-328-92098-3
ISBN-10:   0-328-92098-3

11   20

Welcome!

*my*Perspectives™ *English Language Arts* is a student-centered learning environment where you will analyze text, cite evidence, and respond critically about your learning. You will take ownership of your learning through goal-setting, reflection, independent text selection, and activities that allow you to collaborate with your peers.

Each unit of study includes selections of different genres—including multimedia—all related to a relevant and meaningful Essential Question. As you read, you will engage in activities that inspire thoughtful discussion and debate with your peers allowing you to formulate, and defend, your own perspectives.

*my*Perspectives *ELA* offers a variety of ways to interact directly with the text. You can annotate by writing in your print consumable, or you can annotate in your digital Student Edition. In addition, exciting technology allows you to access multimedia directly from your mobile device and communicate using an online discussion board!

We hope you enjoy using *my*Perspectives *ELA* as you develop the skills required to be successful throughout college and career.

Authors' Perspectives

myPerspectives is informed by a team of respected experts whose experiences working with students and study of instructional best practices have positively impacted education. From the evolving role of the teacher to how students learn in a digital age, our authors bring new ideas, innovations, and strategies that transform teaching and learning in today's competitive and interconnected world.

" The teaching of English needs to focus on engaging a new generation of learners. How do we get them excited about reading and writing? How do we help them to envision themselves as readers and writers? And, how can we make the teaching of English more culturally, socially, and technologically relevant? Throughout the curriculum, we've created spaces that enhance youth voice and participation and that connect the teaching of literature and writing to technological transformations of the digital age."

Ernest Morrell, Ph.D.

is the Macy professor of English Education at Teachers College, Columbia University, a class of 2014 Fellow of the American Educational Research Association, and the Past-President of the National Council of Teachers of English (NCTE). He is also the Director of Teachers College's Institute for Urban and Minority Education (IUME). He is an award-winning author and in his spare time he coaches youth sports and writes poems and plays. Dr. Morrell has influenced the development of *my*Perspectives in Assessment, Writing & Research, Student Engagement, and Collaborative Learning.

Elfrieda Hiebert, Ph.D.

is President and CEO of TextProject, a nonprofit that provides resources to support higher reading levels. She is also a research associate at the University of California, Santa Cruz. Dr. Hiebert has worked in the field of early reading acquisition for 45 years, first as a teacher's aide and teacher of primary-level students in California and, subsequently, as a teacher and researcher. Her research addresses how fluency, vocabulary, and knowledge can be fostered through appropriate texts. Dr. Hiebert has influenced the development of *my*Perspectives in Vocabulary, Text Complexity, and Assessment.

" The signature of complex text is challenging vocabulary. In the systems of vocabulary, it's important to provide ways to show how concepts can be made more transparent to students. We provide lessons and activities that develop a strong vocabulary and concept foundation—a foundation that permits students to comprehend increasingly more complex text."

Kelly Gallagher, M.Ed.

teaches at Magnolia High School in Anaheim, California, where he is in his thirty-first year. He is the former co-director of the South Basin Writing Project at California State University, Long Beach. Mr. Gallagher has influenced the development of *my*Perspectives in Writing, Close Reading, and the Role of Teachers.

" The *my*Perspectives classroom is dynamic. The teacher inspires, models, instructs, facilitates, and advises students as they evolve and grow. When teachers guide students through meaningful learning tasks and then pass them ownership of their own learning, students become engaged and work harder. This is how we make a difference in student achievement—by putting students at the center of their learning and giving them the opportunities to choose, explore, collaborate, and work independently."

" It's critical to give students the opportunity to read a wide range of highly engaging texts and to immerse themselves in exploring powerful ideas and how these ideas are expressed. In *my*Perspectives, we focus on building up students' awareness of how academic language works, which is especially important for English language learners."

Jim Cummins, Ph.D.

is a Professor Emeritus in the Department of Curriculum, Teaching and Learning of the University of Toronto. His research focuses on literacy development in multilingual school contexts as well as on the potential roles of technology in promoting language and literacy development. In recent years, he has been working actively with teachers to identify ways of increasing the literacy engagement of learners in multilingual school contexts. Dr. Cummins has influenced the development of *my*Perspectives in English Language Learner and English Language Development support.

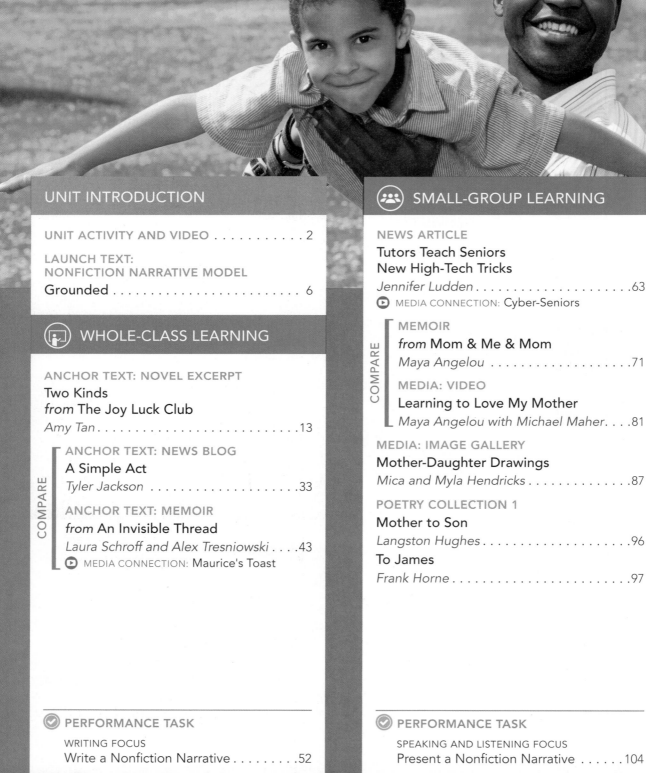

UNIT 1 Generations

DIGITAL PERSPECTIVES

 Use the BouncePage app
whenever you see "Scan
for Multimedia" to access:

- Unit Introduction Videos
- Media Selections
- Modeling Videos
- Selection Audio Recordings

Additional digital resources can be found in:

- Interactive Student Edition
- *my*Perspectives+

UNIT 2 A Starry Home

DIGITAL PERSPECTIVES

 SCAN FOR MULTIMEDIA

Use the BouncePage app whenever you see "Scan for Multimedia" to access:

- Unit Introduction Videos
- Media Selections
- Modeling Videos
- Selection Audio Recordings

Additional digital resources can be found in:

- Interactive Student Edition
- *my*Perspectives+

UNIT 3 Turning Points

INDEPENDENT LEARNING

These selections can be accessed via the Interactive Student Edition.

PERFORMANCE-BASED ASSESSMENT

UNIT REFLECTION

DIGITAL PERSPECTIVES

SCAN FOR MULTIMEDIA

Use the BouncePage app whenever you see "Scan for Multimedia" to access:

- Unit Introduction Videos
- Media Selections
- Modeling Videos
- Selection Audio Recordings

Additional digital resources can be found in:

- Interactive Student Edition
- *my*Perspectives+

UNIT 4 People and the Planet

INDEPENDENT LEARNING

These selections can be accessed via the Interactive Student Edition.

 PERFORMANCE-BASED ASSESSMENT PREP

PERFORMANCE-BASED ASSESSMENT

UNIT REFLECTION

DIGITAL 🖱 PERSPECTIVES

SCAN FOR MULTIMEDIA Use the BouncePage app whenever you see "Scan for Multimedia" to access:

- Unit Introduction Videos
- Media Selections
- Modeling Videos
- Selection Audio Recordings

Additional digital resources can be found in:

- Interactive Student Edition
- *my*Perspectives+

UNIT 5 Facing Adversity

INDEPENDENT LEARNING

These selections can be accessed via the Interactive Student Edition.

 PERFORMANCE-BASED ASSESSMENT PREP

 PERFORMANCE-BASED ASSESSMENT

UNIT REFLECTION

DIGITAL PERSPECTIVES

 SCAN FOR MULTIMEDIA

Use the BouncePage app whenever you see "Scan for Multimedia" to access:

- Unit Introduction Videos
- Media Selections
- Modeling Videos
- Selection Audio Recordings

Additional digital resources can be found in:

- Interactive Student Edition
- *my*Perspectives+

Interactive Student Edition

*my*Perspectives is completely interactive because you can work directly in your digital or print Student Edition.

All activities that you complete in your Interactive Student Edition are saved automatically. You can access your notes quickly so that reviewing work to prepare for tests and projects is easy!

Enter answers to prompts right in your digital Notebook and "turn it in" to your teacher.

The in-line annotation tool allows you to practice close reading by highlighting and adding comments about the text.

Interactivities are available for you to complete and submit directly to your teacher.

the shops in town lowered their shutters in preparation for the storm. Starting early in the morning, my father and brother went around the house nailing shut all the storm-doors, while my mother spent the day in the kitchen cooking emergency provisions. We filled bottles and canteens with water, and packed our most important possessions in rucksacks[2] for possible evacuation. To the adults, typhoons were an annoyance and a threat they had to face almost annually, but to the kids, removed as we were from such practical concerns, it was just a great big circus, a wonderful source of excitement.

12   Just after noon the color of the sky began to change all of a sudden. There was something strange and unreal about it. I stayed outside on the porch, watching the sky, until the wind began to howl and the rain began to beat against the house with a weird dry sound, like handfuls of sand. Then we closed the last storm-door and gathered together in one room of the darkened house, listening to the radio. This particular storm did not have a great deal of rain, it said, but the winds were doing a lot of damage, blowing roofs off houses and capsizing ships. Many people had been killed or injured by flying debris. Over and over again, they warned people against leaving their homes. Every once in a while, the house would creak and shudder as if a huge hand were shaking it, and sometimes there would be a great crash of some heavy-sounding object against a storm-door. My father guessed that these were tiles blowing off the neighbors' houses. For lunch we ate the rice and omelettes my mother had cooked, waiting for the typhoon to blow past.

13   But the typhoon gave no sign of blowing past. The radio said it had lost momentum[3] almost as soon as it came ashore at S. Province, and now it was moving north-east at the pace of a slow runner. The wind kept up its savage howling as it trie[...] stood on land.

14   Perhaps an hour had gone by with the [...] when a hush fell over everything. All of a [...] could hear a bird crying in the distance. M[...] door a crack and looked outside. The win[...] rain had ceased to fall. Thick, gray clouds [...]

NOTES

This sentence is leading up to an exciting story.

CLOSE READ
ANNOTATE: In paragraph 12, annotate at least four vivid details about the storm. Underline those that compare one thing to another.

QUESTION: What is being compared? What picture does each detail create in the reader's mind?

CONCLUDE: How do these descriptions help you visualize the typhoon?

Typhoons are powerful, scary storms that can do a lot of damage.

Use the close-read prompts to guide you through an analysis of the text. You can highlight, circle, and underline the text right in your print Student Edition.

LANGUAGE DEVELOPMENT

THE SEVENTH MAN

Concept Vocabulary

desperate	hallucination	profound
entranced	premonition	meditative

Why These Words? These concept words help to reveal the emotional state of the seventh man. For example, when the wave approaches, the seventh man is *entranced*, waiting for it to attack. After the wave hits, the seventh man believes he sees his friend K. in the wave and claims that this experience was no *hallucination*. Notice that both words relate to experiences that occur only in the mind of the seventh man.

1. How does the concept vocabulary sharpen the reader's understanding of the mental or emotional state of the seventh man?
   These words are descriptive and precise.

2. What other words in the selection connect to this concept?
   ominous, overcome, nightmares

Practice

(notebook icon) **Notebook** The concept vocabulary words appear in "The Seventh Man."

1. Use each concept word in a sentence that demonstrates your understanding of the word's meaning.

2. Challenge yourself to replace the concept word with one or two synonyms. How does the word change affect the meaning of your sentence? For example, which sentence is stronger? Which has a more positive meaning?

Word Study

Latin suffix: -tion The Latin suffix -tion often indicates that a word is a noun. Sometimes this suffix is spelled -ion or -ation. These related suffixes mean "act, state, or condition of." In "The Seventh Man," the word *premonition* means "the state of being forewarned."

1. Record a definition of *hallucination* based on your understanding of its root word and the meaning of the suffix -tion.
   The condition of seeing something that is not real

2. Look back at paragraphs 37–40 and find two other words that use the suffix -tion. Identify the root word that was combined with the suffix. Record a definition for each word.
   cooperate + -tion—the state of working together
   direct + -tion—the state of being guided

Respond to questions and activities directly in your book!

(icon) **WORD NETWORK**
Add interesting survival words from the text to your Word Network.

Digital Resources

You can access digital resources from your print Student Edition, or from Savvas Realize™.

To watch videos or listen to audio from your print Student Edition, all you need is a device with a camera and Pearson's BouncePages app!

ANCHOR TEXT | SHORT STORY

The Seventh Man

Haruki Murakami

BACKGROUND

Hurricanes that originate in the northwest Pacific Ocean are called typhoons. They can stretch up to 500 miles in diameter and produce high winds, heavy rains, enormous waves, and severe flooding. On average, Japan is hit by three severe typhoons each year due to its location and climatic conditions.

SCAN FOR MULTIMEDIA

1 "A huge wave nearly swept me away," said the seventh man, almost whispering. "It happened one September afternoon when I was ten years old."

2 The man was the last one to tell his story that night. The hands of the clock had moved past ten. The small group that huddled in

NOTES

CLOSE READ
ANNOTATE: Mark details in paragraph 2 that

How to watch a video or listen to audio:

1. Download Pearson's BouncePages App from the Apple App or Google Play Store.

2. Open the app on your mobile device.

3. Aim your camera so the page from your Student Edition is viewable on your screen.

4. Tap the screen to scan the page.

5. Press the "Play" button on the page that appears on your device.

6. View the video or listen to the audio directly from your device!

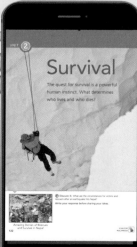

Amazing Stories of Rescues and Survival in Nepal
122

Digital resources, including audio and video, can be accessed in the Interactive Student Edition. Your teacher might also assign activities for you to complete online.

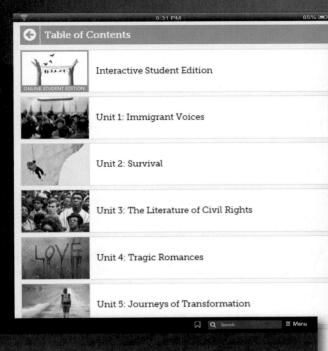

Table of Contents

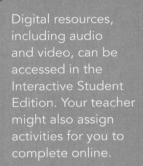 Interactive Student Edition

Unit 1: Immigrant Voices

Unit 2: Survival

Unit 3: The Literature of Civil Rights

Unit 4: Tragic Romances

Unit 5: Journeys of Transformation

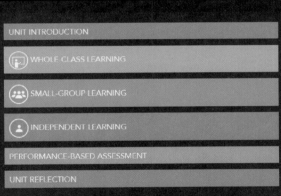

SAVVAS eText 2.0 for Schools

Unit 2: Survival

UNIT 2
Survival

UNIT INTRODUCTION

WHOLE-CLASS LEARNING

SMALL-GROUP LEARNING

INDEPENDENT LEARNING

PERFORMANCE-BASED ASSESSMENT

UNIT REFLECTION

The quest for survival is powerful. It is primitive. What determines who lives and who dies?

You will also find digital novels, interactive lessons, and games!

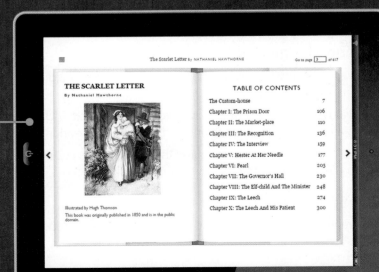

The Scarlet Letter By NATHANIEL HAWTHORNE   Go to page 3 of 617

THE SCARLET LETTER
By Nathaniel Hawthorne

Illustrated by Hugh Thomson
This book was originally published in 1850 and is in the public domain.

TABLE OF CONTENTS

Standards Overview

The following English Language Arts standards will prepare you to succeed in college and your future career. The College and Career Readiness Anchor Standards define what you need to achieve by the end of high school, and the grade-specific Standards define what you need to know by the end of your current grade level.

The following provides an overview of the Standards.

Standards for Reading

College and Career Readiness Anchor Standards for Reading

Key Ideas and Details

1. Read closely to determine what the text says explicitly and to make logical inferences from it; cite specific textual evidence when writing or speaking to support conclusions drawn from the text.

2. Determine central ideas or themes of a text and analyze their development; summarize the key supporting details and ideas.

3. Analyze how and why individuals, events, and ideas develop and interact over the course of a text.

Craft and Structure

4. Interpret words and phrases as they are used in a text, including determining technical, connotative, and figurative meanings, and analyze how specific word choices shape meaning or tone.

5. Analyze the structure of texts, including how specific sentences, paragraphs, and larger portions of the text (e.g., a section, chapter, scene, or stanza) relate to each other and the whole.

6. Assess how point of view or purpose shapes the content and style of a text.

Integration of Knowledge and Ideas

7. Integrate and evaluate content presented in diverse formats and media, including visually and quantitatively, as well as in words.

8. Delineate and evaluate the argument and specific claims in a text, including the validity of the reasoning as well as the relevance and sufficiency of the evidence.

9. Analyze how two or more texts address similar themes or topics in order to build knowledge or to compare the approaches the authors take.

Range of Reading and Level of Text Complexity

10. Read and comprehend complex literary and informational texts independently and proficiently.

Grade 7 Reading Standards for Literature

Standard

Key Ideas and Details

Cite several pieces of textual evidence to support analysis of what the text says explicitly as well as inferences drawn from the text.

Determine a theme or central idea of a text and analyze its development over the course of the text; provide an objective summary of the text.

Analyze how particular elements of a story or drama interact (e.g., how setting shapes the characters or plot).

Craft and Structure

Determine the meaning of words and phrases as they are used in a text, including figurative and connotative meanings; analyze the impact of rhymes and other repetitions of sounds (e.g., alliteration) on a specific verse or stanza of a poem or section of a story or drama.

Analyze how a drama's or poem's form or structure (e.g., soliloquy, sonnet) contributes to its meaning.

Analyze how an author develops and contrasts the points of view of different characters or narrators in a text.

Integration of Knowledge and Ideas

Compare and contrast a written story, drama, or poem to its audio, filmed, staged, or multimedia version, analyzing the effects of techniques unique to each medium (e.g., lighting, sound, color, or camera focus and angles in a film).

Compare and contrast a fictional portrayal of a time, place, or character and a historical account of the same period as a means of understanding how authors of fiction use or alter history.

Range of Reading and Level of Text Complexity

By the end of the year, read and comprehend literature, including stories, dramas, and poems, in the grades 6–8 text complexity band proficiently, with scaffolding as needed at the high end of the range.

Standards Overview

Grade 7 Reading Standards for Informational Text

Standard

Key Ideas and Details

Cite several pieces of textual evidence to support analysis of what the text says explicitly as well as inferences drawn from the text.

Determine two or more central ideas in a text and analyze their development over the course of the text; provide an objective summary of the text.

Analyze the interactions between individuals, events, and ideas in a text (e.g., how ideas influence individuals or events, or how individuals influence ideas or events).

Craft and Structure

Determine the meaning of words and phrases as they are used in a text, including figurative, connotative, and technical meanings; analyze the impact of a specific word choice on meaning and tone.

Analyze the structure an author uses to organize a text, including how the major sections contribute to the whole and to the development of the ideas.

Determine an author's point of view or purpose in a text and analyze how the author distinguishes his or her position from that of others.

Integration of Knowledge and Ideas

Compare and contrast a text to an audio, video, or multimedia version of the text, analyzing each medium's portrayal of the subject (e.g., how the delivery of a speech affects the impact of the words).

Trace and evaluate the argument and specific claims in a text, assessing whether the reasoning is sound and the evidence is relevant and sufficient to support the claims.

Analyze how two or more authors writing about the same topic shape their presentations of key information by emphasizing different evidence or advancing different interpretations of facts.

Range of Reading and Level of Text Complexity

By the end of the year, read and comprehend literary nonfiction in the grades 6–8 text complexity band proficiently, with scaffolding as needed at the high end of the range.

Standards for Writing

College and Career Readiness Anchor Standards for Writing

Text Types and Purposes

1. Write arguments to support claims in an analysis of substantive topics or texts, using valid reasoning and relevant and sufficient evidence.

2. Write informative/explanatory texts to examine and convey complex ideas and information clearly and accurately through the effective selection, organization, and analysis of content.

3. Write narratives to develop real or imagined experiences or events using effective technique, well-chosen details, and well-structured event sequences.

Production and Distribution of Writing

4. Produce clear and coherent writing in which the development, organization, and style are appropriate to task, purpose, and audience.

5. Develop and strengthen writing as needed by planning, revising, editing, rewriting, or trying a new approach.

6. Use technology, including the Internet, to produce and publish writing and to interact and collaborate with others.

Research to Build and Present Knowledge

7. Conduct short as well as more sustained research projects based on focused questions, demonstrating understanding of the subject under investigation.

8. Gather relevant information from multiple print and digital sources, assess the credibility and accuracy of each source, and integrate the information while avoiding plagiarism.

9. Draw evidence from literary or informational texts to support analysis, reflection, and research.

Range of Writing

10. Write routinely over extended time frames (time for research, reflection, and revision) and shorter time frames (a single sitting or a day or two) for a range of tasks, purposes, and audiences.

Grade 7 Writing Standards

Standard

Text Types and Purposes

Write arguments to support claims with clear reasons and relevant evidence.

Introduce claim(s), acknowledge alternate or opposing claims, and organize the reasons and evidence logically.

Standards Overview

Grade 7 Writing Standards

Standard

Text Types and Purposes (continued)

Support claim(s) with logical reasoning and relevant evidence, using accurate, credible sources and demonstrating an understanding of the topic or text.
Use words, phrases, and clauses to create cohesion and clarify the relationships among claim(s), reasons, and evidence.
Establish and maintain a formal style.
Provide a concluding statement or section that follows from and supports the argument presented.
Write informative/explanatory texts to examine a topic and convey ideas, concepts, and information through the selection, organization, and analysis of relevant content.
Introduce a topic clearly, previewing what is to follow; organize ideas, concepts, and information, using strategies such as definition, classification, comparison/contrast, and cause/effect; include formatting (e.g., headings), graphics (e.g., charts, tables), and multimedia when useful to aiding comprehension.
Develop the topic with relevant facts, definitions, concrete details, quotations, or other information and examples.
Use appropriate transitions to create cohesion and clarify the relationships among ideas and concepts.
Use precise language and domain-specific vocabulary to inform about or explain the topic.
Establish and maintain a formal style.
Provide a concluding statement or section that follows from and supports the information or explanation presented.
Write narratives to develop real or imagined experiences or events using effective technique, relevant descriptive details, and well-structured event sequences.
Engage and orient the reader by establishing a context and point of view and introducing a narrator and/or characters; organize an event sequence that unfolds naturally and logically.
Use narrative techniques, such as dialogue, pacing, and description, to develop experiences, events, and/or characters.
Use a variety of transition words, phrases, and clauses to convey sequence and signal shifts from one time frame or setting to another.

Grade 7 Writing Standards

Standard

Text Types and Purposes (continued)

Use precise words and phrases, relevant descriptive details, and sensory language to capture the action and convey experiences and events.

Provide a conclusion that follows from and reflects on the narrated experiences or events.

Production and Distribution of Writing

Produce clear and coherent writing in which the development, organization, and style are appropriate to task, purpose, and audience. (Grade-specific expectations for writing types are defined in standards 1–3 above.)

With some guidance and support from peers and adults, develop and strengthen writing as needed by planning, revising, editing, rewriting, or trying a new approach, focusing on how well purpose and audience have been addressed. (Editing for conventions should demonstrate command of Language standards 1–3 up to and including grade 7.)

Use technology, including the Internet, to produce and publish writing and link to and cite sources as well as to interact and collaborate with others, including linking to and citing sources.

Research to Build and Present Knowledge

Conduct short research projects to answer a question, drawing on several sources and generating additional related, focused questions for further research and investigation.

Gather relevant information from multiple print and digital sources, using search terms effectively; assess the credibility and accuracy of each source; and quote or paraphrase the data and conclusions of others while avoiding plagiarism and following a standard format for citation.

Draw evidence from literary or informational texts to support analysis, reflection, and research.

Apply *grade 7 Reading standards* to literature (e.g., "Compare and contrast a fictional portrayal of a time, place, or character and a historical account of the same period as a means of understanding how authors of fiction use or alter history").

Apply *grade 7 Reading standards* to literary nonfiction (e.g., "Trace and evaluate the argument and specific claims in a text, assessing whether the reasoning is sound and the evidence is relevant and sufficient to support the claims").

Range of Writing

Write routinely over extended time frames (time for research, reflection, and revision) and shorter time frames (a single sitting or a day or two) for a range of discipline-specific tasks, purposes, and audiences.

Standards Overview

Standards for Speaking and Listening

Comprehension and Collaboration

1. Prepare for and participate effectively in a range of conversations and collaborations with diverse partners, building on others' ideas and expressing their own clearly and persuasively.

2. Integrate and evaluate information presented in diverse media and formats, including visually, quantitatively, and orally.

3. Evaluate a speaker's point of view, reasoning, and use of evidence and rhetoric.

Presentation of Knowledge and Ideas

4. Present information, findings, and supporting evidence such that listeners can follow the line of reasoning and the organization, development, and style are appropriate to task, purpose, and audience.

5. Make strategic use of digital media and visual displays of data to express information and enhance understanding of presentations.

6. Adapt speech to a variety of contexts and communicative tasks, demonstrating command of formal English when indicated or appropriate.

Grade 7 Standards for Speaking and Listening

Standard

Comprehension and Collaboration

Engage effectively in a range of collaborative discussions (one-on-one, in groups, and teacher-led) with diverse partners on *grade 7 topics, texts, and issues*, building on others' ideas and expressing their own clearly.

Come to discussions prepared, having read or researched material under study; explicitly draw on that preparation by referring to evidence on the topic, text, or issue to probe and reflect on ideas under discussion.

Follow rules for collegial discussions, track progress toward specific goals and deadlines, and define individual roles as needed.

Pose questions that elicit elaboration and respond to others' questions and comments with relevant observations and ideas that bring the discussion back on topic as needed.

Acknowledge new information expressed by others and, when warranted, modify their own views.

Analyze the main ideas and supporting details presented in diverse media and formats (e.g., visually, quantitatively, orally) and explain how the ideas clarify a topic, text, or issue under study.

Delineate a speaker's argument and specific claims, evaluating the soundness of the reasoning and the relevance and sufficiency of the evidence.

Presentation of Knowledge and Ideas

Present claims and findings, emphasizing salient points in a focused, coherent manner with pertinent descriptions, facts, details, and examples; use appropriate eye contact, adequate volume, and clear pronunciation.

Include multimedia components and visual displays in presentations to clarify claims and findings and emphasize salient points.

Adapt speech to a variety of contexts and tasks, demonstrating command of formal English when indicated or appropriate. (See grade 7 Language standards 1 and 3 for specific expectations.)

Standards Overview

Standards for Language

College and Career Readiness Anchor Standards for Language
Conventions of Standard English
1. Demonstrate command of the conventions of standard English grammar and usage when writing or speaking.
2. Demonstrate command of the conventions of standard English capitalization, punctuation, and spelling when writing.
Knowledge of Language
3. Apply knowledge of language to understand how language functions in different contexts, to make effective choices for meaning or style, and to comprehend more fully when reading or listening.
Vocabulary Acquisition and Use
4. Determine or clarify the meaning of unknown and multiple-meaning words and phrases by using context clues, analyzing meaningful word parts, and consulting general and specialized reference materials, as appropriate.
5. Demonstrate understanding of figurative language, word relationships, and nuances in word meanings.
6. Acquire and use accurately a range of general academic and domain-specific words and phrases sufficient for reading, writing, speaking, and listening at the college and career-readiness level; demonstrate independence in gathering vocabulary knowledge when considering a word or phrase important to comprehension or expression.

Grade 7 Standards for Language
Standard
Conventions of Standard English
Demonstrate command of the conventions of standard English grammar and usage when writing or speaking.
Explain the function of phrases and clauses in general and their function in specific sentences.
Choose among simple, compound, complex, and compound-complex sentences to signal differing relationships among ideas.
Place phrases and clauses within a sentence, recognizing and correcting misplaced and dangling modifiers.
Demonstrate command of the conventions of standard English capitalization, punctuation, and spelling when writing.

Grade 7 Standards for Language

Standard

Conventions of Standard English (continued)

Use a comma to separate coordinate adjectives (e.g., *It was a fascinating, enjoyable movie* but not *He wore an old[,] green shirt)*.

Spell correctly.

Knowledge of Language

Use knowledge of language and its conventions when writing, speaking, reading, or listening.

Choose language that expresses ideas precisely and concisely, recognizing and eliminating wordiness and redundancy.

Vocabulary Acquisition and Use

Determine or clarify the meaning of unknown and multiple-meaning words and phrases based on *grade 7 reading and content,* choosing flexibly from a range of strategies.

Use context (e.g., the overall meaning of a sentence or paragraph; a word's position or function in a sentence) as a clue to the meaning of a word or phrase.

Use common, grade-appropriate Greek or Latin affixes and roots as clues to the meaning of a word (e.g., *belligerent, bellicose, rebel).*

Consult general and specialized reference materials (e.g., dictionaries, glossaries, thesauruses), both print and digital, to find the pronunciation of a word or determine or clarify its precise meaning or its part of speech.

Verify the preliminary determination of the meaning of a word or phrase (e.g., by checking the inferred meaning in context or in a dictionary).

Demonstrate understanding of figurative language, word relationships, and nuances in word meanings.

Interpret figures of speech (e.g., literary, biblical, and mythological allusions) in context.

Use the relationship between particular words (e.g., synonym/antonym, analogy) to better understand each of the words.

Distinguish among the connotations (associations) of words with similar denotations (definitions) (e.g., *refined, respectful, polite, diplomatic, condescending).*

Acquire and use accurately grade-appropriate general academic and domain-specific words and phrases; gather vocabulary knowledge when considering a word or phrase important to comprehension or expression.

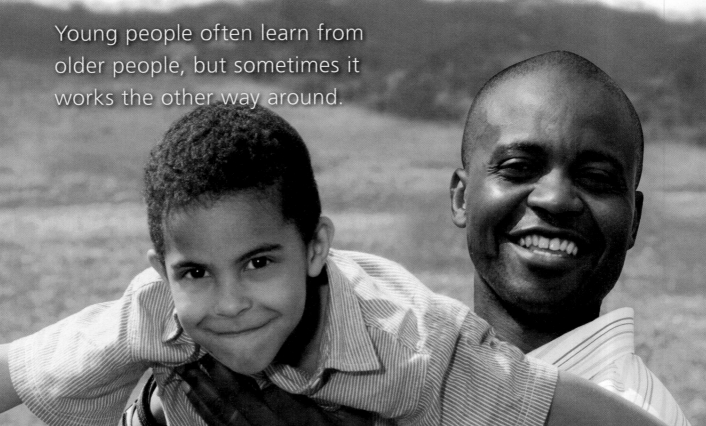

Generations

Young people often learn from older people, but sometimes it works the other way around.

Grizzly Bear Teaches Her Cubs

💬 **Discuss It** What are some examples of things that one generation can learn from another?

Write your response before sharing your ideas.

2

SCAN FOR
MULTIMEDIA

UNIT 1

UNIT INTRODUCTION

ESSENTIAL QUESTION: What can one generation learn from another?

LAUNCH TEXT
NONFICTION
NARRATIVE MODEL
Grounded

WHOLE-CLASS LEARNING

NOVEL EXCERPT

Two Kinds
from The Joy Luck Club
Amy Tan

COMPARE

NEWS BLOG

A Simple Act
Tyler Jackson

MEMOIR

from An Invisible Thread
Laura Schroff and Alex Tresniowski

▶ MEDIA CONNECTION:
Maurice's Toast

 SMALL-GROUP LEARNING

NEWS ARTICLE

Tutors Teach Seniors New High-Tech Tricks
Jennifer Ludden

▶ MEDIA CONNECTION:
Cyber-Seniors

COMPARE

MEMOIR

from Mom & Me & Mom
Maya Angelou

MEDIA: VIDEO

Learning to Love My Mother
Maya Angelou with Michael Maher

MEDIA: IMAGE GALLERY

Mother-Daughter Drawings
Mica and Myla Hendricks

POETRY COLLECTION 1

Mother to Son
Langston Hughes

To James
Frank Horne

INDEPENDENT LEARNING

POETRY COLLECTION 2

Lineage
Margaret Walker

Family
Grace Paley

OPINION PIECE

"Gotcha Day" Isn't a Cause for Celebration
Sophie Johnson

SHORT STORY

The Grandfather and His Little Grandson
Leo Tolstoy

BLOG POST

Bridging the Generational Divide Between a Football Father and a Soccer Son
John McCormick

SHORT STORY

Water Names
Lan Samantha Chang

SHORT STORY

An Hour With Abuelo
Judith Ortiz Cofer

PERFORMANCE TASK

WRITING FOCUS:
Write a Nonfiction Narrative

PERFORMANCE TASK

SPEAKING AND LISTENING FOCUS:
Present a Nonfiction Narrative

PERFORMANCE-BASED ASSESSMENT PREP

Review Evidence for a Nonfiction Narrative

PERFORMANCE-BASED ASSESSMENT

Narration: Nonfiction Narrative and Multimedia Presentation

PROMPT: In what situations can one generation learn from another?

Unit Goals

Throughout this unit you will deepen your perspective about different generations by reading, writing, speaking, listening, and presenting. These goals will help you succeed on the Unit Performance-Based Assessment.

Rate how well you meet these goals right now. You will revisit your ratings later when you reflect on your growth during this unit.

SCALE	1	2	3	4	5
	NOT AT ALL WELL	NOT VERY WELL	SOMEWHAT WELL	VERY WELL	EXTREMELY WELL

READING GOALS   1   2   3   4   5

• Read and analyze how authors express point of view in nonfiction narrative.

• Expand your knowledge and use of academic and concept vocabulary.

WRITING AND RESEARCH GOALS   1   2   3   4   5

• Write a nonfiction narrative in which you develop experiences or events using effective technique.

• Conduct research projects of various lengths to explore a topic and clarify meaning.

LANGUAGE GOAL   1   2   3   4   5

• Develop your voice, or style of writing, with word choice and sentence structure to convey meaning and add variety and interest to your writing and presentations.

SPEAKING AND LISTENING GOALS   1   2   3   4   5

• Collaborate with your team to build on the ideas of others, develop consensus, and communicate.

• Integrate audio, visuals, and text in presentations.

STANDARDS

Language
Acquire and use accurately grade-appropriate general academic and domain-specific words and phrases; gather vocabulary knowledge when considering a word or phrase important to comprehension or expression.

SCAN FOR MULTIMEDIA

Academic Vocabulary: Nonfiction Narrative

Understanding and using academic terms can help you read, write, and speak with precision and clarity. Here are five academic words that will be useful in this unit as you analyze and write narrative texts.

Complete the chart.

1. Review each word, its root, and the mentor sentences.

2. Use the information and your own knowledge to predict the meaning of each word.

3. For each word, list at least two related words.

4. Refer to the dictionary or other resources if needed.

FOLLOW THROUGH

Study the words in this chart, and mark them or their forms wherever they appear in the unit.

WORD	SENTENCES	PREDICT MEANING	RELATED WORDS
dialogue ROOT: **-log-** "word"	1. The television show was known for its well-written *dialogue* between characters. 2. The confusion between Dina and Janet started a *dialogue* that cleared the air.		monologue; logical
consequence ROOT: **-sequ-** "follow"	1. A *consequence* of oversleeping is being late for school. 2. Earning an A on my math test was a positive *consequence* of studying all week.		
perspective ROOT: **-spec-** "look"	1. It's important to keep *perspective* when facing a challenging situation. 2. The personal essay was written from the author's *perspective*.		
notable ROOT: **-not-** "mark"	1. Every *notable* person in the city was invited to the mayor's fund-raising gala. 2. It had been a long week, and nothing particularly *notable* had happened.		
contradict ROOT: **-dict-** "speak" or "assert"	1. The facts of the case remain unclear because the witnesses' statements *contradict* each other. 2. The new test results *contradict* what we once thought to be true about the product.		

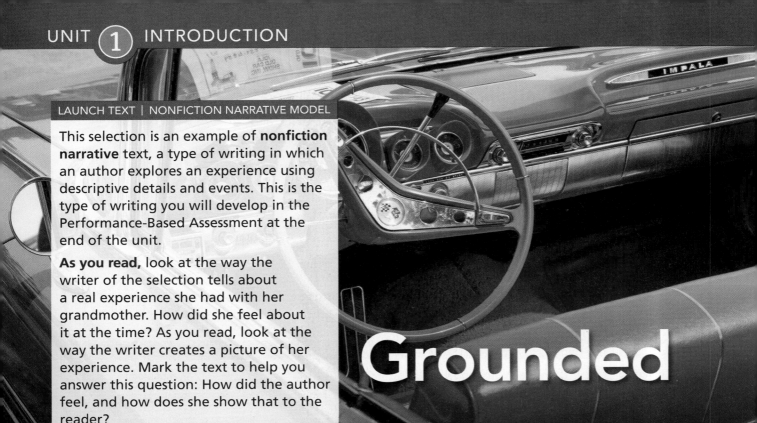

This selection is an example of **nonfiction narrative** text, a type of writing in which an author explores an experience using descriptive details and events. This is the type of writing you will develop in the Performance-Based Assessment at the end of the unit.

As you read, look at the way the writer of the selection tells about a real experience she had with her grandmother. How did she feel about it at the time? As you read, look at the way the writer creates a picture of her experience. Mark the text to help you answer this question: How did the author feel, and how does she show that to the reader?

Grounded

1   Growing up I really didn't know my grandmother. She was a private person, and didn't talk about her past much, but I know she had one. She once told me that before she got married she was a backup singer in a band that I had actually heard of. But that's all she would say about it, no matter how often I prodded.

2   "El pasado es el pasado," she told me. *The past is the past.*

3   To me, she talked in Spanish. I talked back in English. We understood each other.

4   The thing I remember most about Grandma Sofia was how much she loved driving, especially since she came to live with us. She had a 1960s red Chevy Impala convertible that was all her own, a remnant of her band days. She loved driving with the top down, the radio blasting, singing at the top of her lungs when a good song came on. Driving was her independence, her freedom.

5   My parents, however, were concerned that she was getting too old to drive around by herself. One night, I overheard them:

6   "She's okay for now, but how long before she can't manage?"

7   "I'll speak to her tomorrow."

8   I felt sick at the thought of Grandma giving up her car. I knew what driving meant to her. I knew that without her wheels she'd feel ordinary—just another grandma, hovering and wise.

9   Sometimes it felt like Grandma and I were on the sidelines and my parents were in the middle, dragging us toward the center, where we did not want to be. I was often grounded for the smallest things. I didn't really mind, under normal circumstances.

SCAN FOR MULTIMEDIA

NOTES

10   One time—the time I'm writing about—circumstances were not normal. My parents had grounded me for the weekend of Luisa's party, easily the social event of the season. No way was I going to miss it. But my parents weren't even going to be home! They were going to my Aunt Leticia's. It would just be me and Grandma. Me and Grandma and a 1966 red Chevy Impala convertible . . .

11   Saturday night arrived and I was itching to go to the party, so I did the unthinkable: I asked Grandma to drive me to Luisa's. I figured she didn't know about me being grounded. She looked at me quizzically and said she would. I got dressed and ran out to the car. She was waiting for me. I got in.

12   The sky was just beginning to darken, blue clouds against a darker blue sky. Soon it would be nighttime. Grandma looked a little uncomfortable. At first I thought it was because she knew about me being grounded. But then I wondered if maybe she didn't want to drive at night and didn't want to tell me.

13   At that moment I wouldn't have minded getting out and going back home. I felt bad about Grandma. I felt bad about disobeying my parents. But how could I say any of this?

14   We took off. She drove slowly, maybe too slowly. But we didn't get very far. Suddenly she pulled over and stopped the car.

15   We must have been sitting in that car for five minutes, which is a long time if you're sitting in a car not talking. I couldn't ask her if she stopped because she was nervous about driving. And I couldn't ask if she stopped because she knew I was grounded.

16   Finally she turned to me. "Regresamos?" *Shall we turn back?*

17   "Sure," I replied. I was so relieved I could have cried.

18   "Bueno," she said, with a nod. She started the car and turned on the radio. It was a song we both knew by heart. But it was clear that Grandma and I could still learn a lot from each other. ❧

WORD NETWORK FOR GENERATIONS

Vocabulary A Word Network is a collection of words related to a topic. As you read the selections in this unit, identify interesting words related to the idea of generations and add them to your Word Network. For example, you might begin by adding words from the Launch Text, such as *concerned, disobeying,* and *independence.* Continue to add words as you complete this unit.

🔧 **Tool Kit** Word Network Model

concerned

disobeying

independence

GENERATIONS

Summary

Write a summary of "Grounded." A **summary** is a concise, complete, and accurate overview of a text. It should not include a statement of your opinion or an analysis.

Launch Activity

Conduct a Discussion Consider this statement: **Senior citizens can learn a lot from younger people.** Decide your position, and rate your response using this scale.

☐ Strongly Agree ☐ Agree ☐ Disagree ☐ Strongly Disagree

Discuss your ratings with classmates and then participate in a whole-class discussion:

- Give examples from stories you have heard or read in which seniors learn from younger people.
- Exchange ideas and comments about the examples that were discussed.
- As a class, come to consensus about the statement.

QuickWrite

Consider class discussions, the video, and the launch text as you think about the prompt. Record your first thoughts here.

PROMPT: **In what situations can one generation learn from another?**

EVIDENCE LOG FOR GENERATIONS

Review your QuickWrite. Summarize your initial position in one sentence to record in your Evidence Log. Then, record evidence from "Grounded" that supports your initial position.

After each selection you will continue to use your Evidence Log to record the evidence you gather and the connections you make.

 Tool Kit
Evidence Log Model

Title of Text: _____ Date: _____

CONNECTION TO PROMPT	TEXT EVIDENCE/DETAILS	ADDITIONAL NOTES/IDEAS

How does this text change or add to my thinking? Date: _____

 SCAN FOR MULTIMEDIA

ESSENTIAL QUESTION:

What can one generation learn from another?

The famous Indian leader Mahatma Gandhi said, "Learn as if you were to live forever." You are always learning, from peers as well as from teachers, parents, and relatives. You will work with your whole class to explore ways in which generations can learn from each other.

Whole-Class Learning Strategies

Throughout your life, in school, in your community, and in your career, you will continue to learn and work in large-group environments.

Review these strategies and the actions you can take to practice them as you work with your whole class. Add ideas of your own to each step. Get ready to use these strategies during Whole-Class Learning.

STRATEGY	ACTION PLAN
Listen actively	• Eliminate distractions. For example, put your cell phone away. • Keep your eyes on the speaker. •
Clarify by asking questions	• If you're confused, other people probably are, too. Ask a question to help your whole class. • If you see that you are guessing, ask a question instead. •
Monitor understanding	• Notice what information you already know and be ready to build on it. • Ask for help if you are struggling. •
Interact and share ideas	• Share your ideas and answer questions, even if you are unsure. • Build on the ideas of others by adding details or making a connection. •

SCAN FOR MULTIMEDIA

COMPARE TEXTS

PERFORMANCE TASK

WRITING FOCUS

Write a Nonfiction Narrative

The Whole-Class readings illustrate the influence of one generation on another. After reading, you will write a nonfiction narrative about an event in which a person from one generation influenced a person from a different generation.

About the Author

If her mother had gotten her way, **Amy Tan** (b. 1952) would have two professions—doctor and concert pianist. Although Tan showed early promise in music, at 37 she became a successful fiction writer instead. Tan has written many books—most for adults, and some for children. Writing is sometimes tough, Tan admits, but she keeps this in mind: "A story should be a gift." That thought propels Tan to keep creating memorable characters and events.

🔧 Tool Kit
First-Read Guide and Model Annotation

≡ STANDARDS

Reading Literature
By the end of the year, read and comprehend literature, including stories, dramas, and poems, in the grades 6–8 text complexity band proficiently, with scaffolding as needed at the high end of the range.

Two Kinds

Concept Vocabulary

You will encounter the following words as you read "Two Kinds."

Before reading, note how familiar you are with each word. Then, rank the words in order from most familiar (1) to least familiar (6).

WORD	YOUR RANKING
lamented	
indignity	
reproach	
discordant	
squabbling	
devastated	

After completing your first read, come back to the concept vocabulary and review your rankings. Mark changes to your original rankings as needed.

First Read FICTION

Apply these strategies as you conduct your first read. You will have an opportunity to complete the close-read notes after your first read.

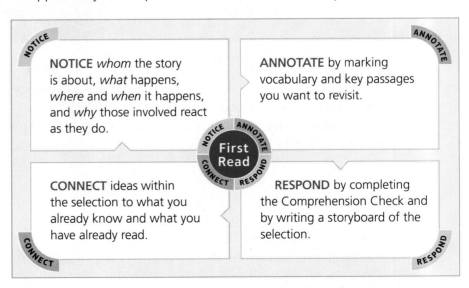

NOTICE *whom* the story is about, *what* happens, *where* and *when* it happens, and *why* those involved react as they do.

ANNOTATE by marking vocabulary and key passages you want to revisit.

CONNECT ideas within the selection to what you already know and what you have already read.

RESPOND by completing the Comprehension Check and by writing a storyboard of the selection.

First Read

Two Kinds

from **The Joy Luck Club**

Amy Tan

BACKGROUND

In 1949, following years of civil war, the Communist Party seized control of China. A number of Chinese who feared Communists—like the mother in "Two Kinds"—fled to the United States. Many lost everything except their hopes for a better future. They placed these hopes on the shoulders of their children born in the new land.

SCAN FOR MULTIMEDIA

1   My mother believed you could be anything you wanted to be in America. You could open a restaurant. You could work for the government and get good retirement. You could buy a house with almost no money down. You could become rich. You could become instantly famous.

2   "Of course, you can be prodigy,[1] too," my mother told me when I was nine. "You can be best anything. What does Auntie Lindo know? Her daughter, she is only best tricky."

3   America was where all my mother's hopes lay. She had come here in 1949 after losing everything in China: her mother and father, her family home, her first husband, and two daughters, twin baby girls. But she never looked back with regret. There were so many ways for things to get better.

❉ ❉ ❉

NOTES

---

1. **prodigy** (PROD uh jee) *n.* child of unusually high talent.

NOTES

CLOSE READ
ANNOTATE: Mark the italicized words in paragraphs 4 and 5.

QUESTION: What is different or unusual about these words?

CONCLUDE: What effect is created by the author's use of these words?

lamented (luh MEHNT ihd) *V.* expressed regret

indignity (ihn DIHG nuh tee) *n.* feeling that one has been disrespected

reproach (rih PROHCH) *n.* criticism or disapproval

4   We didn't immediately pick the right kind of prodigy. At first my mother thought I could be a Chinese Shirley Temple.[2] We'd watch Shirley's old movies on TV as though they were training films. My mother would poke my arm and say, *"Ni kan"*—You watch. And I would see Shirley tapping her feet, or singing a sailor song, or pursing her lips into a very round O while saying, "Oh my goodness."

5   *"Ni kan,"* said my mother as Shirley's eyes flooded with tears. "You already know how. Don't need talent for crying!"

6   Soon after my mother got this idea about Shirley Temple, she took me to a beauty training school in the Mission district and put me in the hands of a student who could barely hold the scissors without shaking. Instead of getting big fat curls, I emerged with an uneven mass of crinkly black fuzz. My mother dragged me off to the bathroom and tried to wet down my hair.

7   "You look like Negro Chinese," she **lamented**, as if I had done this on purpose.

8   The instructor of the beauty training school had to lop off these soggy clumps to make my hair even again. "Peter Pan is very popular these days," the instructor assured my mother. I now had hair the length of a boy's, with straight-across bangs that hung at a slant two inches above my eyebrows. I liked the haircut and it made me actually look forward to my future fame.

9   In fact, in the beginning, I was just as excited as my mother, maybe even more so. I pictured this prodigy part of me as many different images, trying each one on for size. I was a dainty ballerina girl standing by the curtains, waiting to hear the right music that would send me floating on my tiptoes. I was like the Christ child lifted out of the straw manger, crying with holy **indignity**. I was Cinderella stepping from her pumpkin carriage with sparkly cartoon music filling the air.

10 In all of my imaginings, I was filled with a sense that I would soon become *perfect*. My mother and father would adore me. I would be beyond **reproach**. I would never feel the need to sulk for anything.

11 But sometimes the prodigy in me became impatient. "If you don't hurry up and get me out of here, I'm disappearing for good," it warned. "And then you'll always be nothing."

* * *

12 Every night after dinner, my mother and I would sit at the Formica kitchen table. She would present new tests, taking her examples from stories of amazing children that she read in *Ripley's Believe It or Not*, or *Good Housekeeping*, *Reader's Digest*, and a dozen

2. **Shirley Temple** American child star of the 1930s. She starred in her first movie at age three and won an Academy Award at age six.

other magazines she kept in a pile in our bathroom. My mother got these magazines from people whose houses she cleaned. And since she cleaned many houses each week, we had a great assortment. She would look through them all, searching for stories about remarkable children.

13   The first night she brought out a story about a three-year-old boy who knew the capitals of all the states and even most of the European countries. A teacher was quoted as saying the little boy could also pronounce the names of the foreign cities correctly.

14   "What's the capital of Finland?" My mother asked me, looking at the magazine story.

15   All I knew was the capital of California, because Sacramento was the name of the street we lived on in Chinatown. "Nairobi!" I guessed, saying the most foreign word I could think of. She checked to see if that was possibly one way to pronounce "Helsinki" before showing me the answer.

16   The tests got harder—multiplying numbers in my head, finding the queen of hearts in a deck of cards, trying to stand on my head without using my hands, predicting the daily temperatures in Los Angeles, New York, and London.

17   One night I had to look at a page from the Bible for three minutes and then report everything I could remember. "Now Jehoshaphat had riches and honor in abundance and . . . that's all I remember, Ma," I said.

18   And after seeing my mother's disappointed face once again, something inside of me began to die. I hated the tests, the raised hopes and failed expectations. Before going to bed that night, I looked in the mirror above the bathroom sink and when I saw only my face staring back—and that it would always be this ordinary face—I began to cry. Such a sad, ugly girl! I made high-pitched noises like a crazed animal, trying to scratch out the face in the mirror.

19   And then I saw what seemed to be the prodigy side of me—because I had never seen that face before. I looked at my reflection, blinking so I could see more clearly. The girl staring back at me was angry, powerful. This girl and I were the same. I had new thoughts, willful thoughts, or rather thoughts filled with lots of won'ts. I won't let her change me, I promised myself. I won't be what I'm not.

20   So now on nights when my mother presented her tests, I performed listlessly, my head propped on one arm. I pretended to be bored. And I was. I got so bored I started counting the bellows of the foghorns out on the bay while my mother drilled me in other areas. The sound was comforting and reminded me of the cow jumping over the moon. And the next day, I played a game with myself, seeing if my mother would give up on me before

NOTES

CLOSE READ
ANNOTATE: Mark words or phrases in paragraphs 18 and 19 that reveal the narrator's feelings.

QUESTION: Why might the author have chosen to reveal the contrasting emotions of the narrator?

CONCLUDE: What effect does this choice have on the reader?

NOTES

eight bellows. After a while I usually counted only one, maybe two bellows at most. At last she was beginning to give up hope.

21   Two or three months had gone by without any mention of my being a prodigy again. And then one day my mother was watching *The Ed Sullivan Show*[3] on TV. The TV was old and the sound kept shorting out. Every time my mother got halfway up from the sofa to adjust the set, the sound would go back on and Ed would be talking. As soon as she sat down, Ed would go silent again. She got up, the TV broke into loud piano music. She sat down. Silence. Up and down, back and forth, quiet and loud. It was like a stiff embraceless dance between her and the TV set. Finally, she stood by the set with her hand on the sound dial.

22   She seemed entranced by the music, a little frenzied piano piece with this mesmerizing quality, sort of quick passages and then teasing lilting ones before it returned to the quick playful parts.

23   "*Ni kan*," my mother said, calling me over with hurried hand gestures. "Look here."

24   I could see why my mother was fascinated by the music. It was being pounded out by a little Chinese girl, about nine years old, with a Peter Pan haircut. The girl had the sauciness of a Shirley Temple. She was proudly modest like a proper Chinese child. And

_____
3. ***The Ed Sullivan Show*** popular television variety show that ran from 1948 to 1971.

she also did this fancy sweep of a curtsy, so that the fluffy skirt of her white dress cascaded slowly to the floor like the petals of a large carnation.

25 In spite of these warning signs, I wasn't worried. Our family had no piano and we couldn't afford to buy one, let alone reams of sheet music and piano lessons. So I could be generous in my comments when my mother bad-mouthed the little girl on TV.

26 "Play note right, but doesn't sound good! No singing sound," complained my mother.

27 "What are you picking on her for?" I said carelessly. "She's pretty good. Maybe she's not the best, but she's trying hard." I knew almost immediately that I would be sorry I said that.

28 "Just like you," she said. "Not the best. Because you not trying." She gave a little huff as she let go of the sound dial and sat down on the sofa.

29 The little Chinese girl sat down also to play an encore of "Anitra's Dance" by Grieg.[4] I remember the song, because later on I had to learn how to play it.

30 Three days after watching *The Ed Sullivan Show,* my mother told me what my schedule would be for piano lessons and piano practice. She had talked to Mr. Chong, who lived on the first floor of our apartment building. Mr. Chong was a retired piano teacher and my mother had traded housecleaning services for weekly lessons and a piano for me to practice on every day, two hours a day, from four until six.

31 When my mother told me this, I felt as though I had been sent to hell. I whined and then kicked my foot a little when I couldn't stand it anymore.

32 "Why don't you like me the way I am? I'm *not* a genius! I can't play the piano. And even if I could, I wouldn't go on TV if you paid me a million dollars!" I cried.

33 My mother slapped me. "Who ask you be genius?" she shouted. "Only ask you be your best. For you sake. You think I want you be genius? Hnnh! What for! Who ask you!"

34 "So ungrateful," I heard her mutter in Chinese, "If she had as much talent as she has temper, she would be famous now."

35 Mr. Chong, whom I secretly nicknamed Old Chong, was very strange, always tapping his fingers to the silent music of an invisible orchestra. He looked ancient in my eyes. He had lost most of the hair on top of his head and he wore thick glasses and had eyes that always looked tired and sleepy. But he must have been younger than I thought, since he lived with his mother and was not yet married.

36 I met Old Lady Chong once and that was enough. She had this peculiar smell like a baby that had done something in its pants.

---

4. **Grieg** (greeg) Edvard Grieg (1843–1907), Norwegian composer.

NOTES

CLOSE READ

ANNOTATE: Mark the punctuation in paragraphs 32 and 33 that reveals how the mother and daughter communicate.

QUESTION: What does the punctuation suggest about the tone of the conversation?

CONCLUDE: How does the punctuation in these paragraphs help you to better understand the conflict between the mother and the daughter?

Copyright © SAVVAS Learning Company LLC. All Rights Reserved.

Two Kinds **17**

And her fingers felt like a dead person's, like an old peach I once found in the back of the refrigerator; the skin just slid off the meat when I picked it up.

37   I soon found out why Old Chong had retired from teaching piano. He was deaf. "Like Beethoven!"[5] he shouted to me. "We're both listening only in our head!" And he would start to conduct his frantic silent sonatas.

38   Our lessons went like this. He would open the book and point to different things, explaining their purpose: "Key! Treble! Bass! No sharps or flats! So this is C major! Listen now and play after me!"

39   And then he would play the C scale a few times, a simple chord, and then, as if inspired by an old, unreachable itch, he gradually added more notes and running trills and a pounding bass until the music was really something quite grand.

40   I would play after him, the simple scale, the simple chord, and then I just played some nonsense that sounded like a cat running up and down on top of garbage cans. Old Chong smiled and applauded and then said, "Very good! But now you must learn to keep time!"

41   So that's how I discovered that Old Chong's eyes were too slow to keep up with the wrong notes I was playing. He went through the motions in half-time. To help me keep rhythm, he stood behind me, pushing down on my right shoulder for every beat. He balanced pennies on top of my wrists so I would keep them still as I slowly played scales and arpeggios.[6] He had me curve my hand around an apple and keep that shape when playing chords. He marched stiffly to show me how to make each finger dance up and down, staccato[7] like an obedient little soldier.

42   He taught me all these things, and that was how I also learned I could be lazy and get away with mistakes, lots of mistakes. If I hit the wrong notes because I hadn't practiced enough, I never corrected myself. I just kept playing in rhythm. And Old Chong kept conducting his own private reverie.

43   So maybe I never really gave myself a fair chance. I did pick up the basics pretty quickly, and I might have become a good pianist at that young age. But I was so determined not to try, not to be anybody different that I learned to play only the most ear-splitting preludes, the most **discordant** hymns.

discordant (dihs KAWRD uhnt) *adj.* lacking harmony

44   Over the next year, I practiced like this, dutifully in my own way. And then one day I heard my mother and her friend Lindo Jong both talking in a loud bragging tone of voice so others could hear. It was after church, and I was leaning against the

---

5. **Beethoven** (BAY toh vuhn) Ludwig van Beethoven (1770–1827), German composer. Some of his greatest pieces were written when he was completely deaf.
6. **arpeggios** (ahr PEHJ ee ohz) *n.* notes in a chord played separately in quick succession.
7. **staccato** (stuh KAHT oh) *adv.* played crisply, with clear breaks between notes.

brick wall wearing a dress with stiff white petticoats. Auntie Lindo's daughter, Waverly, who was about my age, was standing farther down the wall about five feet away. We had grown up together and shared all the closeness of two sisters **squabbling** over crayons and dolls. In other words, for the most part, we hated each other. I thought she was snotty. Waverly Jong had gained a certain amount of fame as "Chinatown's Littlest Chinese Chess Champion."

45   "She bring home too many trophy," lamented Auntie Lindo that Sunday. "All day she play chess. All day I have no time do nothing but dust off her winnings." She threw a scolding look at Waverly, who pretended not to see her.

46   "You lucky you don't have this problem," said Auntie Lindo with a sigh to my mother.

47   And my mother squared her shoulders and bragged: "Our problem worser than yours. If we ask Jing-mei wash dish, she hear nothing but music. It's like you can't stop this natural talent."

48   And right then, I was determined to put a stop to her foolish pride.

❊ ❊ ❊

49   A few weeks later, Old Chong and my mother conspired to have me play in a talent show which would be held in the church hall. By then, my parents had saved up enough to buy me a secondhand piano, a black Wurlitzer spinet with a scarred bench. It was the showpiece of our living room.

50   For the talent show, I was to play a piece called "Pleading Child" from Schumann's[8] *Scenes from Childhood*. It was a simple, moody piece that sounded more difficult than it was. I was supposed to memorize the whole thing, playing the repeat parts twice to make the piece sound longer. But I dawdled over it, playing a few bars and then cheating, looking up to see what notes followed. I never really listened to what I was playing. I daydreamed about being somewhere else, about being someone else.

51   The part I liked to practice best was the fancy curtsy: right foot out, touch the rose on the carpet with a pointed foot, sweep to the side, left leg bends, look up and smile.

52   My parents invited all the couples from the Joy Luck Club to witness my debut. Auntie Lindo and Uncle Tin were there. Waverly and her two older brothers had also come. The first two rows were filled with children both younger and older than I was. The littlest ones got to go first. They recited simple nursery rhymes, squawked out tunes on miniature violins, twirled Hula

---

8. **Schumann** (SHOO mahn) Robert Alexander Schumann (1810–1856), German composer.

squabbling (SKWAHB blihng) *v.* fighting noisily over small matters

Hoops, pranced in pink ballet tutus, and when they bowed or curtsied, the audience would sigh in unison, "Awww," and then clap enthusiastically.

53   When my turn came, I was very confident. I remember my childish excitement. It was as if I knew, without a doubt, that the prodigy side of me really did exist. I had no fear whatsoever, no nervousness. I remember thinking to myself, This is it! This is it! I looked out over the audience, at my mother's blank face, my father's yawn, Auntie Lindo's stiff-lipped smile, Waverly's sulky expression. I had on a white dress, layered with sheets of lace, and a pink bow in my Peter Pan haircut. As I sat down, I envisioned people jumping to their feet and Ed Sullivan rushing up to introduce me to everyone on TV.

54   And I started to play. It was so beautiful. I was so caught up in how lovely I looked that at first I didn't worry how I would sound. So it was a surprise to me when I hit the first wrong note and I realized something didn't sound quite right. And then I hit another and another followed that. A chill started at the top of my head and began to trickle down. Yet I couldn't stop playing, as though my hands were bewitched. I kept thinking my fingers would adjust themselves back, like a train switching to the right track. I played this strange jumble through two repeats, the sour notes staying with me all the way to the end.

55   When I stood up, I discovered my legs were shaking. Maybe I had just been nervous and the audience, like Old Chong, had seen me go through the right motions and had not heard anything wrong at all. I swept my right foot out, went down on my knee, looked up and smiled. The room was quiet, except for Old Chong, who was beaming and shouting "Bravo! Bravo! Well done!" But then I saw my mother's face, her stricken face. The audience clapped weakly, and as I walked back to my chair, with my whole face quivering as I tried not to cry, I heard a little boy whisper loudly to his mother, "That was awful," and the mother whispered back, "Well, she certainly tried."

56   And now I realized how many people were in the audience, the whole world it seemed. I was aware of eyes burning into my back. I felt the shame of my mother and father as they sat stiffly throughout the rest of the show.

57   We could have escaped during intermission. Pride and some strange sense of honor must have anchored my parents to their chairs. And so we watched it all: the eighteen-year-old boy with a fake moustache who did a magic show and juggled flaming hoops while riding a unicycle. The breasted girl with white makeup who sang from *Madama Butterfly* and got honorable mention. And the eleven-year-old boy who won first prize playing a tricky violin song that sounded like a busy bee.

58   After the show, the Hsus, the Jongs, and the St. Clairs from the Joy Luck Club came up to my mother and father.

59   "Lots of talented kids," Auntie Lindo said vaguely, smiling broadly.

60   "That was somethin' else," said my father, and I wondered if he was referring to me in a humorous way, or whether he even remembered what I had done.

61   Waverly looked at me and shrugged her shoulders. "You aren't a genius like me," she said matter-of-factly. And if I hadn't felt so bad, I would have pulled her braids and punched her stomach.

62   But my mother's expression was what **devastated** me: a quiet, blank look that said she had lost everything. I felt the same way, and it seemed as if everybody were now coming up, like gawkers at the scene of an accident, to see what parts were actually missing. When we got on the bus to go home, my father was humming the busy-bee tune and my mother was silent. I kept thinking she wanted to wait until we got home before shouting at me. But when my father unlocked the door to our apartment, my mother walked in and then went to the back, into the bedroom. No accusations. No blame. And in a way, I felt disappointed. I had been waiting for her to start shouting, so I could shout back and cry and blame her for all my misery.

❋ ❋ ❋

63   I assumed my talent-show fiasco meant I never had to play the piano again. But two days later, after school, my mother came out of the kitchen and saw me watching TV.

64   "Four clock," she reminded me as if it were any other day. I was stunned, as though she were asking me to go through the talent-show torture again. I wedged myself more tightly in front of the TV.

65   "Turn off TV," she called from the kitchen five minutes later.

66   I didn't budge. And then I decided. I didn't have to do what my mother said anymore. I wasn't her slave. This wasn't China. I had listened to her before and look what happened. She was the stupid one.

67   She came out from the kitchen and stood in the arched entryway of the living room. "Four clock," she said once again, louder.

68   "I'm not going to play anymore," I said nonchalantly. "Why should I? I'm not a genius."

69   She walked over and stood in front of the TV. I saw her chest was heaving up and down in an angry way.

devastated (DEH vuh stay tihd) *v.* destroyed; completely upset

70 "No!" I said, and I now felt stronger, as if my true self had finally emerged. So this was what had been inside me all along.

71 "No! I won't!" I screamed.

72 She yanked me by the arm, pulled me off the floor, snapped off the TV. She was frighteningly strong, half pulling, half carrying me toward the piano as I kicked the throw rugs under my feet. She lifted me up and onto the hard bench. I was sobbing by now, looking at her bitterly. Her chest was heaving even more and her mouth was open, smiling crazily as if she were pleased I was crying.

73 "You want me to be someone that I'm not!" I sobbed. "I'll never be the kind of daughter you want me to be!"

74 "Only two kinds of daughters," she shouted in Chinese. "Those who are obedient and those who follow their own mind! Only one kind of daughter can live in this house. Obedient daughter!"

75 "Then I wish I wasn't your daughter. I wish you weren't my mother," I shouted. As I said these things I got scared. It felt like worms and toads and slimy things crawling out of my chest, but it also felt good, as if this awful side of me had surfaced, at last.

76 "Too late change this," said my mother shrilly.

77 And I could sense her anger rising to its breaking point. I wanted to see it spill over. And that's when I remembered the babies she had lost in China, the ones we never talked about. "Then I wish I'd never been born!" I shouted. "I wish I were dead! Like them."

78 It was as if I had said the magic words. Alakazam!—and her face went blank, her mouth closed, her arms went slack, and she backed out of the room, stunned, as if she were blowing away like a small brown leaf, thin, brittle, lifeless.

79 It was not the only disappointment my mother felt in me. In the years that followed, I failed her so many times, each time asserting my own will, my right to fall short of expectations. I didn't get straight A's. I didn't become class president. I didn't get into Stanford. I dropped out of college.

80 For unlike my mother, I did not believe I could be anything I wanted to be. I could only be me.

81 And for all those years, we never talked about the disaster at the recital or my terrible accusations afterward at the piano bench. All that remained unchecked, like a betrayal that was now unspeakable. So I never found a way to ask her why she had hoped for something so large that failure was inevitable.

82 And even worse, I never asked her what frightened me the most: Why had she given up hope?

83 For after our struggle at the piano, she never mentioned my playing again. The lessons stopped. The lid to the piano was closed, shutting out the dust, my misery, and her dreams.

84   So she surprised me. A few years ago, she offered to give me the piano, for my thirtieth birthday. I had not played in all those years. I saw the offer as a sign of forgiveness, a tremendous burden removed.

85   "Are you sure?" I asked shyly. "I mean, won't you and Dad miss it?"

86   "No, this your piano," she said firmly. "Always your piano. You only one can play."

87   "Well, I probably can't play anymore," I said. "It's been years."

88   "You pick up fast," said my mother, as if she knew this was certain. "You have natural talent. You could been genius if you want to."

89   "No I couldn't."

90   "You just not trying," said my mother. And she was neither angry nor sad. She said it as if to announce a fact that could never be disproved. "Take it," she said.

91   But I didn't at first. It was enough that she had offered it to me. And after that, every time I saw it in my parents' living room, standing in front of the bay windows, it made me feel proud, as if it were a shiny trophy I had won back.

❋   ❋   ❋

92   Last week I sent a tuner over to my parents' apartment and had the piano reconditioned, for purely sentimental reasons. My mother had died a few months before and I had been getting things in order for my father, a little bit at a time. I put the jewelry in special silk pouches. The sweaters she had knitted in yellow, pink, bright orange— all the colors I hated—I put those in moth-proof boxes. I found some old Chinese silk dresses, the kind with little slits up the sides. I rubbed the old silk against my skin, then wrapped them in tissue and decided to take them home with me.

93   After I had the piano tuned, I opened the lid and touched the keys. It sounded even richer than I remembered. Really, it was a very good piano. Inside the bench were the same exercise notes with handwritten scales, the same secondhand music books with their covers held together with yellow tape.

94   I opened up the Schumann book to the dark little piece I had played at the recital. It was on the left-hand side of the page, "Pleading Child." It looked more difficult than I remembered. I played a few bars, surprised at how easily the notes came back to me.

95   And for the first time, or so it seemed, I noticed the piece on the right-hand side. It was called "Perfectly Contented." I tried to play this one as well. It had a lighter melody but the same flowing rhythm and turned out to be quite easy. "Pleading Child" was shorter but slower; "Perfectly Contented" was longer, but faster. And after I played them both a few times, I realized they were two halves of the same song. ❧

Comprehension Check

Complete the following items after you finish your first read.

1. In what ways does the mother pressure her daughter to change?

2. How does the mother arrange for her daughter to take piano lessons?

3. How does the narrator prepare for the talent show?

4. What happens when the narrator performs at the talent show?

5. What happens to the piano at the end of the story?

 Notebook Draw a storyboard of key events in "Two Kinds" to confirm your understanding of the story.

- -

RESEARCH

Research to Clarify Choose at least one unfamiliar detail from the text. Briefly research that detail. In what way does the information you learned shed light on an aspect of the story?

Research to Explore Choose something that interested you from the text and formulate a research question.

TWO KINDS

Close Read the Text

1. This model, from paragraph 10 of the text, shows two sample annotations, along with questions and conclusions. Close read the passage, and find another detail to annotate. Then, write a question and conclusion.

ANNOTATE: The author uses italics to emphasize a specific word.

QUESTION: Why is the word *perfect* emphasized?

CONCLUDE: The narrator believes that the only way her parents will be satisfied with her is if she is without fault.

ANNOTATE | QUESTION | CONCLUDE | **Close Read**

In all of my imaginings, I was filled with a sense that I would soon become *perfect*. My mother and father would adore me. I would be beyond reproach. I would never feel the need to sulk for anything.

ANNOTATE: The word *would* is repeated several times.

QUESTION: What idea is stressed by the repetition of *would*?

CONCLUDE: The repetition shows the narrator's hopes for the future. It also shows that she does not feel that her parents adore her, she often feels criticized, and she likely sulks a lot.

🔧 **Tool Kit**
Close-Read Guide and Model Annotation

2. For more practice, go back into the text and complete the close-read notes.

3. Revisit a section of the text you found important. Read this section and **annotate** what you notice. Ask yourself **questions** such as "Why did the author make this choice?" What can you **conclude**?

Analyze the Text

CITE TEXTUAL EVIDENCE
to support your answers.

📓 **Notebook** Respond to these questions.

1. (a) **Compare and Contrast** How are the mother and her daughter similar and different? (b) **Analyze Cause and Effect** How does the difference in their attitudes cause problems?

2. **Draw Conclusions** In this story, **conflict,** or a struggle between the characters, results when a mother pushes her daughter to succeed. Is there a winner in this conflict? Explain.

3. **Make a Judgment** Should the narrator's mother have pushed the daughter as she did? Explain.

4. **Essential Question** *What can one generation learn from another?* What have you learned about how people of different generations interact from reading this story?

STANDARDS
Reading Literature
• Cite several pieces of textual evidence to support analysis of what the text says explicitly as well as inferences drawn from the text.
• Analyze how an author develops and contrasts the points of view of different characters or narrators in a text.

Analyze Craft and Structure

Character and Point of View A **character** is a person or an animal in a literary work.

- **Character traits** are the individual qualities that make each character unique. You can identify character traits by **making inferences**, or educated guesses, about a character based on how he or she thinks, acts, and speaks.

- A **character's motives** are the emotions or goals that drive him or her to act in a certain way.

- A **character's perspective** is how he or she views events based on his or her experiences and emotions.

Point of view is the perspective from which the story is told.

- When a story is told from the **first-person point of view,** the narrator is a character who participates in the action and uses first-person pronouns such as *I* and *me* to refer to himself or herself.

- When a story is told from the **third-person point of view,** the narrator is not a character in the story. The narrator uses third-person pronouns such as *he* and *she* to refer to the characters.

Practice

CITE TEXTUAL EVIDENCE
to support your answers.

Notebook Respond to these questions.

1. Use the diagram to list the daughter's character traits.

2. Reread paragraphs 24–28 of the text. What does this passage show about the difference between the mother's motives and the daughter's motives?

3. How do the different perspectives of the mother and daughter create challenges for each character?

4. (a) From what point of view is the story told? (b) What details in the text enabled you to identify the point of view?

5. How might the story be different if it were told from the mother's point of view?

TWO KINDS

Concept Vocabulary

lamented	reproach	squabbling
indignity	discordant	devastated

Why These Words? These concept vocabulary words relate to the idea of conflict. For example, the narrator fantasizes that she might one day be beyond *reproach*. The word *reproach* describes the heavy criticism that she feels as a result of her mother's actions.

1. Select three of the concept vocabulary words, and explain how each word helps the reader better understand the conflict between the mother and the daughter.

2. What other words in the selection connect to the concept of conflict, or struggle?

Practice

⊟ **Notebook** The concept vocabulary words appear in "Two Kinds." Answer the questions, using the vocabulary words to show your understanding.

1. Why might a person who experiences *indignity* feel upset or angry?
2. Why might a famous chef feel that his or her cooking is beyond *reproach?*
3. Why might someone's neighbors complain about *discordant* music coming from a stereo?
4. What advice can you give people to help them avoid *squabbling* with each other?
5. If a student *lamented* after taking a test, how did the student do?
6. What kind of weather might have *devastated* an apple orchard?

Word Study

Latin Prefix: *in-* The prefix *in-* means "not." When this prefix is added to a base word, the new word takes on the opposite meaning from the original word. Practice your knowledge of this prefix by completing the following activities.

1. When people have *dignity*, they are worthy of honor and respect. Write a definition of the word *indignity* based on your knowledge of the prefix *in-*.

2. Define these words that contain the prefix *in-*: *incorrect, inactive, incomplete.*

⊞ **WORD NETWORK**

Look in the text for words related to the topic of generations, and add them to your Word Network.

▤ **STANDARDS**

Language
• Determine or clarify the meaning of unknown and multiple-meaning words and phrases based on *grade 7 reading and content,* choosing flexibly from a range of strategies.

  b. Use common, grade-appropriate Greek or Latin affixes and roots as clues to the meaning of a word.

• Demonstrate command of the conventions of standard English capitalization, punctuation, and spelling when writing.

Conventions

Nouns and Pronouns A **common noun** names a person, place, thing, or idea. A **proper noun** names a specific person, place, or thing. A **possessive noun** shows ownership.

COMMON NOUNS	PROPER NOUNS	POSSESSIVE NOUNS
mother, daughter, country, street	Mr. Chong, China, Main Street	the audience's reaction Lucas's piano the musicians' bows the children's concert

TIP

CLARIFICATION
Proper nouns are always capitalized. Examples of proper nouns include *Abraham Lincoln, London,* and *Selena.*

A **personal pronoun** takes the place of a noun or several nouns named elsewhere in the text, referring to a specific person or thing. A **possessive pronoun** shows possession or ownership.

Personal Pronouns	I, me, we, us, you, he, him, she, her, it, they, them
Possessive Pronouns	my, mine, our, ours, your, yours, his, hers, its, their, theirs

Read It

Reread paragraph 29 of "Two Kinds." Mark the nouns. Then, classify each noun as common or proper. Finally, identify the possessive noun in the paragraph.

Write It

Revise the sentences. Replace nouns with appropriate pronouns.

1. When the daughter performed, the daughter's playing was sloppy.

2. My father listened patiently, although my father did not want to be there.

3. The youngest children played first. Most of the youngest children were prepared.

📓 **Notebook** Write three sentences about an important scene between the mother and daughter in the selection. Include at least one of each type of noun and pronoun in your sentences.

TWO KINDS

Writing to Sources

Writing an effective narrative, whether fiction or nonfiction, requires creativity and imagination. When developing a narrative, consider the points of view of all the characters, because each one has unique experiences and perspectives. By doing so, you will gain a deeper understanding of how point of view shapes your writing.

Assignment

Choose a scene from the story, and write a **retelling** of the scene from the mother's point of view.

- Review the story, and note important details that can help you identify the mother's character traits and motives. Use these details to ensure that you accurately portray the mother's character.
- Present a clear sequence of events for the scene that you chose.
- Use narrative techniques, such as dialogue and description, to convey the mother's thoughts and feelings.

Vocabulary and Conventions Connection Think about including several of the concept vocabulary words in your retelling. Be sure to correctly use nouns and pronouns to establish a clear point of view and clarify the relationships between characters.

lamented	reproach	squabbling
indignity	discordant	devastated

Reflect on Your Writing

After you have written your retelling, answer the following questions.

1. How did writing from the mother's point of view help you to better understand her perspective?

2. What narrative techniques did you use in your writing? Which narrative technique do you think was most effective in portraying the mother's character?

3. Why These Words? The words you choose make a difference in your writing. Which words did you specifically choose to bring the mother's point of view to life?

STANDARDS

Writing
- Write narratives to develop real or imagined experiences or events using effective technique, relevant descriptive details, and well-structured event sequences.
  a. Engage and orient the reader by establishing a context and point of view and introducing a narrator and/or characters; organize an event sequence that unfolds naturally and logically.
  b. Use narrative techniques, such as dialogue, pacing, and description, to develop experiences, events, and/or characters.
  d. Use precise words and phrases, relevant descriptive details, and sensory language to capture the action and convey experiences and events.

Speaking and Listening
Present claims and findings, emphasizing salient points in a focused, coherent manner with pertinent descriptions, facts, details, and examples; use appropriate eye contact, adequate volume, and clear pronunciation.

Speaking and Listening

A **monologue** is a dramatic speech presented by a single character. The character speaks from the first-person point of view and relates his or her thoughts and feelings about an event.

Assignment

Choose one of the passages listed, and develop a **dramatic monologue** in which the daughter expresses aloud her thoughts and feelings in this moment of the story.

- paragraphs 18–20
- paragraphs 54–56
- paragraphs 84–91

1. Organize Your Monologue Use the following questions to gather ideas and prepare notes.

What happened earlier in the story?	Think about how these events influence the daughter's feelings.
How will your monologue begin?	Choose a strong statement to grab your audience's interest.
What happens during the monologue?	Show how the daughter's thoughts and feelings change during the monologue.
How will your monologue end?	Conclude your monologue with a thought-provoking statement that ends the scene.

2. Prepare Your Delivery Using your notes, practice your monologue.

- Maintain eye contact with members of your audience as you speak.
- Vary the volume of your voice and your pacing to reflect emotion.

3. Evaluate Monologues Use a presentation evaluation guide like the one shown to analyze your classmates' monologues.

PRESENTATION EVALUATION GUIDE

Rate each statement on a scale of 1 (not demonstrated) to 5 (demonstrated).

☐ The speaker communicated events from the daughter's point of view.

☐ The speaker provided details to demonstrate shifts in feeling.

☐ The speaker maintained eye contact with audience members.

☐ The monologue was clear and easy to follow.

✐ EVIDENCE LOG

Before moving on to a new selection, go to your Evidence Log and record what you learned from "Two Kinds."

A SIMPLE ACT

Comparing Texts

In this lesson, you will read and compare "A Simple Act" and an excerpt from *An Invisible Thread*. First you will complete the first-read and close-read activities for "A Simple Act."

from AN INVISIBLE THREAD

About the Author

Tyler Jackson (b. 1981) was raised in England but has traveled extensively, writing about many of the places he has lived. Jackson has survived a hurricane in North Carolina and a flood in Texas, and says, "People pull together in a disaster, but it's remarkable to see the small acts of kindness that usually go unreported."

A Simple Act

Concept Vocabulary

You will encounter the following words as you read "A Simple Act."

Before reading, rate how familiar you are with each word. Indicate how well you know it on a scale of 1 (do not know it) to 5 (know it very well).

WORD	YOUR RANKING
connects	
influence	
encouraged	
bond	

After completing your first read, come back to the concept vocabulary and review your rankings. Mark changes to your original rankings as needed.

First Read NONFICTION

Apply these strategies as you conduct your first read. You will have an opportunity to complete the close-read notes after your first read.

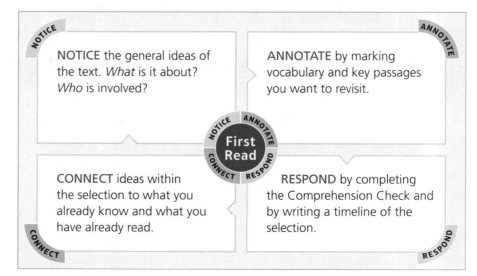

NOTICE the general ideas of the text. *What* is it about? *Who* is involved?

ANNOTATE by marking vocabulary and key passages you want to revisit.

First Read

CONNECT ideas within the selection to what you already know and what you have already read.

RESPOND by completing the Comprehension Check and by writing a timeline of the selection.

STANDARDS

Reading Informational Text
By the end of the year, read and comprehend literary nonfiction in the grades 6–8 text complexity band proficiently, with scaffolding as needed at the high end of the range.

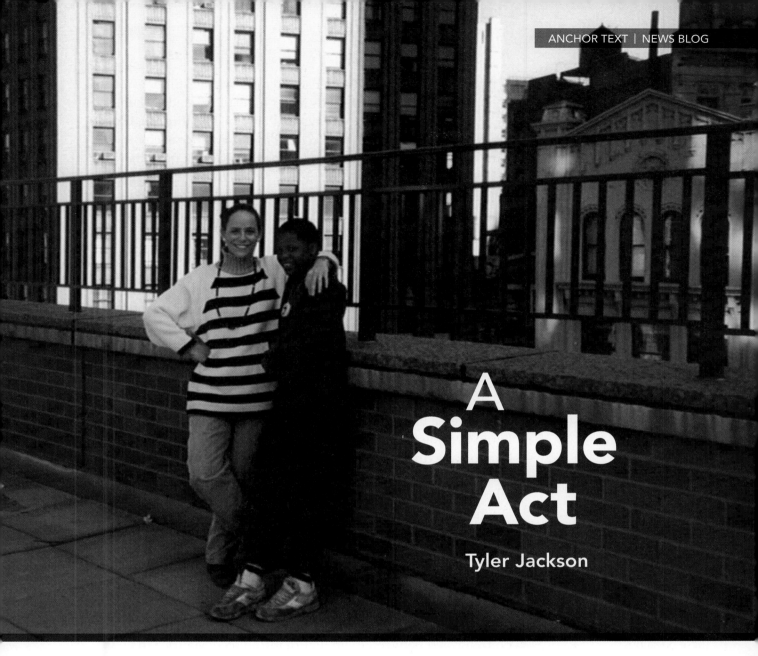

A Simple Act

Tyler Jackson

BACKGROUND

In a big city like New York, thousands of strangers from many different backgrounds cross paths every day. But they rarely stop on the street to get to know each other. When people from very different places make the effort to connect, unexpected friendships can form.

SCAN FOR MULTIMEDIA

1 It was the first day of September in 1986, and the morning rain had given way to bright sunshine. A successful advertising executive made her way across 56th street toward Broadway, on the west side of Manhattan. A young boy—all of eleven years old and dressed in scruffy clothes—asked for some change for something to eat. Laura Schroff lowered her head and walked on; Manhattan was full of panhandlers, and she hardly even noticed them any more.

NOTES

NOTES

connects (kuh NEHKTS) *v.* joins together

influence (IHN floo uhns) *v.* affect someone in an important way

encouraged (ehn KUR ihjd) *v.* inspired; offered support to

bond (BAHND) *n.* uniting connection; link

CLOSE READ

ANNOTATE: Mark the questions included in paragraph 4.

QUESTION: Why might the author have included these questions?

CONCLUDE: What effect do these questions have on Laura?

2   But something drew Laura back to the boy. She still doesn't know what it was, but she calls it an "invisible thread." There's an old Chinese proverb that says that an invisible thread **connects** two people who are destined to meet and **influence** each other. Laura believes she felt that thread. She turned back from the middle of the street and took the boy to lunch.

3   The boy lived in a single room in a welfare hotel with his mother and numerous other relatives. It was only two blocks away from Laura's home, but it might as well have been a different planet. As they talked over their lunch, Laura learned about the boy's life. She herself had not had an easy childhood, but what she heard shocked her, and before she left, she told him to phone her if he was ever hungry. When she didn't hear from him after several days, she returned to the spot they had met— and there he was, in the same clothes and too-tight sneakers. They arranged to meet again the next Monday.

4   Every Monday, Laura Schroff and Maurice Mazyck had dinner together. Some Mondays they ate at Laura's home, and Maurice discovered a life he had only seen on television. Gradually, Laura became the young boy's first role model. She **encouraged** him to have dreams about his future, and got involved in his education. Maurice's teacher was perhaps the only other person who believed in him, and she made Laura take a long hard look at what she was doing. Was she helping Maurice just as a way of helping herself? Could she commit to being there for Maurice even when she didn't feel like it? What kind of damage might it cause Maurice if she were to abandon him after becoming so important to him? Laura thought it through, and came to a decision.

5   The two continued sharing dinner every Monday, and a close **bond** formed between them. Laura introduced Maurice to new places, new ideas, and new possibilities. And Maurice became almost like the child Laura had always wanted. One day, she offered to make lunch for Maurice and leave it with her doorman for him to pick up on his way to school. He asked her if she could put the lunch in a brown paper bag, because then the other kids would know that someone cared about him.

6   Maurice had never left the city until Laura took him to visit her sister's family on Long Island. Her memory of their trip is a favorite one. She had expected Maurice to be amazed by the huge

front lawn and even larger backyard. But what amazed him the most was the large dining room table where they all sat down and talked and ate together. He declared that he wanted a table like that when he had a family of his own. Only months earlier, Maurice had seriously doubted that he would live to be an adult.

7   Laura and Maurice's relationship lasted, and in 1997 a magazine published an article, less than one page long, about it. Laura's friends suggested that she write a book telling the whole story. It was 10 years before she began writing—and another three years before she found a co-writer and started seriously getting down to business. The result of their work, *An Invisible Thread*, reached number one on the *New York Times* best sellers list.

8   Today, Maurice works in construction. He is the first person in his family to earn a paycheck. He has a family of his own, and his children are all very fond of their "Aunt Laurie." If you were to visit the family's apartment, you might notice that there is no couch in the living room. But there is a huge dining room table.

9   The writer Ernest Hemingway said, "The best way to find out if you can trust somebody is to trust them." Over the years, Laura discovered the truth of that statement. She feels that Maurice has given her one of the greatest gifts she has ever had. He repaid her trust by giving her life more meaning than her success at work ever did. He taught her to be grateful for what she has, and for the chance to share it. 🐌

Comprehension Check

Complete the following items after you finish your first read.

1. How did Laura Schroff and Maurice Mazyck meet?

2. What does the old Chinese proverb say connects two people who are destined to meet and influence each other?

3. What weekly ritual do Laura and Maurice begin after their first meeting?

4. What was Maurice's favorite part of the visit to Laura's sister?

5. Describe Maurice's adult life, professionally and personally.

Comprehension Check

6. How did Laura share the story of her relationship with Maurice with an audience?

7. 🗐 **Notebook** Write a timeline of key events in "A Simple Act."

- -

RESEARCH

Research to Clarify Choose at least one unfamiliar detail from the text. Briefly research that detail. In what way does the information you learned shed light on an aspect of the story?

Research to Explore Choose something that interested you from the text and formulate a research question about it.

A SIMPLE ACT

Close Read the Text

1. The model, from paragraph 6 of the essay, shows two sample annotations, along with questions and conclusions. Close read the passage and find another detail to annotate. Then, write a question and your conclusion.

> **ANNOTATE:** This passage describes what most impressed Maurice.
>
> **QUESTION:** Why does the writer include this information in the text?
>
> **CONCLUDE:** The writer shows that Maurice yearns for a close family, which he doesn't currently have.

Close Read
ANNOTATE · QUESTION · CONCLUDE

> **ANNOTATE:** The word *amazed* is repeated.
>
> **QUESTION:** Why does the author repeat this word?
>
> **CONCLUDE:** The author wants to emphasize that Maurice has a stronger interest in how the family spends time together than in property size.

> She had expected Maurice to be amazed by the huge front lawn and even larger backyard. But what amazed him the most was the large dining room table where they all sat down and talked and ate together. He declared that he wanted a table like that when he had a family of his own.

2. For more practice, go back into the text and complete the close-read notes.

3. Revisit a section of the text you found important during your first read. Read this section closely and **annotate** what you notice. Ask **questions** such as "Why did the author make this choice?" What can you **conclude**?

Analyze the Text

CITE TEXTUAL EVIDENCE
to support your answers.

📓 **Notebook** Respond to these questions.

1. (a) Analyze How does Maurice surprise Laura when he explains in paragraph 6 what he liked most about visiting Laura's sister? **(b) Infer** What do readers learn about Maurice's values?

2. Draw Conclusions How do both Laura and Maurice benefit from their relationship?

3. Evaluate In paragraph 7 the author mentions that a book about Laura and Maurice's friendship became a best-seller. Why do you think people became so interested in this friendship?

4. Essential Question *What can one generation learn from another?* What have you learned about how people of different generations learn from each other?

⊞ STANDARDS
Reading Informational Text
• Cite several pieces of textual evidence to support analysis of what the text says explicitly as well as inferences drawn from the text.
• Determine an author's point of view or purpose in a text and analyze how the author distinguishes his or her position from that of others.

Analyze Craft and Structure

Author's Point of View The attitudes and approach that an author takes in an informational text show the **author's point of view.** In some informational texts, authors take an objective approach, avoiding opinions and other biases. These texts are based almost entirely on factual information.

In other informational texts, authors are more subjective—mixing facts with their own commentary and interpretation. The commentary may take the form of direct opinions, or it may involve using **weighted words**—words that have strong emotional associations beyond their basic meanings.

- In "A Simple Act," the phrase "all of eleven years old" in paragraph 1 shows that the author is concerned that the boy was too young to be begging for money on the streets.
- In paragraph 4, the author writes that Maurice's teacher "made Laura take a long hard look at what she was doing" to show that the teacher took Maurice's situation very seriously.

In these paragraphs, the author uses weighted words to create sympathy for Maurice in the reader's mind.

Practice

CITE TEXTUAL EVIDENCE to support your answers.

Notebook Respond to these questions.

1. Reread paragraph 3, and use the chart to analyze the author's use of weighted words and phrases, and the effect these word choices have on readers.

WORD OR PHRASE	PRECISE MEANING	EFFECT

2. Explain how the weighted words in paragraph 3 affect the reader's understanding of the differences between Maurice's life and Laura's life.

3. Find an additional example of weighted words in paragraphs 5–9, and explain why the author might have chosen such language.

4. How would the reader's understanding of the article differ if the author had avoided using weighted words and used more objective language?

A SIMPLE ACT

Concept Vocabulary

connects	encouraged
influence	bond

Why These Words? The concept vocabulary words help to show relationships between people. For example, the old Chinese proverb says that an invisible thread *connects*, or joins together, two people who are destined to meet. In turn, these two people will *influence* each other, or affect each other in an important way. Notice that both words relate to the relationship between Laura and Maurice.

1. How does the concept vocabulary sharpen the reader's understanding of the relationship between Laura and Maurice?

2. Identify two other words in the selection that are related to this concept, and explain how they are related.

WORD NETWORK

Look in the text for words related to the topic of generations, and add them to your Word Network.

Practice

Notebook The concept words appear in "A Simple Act."

1. Use each concept word in a sentence that shows your understanding of each word's meaning.

2. Work with a partner, and take turns trying to list as many words as you can about interpersonal relationships.

Word Study

Multiple-Meaning Words A multiple-meaning word is a word with more than one definition. Sometimes the definitions of multiple-meaning words are similar, but in other cases they may be completely unrelated. For example, the word *bond*, which appears in "A Simple Act," has several different meanings. Write the meaning of *bond* as it is used in the fifth paragraph. Then, use a dictionary to find two more definitions of the word *bond*.

STANDARDS

Language
• Demonstrate command of the conventions of standard English grammar and usage when writing or speaking.
• Determine or clarify the meaning of unknown and multiple-meaning words and phrases based on *grade 7 reading and content,* choosing flexibly from a range of strategies.

Conventions

Adverbs An **adverb** is a word that modifies or describes a verb, adjective, or another adverb. These words provide information by answering the question *How? When? Where? How often?* or *To what extent?* Many adverbs end in the suffix *-ly*. This chart shows examples:

How?	Maurice asked *politely* for change.
When?	Laura said no, but *soon* changed her mind.
Where?	They went *inside* for a meal.
How often?	They *usually* met for dinner on Monday night.
To what extent?	Today, Maurice and Laura are *extremely* good friends.

Read It

1. Identify the adverb or adverbs in each sentence. Then, identify the word each adverb modifies or describes.

   a. Maurice and Laura shared meals regularly and enthusiastically.

   b. They often exchanged opinions and frequently agreed.

   c. Later, Laura befriended Maurice's children, too.

   d. Laura's book was very popular and deeply affected many readers.

2. Reread paragraphs 4–7 of the text. Mark the adverbs, identify the verbs they modify, and tell how these words clarify information.

Write It

📓 **Notebook** The sample sentence here was revised by adding an adverb that addresses the question in parentheses. Add adverbs to the sentences provided, based on the questions in parentheses.

> EXAMPLE
> Laura was glad she went back to meet Maurice. (To what extent was she glad?)
> Laura was **extremely** glad she went back to meet Maurice.

1. Maurice and Laura became good friends. (When did they become friends?)

2. Maurice confided in his new friend. (How did he confide?)

3. They pushed each other to try new things. (How often did they push each other?)

A SIMPLE ACT

Comparing Texts

You will now read an excerpt from *An Invisible Thread*. First, complete the first-read and close-read activities. Then, compare the point of view of "A Simple Act" with the point of view of *An Invisible Thread*.

from AN INVISIBLE THREAD

About the Authors

Laura Schroff had a career in advertising sales for more than 30 years and helped launch *USA Today* and several other highly successful publications. She is now a motivational speaker and encourages people to make a difference in the lives of others.

Alex Tresniowski is a writer based in New York City. He has been a senior writer for *People* magazine, writing human-interest, crime, and sports articles, and he is the co-author of several books, including *An Invisible Thread* and *The Vendetta*.

STANDARDS

Reading Informational Text
By the end of the year, read and comprehend literary nonfiction in the grades 6–8 text complexity band proficiently, with scaffolding as needed at the high end of the range.

from *An Invisible Thread*
Concept Vocabulary

You will encounter the following words as you read an excerpt from *An Invisible Thread*.

Before reading, note how familiar you are with each word. Then, rank the words in order from most familiar (1) to least familiar (3).

WORD	YOUR RANKING
resilience	
perseverance	
generosity	

After completing the first read, come back to the concept vocabulary and review your rankings. Mark changes to your original rankings as needed.

First Read NONFICTION

Apply these strategies as you conduct your first read. You will have an opportunity to complete the close-read notes after your first read.

NOTICE the general ideas of the text. *What* is it about? *Who* is involved?

ANNOTATE by marking vocabulary and key passages you want to revisit.

First Read

CONNECT ideas within the selection to what you already know and what you have already read.

RESPOND by competing the Comprehension Check and by writing a brief summary of the selection.

from An Invisible Thread

Laura Schroff and Alex Tresniowski

BACKGROUND

Laura Schroff and Maurice Mazyck had been friends for 15 years when he gave the final toast at the celebration of her 50th birthday. Maurice's words, and Laura's reaction to them, reveal what each had gained from their long friendship.

SCAN FOR MULTIMEDIA

1   Then came the final toast. The speaker was in a sharp black tuxedo with spectacular black-and-white shoes, and his wife was in a stunning navy blue gown, her hair swept up. Nearly everyone in the room had met him or at least knew his story, and so everyone was excited to see him and hear him speak. He kissed his wife, walked up and took the microphone, and began his toast.

2   "Laurie, where can I start," Maurice began. "We met . . . the way we met was so special to me. I was a young boy on the street with barely nothing, and I was very hungry that day and I asked this lady, 'Miss, can you spare some change?' And she walked away. And then she stopped. She was in the middle of the street— she almost got hit—and she looked and came back and took me to McDonald's. We ate and then walked around Central Park; she took me to Haagen-Dazs and then we played some games.

3   "You know, at that moment she saved my life. 'Cause I was going down the wrong road, the wrong hill, and, you know, my mother—bless her soul, my mother died—and the Lord sent me an angel. And my angel was Laurie.

4   "Without you," Maurice said, raising his glass, "I could not be the man I am today."

5   I was so incredibly moved when I heard Maurice say I saved his life. Heck, I nearly lost it throughout his whole darn toast. Whenever I hear someone tell me how lucky Maurice is to have

NOTES

CLOSE READ

ANNOTATE: In paragraphs 3 and 4, mark the punctuation.

QUESTION: Why do you think the author uses this type of punctuation in transcribing Maurice's words?

CONCLUDE: Would this passage have the same effect if it had just summarized what Maurice said? Explain.

resilience (rih ZIHL yuhns) *n.* ability to recover quickly

perseverance (pur suh VIHR uhns) *n.* continued, patient effort

generosity (jehn uhr AHS uh tee) *n.* willingness to give or share

met me, I have to stop them and correct them. The truth is that the lucky one is me.

6   Maurice taught me so many things; I can't possibly list them all. He taught me how to live. He taught me one of the most important lessons a person can hope to learn—he taught me to be grateful for what I have. He taught me about **resilience**, courage, **perseverance**, and about the special strength that comes from overcoming adversity. He taught me the true value of money, the real meaning of lunch in a brown paper bag, the importance of a silly ritual like baking cookies. He taught me, more than I ever taught him, what it means to be a friend.

7   Everything I ever gave to Maurice, he gave back to me tenfold. Every meal, every shirt, every bike or toothbrush, was matched by Maurice with a more genuine appreciation than I have ever known. Every hand I ever lent him was returned with a hug; every kindness was paid back with an impossibly optimistic smile. If love is the greatest gift of all—and I believe it is—then the greatest privilege of all is to be able to love someone. Maurice appeared out of nowhere and allowed me to love him, and for that, I simply can never thank him enough. His **generosity** of spirit continues to astound me, and to this day my relationship with him is the relationship I am most proud of in my life. ❧

MEDIA CONNECTION

Maurice's Toast

💬 **Discuss It** In what way does this video of Maurice's toast deepen your understanding of and appreciation for the text?

Write your response before sharing your ideas.

SCAN FOR MULTIMEDIA

Comprehension Check

Complete the following items after you finish your first read.

1. At what stage of his life does Maurice give a toast explaining how he and Laura met?

2. What statement does Maurice make that makes Laura "nearly lose it"?

3. How does Laura respond when people say that Maurice was lucky to meet her?

4. What does Laura say she learned from knowing Maurice?

5. According to Laura, what are the greatest gift and greatest privilege of all?

6. 🗐 **Notebook** Write a summary of the excerpt from *An Invisible Thread* to confirm your understanding of the selection.

- -

RESEARCH

Research to Clarify Choose at least one unfamiliar detail from the text. Briefly research that detail. In what way does the information you learned shed light on an aspect of the story?

Research to Explore Choose something that interests you from the text and formulate a research question.

from AN INVISIBLE THREAD

Close Read the Text

1. The model, from paragraph 1 of the essay, shows two sample annotations, along with questions and conclusions. Close read the passage, and find another detail to annotate. Then, write a question and your conclusion.

ANNOTATE: This phrase has unusual word order.

QUESTION: Why did the author choose to put the verb before the noun?

CONCLUDE: Using this word order makes the sentence seem more formal, which suits the setting of the scene.

ANNOTATE: The author uses vivid language here.

QUESTION: Why does the author provide so much detail about the speaker and his wife?

CONCLUDE: These details emphasize that Maurice has become successful.

> Then came the final toast. The speaker was in a sharp black tuxedo with spectacular black-and-white shoes, and his wife was in a stunning navy blue gown, her hair swept up.

2. For more practice, go back into the text and complete the close-read notes.

3. Revisit a section of the text you found important and **annotate** what you notice. Ask **questions** such as "Why did the author make this choice?" What can you **conclude**?

Analyze the Text

CITE TEXTUAL EVIDENCE to support your answers.

Notebook Respond to these questions.

1. Analyze In the first paragraph of the excerpt from her memoir, Laura Schroff gives the reader a positive impression of Maurice. Which of her word choices contribute most to this positive tone?

2. Draw Conclusions In his toast, Maurice says that when he asked Laura for spare change, at first she walked past him. Then, she stopped in the middle of the street, almost got hit by a car, and then walked back to him. Why do you think Laura turned around?

3. Interpret In paragraph 7, Laura says, "Everything I ever gave to Maurice, he gave back to me tenfold." What does this statement suggest about her friendship with Maurice?

4. Make Inferences Why do you think Maurice gave the final toast?

5. Essential Question: *What can one generation learn from another?* How did reading this excerpt affect your understanding of how people from different generations can learn from one another?

STANDARDS

Reading Informational Text
Determine an author's point of view or purpose in a text and analyze how the author distinguishes his or her position from that of others.

Analyze Craft and Structure

Narrative Point of View *An Invisible Thread* is a memoir written from the **first-person point of view.** You can tell a work of nonfiction is written from the first-person point of view by looking for the following clues.

- The author uses the pronoun *I* to refer to himself or herself.
- The author is involved in the events being described.
- Authors often use **direct quotations,** or a person's exact words, to reflect the views of other people involved in the narrative.

Memoirs are usually written from the first-person point of view. Authors of memoirs use the first-person point of view because they are describing events and experiences in their *own* lives—both what happened as well as personal reactions and emotions.

Practice

CITE TEXTUAL EVIDENCE to support your answers.

⊜ **Notebook** **Respond to these questions.**

1. Record two examples of first-person point of view in paragraphs 5–7 of the text. Rewrite each example to change the point of view to third person by using the pronoun *she*. An example is shown.

   Example: "**I** was so incredibly moved when **I** heard Maurice say **I** saved his life."
   She was so incredibly moved when **she** heard Maurice say **she** saved his life.

ORIGINAL PASSAGE	REWRITTEN PASSAGE

2. **(a)** When the text begins, the point of view is unclear. At what point in the text is it evident that it is written in the first-person point of view? **(b)** What clues in the text helped you to recognize point of view?

3. **(a)** What strategy do the writers of *An Invisible Thread* use to present Maurice's point of view? **(b)** Do you think this strategy is effective? Why or why not?

4. How do the ideas expressed by the first-person narrator in *An Invisible Thread* deepen your understanding of relationship between Laura and Maurice?

from AN INVISIBLE THREAD

Concept Vocabulary

| resilience | perseverance | generosity |

Why These Words? These concept vocabulary words show positive qualities or personality traits. Maurice and Laura demonstrate these qualities in their relationship with each other. For example, the way Maurice overcomes adversity teaches Laura about *resilience* and *perseverance*. Notice that both of these words show positive aspects of Maurice's personality.

1. How does the concept vocabulary sharpen your understanding of how both Laura and Maurice benefited from their relationship?

2. What other words in the selection connect to the concept of positive personality traits?

Practice

📓 **Notebook** The concept vocabulary words appear in the excerpt from *An Invisible Thread*.

1. Use each word in a sentence that demonstrates your understanding of the word's meaning.

2. Work with a partner, and take turns coming up with as many **synonyms,** or words with similar meanings, and **antonyms,** or words with opposite meanings, as you can for each concept vocabulary word.

Word Study

Latin Suffix: *-ity* The Latin suffix *-ity* means the "state, quality, or condition of." In the selection, the author refers to Maurice's "*generosity* of spirit."

1. Explain how the suffix *-ity* contributes to the meaning of the concept vocabulary word *generosity*.

2. Look at paragraph 6, and find another word that uses the suffix *-ity*. Identify the base word that was combined with the suffix. Write a definition for that word.

🔲 WORD NETWORK

Add words related to generations from the text to your Word Network.

☰ STANDARDS

Language
• Demonstrate command of the conventions of standard English capitalization, punctuation, and spelling when writing.
   a. Use a comma to separate coordinate adjectives.
• Determine or clarify the meaning of unknown and multiple-meaning words and phrases based on grade 7 reading and content, choosing flexibly from a range of strategies.
   b. Use common, grade-appropriate Greek or Latin affixes and roots as clues to the meaning of a word.
• Demonstrate understanding of figurative language, word relationships, and nuances in word meanings.
   b. Use the relationship between particular words to better understand each of the words.

Conventions

Adjectives An **adjective** is a word that modifies or describes a noun or pronoun. Adjectives may answer the question *What kind? How many? Which one?* or *Whose?* Possessive nouns and pronouns are used as adjectives to answer the question *Whose?*

What kind?	The young boy had a genuine smile.	Which one?	Have you read that book?
How many?	They talked for fifty minutes.	Whose?	I greatly admired Maurice's speech.

Two or More Adjectives Coordinate adjectives are two or more adjectives that modify the same noun and are separated by a comma. You can tell whether adjectives are coordinate if the word *and* could be used in place of the comma and you could reverse the adjectives. **Cumulative adjectives** also modify the same noun, but they are not separated by a comma. Cumulative adjectives cannot be reversed.

COORDINATE ADJECTIVES	CUMULATIVE ADJECTIVES
They became lifelong, devoted friends. You could say: *They became devoted and lifelong friends.*	She wore a light blue sweater. (*She wore a blue light sweater* does not mean the same thing.)

Read It

Identify the adjectives in each sentence, and name the nouns they modify. Then tell whether the adjectives are coordinate or cumulative and explain why.

1. Maurice gave an emotional, heartfelt speech.
2. His warm good nature inspired many listeners.
3. The book teaches many valuable life lessons.

Write It

The original sentence in the example below was revised by adding two adjectives. Review the example, and then add two adjectives to each practice sentence. Separate the adjectives with commas if needed.

> EXAMPLE
> **Original:** Laura wrote a memoir.
> **Revision:** Laura wrote an *unforgettable personal* memoir.

1. Maurice shared a story with the audience.

2. Laura wore a dress.

🔲 **Notebook** Write a paragraph describing Laura and Maurice's relationship. Include at least one pair of coordinate and one pair of cumulative adjectives.

A SIMPLE ACT

from AN INVISIBLE THREAD

Writing to Compare

You have read two selections about the friendship between Laura Stroff and Maurice Mazyck: the news blog "A Simple Act" and the excerpt from the memoir *An Invisible Thread*. Now, deepen your analysis and express your observations in writing.

Assignment

The news blog and the memoir tell about how Laura and Maurice's friendship helped them both. To prepare for your assignment, consider the following:

- How the friendship started and grew
- Why the friendship lasted so long

Write an **explanatory essay** in which you analyze ways in which the authors of the two pieces present information about the same topic: the friendship between Laura and Maurice.

Analyze the Texts

Gather Evidence Reread both "A Simple Act" and the excerpt from *An Invisible Thread* to examine the key information that the two authors provide when describing their friendship. Use the chart to record your notes.

As you gather evidence, ask yourself the following questions:

- What descriptive details do the two texts provide?
- What quotations, if any, are used?
- Does the text focus on a series of events or more on the quality of the friendship?

	Types of Details Used	Overall Effect of the Text
A Simple Act		
from An Invisible Thread		

Copyright © SAVVAS Learning Company LLC. All Rights Reserved.

▤ STANDARDS

Reading Informational Text
Analyze how two or more authors writing about the same topic shape their presentations of key information by emphasizing different evidence or advancing different interpretations of facts.

Writing
Draw evidence from literary or informational texts to support analysis, reflection, and research.

🖸 **Notebook** Respond to these questions.

1. How do the two texts differ in their presentation of the benefits of friendship?

2. What key information is the same across the two texts?

3. In which text is the emphasis on friendship more apparent? Explain your response.

Planning and Prewriting

Determine Your Central Idea In one sentence, write the central idea, or thesis, you will develop in your essay:

Central Idea/Thesis:_____

_____

Create an Outline To help you structure your essay, create an outline to organize your ideas.

Outline

I. Types of Details Used

    A. "A Simple Act"

    B. excerpt from *An Invisible Thread*

II. Overall Effect of the Text

    A. "A Simple Act"

    B. excerpt from *An Invisible Thread*

Drafting

Write a First Draft Use your completed outline to write your first draft. Develop your essay with details from the texts and present a smooth and logical explanation of your ideas. Use clear language and transitions to connect your ideas.

Use Transition Words Using transition words can help you present your ideas in a logical sequence and you make your essay flow more smoothly. There are several types of transitional words and phrases.
- Words and phrases that show **similarities:** *also, in addition, likewise*
- Words and phrases that show **differences:** *but, however, yet*
- Words and phrases that show **sequence:** *first, next, then, finally*
- Words and phrases that show **examples:** *for example, for instance*

Review and Revise

Once you are done writing, critically review your essay. Make sure you have given specific examples to support your ideas. Then, check to be sure you have used transitions to link those ideas. Finally, proofread your work to ensure it is free from errors in grammar, spelling, and punctuation.

✐ EVIDENCE LOG

Before moving on to a new selection, go to your Evidence Log and record what you learned from these selections.

☰ STANDARDS

Writing
Write informative/explanatory texts to examine a topic and convey ideas, concepts, and information through the selection, organization, and analysis of relevant content.
  b. Develop the topic with relevant facts, definitions, concrete details, quotations, or other information and examples.
  c. Use appropriate transitions to create cohesion and clarify the relationships among ideas and concepts.

Language
Demonstrate command of the conventions of standard English capitalization, punctuation, and spelling when writing.
  b. Spell correctly.

- TWO KINDS

- A SIMPLE ACT

- *from* AN INVISIBLE THREAD

🔧 **Tool Kit**

Student Model of a
Nonfiction Narrative

ACADEMIC VOCABULARY

As you craft your
argument, consider using
some of the academic
vocabulary you learned in
the beginning of the unit.

dialogue
consequence
perspective
notable
contradict

☷ STANDARDS

Writing
• Write narratives to develop
real or imagined experiences or
events using effective technique,
relevant descriptive details, and
well- structured event sequences.
• Write routinely over extended time
frames and shorter time frames for
a range of discipline-specific tasks,
purposes, and audiences.

Write a Nonfiction Narrative

You have just read texts in which people of different generations have an
influence on each other's lives. In "Two Kinds," an ambitious mother ends
up teaching her child unexpected but valuable lessons. "A Simple Act"
and the excerpt from *An Invisible Thread* present the story of two friends
whose chance meeting enriched both of their lives. Now you will use your
knowledge of these texts to write a nonfiction narrative about the ways
in which people of different generations can influence each other.

Assignment

Write a **nonfiction narrative** about the influence someone from
a different generation has had on you or someone you know. In
your narrative, draw on the texts you have read in this section. Your
narrative should answer this question:

> What unexpected event shows how a person can
> influence someone from a different generation?

Elements of a Nonfiction Narrative

A **nonfiction narrative** is a story of something that actually happened.
In a personal narrative, the writer uses the first-person point of view
(employing pronouns *I* and *me*) to tell the true story of something that he
or she has experienced. Other nonfiction narratives, such as biography,
are written from the third-person point of view.

An engaging nonfiction narrative contains these elements:

- well-developed major and minor characters as well as a narrator, who
  is you, the writer

- a problem or conflict

- a clear sequence of events that unfolds naturally and logically

- narrative techniques such as dialogue, description, and pacing

- a variety of transitional words, phrases, and clauses to convey
  sequence and signal shifts from one setting or time frame to another

- precise words, well-chosen quotations, vivid descriptive details, and
  powerful sensory language

- a conclusion that follows from and reflects on the experiences in
  the narrative

Model Nonfiction Narrative For a model of a
well-crafted nonfiction narrative, see the Launch
Text, "Grounded."

Challenge yourself to find all of the elements of an
effective nonfiction narrative in the text. You will
have an opportunity to review these elements as
you prepare to write your own nonfiction narrative.

Prewriting / Planning

Focus Your Topic Reread the assignment. Consider the person and event you would like to highlight in your narrative. State your main idea in a sentence:

_____ helped to influence _____
     (person from generation 1)   (person from generation 2)

by _____.
            (action that influenced person from generation 2)

Develop Characters Realistic, engaging characters make a narrative come alive. Think about each character you will include in your narrative. List traits and descriptive details that make him or her unique and interesting. Consider the ways in which dialogue between the characters will help propel the action in your narrative. Don't forget to include yourself as the narrator!

CHARACTERS	TRAITS	DETAILS/DIALOGUE

Gather Details Details for a nonfiction narrative come mainly from your own memories and experiences. A photo album or a conversation with a relative may stimulate your memory and help you find a topic.

There are many different types of details you can use to craft your nonfiction narrative:

- **anecdotes:** brief stories that illustrate a point or key idea
- **dialogue/quotations:** statements from personal interviews or conversations with the people who are featured in your narrative
- **examples:** facts, ideas, and events that support an idea or insight

Study the Launch Text to identify ways in which the writer uses various types of details to develop characters and ideas.

EVIDENCE LOG

Review your Evidence Log and identify types of details you may want to cite in your nonfiction narrative.

STANDARDS

Writing
Write narratives to develop real or imagined experiences or events using effective technique, relevant descriptive details, and well-structured event sequences.

   b. Use narrative techniques, such as dialogue, pacing, and description, to develop experiences, events, and/or characters.

Drafting

Organize a Sequence of Events In a nonfiction narrative, the writer often sequences events in **chronological order**, so that one event proceeds to the next in the order in which they actually happened.

Use a timeline to organize your narrative so that it flows in chronological order. Then, add details to elaborate on the action. The timeline here shows key events in the Launch Text. Use it as a model to construct a timeline of your own narrative.

MODEL: "Grounded" Timeline

INTRODUCTION
Narrator, Grandma, and their relationship are described.

1. Parents talk about Grandma's driving.

2. Narrator is grounded.

3. Narrator asks Grandma for a ride to a party.

4. Narrator and Grandma feel bad on the ride.

5. Grandma asks to turn back; narrator agrees.

CONCLUSION
Grandma and narrator have learned from each other and share an understanding.

Nonfiction Narrative Timeline

INTRODUCTION

1.

2.

3.

4.

5.

CONCLUSION

STANDARDS

Writing
• Engage and orient the reader by establishing a context and point of view and introducing a narrator and/or characters; organize an event sequence that unfolds naturally and logically.
• Use a variety of transition words, phrases, and clauses to convey sequence and signal shifts from one time frame or setting to another.

Use Transitions To make the sequence of events in your narrative clear to readers, use transition words, such as *first, then, next, later,* and *finally,* to establish a clear chronological order. Use the numbered events in your timeline to help you determine which transition words to use and where in your writing to use them.

Write a First Draft Refer to your timeline as you write your first draft. As you draft your narrative, refer to the elements of nonfiction narrative writing as well as your Prewriting/Planning notes.

Develop Technique: Finding Your Voice

Voice A writer's distinctive style is referred to as **voice**, and it can be influenced by word choice, **sentence structure** (the way the author constructs a sentence), and **tone**—the writer's attitude toward his or her subject. Developing a unique voice can take time. These tips and activities will help get you started.

Read It

This chart shows examples from the Launch Text that contribute to the author's voice.

Word Choice	*singing at the top of her lungs; just beginning to darken with blue clouds against a darker blue sky*
Varied Sentence Structure and Dialogue	*We took off. She drove slowly, maybe too slowly. "Bueno," she said, with a nod.*
Reflective, Genuine Tone	*But how could I say any of this? I was so relieved I could have cried.*

Write It

As you draft your nonfiction narrative, think of ways in which you can develop your voice. To do so, ask yourself questions such as: *What should the tone of my narrative be? What emotions do I want the audience to experience?* and *How can I make my personality as narrator more authentic?*

Also pay close attention to your sentence structures, and strive to mimic real speech patterns. When writing from the first-person point of view, you might be inclined to begin many of your sentences with the pronoun *I*, which will create a repetitive, dull pattern. This chart provides strategies to help you avoid repetitive sentence beginnings and create variety.

STANDARDS

Writing
Write narratives to develop real or imagined experiences or events using effective technique, relevant descriptive details, and well-structured event sequences.

d. Use precise words and phrases, relevant descriptive details, and sensory language to capture the action and convey experiences and events.

ORIGINAL	STRATEGY TO ADD VARIETY	REVISION
I was surprised to see my sister on the stage.	*Start your sentence with a word that describes your emotion or mood.*	Startled, I noticed the familiar figure of my sister on the stage.
I rushed to congratulate her after the play ended.	*Move another part of the sentence to the beginning.*	After the play ended, I rushed to congratulate her.
I said her portrayal of the character was so realistic I forgot she was my sister.	*Start with a real quotation instead of writing that someone said something.*	"Great job!" I exclaimed. "You really made me believe you were Alice."

Revising

Evaluating Your Draft

Use the following checklist to evaluate the effectiveness of your first draft. Then, use your evaluation and the instruction on this page to guide your revision.

FOCUS AND ORGANIZATION	EVIDENCE AND ELABORATION	CONVENTIONS
☐ Provides an introduction that establishes a clear context and point of view.	☐ Effectively uses narrative techniques, such as dialogue, pacing, and description.	☐ Attends to the norms and conventions of the discipline.
☐ Presents a clear chronological sequence of events that are linked by clarifying transitions.	☐ Uses descriptive details, sensory language, and precise words and phrases.	
☐ Provides a conclusion that follows from and reflects on the events and experiences in the narrative.	☐ Establishes voice through word choice, sentence structure, and tone.	

🔀 WORD NETWORK

Include interesting words from your Word Network in your personal narrative.

☰ STANDARDS

Writing
• Write narratives to develop real or imagined experiences or events using effective technique, relevant descriptive details, and well-structured event sequences.
  a. Engage and orient the reader by establishing a context and point of view and introducing a narrator and/or characters; organize an event sequence that unfolds naturally and logically.
  d. Use precise words and phrases, relevant descriptive details, and sensory language to capture the action and convey experiences and events.
  e. Provide a conclusion that follows from and reflects on the narrated experiences or events.
• Produce clear and coherent writing in which the development, organization, and style are appropriate to task, purpose, and audience.

Revising for Focus and Organization

Provide a Clear Conclusion The conclusion of a nonfiction narrative clarifies the overall message and provides readers with a sense of **resolution**, or completion. It resolves any conflicts or questions presented in the narrative. To increase the clarity of your conclusion, check to be sure that it follows logically from the body of your essay. Then, consider whether your conclusion provides a fresh insight on your topic.

Revising for Evidence and Elaboration

Use Precise Language In order to craft a lively narrative that engages readers, avoid words and language that leave the reader with questions such as *What kind? How? In what way? How often?* and *To what extent?* As you review your draft, identify vague words that do not provide specific answers to questions such as those in the previous sentence. As you revise, replace these vague words with specific, precise words that convey your ideas more vividly and accurately. Here are some examples:

vague noun: *stuff*	use	*souvenirs, gifts, photos*
vague verb: *said*	use	*exclaimed, whispered, declared*
vague adjective: *pretty*	use	*attractive, exquisite, adorable*
vague adverb: *greatly*	use	*enormously, incredibly, remarkably*

Adjust Pacing Read through your draft. If part of your story seems to lag or feel boring, try one of the following: Cut unneeded plot events; put dialogue in place of description; or shorten the sentences so that events seem to happen more rapidly.

PEER REVIEW

Exchange narratives with a classmate. Use the checklist to evaluate your classmate's narrative, and provide supportive feedback.

1. Is the point of view clear, and are the characters well developed?

☐ yes   ☐ no   If no, suggest how the writer might improve them.

2. Is there a clear sequence of events that unfolds chronologically and is clarified by transitions?

☐ yes   ☐ no   If no, explain what confused you.

3. Does the narrative end with a conclusion that connects to and reflects on the events and experiences presented?

☐ yes   ☐ no   If no, tell what you think might be missing.

4. What is the strongest part of your classmate's narrative? Why?

_____

_____

Editing and Proofreading

Edit for Conventions Reread your draft for accuracy and consistency. Correct errors in grammar and word usage. Be sure you have included a variety of sentence structures and word choices that reflect your unique voice.

Proofread for Accuracy Read your draft carefully, looking for errors in spelling and punctuation. As you proofread, make sure that any **dialogue**—the actual words spoken by a character—is enclosed in quotation marks. A split dialogue is a quotation that is interrupted by the inclusion of additional information, such as the identification of the speaker. Refer to the Launch Text for examples of each type of dialogue.

Publishing and Presenting

Create a final version of your narrative. Share it with a small group so that your classmates can read it and make comments. In turn, review and comment on your classmates' work. As a group, discuss what your narratives have in common and the ways in which they are different.

Reflecting

Reflect on what you learned as you wrote your narrative. In what ways did writing about past experiences and events help to heighten your understanding of them? What was the most challenging aspect of composing your narrative? Did you learn something from reviewing the work of others and discussing your narrative that might inform your narrative writing process in the future?

▤ STANDARDS

Writing
With some guidance and support from peers and adults, develop and strengthen writing as needed by planning, revising, editing, rewriting, or trying a new approach, focusing on how well purpose and audience have been addressed.

ESSENTIAL QUESTION:

What can one generation learn from another?

What people value can change from one generation to the next, but there are always some common threads despite these differences. You can gain new insight and knowledge when you understand the values and challenges facing other generations. You will work in a group to continue your exploration of the relationship between generations.

Small-Group Learning Strategies

Throughout your life, you'll continue to develop strategies that make you a better learner. In school, in your community, in college, and in your career, you will continue to learn and work in teams.

Look at these strategies and the actions you can take to practice them. Add ideas of your own for each step. Get ready to use these strategies during Small-Group Learning.

STRATEGY	ACTION PLAN
Prepare	• Complete your assignments so that you are prepared for group work. • Organize your thinking so you can contribute to your group's discussions. •
Participate fully	• Make eye contact to signal that you are listening and taking in what is being said. • Use text evidence when making a point. •
Support others	• Build off ideas from others in your group. • Invite others who have not yet spoken to do so. •
Clarify	• Paraphrase the ideas of others to ensure that your understanding is correct. • Ask follow-up questions. •

SCAN FOR
MULTIMEDIA

CONTENTS

PERFORMANCE TASK

SPEAKING AND LISTENING FOCUS
Present a Nonfiction Narrative

The Small-Group readings explore the insights that people of different generations share with each other. After reading, your group will plan and deliver a multimedia presentation about a lesson one generation can learn from another.

Working as a Team

1. Discuss the Topic In your group, discuss the following question:

> **What kinds of ideas and experiences can young people and adults share?**

As you take turns sharing your thoughts, be sure to provide examples for your response. After all group members have shared, discuss the similarities and differences among your responses.

2. List Your Rules As a group, decide on the rules that you will follow as you work together. Two samples are provided. Add two more of your own. You may add or revise rules based on your experience together.

- Everyone should participate in group discussions.
- People should not interrupt.

- _____

  _____

- _____

  _____

3. Apply the Rules Before you engage in group discussions or activities, review the rules and adapt them as needed based on your group's experience.

4. Name Your Group Choose a name that reflects the unit topic.

Our group's name: _____

5. Create a Communication Plan Decide how you want to communicate with one another. For example, you might use online collaboration tools, email, or instant messaging.

Our group's decision: _____

_____

Making a Schedule

First, find out the due dates for the small-group activities. Then, preview the texts and activities with your group and make a schedule for completing the tasks.

SELECTION	ACTIVITIES	DUE DATE
Tutors Teach Seniors New High-Tech Tricks		
from Mom & Me & Mom Learning to Love My Mother		
Mother-Daughter Drawings		
Mother to Son To James		

Working on Group Projects

Different projects require different roles. As your group works together, you'll find it more effective if each person has a specific role. Before beginning a project, decide among yourselves on each group member's role. Here are some possible roles; add your own ideas.

Project Manager: monitors the schedule and keeps everyone on task

Researcher: organizes research activities

Recorder: takes notes during group meetings

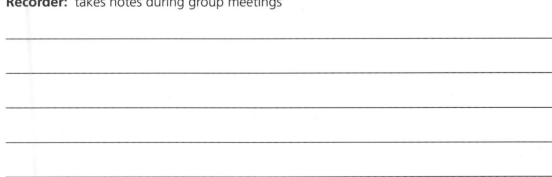

 SCAN FOR MULTIMEDIA

About the Author

Jennifer Ludden (b. 1967) is a correspondent for National Public Radio (NPR). Ludden has won and shared in several awards for her work as a foreign reporter covering the Middle East, Europe, and West and Central Africa. She graduated from Syracuse University in 1988.

Tutors Teach Seniors New High-Tech Tricks

Concept Vocabulary

You will encounter the following words as you read "Tutors Teach Seniors New High-Tech Tricks."

struggling	impairments	frustrated

Context Clues To find the meaning of unfamiliar words, look for clues in the context, which is made up of the surrounding words and phrases.

> **Example:** To edit the photo on her laptop, Sigrid had to **download** a new program.
>
> **Context clue:** To get a new program on your computer, you need to **download** it.
>
> **Possible meaning:** To **download** means "to transfer data to your computer."
>
> **Example:** My computer is infected with a nasty **worm**.
>
> **Context clues:** The word *nasty* means "unpleasant," and it describes the worm that has *infected* a *computer*.
>
> **Possible meaning:** A **worm** means "a computer bug" or "problem."

Apply your knowledge of context clues and other vocabulary strategies to determine the meanings of unfamiliar words you encounter during your first read.

First Read NONFICTION

Apply these strategies as you conduct your first read. You will have an opportunity to complete a close read after your first read.

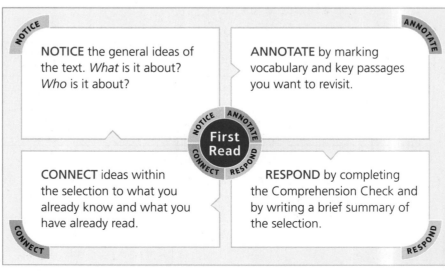

NOTICE the general ideas of the text. *What* is it about? *Who* is it about?

ANNOTATE by marking vocabulary and key passages you want to revisit.

First Read

CONNECT ideas within the selection to what you already know and what you have already read.

RESPOND by completing the Comprehension Check and by writing a brief summary of the selection.

▤ **STANDARDS**

Reading Informational Text
By the end of the year, read and comprehend literary nonfiction in the grades 6–8 text complexity band proficiently, with scaffolding as needed at the high end of the range.

Language
Determine or clarify the meaning of unknown and multiple-meaning words and phrases based on *grade 7 reading and conten*t, choosing flexibly from a range of strategies.

  a. Use context as a clue to the meaning of a word or phrase.

Tutors Teach Seniors
New High-Tech Tricks
Jennifer Ludden

BACKGROUND

Modern technology allows us to easily connect with one another. People can instantaneously share photographs and have face-to-face conversations with friends and family both down the street and on the other side of the world. However, technology changes so quickly that senior citizens are often left behind.

SCAN FOR
MULTIMEDIA

1   A week after Christmas, many Americans are no doubt trying to figure out how to use the high-tech gadgets they got as gifts. This can be especially challenging for seniors. But a number of programs across the country are finding just the right experts to help usher older adults into the digital age.

2   For Pamela Norr, of Bend, Ore., the light bulb went off as she, yet again, was trying to help her own elder parents with a tech problem. To whom did she turn?

3   "My teenage kids," she says.

4   Norr happens to head the Central Oregon Council on Aging, and thus was born TECH—Teenager Elder Computer Help.

5   "I thought if my parents need it, probably other seniors need it, too," she says.

6   High school students studying computer tech or involved with the National Honor Society sign up to teach local senior citizens about Facebook, Skype, smartphones, even something as seemingly simple as a camera. Norr discovered that many seniors had been given digital cameras by their children.

7   "They were going around town taking all these great pictures that they wanted to send to their family members," she says. But

NOTES

they "couldn't figure out how to connect to the USB port[1] or take out the SIM card.[2]"

8　　Many elders have moved to central Oregon to retire. Sigrid Scully, 84, signed up for a TECH class because she was **struggling** to stay connected with far-flung family.

9　　"My kids were not returning calls," she says. "They don't write letters. They are so knowledgeable about texting and email, and so I needed to get to know how to do that."

10　　Scully worried she'd never catch on. She'd read a computer manual once, but didn't understand words like "icon" or "cookies." She says her teen tutor was personable and used plain language.

11　　"So many teenagers think that seniors are just old people that don't know anything," she says. "And actually, the camaraderie and knowledge that we can transmit to one another is so wonderful and so helpful. I had that feeling with this class."

Sensitivity Training

12　　"It has made me think about what life was like without Facebook and the Internet," says 15-year-old Tucker Rampton, who's helped train about a dozen Oregon seniors. He's been surprised to have to explain email, something he thought everyone had mastered. Then again, a lot of seniors ask him about Twitter, which Rampton admits he knows nothing about. He says teaching tech to seniors has changed his perspective.

13　　"I think it's a very good idea to work on your patience," he says, "and be more understanding when it comes to what's going on in their minds."

14　　At Pace University in New York, college students who tutor seniors in local retirement homes are prepped with sensitivity training.

15　　"They get to feel what it's like to be 70, 80, 90 years old," says associate professor Jean Coppola, who directs the program. "They wear specially prepared glasses that give them different visual **impairments.**"

16　　Coppola also has students do things like tape two fingers together—to simulate the effects of arthritis or a stroke—then try to navigate a mouse. By the time they're at the computer with an elder, she says, they're not **frustrated** at all.

17　　"They'll say something a hundred times because they've worn cotton balls or earplugs in their ear," she says. "They understand that they have to speak up, articulate their words."

---

1. **USB port** *n.* computer hardware for connecting other devices to computers.
2. **SIM card** *n.* smart card used in cell phones to store identification information.

18   Coppola says the whole thing is a bonding experience for both generations. Applause often breaks out the first time a senior receives an email. Some have been able to see new grandchildren for the first time through emailed photos.

19   Pamela Norr, in Oregon, says young trainers also gain new confidence. They see that the seniors are "not criticizing me for the way I dress," she says, "or clucking their tongue. They're actually respecting me for the knowledge base that I have."

20   Perhaps most unexpected, some teen trainers and seniors have even become friends. They keep in touch long after class ends— through Facebook, of course. ❧

MEDIA CONNECTION

Cyber-Seniors

💬 **Discuss It** What benefits do young people get when they teach seniors about technology and the Internet?

Write your response before sharing your ideas.

SCAN FOR MULTIMEDIA

Comprehension Check

📓 **Notebook** Complete the following items after you finish your first read. Review and clarify details with your group.

1. What situation led Pamela Norr to start TECH—Teenager Elder Computer Help?

2. What kinds of things do seniors want to do with computers and other tech devices?

3. In the Pace University program, how did teenagers experience what it is like to be an older person?

4. Write a summary of the selection that answers *Who, What, Where, When, Why,* and *How?*

- -

RESEARCH

Research to Clarify Briefly research at least one unfamiliar detail from the selection. In what way does the information shed light on an aspect of the article?

TIP

GROUP DISCUSSION

If you do not fully understand a classmate's comment, don't hesitate to ask for clarification. Use a friendly and respectful tone when you ask.

🔀 WORD NETWORK

Look in the text for words related to the topic of generations, and add them to your Word Network.

⠿ STANDARDS

Reading Informational Text
• Cite several pieces of textual evidence to support analysis of what the text says explicitly as well as inferences drawn from the text.
• Determine two or more central ideas in a text and analyze their development over the course of the text; provide an objective summary of the text.

Language
Determine or clarify the meaning of unknown and multiple-meaning words and phrases based on *grade 7 reading and content,* choosing flexibly from a range of strategies.
c. Consult general and specialized reference materials, both print and digital, to find the pronunciation of a word or determine or clarify its precise meaning or its part of speech.

Close Read the Text

With your group, revisit sections of the text you marked during your first read. **Annotate** details that you notice. What **questions** do you have? What can you **conclude**?

Analyze the Text

> **CITE TEXTUAL EVIDENCE**
> to support your answers.

📓 **Notebook** Complete the activities.

1. **Review and Clarify** With your group, reread paragraphs 12–13 of the selection. Discuss how helping seniors with tech problems has changed the perspective of Tucker Rampton. In what way has reading this selection changed your own perspective?

2. **Present and Discuss** Share with your group the passages from the selection that you found especially important. Take turns presenting your passages. Discuss what you noticed in the selection, what questions you asked, and what conclusions you reached.

3. **Essential Question:** *What can one generation learn from another?* What has this article taught you about how different generations can learn from one another? Discuss with your group.

LANGUAGE DEVELOPMENT

Concept Vocabulary

struggling	impairments	frustrated

Why These Words? The concept vocabulary words from the text are related. With your group, determine what the words have in common. Write your ideas and add another word that fits the category.

Practice

📓 **Notebook** Confirm your understanding of the concept vocabulary words by using each word in a sentence that demonstrates your understanding of the word.

Word Study

📓 **Notebook** **Suffix: -*ment*** The suffix -*ment* means "the result of an action." When added to a verb (the action), the suffix creates a noun. Use a dictionary to find the meaning of the following words that contain the suffix -*ment: advertisement, amusement, settlement.* Explain how the suffix -*ment* contributes to the meaning of each word.

Analyze Craft and Structure

Development of Central Ideas The **central idea,** or **main idea,** is the most important point in a text. Sometimes the writer directly states the central idea of a text. More often, the central idea is unstated, or implied. When a central idea is implied, readers must **make inferences,** or educated guesses, from the details included in the text in order to determine the central idea.

When you read nonfiction, adjust your reading rate to help you recognize the central idea.

- **Skim,** or look over the text quickly, to get a sense of important ideas before you begin reading.
- **Read closely** to learn what the central ideas are.
- **Scan,** or run your eyes over the text, to find answers to questions, to clarify, or to find supporting details.

Practice

> **CITE TEXTUAL EVIDENCE** to support your answers.

📝 **Notebook** Respond to these questions.

1. What details does the article provide to support the central idea that teens are well-suited to help seniors with technology?

2. (a) Complete the chart below to help you analyze the development of central ideas in the article. Identify the needs of each group, what group members provided for each other, and how they benefited from each other.

	WHAT THEY NEED	WHAT THEY PROVIDE	HOW GROUP BENEFITS
Seniors	Seniors have difficulty with high-tech gadgets.		
Teens		Teens share technology expertise.	Teens gain confidence.

(b) Review your chart entries. How well do the needs of each group match what the other group is able to provide? Explain.

3. How does the author's use of quotations from program participants contribute to the development of central ideas?

4. At the end of the article, the author describes how seniors and teens continue to maintain their friendships through Facebook. In what way does this detail connect with the central idea of the text?

TUTORS TEACH SENIORS NEW
HIGH-TECH TRICKS

Conventions

Conjunctions connect parts of a sentence. Coordinating and subordinating conjunctions both clarify relationships between ideas. **Coordinating conjunctions** connect words, phrases, and clauses of equal importance. **Subordinating conjunctions** connect a less important clause to a more important clause.

TYPE OF CONJUNCTION	CONJUNCTIONS	EXAMPLES
coordinating	*and, but, for, nor, or, so, yet*	**Original:** Tommy was tired. He watched the movie anyway. **Revised:** *Tommy was tired but watched the movie anyway.*
subordinating	*after, although, as, as if, as long as, because, before, even though, how, if, in order that, since, so that, than, that, though, till, unless, until, when, whenever, where, whereas, wherever, whether, while, why*	**Original:** Gabby made her bed. It was evening. **Revised:** *Gabby made her bed even though it was evening.*

Read It

Identify the conjunction in each sentence. Label each conjunction as coordinating or subordinating.

1. Sigrid joined the program because she had no idea how to send email.

2. Today, Omar will teach seniors how to email or how to use a digital camera.

Write It

📝 **Notebook** Sometimes, too many short sentences in a row can seem choppy and unclear. Using conjunctions can create a smoother writing style. To fix short and choppy sentences, rewrite them by following these steps. First, identify whether the ideas in the sentences are of equal importance or unequal importance. Then, combine the sentences using either coordinating or subordinating conjunctions. Look at the example, and then revise the sentences provided.

> EXAMPLE
>
> **Original:** Pamela couldn't download an app. She asked her teenaged son for help.
>
> **Revised:** *Pamela couldn't download an app until she asked her teenaged son for help.*

1. Edward's tech class ended. He enrolled in additional computer classes.

2. Marsha mumbled. Steve understood every word she said.

STANDARDS

Language
• Demonstrate command of the conventions of standard English grammar and usage when writing or speaking.
• Use knowledge of language and its conventions when writing, speaking, reading, or listening.

  a. Choose language that expresses ideas precisely and concisely, recognizing and eliminating wordiness and redundancy.

Speaking and Listening

Assignment

Work with your group to create a **multimedia presentation** in which you incorporate text, charts, images, videos, music, or other media that help you to convey your ideas effectively. Choose from the following topics:

☐ an **instructional brochure** in which you explain to seniors how to use a technology application

☐ a **program proposal** in which you present an idea for a program that would connect teens and seniors in new ways

EVIDENCE LOG

Before moving on to a new selection, go to your log and record what you learned from "Tutors Teach Seniors New High-Tech Tricks."

Project Plan Make a list of tasks that your group will need to carry out. Assign individual group members to carry out each task. Determine how you will obtain or create multimedia items for your presentation. Use this chart to organize your plans.

TASK	WHO	QUESTIONS TO ANSWER

Organize and Practice Organize your project plan by making a script that includes speakers' lines and indicates media cues. Then, practice your presentation before you present it to your class. Use the following techniques:

- Record each speaker and then play the recording to ensure all are speaking clearly and with adequate volume.

- Work on transitions between speakers and various media to ensure the presentation flows smoothly.

- Time your presentation to ensure that it is paced appropriately. Slow down when necessary so that your audience can understand what you are saying.

Present and Evaluate Present your work to the class, and invite questions when you are finished. Listen to the presentations of other groups, and ask questions if anything is unclear. Note presentation techniques and creative ideas in other groups' presentations that you found interesting.

STANDARDS

Speaking and Listening
- Engage effectively in a range of collaborative discussions with diverse partners on *grade 7 topics, texts, and issues,* building on others' ideas and expressing their own clearly.
  - b. Follow rules for collegial discussions, track progress toward specific goals and deadlines, and define individual roles as needed.
  - c. Pose questions that elicit elaboration and respond to others' questions and comments with relevant observations and ideas that bring the discussion back on topic as needed.
  - d. Acknowledge new information expressed by others and, when warranted, modify their own views.
- Present claims and findings, emphasizing salient points in a focused, coherent manner with pertinent descriptions, facts, details, and examples; use appropriate eye contact, adequate volume, and clear pronunciation.
- Include multimedia components and visual displays in presentations to clarify claims and findings and emphasize salient points.

Writing
Conduct short research projects to answer a question, drawing on several sources and generating additional related, focused questions for further research and investigation.

from MOM & ME & MOM

Comparing Text to Media

In this lesson, you will read an excerpt from Maya Angelou's memoir *Mom & Me & Mom*. Then, you will watch a video in which Angelou discusses her relationship with her mother. The work your group does on this selection will prepare you to compare it with the video.

LEARNING TO LOVE MY MOTHER

About the Author

Born Marguerite Johnson, **Maya Angelou** (1928–2014) struggled with racism, poverty, and ill treatment early in her life. Across her long career she was a dancer, actress, singer, teacher, and writer. Angelou became one of the best-known African American authors in the world, and she was an activist for women and for the African American community.

STANDARDS

Reading Informational Text
By the end of the year, read and comprehend literary nonfiction in the grades 6–8 text complexity band proficiently, with scaffolding as needed at the high end of the range.

Language
Determine or clarify the meaning of unknown and multiple-meaning words and phrases based on *grade 7 reading and content,* choosing flexibly from a range of strategies.

70 UNIT 1 • GENERATIONS

from Mom & Me & Mom

Concept Vocabulary

As you perform your first read of the excerpt from *Mom & Me & Mom,* you will encounter these words.

| supervision | charitable | philanthropist |

Base Words Use your knowledge of the "inside," or base, word along with context to determine the meaning of an unfamiliar word. Here is an example of how to apply the strategy.

> **Unfamiliar Word** *artisan*
>
> **Familiar "Inside" Word** *art,* which means "something made through skill and creativity."
>
> **Context** The beautiful ceramic jug was created by an **artisan** in the town next to ours.
>
> **Conclusion** The jug was a beautiful ceramic piece made by someone. *Artisan* must mean "someone who creates a type of art."

Apply your knowledge of base words and other vocabulary strategies to determine the meanings of unfamiliar words you encounter during your first read.

First Read NONFICTION

Apply these strategies as you conduct your first read. You will have an opportunity to complete a close read after your first read.

NOTICE the general ideas of the text. *What* is it about? *Who* is involved?

ANNOTATE by marking vocabulary and key passages you want to revisit.

First Read

CONNECT ideas within the selection to other knowledge and other selections you have read.

RESPOND by completing the Comprehension Check and by writing a brief summary of the selection.

from Mom & Me & Mom

Maya Angelou

BACKGROUND

When Maya Angelou was 3 years old and her brother Bailey was 5, her parents divorced and sent the children off to live with their grandmother in Stamps, Arkansas. When Maya was 13, she and Bailey were sent back to San Francisco to live with their mother, Vivian Baxter.

SCAN FOR
MULTIMEDIA

Chapter 3

1   My grandmother made arrangements with two Pullman car[1] porters and a dining car waiter for tickets for herself, my brother, and me. She said she and I would go to California first and Bailey would follow a month later. She said she didn't want to leave me without adult **supervision**, because I was a thirteen-year-old girl. Bailey would be safe with Uncle Willie. Bailey thought he was looking after Uncle Willie, but the truth was, Uncle Willie was looking after him.

2   By the time the train reached California, I had become too frightened to accept the idea that I was going to meet my mother at last.

3   My grandmother took my hands. "Sister, there is nothing to be scared for. She is your mother, that's all. We are not surprising her.

> ### NOTES
>
> Mark base words or indicate another strategy you used that helped you determine meaning.
>
> **supervision**
> (soo pehr VIH zhun) *n.*
> MEANING:

---

1. **Pullman car** *n.* type of railroad sleeping car built by the Pullman Company.

When she received my letter explaining how Junior was growing up, she invited us to come to California."

4   Grandmother rocked me in her arms and hummed. I calmed down. When we descended the train steps, I looked for someone who could be my mother. When I heard my grandmother's voice call out, I followed the voice and I knew she had made a mistake, but the pretty little woman with red lips and high heels came running to my grandmother.

5   "Mother Annie! Mother Annie!"

6   Grandmother opened her arms and embraced the woman. When Momma's arms fell, the woman asked, "Where is my baby?"

7   She looked around and saw me. I wanted to sink into the ground. I wasn't pretty or even cute. That woman who looked like a movie star deserved a better-looking daughter than me. I knew it and was sure she would know it as soon as she saw me.

8   "Maya, Marguerite, my baby." Suddenly I was wrapped in her arms and in her perfume. She pushed away and looked at me. "Oh baby, you're beautiful and so tall. You look like your daddy and me. I'm so glad to see you."

9   She kissed me. I had not received one kiss in all the years in Arkansas. Often my grandmother would call me and show me off to her visitors. "This is my grandbaby." She would stroke me and smile. That was the closest I had come to being kissed. Now Vivian Baxter was kissing my cheeks and my lips and my hands. Since I didn't know what to do, I did nothing.

10   Her home, which was a boardinghouse,[2] was filled with heavy and very uncomfortable furniture. She showed me a room and said it was mine. I told her I wanted to sleep with Momma. Vivian said, "I suppose you slept with your grandmother in Stamps, but she will be going home soon and you need to get used to sleeping in your own room."

11   My grandmother stayed in California, watching me and everything that happened around me. And when she decided that everything was all right, she was happy. I was not. She began to talk about going home, and wondering aloud how her crippled son was getting along. I was afraid to let her leave me, but she said, "You are with your mother now and your brother will be coming soon. Trust me, but more than that trust the Lord. He will look after you."

12   Grandmother smiled when my mother played jazz and blues very loudly on her record player. Sometimes she would dance just because she felt like it, alone, by herself, in the middle of the floor. While Grandmother accepted behavior so different, I just couldn't get used to it.

---

2. **boardinghouse** *n.* house where people rent one or more rooms for either short or long periods of time.

13　My mother watched me without saying much for about two weeks. Then we had what was to become familiar as "a sit-down talk-to."

14　She said, "Maya, you disapprove of me because I am not like your grandmother. That's true. I am not. But I am your mother and I am working some part of my anatomy³ off to pay for this roof over your head. When you go to school, the teacher will smile at you and you will smile back. Students you don't even know will smile and you will smile. But on the other hand, I am your mother. If you can force one smile on your face for strangers, do it for me. I promise you I will appreciate it."

15　She put her hand on my cheek and smiled. "Come on, baby, smile for Mother. Come on. Be **charitable**."

16　She made a funny face and against my will, I smiled. She kissed me on my lips and started to cry. "That's the first time I have seen you smile. It is a beautiful smile. Mother's beautiful daughter can smile."

17　I was not used to being called beautiful.

18　That day, I learned that I could be a giver simply by bringing a smile to another person. The ensuing⁴ years have taught me that a kind word or a vote of support can be a charitable gift. I can move over and make another place for another to sit. I can turn my music up if it pleases, or down if it is annoying.

19　I may never be known as a **philanthropist**, but I certainly want to be known as charitable.

✳   ✳   ✳

20　I was beginning to appreciate her. I liked to hear her laugh because I noticed that she never laughed at anyone. After a few weeks it became clear that I was not using any title when I spoke to her. In fact, I rarely started conversations. Most often, I simply responded when I was spoken to.

2!　She asked me into her room. She sat on her bed and didn't invite me to join her.

22　"Maya, I am your mother. Despite the fact that I left you for years, I am your mother. You know that, don't you?"

23　I said, "Yes, ma'am." I had been answering her briefly with a few words since my arrival in California.

24　"You don't have to say 'ma'am' to me. You're not in Arkansas."

25　"No, ma'am. I mean no."

26　"You don't want to call me 'Mother,' do you?"

27　I remained silent.

---

3. **anatomy** (uh NAT uh mee) *n.* the structure of the body.
4. **ensuing** *adj.* following.

NOTES

Mark base words or indicate another strategy you used that helped you determine meaning.

charitable (CHAIR ih tuh buhl) *adj.*

MEANING:

philanthropist (fih LAN thruh pihst) *n.*

MEANING:

28 "You have to call me something. We can't go through life without you addressing me. What would you like to call me?"

29 I had been thinking of that since I first saw her. I said, "Lady."

30 "What?"

31 "Lady."

32 "Why?"

33 "Because you are beautiful, and you don't look like a mother."

34 "Is Lady a person you like?"

35 I didn't answer.

36 "Is Lady a person you might learn to like?"

37 She waited as I thought about it.

38 I said, "Yes."

39 "Well, that's it. I am Lady, and still your mother."

40 "Yes, ma'am. I mean yes."

41 "At the right time I will introduce my new name."

42 She left me, turned up the player, and sang loudly with the music. The next day I realized she must have spoken to my grandmother.

43 Grandmother came into my bedroom. "Sister, she is your mother and she does care for you."

44 I said, "I'll wait until Bailey gets here. He will know what to do, and whether we should call her Lady."

Chapter 4

45   Mother, Grandmother, and I waited at the railway station. Bailey descended from the train and saw me first. The smile that took over his face made me forget all the discomfort I had felt since coming to California.

46   His eyes found Grandmother and his smile changed to a grin, and he waved to her. Then he saw Mother and his response broke my heart. Suddenly he was a lost little boy who had been found at last. He saw his mother, his home, and then all his lonely birthdays were gone. His nights when scary things made noise under the bed were forgotten. He went to her as if hypnotized. She opened her arms and she clasped him into her embrace. I felt as if I had stopped breathing. My brother was gone, and he would never come back.

47   He had forgotten everything, but I remembered how we felt on the few occasions when she sent us toys. I poked the eyes out of each doll, and Bailey took huge rocks and smashed to bits the trucks or trains that came wrapped up in fancy paper.

48   Grandmother put her arm around me and we walked ahead of the others back to the car. She opened the door and sat in the backseat. She looked at me and patted the seat beside her. We left the front seat for the new lovers.

49   The plan was that Grandmother would return to Arkansas two days after Bailey arrived. Before Lady and Bailey Jr. reached the car I said to Grandmother, "I want to go back home with you, Momma."

50   She asked, "Why?"

51   I said, "I don't want to think of you on that train all alone. You will need me."

52   "When did you make that decision?" I didn't want to answer.

53   She said, "When you saw the reunion of your brother and his mother?" That she should have such understanding, being an old woman and country, too: I thought it was amazing. It was just as well that I had no answer, because Bailey and his mother had already reached the car.

54   Vivian said to Grandmother, "Mother Annie, I didn't look for you two. I knew you would go to the car." Bailey didn't turn to look at me. His eyes were glued to his mother's face. "One thing about you that cannot be denied, you are a true sensible woman."

55   Grandmother said, "Thank you, Vivian. Junior?"

56   She had to call twice to get his attention, "Junior, how was the train? Did somebody make food for your trip? How did you leave Willie?"

57   Suddenly he remembered there was someone else in the world. He grinned for Grandmother. "Yes, ma'am, but none of them can cook like you."

NOTES

58   He turned to me and asked, "What's happening, My? Has California got your tongue? You haven't said a word since I got in the car."

59   I made my voice as cold as possible. I said, "You haven't given me a chance."

60   In a second he said, "What's the matter, My?"

61   I had hurt him and I was glad. I said, "I may go back to Stamps with Momma." I wanted to break his heart.

62   "No, ma'am, you will not." My grandmother's voice was unusually hard.

63   My mother asked, "Why would you leave now? You said all you were waiting on was your brother. Well, here he is." She started the car and pulled out into traffic.

64   Bailey turned back to her. He added, "Yep, I'm in California."

65   Grandmother held my hand and patted it. I bit the inside of my mouth to keep from crying.

66   No one spoke until we reached our house. Bailey dropped his hand over the back of the front seat. When he wiggled his fingers, I grabbed them. He squeezed my fingers and let them go and drew his hand back to the front seat. The exchange did not escape Grandmother's notice, but she said nothing. ❧

❊   ❊   ❊

Comprehension Check

Complete the following items after you finish your first read. Review and clarify details with your group.

1. What was Angelou frightened of at the beginning of the story?

2. Why did Angelou think her grandmother had been mistaken in identifying the woman on the train platform as her mother?

3. What lesson does Angelou learn from her mother when she finally smiles for her?

4. 🖺 **Notebook** Write a summary of the excerpt from *Mom & Me & Mom* to confirm your understanding of the memoir.

Close Read the Text

With your group, revisit sections of the text you marked during your first read. **Annotate** details that you notice. What **questions** do you have? What can you **conclude**?

Analyze the Text

> **CITE TEXTUAL EVIDENCE**
> to support your answers.

Notebook Complete the activities.

1. **Review and Clarify** With your group, reread paragraphs 45–48 of the excerpt. How does Angelou describe her brother Bailey's reunion with their mother? What was Angelou's response to seeing their reunion? Why might she have responded this way?

2. **Present and Discuss** Now, work with your group to share passages from the memoir that you found especially important. Take turns presenting your passages. Discuss what you noticed in the text, what questions you asked, and what conclusions you reached.

3. **Essential Question:** *What can one generation learn from another?* What has this excerpt taught you about the ways in which people of different generations can learn from each other?

TIP

GROUP DISCUSSION
Be sure to identify specific events or passages so your classmates can follow your thinking. Use precise words and specific details to express your thoughts.

LANGUAGE DEVELOPMENT

Concept Vocabulary

| charitable | philanthropist | supervision |

Why These Words? The three concept words from the text are related. With your group, determine what the words have in common. Write your ideas and add another word that fits the category.

Practice

Notebook Confirm your understanding of the concept vocabulary words from the text by using them in sentences. Be sure to use context clues that signal the meaning of the words.

Word Study

Latin Prefix: *super-* The Latin prefix *super-* means "above," "over," or "beyond." Angelou's grandmother did not want Maya to leave without adult *supervision;* she wanted an adult to be watching *over* Maya. Using your knowledge of the prefix *super-,* determine the meanings of the following words: *superhuman, superstructure, supersonic.* Then, use a dictionary to find the precise meaning of each word.

⬡ WORD NETWORK

Identify words from the memoir that relate to generations. Add these words to your Word Network.

STANDARDS

Speaking and Listening
Engage effectively in a range of collaborative discussions (one-on-one, in groups, and teacher-led) with diverse partners on grade 7 topics, texts, and issues, building on others' ideas and expressing their own clearly.

Language
Determine or clarify the meaning of unknown and multiple-meaning words and phrases based on *grade 7 reading and content,* choosing flexibly from a range of strategies.
  b. Use common, grade-appropriate Greek or Latin affixes and roots as clues to the meaning of a word.
  d. Verify the preliminary determination of the meaning of a word or phrase.

from MOM & ME & MOM

TIP

CLOSE READING

When analyzing characterization, pay attention to the words the author uses to describe *how* the characters speak.

STANDARDS

Reading Informational Text
• Cite several pieces of textual evidence to support analysis of what the text says explicitly as well as inferences drawn from the text.
• Analyze the interactions between individuals, events, and ideas in a text.

Analyze Craft and Structure

Narrative Nonfiction: Characterization Authors of nonfiction use descriptions and details to help a reader understand the people about whom they are writing. These descriptions help reveal **character traits,** the qualities that make people unique. For example, a person may have the character traits of intelligence and friendliness.

Characterization is the process that writers use to develop their descriptions of people. For instance, in describing a person, a writer might focus on one type of character trait early in a piece of writing and switch to another character trait later in the piece to further develop the portrayal. There are two types of characterization:

- **Direct characterization:** The writer directly describes a person's character traits.
- **Indirect characterization:** The writer reveals a person's character traits through the person's own words and actions and from the words and actions of other people. Readers must **make inferences,** or educated guesses, to determine character traits from indirect characterization.

Practice

CITE TEXTUAL EVIDENCE
to support your answers.

Use the chart to analyze indirect characterization in *Mom & Me & Mom.* First, write down some of the person's words and actions that are revealed in the text. Then, make an inference about a character trait of the person, based on these words and actions. The first row has been done for you.

PERSON	WORDS AND ACTIONS IN TEXT	INFERENCE ABOUT CHARACTER TRAIT
Grandmother	*My grandmother took my hands. "Sister, there is nothing to be scared for. She is your mother, that's all. We are not surprising her."* (paragraph 3)	nurturing
Maya		
Mother		

Conventions

Independent and Dependent Clauses A **clause** is a group of words that has both a subject and a verb. An **independent clause** has a subject and a verb, and it can stand by itself as a sentence. A **dependent,** or **subordinate, clause** has a subject and a verb, but it cannot stand alone as a complete sentence.

TYPE OF CLAUSE	EXAMPLES
Independent Clause	• My grandmother took my hands • Grandmother rocked me in her arms and hummed • She asked me into her room • Mother, Grandmother, and I waited at the railway station
Dependent Clause	• Because I was a thirteen-year-old girl • Since I didn't know what to do • While Grandmother accepted behavior so different • When he wiggled his fingers

Read It

1. Identify each group of words as an independent clause or a dependent clause.

   a. I had not received one kiss in all the years in Arkansas

   b. That woman who looked like a movie star

   c. I was beginning to appreciate her

   d. Before Lady and Bailey Jr. reached the car

2. Reread paragraph 20 of *Mom & Me & Mom*. Mark and then label one example of an independent clause and one example of a dependent clause.

Write It

📓 **Notebook** Write a brief paragraph that describes how Maya's interactions with her mother changed before Bailey's arrival. Include two independent clauses and two dependent clauses in your writing. Then label these types of clauses in your finished paragraph.

✎ EVIDENCE LOG

Before moving on to a new selection, go to your Evidence Log and record what you learned from the excerpt from *Mom & Me & Mom.*

⊞ STANDARDS

Language
Demonstrate command of the conventions of standard English grammar and usage when writing or speaking.

a. Explain the function of phrases and clauses in general and their function in specific sentences.

from MOM & ME & MOM

Comparing Text to Media

The video interview you will watch features Maya Angelou, the author of *Mom & Me & Mom,* describing some of the experiences she wrote about in her memoir. While watching this video, think about ways in which both written text and spoken words can tell a story.

LEARNING TO LOVE MY MOTHER

About the Interviewer

Michael Maher has produced and filmed numerous videos, including many for *BBC News Magazine.* In most of his work—even when he is the interviewer—he is not very visible, and the focus of the video doesn't stray from the subject.

Learning to Love My Mother

Media Vocabulary

The following words or concepts will be useful to you as you analyze, discuss, and write about video interviews.

set: where the interview takes place	• The set of an interview is usually free of noise and other distractions. • The set may be in a location that suits the subject matter of the interview.
questions: what the interviewer chooses to ask an interviewee to elicit specific information	• The questions may ask for factual responses or encourage the subject to reflect on a particular topic or experience. • "Leading" questions suggest the particular answer an interviewer wants to hear.
tone: the attitude of an interviewer or interviewee toward the subject matter or audience	• The overall tone of an interview may vary depending on the topic and interviewer's purpose. • Word choice, vocal qualities, and facial expressions set the tone of the interview.

First Review MEDIA: VIDEO

Apply these strategies as you watch the video interview. Be sure to note time codes so you can more easily revisit specific sections of the video.

WATCH *who* speaks, *what* they say, and *how* they say it.

NOTE elements that you find interesting and want to revisit.

First Review
WATCH · NOTE · CONNECT · RESPOND

CONNECT details in the interview to other texts you've read or images you've seen.

RESPOND by completing the Comprehension Check at the end.

STANDARDS

Reading Informational Text
By the end of the year, read and comprehend literary nonfiction in the grades 6–8 text complexity band proficiently, with scaffolding as needed at the high end of the range.

Language
Acquire and use accurately grade-appropriate general academic and domain-specific words and phrases; gather vocabulary knowledge when considering a word or phrase important to comprehension or expression.

Learning to Love My Mother

Maya Angelou with Michael Maher

BACKGROUND

When Maya Angelou was three years old, she and her brother were sent to live with their grandmother. Their mother, Vivian Baxter, was not ready to be tied down with a family. Ten years later, the two children returned to live with their mother. More than 70 years later, Angelou wrote about this transition in her memoir *Mom & Me & Mom*. In this interview, she tells Michael Maher some of the lessons she learned from her experiences.

SCAN FOR MULTIMEDIA

NOTES

Comprehension Check

Compete the following items after you finish your first review. Review and clarify details with your group.

1. What are some of the ways in which Vivian Baxter was unlike Maya Angelou's grandmother?

2. How did Vivian Baxter react to her daughter's calling her *Lady*?

3. According to Angelou, what would Vivian Baxter have thought about there being an African American president?

4. What are two life lessons Angelou thinks people should learn?

5. What is one reason Angelou forgives her mother for abandoning her?

6. Explain how Maya Angelou overcame her problems with her mother, and describe how she based her advice to others on her own experience.

Close Review

Watch the interview again. Write down any new observations that seem important. What **questions** do you have? What can you **conclude**?

REVIEW · QUESTION · Close Review · CONCLUDE

LEARNING TO LOVE MY MOTHER

Analyze the Media

📓 **Notebook** Complete the activities.

1. **Present and Discuss** Choose a section of the interview that you find most interesting and powerful. Share your choice with your group and discuss why you chose it. Explain what you noticed in the section, what questions it raised for you, and what conclusions you reached about it.

2. **Review and Synthesize** With your group, review the video. What impact do the old photographs of Angelou and her family create? How do they affect your understanding of Angelou and her experiences? Discuss with your group.

3. **Essential Question:** *What can one generation learn from another?* What did Maya Angelou learn from her mother and grandmother? What does Angelou hope future generations will take away from her story? Discuss your response with the group.

LANGUAGE DEVELOPMENT

Media Vocabulary

Use these words in your responses to the questions.

set	questions	tone

1. If you were conducting this interview, what location would you have chosen?

2. Would you have asked Maya Angelou anything that the interviewer did not?

3. How did the interviewer relate to Maya Angelou on a personal level? How does the tone of both speakers affect your viewing of the interview?

▤ STANDARDS

Speaking and Listening
Analyze the main ideas and supporting details presented in diverse media and formats and explain how the ideas clarify a topic, text, or issue under study.

Language
Acquire and use accurately grade-appropriate general academic and domain-specific words and phrases; gather vocabulary knowledge when considering a word or phrase important to comprehension or expression.

from MOM & ME & MOM

LEARNING TO LOVE MY MOTHER

Writing to Compare

Both *Mom & Me & Mom* and the interview with Maya Angelou, "Learning to Love My Mother," discuss Angelou's relationship with her mother. Review the selections and consider how the medium in which information is provided—text and audiovisual—affects what you learn about the subject.

Assignment

Write a **comparison-and-contrast essay** in which you analyze the similarities and differences in the way each medium portrays Maya Angelou and her relationship with her mother.

Prewriting and Planning

You will complete the Prewriting and Planning sections as a group, and work individually to write your essay. After you finish your first draft, you will work with your group to revise your essay before handing it in.

Compare the Text and Video With your group, compare the ways in which the text and the video provide information. Use the chart to record your findings.

ANGELOU'S EXPERIENCES	WHAT I LEARNED FROM *MOM & ME & MOM*	WHAT I LEARNED FROM "LEARNING TO LOVE MY MOTHER"	HOW THE TEXT COMPARES WITH THE VIDEO INTERVIEW
Maya's first impressions of her mother			
Why Maya calls her mother *Lady*			
How Maya's feelings about her mother change			

📓 **Notebook Respond to these questions.**

1. Does the video reveal aspects of the mother-daughter relationship that the text does not?

2. Does the text provide information not found in the video?

STANDARDS

Reading Informational Text
Compare and contrast a text to an audio, video, or multimedia version of the text, analyzing each medium's portrayal of the subject.

Writing
Draw evidence from literary or informational texts to support analysis, reflection, and research.

b. Apply *grade 7 Reading standards* to literary nonfiction.

Assign Tasks Make a list of tasks that members of your group will need to complete for your project. Assign each task to a different group member.

Organize Your Essay Before you begin drafting, decide how you will organize information for your comparison-and-contrast essay. Choose the method that will best suit your purpose.

- **Block Method:** Present all details about one of your subjects. Then, present all details about your next subject. This method emphasizes the subjects being discussed, since each gets its own treatment.
- **Point-by-Point Method:** Discuss one aspect of both subjects, then another aspect of both subjects, and so on. This method emphasizes the points of comparison rather than the subjects being compared.

Regardless of the method you choose, be sure that each of your main points is stated clearly and supported by evidence from the selections.

Drafting

Using Transitions Once you have gathered details and decided on an organizing structure, draft the essay. As you draft, use words and phrases to show the relationships between ideas in your essay. Transition words and phrases can emphasize points of comparison and of contrast.

	TRANSITION WORDS AND PHRASES
Comparisons	*similarly, also, in addition, furthermore*
Contrasts	*although, however, but, on the other hand*

Review, Revise, and Edit

Work with your group to critically review and then revise and edit your essay. If the answer to any of these questions is no, edit your work before submitting a final draft.

- Are the main points of the essay clearly stated? Is each point supported with evidence in the text?
- Is the essay clearly organized using either the block method or the point-by-point method?
- Are the relationships between ideas clarified by transition words and phrases?
- Is your essay free from errors in grammar, spelling, and punctuation?

📝 EVIDENCE LOG

Before moving on to a new selection, go to your Evidence Log and record what you learned from *Mom & Me & Mom* and "Learning to Love My Mother."

☰ STANDARDS

Reading Informational Text
Compare and contrast a text to an audio, video, or multimedia version of the text, analyzing each medium's portrayal of the subject.

Writing
• Write informative/explanatory texts to examine a topic and convey ideas, concepts, and information through the selection, organization, and analysis of relevant content.
  a. Introduce a topic clearly, previewing what is to follow; organize ideas, concepts, and information, using strategies such as definition, classification, comparison/contrast, and cause/effect; include formatting, graphics, and multimedia when useful to aiding comprehension.
  b. Develop the topic with relevant facts, definitions, concrete details, quotations, or other information and examples.
  c. Use appropriate transitions to create cohesion and clarify the relationships among ideas and concepts.

• Use technology, including the Internet, to produce and publish writing and link to and cite sources as well as to interact and collaborate with others, including linking to and citing sources.

About the Artist

Mica Angela Hendricks was born into a military family and traveled to many countries. As a child, she would carry a sketchbook everywhere she went. People who didn't know her well would simply call her "that girl that draws." Hendricks is now an illustrator and has collaborated with her four-year-old daughter, Myla, on the sketchbook "Share With Me."

Mother-Daughter Drawings

Media Vocabulary

These words will be useful to you as you analyze, discuss, and write about drawings.

composition: arrangement of elements in a drawing	• The elements of a drawing's composition include color, line, shape, space, form, and texture. • The way an artist arranges the elements may create emphasis on one part of the drawing over others.
light and shadow: techniques that add depth to a drawing and make it more realistic	• Light and shadow can turn a two-dimensional shape, such as a circle, into a three-dimensional form, such as a sphere. • Light and shadow help create perspective and mood
perspective: technique used to create the illusion of a three-dimensional world on a two-dimensional surface, such as a piece of paper	• Correct proportion helps a drawing look realistic, taking into account how close or far objects in it are meant to be. • Smaller objects in a drawing appear to be farther way, and larger ones closer.

First Review MEDIA: ART AND PHOTOGRAPHY

Apply these strategies as you study each drawing.

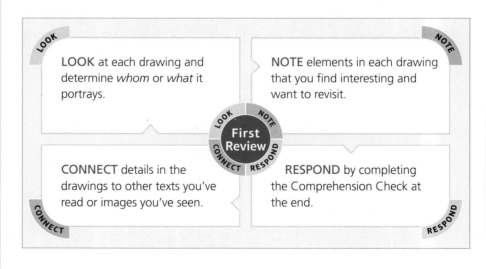

LOOK at each drawing and determine *whom* or *what* it portrays.

NOTE elements in each drawing that you find interesting and want to revisit.

CONNECT details in the drawings to other texts you've read or images you've seen.

RESPOND by completing the Comprehension Check at the end.

First Review

STANDARDS

Reading Informational Text
By the end of the year, read and comprehend literary nonfiction in the grades 6–8 text complexity band proficiently, with scaffolding as needed at the high end of the range.

Language
Acquire and use accurately grade-appropriate general academic and domain-specific words and phrases; gather vocabulary knowledge when considering a word or phrase important to comprehension or expression.

Mother-Daughter Drawings

Mica and Myla Hendricks

BACKGROUND

Artist Mica Angela Hendricks had always tried to teach her four-year-old daughter Myla the importance of sharing. But it's easier to talk about sharing than to do it. Mica found that out when Myla noticed her mother drawing in a sketchbook and asked if she could draw in it too. Mica was afraid Myla would ruin her drawings, but decided she had to set a good example by practicing what she preached, especially after Myla quoted her words back to her: "If you can't share, we might have to take it away."

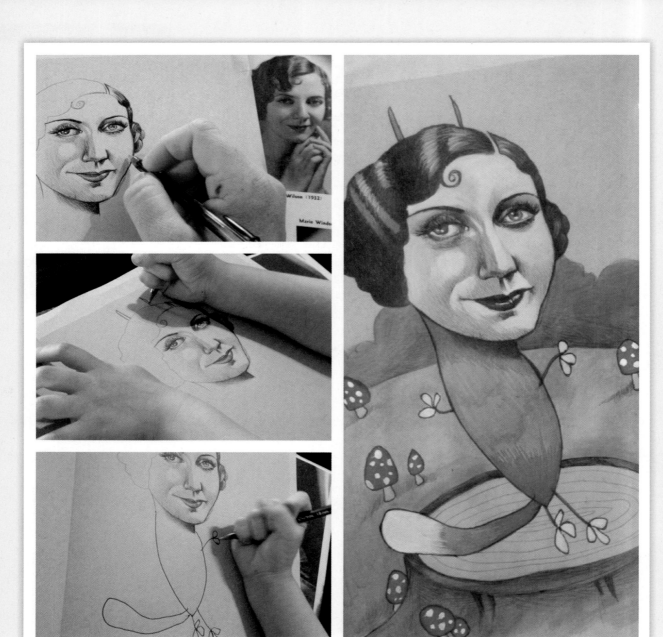

IMAGE 1: Mica had just drawn a woman's face from an old photograph.
She let Myla draw the woman's body and then used acrylic paint to add
color, highlights, and texture to the entire piece.

NOTES

IMAGE 2: Mica was impressed that her collaboration with her daughter turned out so well and wanted to try it again.

NOTES

IMAGE 3: Mica began filling her sketchbook with drawings of heads and letting Myla draw the bodies.

NOTES

IMAGE 4: At first, Mica tried telling Myla what kind of bodies to draw. She soon realized the drawings turned out better when Myla did what she wanted. "In most instances, kids' imaginations *way* outweigh a grown-up's," Mica says.

NOTES

IMAGE 5: Working with her daughter taught Mica that giving up control is not just fun, but necessary. "Those things you hold so dear cannot change and grow and expand unless you loosen your grip on them a little," she says.

NOTES

Comprehension Check

The image gallery uses both words and images to tell a story. Use the chart below to note specific details about each image, then describe how each image relates to the text that accompanies it. Share your responses with your group.

IMAGE	WHAT THE IMAGE SHOWS	HOW THE IMAGE RELATES TO THE TEXT
IMAGE 1 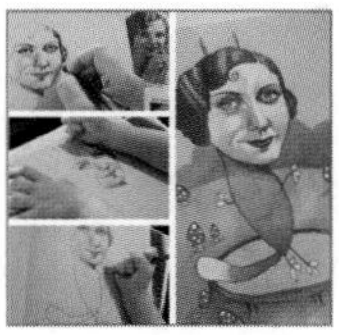		
IMAGE 2 		
IMAGE 3 		
IMAGE 4 		
IMAGE 5 		
NOTES		

MOTHER-DAUGHTER DRAWINGS

Close Review

With your group, revisit the images and your first-review notes. Record any new observations that seem important. What **questions** do you have? What can you **conclude**?

Analyze the Media

Notebook Complete the activities.

1. **Present and Discuss** Choose the image you find most interesting or powerful. Share your choice with the group and discuss why you chose it. Explain what you noticed in the image, what questions it raised for you, and what conclusions you reached about it.

2. **Review and Synthesize** With your group, review all the images. What does Mica Hendricks's experience drawing with her daughter reveal about how art is created?

3. **Notebook Essential Question: *What can one generation learn from another?*** What do you think the mother and daughter might have learned from each other by drawing together? What has learning about the Hendricks' process taught you about the ways in which one generation can learn from another?

WORD NETWORK

Look in the image gallery for words related to the topic of generations, and add them to your Word Network.

LANGUAGE DEVELOPMENT

Media Vocabulary

| composition | light and shadow | perspective |

Use the concept vocabulary words in your responses to the following questions.

1. Why might Image 1 be made up of four separate photographs?

2. What mood is suggested by Image 4? How is that mood created?

3. In Image 5, what is the primary focus and what constitutes the background?

STANDARDS

Speaking and Listening
Analyze the main ideas and supporting details presented in diverse media and formats and explain how the ideas clarify a topic, text, or issue under study.

Language
Acquire and use accurately grade-appropriate general academic and domain-specific words and phrases; gather vocabulary knowledge when considering a word or phrase important to comprehension or expression.

EFFECTIVE EXPRESSION

Speaking and Listening

Assignment

Sharing her sketchbook with her four-year-old daughter taught Mica Angela Hendricks that giving up control can help people grow. Write a brief narrative of an event that taught you a lesson about life, and share it with your group. Then, work together to create a **multimedia slideshow.** Choose one description on which to focus and combine it with at least four images, such as photos, illustrations, or other types of visual multimedia.

Choose Your Images As your group researches images for your slideshow, consider what you have learned about the ways in which **composition, perspective,** and **light and shadow** affect an image. Discuss these questions with your group:

- What mood or feeling do you want your images to convey?
- Which images should be photographs, which should be illustrations, and which should be a combination of both?
- What materials, props, and locations do you need to create your images?

Plan the Project Once you have considered these questions, make a storyboard. Decide which part of the narrative each image will represent. Arrange the images in a logical sequence.

STORYBOARD TEMPLATE

Draft and Rehearse Work with your group to finalize the narrative and slideshow. Assign roles for presenting, and rehearse to ensure that speakers are prepared and that the media is integrated smoothly.

Present and Discuss Read the narrative for the class and then present the slideshow. Discuss which aspects of the narrative are best told in words and which are best told in pictures.

Reflect With Your Group In the caption that accompanies the last image of the gallery, Mica Hendricks says, "Those things you hold so dear cannot change and grow and expand unless you loosen your grip on them a little." How did the process of working with your group to develop the slideshow influence your ideas about this quote? Did you find that it was difficult to "loosen your grip" and work collaboratively? What did you learn from the experience?

 TIP

GROUP DISCUSSION
Think about the relationship between your images with your group. Should they have a similar look, or should they contrast with each other? Why?

✏ EVIDENCE LOG

Before moving on to a new selection, go to your Evidence Log and record what you learned from "Mother-Daughter Drawings."

STANDARDS

Speaking and Listening
• Engage effectively in a range of collaborative discussions with diverse partners on *grade 7 topics, texts, and issues,* building on others' ideas and expressing their own clearly.
  a. Come to discussions prepared, having read or researched material under study; explicitly draw on that preparation by referring to evidence on the topic, text, or issue to probe and reflect on ideas under discussion.
• Include multimedia components and visual displays in presentations to clarify claims and findings and emphasize salient points.

Language
Acquire and use accurately grade-appropriate general academic and domain-specific words and phrases; gather vocabulary knowledge when considering a word or phrase important to comprehension or expression.

POETRY COLLECTION 1

Mother to Son

To James

Concept Vocabulary

As you perform your first read of these two poems, you will encounter the following words.

flung	catapulted	lurched

Context Clues If these words are unfamiliar to you, try using **context clues**—other words and phrases that appear in a text—to help you determine their meanings. There are various types of context clues that you might encounter as you read.

Restatement of Idea: As they fought to get past the finish line, one runner **hurled** himself forward, throwing his body over the line.

Synonym: At the beginning of the race, he **launched,** or propelled, himself over the start line.

Contrast of Idea: The winners of the race glided across the finish line, while the remaining competitors **stumbled** behind them.

Apply your knowledge of context clues and other vocabulary strategies to determine the meanings of unfamiliar words you encounter during your first read of the two poems.

First Read POETRY

Refer to these strategies as you conduct your first read. You will have an opportunity to complete a close read after your first read.

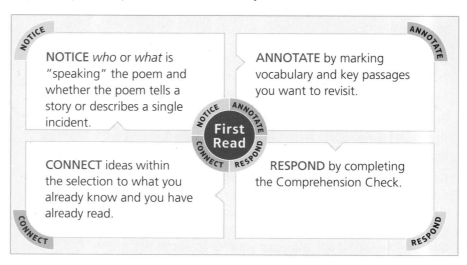

NOTICE who or what is "speaking" the poem and whether the poem tells a story or describes a single incident.

ANNOTATE by marking vocabulary and key passages you want to revisit.

CONNECT ideas within the selection to what you already know and you have already read.

RESPOND by completing the Comprehension Check.

STANDARDS

Reading Literature
By the end of the year, read and comprehend literature, including stories, dramas, and poems, in the grades 6–8 text complexity band proficiently, with scaffolding as needed at the high end of the range.

Language
Determine or clarify the meaning of unknown and multiple-meaning words and phrases based on *grade 7 reading and content,* choosing flexibly from a range of strategies.

a. Use context as a clue to the meaning of a word or phrase.

About the Poets

Langston Hughes (1902–1967) was an African American writer known for jazz-inspired poems that portrayed African American life in America. His work was controversial. Some critics worried that it played into racial stereotypes. Others praised Hughes for reaching everyday people by using language and themes "familiar to anyone who had the ability simply to read."

Frank Horne (1899–1974) was an African American writer and activist. As a director at the U.S. Housing Authority, he fought to end segregated housing. As a poet, he fought discrimination with poems that conveyed dignity and pride.

Backgrounds

Mother to Son

Even after the abolition of slavery, life was very hard for most African Americans. Poetry, music, and the other arts were creative outlets that allowed them to express the hardships of their lives and to find inspiration.

To James

From 1914 through 1937, Harlem, a neighborhood in New York City, was the setting for an awakening of African American culture that came to be known as the Harlem Renaissance. During this period, African American writers such as Langston Hughes and Frank Horne searched for the truest way to express their experiences. Each developed a unique style that ultimately helped shape not just African American culture but also world culture.

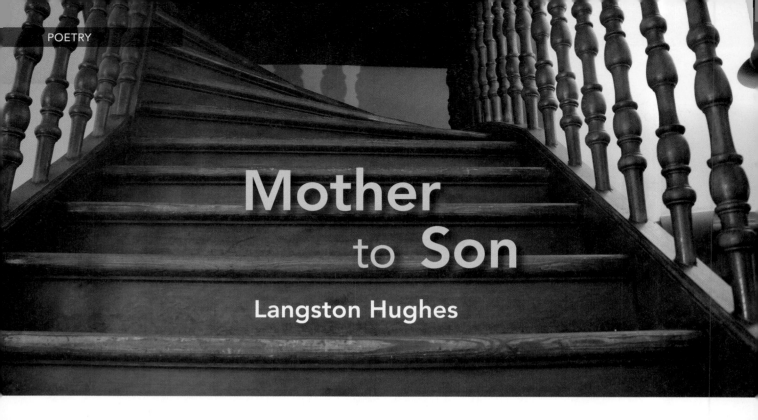

Mother to Son

Langston Hughes

SCAN FOR
MULTIMEDIA

NOTES

Well, son, I'll tell you:
Life for me ain't been no crystal stair.
It's had tacks in it,
And splinters,
5   And boards torn up,
And places with no carpet on the floor—
Bare.
But all the time
I'se been a-climbin' on,
10 And reachin' landin's,
And turnin' corners,
And sometimes goin' in the dark
Where there ain't been no light.
So boy, don't you turn back.
15 Don't you set down on the steps
'Cause you finds it's kinder hard.
Don't you fall now—
For I'se still goin', honey,
I'se still climbin',
20 And life for me ain't been no crystal stair.

To James

Frank Horne

SCAN FOR
MULTIMEDIA

NOTES

Mark context clues or indicate
another strategy you used that
helped you determine meaning.

flung (FLUHNG) *v.*

MEANING:

catapulted
(KA tuh puhl tihd) *v.*

MEANING:

lurched (LURCHT) *v.*

MEANING:

Do you remember
How you won
That last race . . . ?
How you **flung** your body
5 At the start . . .
How your spikes
Ripped the cinders[1]
In the stretch . . .
How you **catapulted**
10 Through the tape . . .
Do you remember . . . ?
Don't you think
I **lurched** with you
Out of those starting holes . . . ?
15 Don't you think
My sinews[2] tightened
At those first
Few strides . . .
And when you flew into the stretch

1. **cinders** *n.* ashes.
2. **sinews** *n.* strong tissue that connects muscle to bone.

20 Was not all my thrill
Of a thousand races
In your blood . . . ?
At your final drive
Through the finish line
25 Did not my shout
Tell of the
Triumphant ecstasy
Of victory . . . ?
Live
30 As I have taught you
To run, Boy—
It's a short dash
Dig your starting holes
Deep and firm
35 Lurch out of them
Into the straightaway
With all the power
That is in you
Look straight ahead
40 To the finish line
Think only of the goal
Run straight
Run high
Run hard
45 Save nothing
And finish
With an ecstatic burst
That carries you
Hurtling
50 Through the tape
To victory. . . .

Comprehension Check

Complete the following items after you finish your first read. Review and clarify details with your group.

MOTHER TO SON

1. Identify three words or phrases from the poem that describe the staircase.

2. What does the speaker tell her son NOT to do?

TO JAMES

1. What event does the speaker refer to at the poem's start?

2. What goal does the speaker of the poem identify?

3. Which actions repeat throughout the poem?

RESEARCH

Research to Explore These poems may spark your curiosity to learn more. Briefly research a topic related to one of the poems. Then, share what you have learned with your group.

POETRY COLLECTION 1

Close Read the Text

With your group, revisit sections of the text that you marked during your first read. **Annotate** details that you notice. What **questions** do you have? What can you **conclude**?

Analyze the Text

CITE TEXTUAL EVIDENCE to support your answers.

🔲 **Notebook** Complete the activities.

1. **Review and Clarify** With your group, reread "Mother to Son." What qualities does the mother demonstrate through her words and actions? Why does the mother need these qualities?

2. **Present and Discuss** Now, work with your group to share lines from the poems that you found especially important. Take turns presenting your lines. Discuss what you noticed in the lines, what questions you asked, and what conclusions you reached.

3. **Essential Question:** *What can one generation learn from another?* What have these poems revealed about what one generation teaches another? Discuss your ideas with the group.

🔗 WORD NETWORK

Look in the text for words related to the topic of generations, and add them to your Word Network.

☰ STANDARDS

Reading Literature
• Cite several pieces of textual evidence to support analysis of what the text says explicitly as well as inferences drawn from the text.
• Determine a theme or central idea of a text and analyze its development over the course of the text; provide an objective summary of the text.
• Determine the meaning of words and phrases as they are used in a text, including figurative and connotative meanings; analyze the impact of rhymes and other repetitions of sounds on a specific verse or stanza of a poem or section of a story or drama.

Language
Demonstrate understanding of figurative language, word relationships, and nuances in word meanings.
  c. Distinguish among the connotations of words with similar denotations.

LANGUAGE DEVELOPMENT

Concept Vocabulary

flung	catapulted	lurched

Why These Words? The concept vocabulary words from the poems are related. With your group, determine what the words have in common. Write your ideas and add another word that fits the category.

Practice

🔲 **Notebook** To gain a better understanding of the concept vocabulary words, write a sentence for each word that demonstrates your understanding of the word's meaning.

Word Study

Connotations and Denotations A **connotation** is an association or feeling that a word suggests in addition to its literal dictionary definition, or **denotation**. Two words can have similar denotations but different connotations. For example, the words *mother* and *matriarch* have the same basic denotation. However, *mother* has positive connotations of warmth and security, whereas *matriarch* suggests a feeling of distance and formality.

Find two synonyms in a thesaurus for the concept vocabulary word *flung*. Write an explanation of how the connotations of the three words differ.

Analyze Craft and Structure

Figurative Language: Symbolism A **symbol** is anything—an object, person, animal, place, or situation—that represents something else. A symbol has its own meaning, but it also stands for something larger than itself, usually an abstract idea. For example, a dove is a type of bird that symbolizes peace.

In poetry, an author's use of symbolism can often reveal the **theme**, or insight about life, of a poem. To determine the theme of a poem that incorporates symbolism, **make inferences**, or educated guesses, as to what the symbol might represent based on the details in the poem. Then, consider the meaning of the symbol and how it suggests the theme.

Practice

CITE TEXTUAL EVIDENCE
to support your answers.

Gather your notes in this chart and share with your group.

	MOTHER TO SON	TO JAMES
How is symbolism used in the poem? What is the symbol?		
What impression of life does this symbol create? What details from the poem suggest this impression?		
What does this symbol suggest about how people should live their lives?		
What is the theme of the poem? What details from your analysis of the author's use of symbolism support this inference?		

POETRY COLLECTION 1

TIP

GROUP DISCUSSION
Take turns presenting portions of each poem aloud. Discuss how listening to a poem read aloud helps you to hear rhythm, rhyme, and other sound devices. Discuss the connection between the sound of a poem and its meaning.

Author's Style

Rhythm and Repetition Rhythm is the pattern of strong and weak beats in spoken or written language.

In free verse poems such as "To James" by Frank Horne and "Mother to Son" by Langston Hughes, the structural pattern can be irregular and closer to the natural rising and falling of spoken language. The term "free verse" refers to poetry that has no standard pattern of rhyme or rhythm.

Repetition is the repeated use of any element of language. Poets can repeat a sound, a word, a phrase, a sentence, a rhyme, a rhythm, or all of these elements to emphasize ideas and create musical effects. Here are some examples:

- *The sun sank in the sea.*
- *We didn't look, we didn't listen, we only were.*
- *I gallop'd, Dirck gallop'd, we gallop'd all three;*

Notice that in these examples, both words and sounds are repeated.

Read It

Test your understanding of repetition with a game. Working individually, make a list of the repeated elements in "To James" and "Mother to Son." Identify as many examples as you can; then rejoin your group and compare lists.

Write It

Choose one poem from the collection and write a paragraph describing how the poet uses rhythm and repetition to emphasize certain ideas.

▦ STANDARDS
Reading Literature
Determine the meaning of words and phrases as they are used in a text, including figurative and connotative meanings; analyze the impact of rhymes and other repetitions of sounds on a specific verse or stanza of a poem or section of a story or drama.

Language
Demonstrate understanding of figurative language, word relationships, and nuances in word meanings.

Writing to Sources

Assignment

Write a **narrative poem** in which the speaker shares with readers a lesson learned through personal experience. Include at least one symbol in your poem.

You will work individually to craft your poem. After you have completed your poems, you will revise and discuss them as a group.

Analyze Sources for Inspiration As you brainstorm ideas for your poem, review the poems by Hughes and Horne. Note the ways in which the poets use symbols to convey the experience of the speaker and to develop the theme of the poem. Also, note other techniques, such as description, that the poets use to capture the experiences of the speaker and the subjects. Studying the ways poets effectively use symbols and narrative techniques can help you better apply them to your own writing.

Organize Your Ideas Consider the following questions to organize your thoughts and add interest to your poem:

- What experience will my poem describe? What symbol will I use to convey this experience?

- Who is the speaker of my poem? Whom will the speaker be addressing, and what is their relationship?

- What is the setting of my poem? What specific details describe the setting?

- How can I use **sensory language,** or language that appeals to one or more of the five senses, to vividly describe my speaker, subjects, setting, and experience?

- What is the theme of my poem? What lesson is the experience in my poem meant to convey?

Draft Your Poem Once you have planned your poem, write it down. Try not to self-edit at this point; strive to get it written in one sitting so that you can maintain your flow of ideas.

Revise and Evaluate Exchange the first draft of your poem with a group member. See if you can determine the subject, symbol, and theme of your classmate's poem. Also, consider your classmate's use of sensory language and descriptive details: *Is any sensory language confusing or inaccurate? Are there places where descriptive details would make the poem more interesting?* Provide feedback to your classmate politely and respectfully.

Discuss as a Group Read the final version of your poem to your group. After all members have recited their poems, discuss the similarities and differences between them. Discuss the process of writing a poem and creating a symbol: *How was this challenging? How did the process increase your understanding of the ways in which symbols can be effective in poetry?*

✍ EVIDENCE LOG

Before moving on to a new selection, go to your log and record what you learned from "Mother to Son" and "To James."

▤ STANDARDS

Writing

- Write narratives to develop real or imagined experiences or events using effective technique, relevant descriptive details, and well-structured event sequences.
  a. Engage and orient the reader by establishing a context and point of view and introducing a narrator and/or characters; organize an event sequence that unfolds naturally and logically.
  b. Use narrative techniques, such as dialogue, pacing and description, to develop experiences, events, and/or characters.
  d. Use precise words and phrases, relevant descriptive details, and sensory language to capture the action and convey experiences and events.
- With some guidance and support from peers and adults, develop and strengthen writing as needed by planning, revising, editing, rewriting, or trying a new approach, focusing on how well purpose and audience have been addressed.
- Draw evidence from literary or informational texts to support analysis, reflection, and research.
  a. Apply *grade 7 Reading standards* to literature.

SOURCES

- TUTORS TEACH SENIORS NEW HIGH-TECH TRICKS
- *from* MOM & ME & MOM
- LEARNING TO LOVE MY MOTHER
- MOTHER TO SON
- TO JAMES

Present a Nonfiction Narrative

Assignment

Work with your group to present a **panel discussion** in which you tell stories and give examples that relate to the following question.

> What new knowledge or skills can you learn from someone of a different generation?

Plan With Your Group

Analyze the Texts With your group, identify a key lesson about life taught in each text listed. Summarize your ideas on this chart.

TITLE	LESSON TAUGHT / SUPPORTING DETAILS
Tutors Teach Seniors New High-Tech Tricks	
from Mom & Me & Mom	
Learning to Love My Mother	
Mother to Son	
To James	

Assign Roles When the chart is complete, review with your group. Then, identify one group member to act as moderator and the other group members to represent one narrator or one speaker in the panel discussion.

STANDARDS

Speaking and Listening
- Engage effectively in a range of collaborative discussions with diverse partners on *grade 7 topics, texts, and issues,* building on others' ideas and expressing their own clearly.
  a. Come to discussions prepared, having read or researched material under study; explicitly draw on that preparation by referring to evidence on the topic, text, or issue to probe and reflect on ideas under discussion.
  b. Follow rules for collegial discussions, track progress toward specific goals and deadlines, and define individual roles as needed.

- Analyze the main ideas and supporting details presented in diverse media and formats and explain how the ideas clarify a topic, text, or issue under study.

Plan Your Panel Discussion Allow time for the moderator to prepare questions for the discussion about life lessons that are passed on between generations. Other group members should use this time to become expert on the speaker or narrator of a given text. Keep the following in mind:

- The moderator's questions should lead responders to relate **anecdotes,** or short, true-life stories, about their experiences.
- Panel members should be prepared to respond to the moderator's questions with stories about what they learned from another generation.

Rehearse With Your Group

Review Requirements As you practice your panel discussion, use this checklist to evaluate the effectiveness of your first run-through. Then, use your evaluation and these instructions to guide any changes you make to the format of the panel discussion.

CONTENT	PRESENTATION TECHNIQUES
☐ The questions posed are meaningful and answerable.	☐ Speakers make eye contact and speak clearly.
☐ The responses should be in the form of a narrative.	☐ Speakers adjust volume and pacing as appropriate.
	☐ Speakers use their tone of voice to emphasize main points.

Fine-Tune the Content If the connection between the moderator's questions and the panel members' responses are not yet clear, work as a group to make the connections stronger. You may need to perform further analysis of the source texts to strengthen the content.

Brush Up on Your Presentation Techniques Practice making eye contact with the moderator and with other panel members as they speak. Avoid multitasking during the discussion so that the focus remains on the person speaking.

Present and Evaluate

Remember that you must use teamwork to make this presentation effective. As you listen to other groups present, take notes and be ready to ask questions and provide feedback at the conclusion of their discussion.

::: STANDARDS

Speaking and Listening
- Present claims and findings, emphasizing salient points in a focused, coherent manner with pertinent descriptions, facts, details, and examples; use appropriate eye contact, adequate volume, and clear pronunciation.
- Adapt speech to a variety of contexts and tasks, demonstrating command of formal English when indicated or appropriate.

ESSENTIAL QUESTION:

What can one generation learn from another?

People from different generations sometimes have very different ways of looking at the world. For your final reading selection in this unit, you will choose one additional text about generations. Follow these steps to help you choose.

Look Back Think about the selections you have already read. What more do you want to know about the topic of generations?

Look Ahead Preview the selections by reading the descriptions. Which one seems most interesting and appealing to you?

Look Inside Take a few minutes to scan through the text you chose. Make another selection if this text doesn't meet your needs.

Independent Learning Strategies

Throughout your life, in school, in your community, and in your career, you will need to rely on yourself to learn and work on your own. Review these strategies and the actions you can take to practice them during Independent Learning. Add ideas of your own for each category.

STRATEGY	ACTION PLAN
Create a schedule	• Make a plan for what to do each day. • Understand your goals and deadlines. •
Practice what you've learned	• Use first-read and close-read strategies to deepen your understanding. • Evaluate the usefulness of the evidence to help you understand the topic. • Consider the quality and reliability of the source. •
Take notes	• Record important ideas and information. • Review notes before preparing to share with a group. •

SCAN FOR
MULTIMEDIA

Choose one selection. Selections are available online only.

SCAN FOR
MULTIMEDIA

First-Read Guide

Use this page to record your first-read ideas.

Selection Title: _____

🔧 **Tool Kit**
First-Read Guide and
Model Annotation

NOTICE

NOTICE new information or ideas you learn about the unit topic as you first read this text.

ANNOTATE

ANNOTATE by marking vocabulary and key passages you want to revisit.

First Read
NOTICE · ANNOTATE · CONNECT · RESPOND

CONNECT

CONNECT ideas within the selection to other knowledge and the selections you have read.

RESPOND

RESPOND by writing a brief summary of the selection.

≡ STANDARD

Reading Read and comprehend complex literary and informational texts independently and proficiently.

Close-Read Guide

Use this page to record your close-read ideas.

Selection Title: _____

Textual Evidence

Annotate • Question • Conclude
Revisit sections of the text you marked during your first read. Read the sections closely and annotate what you notice. Ask yourself questions about the text. What can you conclude? Write your ideas.

Focus on Big Ideas

Think about the author's choice of patterns, structure, techniques, and ideas included in the text. Select one and record your thoughts about what this choice conveys.

QuickWrite

Pick a paragraph from the text that grabbed your interest. Explain the power of this passage.

STANDARD

Reading Read and comprehend complex literary and informational texts independently and proficiently.

Share Your Independent Learning

Prepare to Share

What can one generation learn from another?

When you read something independently, you can continue to grow by sharing what you have learned with others. Reflect on the text you explored independently, and write notes about its connection to the unit. In your notes, consider why this text belongs in this unit.

Learn From Your Classmates

💬 **Discuss It** Share your ideas about the text you explored on your own. As you talk with your classmates, jot down ideas that you learn from them.

Reflect

Review your notes, and mark the most important insight you gained from these writing and discussion activities. Explain how this idea adds to your understanding of the topic of generations.

Review Evidence for a Nonfiction Narrative

At the beginning of the unit, you expressed your own ideas in response to the following question:

In what situations can one generation learn from another?

✐ EVIDENCE LOG

Review your Evidence Log and your QuickWrite from the beginning of the unit. Did you learn anything new?

NOTES

Identify at least three pieces of evidence that interested you about the relationships between generations.

1.

2.

3.

Identify a real-life experience that illustrates one of your current ideas about the ways in which people of different generations can learn from each other.

_____

To develop your thoughts into a topic for your nonfiction narrative, complete this sentence starter:

I learned a great deal about the ways in which people from different generations can learn from each other when

_____

_____

Evaluate Your Evidence Consider your original ideas and thoughts on the subject. How did the selections you read and watched impact your ideas and opinions?

☰ STANDARDS

Writing
• Write narratives to develop real or imagined experiences or events using effective technique, relevant descriptive details, and well-structured event sequences.

 a. Engage and orient the reader by establishing a context and point of view and introducing a narrator and/or characters; organize an event sequence that unfolds naturally and logically.

• Draw evidence from literary or informational texts to support analysis, reflection, and research.

PART 1

Writing to Sources: Nonfiction Narrative

In this unit, you read about a variety of characters who influenced one another across generations. Often, the insight went both ways, as older people learned from younger people, just as children learned from adults.

Assignment

Write a nonfiction narrative in which you use dialogue, description, and precise words to develop and convey experiences and events. Your narrative should respond to the following prompt:

> In what situations can one generation learn from another?

Your narrative might be about an experience that you had with an older relative or another person from a different generation. As an alternative, you could write about an experience one of your friends or family members had with someone from a different generation. Conclude your narrative by reflecting on the ways in which the selections in this unit and the process of writing this narrative have deepened your understanding of the relationships between people of different generations.

 WORD NETWORK

As you write and revise your nonfiction narrative, use your Word Network to help vary your word choices.

Reread the Assignment Review the assignment to be sure you fully understand it. The assignment may reference some of the academic words presented at the beginning of the unit. Be sure you understand each of the words here in order to complete the assignment correctly.

Academic Vocabulary

dialogue	consequence	perspective
notable	contradict	

Review the Elements of a Nonfiction Narrative Before you begin writing, read the Nonfiction Narrative Rubric. Once you have completed your first draft, check it against the rubric. If one or more of the elements is missing or not as strong as it could be, revise your narrative to add or strengthen that component.

Connect to the Selections In your narrative, make connections to the selections in this unit by including details and examples that clarify the ideas in your narrative. Review the literary techniques, such as description and dialogue, that the authors use in the selections to engage readers. You may use the authors' examples as a model to develop the use of literary techniques in your own narrative.

STANDARDS

Writing
- Write narratives to develop real or imagined experiences or events using effective technique, relevant descriptive details, and well-structured event sequences.
- Draw evidence from literary or informational texts to support analysis, reflection, and research.
- Write routinely over extended time frames and shorter time frames for a range of discipline-specific tasks, purposes, and audiences.

Nonfiction Narrative Rubric

	Focus and Organization	Evidence and Elaboration	Language Conventions
4	The introduction is engaging and introduces the characters and situation in a way that appeals to readers. Events in the narrative progress in logical order and are linked by clear transitions. The conclusion follows the events in the narrative and provides insightful reflection on the related experiences in the narrative.	Narrative techniques, such as dialogue, pacing, and description, are used to add interest to the narrative and to develop the characters and events. Precise, vivid words and sensory language are frequently used to convey the experiences in the narrative and to help the reader imagine the characters and scenes.	The narrative intentionally uses standard English conventions of usage and mechanics.
3	The introduction is engaging and clearly introduces the characters and situation. Events in the narrative progress logically, and transition words are used frequently. The conclusion follows the rest of the narrative and provides some reflection on the experiences related in the narrative.	Narrative techniques, such as dialogue, pacing, and description, are often used to add interest to the narrative and to develop experiences and events. Precise, vivid words and sensory language are usually used to convey the experiences in the narrative and to describe the characters and events.	The narrative demonstrates accuracy in standard English conventions of usage and mechanics.
2	The introduction introduces the characters. Events in the narrative progress somewhat logically, and some transition words are used. The conclusion adds little to the narrative and does not provide reflection on the experiences in the narrative.	Narrative techniques, such as dialogue and description, are sometimes used in the narrative. Precise, vivid words and sensory language are sometimes used to convey experiences.	The narrative demonstrates some accuracy in standard English conventions of usage and mechanics.
1	The introduction does not introduce the characters and situation, or there is no introduction. Events in the narrative do not progress logically. The ideas seem disconnected and are not linked by transitional words and phrases. The conclusion does not connect to the narrative, or there is no conclusion.	Few, if any, narrative techniques are used in the narrative. The narrative fails to incorporate sensory language and precise words to convey experiences and to develop characters.	The narrative contains mistakes in standard English conventions of usage and mechanics.

PART 2
Speaking and Listening: Multimedia Presentation

Assignment

After completing the final draft of your nonfiction narrative, use it as the foundation for a **multimedia presentation**.

Do not simply read your narrative aloud. Take the following steps to make your multimedia presentation lively and engaging.

- Review your narrative, and concentrate your presentation on the parts of your narrative that provide reflection on the events and experiences presented.
- Include different types of media that will help emphasize the main points of your presentation.
- Use appropriate eye contact, adequate volume, and clear pronunciation.

Review the Rubric Before you deliver your presentation, check your plans against this rubric. If one or more of the elements is missing or not as strong as it could be, revise your presentation.

STANDARDS

Speaking and Listening
- Present claims and findings, emphasizing salient points in a focused, coherent manner with pertinent descriptions, facts, details, and examples; use appropriate eye contact, adequate volume, and clear pronunciation.
- Include multimedia components and visual displays in presentations to clarify claims and findings and emphasize salient points.

	Content	Use of Media	Presentation Technique
3	The narrative effectively establishes a point of view and follows a logical sequence. The speaker effectively uses narrative techniques and a variety of transitions for cohesion and clarity. The speaker includes relevant descriptive details.	The media connect to all parts of the narrative. The media enhance and add interest to the narrative. The timing of the media matches the timing of the narrative.	The speaker makes eye contact and speaks clearly. The speaker adjusts volume and pacing effectively.
2	The narrative establishes a point of view and generally follows a logical sequence. The speaker uses some narrative techniques and some transitions. The speaker includes some descriptive details.	The media connect to some parts of the narrative. The media add interest to the narrative. The timing of the media sometimes matches the timing of the narrative.	The speaker sometimes makes eye contact and speaks clearly. The speaker somtimes adjusts volume and pacing.
1	The narrative does not establish a point of view and does not follow a logical sequence. The speaker does not use narrative techniques and transitions. The speaker does not include descriptive details.	The media do not connect to the narrative. The media do not add interest to the narrative. The timing of the media does not match the timing of the narrative.	The speaker does not make eye contact and does not speak clearly. The speaker does not adjust volume and pacing.

Reflect on the Unit

Now that you've completed the unit, take a few moments to reflect on your learning.

Reflect on the Unit Goals

Look back at the goals at the beginning of the unit. Use a different-colored pen to rate yourself again. Then, think about readings and activities that contributed the most to the growth of your understanding. Record your thoughts.

Reflect on the Learning Strategies

Discuss It Write a reflection on whether you were able to improve your learning based on your Action Plans. Think about what worked, what didn't, and what you might do to keep working on these strategies. Record your ideas before a class discussion.

Reflect on the Text

Choose a selection that you found challenging, and explain what made it difficult.

Describe something that surprised you about a text in the unit.

Which activity taught you the most about generations? What did you learn?

SCAN FOR
MULTIMEDIA

A Starry Home

Are there worlds beyond our galaxy? Should we find out?

Earth Views

💬 **Discuss It** Why are people curious about our galaxy and what lies beyond?

Write your response before sharing your ideas.

SCAN FOR
MULTIMEDIA

UNIT 2

UNIT INTRODUCTION

ESSENTIAL QUESTION:

Should we make a home in space?

LAUNCH TEXT
ARGUMENT MODEL
Leaving Main Street

WHOLE-CLASS LEARNING

ANCHOR TEXT: SHORT STORY

Dark They Were, and Golden-Eyed
Ray Bradbury

COMPARE

MEDIA: RADIO PLAY

Dark They Were, and Golden-Eyed
Ray Bradbury, and
Michael McDonough
(producer)

ANCHOR TEXT: NEWS ARTICLE

Danger! This Mission to Mars Could Bore You to Death!
Maggie Koerth-Baker

PERFORMANCE TASK

WRITING FOCUS:
Write an Argument

SMALL-GROUP LEARNING

NEWS ARTICLE

Future of Space Exploration Could See Humans on Mars, Alien Planets
Nola Taylor Redd

▶ MEDIA CONNECTION:
Starship

SHORT STORY

The Last Dog
Katherine Paterson

MEDIA: VIDEO

Ellen Ochoa: Director, Johnson Space Center
Ellen Ochoa

INTERVIEW

Neil deGrasse Tyson on the Future of U.S. Space Exploration After *Curiosity*
Keith Wagstaff

PERFORMANCE TASK

SPEAKING AND LISTENING FOCUS:
Present an Argument

INDEPENDENT LEARNING

POETRY

Science-Fiction Cradlesong
C. S. Lewis

WEB ARTICLE

UFO Sightings and News
Benjamin Radford

PERSUASIVE ESSAY

from **Packing for Mars**
Mary Roach

SCIENCE ARTICLE

Trip to Mars Could Damage Astronauts' Brains
Laura Sanders

PERFORMANCE-BASED ASSESSMENT PREP

Review Evidence for an Argument

PERFORMANCE-BASED ASSESSMENT

Argument: Essay and Oral Presentation

PROMPT:

Should we spend valuable resources on space exploration?

Unit Goals

Throughout this unit you will deepen your perspective about space exploration by reading, writing, speaking, listening, and presenting. These goals will help you succeed on the Unit Performance-Based Assessment.

Rate how well you meet these goals right now. You will revisit your ratings later, when you reflect on your growth during this unit.

SCALE					
	1	2	3	4	5
	NOT AT ALL WELL	NOT VERY WELL	SOMEWHAT WELL	VERY WELL	EXTREMELY WELL

READING GOALS   1   2   3   4   5

- Evaluate written arguments by analyzing how authors state and support their claims.

- Expand your knowledge and use of academic and concept vocabulary.

WRITING AND RESEARCH GOALS   1   2   3   4   5

- Write an argumentative essay in which you effectively incorporate the key elements of an argument.

- Conduct research projects of various lengths to explore a topic and clarify meaning.

LANGUAGE GOAL   1   2   3   4   5

- Demonstrate command of the proper use of verb tenses.

SPEAKING AND LISTENING GOALS   1   2   3   4   5

- Collaborate with your team to build on the ideas of others, develop consensus, and communicate.

- Integrate audio, visuals, and text in presentations.

STANDARDS

Language
Acquire and use accurately grade appropriate general academic and domain-specific words and phrases; gather vocabulary knowledge when considering a word or phrase important to comprehension or expression.

SCAN FOR MULTIMEDIA

Academic Vocabulary: Argument

Academic terms appear in all subjects and can help you read, write, and discuss with more precision. Here are five academic words that will be useful to you in this unit as you analyze and write arguments.

Complete the chart.

1. Review each word, its root, and the mentor sentences.

2. Use the information and your own knowledge to predict the meaning of each word.

3. For each word, list at least two related words.

4. Refer to the dictionary or other resources if needed.

TIP

FOLLOW THROUGH
Study the words in this chart, and mark them or their forms wherever they appear in the unit.

WORD	MENTOR SENTENCES	PREDICT MEANING	RELATED WORDS
justify ROOT: **-jus-** "law"; "right"	1. Raymond had to *justify* his position on a controversial subject during the debate. 2. Lucy decided to *justify* her lateness by saying she was stuck in traffic.		justice; justification
alternative ROOT: **-alt-** "other"	1. The guest speaker presented an *alternative* point of view. 2. Tania developed an *alternative* way to study for math tests.		
certainty ROOT: **-cert-** "sure"	1. Winning a scholarship seemed to be a *certainty* for the valedictorian. 2. The astronomers knew with *certainty* that the comet would return again in ten years.		
discredit ROOT: **-cred-** "believe"	1. The scientist had to *discredit* his partner's work because the correct procedure was not followed. 2. The lawyer used facts to *discredit* the testimony of the star witness.		
assumption ROOT: **-sum-** "take up"	1. The scientist made an *assumption* about life on Mars based on his experiments. 2. It is not a good idea to make an *assumption* if you do not have all the facts and research.		

This selection is an example of an **argumentative text**, a type of writing in which an author states and defends a position on a topic. This is the type of writing you will develop in the Performance-Based Assessment at the end of the Unit.

As you read, look at the way the writer presents the argument that people are born to explore the unknown.

Leaving Main Street

NOTES

1 In July, 2015, the world watched in awe as close-up photographs of Pluto streamed back to Earth from three billion miles away. The spacecraft *New Horizons* had traveled nine years to study the dwarf planet at the edge of our solar system.

2 As a result of the mission, scientists discovered that Pluto is not just a giant ball of ice. It has a molten core, tectonic plates, and volcanic activity, just as Earth does. It may even support some form of life. The *New Horizons* mission has been hailed as a triumph of human ingenuity, and a huge leap forward for the future of space exploration.

3 Yet it almost didn't happen. The mission had to overcome some serious challenges before it could get underway—such as repeated threats to defund it.

4 There have always been naysayers who've questioned the need for space exploration. The argument goes that the United States has more important things to spend its money on, such as ending hunger and poverty.

5 Others argue that a successful space program adds to our national prestige, helps the economy, creates jobs, and improves national security. It inspires students to pursue innovative projects and careers in science and technology. At a cost of six-tenths of a percent of the federal budget, it's well worth the price: The cost of exploration is vastly outweighed by the idea of extending humankind's sphere of influence to outer space.

6 But these are not the real reasons for continuing the space program, says Michael Griffin in *Air & Space Magazine*. Griffin makes the point that people go to space for reasons that are not necessarily logical. In other words, money doesn't have much

SCAN FOR
MULTIMEDIA

to do with it. "When we contemplate committing large sums of money to a project, we tend to dismiss reasons that are emotional or value-driven," Griffin says. He goes on to say that Americans need the prospect of exploring space.

7   Humans explore space because it's in our genes. We're hardwired with certain built-in features that compel us in that direction. Here's how it breaks down:

8   First, there is something about the human condition that strives to be the best, or the first, at something. Our ancestors survived by outperforming others.

9   Second, humans are by nature curious about exploring new places. Everyone remembers being a kid and wanting to see what's "over there." Humans will not tolerate boundaries; their dream is to explore what's beyond.

10   Third, humans have always created monuments to commemorate their great achievements, so that the next generation will remember who they are and how they spent their time here. What we want to be remembered for is finding life on other worlds, maybe even for landing on Mars.

11   Finally, NASA's space program inspires competition and innovation. The Hubble Space Telescope and the robotic missions to the planets have been shining examples of what can be achieved when a project is based on goals set by scientists rather than by politicians.

12   If we stop exploring space, soon society will have forgotten what it's like to be human. It's human to wonder about things we can't see, to look for what's over the horizon. And how can we be so narrow-minded as to think we're the only ones out there? ❧

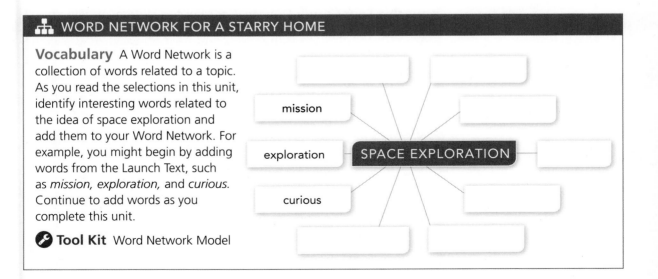

⚎ WORD NETWORK FOR A STARRY HOME

Vocabulary A Word Network is a collection of words related to a topic. As you read the selections in this unit, identify interesting words related to the idea of space exploration and add them to your Word Network. For example, you might begin by adding words from the Launch Text, such as *mission*, *exploration*, and *curious*. Continue to add words as you complete this unit.

🛠 **Tool Kit** Word Network Model

mission

exploration

curious

SPACE EXPLORATION

Summary

Write a summary of "Leaving Main Street." A **summary** is a concise, complete, and accurate overview of a text. It should not include a statement of your opinion or an analysis.

Launch Activity

Launch a Four-Corner Debate Consider this statement: **We should stop exploring space because the money spent on space missions could be put to better use here on Earth.**

- Record your position on the statement and explain your thinking.

  ☐ Strongly Agree ☐ Agree ☐ Disagree ☐ Strongly Disagree

- Form a group with like-minded students in one corner of the classroom.

- Discuss questions such as "What examples from the text or your own prior knowledge led you to take this position?"

- After your discussion, have a representative from each group present a brief two- or three-minute summary of the group's position.

- After all the groups have presented their views, move into the four corners again. If you change your corner, be ready to explain why.

QuickWrite

Consider class discussions, presentations, the video, and the Launch Text as you think about the prompt. Record your first thoughts here.

PROMPT: **Should we spend valuable resources on space exploration?**

✐ EVIDENCE LOG FOR A STARRY HOME

Review your QuickWrite and summarize your point of view to record in your Evidence Log. Then, record evidence from "Leaving Main Street" that supports your point of view.

After each selection, you will continue to use your Evidence Log to record the evidence you gather and the connections you make. This graphic shows what your Evidence Log looks like.

🔧 **Tool Kit** Evidence Log Model

Title of Text: _____   Date: _____

CONNECTION TO PROMPT	TEXT EVIDENCE/DETAILS	ADDITIONAL NOTES/IDEAS

How does this text change or add to my thinking?   Date: _____

SCAN FOR
MULTIMEDIA

ESSENTIAL QUESTION:

Should we make a home in space?

Some people gaze up at a starry sky and think it is beautiful. Some people look up at the same sky and want to find out who or what is up there. You will work with your whole class to explore the pros and cons of space exploration.

Whole-Class Learning Strategies

Throughout your life, in school, in your community, and in your career, you will continue to learn and work in large-group environments.

Review these strategies and the actions you can take to practice them as you work with your whole class. Add ideas of your own for each category for each step. Get ready to use these strategies during Whole-Class Learning.

STRATEGY	ACTION PLAN
Listen actively	• Eliminate distractions. For example, put your cellphone away. • Keep your eyes on the speaker. •
Clarify by asking questions	• If you're confused, other people probably are, too. Ask a question to help your whole class. • If you see that you are guessing, ask a question instead. •
Monitor understanding	• Notice what information you already know and be ready to build on it. • Ask for help if you are struggling. •
Interact and share ideas	• Share your ideas and answer questions, even if you are unsure. • Build on the ideas of others by adding details or making a connection. •

SCAN FOR MULTIMEDIA

CONTENTS

COMPARE

Comparing Text to Media

In this lesson, you will read the short story "Dark They Were, and Golden-Eyed" and listen to a radio play performance of it. You will then compare the text to the radio play.

DARK THEY WERE, AND
GOLDEN-EYED
(short story)

DARK THEY WERE, AND
GOLDEN-EYED
(radio play)

About the Author

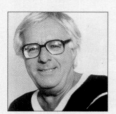

As a boy, **Ray Bradbury** (1920–2012) loved magicians, circuses, and science fiction stories. He began writing at the age of 12 and went on to become one of the most celebrated writers of science fiction and fantasy. *The Martian Chronicles,* a collection of Bradbury's stories about Earth's colonization of Mars, was published in 1950 and is considered a classic today.

🔧 Tool Kit
First-Read Guide and Model Annotation

☷ STANDARDS
Reading Literature
By the end of the year, read and comprehend literature, including stories, dramas, and poems, in the grades 6–8 text complexity band proficiently, with scaffolding as needed at the high end of the range.

Dark They Were, and Golden-Eyed

Concept Vocabulary

You will encounter the following words as you read the short story. Before reading, note how familiar you are with each word. Then, rank the words in order from most familiar (1) to least familiar (6).

WORD	YOUR RANKING
submerged	
forlorn	
canals	
immense	
atmosphere	
mosaic	

After completing your first read, come back to the concept vocabulary and review your rankings. Mark changes to your rankings as needed.

First Read FICTION

Apply these strategies during your first read. You will have an opportunity to complete the close-read notes after your first read.

NOTICE *whom* the story is about, *what* happens, *where* and *when* it happens, and *why* those involved react as they do.

ANNOTATE by marking vocabulary and key passages you want to revisit.

First Read

CONNECT ideas within the selection to what you already know and what you have already read.

RESPOND by completing the Comprehension Check and by writing a brief summary of the selection.

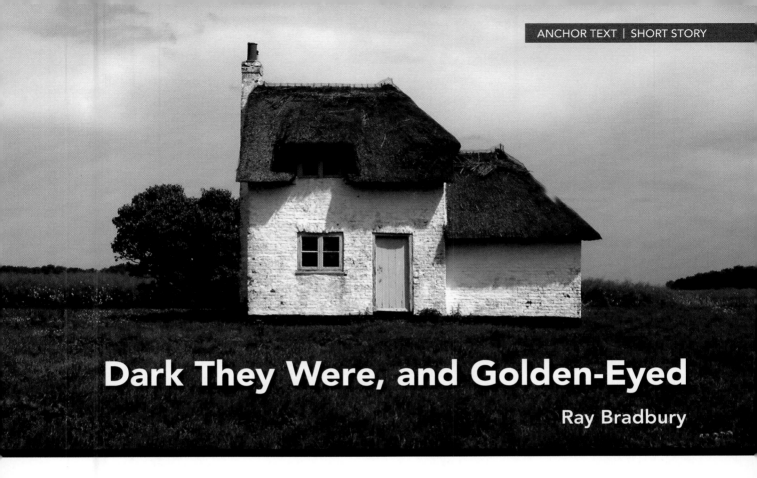

Dark They Were, and Golden-Eyed

Ray Bradbury

BACKGROUND

The astronomer Carl Sagan once wrote, "Mars has become a kind of mythic arena onto which we have projected our earthly hopes and fears." People have always been fascinated by the possibility of alien life on Mars. In this story, author Ray Bradbury does away with hard science, choosing instead to explore the aura of mystery that has always surrounded the Red Planet.

SCAN FOR MULTIMEDIA

1 The rocket metal cooled in the meadow winds. Its lid gave a bulging *pop*. From its clock interior stepped a man, a woman, and three children. The other passengers whispered away across the Martian meadow, leaving the man alone among his family.

2 The man felt his hair flutter and the tissues of his body draw tight as if he were standing at the center of a vacuum. His wife, before him, seemed almost to whirl away in smoke. The children, small seeds, might at any instant be sown to all the Martian climes.

3 The children looked up at him, as people look to the sun to tell what time of their life it is. His face was cold.

4 "What's wrong?" asked his wife.

5 "Let's get back on the rocket."

6 "Go back to Earth?"

7 "Yes! Listen!"

8 The wind blew as if to flake away their identities. At any moment the Martian air might draw his soul from him, as marrow

NOTES

CLOSE READ

ANNOTATE: In paragraph 2, mark the things that are being compared.

QUESTION: What is unusual about these comparisons?

CONCLUDE: What mood or overall impression has Bradbury created with these comparisons?

comes from a white bone. He felt **submerged** in a chemical that could dissolve his intellect and burn away his past.

9 They looked at Martian hills that time had worn with a crushing pressure of years. They saw the old cities, lost in their meadows, lying like children's delicate bones among the blowing lakes of grass.

10 "Chin up, Harry," said his wife. "It's too late. We've come over sixty million miles."

11 The children with their yellow hair hollered at the deep dome of Martian sky. There was no answer but the racing hiss of wind through the stiff grass.

12 He picked up the luggage in his cold hands. "Here we go," he said—a man standing on the edge of a sea, ready to wade in and be drowned.

13 They walked into town.

14 Their name was Bittering. Harry and his wife Cora; Dan, Laura, and David. They built a small white cottage and ate good breakfasts there, but the fear was never gone. It lay with Mr. Bittering and Mrs. Bittering, a third unbidden partner at every midnight talk, at every dawn awakening.

15 "I feel like a salt crystal," he said, "in a mountain stream, being washed away. We don't belong here. We're Earth people. This is Mars. It was meant for Martians. For heaven's sake, Cora, let's buy tickets for home!"

16 But she only shook her head. "One day the atom bomb will fix Earth. Then we'll be safe here."

17 "Safe and insane!"

18 *Tick-tock, seven o'clock* sang the voice-clock; *time to get up.* And they did.

19 Something made him check everything each morning—warm hearth, potted blood-geraniums—precisely as if he expected something to be amiss. The morning paper was toast-warm from the 6 A.M. Earth rocket. He broke its seal and tilted it at his breakfast place. He forced himself to be convivial.[1]

20 "Colonial days all over again," he declared. "Why, in ten years there'll be a million Earthmen on Mars. Big cities, everything! They said we'd fail. Said the Martians would resent our invasion. But did we find any Martians? Not a living soul! Oh, we found their empty cities, but no one in them. Right?"

21 A river of wind submerged the house. When the windows ceased rattling Mr. Bittering swallowed and looked at the children.

22 "I don't know," said David. "Maybe there're Martians around we don't see. Sometimes nights I think I hear 'em. I hear the wind. The sand hits my window. I get scared. And I see those towns way

---

1. **convivial** (kuhn VIHV ee uhl) *adj.* social and friendly.

up in the mountains where the Martians lived a long time ago. And I think I see things moving around those towns, Papa. And I wonder if those Martians *mind* us living here. I wonder if they won't do something to us for coming here."

23   "Nonsense!" Mr. Bittering looked out the windows. "We're clean, decent people." He looked at his children. "All dead cities have some kind of ghosts in them. Memories, I mean." He stared at the hills. "You see a staircase and you wonder what Martians looked like climbing it. You see Martian paintings and you wonder what the painter was like. You make a little ghost in your mind, a memory. It's quite natural. Imagination." He stopped. "You haven't been prowling up in those ruins, have you?"

24   "No, Papa." David looked at his shoes.

25   "See that you stay away from them. Pass the jam."

26   "Just the same," said little David, "I bet something happens. "

27   Something happened that afternoon.

28   Laura stumbled through the settlement, crying. She dashed blindly onto the porch.

29   "Mother, Father—the war, Earth!" she sobbed. "A radio flash just came. Atom bombs hit New York! All the space rockets blown up. No more rockets to Mars, ever!"

30   "Oh, Harry!" The mother held onto her husband and daughter.

31   "Are you sure, Laura?" asked the father quietly.

32   Laura wept. "We're stranded on Mars, forever and ever!"

33   For a long time there was only the sound of the wind in the late afternoon.

34   Alone, thought Bittering. Only a thousand of us here. No way back. No way. No way. Sweat poured from his face and his hands and his body; he was drenched in the hotness of his fear. He wanted to strike Laura, cry, "No, you're lying! The rockets will come back!" Instead, he stroked Laura's head against him and said, "The rockets will get through someday."

35   "Father, what will we do?"

36   "Go about our business, of course. Raise crops and children. Wait. Keep things going until the war ends and the rockets come again."

37   The two boys stepped out onto the porch.

38   "Children," he said, sitting there, looking beyond them, "I've something to tell you."

39   "We know," they said.

40   In the following days, Bittering wandered often through the garden to stand alone in his fear. As long as the rockets had spun a silver web across space, he had been able to accept Mars. For he had always told himself: Tomorrow, if I want, I can buy a ticket and go back to Earth.

NOTES

CLOSE READ

ANNOTATE: Mark details in the beginning of paragraph 34 that describe Bittering's inner thoughts.

QUESTION: Why are these thoughts expressed in incomplete sentences, with a lot of repetition?

CONCLUDE: What does this use of language help reveal about Bittering's emotional state?

CLOSE READ

ANNOTATE: Mark examples of descriptive language in paragraph 41.

QUESTION: What idea about Mars does this use of language suggest?

CONCLUDE: How does this passage build suspense?

41   But now: The web gone, the rockets lying in jigsaw heaps of molten girder and unsnaked wire. Earth people left to the strangeness of Mars, the cinnamon dusts and wine airs, to be baked like gingerbread shapes in Martian summers, put into harvested storage by Martian winters. What would happen to him, the others? This was the moment Mars had waited for. Now it would eat them.

42   He got down on his knees in the flower bed, a spade in his nervous hands. Work, he thought, work and forget.

43   He glanced up from the garden to the Martian mountains. He thought of the proud old Martian names that had once been on those peaks. Earthmen, dropping from the sky, had gazed upon hills, rivers, Martian seats left nameless in spite of names. Once Martians had built cities, named cities; climbed mountains, named mountains; sailed seas, named seas. Mountains melted, seas drained, cities tumbled. In spite of this, the Earthmen had felt a silent guilt at putting new names to these ancient hills and valleys.

44   Nevertheless, man lives by symbol and label. The names were given.

45   Mr. Bittering felt very alone in his garden under the Martian sun, anachronism² bent here, planting Earth flowers in a wild soil.

46   Think. Keep thinking. Different things. Keep your mind free of Earth, the atom war, the lost rockets.

47   He perspired. He glanced about. No one watching. He removed his tie. Pretty bold, he thought. First your coat off, now your tie. He hung it neatly on a peach tree he had imported as a sapling from Massachusetts.

48   He returned to his philosophy of names and mountains. The Earthmen had changed names. Now there were Hormel Valleys, Roosevelt Seas, Ford Hills, Vanderbilt Plateaus, Rockefeller Rivers,³ on Mars. It wasn't right. The American settlers had shown wisdom, using old Indian prairie names: Wisconsin, Minnesota, Idaho, Ohio, Utah, Milwaukee, Waukegan, Osseo. The old names, the old meanings.

49   Staring at the mountains wildly, he thought: Are you up there? All the dead ones, you Martians? Well, here we are, alone, cut off! Come down, move us out! We're helpless!

50   The wind blew a shower of peach blossoms.

51   He put out his sun-browned hand and gave a small cry. He touched the blossoms and picked them up. He turned them, he touched them again and again. Then he shouted for his wife.

52   "Cora!"

53   She appeared at a window. He ran to her.

---

2. **anachronism** (uh NA kruh nih zuhm) *n.* something that seems to belong to the past instead of the present.
3. **Hormel Valleys . . . Rockefeller Rivers** the colonists have named places on Mars after well-known families from mid-twentieth-century America.

54 "Cora, these blossoms!"

55 She handled them.

56 "Do you see? They're different. They've changed! They're not peach blossoms any more!"

57 "Look all right to me," she said.

58 "They're not. They're wrong! I can't tell how. An extra petal, a leaf, something, the color, the smell!"

59 The children ran out in time to see their father hurrying about the garden, pulling up radishes, onions, and carrots from their beds.

60 "Cora, come look!"

61 They handled the onions, the radishes, the carrots among them.

62 "Do they look like carrots?"

63 "Yes . . . no." She hesitated. "I don't know."

64 "They're changed."

65 "Perhaps."

66 "You know they have! Onions but not onions, carrots but not carrots. Taste: the same but different. Smell: not like it used to be." He felt his heart pounding, and he was afraid. He dug his fingers into the earth. "Cora, what's happening? What is it? We've got to get away from this." He ran across the garden. Each tree felt his touch. "The roses. The roses. They're turning green!"

67 And they stood looking at the green roses.

68 And two days later Dan came running. "Come see the cow. I was milking her and I saw it. Come on!"

69 They stood in the shed and looked at their one cow.

70 It was growing a third horn.

NOTES

71   And the lawn in front of their house very quietly and slowly was coloring itself like spring violets. Seed from Earth but growing up a soft purple.

72   "We must get away," said Bittering. "We'll eat this stuff and then we'll change—who knows to what? I can't let it happen. There's only one thing to do. Burn this food!"

73   "It's not poisoned."

74   "But it is. Subtly, very subtly. A little bit. A very little bit. We mustn't touch it."

75   He looked with dismay at their house. "Even the house. The wind's done something to it. The air's burned it. The fog at night. The boards, all warped out of shape. It's not an Earthman's house any more."

76   "Oh, your imagination!"

77   He put on his coat and tie. "I'm going into town. We've got to do something now. I'll be back."

78   "Wait, Harry!" his wife cried.

79   But he was gone.

80   In town, on the shadowy step of the grocery store, the men sat with their hands on their knees, conversing with great leisure and ease.

81   Mr. Bittering wanted to fire a pistol in the air.

82   What are you doing, you fools! he thought. Sitting here! You've heard the news—we're stranded on this planet. Well, move! Aren't you frightened? Aren't you afraid? What are you going to do?

83   "Hello, Harry," said everyone.

84   "Look," he said to them. "You did hear the news, the other day, didn't you?"

85   They nodded and laughed. "Sure. Sure, Harry."

86   "What are you going to do about it?"

87   "Do, Harry, do? What *can* we do?"

88   "Build a rocket, that's what!"

89   "A rocket, Harry? To go back to all that trouble? Oh, Harry!"

90   "But you *must* want to go back. Have you noticed the peach blossoms, the onions, the grass?"

91   "Why, yes, Harry, seems we did," said one of the men.

92   "Doesn't it scare you?"

93   "Can't recall that it did much, Harry."

94   "Idiots!"

95   "Now, Harry."

96   Bittering wanted to cry. "You've got to work with me. If we stay here, we'll all change. The air. Don't you smell it? Something in the air. A Martian virus, maybe; some seed, or a pollen. Listen to me!"

97   They stared at him.

CLOSE READ

ANNOTATE: Mark details in paragraphs 83–85 that indicate disagreement between Bittering and the other men.

QUESTION: Why might Bradbury have chosen to build conflict through the use of dialogue?

CONCLUDE: Would this passage be as effective if it had been written as description rather than dialogue? Explain.

98   "Sam," he said to one of them.

99   "Yes, Harry?"

100   "Will you help me build a rocket?"

101   "Harry, I got a whole load of metal and some blueprints. You want to work in my metal shop on a rocket, you're welcome. I'll sell you that metal for five hundred dollars. You should be able to construct a right pretty rocket, if you work alone, in about thirty years."

102   Everyone laughed.

103   "Don't laugh."

104   Sam looked at him with quiet good humor.

105   "Sam," Bittering said. "Your eyes—"

106   "What about them, Harry?"

107   "Didn't they used to be gray?"

108   "Well now, I don't remember."

109   "They were, weren't they?"

110   "Why do you ask, Harry?"

111   "Because now they're kind of yellow-colored."

112   "Is that so, Harry?" Sam said, casually.

113   "And you're taller and thinner—"

114   "You might be right, Harry."

115   "Sam, you shouldn't have yellow eyes."

116   "Harry, what color eyes have *you* got?" Sam said.

117   "My eyes? They're blue, of course."

118   "Here you are, Harry." Sam handed him a pocket mirror. "Take a look at yourself."

119   Mr. Bittering hesitated, and then raised the mirror to his face.

120   There were little, very dim flecks of new gold captured in the blue of his eyes.

121   "Now look what you've done," said Sam a moment later. "You've broken my mirror."

122   Harry Bittering moved into the metal shop and began to build the rocket. Men stood in the open door and talked and joked without raising their voices. Once in a while they gave him a hand on lifting something. But mostly they just idled and watched him with their yellowing eyes.

123   "It's suppertime, Harry," they said.

124   His wife appeared with his supper in a wicker basket.

125   "I won't touch it," he said. "I'll eat only food from our Deepfreeze. Food that came from Earth. Nothing from our garden."

126   His wife stood watching him. "You can't build a rocket."

127   "I worked in a shop once, when I was twenty. I know metal. Once I get it started, the others will help," he said, not looking at her, laying out the blueprints.

forlorn (fawr LAWRN) *adj.*
abandoned or deserted

CLOSE READ

ANNOTATE: Mark the Martian word Mr. Bittering says in paragraph 135.

QUESTION: Why does the author have Bittering speak Martian at this point in the story?

CONCLUDE: In what way is this event significant?

128   "Harry, Harry," she said, helplessly.

129   "We've got to get away, Cora. We've *got* to!"

130   The nights were full of wind that blew down the empty moonlit sea meadows past the little white chess cities lying for their twelve-thousandth year in the shallows. In the Earthmen's settlement, the Bittering house shook with a feeling of change.

131   Lying abed, Mr. Bittering felt his bones shifted, shaped, melted like gold. His wife, lying beside him, was dark from many sunny afternoons. Dark she was, and golden-eyed, burnt almost black by the sun, sleeping, and the children metallic in their beds, and the wind roaring **forlorn** and changing through the old peach trees, the violet grass, shaking out green rose petals.

132   The fear would not be stopped. It had his throat and heart. It dripped in a wetness of the arm and the temple and the trembling palm.

133   A green star rose in the east.

134   A strange word emerged from Mr. Bittering's lips.

135   "*Iorrt. Iorrt.*" He repeated it.

136   It was a Martian word. He knew no Martian.

137   In the middle of the night he arose and dialed a call through to Simpson, the archaeologist.

138   "Simpson, what does the word *Iorrt* mean?"

139   "Why that's the old Martian word for our planet Earth. Why?"

140   "No special reason."

141   The telephone slipped from his hand.

142   "Hello, hello, hello, hello," it kept saying while he sat gazing out at the green star. "Bittering? Harry, are you there?"

143   The days were full of metal sound. He laid the frame of the rocket with the reluctant help of three indifferent men. He grew very tired in an hour or so and had to sit down.

144   "The altitude," laughed a man.

145   "Are you *eating*, Harry?" asked another.

146   "I'm eating," he said, angrily.

147   "From your Deepfreeze?"

148   "Yes!"

149   "You're getting thinner, Harry."

150   "I'm not."

151   "And taller."

152   "Liar!"

153   His wife took him aside a few days later. "Harry, I've used up all the food in the Deepfreeze. There's nothing left. I'll have to make sandwiches using food grown on Mars."

154   He sat down heavily.

155   "You must eat," she said. "You're weak."

156   "Yes," he said.

157   He took a sandwich, opened it, looked at it, and began to nibble at it.

158   "And take the rest of the day off," she said. "It's hot. The children want to swim in the **canals** and hike. Please come along."

159   "I can't waste time. This is a crisis!"

160   "Just for an hour," she urged. "A swim'll do you good."

161   He rose, sweating. "All right, all right. Leave me alone. I'll come."

162   "Good for you, Harry."

163   The sun was hot, the day quiet. There was only an **immense** staring burn upon the land. They moved along the canal, the father, the mother, the racing children in their swimsuits. They stopped and ate meat sandwiches. He saw their skin baking brown. And he saw the yellow eyes of his wife and his children, their eyes that were never yellow before. A few tremblings shook him, but were carried off in waves of pleasant heat as he lay in the sun. He was too tired to be afraid.

164   "Cora, how long have your eyes been yellow?"

165   She was bewildered. "Always, I guess."

166   "They didn't change from brown in the last three months?"

167   She bit her lips. "No. Why do you ask?"

168 "Never mind."

169 They sat there.

170 "The children's eyes," he said. "They're yellow, too."

171 "Sometimes growing children's eyes change color."

172 "Maybe *we're* children, too. At least to Mars. That's a thought." He laughed. "Think I'll swim."

173 They leaped into the canal water, and he let himself sink down and down to the bottom like a golden statue and lie there in green silence. All was water-quiet and deep, all was peace. He felt the steady, slow current drift him easily.

174 If I lie here long enough, he thought, the water will work and eat away my flesh until the bones show like coral. Just my skeleton left. And then the water can build on that skeleton— green things, deep water things, red things, yellow things. Change. Change. Slow, deep, silent change. And isn't that what it is up *there*?

175 He saw the sky submerged above him, the sun made Martian by **atmosphere** and time and space.

atmosphere (AT muhs fihr) *n.* the gas surrounding the earth; the air

176 Up there, a big river, he thought, a Martian river; all of us lying deep in it, in our pebble houses, in our sunken boulder houses, like crayfish hidden, and the water washing away our old bodies and lengthening the bones and—

177 He let himself drift up through the soft light.

178 Dan sat on the edge of the canal, regarding his father seriously.

179 "*Utha*," he said.

180 "What?" asked his father.

181 The boy smiled. "You know. *Utha's* the Martian word for 'father.'"

182 "Where did you learn it?"

183 "I don't know. Around. *Utha!*"

184 "What do you want?"

185 The boy hesitated. "I—I want to change my name."

186 "Change it?"

187 "Yes."

188 His mother swam over. "What's wrong with Dan for a name?"

189 Dan fidgeted. "The other day you called Dan, Dan, Dan. I didn't even hear. I said to myself, That's not my name. I've a new name I want to use."

190 Mr. Bittering held to the side of the canal, his body cold and his heart pounding slowly. "What is this new name?"

191 "Linnl. Isn't that a good name? Can I use it? Can't I, please?"

192 Mr. Bittering put his hand to his head. He thought of the silly rocket, himself working alone, himself alone even among his family, so alone.

193 He heard his wife say, "Why not?"

194 He heard himself say, "Yes, you can use it."

195   "Yaaa!" screamed the boy. "I'm Linnl, Linnl!"

196   Racing down the meadowlands, he danced and shouted.

197   Mr. Bittering looked at his wife. "Why did we do that?"

198   "I don't know," she said. "It just seemed like a good idea."

199   They walked into the hills. They strolled on old **mosaic** paths, beside still pumping fountains. The paths were covered with a thin film of cool water all summer long. You kept your bare feet cool all the day, splashing as in a creek, wading.

200   They came to a small deserted Martian villa with a good view of the valley. It was on top of a hill. Blue marble halls, large murals, a swimming pool. It was refreshing in this hot summertime. The Martians hadn't believed in large cities.

201   "How nice," said Mrs. Bittering, "if we could move up here to this villa for the summer."

202   "Come on," he said. "We're going back to town. There's work to be done on the rocket."

203   But as he worked that night, the thought of the cool blue marble villa entered his mind. As the hours passed, the rocket seemed less important.

204   In the flow of days and weeks, the rocket receded and dwindled. The old fever was gone. It frightened him to think he had let it slip this way. But somehow the heat, the air, the working conditions—

205   He heard the men murmuring on the porch of his metal shop.

206   "Everyone's going. You heard?"

207   "All going. That's right."

208   Bittering came out. "Going where?" He saw a couple of trucks, loaded with children and furniture, drive down the dusty street.

209   "Up to the villas," said the man.

210   "Yeah, Harry. I'm going. So is Sam. Aren't you Sam?"

211   "That's right, Harry. What about you?"

212   "I've got work to do here. "

213   "Work! You can finish that rocket in the autumn, when it's cooler."

214   He took a breath. "I got the frame all set up."

215   "In the autumn is better." Their voices were lazy in the heat.

216   "Got to work," he said.

217   "Autumn," they reasoned. And they sounded so sensible, so right.

218   "Autumn would be best," he thought. "Plenty of time, then."

219   No! cried part of himself, deep down, put away, locked tight, suffocating. No! No!

220   "In the autumn," he said.

221   "Come on, Harry," they all said.

222   "Yes," he said, feeling his flesh melt in the hot liquid air. "Yes, in the autumn. I'll begin work again then."

NOTES

mosaic (moh ZAY ihk) *adj.* made of many small pieces of colored glass or stone

CLOSE READ

ANNOTATE: Mark the words or ideas that are repeated in paragraphs 212–222.

QUESTION: Why are these words or ideas repeated so often? What is happening to Bittering as the discussion progresses?

CONCLUDE: What important change has occurred as Bittering echoes the words of others?

223   "I got a villa near the Tirra Canal," said someone.

224   "You mean the Roosevelt Canal, don't you?"

225   "Tirra. The old Martian name."

226   "But on the map—"

227   "Forget the map. It's Tirra now. Now I found a place in the Pillan Mountains—"

228   "You mean the Rockefeller Range," said Bittering.

229   "I mean the Pillan Mountains," said Sam.

230   "Yes," said Bittering, buried in the hot, swarming air. "The Pillan Mountains."

231   Everyone worked at loading the truck in the hot, still afternoon of the next day.

232   Laura, Dan, and David carried packages. Or, as they preferred to be known, Ttil, Linnl, and Werr carried packages.

233   The furniture was abandoned in the little white cottage.

234   "It looked just fine in Boston," said the mother. "And here in the cottage. But up at the villa? No. We'll get it when we come back in the autumn."

235   Bittering himself was quiet.

236   "I've some ideas on furniture for the villa," he said after a time. "Big, lazy furniture."

237   "What about your encyclopedia? You're taking it along, surely?"

238   Mr. Bittering glanced away. "I'll come and get it next week."

239   They turned to their daughter. "What about your New York dresses?"

240   The bewildered girl stared. "Why, I don't want them any more."

241   They shut off the gas, the water, they locked the doors and walked away. Father peered into the truck.

242   "Gosh, we're not taking much," he said. "Considering all we brought to Mars, this is only a handful!"

243   He started the truck.

244   Looking at the small white cottage for a long moment, he was filled with a desire to rush to it, touch it, say good-bye to it, for he felt as if he were going away on a long journey, leaving something to which he could never quite return, never understand again.

245   Just then Sam and his family drove by in another truck.

246   "Hi, Bittering! Here we go!"

247   The truck swung down the ancient highway out of town. There were sixty others traveling in the same direction. The town filled with a silent, heavy dust from their passage. The canal waters lay blue in the sun, and a quiet wind moved in the strange trees.

248   "Good-bye, town!" said Mr. Bittering.

249   "Good-bye, good-bye," said the family, waving to it.

250   They did not look back again.

251   Summer burned the canals dry. Summer moved like flame upon the meadows. In the empty Earth settlement, the painted houses flaked and peeled. Rubber tires upon which children had swung in back yards hung suspended like stopped clock pendulums in the blazing air.

252   At the metal shop, the rocket frame began to rust.

253   In the quiet autumn Mr. Bittering stood, very dark now, very golden-eyed, upon the slope above his villa, looking at the valley.

254   "It's time to go back," said Cora.

255   "Yes, but we're not going," he said quietly. "There's nothing there any more."

256   "Your books," she said. "Your fine clothes.

257   "Your *Illes* and your fine *ior uele rre*," she said.

258   "The town's empty. No one's going back," he said. "There's no reason to, none at all."

259   The daughter wove tapestries and the sons played songs on ancient flutes and pipes, their laughter echoing in the marble villa.

260   Mr. Bittering gazed at the Earth settlement far away in the low valley. "Such odd, such ridiculous houses the Earth people built."

261   "They didn't know any better," his wife mused. "Such ugly people. I'm glad they've gone."

262   They both looked at each other, startled by all they had just finished saying. They laughed.

263   "Where did they go?" he wondered. He glanced at his wife. She was golden and slender as his daughter. She looked at him, and he seemed almost as young as their eldest son.

264   "I don't know," she said.

265   "We'll go back to town maybe next year, or the year after, or the year after that," he said, calmly. "Now—I'm warm. How about taking a swim?"

266   They turned their backs to the valley. Arm in arm they walked silently down a path of clear-running spring water.

✳ ✳ ✳

267   Five years later a rocket fell out of the sky. It lay steaming in the valley. Men leaped out of it, shouting.

268   "We won the war on Earth! We're here to rescue you! Hey!"

269   But the American-built town of cottages, peach trees, and theaters was silent. They found a flimsy rocket frame rusting in an empty shop.

270   The rocket men searched the hills. The captain established headquarters in an abandoned bar. His lieutenant came back to report.

271   "The town's empty, but we found native life in the hills, sir. Dark people. Yellow eyes. Martians. Very friendly. We talked a bit,

NOTES

CLOSE READ

ANNOTATE: Mark details in paragraphs 269–278 that reveal the findings of the rescue mission from Earth.

QUESTION: Why has Bradbury chosen to include this scene? What clues to the colonists' fate are hinted at?

CONCLUDE: Does this lingering mystery improve or weaken the story? Explain.

not much. They learn English fast. I'm sure our relations will be most friendly with them, sir."

272   "Dark, eh?" mused the captain. "How many?"

273   "Six, eight hundred, I'd say, living in those marble ruins in the hills, sir. Tall, healthy. Beautiful women."

274   "Did they tell you what became of the men and women who built this Earth settlement, Lieutenant?"

275   "They hadn't the foggiest notion of what happened to this town or its people."

276   "Strange. You think those Martians killed them?"

277   "They look surprisingly peaceful. Chances are a plague did this town in, sir."

278   "Perhaps. I suppose this is one of those mysteries we'll never solve. One of those mysteries you read about."

279   The captain looked at the room, the dusty windows, the blue mountains rising beyond, the canals moving in the light, and he heard the soft wind in the air. He shivered. Then, recovering, he tapped a large fresh map he had thumbtacked to the top of an empty table.

280   "Lots to be done, Lieutenant." His voice droned on and quietly on as the sun sank behind the blue hills. "New settlements. Mining sites, minerals to be looked for. Bacteriological specimens taken. The work, all the work. And the old records were lost. We'll have a job of remapping to do, renaming the mountains and rivers and such. Calls for a little imagination.

281   "What do you think of naming those mountains the Lincoln Mountains, this canal the Washington Canal, those hills—we can name those hills for you, Lieutenant. Diplomacy. And you, for a favor, might name a town for me. Polishing the apple. And why not make this the Einstein Valley, and farther over . . . are you *listening*, Lieutenant?"

282   The lieutenant snapped his gaze from the blue color and the quiet mist of the hills far beyond the town.

283   "What? Oh, *yes*, sir!" ❧

Comprehension Check

Complete the following items after you finish your first read.

1. What is the story's setting?

2. What causes the people from Earth to become stranded on Mars?

3. What change does Harry first notice in the world around him?

4. What does the rescue crew find when they arrive on Mars after five years?

5. 🗒 **Notebook** Write a summary of "Dark They Were, and Golden-Eyed."

- -

RESEARCH

Research to Clarify Choose at least one unfamiliar detail from the text. Briefly research that detail. In what way does the information you learned shed light on an aspect of the story?

DARK THEY WERE, AND
GOLDEN-EYED

Close Read the Text

1. This model, from paragraph 251 of the text, shows two sample annotations, along with questions and conclusions. Close read the passage, and find another detail to annotate. Then, write a question and your conclusion.

ANNOTATE: I notice that many words contain the letter *m*.

QUESTION: What effect does this repetition create?

CONCLUDE: The repeated sound creates a drowsy mood.

> Summer burned the canals dry. Summer moved like flame upon the meadows. In the empty Earth settlement, the painted houses flaked and peeled. Rubber tires upon which children had swung in back yards hung suspended like stopped clock pendulums in the blazing air.

ANNOTATE: I notice that an unusual comparison is made.

QUESTION: What effect is created with this simile?

CONCLUDE: It emphasizes the heat and desolation of the setting.

Close Read
ANNOTATE · QUESTION · CONCLUDE

2. For more practice, go back into the text and complete the close-read notes.

3. Revisit a section of the text you found important during your first read. Read this section closely and **annotate** what you notice. Ask yourself **questions** such as "Why did the author make this choice?" What can you **conclude**?

🔧 Tool Kit
Close-Read Guide and Model Annotation

Analyze the Text

CITE TEXTUAL EVIDENCE
to support your answers.

📓 **Notebook** Respond to these questions.

1. Analyze What might the constantly blowing wind represent?

2. Analyze In what ways does the author indicate that the Bittering family has begun to change significantly?

3. Speculate The fate of the original colonists is not specifically described. What do you think will become of the rescue team? What story details support your idea?

4. Essential Question: *Should we make a home in space?* What idea about living in space is suggested by this story?

📋 STANDARDS

Reading Literature
Determine the meaning of words and phrases as they are used in a text, including figurative and connotative meanings; analyze the impact of rhymes and other repetitions of sounds on a specific verse or stanza of a poem or section of a story or drama.

Language
Demonstrate understanding of figurative language, word relationships, and nuances in word meaning.
  a. Interpret figures of speech in context.

Analyze Craft and Structure

Figurative Language: Metaphor and Simile Figurative language is writing or speech that is not meant to be taken literally. The use of figurative language creates layers of meaning and helps readers see things in new ways.

- A **simile** compares two apparently unlike things using the words *like* or *as*: *The rocket was like a speeding bullet that tore through the sky.*

- A **metaphor** compares two apparently unlike things by saying that one thing *is* another: *The rocket was a speeding bullet that tore through the sky.*

- **Personification** is a comparison in which a nonhuman subject is given human characteristics: *The rocket gently enfolded its passengers as it tore through the sky.*

Practice

CITE TEXTUAL EVIDENCE to support your answers.

📓 **Notebook** Respond to these questions.

1. Read each passage from the story shown in the chart. Identify each as an example of simile, metaphor, or personification. Some passages may contain more than one type of figurative language. In the final column of the chart, give reasons for your answers.

TEXT PASSAGE	TYPE(S) OF FIGURATIVE LANGUAGE	EXPLANATION
The children, small seeds, might at any instant be sown to all the Martian climes. (paragraph 2)		
They saw the old cities, . . . lying like children's delicate bones among the blowing lakes of grass. (paragraph 9)		
This was the moment Mars had waited for. Now it would eat them. (paragraph 41)		

2. Rewrite a simile you identified in the chart as a metaphor.

_____

_____

3. Write a sentence in which you personify the blowing wind that is described throughout the story.

_____

_____

DARK THEY WERE, AND
GOLDEN-EYED

Concept Vocabulary

submerged	canals	atmosphere
forlorn	immense	mosaic

Why These Words? The concept vocabulary words from the text describe Bradbury's vision of Mars. For example, the Bitterings' house is *submerged* by a river of wind, which also roars "*forlorn* and changing through the old peach tree."

1. How does the concept vocabulary sharpen the reader's understanding of what it is like for the Bitterings to live on Mars?

2. What other words in the selection connect to the concept of describing an alien world?

Practice

📘 **Notebook** The concept vocabulary words appear in "Dark They Were, and Golden-Eyed."

1. Use each concept word in a sentence that demonstrates your understanding of the word's meaning.
2. Challenge yourself to replace each concept word with one or two synonyms. How does the word change affect the meaning of your sentence? For example, which sentence is stronger? Which has a more positive meaning?

Word Study

Synonyms and Nuance Words that have the same basic meaning are called **synonyms.** Often, however, there are subtle shades of meaning, or **nuances,** between synonyms. For example, the basic meaning of *forlorn* is "sad," but its nuances indicate that it is a type of sadness caused by abandonment or loneliness.

1. Identify the basic meaning of these synonyms, and then describe their differences in nuance: *immense / colossal.*

2. Using a thesaurus, find two other words related to *forlorn*. Record a definition for each synonym, and then use each word in a sentence that reflects its nuances, or shades of meaning.

⬡ WORD NETWORK

Add interesting words related to space exploration from the text to your Word Network.

▦ STANDARDS

Language
• Determine or clarify the meaning of unknown and multiple-meaning words and phrases based on *grade 7 reading and content,* choosing flexibly from a range of strategies.
• Demonstrate understanding of figurative language, word relationships, and nuances in word meanings.

144 UNIT 2 • A STARRY HOME

Conventions

Comparisons Using Adjectives and Adverbs **Adjectives** modify, or describe, nouns or pronouns. **Adverbs** modify verbs, adjectives, and other adverbs. Most adjectives and adverbs have three degrees of comparison.

- The **positive degree** is used when no comparison is made. For example: "Jackson Avenue is a *long* street." "We progressed *quickly*."

- The **comparative degree** is used when two things are being compared. The comparative degree of most one- or two-syllable modifiers ends with *-er*. The word *more* is used to form the comparative degree of most longer modifiers or adverbs that end with *-ly*. For example: "Washington Avenue is *longer* than Jackson Avenue." "We progressed *more quickly* than they did."

- The **superlative degree** is used when three or more things are being compared. The superlative degree of most one- or two-syllable modifers ends with *-est*. The word *most* is used to form the superlative degree of most longer modifiers or adverbs that end with *-ly*. For example: "Lincoln Avenue is the *longest* street in town." "We progressed the *most quickly* of all."

Read It

1. Mark the adjectives and adverbs in these sentences. Label each one *positive*, *comparative*, or *superlative*.

   a. They were determined to build the strongest rocket that they possibly could.

   b. It was a cold, dreary night on the quiet, red planet.

   c. Everybody thought it was odd that Harry's eyes turned gold more quickly than Cora's eyes did.

2. Reread paragraph 275 of "Dark They Were, and Golden-Eyed." Identify the superlative adjective.

Write It

Respond to these items.

1. Rewrite each sentence below twice. Replace each positive, comparative, or superlative adjective or adverb with the forms of the other two degrees of comparison for that word—whichever two forms are not used in the original sentence.

   a. James drew a funny picture.

   b. This room has been repainted with a darker shade of green.

   c. It rained heavily through the night.

2. **Notebook** Write a brief paragraph that includes at least one positive, one comparative, and one superlative adjective or adverb.

TIP

FOLLOW THROUGH
Refer to the Grammar Handbook to learn more about adjectives and adverbs.

📝 **EVIDENCE LOG**

Before moving on to a new selection, go your Evidence Log and record what you've learned from "Dark They Were, and Golden-Eyed."

STANDARDS
Language
Demonstrate command of the conventions of standard English grammar and usage when writing or speaking.

Comparing Text to Media

DARK THEY WERE, AND
GOLDEN-EYED
(short story)

In this lesson, you will listen to a radio play of "Dark They Were, and Golden-Eyed." You will then compare the story and the performance of the radio play.

DARK THEY WERE, AND
GOLDEN-EYED
(radio play)

About the Producer

Michael McDonough is a professional sound designer and the producer of the *Bradbury 13* series. For *Bradbury 13*, McDonough wrote all the scripts and created spectacular original sound effects. McDonough first learned sound design as a student at Brigham Young University and went on to work on dozens of films and television shows.

Dark They Were, and Golden-Eyed

Media Vocabulary

These words will be useful to you as you analyze, discuss, and write about the radio play.

sound effects: sounds produced artificially for a radio production	• Sound effects indicate settings and actions (city noises; the dropping of a book). • Certain sound effects also help create mood and atmosphere (a rusty door; the screech of an owl).
human voice: the central conveyor of events and interactions in a radio play	• Voices in a radio play need to be distinct so listeners know which character is speaking. • A speaker's pitch, volume, and pacing take on even more importance in a radio play.
silence: the absence of sound	• Silence after rapid dialogue can heighten suspense. • Silence or near silence can focus listeners' attention on characters' probable inner thoughts or on something ominous, such as the over-loud ticking of a clock.

First Review MEDIA: AUDIO

Study the radio play using these strategies. Take note of time codes as you listen so that you can go back and analyze sections you find interesting.

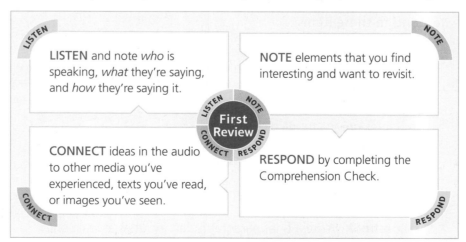

LISTEN and note *who* is speaking, *what* they're saying, and *how* they're saying it.

NOTE elements that you find interesting and want to revisit.

First Review

CONNECT ideas in the audio to other media you've experienced, texts you've read, or images you've seen.

RESPOND by completing the Comprehension Check.

⊟ STANDARDS

Reading Literature
By the end of the year, read and comprehend literature, including stories, dramas, and poems, in the grades 6–8 text complexity band proficiently, with scaffolding as needed at the high end of the range.

Language
Acquire and use accurately grade-appropriate general academic and domain-specific words and phrases; gather vocabulary knowledge when considering a word or phrase important to comprehension or expression.

Dark They Were, and Golden-Eyed

Michael McDonough, Producer

BACKGROUND

During the 1930s and 1940s, radio plays were a highly popular form of entertainment. However, with the rise of television, radio plays all but disappeared. In 1984, National Public Radio aired *Bradbury 13*, a series of radio adaptations of Ray Bradbury's works that re-create the feel of classic radio drama.

SCAN FOR MULTIMEDIA

NOTES

Comprehension Check

Complete the following items after you finish your first review.

1. What two speakers that are not in the original text begin the radio broadcast?

2. What additional details about the bombs on Earth are revealed in the radio play?

3. The Bitterings relocate to the villa toward the end of the story. In what way does the restructuring of description and dialogue from the original text to the radio play aid in your understanding of the characters' changing attitudes?

- -

RESEARCH

Research to Explore Choose one of the following to research: the story's author, the series called *Bradbury 13,* or the history of radio plays in general. How does this new knowledge help deepen your appreciation of this selection?

Close Review

Listen again to the radio play. Write any new observations that seem important. What **questions** do you have? What can you **conclude**?

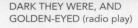

DARK THEY WERE, AND GOLDEN-EYED (radio play)

Analyze the Media

Notebook Respond to these questions.

1. **Compare and Contrast (a)** In what way is the opening scene of the radio play similar to the story's opening scene? **(b)** In what way does the opening scene differ from the story?

2. **Evaluate** Which version of the story did you enjoy more, the text or the audio? Give reasons for your response.

3. **Connect** If you were to cast the radio play, what actor would you choose to play each part? Explain your choices.

4. **Essential Question:** *Should we make a home in space?* What have you learned about living in space by listening to this radio play?

POINT OF COMPARISON

The text and the audio version of "Dark They Were, and Golden-Eyed" tell the same story. Pay attention to how experiencing the story is different when you read it and when you listen to it.

LANGUAGE DEVELOPMENT

Media Vocabulary

Use media vocabulary words in your responses to the following:

sound effects	human voice	silence

1. In what way has the Martian atmosphere been brought to life in the radio play?

2. Do the characters sound the way you thought they would sound, based on your reading of the story?

3. How are changes of scene indicated in the radio play?

STANDARDS
Speaking and Listening
Analyze the main ideas and supporting details presented in diverse media and formats and explain how the ideas clarify a topic, text, or issue under study.

DARK THEY WERE, AND
GOLDEN-EYED
(short story)

DARK THEY WERE, AND
GOLDEN-EYED
(radio play)

STANDARDS

Reading Literature
Compare and contrast a written story, drama, or poem to its audio, filmed, staged, or multimedia version, analyzing the effects of techniques unique to each medium.

Writing
• Write informative/explanatory texts to examine a topic and convey ideas, concepts, and information through the selection, organization, and analysis of relevant content.
• Draw evidence from literary or informational texts to support analysis, reflection, and research.
  a. Apply *grade 7 Reading standards* to literature.

Writing to Compare

You have read Ray Bradbury's science fiction tale "Dark They Were, and Golden-Eyed" and listened to a radio play adaptation of the story. Now, deepen your analysis and express your observations in writing.

Assignment

Both the story and the radio play describe the experiences of the Bittering family and other people from Earth living in a colony on Mars. To prepare for your assignment, consider the following:

• How are the story and radio play similar?
• What are the most important differences between the two?

Write a **comparison-and-contrast essay** in which you analyze the techniques each version uses to bring this tale to life. Conclude with an evaluation that tells which version is more effective.

Prewriting

Notebook Analyze Author's Purpose Skim Bradbury's story. Consider what his goals might have been when he was writing it in 1949. Then, think about the goals of Michael McDonough, the producer of the radio play. How might his goals have differed? Write your thoughts below.

Bradbury's goals	
McDonough's goals	

Compare Elements Both versions tell the same story, but they use techniques specific to their mediums. A short story uses language to develop plot, characters, and mood. A radio play uses voices, sound effects, and music to develop the same elements. Use a chart like this one to compare.

DARK THEY WERE, AND GOLDEN-EYED		
	SHORT STORY	RADIO PLAY
Plot How are events presented?		
Characters Who are the main characters, and how are they depicted?		
Mood What is the atmosphere of the work? What creates this mood?		

⊟ Notebook **Respond to these questions.**

1. Which narrative elements are stronger in Bradbury's short story?

2. Which elements have a greater impact in the radio play?

3. Which version of the tale is more effective? Why?

Drafting

Draft a strong introduction, body, and conclusion for your comparison-and-contrast essay. Follow an outline that includes details you collected. Write one paragraph for each numbered section in your outline.

Introduction	
I. Opening	Describe the narrative and mediums you are comparing.
Body	
II. Plot	Explain how the plot is developed in each version.
III. Characters	Tell how characters are presented in each version.
IV. Mood	Identify the mood created by each version.
Conclusion	
V. Evaluation	State which version is more effective.

Use Transitions Clearly identify which version of the tale you are writing about in each sentence. Transitions such as the following can help to distinguish versions and identify comparisons and contrasts:

In Bradbury's story . . .	*However,* in the radio play . . .
The language of the story . . .	*On the other hand,* the radio play . . .
The story's characters . . .	*Similarly,* the settlers in the radio play . . .

Where the story uses _____, the radio play employs _____.

Whereas the radio play takes advantage of _____, the story benefits from _____.

Support Your Conclusion Cite specific evidence from both versions of "Dark They Were, and Golden-Eyed" to support the evaluation in your conclusion. You may wish to describe the strengths of both versions, but emphasize why one version has a greater overall impact.

Review, Revise, and Edit

When you are done drafting, review and revise your essay. Make sure your essay presents information in a logical way. Make sure the points of comparison and contrast are clearly identified, and a concluding evaluation is supported by effective evidence. Proofread your draft for spelling and grammar errors. Finally, work with a partner to have a peer review of each other's essays.

✍ EVIDENCE LOG

Before moving on to a new selection, go to your Evidence Log and record what you've learned from the text and audio versions of "Dark They Were, and Golden-Eyed."

☰ STANDARDS

Writing
Write informative/explanatory texts to examine a topic and convey ideas, concepts, and information through the selection, organization, and analysis of relevant content.
 a. Introduce a topic clearly, previewing what is to follow; organize ideas, concepts, and information, using strategies such as definition, classification, comparison/contrast, and cause/effect; include formatting, graphics, and multimedia when useful to aiding comprehension.
 b. Develop the topic with relevant facts, definitions, concrete details, quotations, or other information and examples.
 d. Use precise language and domain-specific vocabulary to inform about or explain the topic.
 f. Provide a concluding statement or section that follows from and supports the information or explanation presented.

About the Author

Maggie Koerth-Baker
(b. 1981) is an American science journalist and author. She is the science editor at *BoingBoing*, a general-interest blog, and has contributed articles to the *New York Times Magazine*. Koerth-Baker writes about the relationship between science, culture, and human behavior.

Danger! This Mission to Mars Could Bore You to Death!

Concept Vocabulary

You will encounter the following words as you read "Danger! This Mission to Mars Could Bore You to Death!" Before reading, note how familiar you are with each word. Then, rank the words in order from most familiar (1) to least familiar (6).

WORD	YOUR RANKING
chronic	
stimulus	
subconsciously	
excruciatingly	
monotony	
catastrophic	

After completing the first read, come back to the concept vocabulary and review your rankings. Mark changes to your original rankings as needed.

First Read NONFICTION

Apply these strategies as you conduct your first read. You will have an opportunity to complete the close-read notes after your first read.

NOTICE the general ideas of the text. *What* is it about? *Who* is involved?

ANNOTATE by marking vocabulary and key passages you want to revisit.

First Read

CONNECT ideas within the selection to what you already know and what you have already read.

RESPOND by completing the Comprehension Check and by writing a brief summary of the selection.

STANDARDS
Reading Informational Text
By the end of the year, read and comprehend literary nonfiction in the grades 6–8 text complexity band proficiently, with scaffolding as needed at the high end of the range.

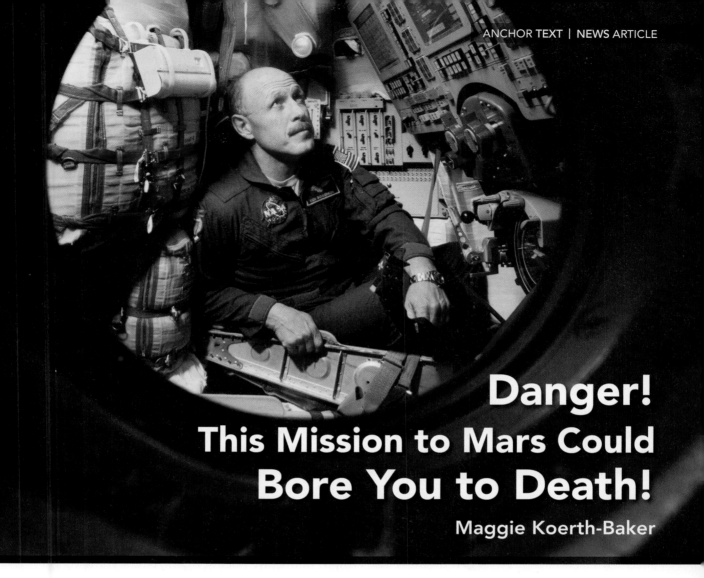

Danger!
This Mission to Mars Could
Bore You to Death!

Maggie Koerth-Baker

BACKGROUND

This article mentions Ernest Shackleton, who led several expeditions to the South Pole in the early 1900s. While these icy voyages took a huge toll on the crew's bodies, crew members also struggled with the mental stress of being isolated from society for months on end. On a mission to Mars, astronauts would also have to endure long periods of isolation and boredom.

SCAN FOR
MULTIMEDIA

1   Right now, six people are living in a nearly windowless, white geodesic dome[1] on the slopes of Hawaii's Mauna Loa volcano. They sleep in tiny rooms, use no more than eight minutes of shower time a week and subsist on a diet of freeze-dried, canned or preserved food. When they go outside, they exit through a mock air lock, clad head to toe in simulated spacesuits. The dome's occupants are playing a serious version of the game of pretend—what if we lived on Mars?

NOTES

---

1. **geodesic dome** round building that is inexpensive to build and is known for its structural strength, efficiency, and durability.

chronic (KRON ihk) *adj.*
lasting a long time or
recurring often

CLOSE READ

ANNOTATE: Mark
descriptive details you find
in paragraph 4.

QUESTION: What point
is the author making by
listing such details?

CONCLUDE: Do the details
effectively support the
topic sentence of the
paragraph?

stimulus (STIHM yuh luhs) *n.*
something that causes
action or reaction

2   Research at the Hawaii Space Exploration Analog and
Simulation (HI-SEAS) project, funded in part by NASA, is a
continuation of a long history of attempts to understand what will
happen to people who travel through outer space for long periods
of time. It's more than a technical problem. Besides multistage
rockets to propel a spacecraft out of Earth's atmosphere, years
of planning and precise calculations and massive amounts of
fuel, traveling the tens of millions of miles to Mars will take a
tremendous amount of time. With current technology, the journey
takes more than eight months each way.

3   Which means that astronauts will get bored. In fact, a number
of scientists say that—of all things—boredom is one of the biggest
threats to a manned Mars mission, despite the thrill inherent in
visiting another planet. And so, attention is being paid to the
effects of boredom at HI-SEAS, and on the International Space
Station. But because of the causes of **chronic** boredom, scientists
say, research facilities in Antarctica might actually provide a better
simulation of the stress of a journey to Mars.

4   Most living things constantly seek out sensory stimulation—
new smells, tastes, sights, sounds or experiences. Even
single-celled amoebas will move to investigate new sources of
light or heat, says Sheryl Bishop, who studies human performance
in extreme environments at the University of Texas Medical
Branch. Animals deprived of naturalistic environments and the
mental stimulation that comes with them can fall into repetitive,
harmful patterns of behavior. Anybody of a certain age will
remember zoos full of manically pacing tigers, bears gnawing on
their metal cages and birds that groomed themselves bald—all a
result, we now know, of their rather unstimulating lifestyles.

5   Human boredom isn't quite as well understood, says James
Danckert, a professor of cognitive neuroscience at the University
of Waterloo. He's currently working on what he says may be the
first study of how our brain activity changes when we're bored.
Danckert is hoping to find out whether boredom is connected to
a phenomenon called the "default network"—a background hum
of brain activity that seems to remain on even when you aren't
directly focused on something. There's a lot of observable activity
in the brains of people who are staring at a blank screen—way
more than anybody expected, Danckert says. The default network
maps closely to the brain-activity patterns scientists see when
someone's mind is wandering. It suggests that what we call a
restless mind is just that—a mind desperate for something to
amuse it, searching frantically for **stimulus**.

6   Boredom, it turns out, is a form of stress. Psychologically, it's
the mirror image of having too much work to do, says Jason
Kring, president of the Society of Human Performance in Extreme

Environments, an organization that studies how people live and work in space, underwater, on mountaintops and other high-risk places. If your brain does not receive sufficient stimulus, it might find something else to do—it daydreams, it wanders, it thinks about itself. If this goes on too long, it can affect your mind's normal functioning. Chronic boredom correlates with depression and attention deficits.

7   Astronaut candidates go through two years of training before they're even approved to fly. And before they are chosen to be candidates, they have to compete against thousands of other applicants. The 2013 class, for instance, had more than 6,000 applicants and only 8 were chosen. Astronauts are rigorously tested for psychological as well as physical fitness. But no mission in NASA's history has raised the specter of chronic boredom to the degree that a Mars mission does, because none have involved such a long journey through nothingness.

8   What if, millions of miles from home, a chronically bored astronaut forgets a certain safety procedure? What if he gets befuddled while reading an oxygen gauge? More important, Danckert and Kring say, bored people are also prone to taking risks, **subconsciously** seeking out stimulation when their environment bores them.

9   The cognitive and social psychologist Peter Suedfeld says that people will sometimes do reckless, stupid things when they suffer from chronic boredom. In Antarctica, where winter can cut scientists and crew off from the rest of the world for as long as nine months, the isolation can lead to strange behavior. Suedfeld told me he has heard about Antarctic researchers venturing outside in 40-below weather without proper clothing and without telling anyone else they were going out.

10   The diaries of early polar explorers are full of tales of extreme boredom, depression and desperate attempts at entertainment reminiscent of prisoners' stories from solitary confinement. An important lesson that Antarctica can impart on a Mars expedition is this: even scientists on important missions can get **excruciatingly** bored.

11   One effective way astronauts combat boredom is by staying busy with work. That's a strategy at HI-SEAS, where the crew member Kate Greene told me that her schedule is packed—every hour planned and accounted for, from the time she wakes up to the time she goes to bed at night. Life on the International Space Station is similar. (In fact, historically, NASA's problem has been overworking people: in 1973, the exhausted crew of Skylab 4[2] actually staged a relaxation rebellion and took an unscheduled day off.) But Antarctica is different from HI-SEAS or the

2. **Skylab 4** mission aboard United States space station Skylab.

NOTES

CLOSE READ
ANNOTATE: Mark facts in paragraph 7 that show the challenges with which astronauts are faced.

QUESTION: Why did the author include these facts?

CONCLUDE: How do these facts help you to better understand the reason that chronic boredom is especially problematic for a Mars mission?

subconsciously (suhb KON shuhs lee) *adv.* occurring in the mind without one's full awareness

excruciatingly (ehk SKROO shee ay tihng lee) *adv.* painfully; miserably

monotony (muh NOT uh nee) *n.* sameness; boredom

International Space Station. Communications are limited. There's nobody outside the base directing your day. Spectacular views vanish in a haze of white. It's just you, the people you came in with, no way out and little to break up the **monotony**.

12   And so some researchers there have learned to actively fend off boredom by creating what you might call a unique office culture. They celebrate a ridiculous number of holidays, both traditional and invented. You need something to look forward to, Suedfeld says, and planning the events helps change the routine. Even Ernest Shackleton's Antarctic crew found ways to put on skits and concerts. On one expedition, Shackleton brought a small printing press. At McMurdo Station,[3] the 1983 winter crew created costumes, learned lines and acted out scenes from the movie *Escape From New York.* It's possible that we may, someday, watch recordings of Mars-bound astronauts acting out other John Carpenter films. (It's not so far-fetched. Chris Hadfield, a Canadian astronaut, made a tribute to David Bowie's "Space Oddity" that racked up more than 16 million views on YouTube.)

13   It might sound absurd, but many scientists say strategies like this are necessary because, without proper mental stimulus, we risk making a physically and technologically challenging endeavor into a psychologically grueling one. It would be **catastrophic** if humanity's greatest voyage were brought low by the mind's tendency to wander when left to its own devices. ❧

catastrophic (kat uh STROF ihk) *adj.* disastrous

---

3. **McMurdo Station** Antarctic research station.

Comprehension Check

Complete the following items after you finish your first read.

1. Why are six people living in a geodesic dome on the slopes of a volcano in Hawaii?

2. With our current technology, how long will a journey to Mars take?

3. According to scientists, what is one of the biggest threats to a manned Mars mission?

4. 📓 **Notebook** Write a brief summary of "Danger! This Mission to Mars Could Bore You to Death!"

- -

RESEARCH

Research to Clarify Choose at least one unfamiliar detail from the news article. Briefly research that detail. In what way does the information you learned shed light on an aspect of the article?

DANGER! THIS MISSION
TO MARS COULD BORE
YOU TO DEATH!

Close Read the Text

1. This model, from paragraph 8 of the text, shows two sample annotations, along with questions and conclusions. Close read the passage, and find another detail to annotate. Then, write a question and conclusion.

Close Read
ANNOTATE · QUESTION · CONCLUDE

> **ANNOTATE:** The author begins this paragraph with two questions that introduce possible situations.
>
> **QUESTION:** Why does the author ask two questions without providing answers to them?
>
> **CONCLUDE:** The author is showing that there are many other potential risks resulting from astronaut boredom.

> What if, millions of miles from home, a chronically bored astronaut forgets a certain safety procedure? What if he gets befuddled while reading an oxygen gauge? More important, Danckert and Kring say, bored people are also prone to taking risks, subconsciously seeking out stimulation when their environment bores them.

> **ANNOTATE:** The author includes information from subject-matter experts.
>
> **QUESTION:** Why does the author include this information?
>
> **CONCLUDE:** Expert information supports and strengthens the author's explanation.

🔧 **Tool Kit**
Close-Read Guide and
Model Annotation

2. For more practice, go back into the text and complete the close-read notes.

3. Revisit a section of the text you found important during your first read. Read this section closely and **annotate** what you notice. Ask yourself **questions** such as "Why did the author make this choice?" What can you **conclude**?

Analyze the Text

CITE TEXTUAL EVIDENCE
to support your answers.

📓 **Notebook** Respond to these questions.

1. **Connect** How is chronic boredom a form of stress?

2. **Classify** (a) Which details about the dangers of boredom were most convincing? (b) Which details were least convincing?

3. **Essential Question** *Should we make a home in space?* What have you learned about the benefits and drawbacks of space travel from reading this article?

☰ **STANDARDS**
Reading Informational Text
Analyze the structure an author uses to organize a text, including how the major sections contribute to the whole and to the development of the ideas.

Analyze Craft and Structure

Text Structure: Informative Writing Any kind of writing that teaches, informs, or explains is called **informative writing.** Effective informative texts present numerous aspects of a topic in a way that is easy to follow and understand.

- The topic of the text is introduced and then developed in related sections or paragraphs. These sections or paragraphs build on one another to present a clear picture of the topic.

- The author provides support for his or her ideas with facts, statistics, and other details that describe and elaborate on the topic; the support may also include quotations from experts on the topic.

- Transition words and phrases, such as *finally, since,* and *in fact,* are often used to show how ideas are connected.

Practice

CITE TEXTUAL EVIDENCE
to support your answers.

📓 **Notebook** Respond to these questions.

1. Use the chart to identify key information provided in the article.

What details are provided in the introduction?	
What aspects of the topic are explored in the body paragraphs?	
What key idea is reinforced in the conclusion?	

2. (a) Identify three transition words or phrases in paragraph 3 of the article. (b) How do these words and phrases link the ideas in this paragraph together?

3. How effectively has the author introduced ideas and supported them? Cite details to support your response.

DANGER! THIS MISSION TO MARS COULD BORE YOU TO DEATH!

WORD NETWORK

Add interesting words related to space exploration from the text to your Word Network.

Concept Vocabulary

chronic	subconsciously	monotony
stimulus	excruciatingly	catastrophic

Why These Words? The concept vocabulary words from the text are related to boredom. For example, when we are bored, we might *subconsciously* seek some sort of *stimulus*.

1. How does the concept vocabulary sharpen your understanding of how people respond to boredom?

2. What other words in the selection connect to the condition of boredom or the potential risks it poses?

Practice

Notebook **Respond to these questions.**

1. Why might a doctor be concerned if a patient had a *chronic* cough?

2. What sort of *stimulus* might a person seek if he or she were sleepy?

3. What might happen if someone were *subconsciously* nervous about speaking in front of people?

4. What might it feel like to have an *excruciatingly* painful headache?

5. Why might many people find *monotony* in household chores?

6. What might happen to a ship in a *catastrophic* disaster at sea?

Word Study

Latin Prefix: *sub-* The Latin prefix *sub-* means "under" or "below." The word *subconsciously* means "in a way that is below consciousness"; that is, it refers to a thought or action that occurs in a way in which a person is not directly aware of having the thought or performing the action. In the article, the author says that when people become bored, they *subconsciously* seek out stimulation, or they look for things to stimulate them without even being aware that they are doing so.

1. Write a sentence that correctly uses the word *subconsciously*.

2. Using a dictionary or thesaurus, find three other words that have the prefix *sub-*. Record the definition for each word, and write a sentence that correctly uses each word.

STANDARDS

Language
• Demonstrate command of the conventions of standard English grammar and usage when writing or speaking.
• Determine or clarify the meaning of unknown and multiple-meaning words and phrases based on *grade 7 reading and content*, choosing flexibly from a range of strategies.
  b. Use common, grade-appropriate Greek or Latin affixes and roots as clues to the meaning of a word.

Conventions

Action Verbs and Linking Verbs A **verb** is a word that expresses an action or a state of being. A complete sentence must have at least one verb.

- An **action verb** tells what action someone or something is doing.
- A **linking verb** joins the subject of a sentence with a word or phrase that describes or renames the subject. The most common linking verbs are forms of *be,* such as *am, is, are, was, were, has been,* and *will be.* Other linking verbs include *seem, become, stay,* and *feel.*

Several verbs can be used either as action verbs or as linking verbs. The examples in this chart will help you tell the difference between action and linking verbs.

ACTION VERBS	LINKING VERBS
Manny *tastes* the apple. *(The subject,* Manny, *is eating an apple.)*	The apple *tastes* sour. *(The adjective,* sour, *describes the subject,* apple.)
The farmer *grows* corn. *(The subject, the* farmer, *is raising corn.)*	The corn *grows* tall. *(The adjective,* tall, *describes the subject,* corn.)
Jeri *felt* the turtle's shell. *(The subject,* Jeri, *was touching the shell.)*	The turtle's shell *felt* hard. (Hard *describes the subject, the turtle's* shell.)

Read It

Mark the verbs in these excerpts from the news article, and label each as an action verb or a linking verb.

1. When they go outside, they exit through a mock air lock. . . .

2. The diaries of early polar explorers are full of tales of extreme boredom, depression and desperate attempts at entertainment reminiscent of prisoners' stories from solitary confinement.

3. . . . astronauts will get bored.

Write It

🗐 **Notebook** Write a sentence for each item, using the subject indicated and the action or linking verb in parentheses. If a verb can be either action or linking, choose which form to use, and label it next to your sentence.

1. astronaut (look)

2. scientists (research)

3. boredom (stimulate)

4. International Space Station (will be)

DANGER! THIS MISSION
TO MARS COULD BORE
YOU TO DEATH!

STANDARDS

Writing
• Write arguments to support claims with clear reasons and relevant evidence.
  a. Introduce claim(s), acknowledge alternate or opposing claims, and organize the reasons and evidence logically.
  b. Support claim(s) with logical reasoning and relevant evidence, using accurate, credible sources and demonstrating an understanding of the topic or text.
  d. Establish and maintain a formal style.
  e. Provide a concluding statement or section that follows from and supports the argument presented.
• Conduct short research projects to answer a question, drawing on several sources and generating additional related, focused questions for further research and investigation.

Speaking and Listening
• Present claims and findings, emphasizing salient points in a focused, coherent manner with pertinent descriptions, facts, details, and examples; use appropriate eye contact, adequate volume, and clear pronunciation.
• Include multimedia components and visual displays in presentations to clarify claims and findings and emphasize salient points.

Writing to Sources

A **blog post** is a piece of writing added to an online journal called a **blog,** in which someone provides information about or expresses his or her thoughts on various subjects.

Assignment

Write an argument in the form of a **blog post** in response to "Danger! This Mission to Mars Could Bore You to Death!" In your post, state your position on the topic of combating astronauts' boredom while traveling to Mars. Is the effort to combat boredom worth the expense? Briefly research different perspectives on the topic, and then make and support your claim in your blog post.

- Identify your claim, and decide on a research plan.
- Conduct research—using accurate, credible sources—to compile evidence to support your argument.
- Organize the information you will use in your blog post so that your reasons and evidence are clearly connected and flow logically.
- Acknowledge and address alternative or opposing claims.
- Provide a concluding statement that follows from and supports your argument.

Vocabulary and Conventions Connection Think about including several of the concept vocabulary words in your writing. You may also want to be aware of your use of action and linking verbs. Using too many linking verbs may make your writing dull.

chronic	subconsciously	monotony
stimulus	excruciatingly	catastrophic

Reflect on Your Writing

After you have written your blog post, answer these questions.

1. Was it easy or difficult to support your claim?

2. What is the most surprising thing you learned during your research?

3. Why These Words? The words you choose make a difference in your writing. Which words did you specifically choose to strengthen your argument?

Speaking and Listening

A **visual presentation** is a way of conveying information through the use of visual aids such as charts, diagrams, illustrations, photos, or video clips.

Assignment

Briefly research activities that are designed to combat boredom. Use these ideas, as well as those in the article, to create an activity that could help astronauts combat boredom during an eight-month journey to Mars. Share your idea with the class in a **visual presentation**. Be sure to clearly explain why your activity will effectively combat the boredom that astronauts will face.

1. Plan Your Presentation
- Consult several print and digital sources to gather information.
- Gather or create a variety of visual aids.

2. Organize Your Presentation
- Create a script that flows logically. Indicate in the script the point at which you will show visuals.
- Arrange the visuals in the order in which you will show them.
- Rehearse your presentation. You may want to work with a peer and get feedback.

3. Deliver Your Presentation
- Maintain appropriate eye contact with your audience.
- Speak clearly and at an appropriate volume.
- Ensure that your classmates can clearly see and examine the visuals you display.

4. Evaluate Presentations Use a presentation evaluation guide like the one shown to evaluate your own as well as your classmates' presentations.

PRESENTATION EVALUATION GUIDE

Rate each statement on a scale of 1 (not demonstrated) to 5 (demonstrated).

☐ The idea for an activity was creative and original.

☐ The speaker supported his or her ideas with details, descriptions, and examples.

☐ The presentation was well organized and easy to follow.

☐ The presentation included a variety of visual aids.

☐ The speaker maintained eye contact with the audience.

☐ The speaker spoke clearly and at an appropriate volume.

📝 EVIDENCE LOG

Before moving on to a new selection, go to your Evidence Log and record what you've learned from "Danger! This Mission to Mars Could Bore You to Death!"

Tool Kit

Student Model of an Argument

ACADEMIC VOCABULARY

As you craft your argument, consider using some of the academic vocabulary you learned in the beginning of the unit.

justify
alternative
certainty
discredit
assumption

STANDARDS

Writing
- Write arguments to support claims with clear reasons and relevant evidence.
- Write routinely over extended time frames and shorter time frames for a range of discipline-specific tasks, purposes, and audiences.

Write an Argument

The texts and radio play in this section all relate to the exploration of Mars. In "Dark They Were, and Golden-Eyed," a family faces enormous changes on Mars. "Danger! This Mission to Mars Could Bore You to Death!" examines the challenges that chronic boredom poses to astronauts on very long space missions. Now, you will use your knowledge of these texts to write an argument about space exploration, in the form of an editorial.

Assignment

Based on the texts and audio you've encountered in this unit, as well as outside reading and prior knowledge, write an **editorial** in which you respond to the following question:

> Do the benefits of exploring Mars outweigh the risks?

Elements of an Argument

An **editorial** is a type of argument that typically appears in a newspaper and takes a position on a specific topic or issue. In an argument, the writer states and supports a **claim**, or position, based on factual evidence and logical reasoning. Editorials usually include the writer's opinions as well, revealing personal viewpoints.

An effective argument contains these elements:

- a clear statement of your claim on an issue that has more than one side
- information about the issue
- persuasive evidence and logical reasoning that support the claim
- statements that acknowledge opposing views and offer counterarguments to these views
- a clear organizational structure
- words, phrases, and clauses that show the relationships among claims, reasons, and evidence
- a formal style

Model Argument For a model of a well-crafted argument, see the Launch Text, "Leaving Main Street."

Challenge yourself to find all of the elements of an effective argument in the text. You will have an opportunity to review these elements as you prepare to write your own argument.

Prewriting / Planning

Develop a Claim To determine the claim you will make in your editorial, begin by reviewing the texts to evaluate the benefits and risks of exploring Mars. Make a two-column list in which you write benefits in one column and risks in the other. Then, decide which position you will defend in your editorial.

Write a Claim To make your position clear to readers, review your notes and develop a **thesis statement**—one strong sentence that states your claim. Include this sentence in your introduction.

Consider Possible Counterclaims In order to effectively make your claim, you must consider all sides of an issue. This means that you must identify **counterclaims,** or views that oppose your position, and explain why these views are flawed. Addressing counterclaims to your argument will make your claim more persuasive and powerful. To anticipate counterclaims to your argument, complete these sentences:

Another reader might say that _____ .

The reason he or she might think this is because _____ .

The evidence that supports this alternative position is _____ .

However, my position is stronger because _____ .

Gather Evidence Reread the texts to find evidence that supports your ideas. Supporting evidence includes facts, statistics, quotations, examples, and other details. For example, the author of the Launch Text uses the following example as evidence to support a claim:

> *. . . there is something about the human condition that strives to be the best, or the first, at something. Our ancestors survived by outperforming others.*
>
> —from "Leaving Main Street"

Connect Across Texts To effectively present and support your argument with evidence from the Anchor Texts, review the texts and note key ideas. You can **paraphrase**, or restate in your own words, ideas and insights from the texts. You can also use **direct quotations**, or an author's exact words. If you quote an author, be sure you put the words in quotation marks and name the author and work from which you are quoting.

Note how the author of the Launch Text presents and supports an argument. Ask questions such as:

- How does the author state and support a claim?
- How does the author connect the claims, evidence, and reasons in the argument?

EVIDENCE LOG

Review your Evidence Log and identify key details you may want to include in your argument.

STANDARDS

Writing
Write arguments to support claims with clear reasons and relevant evidence.
  a. Introduce claim(s), acknowledge alternate or opposing claims, and organize the reasons and evidence logically.
  b. Support claim(s) with logical reasoning and relevant evidence, using accurate, credible sources and demonstrating an understanding of the topic or text.

Drafting

Organize Your Argument Most arguments are composed of three parts:

- the **introduction**, in which you state your claim
- the **body**, in which you provide analysis, supporting reasons, and evidence
- the **conclusion**, in which you summarize or restate your claim

Each part of your argument should build on the part that came before, and every point should connect directly to your main claim. This outline shows the key sections of the Launch Text. Notice that each paragraph fulfills a specific purpose.

LAUNCH TEXT

MODEL: "Leaving Main Street"	**My Argument**
INTRODUCTION AND CLAIM	INTRODUCTION
Author presents first set of arguments and supporting details	
	BODY
Author addresses counterarguments	
Author presents strongest argument	
	CONCLUSION
Author concludes the argument	

Clearly Connect Your Ideas In order for an argument to be effective, it must show clear connections between claims, counterclaims, reasoning, and evidence. Some transitional words and phrases show the connections between similar ideas, whereas others show the connections between opposing ideas. Refer to the examples as you draft. First, determine the relationship between two ideas. Then, choose an appropriate word that will clarify this relationship.

> **Similar Ideas:** *because, in addition, also, likewise, moreover, as well as, similarly, furthermore*
> **Opposing Ideas:** *although, but, in contrast, even though, despite, whereas, regardless, however*

Write a Strong Conclusion You should conclude your editorial with a powerful conclusion that follows the logic of your reasoning and supports the position you defined in your thesis statement. Do not introduce new ideas or information in your conclusion. Because your conclusion is your last chance to make your case to your audience, it should be clear and persuasive.

Write a First Draft As you draft your editorial, review the elements of an argument, as well as the information you gathered in the Prewriting/Planning section of this Performance Task.

STANDARDS

Writing
Write arguments to support claims with clear reasons and relevant evidence.
a. Introduce claim(s), acknowledge alternate or opposing claims, and organize the reasons and evidence logically.
c. Use words, phrases, and clauses to create cohesion and clarify the relationships among claim(s), reasons, and evidence.
e. Provide a concluding statement or section that follows from and supports the argument presented.

LANGUAGE DEVELOPMENT: CONVENTIONS

Revising for Correct Verb Tense

A **verb** expresses an action or a state of being. Verbs have **tenses,** or different forms, that tell when something happens or exists.

Present tense indicates an action that happens regularly or indicates a general truth.

Past tense indicates an action that has already happened.

Future tense indicates an action that will happen.

Present perfect tense indicates an action that happened sometime in the past or an action that happened in the past and is still happening now.

Past perfect tense indicates an action that was completed before another action in the past.

Future perfect tense indicates an action that will have been completed before another.

Read It

These sentences from the Launch Text show different verb tenses.

- *It <u>has</u> a molten core, tectonic plates, and volcanic activity. . . .* (present tense)
- *Our ancestors <u>survived</u> by outperforming others.* (past tense)
- *Humans <u>will</u> not <u>tolerate</u> boundaries. . . .* (future tense)
- *Humans <u>have</u> always <u>created</u> monuments to commemorate achievements. . . .* (present perfect)
- *The spacecraft* New Horizons *<u>had traveled</u> nine years to study the dwarf planet at the edge of our solar system.* (past perfect)
- *If we stop exploring space, soon society <u>will have forgotten</u> what it's like to be human.* (future perfect)

Write It

To fix an incorrect form of a verb, first identify any questionable verbs in your editorial. Then, verify the correct form using one of the following methods:

1. **Review the basic forms of the six tenses.** First, identify the time—present, past, or future—in which the action occurs. Then, review the examples in Read It to determine which verb form corresponds with that time. Avoid shifting from one tense to another unnecessarily.

2. **Rewrite the sentence.** Consider which verb tense will make your ideas as precise as possible. Then, revise the sentence using that tense.

PUNCTUATION

Use periods or semicolons to separate complete sentences or ideas. Semicolons are appropriate if two complete ideas are closely related.

≡ STANDARDS

Language
- Demonstrate command of the conventions of standard English grammar and usage when writing or speaking.
- Demonstrate command of the conventions of standard English capitalization, punctuation, and spelling when writing.
- Use knowledge of language and its conventions when writing, speaking, reading, or listening.
  a. Choose language that expresses ideas precisely and concisely, recognizing and eliminating wordiness and redundancy.

Revising

Evaluating Your Draft

Use the following checklist to evaluate the effectiveness of your first draft. Then, use your evaluation and the instruction on this page to guide your revision.

FOCUS AND ORGANIZATION	EVIDENCE AND ELABORATION	CONVENTIONS
☐ Provides a clearly stated claim and context surrounding the issue.	☐ Supports claims with logical reasoning and persuasive evidence from credible sources.	☐ Uses a formal style.
☐ Establishes a clear organizational structure.		☐ Attends to the norms and conventions of the discipline.
☐ Uses words, phrases, and clauses that help tie together ideas and make the relationships among ideas clear.		
☐ Acknowledges opposing claims and offers counterarguments.		
☐ Provides a conclusion that follows from and supports the argument.		

Highlight Your Main Points To be sure that your editorial is organized clearly, use the following strategies as you revise your writing.

- If a reader needs to know one main point to understand a second one, make sure the first main point comes *before* the second.
- If one main point is essentially the same as another, combine these points or combine the paragraphs in which they appear.
- If one main point is stronger than the others, move it to the end of the body of your editorial. This will ensure that your editorial progresses logically, with your strongest point preceding your conclusion.

Tone

- Make use of academic vocabulary whenever possible.
- A pure argument is not written in the "I" form. Instead of writing "I think that humans explore space because it's in our genes," shorten and strengthen the thought: "Humans explore space because it's in our genes."

Choose Precise Words When you evaluate your draft, check to see that you have used precise language. Precise language helps convey your point and builds support for your position. Create an authoritative voice by using precise, lively words that will appeal to readers' sense of reason.

Vague: a *good* mission

Precise: a *life-changing* mission

⊞ WORD NETWORK

Include appropriate words from your Word Network in your argument.

☷ STANDARDS

Writing

Write arguments to support claims with clear reasons and relevant evidence.

    a. Introduce claim(s), acknowledge alternate or opposing claims, and organize the reasons and evidence logically.

    d. Establish and maintain a formal style.

PEER REVIEW

Exchange editorials with a classmate. Use the checklist to evaluate your classmate's editorial and provide supportive feedback.

1. Is there a clearly stated claim?

[ ] yes   [ ] no   If no, suggest ways in which the writer might clarify it.

2. Is there support for the claim based on logical reasoning and relevant evidence from accurate, credible sources?

[ ] yes   [ ] no   If no, point out where the writer should provide support.

3. Is there a concluding statement that follows from and supports the argument?

[ ] yes   [ ] no   If no, suggest that the writer include one.

4. What is the strongest part of your classmate's editorial? Why?

_____

_____

Editing and Proofreading

Edit for Conventions Reread your draft for accuracy and consistency. Correct errors in grammar and word usage. Make sure you have maintained a formal style—free of contractions, slang, and other casual language—throughout your writing. Be sure you have included a variety of transition words and phrases that connect your ideas. Also check to ensure your verb tenses are consistent.

Proofread for Accuracy Read your draft carefully, correcting errors in spelling and punctuation. Pay particular attention to end-sentence and mid-sentence punctuation. Reading your draft aloud will help you see where sentences end, which is where you need appropriate end-sentence punctuation.

Publishing and Presenting

Create a final version of your editorial. Share it with your class or a small group of classmates, so they can read it and make comments. In turn, review and comment on your classmates' work. As a group, discuss what your editorials have in common and the ways in which they are different. Always maintain a polite and respectful tone when commenting on someone else's work.

Reflecting

Think about what you learned by writing your editorial. What could you do differently the next time you write an argument to make the writing experience easier and to make your argument stronger?

STANDARDS
Writing
• Write arguments to support claims with clear reasons and relevant evidence.
  c. Use words, phrases, and clauses to create cohesion and clarify the relationships among claim(s), reasons, and evidence.
  d. Establish and maintain a formal style.
• With some guidance and support from peers and adults, develop and strengthen writing as needed by planning, revising, editing, rewriting, or trying a new approach, focusing on how well purpose and audience have been addressed.

ESSENTIAL QUESTION:

Should we make a home in space?

Some people think that space exploration is the biggest thrill of all. Others think it is a big waste of time and money. You will read selections that examine different aspects of this subject. Work in a small group to continue your investigation into the concept of space travel.

Small-Group Learning Strategies

Throughout your life, in school, in your community, and in your career, you will continue to learn and work with others.

Look at these strategies and the actions you can take to practice them as you work in teams. Add ideas of your own for each step. Use these strategies during Small-Group Learning.

STRATEGY	ACTION PLAN
Prepare	• Complete your assignments so that you are prepared for group work. • Organize your thinking so you can contribute to your group's discussions. •
Participate fully	• Make eye contact to signal that you are listening and taking in what is being said. • Use text evidence when making a point. •
Support others	• Build off ideas from others in your group. • Invite others who have not yet spoken to do so. •
Clarify	• Paraphrase the ideas of others to ensure that your understanding is correct. • Ask follow-up questions. •

SCAN FOR
MULTIMEDIA

CONTENTS

PERFORMANCE TASK

SPEAKING AND LISTENING FOCUS

Present an Argument

The small-group readings present different perspectives on exploring and colonizing outer space. After reading, your group will create a multimedia presentation about the pros and cons of the space program.

Working as a Team

1. Take a Position In your group, discuss the following question:

> **Would you rather stay here on Earth or experience life on another planet?**

As you take turns sharing your positions, be sure to provide examples for your choice. After all group members have shared, discuss the challenges you might encounter if you were living on another planet.

2. List Your Rules As a group, decide on the rules that you will follow as you work together. Two samples are provided. Add two more of your own. You may add or revise rules based on your experience together.

- Everyone should participate in group discussions.
- People should not interrupt.

- _____

  _____

- _____

  _____

3. Apply the Rules Practice working as a group. Share what you have learned about living in space. Make sure each person in the group contributes. Take notes and be prepared to share with the class one thing that you heard from another member of your group.

4. Name Your Group Choose a name that reflects the unit topic.

Our group's name: _____

5. Create a Communication Plan Decide how you want to communicate with one another. For example, you might use online collaboration tools, email, or instant messaging.

Our group's decision: _____

_____

Making a Schedule

First, find out the due dates for the small-group activities. Then, preview the texts and activities with your group and make a schedule for completing the tasks.

SELECTION	ACTIVITIES	DUE DATE
Future of Space Exploration Could See Humans on Mars, Alien Planets		
The Last Dog		
Ellen Ochoa: Director, Johnson Space Center		
Neil deGrasse Tyson on the Future of U.S. Space Exploration After *Curiosity*		

Working on Group Projects

As your group works together, you'll find it more effective if each person has a specific role. Different projects require different roles. Before beginning a project, discuss the necessary roles and choose one for each group member. Some possible roles are listed here. Add your own ideas to the list.

Project Manager: monitors the schedule and keeps everyone on task

Researcher: organizes research activities

Recorder: takes notes during group meetings

_____

_____

_____

_____

SCAN FOR MULTIMEDIA

About the Author

Nola Taylor Redd is a science and astronomy writer. Redd's work has been featured in *Scientific American, Astronomy Magazine,* and *Sky & Telescope Magazine,* as well as on Space.com.

Future of Space Exploration Could See Humans on Mars, Alien Planets

Concept Vocabulary

As you perform your first read of "Future of Space Exploration Could See Humans on Mars, Alien Planets," you will encounter these words.

| colonize | planetary | interstellar |

Context Clues If these words are unfamiliar to you, try using **context clues**—other words and phrases that appear near the unfamiliar words—to help you determine their meanings. There are various types of context clues that you may encounter as you read.

> **Synonyms:** If the satellite is knocked out of **orbit**, scientists will have to recalculate its path.
>
> **Restatement of an Idea:** The rocket **boost** gave the ship the extra power it needed to launch.
>
> **Contrast of Ideas:** We knew the **blackout** had ended because we regained radio communication with our team.

Apply your knowledge of context clues and other vocabulary strategies to determine the meanings of unfamiliar words you encounter during your first read.

First Read NONFICTION

Apply these strategies as you conduct your first read. You will have an opportunity to complete a close read after your first read.

NOTICE the general ideas of the text. *What* is it about? *Who* is involved?

ANNOTATE by marking vocabulary and key passages you want to revisit.

First Read

CONNECT ideas within the selection to what you already know and what you have already read.

RESPOND by completing the Comprehension Check and by writing a brief summary of the selection.

STANDARDS

Reading Informational Text
By the end of the year, read and comprehend literary nonfiction in the grades 6–8 text complexity band proficiently, with scaffolding as needed at the high end of the range.

Language
Determine or clarify the meaning of unknown and multiple-meaning words and phrases based on *grade 7 reading and content*, choosing flexibly from a range of strategies.

a. Use context as a clue to the meaning of a word or phrase.

Future of Space Exploration Could See Humans on Mars, Alien Planets

Nola Taylor Redd

BACKGROUND

In 1969, Neil Armstrong became the first astronaut to walk on Earth's moon. The next big step in space exploration is to put a person on another planet, such as Mars. In this article, former astronaut Mae Jemison and NASA engineer Adam Steltzner discuss the future of space exploration and what is needed to make it possible.

SCAN FOR MULTIMEDIA

"An inclusive journey"

1   Mars may be one of the closest planets humans want to **colonize**, but it certainly isn't the only one. Mae Jemison described the 100-Year Starship project to an interested audience.

2   Funded by NASA's Ames Research Center and the Defense Advanced Research Projects Agency (DARPA), the 100-Year Starship project aims to develop the tools and technology necessary to build and fly a spaceship to another **planetary** system within the next 100 years. The program isn't necessarily concerned with building the ship itself as much as it seeks to foster innovation and enthusiasm for **interstellar** travel.

3   "The reason we're not on the moon has nothing to do with technology and everything to do with public will and commitment," Jemison said.

4   As a result, the project, which Jemison heads, seeks to increase public enthusiasm for space as well. The 100-Year Starship

NOTES

Mark context clues or indicate another strategy you used that helped you determine meaning.

colonize (KOL uh nyz) *v.*

MEANING:

planetary (PLAN uh tehr ee) *adj.*

MEANING:

interstellar (ihn tuhr STEHL uhr) *adj.*

MEANING:

program not only includes engineers and astrophysicists,[1] but also artists and science fiction writers.

5   "It has to be an inclusive journey," she said.

6   Though many people object to funding the space program when there are humanitarian needs that have to be met on Earth, Jemison points out that such exploration often leads to innovation and unexpected technology that make an impact on Earth-based programs.

7   "I believe that pursuing an extraordinary tomorrow will create a better world today," she said.

8   Traveling to another star takes far more time than just developing the necessary technology. Jemison compares the distance to Proxima Centauri, the nearest star, to that between New York City and Los Angeles. If NASA's *Voyager 1* spacecraft, which launched in 1977, was en route, it would have traveled only 1 mile in the past four decades.

9   At that rate, it would take 70,000 years to reach Proxima Centauri.

10   Speaking to the long time frames of space travel, Steltzner said, "I can't really think of a country that's been stable for 1,000 years."

11   Without the development of a method to warp or shrink space-time, or a new propulsion system[2]—both ideas that the 100-Year Starship program is exploring—humanity would need to find a way to overcome some of its instability problems.

12   To get there, Jemison emphasized that everyone must be involved in the process.

13   "The public did not leave space," she said while discussing the reduced enthusiasm. "The public was left out of space." ❧

---

1. **astrophysicists** scientists who study how objects in space behave.
2. **propulsion system** parts of a rocket that push it through air and space.

MEDIA CONNECTION

Starship

💬 **Discuss It** What skills and talents would benefit the space program?

Write your response before sharing your ideas.

SCAN FOR MULTIMEDIA

Comprehension Check

Complete the following items after you finish your first read. Review and clarify
details with your group.

1. What is the goal of the 100-Year Starship project?

2. What does Jemison mean when she says that the project must be inclusive?

3. What is one of the challenges faced by the project?

4. 🗐 **Notebook** Confirm your understanding of the news article by writing a brief
summary of its main points.

- -

RESEARCH

Research to Clarify Choose at least one unfamiliar scientific detail in the text, such as
Proxima Centauri or possible methods to warp space-time. Briefly research that detail. In
what way does this information deepen your understanding of the news article? Share your
findings with your group.

FUTURE OF SPACE
EXPLORATION COULD SEE
HUMANS ON MARS, ALIEN
PLANETS

TIP

GROUP DISCUSSION

Come to group discussions
prepared to contribute. Be
sure you have read and
understood the selection
in advance, verifying the
meanings of any unfamiliar
words.

⊞ WORD NETWORK

Add interesting words
related to space exploration
from the text to your
Word Network.

☰ STANDARDS

Speaking and Listening
Engage effectively in a range of
collaborative discussions with
diverse partners on *grade 7 topics,
texts, and issues,* building on
others' ideas and expressing their
own clearly.

Language
Determine or clarify the meaning
of unknown and multiple-meaning
words and phrases based on *grade 7
reading and content,* choosing
flexibly from a range of strategies.
  b. Use common, grade-
  appropriate Greek or Latin affixes
  and roots as clues to the meaning
  of a word.
  d. Verify the preliminary
  determination of the meaning of
  a word or phrase.

Close Read the Text

With your group, revisit sections of the text you marked
during your first read. **Annotate** what you notice. What
questions do you have? What can you **conclude**?

Analyze the Text

CITE TEXTUAL EVIDENCE
to support your answers.

1. **Review and Clarify** With your group, review the article. Discuss
   Jemison's goals. Why do you think she believes it is important for the
   public to be enthusiastic about space travel?

2. **Present and Discuss** Now, work with your group to share passages
   from the article that you found especially important. Take turns
   presenting your passages. Discuss what you noticed in the text, the
   questions you asked, and the conclusions you reached.

3. **Essential Question:** *Should we make a home in space?* What has
   this selection taught you about the possibility of making a home in
   space? Discuss with your group.

Concept Vocabulary

colonize	planetary	interstellar

Why These Words? The concept vocabulary words from the text are
related. With your group, determine what the words have in common.
Write your ideas and add another word that fits the category.

Practice

Use the concept vocabulary words in a group discussion of this question:
*What would it take to convince people to participate in a space mission
to another planet?*

Word Study

🗐 **Notebook Latin Suffix: -ary** According to the article, the
100-Year Starship project wants to fly a spaceship to another planetary
system. The word *planetary* ends with the Latin suffix *-ary,* meaning
"belonging to" or "relating to." Using your knowledge of the suffix *-ary,*
determine the meanings of the following words: *customary, honorary,
revolutionary.* Then, use a dictionary to find the precise meaning of each
word.

Analyze Craft and Structure

Development of Ideas: Text Structure Authors not only consider what they want to write about, but also the best way to present that information. In "Future of Space Exploration Could See Humans on Mars, Alien Planets," Nola Taylor Redd has organized details from an interview she conducted with Mae Jemison and Adam Steltzner into a cohesive text.

To develop the ideas in her article Redd:

- Sets the context and background for the interview
- Arranges the details from the interview into a logical order
- Uses transitions to link ideas
- Concludes with a strong quotation from an interview subject

≡ STANDARDS

Reading Informational Text
Analyze the structure an author uses to organize a text, including how the major section contribute to the whole and to the development of the ideas.

Practice

CITE TEXTUAL EVIDENCE
to support your answers.

1. Work with your group to identify various types of details used in the article. Reread sections of the text as necessary, and record your findings in this chart.

   Topic: _____

	TEXT EXAMPLE(S)	NOTES
Context and Background		
Use of Quotations		
Use of Paraphrases From Interview		
Use of Transitions to Link Ideas		
Concluding Idea		

2. When you have completed the chart, discuss with your group the overarching central idea that Redd conveys. Provide support for your responses.

3. Then, working alone, rate the effectiveness of the overall structure of the article using this scale. A "1" is least effective; a "5" is most effective. Then, compare your ratings with the group and discuss.

1	2	3	4	5

Conventions

The Principal Parts of Verbs A verb has four **principal parts: present, present participle, past,** and **past participle.**

The chart shows the four principal parts of the regular verb *walk*. It also includes the principal parts of some commonly misused irregular verbs. Notice that present and past participles are used with helping verbs such as *has, have, had, am, is, are,* and *were.* A verb together with its helping verb or verbs is called a **verb phrase.**

PRESENT	PRESENT PARTICIPLE	PAST	PAST PARTICIPLE
walk	(is) walking	walked	(has) walked
am, is, are	(is) being	was, were	(has) been
go	(is) going	went	(has) gone
begin	(is) beginning	began	(has) begun

Read It

Identify the verb or verb phrase in each sentence. Label each as either *present, present participle, past,* or *past participle.*

1. Jemison is an astronaut.

2. People have imagined trips to other planets.

3. Hillary planned the construction of a spaceship.

4. Scientists are working constantly on the problem.

Write It

📝 **Notebook** Should we spend money to send a spaceship to another planetary system, or should we use that money to solve problems closer to home? Write a paragraph in which you persuade readers either to fund or not to fund the 100-Year Starship project. Include an example of each of the four principal parts of verbs in your paragraph.

Speaking and Listening

Assignment

Create a **multimedia presentation** in which you incorporate text and images to explain a topic. Choose from the following topics:

☐ An **illustrated biography** about Mae Jemison that includes the highlights of her career and her interest in the 100-Year Starship project

☐ An **informational brochure** in which you explain the requirements necessary for achieving the goals of the 100-Year Starship project, including various spaceship designs that would allow people to "warp" time in space

Project Plan Assign a role for each member of your group. Roles can include text researcher, multimedia researcher, note taker, and presenter.

Here are some questions to consider as you plan your presentation.

- What reliable print and digital sources will I use in addition to the selection?
- What information will be better conveyed with text?
- What information will be better conveyed with multimedia?
- What materials and equipment will the group need for the presentation?

Once you have completed your research and considered these questions, work collaboratively to make a plan, or storyboard, for your visual presentation.

Credit Sources It is important to properly credit the research sources you used for your presentation. Ask your teacher what method of citation you should use, and be sure to include accurate citations for all of your sources to avoid **plagiarism,** or presenting someone else's ideas as if they were your own. When you deliver your presentation, credit sources by using phrases such as "According to . . ." or "In the article by. . . ."

Rehearse and Present Decide on the presentation roles for your group, and set aside time to rehearse.

- Make sure that any equipment is working properly before you begin your presentation.
- Speak clearly and with enough volume so that everyone in the audience can hear.
- Make sure audience members can see images clearly.

☑ EVIDENCE LOG

Before moving on to a new selection, go to your log and record what you learned from "Future of Space Exploration Could See Humans on Mars, Alien Planets."

☰ STANDARDS

Writing
- Conduct short research projects to answer a question, drawing on several sources and generating additional related, focused questions for further research and investigation.
- Gather relevant information from multiple print and digital sources, using search terms effectively; assess the credibility and accuracy of each source; and quote or paraphrase the data and conclusions of others while avoiding plagiarism and following a standard format for citation.

Speaking and Listening
Include multimedia components and visual displays in presentations to clarify claims and findings and emphasize salient points.

About the Author

The daughter of two American missionaries, **Katherine Paterson** (b. 1932) was born in China and lived there during her early childhood years. Paterson became a renowned writer of children's novels. She has twice won the Newbery Medal and National Book Award.

The Last Dog

Concept Vocabulary

As you perform your first read of "The Last Dog," you will encounter these words.

threatening	extinct	mutation

Context Clues To find the meaning of unfamiliar words, look for clues in the context, which is made up of the words, punctuation, and images that surround the unknown word.

> **Example:** The **inquisitive** dog searched the unknown surroundings.
>
> **Context Clue:** The dog is described as *inquisitive* and is searching unknown areas.
>
> **Possible Meaning:** *Inquisitive* means "curious."
>
> **Example:** The **deviant** robot was taken out of service for its strange behavior.
>
> **Context Clue:** A robot described as *deviant* is taken out of service because of its strange behavior.
>
> **Possible Meaning:** *Deviant* means "considered strange by others."

Apply your knowledge of context clues and other vocabulary strategies to determine the meanings of unfamiliar words you encounter during your first read of "The Last Dog."

First Read FICTION

Apply these strategies as you conduct your first read. You will have an opportunity to complete a close read after your first read.

NOTICE *whom* the story is about, *what* happens, *where* and *when* it happens, and *why* those involved react as they do.

ANNOTATE by marking vocabulary and key passages you want to revisit.

First Read

NOTICE • ANNOTATE • CONNECT • RESPOND

CONNECT ideas within the selection to what you already know and what you have already read.

RESPOND by completing the Comprehension Check and by writing a brief summary of the selection.

STANDARDS

Reading Literature
By the end of the year, read and comprehend literature, including stories, dramas, and poems, in the grades 6–8 text complexity band proficiently, with scaffolding as needed at the high end of the range.

Language
Determine or clarify the meaning of unknown and multiple-meaning words and phrases based on *grade 7 reading and content*, choosing flexibly from a range of strategies.
  a. Use context as a clue to the meaning of a word or phrase.

The Last Dog

Katherine Paterson

BACKGROUND

In this science fiction story, the author imagines a future in which people live in a sealed dome and believe that the outside world is unsafe and in ruins. The story's main character discovers something that everyone thinks can't exist—and it changes everything.

SCAN FOR MULTIMEDIA

NOTES

1   Brock approached the customs gate. Although he did not reach for the scanner, a feeling it might have labeled "excitement" made him tremble. His fingers shook as he punched in his number on the inquiry board. "This is highly irregular, Brock 095670038," the disembodied voice said. "What is your reason for external travel?"

2   Brock took a deep breath. "Scientific research," he replied. He didn't need to be told that his behavior was "irregular." He'd never heard of anyone doing research outside the dome—actual rather than virtual research. "I—I've been cleared by my podmaster and the Research Team. . . ."

3   "Estimated time of return?" So, he wasn't to be questioned further.

4   "Uh, 1800 hours."

5   "Are you wearing the prescribed dry suit with helmet and gloves?"

6   "Affirmative."

7   "You should be equipped with seven hundred fifty milliliters of liquid and food tablets for one day travel."

8   "Affirmative." Brock patted the sides of the dry suit to be sure.

9   "Remember to drink sparingly. Water supply is limited." Brock nodded. He tried to lick his parched lips, but his whole mouth felt dry. "Is that understood?"

10   "Affirmative." Was he hoping customs would stop him? If he was, they didn't seem to be helping him. Well, this was what he wanted, wasn't it? To go outside the dome.

11   "Turn on the universal locator, Brock 095670038, and proceed to gate."

12   Why weren't they questioning him further? Were they eager for him to go? Ever since he'd said out loud in group speak that he wanted to go outside the dome, people had treated him strangely—that session with the podmaster and then the interview with the representative from Research. Did they think he was a deviant?[1] Deviants sometimes disappeared. The word was passed around that they had "gone outside," but no one really knew. No deviant had ever returned.

13   The gate slid open. Before he was quite ready for it, Brock found himself outside the protection of the dome. He blinked. The sun—at least it was what was called "the sun" in virtual lessons—was too bright for his eyes even inside the tinted helmet. He took a deep breath, one last backward look at the dome, which, with the alien sun gleaming on it, was even harder to look at than the distant star, and started across an expanse of brown soil [was it?] to what he recognized from holograms as a line of purplish mountains in the distance.

14   It was, he pulled the scanner from his outside pouch and checked it, "hot." Oh, that was what he was feeling. Hot. He remembered "hot" from a virtual lesson he'd had once on deserts. He wanted to take off the dry suit, but he had been told since he could remember that naked skin would suffer irreparable burning outside the protection of the dome. He adjusted the control as he walked so that the unfamiliar perspiration would evaporate. He fumbled a bit before he found the temperature adjustment function. He put it on twenty degrees centigrade and immediately felt more comfortable. No one he really knew had ever left the dome (stories of deviants exiting the dome being hard to verify), but there was all this equipment in case someone decided to venture out. He tried to ask the clerk who outfitted him, but the woman was evasive. The equipment was old, she said. People used to go out, but the outside environment was **threatening**, so hardly anyone (she looked at him carefully now), hardly anyone ever used it now.

15   Was Brock, then, the only normal person still curious about the outside? Or had all those who had dared to venture out perished, discouraging further forays? Perhaps he *was* a deviant for wanting to see the mountains for himself. When he'd mentioned it to others, they had laughed, but there was a hollow sound to the laughter.

Mark context clues or indicate another strategy you used that helped you determine meaning.

threatening (THREHT uhn ihng) *adj.*

MEANING:

---

1. **deviant** (DEE vee uhnt) *n.* strange, irregular person.

16   If he never returned, he'd have no one to blame but himself. He knew that. While his podfellows played virtual games, he'd wandered into a subsection of the historical virtuals called "ancient fictions." Things happened in these fictions more—well, more densely than they did in the virtuals. The people he met there—it was hard to describe—but somehow they were more *actual* than dome dwellers. They had strange names like Huck Finn and M. C. Higgins the Great. They were even a little scary. It was their insides. Their insides were very loud. But even though the people in the ancient fictions frightened him a bit, he couldn't get enough of them. When no one was paying attention, he went back again and again to visit them. They had made him wonder about that other world—that world outside the dome.

17   Perhaps, once he had realized the danger the ancient fictions posed, he should have left them alone, but he couldn't help himself. They had made him feel hollow, hungry for something no food pellet or even virtual experience could satisfy. And now he was in that world they spoke of and the mountains of it were in plain view.

18   He headed for the purple curves. Within a short distance from the dome, the land was clear and barren, but after he had been walking for an hour or so he began to pass rusting hulks and occasional ruins of what might have been the dwellings of ancient peoples that no one in later years had cleared away for recycling or vaporization.

19   He checked the emotional scanner for an unfamiliar sensation. "Loneliness," it registered. He rather liked having names for these new sensations. It made him feel a bit "proud," was it? The scanner was rather interesting. He wondered when people had stopped using them. He hadn't known they existed until, in that pod meeting, he had voiced his desire to go outside.

20   The podmaster had looked at him with a raised eyebrow and a sniff. "Next thing you'll be asking for a scanner," he said.

21   "What's a scanner?" Brock asked.

22   The podmaster requisitioned one from storage, but at the same time, he must have alerted Research, because it was the representative from Research who had brought him the scanner and questioned him about his expressed desired for an Actual Adventure—a journey outside the dome.

23   "What has prompted this, uh—unusual ambition?" the representative had asked, his eyes not on Brock but on the scanner in his hand. Brock had hesitated, distracted by the man's fidgeting with the strange instrument. "I—I'm interested in scientific research," Brock said at last.

24   So here he was out of the pod, alone for the first time in his life. Perhaps, though, he should have asked one of his podfellows to

come along. Or even the pod robopet. But the other fellows all laughed when he spoke of going outside, their eyes darting back and forth. Nothing on the outside, they said, could equal the newest Virtual Adventure. He suddenly realized that ever since he started interfacing with the ancient fictions, his fellows had given him that look. They did think he was odd—not quite the same as a regular podfellow. Brock didn't really vibe with the pod robopet. It was one of the more modern ones, and when they'd programmed its artificial intelligence they'd somehow made it too smart. The robopet in the children's pod last year was older, stupider, and more "fun" to have around.

25   He'd badly underestimated the distance to the mountains. The time was well past noon, and he had at least three kilometers to go. Should he signal late return or turn about now? He didn't have much more than one day's scant supply of water and food tablets. But he was closer to the hills than to the dome. He felt a thrill ["excitement"] and pressed on.

26   There were actual trees growing on the first hill. Not the great giants of virtual history lessons, more scrubby and bent. But they were trees, he was sure of it. The podmaster had said that trees had been **extinct** for hundreds of years. Brock reached up and pulled off a leaf. It was green and had veins. In some ways it looked like his own hand. He put the leaf in his pack to study later. He didn't want anyone accusing him of losing his scientific objectivity.[2] Only deviants did that. Farther up the hill he heard an unfamiliar burbling sound. No, he knew that sound. It was water running. He'd heard it once when the liquid dispenser had malfunctioned. There'd been a near panic in the dome over it. He checked the scanner. There was no caution signal, so he hurried toward the sound.

27   It was a—a "brook"—he was sure of it! Virtual lessons had taught that there were such things outside in the past but that they had long ago grown poisonous, then in the warming climate had dried up. But here was a running brook, not even a four-hour journey from his dome. His first impulse was to take off his protective glove and dip a finger in it, but he drew back. He had been well conditioned to avoid danger. He sat down clumsily on the bank. Yes, this must be grass. There were even some tiny flowers mixed in the grass. Would the atmosphere poison him if he unscrewed his helmet to take a sniff? He punched the scanner to read conditions, but the characters on the scanner panel danced about uncertainly until, at length, the disembodied voice said "conditions unreadable." He'd better not risk it.

28   He pushed the buttons now for liquid and pellets. A tube appeared in his mouth. It dropped a pellet on his tongue. From

Mark context clues or indicate another strategy you used that helped you determine meaning.

extinct (ehk STIHNGKT) *adj.*

MEANING:

2. **objectivity** (ob jehk TIHV uh tee) *n.* perspective based on facts, not feelings or opinions.

the tube he sucked liquid enough to swallow his meal. What was it they called outside nourishment in the history virtuals? *Pecnec*? Something like that. He was having a *pecnec* in the *woods* by a *brook*. A hasty consulting of the scanner revealed that what he was feeling was "pleasure." He was very glad he hadn't come with an anxious podfellow or, worse, an advanced robopet that would, no doubt, be yanking at his suit already, urging him back toward the dome.

29   It was then, in the middle of the post-*pecnec* satisfaction, that he heard the new sound. Like that programmed into a robopet, yet different. He struggled to his feet. The dry suit from storage was certainly awkward when you wanted to stand up or sit down. Nothing on the scanner indicated danger, so he went into the scrubby woods toward the sound. And stopped abruptly.

30   Something was lying under the shadow of a tree. Something about a meter long. It was furred and quite still. The sound was not coming from it. And then he saw the small dog—the puppy. He was sure it was a puppy, nosing the stiff body of what must once have been its mother, making the little crying sounds that he'd heard from the brook. Later, much later, he realized that he should have been wary. If the older dog had died of some extradomal[3] disease, the puppy might have been a carrier. But at the time, all he could think of was the puppy, a small creature who had lost its mother.

31   He'd found out about mothers from the Virtuals. Mothers were extinct in the dome. Children were conceived and born in the lab and raised in units of twelve in the pods, presided over by a bank of computers and the podmaster. Nuclear families,[4] as everyone knew, had been wasteful of time, energy, and space. There was an old proverb: The key to survival is efficiency. So though Brock could guess the puppy was "sad" (like that fictions person, Jo, whose podmate expired), he didn't know what missing a mother would feel like. And who would whimper for a test tube?

32   Brock had never seen a dog, of course, but he'd seen plenty of dog breed descriptions on the science/history virtuals. Dogs had been abundant once. They filled the ancient fictions. They even had names there—Lassie, Toto, Sounder. But now dogs were extinct, gone during the dark ages when the atmosphere had become warm and poisonous. The savages who had not had the intelligence or wealth to join the foresighted dome crafters had killed all animals wild or domesticated for food before they had eventually died out themselves. It was all in one of the very first virtual lessons. He had seen that one many times. He never confessed to anyone how, well, sad it made him feel.

---

3. **extradomal** *adj.* from outside the dome.
4. **nuclear families** groups consisting of parents and their children.

33   But obviously, dogs were not quite extinct. Cautiously, he moved toward the small one.

34   "Alert. Alert. Scanning unknown object."

35   Brock pushed the off button. "Are you sure you want to turn off scanner?"

36   "Affirmative." He stuck the scanner into his pouch.

37   The puppy had lifted its head at the sound of his voice. It looked at him, head cocked, as though deciding whether to run or stay.

38   "It's all right, dog," Brock said soothingly. "I won't hurt you." He stayed still. He didn't want to frighten the little beast. If it ran, he wasn't sure he'd be able to catch it in his clumsy dry suit.

39   Slowly he extended his gloved hand. The dog backed away anxiously, but when Brock kept the hand extended, the puppy slowly crept toward him and sniffed, making whimpering sounds. It wasn't old enough to be truly afraid, it seemed. The pup licked his glove tentatively, then backed away again. It was looking for food, and plasticine gloves weren't going to satisfy.

40   Brock looked first at the dead mother, whose source of nourishment must have long dried up, then around the landscape. What would a dog eat? A puppy on its own? He took off his glove and reached through his pouch into the inside pocket that held his pellet supply. Making every move slow and deliberate so as not to startle the dog, he held out a pellet. The dog came to his hand, licked it, then the pellet. It wrinkled its nose. Brock laughed. He didn't need the scanner now to tell him that what he felt was "pleasure." He loved the feel of the rough tongue on his palm and the little furred face, questioning him.

41   "It's all right, fellow. You can eat it."

42   As though understanding, the pup gulped down the pellet. Then looked around for more, not realizing that it had just bolted

down a whole meal. When the dog saw there was no more coming, it ran over to the brook. Brock watched in horror as it put its head right down into the poisonous stream and lapped noisily.

43   "Don't!" Brock cried.

44   The puppy turned momentarily at the sound, then went back to drinking, as though it was the most normal thing in the world. Well, it was, for the dog. Where else would a creature in the wild get liquid? If the streams were not all dried up, they must have learned to tolerate the water. But then, it was breathing the poisoned atmosphere, wasn't it? Why hadn't it hit Brock before? This was a fully organic creature on the outside *without any life support system*. What could that mean? Some amazing **mutation** must have occurred, making it possible for at least some creatures to breathe the outside atmosphere and drink its poisoned water. Those who couldn't died, those who could survived and got stronger. Even the ancient scientist Darwin[5] knew that. And Brock had come upon one of these magnificent mutants!

45   The puppy whimpered and looked up at Brock with large, trusting eyes. How could he think of it as a mutant specimen? It was a puppy. One who had lost its mother. What would it eat? There was no sign of food for a carnivore. Perhaps way back in the mountains some small mammals had also survived, keeping the food chain going, but the puppy would not live long enough to find its way there, much less know how to hunt with its mother gone. For the first time in his life something deep inside Brock reached out toward another creature. The thought of the puppy languishing here by the side of its dead parent until it, too . . .

46   "Your name is Brog, all right?" The ancient astronomers had named stars after themselves. He had discovered something just as wonderful. Didn't he have the right to name it sort of after himself while preserving the puppy's uniqueness? "Don't worry, Brog. I won't let you starve."

47   Which is why Brock appeared at the customs portal after dark, the front of his dry suit stained, carrying a wriggling *Canis familiaris*[6] of uncertain breed.

48   If there had been any way to smuggle the dog in, Brock would have. But he couldn't for the life of him figure out how. As it was, every alarm in the area went off when he stepped into the transitional cubicle. The disembodied voice of the monitor queried him.

49   "Welcome back, Brock 095670038. You're late."

50   "Affirmative."

51   "And you are carrying contraband."

52   "I pulled a leaf."

---

5. **Darwin** Charles Darwin (1809–1882); scientist who first formulated the theory of evolution.
6. *Canis familiaris* (KAY nihs fuh mihl ee AR ihs) scientific name for a dog.

Mark context clues or indicate another strategy you used that helped you determine meaning.

mutation (myoo TAY shuhn) *n.*

MEANING:

53 "Deposit same in quarantine bins."

54 "Affirmative."

55 "Sensors denote warm-blooded presence not on official roster."

56 "I found a dog," Brock mumbled.

57 "Repeat."

58 "A dog."

59 "*Canis familiaris* is extinct."

60 "Well, maybe it's just a robopet that got out somehow."

61 "Correction. Robopets are bloodless. Leave dry suit for sterilization and proceed to quarantine inspection."

62 The officials in quarantine inspection, who rarely had anything to inspect, were at first nervous and then, as they watched the puppy happily licking Brock's face, interested despite themselves. An actual dog! None of them had ever seen one, of course, and Brock's dog was so much, well, more vital than a robopet. And although, on later reflection, they knew they should have terminated or expelled it, they couldn't quite bring themselves to do so that night.

63 "It will have to go to Research," the chief inspector finally declared.

64 "Permission requested to hand carry the dog known as Brog to Research," Brock said. There was a bit of an argument about that. Several inspectors sought the honor, but the chief declared that Brock, having shed his dry suit and being already contaminated, should be placed with the dog in a hermetically sealed air car and transported to Research.

65 The scientists in Research were predictably amazed to see a live *Canis familiaris*. But being scientists and more objective than the lower-grade quarantine inspectors, they kept a safe distance both physically and psychically from the creature. Only the oldest scientist, dressed in proper protective clothing, came into the laboratory with Brock and the dog. He scanned and poked and prodded the poor little fellow until it began to whimper in protest.

66 "Brog needs to rest," said Brock, interrupting the scientist in the midst of his inspection. "She's (for by this time gender had been indisputably established) had a hard day. And if there's some actual food available—she's not used to pellets."

67 "Of course, of course," said one of the researchers through the speaker in the observation booth. "How thoughtless. Send someone out for a McLike burger without sauce. She may regard it as meat. Anyhow, it will seem more like food to her than a pellet, affirmative, Brock?"

68 The scientists, Brock soon realized, were looking to him for advice. He was, after all, the discoverer of the last dog. It gave him sudden scientific status. Brock had sense enough to take advantage of this. After Brog had swallowed the McLike burger in three quick gulps, Brock insisted that he be allowed to stay

with Brog, so that he might interact and sleep with her. "She's not like us," he explained. "She's used to tumbling about and curling up with other warm bodies. In the old myths," he added, "puppies separated from their litters cried all night long. She will need constant interaction with another warm-blooded creature or she might well die of," he loved using his new vocabulary, "loneliness."

69   The scientists agreed. After all, research was rather like quarantine, and since Brock had touched the dog ungloved and unprotected, he might well have picked up some germ from her. It was better to keep them both isolated in the research lab where proper precautions would be taken.

70   For nearly a week, Brock lived with Brog in the research center, eating McLike burgers, playing "fetch," teaching Brog to "sit," "heel," "come"—all the commands he could cull from the ancient texts. The dog quickly learned to obey Brock's commands, but it wasn't the automatic response of a robopet. Brog delighted in obedience. She wanted to please Brock, and those few times when she was too busy nosing about the lab and failed to obey instantly, those times when Brock's voice took on a sharp tone of reproof, the poor little thing put her tail between her legs, looked up at him with sorrowful eyes, begging to be forgiven. Brock was tempted to speak sharply to her even when there was no need, for the sight of her drooping ears and tail, her mournful eyes, was so dear to him that he did what Travis Coates had done to Old Yeller. He hugged her. There was no other way to explain it. He simply put his arms around her and held her to his chest while she beat at him with her tail and licked his face raw. Out of the corner of his eye he was aware that one of the scientists was watching. Well, let him watch. Nothing was as wonderful as feeling this warmth toward another creature.

71   For the first week, the researchers seemed quite content to observe dog and boy from their glass-paneled observation booth and speak copious notes into their computers. Only the oldest of them would come into the lab and actually touch the alien creature, and he always wore a sterile protective suit with gloves. The others claimed it would interfere with objectivity if they got close to the dog, but they all seemed to behave positively toward Brog. No mention was made to Brock of his own less than-objective behavior. So Brock was astounded to awake in the middle of the night to the sounds of an argument. Someone had forgotten to turn off the communication system.

72   "Cloning—it's the only thing to do. If she's the last, we owe it to posterity to keep the line going."

73   "And how are we going to raise a pack of dogs in a dome? One is nearly eating and drinking us out of test tube and petri dish. We can't go on this way. As drastic as it may seem, we have

to be realistic. Besides, no one has had the chance to do actual experiments since the dark ages. Haven't you ever, just once, yearned to compare virtual research with actual?"

74   "What about the boy? He won't agree. Interfacing daily with the dog, he's become crippled by primal urges."

75   "Can you think what chaos might ensue if a flood of primordial[7] emotions were to surface in a controlled environment such as ours?" another asked. "Apparently, emotions are easily triggered by interactions with primitive beasts, like dogs."

76   "Shh. Not now. The speaker is—" The system clicked off.

77   But Brock had already heard. He knew he had lost anything resembling scientific objectivity. He was no longer sure objectivity was a desirable trait. He rather enjoyed being flooded by "primordial emotions." But he was more worried for Brog than for himself. It wasn't hard to figure out what the scientists meant by "actual experiments." Cloning would be bad enough. Ten dogs who looked just like Brog so no one would know how special, how truly unique Brog was. But experiments! They'd cut her open and examine her internal organs, the way scientists had in the dark ages. They'd prod her with electric impulses and put chips in her brain. They'd try to change her personality or modify her behavior. They'd certainly try to make her eat and drink less!

78   In the dark, he put his arm around Brog and drew her close. He loved the terrible smell of her breath and the way she snored when she slept. They'd probably fix that, too.

79   The next day he played sick. Brog, faithful dog that she was, hung around him whimpering, licking his face. The scientists showed no particular concern. They were too busy plotting what they might do with Brog.

80   Brock crept to the nearest terminal[8] in the lab. It was already logged in. The scientists had been doing nothing but research on *Canis familiaris*. COMMON CANINE DISEASES. Brock scrolled down the list with descriptions. No, *distemper* wouldn't do. The first symptom was loss of appetite. He couldn't make Brog fake that. On and on it went—no, *heartworms* wouldn't do. What he needed was a disease that might affect *Homo sapiens* as well as *Canis familiaris*. Here it was! "Rabies: A viral disease occurring in animals and humans, especially in dogs and wolves. Transmitted by bite or scratch. The early stages of the disease are most dangerous, for an otherwise healthy and friendly appearing animal will suddenly bite without provocation."

81   Rabies was it! Somehow he would have to make Brog bite him. There was no antirabies serum in the dome, he felt sure. There were no animals in the dome. Why would they use precious space

---

7. **primordial** (pry MAWR dee uhl) *adj.* very ancient and basic.
8. **terminal** *n.* computer.

to store an unneeded medication? So they'd have to expel him as well as Brog for fear of spreading the disease. He shivered, then shook himself. No matter what lay on the outside, he could not stand to go back to the life he had lived in the dome before he met Brog.

82   He crept back to bed, pulling the covers over Brog. When one of the scientists came into the observation booth, Brock pinched Brog's neck as hard as he could. Nothing. He pinched again, harder. Brog just snuggled closer, slobbering on his arm.

83   Disgusted, Brock got out of bed. Brog hopped down as well, rubbing against his leg. Pinching obviously was not going to do it. While the scientist on duty in the booth was bending over a computer terminal, Brock brought his foot down on Brog's paw. A tiny *yip* was all he got from that cruel effort—not enough sound even to make the man look up.

84   "Feeling better, Brock 095670038?" The oldest researcher had come into the lab.

85   "Affirmative," Brock answered.

86   "And how are you, puppy-wuppy?" The old man tickled Brog under her chin with his gloved hand. *If I were a dog, I'd bite someone like that*, thought Brock, but Brog, of course, simply licked the researcher's glove and wagged her tail.

87   That was when he got his great idea. He waited to execute it until the proper moment. For the first time, all the scientists had gathered in the lab, all of them in protective garb, some of them twitching nervously in their chairs. They were sitting in a circle around Brock and Brog, explaining what must be done.

88   "It has to be done for the sake of science," they began. Then they went on to, "For the sake of the dome community, which is always, as you well know, short on food, and particularly short on water." Brock listened to their arguments, nodding solemnly, pretending to agree. "It won't be as if she'll really be gone, you know. We've made virtuals of her—a special series just for you to keep. You can virtually play with her whenever you like."

89   That was the cue. Brock turned and bit Brog on the tail so hard that the blood started. Brog, surprised and enraged, spun around and bit Brock on the nose.

90   There was a shocked silence. Every scientist leaned backward, body pressed hard against his or her chair back. Every eye was on the two of them.

91   "I—I don't know what got into me," Brock said. "I've been feeling very weird." The scientists continued to stare. "I was checking the historical records. . . ."

92   All of the scientists fled the room. Someone ran to a computer terminal. When Brock offered to take Brog out of the dome and let her loose in the mountains, no one argued. Neither did they

The Last Dog   **193**

say, "Hurry back," or even, "Take care." No one came close as he loaded his pouch with water and food pellets. The customs gate monitor asked no questions.

93   Out of sight of the dome, Brog was delirious with joy, jumping and running about in circles around Brock's boots. Why wasn't the atmosphere choking Brog if it was as poisonous as the dome dwellers claimed? His heart beating rapidly, Brock unscrewed his helmet just enough to let in a little of the outside atmosphere. Nothing happened. In fact, he seemed to be breathing perfectly normally. He took off the helmet entirely. He was still breathing freely. But his heart was beating so hard, he couldn't be sure. He waited for the choking sensation he had been warned of. It didn't occur. Could they be wrong? Could the outside world have healed itself? Perhaps—perhaps the reason the scanner had so much trouble reading the outside atmosphere was because it wasn't within the range of computerized expectations.

94   Could it be? Could it be that fear had kept the dome dwellers prisoner many years longer than a poisoned environment would have?

95   He unfastened the dry suit and slowly stepped out of it into the sunlight.

96   It was wonderful how much faster he could walk without the clumsy suit. "Who knows?" Brock said to a frisking Brog. "Who knows, maybe out here you aren't the last dog. Your mother had to come from somewhere."

97   Brog barked happily in reply.

98   "And maybe, just maybe, where there are dogs, there are humans as well."

99   They stopped at the brook where they'd met, and both of them had a long drink. Brock no longer carried a scanner, but he knew what he felt was excitement. The water was delicious. ❧

Comprehension Check

Complete the following items after you finish your first read. Review and clarify details with your group.

1. Where does Brock live?

2. What do people believe about the world outside the dome?

3. What does Brock discover about the world outside the dome?

4. 🗐 **Notebook** Confirm your understanding of the text by writing a brief plot summary. Your summary should include only the most important events in the story.

- -

RESEARCH

Research to Clarify Choose at least one unfamiliar detail from the story. Briefly research that detail. In what way does the information you learned shed light on an aspect of the story?

Research to Explore Research Biosphere 2, a scientific research facility in Arizona. Formulate two research questions about it. For instance, questions could include: What is the purpose of Biosphere 2? What was its first mission? What challenges has it faced? Briefly research the answer to your question and share your findings with your group.

Close Read the Text

With your group, revisit sections of the text you marked during your first read. **Annotate** what you notice. What **questions** do you have? What can you **conclude**?

Analyze the Text

CITE TEXTUAL EVIDENCE to support your answers.

📝 **Notebook** Complete the activities.

1. **Review and Clarify** With your group, reread paragraph 16 of the story. Then, identify the author's use of **allusion,** or references to well-known people, events, or literary works. Discuss the ways in which the use of allusion improves or weakens the story.

2. **Present and Discuss** Now, work with your group to share the passages from the text that you found especially important. Discuss what you noticed in the text, the questions you asked, and the conclusions you reached.

3. **Essential Question:** *Should we make a home in space?* What has this selection taught you about the problems of making a home in space?

LANGUAGE DEVELOPMENT

Concept Vocabulary

| threatening | extinct | mutation |

Why These Words? The concept vocabulary words from the text are related. With your group, determine what the words have in common. Write your ideas and add another word that fits the category.

Practice

📝 **Notebook** Confirm your understanding of these words by using them in sentences. Include context clues that hint at each word's meaning.

Word Study

Latin Suffix: -tion In the story, Brock thinks that the puppy is the product of a *mutation* that enables her to survive in the outside world. The word *mutation* is built from the verb *mutate*, meaning "to change," and the Latin suffix -tion, which turns a verb into a noun. Based on that information, identify the meaning and part of speech of *mutation*.

TIP

GROUP DISCUSSION

When you work in your group to answer the Analyze the Text questions, be sure to support your opinions and ideas with evidence from the text.

🕸 WORD NETWORK

Add interesting words related to space exploration from the text to your Word Network.

⠿ STANDARDS

Language
• Determine or clarify the meaning of unknown and multiple-meaning words and phrases based on *grade 7 reading and content,* choosing flexibly from a range of strategies.
   a. Use context as a clue to the meaning of a word or phrase.
• Demonstrate understanding of figurative language, word relationships, and nuances in word meanings.
   a. Interpret figures of speech in context.

Analyze Craft and Structure

Elements of a Short Story: Conflict and Resolution In most stories, the plot centers on a **conflict**, or struggle between opposing forces. There are two types of conflict.

- **External conflict** is a struggle between a character and an outside force, such as another character or nature.
- **Internal conflict** is a struggle within a character as he or she wrestles with opposing feelings, beliefs, needs, or desires.

A story often has more than one conflict and may include both an external and an internal conflict. In most stories, a series of small conflicts contribute to the main conflict. The **resolution**, or outcome, often comes toward the end of the story when the conflicts, or problems, are settled in some way.

STANDARDS

Reading Literature
Analyze how particular elements of a story or drama interact.

Practice

CITE TEXTUAL EVIDENCE to support your answers.

Use this graphic organizer to analyze the conflicts and resolution in "The Last Dog." Work individually to complete the graphic organizer.

CONFLICT AND RESOLUTION IN "THE LAST DOG"	
Conflict(s): What does the main character struggle with? What other conflicts exist?	
Type(s) of Conflict: External or internal?	
Resolution: How are the conflicts settled, or resolved?	

When you have finished, share your completed chart with your group and discuss the following questions:

- Is there a main conflict that stands out in the story? Explain.
- How are the external conflicts and the internal conflicts related?
- Did the resolution settle the conflicts in the story? Did you find the resolution satisfying?

THE LAST DOG

Conventions

Simple and Compound Subjects and Predicates Every sentence has a subject and a predicate and expresses a complete thought. The **subject** tells whom or what the sentence is about. The **predicate** tells what the subject is, does, or has done to it.

PART OF SENTENCE	EXAMPLE
A **simple subject** is a single main noun or pronoun.	<u>Brog</u> drinks water from the brook.
A **compound subject** is two or more nouns or pronouns that share the same verb. The subjects are joined by a conjunction such as *and* or *or*.	<u>Brock</u> and <u>Brog</u> drink water from the brook.
A **simple predicate** is a single main verb or verb phrase.	Brog <u>drinks</u> water from the brook.
A **compound predicate** contains two or more main verbs that share the same subject. The verbs are joined by a conjunction such as *and* or *or*.	Brog <u>drinks</u> and <u>laps</u> water from the brook.

Read It

Work with your group to identify an example of a simple subject and an example of a compound predicate in "The Last Dog." Write your examples in the chart.

PART OF SENTENCE	EXAMPLE
Simple Subject	
Compound Predicate	

Write It

Notebook Sometimes too many short, simple sentences in a row can make your writing choppy and repetitive. Try adding sentence variety by combining simple subjects and predicates into compound subjects and predicates. Revise the following passage so that it includes at least one more compound predicate and one more compound subject.

My sister and I take care of our dogs. I feed them. My sister feeds them. I also walk them. I give them water. My sister also walks them and gives them water. My sister sometimes brushes their coats. I also sometimes brush their coats. Taking care of dogs is a lot of work!

STANDARDS

Language
• Demonstrate command of the conventions of standard English grammar and usage when writing or speaking.
• Use knowledge of language and its conventions when writing, speaking, reading, or listening.
   a. Choose language that expresses ideas precisely and concisely, recognizing and eliminating wordiness and redundancy.

Writing to Sources

A fictional narrative uses a combination of narrative strategies to tell a story and engage readers. These strategies include characterization, description, dialogue, figurative language, and imagery.

Assignment

Use your imagination to write your own version of the last seven paragraphs of this story. Begin your **revised ending** with the words "Out of sight of the dome, . . ." For your revision, choose one of the following options:

☐ Change the narrator, and write from the perspective of the puppy, Brog, giving her a human voice.

☐ Add a character to the story, who influences the story's resolution.

Develop Your Story Choose an option for your revision of the end of the story. How will it be similar to or different from the author's resolution to the story?

Think carefully about how your choice will affect the resolution of the narrative. For example, how would writing from the puppy's perspective affect the end of the story? How might introducing a new character change the story's ending?

Carefully choose words and descriptive details that engage the reader and bring your revised ending to life. Take notes in a chart like the one shown, and then draft your revised ending.

	NOTES FOR MY VERSION
Narrator	
Plot Events	
Resolution	

Reflect on Your Writing When your draft is completed, share it with others in your group. Then, as a group, discuss the following questions.

- What purpose does the narrator's perspective serve in a story?
- What effects do different resolutions have on a story?
- What type of resolution do you find most satisfying?

✐ EVIDENCE LOG

Before moving on to a new selection, go to your Evidence Log and record what you learned from "The Last Dog."

☰ STANDARDS

Writing
- Write narratives to develop real or imagined experiences or events using effective technique, relevant descriptive details, and well-structured event sequences.
  b. Use narrative techniques, such as dialogue, pacing, and description, to develop experiences, events, and/or characters.
  e. Provide a conclusion that follows from and reflects on the narrated experiences or events.
- Write routinely over extended time frames and shorter time frames for a range of discipline-specific tasks, purposes, and audiences.

About the Narrator

Ellen Ochoa, Ph.D, (b. 1958) was born in Los Angeles, California. She became the first Latina astronaut to go to space, as a crewmember aboard the space shuttle *Discovery*. In 2012, Dr. Ochoa was named Director of NASA's Johnson Space Center. "Don't be afraid to reach for the stars," Dr. Ochoa says. "I believe a good education can take you anywhere on Earth and beyond."

Ellen Ochoa: Director, Johnson Space Center

Technical Vocabulary

These words will be useful to you as you analyze, discuss, and write about the video. Context sentences are provided to the right of each word.

aptitude: natural ability or talent	• Carla's math teacher encouraged her to do extra credit work because of Carla's aptitude for math.
calculus: math used to study change	• Carla thinks that studying calculus is challenging but fascinating.
mission control: a command center for the control, monitoring, and support of activities connected with manned space flight	• Carla is hoping to visit mission control one day in order to see the technology of manned space flight at work.

First Review MEDIA: VIDEO

Study the video using these strategies.

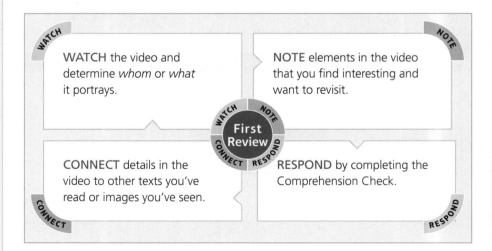

WATCH the video and determine *whom* or *what* it portrays.

NOTE elements in the video that you find interesting and want to revisit.

CONNECT details in the video to other texts you've read or images you've seen.

RESPOND by completing the Comprehension Check.

Ellen Ochoa: Director, Johnson Space Center

BACKGROUND

In this interview, Johnson Space Center Director Dr. Ellen Ochoa talks about how she came to be an astronaut with NASA. She mentions Sally Ride as one of her influences. In 1983, Ride became the first woman from the United States to launch into outer space when she joined the team aboard the space shuttle *Challenger*. Since then, more than 50 women scientists have joined Ride in making the journey to space.

SCAN FOR MULTIMEDIA

NOTES

Comprehension Check

Complete the following items after you finish your first review. Review and clarify details with your group.

1. Identify at least one thing that inspired Ochoa to become an astronaut.

2. How did Ochoa make history?

3. How did Sally Ride influence Ochoa?

TECHNICAL VOCABULARY

Use these words as you discuss and write about the video.

aptitude
calculus
mission control

⊞ **WORD NETWORK**

Add interesting words related to space exploration from the video to your Word Network.

Close Review

Watch the video again. Write any new observations that seem important. What **questions** do you have? What can you **conclude**?

Analyze the Media

CITE TEXTUAL EVIDENCE to support your answers.

🗐 **Notebook** Complete the activities.

1. Present and Discuss Choose the section of the video you find most interesting or powerful. Share your choice with the group and discuss why you chose it. Explain what you noticed in that part of the video, the questions it raised for you, and the conclusions you reached.

2. Review and Synthesize With your group, review the video. How is Ochoa's experience as an astronaut similar to and different from what you might expect? Explain.

3. Essential Question: *Should we make a home in space?* What has this video taught you about space exploration by humans? Discuss with your group.

Speaking and Listening

Assignment

Work as a group to write and present a short **biography** of Ochoa's life. Watch the video again and have each member of the group take notes. Then, briefly research Ellen Ochoa's career. Afterward, hold a group discussion to decide which details from the video and from your research to include in the biography.

ELLEN OCHOA: DIRECTOR, JOHNSON SPACE CENTER

Define Individual Roles Before viewing, writing, and discussing, assign tasks to group members. These might include:

- leading the planning discussion
- integrating research into the draft
- typing the final draft
- presenting the biography to the class

Analyze and Discuss Use these tips to guide your note-taking, discussion, and presentation:

- Watch the video several times in order to catch and note important details about Ochoa's life and her motivations for becoming an astronaut. Pause the video as needed.
- Don't write down everything you hear. Focus on specific dates and facts. Fill in details in later viewings. Use a chart like the one shown.

VIDEO TIME CODE	DETAILS FROM VIDEO
Additional Details From Research	

Plan Once you have gathered details, discuss with your group each item to include in the biography. Work collaboratively to determine a logical order in which to present your information. You may want to create a timeline to accompany your presentation.

Present Rehearse and then present your finished biography to the class. Invite questions and feedback from the class after your presentation.

EVIDENCE LOG

Before moving on to a new selection, go to your Evidence Log and record what you learned from the video.

STANDARDS

Speaking and Listening
Engage effectively in a range of collaborative discussions (one-on-one, in groups, and teacher-led) with diverse partners *on grade 7 topics, texts, and issues,* building on others' ideas and expressing their own clearly.

a. Come to discussions prepared, having read or researched material under study; explicitly draw on that preparation by referring to evidence on the topic, text, or issue to probe and reflect on ideas under discussion.
b. Follow rules for collegial discussions, track progress toward specific goals and deadlines, and define individual roles as needed.
c. Pose questions that elicit elaboration and respond to others' questions and comments with relevant observations and ideas that bring the discussion back on topic as needed.
d. Acknowledge new information expressed by others and, when warranted, modify their own views.

About the Author
Keith Wagstaff is a science and technology journalist. He has written for *Time* magazine, *NBC News*, and other outlets.

Neil deGrasse Tyson on the Future of U.S. Space Exploration After *Curiosity*

Concept Vocabulary

As you perform your first read, you will encounter these words.

cede	enterprise	capitalistic

Base Words If these words are unfamiliar to you, analyze each one to see whether it contains a **base word** you know. Then, use your knowledge of the "inside" word, along with context, to determine the meaning of the concept word. Here is an example of how to apply the strategy.

> **Unfamiliar Word:** *investment*
>
> **Familiar "Inside" Word:** *invest*, meaning "to spend money in hopes of earning more back"
>
> **Context:** "It's an investment, not a handout."
>
> **Conclusion:** The item being discussed is not given out freely; a return is expected. *Investment* might mean "something bought with the expectation of making money or getting something out of it."

Apply your knowledge of base words and other vocabulary strategies to determine the meanings of unfamiliar words you encounter during your first read.

First Read NONFICTION

Apply these strategies as you conduct your first read. You will have an opportunity to complete a close read after your first read.

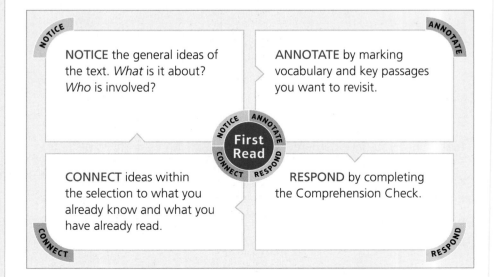

NOTICE the general ideas of the text. *What* is it about? *Who* is involved?

ANNOTATE by marking vocabulary and key passages you want to revisit.

CONNECT ideas within the selection to what you already know and what you have already read.

RESPOND by completing the Comprehension Check.

First Read

STANDARDS

Reading Informational Text
By the end of the year, read and comprehend literary nonfiction in the grades 6–8 text complexity band proficiently, with scaffolding as needed at the high end of the range.

Language
Determine or clarify the meaning of unknown and multiple-meaning words and phrases based on *grade 7 reading and content*, choosing flexibly from a range of strategies.

Neil deGrasse Tyson
on the Future of U.S. Space Exploration After *Curiosity*

Keith Wagstaff

BACKGROUND

NASA's *Curiosity* is a robotic rover that landed on Mars in 2012. Since then, *Curiosity* has been roaming Mars, collecting data and looking for signs of microbial life. In this interview, astrophysicist Neil deGrasse Tyson discusses the *Curiosity* mission and the possibility of people's traveling to Mars.

SCAN FOR MULTIMEDIA

Some people are questioning the need to fund a government space program. Why do we still need NASA?

1   The people who say that all we need is private space travel are simply delusional. My book on space, *Space Chronicles: Facing the Ultimate Frontier,* was originally titled *Failure to Launch: The Dreams and Delusions of Space Enthusiasts.* Space enthusiasts are the most susceptible demographic to delusion that I have ever seen.

2   Private enterprise can never lead a space frontier. It's not possible because a space frontier is expensive, it has unknown risks, and it has unquantified risks. Historically, governments have done this. They have drawn the maps, they have found where the trade winds[1] are, they have invented the new tools to go where no one has gone before. Then, when the routines are set up, you **cede** that to private **enterprise**.

3   That's why I don't know what they're thinking. The first colony on Mars is not going to be built by a private company. How are you going to make money? You're not.

4   Look what's going on now. Private enterprise is giving us access to low-Earth orbit for less than what NASA was providing. That should have been happening decades ago. Why is that happening now? Because low-Earth orbit is no longer the frontier. NASA has been going in and out of low-Earth orbit since 1962.

NOTES

Mark base words or indicate another strategy you used that helped you determine meaning.

cede (seed) *v.*

MEANING:

enterprise (EHN tuhr pryz) *n.*

MEANING:

---

1. **trade winds** reliable winds that captains of sailing ships have traditionally used to cross the oceans.

5   I see private enterprise as a fundamental part of creating a space industry, but there will always be the frontier.

When *Curiosity* touches down,[2] will that be enough to inspire young people to go into the STEM fields (science, technology, engineering, and mathematics) and to get the American people behind a manned mission to Mars?

6   Anything NASA does in space that has never been done before drums up interest in science. Images from the Hubble Telescope, the *Spirit* and *Opportunity* rovers, broadcasts from the International Space Station—anything NASA does accomplishes this.

7   Whether that's enough to get humans on Mars, I don't think so. *Curiosity* is cheap compared to sending humans out of low-Earth orbit. A different kind of understanding of the value of sending humans into space needs to be had before that happens. I don't think *Curiosity* is a stepping stone to that.

Are the barriers to sending humans to Mars political?

8   No. It's an understanding—that the public does not yet have—of the role of NASA as a flywheel[3] of innovation, influencing not only direct spin-offs but also the culture itself. When you feel that you are part of an innovation nation, you think innovatively, no matter your field.

9   You start thinking that the science fiction story you just read or movie you just saw is maybe in reach. Maybe it's possible. For example, in the movie *Prometheus*, they have these flying spheres that go up and down caves and use laser tomography to map their structure. We don't have that, but that's really cool and I can imagine having that.

10   That idea might inspire me to try and create it instead of just sitting back and saying, "Oh, that's the future and it will probably never happen. Now let me go back and watch Snooki."[4]

11   I am certain that once that flywheel is set into motion and the discoveries of NASA become writ large in the newspapers, that people will come to understand that innovations in science and technology—brought to you by the force of nature we call NASA—are the engines of 21st Century economies. It's an investment, not a handout.

What is it going to mean to the human race if we land on Mars?

12   Here's the problem. I don't know how old you are, but I'm guessing you were born after we landed on the Moon. Now, given that fact, I'm guessing that there is no single event in your life that is positive where you say, "I remember where I was at that moment." Is there?

No.

---

2. **When *Curiosity* touches down** This interview took place four days before *Curiosity* was scheduled to land on Mars.
3. **flywheel** *n.* wheel that controls a machine's speed and power.
4. **Snooki** star of a reality television show.

13 I have the benefit of being able to say I know where I was when Neil Armstrong walked on the Moon. You don't have it. You don't have that moment. We have bred multiple generations of people who have not experienced knowing where you are the moment a news story broke, with that news story being great and grand and something that elevates society instead of diminishes it. If we land on Mars, you'll know where you were the day that happened. Landing on Mars expands the space frontier and that makes headlines.

14 Boldly going where hundreds have gone before does not make headlines. If you make the headlines, that's what stimulates STEM interest. You won't need a program to excite people to get into the sciences. You won't need tariffs[5] to keep your factories stateside, because you'll be innovating at a pace where you're making products the rest of the world hasn't figured out how to make yet.

15 When an industry matures, it means it's not advancing and of course the jobs go overseas. That's the obligation of the multi-national corporation, to put the factory where it can make the widget as cheap as possible. Don't get angry when a corporation does that, we've all bought into this concept. We live in a **capitalistic** society. That's how it works.

16 You don't complain. You say "Let's innovate so we can make things that [other countries] can't." All of that is possible when you have a healthy NASA exploring the cosmos. All of that. ❧

5. **tariffs** (TAIR ihfs) *n.* taxes on goods imported from other countries.

Mark base words or indicate another strategy you used that helped you determine meaning.

capitalistic (kap uh tuh LIHS tihk) *adj.*

MEANING:

Comprehension Check

Complete the following items after you finish your first read. Review and clarify details with your group.

1. In Neil deGrasse Tyson's opinion, who can best lead the exploration of frontiers?

2. What role does deGrasse Tyson see for private companies?

RESEARCH

Research to Clarify Choose at least one unfamiliar detail in the selection. Briefly research that detail. In what way does the information you learned shed light on the selection?

NEIL deGRASSE TYSON ON
THE FUTURE OF U.S. SPACE
EXPLORATION AFTER *CURIOSITY*

TIP

GROUP DISCUSSION

If you disagree with a group
member's opinion, do so
respectfully. Be prepared to
support your own opinion
with details from the
selection.

🔀 WORD NETWORK

Add interesting words
related to space exploration
from the text to your
Word Network.

Close Read the Text

With your group, revisit sections of the text you marked
during your first read. **Annotate** details that you notice.
What **questions** do you have? What can you **conclude**?

Analyze the Text

> **CITE TEXTUAL EVIDENCE**
> to support your answers.

📓 **Notebook** Complete the activities.

1. **Review and Clarify** With your group, review paragraphs 1–5 of the
   interview. According to deGrasse Tyson, why are people who say that
   we only need private space travel "simply delusional"?

2. **Present and Discuss** Now, work with your group to share the
   passages from the selection that you found especially important.
   Take turns presenting your passages. Discuss what you noticed in the
   selection, the questions you asked, and the conclusions you reached.

3. **Essential Question: *Should we make a home in space?*** What
   has this selection taught you about humans making a home in space?
   Discuss with your group.

LANGUAGE DEVELOPMENT

Concept Vocabulary

cede	enterprise	capitalistic

Why These Words? The concept vocabulary words from the text are
related. With your group, determine what the words have in common.
Write your ideas and add another word that fits the category.

Practice

📓 **Notebook** Confirm your understanding of the concept vocabulary
words by using them in a discussion of the role of money in space
exploration. Should the government play the leading role in funding
space travel, or should space travel be handled by private companies?

Word Study

Multiple-Meaning Words In the interview, deGrasse Tyson discusses
the role of private enterprise in exploring space. The word *enterprise*
has several meanings. Use a dictionary to find all of the definitions of
enterprise. Then, determine which meaning is the correct meaning for
enterprise as it is used in the interview.

📑 STANDARDS

Language
Determine or clarify the meaning
of unknown and multiple-meaning
words and phrases based on
grade 7 reading and content,
choosing flexibly from a range of
strategies.
  c. Consult general and
  specialized reference materials,
  both print and digital, to find
  the pronunciation of a word or
  determine or clarify its precise
  meaning or its part of speech.

Analyze Craft and Structure

Evaluate Argument and Claims An **argument** is a logical way of presenting a specific belief, conclusion, or perspective on an issue or action. A good argument provides logical reasons and relevant evidence in support of a **claim,** or position on the topic or action at hand.

- **relevant evidence: facts,** or statements that can be proved true, from credible sources that are current
- **logical reasons:** conclusions that are reached based on an analysis of the relevant evidence

Word choice, or the words, phrases, and expressions an author uses, can strengthen an argument. Most arguments are characterized by precise, formal language that clearly shows the connections between claims, reasons, and evidence. However, an author may use **figurative language,** or language that is not meant literally, to appeal to his or her audience or to simplify a complex idea.

:≡ STANDARDS

Reading Informational Text
- Determine the meaning of words and phrases as they are used in a text, including figurative, connotative, and technical meanings; analyze the impact of a specific word choice on meaning and tone.
- Determine an author's point of view or purpose in a text and analyze how the author distinguishes his or her position from that of others.
- Trace and evaluate the argument and specific claims in a text, assessing whether the reasoning is sound and the evidence is relevant and sufficient to support the claims.

Practice

CITE TEXTUAL EVIDENCE to support your answers.

🔁 **Notebook** Work with your group to analyze Neil deGrasse Tyson's argument. Use a chart such as the one shown to record your notes. Then, answer the questions that follow.

CLAIM	EVIDENCE	REASONS

1. (a) What is deGrasse Tyson's main claim? (b) What evidence and reasons support his argument?

2. A **metaphor** is a type of figurative language that compares two unlike things by saying that one thing is another. (a) What is the metaphor deGrasse Tyson uses in paragraphs 8–11? (b) How does the use of this metaphor affect his argument?

3. Based on your analysis, is deGrasse Tyson's argument effective and convincing? Why or why not?

Conventions

Sentence Functions and End Marks There are four types of sentences, which can be classified according to how they function. End marks vary according to the function of the sentence.

TYPE OF SENTENCE	FUNCTION	END MARK	EXAMPLE
Declarative	To make statements	period (.)	I have no desire to ride in a spaceship.
Interrogative	To ask questions	question mark (?)	Would you want to travel to another planet?
Imperative	To give commands or directions	exclamation point (!) or period (.)	Put on your seatbelt. Sit down, now!
Exclamatory	To call out or exclaim	exclamation point (!)	What a thrill!

Read It

Work with your group to fill in the chart with an example from the selection of each type of sentence. If you cannot find an example, write a sentence of your own.

TYPE OF SENTENCE	EXAMPLE
Declarative	
Interrogative	
Imperative	
Exclamatory	

Write It

⊟ Notebook Using different types of sentences can make your writing more interesting to read. Write a paragraph about space exploration in which you use each type of sentence and end mark at least once. Share your paragraph with your group.

Research

Assignment

Work with your group to conduct research and write a short **informational report** on one of the following topics:

- [ ] the life and work of Neil deGrasse Tyson
- [ ] the planet Mars
- [ ] the robotic rover *Curiosity*

Your group should formulate a research question; gather information from multiple, reliable sources; and present the information in a clear, organized way.

Project Plan With your group, choose a topic and then formulate your research plan. Use this chart to help gather details.

Topic and Research Plan: _____

SOURCE (TITLE, AUTHOR, AND DATE)	WHAT I LEARNED

Organize and Draft Share your research findings with the group, and decide which details to use in your group report. Organize the details logically, and create a first draft. Be sure to cite the sources you used.

Reflect on Your Research Project After you have presented your project, reflect on the experience by asking yourself these questions.

- What did I learn?
- Was it challenging to work in a group on a written project?
- What parts of the group's process worked well?
- What might I do differently when working on group projects?

✎ EVIDENCE LOG

Before moving on to a new selection, go to your Evidence Log and record what you learned from "Neil deGrasse Tyson on the Future of U.S. Space Exploration After *Curiosity*."

▤ STANDARDS

Writing
- Write informative/explanatory texts to examine a topic and convey ideas, concepts, and information through the selection, organization, and analysis of relevant content.
- Conduct short research projects to answer a question, drawing on several sources and generating additional related, focused questions for further research and investigation.
- Gather relevant information from multiple print and digital sources, using search terms effectively; assess the credibility and accuracy of each source; and quote or paraphrase the data and conclusions of others while avoiding plagiarism and following a standard format for citation.

Present an Argument

Assignment

You have read different selections that address the benefits and drawbacks of space exploration. With your group, develop and deliver a **multimedia presentation** that addresses this question:

> Should space exploration be a priority for our country?

Plan With Your Group

Analyze the Text With your group, discuss the various ideas and opinions about space exploration that are presented in the texts you have read. Use the chart to list your ideas. For each selection, identify benefits and drawbacks of space exploration. Then, come to a consensus, or agreement, about whether the benefits of space exploration by our country outweigh the drawbacks.

TITLE	SPACE EXPLORATION BENEFITS AND DRAWBACKS
Future of Space Exploration Could See Humans on Mars, Alien Planets	
The Last Dog	
Ellen Ochoa: Director, Johnson Space Center	
Neil deGrasse Tyson on the Future of U.S. Space Exploration After *Curiosity*	

Gather Evidence and Media Examples Review the selections and note specific examples that support your group's claim. Once the chart is complete, do some additional research to learn more about current NASA programs and to find relevant media to include in the group presentation. Consider photographs, illustrations, music, charts, graphs, and video clips. Allow each group member to make suggestions.

Organize Your Ideas Use a script outline, such as the one shown, to organize your presentation. Assign roles for each part of the presentation, note when each part begins, and record what each presenter will say.

MULTIMEDIA PRESENTATION SCRIPT		
	Media Cues	Script
Presenter 1		
Presenter 2		
Presenter 3		

Rehearse With Your Group

Practice With Your Group As you practice delivering your portion of the presentation, use this checklist to evaluate the effectiveness of your group's rehearsal. Then, use your evaluation and the instruction here to guide revisions to your presentation.

CONTENT	USE OF MEDIA	PRESENTATION TECHNIQUES
☐ The claims of the presentation are clear. ☐ The claims are supported with evidence from the texts in this section.	☐ The media support the claim. ☐ The media communicate key ideas. ☐ The media are sequenced effectively. ☐ The equipment functions properly.	☐ The media are visible and audible. ☐ The transitions between the media segments are smooth. ☐ The speaker uses eye contact and speaks clearly.

Fine-Tune the Content To make your argument strong, you may need to go back into the texts and your research sources to find more support for your claims. Work with your group to identify any points that are confusing and need clarification.

Improve Your Use of Media Double-check that media equipment is in working order, and make a backup plan in case your equipment fails. If the media are not well distributed through the presentation, work to change the pacing.

Brush Up on Your Presentation Techniques Practice delivering your presentation several times as a group until you are comfortable. Give each other feedback and encouragement to improve and polish your presentation.

Present and Evaluate

When you present as a group, be sure that each member has taken into account each of the checklist items. As you watch other groups, evaluate how well they meet the checklist criteria.

▤ STANDARDS

Speaking and Listening
• Present claims and findings, emphasizing salient points in a focused, coherent manner with pertinent descriptions, facts, details, and examples; use appropriate eye contact, adequate volume, and clear pronunciation.
• Include multimedia components and visual displays in presentations to clarify claims and findings and emphasize salient points.

ESSENTIAL QUESTION:

Should we make a home in space?

There is much we don't know about the universe. Some people are eager to support further space exploration, whereas others would prefer to devote time and money to improving conidtions on our own planet. In this section, you will choose one additional selection about outer space for your final reading experience in this unit. Follow these steps to help you choose.

Look Back Think about the selections you have already read. What more do you want to know about outer space?

Look Ahead Preview the selections by reading the descriptions. Which one seems most interesting and appealing to you?

Look Inside Take a few minutes to scan through the text you chose. Make another selection if this text doesn't meet your needs.

Independent Learning Strategies

Throughout your life, in school, in your community, and in your career, you will need to rely on yourself to learn and work on your own. Review these strategies and the actions you can take to practice them during Independent Learning. Add ideas of your own for each category.

STRATEGY	ACTION PLAN
Create a schedule	• Understand your goals and deadlines. • Make a plan for what to do each day. •
Take notes	• Record important ideas and information. • Review your notes before preparing to share with a group. •
Practice what you've learned	• Use first-read and close-read strategies to deepen your understanding. • After you read, evaluate the usefulness of the evidence to help you understand the topic. • Consider the quality and reliability of the source. •

SCAN FOR
MULTIMEDIA

CONTENTS

Choose one selection. Selections are available online only.

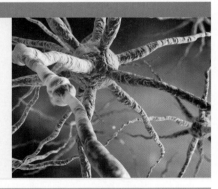
PERFORMANCE-BASED ASSESSMENT PREP

Review Evidence for an Argument

Complete your Evidence Log for the unit by evaluating what you've learned and synthesizing the information you've recorded.

SCAN FOR MULTIMEDIA

First-Read Guide

Use this page to record your first-read ideas.

Tool Kit
First-Read Guide and
Model Annotation

Selection Title: _____

NOTICE

NOTICE new information or ideas you learn about the unit topic as you first read this text.

ANNOTATE

ANNOTATE by marking vocabulary and key passages you want to revisit.

NOTICE ANNOTATE
First Read
CONNECT RESPOND

CONNECT

CONNECT ideas within the selection to other knowledge and the selections you have read.

RESPOND

RESPOND by writing a brief summary of the selection.

STANDARD

Reading Read and comprehend complex literary and informational texts independently and proficiently.

Close-Read Guide

Use this page to record your close-read ideas.

Selection Title: _____

Tool Kit
Close-Read Guide and
Model Annotation

Close Read the Text

Revisit sections of the text you marked during your first read. Read these sections closely and **annotate** what you notice. Ask yourself **questions** about the text. What can you **conclude**? Write down your ideas.

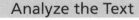

Analyze the Text

Think about the author's choices of patterns, structure, techniques, and ideas included in the text. Select one and record your thoughts about what this choice conveys.

QuickWrite

Pick a paragraph from the text that grabbed your interest. Explain the power of this passage.

_____
_____
_____
_____
_____
_____
_____
_____
_____
_____

STANDARD

Reading Read and comprehend complex literary and informational texts independently and proficiently.

Share Your Independent Learning

Prepare to Share

Should we make a home in space?

Even when you read something independently, your understanding continues to grow when you share what you have learned with others. What did you learn about making a home in space? Reflect on the text you explored independently and write notes about its connection to the unit. In your notes, consider why this text belongs in this unit.

Learn From Your Classmates

💬 **Discuss It** Share your ideas about the text you explored on your own. As you talk with others in your class, jot down a few ideas that you learned from them.

Reflect

Review your notes, and mark the most important insight you gained from these writing and discussion activities. Explain how this idea adds to your understanding of space exploration.

▤ STANDARDS

Speaking and Listening
Engage effectively in a range of collaborative discussions with diverse partners on *grade 7 topics, texts, and issues,* building on others' ideas and expressing their own clearly.

Review Evidence for an Argument

At the beginning of this unit, you took a position on the following question:

Should we spend valuable resources on space exploration?

✐ EVIDENCE LOG

Review your Evidence Log and your QuickWrite from the beginning of the unit. Did your opinion change?

☐ YES	☐ NO
Identify at least three pieces of evidence that convinced you to change your mind.	Identify at least three pieces of evidence that reinforced your initial position.
1.	**1.**
2.	**2.**
3.	**3.**

State your position now:

_____

_____

Identify a possible counterclaim:

_____

_____

Evaluate the Strength of Your Evidence Consider your point of view. How did the texts you read impact your point of view?

☐ Do more research   ☐ Talk with my classmates

☐ Reread a selection   ☐ Ask an expert

☐ Other: _____

≣ STANDARDS

Writing
Write arguments to support claims with clear reasons and relevant evidence.
  a. Introduce claim(s), acknowledge alternate or opposing claims, and organize the reasons and evidence logically.
  b. Support claim(s) with logical reasoning and relevant evidence, using accurate, credible sources and demonstrating an understanding of the topic or text.

SOURCES

• WHOLE-CLASS SELECTIONS

• SMALL-GROUP SELECTIONS

• INDEPENDENT-LEARNING
SELECTION

WORD NETWORK

As you write and revise your argument, use your Word Network to help vary your word choices.

PART 1
Writing to Sources: Argument

In this unit you read about space exploration, real and imagined, from various perspectives. Some authors argued in favor of continued or increased exploration of the frontiers of space. Other authors warned of the dangers that may come as a result of it.

Assignment

Write an **argument** in which you state and defend a claim in response to the following question:

> Should we spend valuable resources on space exploration?

Use credible evidence from the selections that you read and researched in this unit to justify your claim. Support your claim with logical reasoning and relevant evidence, and organize your ideas effectively so that your argument is easy to follow. Remember to address counterclaims, or alternative viewpoints, to your position. Use a formal tone in your writing.

Reread the Assignment Review the assignment to be sure you fully understand it. The assignment may reference some of the academic words presented at the beginning of the unit. Be sure you understand each of the words given below to complete the assignment correctly.

Academic Vocabulary

justify	alternative	certainty
discredit	assumption	

Review the Elements of Effective Argument Before you begin writing, read the Argument Rubric. Once you have completed your first draft, check it against the rubric. If one or more of the elements is missing or not as strong as it could be, revise your essay to add or strengthen that component.

STANDARDS

Writing
• Write arguments to support claims with clear reasons and relevant evidence.
• Write routinely over extended time frames and shorter time frames for a range of discipline-specific tasks, purposes, and audiences.

Argument Rubric

	Focus and Organization	Evidence and Elaboration	Conventions
4	The introduction is engaging and states the claim in a persuasive way. The claim is supported by logical reasons and relevant evidence, and opposing claims are addressed. Reasons and evidence are logically organized so that the argument is easy to follow. Words, phrases, and clauses create cohesion and clearly show the relationships between claims, reasons, and evidence. The conclusion supports the argument and offers a fresh insight into the topic.	Each claim and reason is clearly and logically supported by evidence from the texts. The tone of the argument is formal and objective. Words are carefully chosen and suited to purpose and audience.	The argument intentionally uses standard English conventions of usage and mechanics.
3	The introduction is somewhat engaging and states the claim clearly. The claim is supported by reasons and evidence, and opposing claims are acknowledged. Reasons and evidence are organized so that the argument is easy to follow. Words, phrases, and clauses clearly show the relationships between claims, reasons, and evidence. The conclusion supports the argument.	Each claim and reason is supported by evidence from the texts. The tone of the argument is mostly formal and objective. Words are generally suited to purpose and audience.	The argument demonstrates accuracy in standard English conventions of usage and mechanics.
2	The introduction states the claim. The claim is supported by some reasons and evidence, and opposing claims may be briefly acknowledged. Reasons and evidence are organized somewhat logically with a few words and phrases that create cohesion. The conclusion relates to the claim.	Most claims and reasons are supported by evidence from the texts. The tone of the argument is occasionally formal and objective. Words are somewhat suited to purpose and audience.	The argument demonstrates some accuracy in standard English conventions of usage and mechanics.
1	The claim is not clearly stated. The claim is not supported by reasons and evidence, and opposing claims are not acknowledged. Reasons and evidence are disorganized and the argument is difficult to follow. The conclusion does not relate to the argument or is missing entirely.	Claims and reasons are not supported by evidence from the texts. The tone is informal. Words are not suited to purpose and audience.	The argument contains mistakes in standard English conventions of usage and mechanics.

PART 2
Speaking and Listening: Oral Presentation

Assignment

After completing the final draft of your argument, use it as the foundation for a brief **oral presentation**. Do not simply read your argument aloud. Take the following steps to make your presentation lively and engaging.

- Review your argument, and mark key reasons and evidence that support your claim. Use these annotations as a guide for your presentation script.
- Choose visuals that add interest to your presentation.
- Prepare a final draft of your presentation, and deliver to the class.

Review the Rubric Before you deliver your presentation, check your plans against this rubric.

	Content	Organization	Presentation Techniques
3	The introduction is engaging and establishes the claim in a persuasive way.	The speaker uses time effectively, spending the right amount on each part.	The speaker maintains eye contact and speaks clearly and with adequate volume.
	The presentation includes strong, valid reasons and evidence to support the claim and address counterclaims.	Ideas progress logically, with clear transitions among ideas so the argument is easy for listeners to follow.	The speaker presents the argument with energy and strong conviction.
	Conclusion offers fresh insight into the claim.	The sequence of the visuals matches the timing of the speaker.	
2	The introduction establishes a claim.	The speaker uses time somewhat effectively, spending the right amount of time on most parts.	The speaker sometimes maintains eye contact and speaks somewhat clearly and with adequate volume.
	The presentation includes some reasons and evidence to support the claim and vaguely acknowledges counterclaims.	Ideas progress logically with some transitions among ideas.	The speaker presents with some energy and conviction.
	The conclusion offers some insight and restates important information.	The sequence of visuals sometimes matches the timing of the speaker.	
1	The introduction does not clearly state a claim.	The speaker does not use time effectively and focuses too much time on some parts and too little on others.	The speaker does not maintain eye contact or speak clearly with adequate volume.
	The presentation does not include reasons or evidence to support a claim or acknowledge counterclaims.	Ideas do not progress logically.	The speaker's argument lacks energy or conviction.
	The conclusion does not restate important information about a claim.	The sequence of visuals does not match the timing of the speaker.	

Reflect on the Unit

Now that you've completed the unit, take a few moments to reflect on your learning.

Reflect on the Unit Goals

Look back at the goals at the beginning of the unit. Use a different-colored pen to rate yourself again. Think about readings and activities that contributed the most to the growth of your understanding. Record your thoughts.

Reflect on the Learning Strategies

Discuss It Write a reflection on whether you were able to improve your learning based on your Action Plans. Think about what worked, what didn't, and what you might do to keep working on these strategies. Record your ideas before joining in a class discussion.

Reflect on the Text

Choose a selection that you found challenging and explain what made it difficult.

Explain something that surprised you about a text in the unit.

Which activity taught you the most about making a home in outer space? What did you learn?

SCAN FOR
MULTIMEDIA

Turning Points

Life is filled with little moments and big moments. Most of the time they just pass by, but sometimes an event or experience can change someone's life in an instant.

A Transformation

💬 **Discuss It** What sorts of turning points occur in nature and in the human experience?

Write your response before sharing your ideas.

SCAN FOR MULTIMEDIA

UNIT 3

UNIT INTRODUCTION

ESSENTIAL QUESTION: What can cause a sudden change in someone's life?

LAUNCH TEXT
EXPLANATORY
ESSAY MODEL
At the
Crossroads

WHOLE-CLASS LEARNING

ANCHOR TEXT: DRAMA

A Christmas Carol: Scrooge and Marley, Act I
Israel Horovitz

ANCHOR TEXT: DRAMA

A Christmas Carol: Scrooge and Marley, Act II
Israel Horovitz

COMPARE

MEDIA: FILM

from *Scrooge*
directed by
Henry Edwards

SMALL-GROUP LEARNING

SHORT STORY

Thank You, M'am
Langston Hughes

MEMOIR

from An American
Childhood
Annie Dillard

MEDIA: PHOTO GALLERY

Urban Farming Is
Growing a Greener
Future
Hillary Schwei

INDEPENDENT LEARNING

REFLECTIVE ESSAY

Little Things Are Big
Jesús Colón

NEWS ARTICLE

Profile: Malala
Yousafzai
BBC

BIOGRAPHY

Noor Inayat Khan
from Women Heroes of
WWII
Kathryn J. Atwood

SHORT STORY

A Retrieved
Reformation
O. Henry

PERFORMANCE TASK

WRITING FOCUS:
Write an Explanatory Essay

PERFORMANCE TASK

SPEAKING AND LISTENING FOCUS:
Present an Explanatory Essay

PERFORMANCE-BASED ASSESSMENT PREP

Review Evidence for an Explanatory
Essay

PERFORMANCE-BASED ASSESSMENT

Explanatory Text: Essay and Oral Presentation

PROMPT:
What can cause a significant change in someone's life?

Unit Goals

Throughout this unit you will deepen your perspective about turning points in people's lives by reading, writing, speaking, listening, and presenting. These goals will help you succeed on the Unit Performance-Based Assessment.

Rate how well you meet these goals right now. You will revisit your ratings later when you reflect on your growth during this unit.

SCALE

1	2	3	4	5
NOT AT ALL WELL	NOT VERY WELL	SOMEWHAT WELL	VERY WELL	EXTREMELY WELL

READING GOALS   1 2 3 4 5

- Read and analyze explanatory texts.

- Expand your knowledge and use of academic and concept vocabulary.

WRITING AND RESEARCH GOALS   1 2 3 4 5

- Write an explanatory text to examine a topic and convey ideas.

- Conduct research projects of various lengths to explore a topic and clarify meaning.

LANGUAGE GOAL   1 2 3 4 5

- Choose language that expresses ideas precisely and concisely, recognizing and eliminating wordiness and redundancy.

SPEAKING AND LISTENING GOALS   1 2 3 4 5

- Collaborate with your team to build on the ideas of others, develop consensus, and communicate.

- Integrate audio, visuals, and text in presentations.

☰ STANDARDS

Language
Acquire and use accurately grade appropriate general academic and domain-specific words and phrases; gather vocabulary knowledge when considering a word or phrase important to comprehension or expression.

SCAN FOR MULTIMEDIA

Academic Vocabulary: Explanatory Text

Academic terms appear in all subjects and can help you read, write, and discuss with more precision. Explanatory writing relies on facts to inform or explain. Here are five academic words that will be useful to you in this unit as you analyze and write explanatory texts.

Complete the chart.

1. Review each word, its root, and mentor sentences.

2. Use the information and your own knowledge to predict the meaning of each word.

3. For each word, list at least two related words.

4. Refer to the dictionary or other resources if needed.

TIP

FOLLOW THROUGH
Study the words in this chart, and mark them or their forms wherever they appear in the unit.

WORD	MENTOR SENTENCES	PREDICT MEANING	RELATED WORDS
contribute ROOT: **-trib-** "give"	1. Jennifer likes to *contribute* to the discussion when she has something meaningful to add. 2. Julio wants to *contribute* a short story to the school literary magazine.		tribute; attribute
consistent ROOT: **-sist-** "stand"	1. Keeping *consistent* pressure on a wound helps stop bleeding. 2. The runner kept a *consistent* routine to prepare for the race.		
maintain ROOT: **-tain-** "hold"	1. The disabled train struggled to *maintain* speed. 2. The veterinarian *maintained* her belief that dogs need grooming.		
observation ROOT: **-serv-** "watch over"	1. Watching the rat every day, the scientist learned about it through *observation*. 2. *Observation* of the moon was impossible because it was a cloudy night.		
sufficient ROOT: **-fic-** "make do"	1. In order to prove your point, you must provide *sufficient* evidence. 2. I don't have *sufficient* money to buy that shirt.		

At the Crossroads

NOTES

1   In April of 2012, 25-year-old Nick Kleckner was working as an electrician and cabdriver in northern California. And then, suddenly, he found himself at a crossroads. He left it all—his job, his family, his friends—and bought a one-way plane ticket to Jacksonville, Florida. He had a bold plan in mind. He was going to walk to California with virtually nothing on his back. He hoped the journey would change his life, but he had no idea how!

2   Nick, who was not exactly prepared, had nothing in the way of survival skills, so he planned to survive on the goodness of the people he met on the road.

3   Using the handle "Hobo Nick," Nick began his journey on April 5, leaving Jacksonville with a backpack, a sleeping bag, and a travel kit. He also had an iPod and the ability to receive Internet service. Throughout the journey, he would document his experience in minute detail and send daily updates to his mother, who'd post them on his blog.

4   The question is: Why? What would make someone take off like that? Nick had a comfortable life. He had a good income, a house, a new car, and a new motorcycle. He was moving forward with his life. By society's standards he should have been happy—but he wasn't.

5   Nick was in a rut. His life felt repetitive and boring. It lacked a higher purpose. He felt he wasn't growing as a person. He had "things" but didn't appreciate them. "It got to the point where I couldn't deal with everything anymore," Nick said later. "I felt a lot of pressure, stress, and anxiety and decided to get out."

6   As Hobo Nick, he trekked across miles of scorched desert and endured nights of pounding rain. In the towns and cities, he

SCAN FOR MULTIMEDIA

slept on the street, where he knew that there were people to help him out.

7   Even with help, it was a hard journey. Nick would sometimes go days without food, or search dumpsters for things to eat. But whenever he felt that he had more than he needed, he decided to "pay it forward" by giving to other folks he encountered on his way. Paying it forward was one of Nick's goals on his journey—giving more than he received. If he was offered money or a gift card he didn't need, he gave it away to people who did. He was surprised at people's generosity along the way. There was a time in Mississippi when the cars actually pulled over to the side of the road to check on him and give him money. The experience taught him a valuable lesson: if you share what you have, and help others as much as possible, you will never be stranded.

8   In his blog, Nick chronicled the important changes brought about by his selfless lifestyle and rejection of material things. He has learned to live in the moment and to be thankful for everything he has.

9   On September 29, after an epic 2,500-mile walk across the North American continent, Nick managed to make it all the way to Huntington Beach, California. More than a hundred family members, friends and well-wishers were waiting for him. During the six months of his journey, he destroyed five pairs of shoes and lost about 55 pounds.

10   In the future, Nick plans to do another cross-country trip. "The point is always to give more than you take," he says, adding that "the biggest takeaway from this experience is to have realized that mankind is better than I ever dreamed." 🍃

NOTES

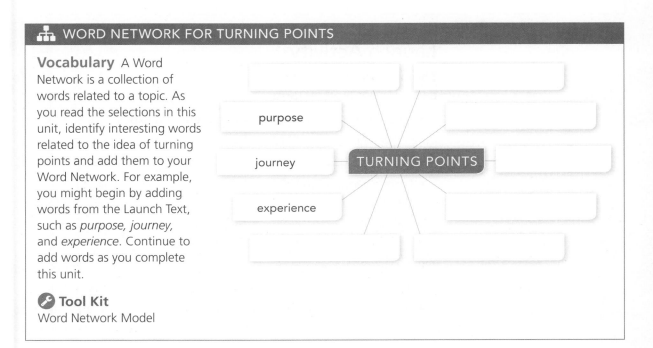

🗂 WORD NETWORK FOR TURNING POINTS

Vocabulary A Word Network is a collection of words related to a topic. As you read the selections in this unit, identify interesting words related to the idea of turning points and add them to your Word Network. For example, you might begin by adding words from the Launch Text, such as *purpose, journey,* and *experience.* Continue to add words as you complete this unit.

🔧 **Tool Kit**
Word Network Model

purpose

journey

experience

TURNING POINTS

Summary

Write a summary of "At the Crossroads." A **summary** is a concise, complete, and accurate overview of a text. It should not include a statement of your opinion or an analysis.

Launch Activity

Thumbs Up/Thumbs Down Consider this statement: **A person's life can change in an instant.**

- Record your position on the statement and explain your thinking.

  ☐ Strongly Agree ☐ Agree ☐ Disagree ☐ Strongly Disagree

- Form a group with like-minded students in one corner of the classroom.

- Discuss questions such as "What examples from the text or your own prior knowledge led you to take this position?"

- After your discussion, have a representative from each group present a brief two- or three-minute summary of the group's position.

- After all the groups have presented their views, move into the four corners again. If you change your corner, be ready to explain why.

QuickWrite

Consider class discussions, presentations, the video, and the Launch Text as you think about the prompt. Record your first thoughts here.

PROMPT: **What can cause a significant change in someone's life?**

EVIDENCE LOG FOR TURNING POINTS

Review your QuickWrite. Summarize your point of view in one sentence to record in your Evidence Log. Then, record evidence from "At the Crossroads" that supports your point of view.

After each selection, you will continue to use your Evidence Log to record the evidence you gather and the connections you make. This graphic shows what your Evidence Log looks like.

🔧 **Tool Kit**
Evidence Log Model

Title of Text: _____ Date: _____

CONNECTION TO PROMPT	TEXT EVIDENCE/DETAILS	ADDITIONAL NOTES/IDEAS

How does this text change or add to my thinking?   Date: _____

SCAN FOR
MULTIMEDIA

ESSENTIAL QUESTION:

What can cause a sudden change in someone's life?

People change a little bit every day as they learn and enjoy new experiences, but is it possible for a person to change in an instant? You will work with your whole class to explore the concept of turning points. The selections you are going to read provide some interesting insights.

Whole-Class Learning Strategies

Throughout your life, in school, in your community, and in your career, you will continue to learn and work in large-group environments.

Review these strategies and the actions you can take to practice them as you work with your whole class. Add ideas of your own for each category for each step. Get ready to use these strategies during Whole-Class Learning.

STRATEGY	ACTION PLAN
Listen actively	• Eliminate distractions. For example, put your cellphone away. • Keep your eyes on the speaker. •
Clarify by asking questions	• If you're confused, other people probably are, too. Ask a question to help your whole class. • If you see that you are guessing, ask a question instead. •
Monitor understanding	• Notice what information you already know and be ready to build on it. • Ask for help if you are struggling. •
Interact and share ideas	• Share your ideas and answer questions, even if you are unsure. • Build on the ideas of others by adding details or making a connection. •

SCAN FOR MULTIMEDIA

CONTENTS

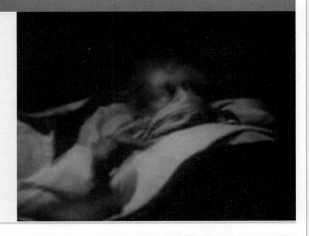
COMPARE

PERFORMANCE TASK

WRITING FOCUS

Write an Explanatory Essay

The Whole-Class readings dramatize a moment of truth for Ebenezer Scrooge. After reading, you will write an essay in which you describe Scrooge's transformation over the course of the play.

About the Playwright

As a teenager, **Israel Horovitz** (b. 1939) did not like books by Charles Dickens. As he got older, however, he came to appreciate Dickens's style and stories. Today, Horovitz refers to Dickens as "a masterful storyteller." He imagines that if Dickens were alive today, he would be "our greatest television writer, or perhaps screenwriter." As Horovitz adapted Dickens's novel into a play, he thought about which character was his favorite. Surprisingly, it is Scrooge, who reminds Horovitz of his own father.

 **Tool Kit**
First-Read Guide and Model Annotation

STANDARDS

Reading Literature
By the end of the year, read and comprehend literature, including stories, dramas, and poems, in the grades 6–8 text complexity band proficiently, with scaffolding as needed at the high end of the range.

A Christmas Carol: Scrooge and Marley, Act I

Concept Vocabulary

You will encounter the following words as you read *A Christmas Carol: Scrooge and Marley,* Act I. Before reading, note how familiar you are with each word. Then, rank the words in order from most familiar (1) to least familiar (6).

WORD	YOUR RANKING
covetous	
morose	
resolute	
impossible	
malcontent	
miser	

After completing the first read, come back to the concept vocabulary and review your rankings. Mark changes to your original rankings as needed.

First Read DRAMA

Apply these strategies as you conduct your first read. You will have an opportunity to complete the close-read notes after your first read.

NOTICE *whom* the play is about, *what* happens, *where* and *when* it happens, and *why* those involved react as they do.

ANNOTATE by marking vocabulary and key passages you want to revisit.

CONNECT ideas within the selection to what you already know and what you have already read.

RESPOND by completing the Comprehension Check and by writing a brief summary of the selection.

First Read

A Christmas Carol: Scrooge and Marley

Act I

Israel Horovitz

SCAN FOR
MULTIMEDIA

BACKGROUND

Charles Dickens's novella, *A Christmas Carol,* from which this play was adapted, shows sympathy for the struggles of the poor. The story is set in England during the nineteenth century, a time of rapid industrial growth. In this booming economy, the wealthy lived in luxury, but the poor and the working class suffered.

CHARACTERS

Jacob Marley, a specter

Ebenezer Scrooge, not yet dead, which is to say still alive

Bob Cratchit, Scrooge's clerk

Fred, Scrooge's nephew

Thin Do-Gooder

Portly Do-Gooder

Specters (Various), carrying money-boxes

The Ghost of Christmas Past

Four Jocund Travelers

A Band of Singers

A Band of Dancers

Little Boy Scrooge

Young Man Scrooge

Fan, Scrooge's little sister

The Schoolmaster

Schoolmates

Fezziwig, a fine and fair employer

Dick, young Scrooge's co-worker

Young Scrooge

A Fiddler

More Dancers

Scrooge's Lost Love

Scrooge's Lost Love's Daughter

Scrooge's Lost Love's Husband

The Ghost of Christmas Present

Some Bakers

Mrs. Cratchit, Bob Crachit's wife

Belinda Cratchit, a daughter

Martha Cratchit, another daughter

Peter Cratchit, a son

Tiny Tim Cratchit, another son

Scrooge's Niece, Fred's wife

The Ghost of Christmas Future, a mute Phantom

Three Men of Business

Drunks, Scoundrels, Women of the Streets

A Charwoman

Mrs. Dilber

Joe, an old second-hand goods dealer

A Corpse, very like Scrooge

An Indebted Family

Adam, a young boy

A Poulterer

A Gentlewoman

Some More Men of Business

THE PLACE OF THE PLAY Various locations in and around the City of London, including Scrooge's Chambers and Offices; the Cratchit Home; Fred's Home; Scrooge's School; Fezziwig's Offices; Old Joe's Hide-a-Way.

THE TIME OF THE PLAY The entire action of the play takes place on Christmas Eve, Christmas Day, and the morning after Christmas, 1843.

Scene 1

1 [*Ghostly music in auditorium. A single spotlight on* Jacob Marley, *D.C. He is ancient; awful, dead-eyed. He speaks straight out to auditorium.*]

2 **Marley.** [*Cackle-voiced*] My name is Jacob Marley and I am dead. [*He laughs.*] Oh, no, there's no doubt that I am dead. The register of my burial was signed by the clergyman, the clerk, the undertaker . . . and by my chief mourner . . . Ebenezer Scrooge . . . [*Pause; remembers*] I am dead as a doornail.

3 [*A spotlight fades up, Stage Right, on* Scrooge, *in his counting-house*[1] *counting. Lettering on the window behind* Scrooge *reads: "Scrooge and Marley, Ltd." The spotlight is tight on* Scrooge's *head and shoulders. We shall not yet see into the offices and setting. Ghostly music continues, under.* Marley *looks across at* Scrooge; *pitifully. After a moment's pause*]

4 I present him to you: Ebenezer Scrooge . . . England's most tightfisted hand at the grindstone, Scrooge! a squeezing, wrenching, grasping, scraping, clutching, **covetous**, old sinner! secret, and self-contained, and solitary as an oyster. The cold within him freezes his old features, nips his pointed nose, shrivels his cheek, stiffens his gait; makes his eyes red, his thin lips blue; and speaks out shrewdly in his grating voice. Look at him. Look at him . . .

5 [Scrooge *counts and mumbles.*]

6 **Scrooge.** They owe me money and I will collect. I will have them jailed, if I have to. They owe me money and I will collect what is due me.

7 [Marley *moves towards* Scrooge; *two steps. The spotlight stays with him.*]

---

1. **counting-house** *n.* office for keeping financial records and writing business letters.

covetous (KUHV uh tuhs) *adj.* greedy and jealous

CLOSE READ

ANNOTATE: Mark the use of descriptive words in paragraph 4.

QUESTION: Why might the playwright have chosen these words?

CONCLUDE: How does the playwright's word choice affect the reader's understanding of Scrooge's character?

8 **Marley.** [*Disgusted*] He and I were partners for I don't know how many years. Scrooge was my sole executor, my sole administrator, my sole assign, my sole residuary legatee,[2] my sole friend and my sole mourner. But Scrooge was not so cut up by the sad event of my death, but that he was an excellent man of business on the very day of my funeral, and solemnized[3] it with an undoubted bargain. [*Pauses again in disgust*] He never painted out my name from the window. There it stands, on the window and above the warehouse door: Scrooge and Marley. Sometimes people new to our business call him Scrooge and sometimes they call him Marley. He answers to both names. It's all the same to him. And it's cheaper than painting in a new sign, isn't it? [*Pauses; moves closer to* Scrooge] Nobody has ever stopped him in the street to say, with gladsome looks, "My dear Scrooge, how are you? When will you come to see me?" No beggars implored him to bestow a trifle, no children ever ask him what it is o'clock, no man or woman now, or ever in his life, not once, inquire the way to such and such a place. [Marley *stands next to* Scrooge *now. They share, so it seems, a spotlight.*] But what does Scrooge care of any of this? It is the very thing he likes! To edge his way along the crowded paths of life, warning all human sympathy to keep its distance.

9 [*A ghostly bell rings in the distance.* Marley *moves away from* Scrooge, *now, heading* D. *again. As he does, he "takes" the light:* Scrooge *has disappeared into the black void beyond.* Marley *walks* D.C., *talking directly to the audience. Pauses*]

10 The bell tolls and l must take my leave. You must stay a while with Scrooge and watch him play out his scroogey life. It is now the story: the once-upon-a-time. Scrooge is busy in his counting-house. Where else? Christmas eve and Scrooge is busy in his counting-house. It is cold, bleak, biting weather outside: foggy withal: and, if you listen closely, you can hear the people in the court go wheezing up and down, beating their hands upon their breasts, and stamping their feet upon the pavement stones to warm them . . .

11 [*The clocks outside strike three.*]

12 Only three! and quite dark outside already: it has not been light all day this day.

13 [*This ghostly bell rings in the distance again.* Marley *looks about him. Music in.* Marley *flies away.*]

14 [*N.B.* Marley's *comings and goings should, from time to time, induce the explosion of the odd flash-pot,* I.H.]

NOTES

2. **sole residuary legatee** *n.* legal term for a person who inherits someone's home after he or she dies.

3. **solemnized** *v.* honored or remembered. Marley is being sarcastic.

A Christmas Carol: Scrooge and Marley, Act I **237**

Scene 2

1   [*Christmas music in, sung by a live chorus, full. At conclusion of song, sound fades under and into the distance. Lights up in set: offices of Scrooge and Marley, Ltd.* Scrooge *sits at his desk, at work. Near him is a tiny fire. His door is open and in his line of vision, we see* Scrooge's *clerk,* Bob Cratchit, *who sits in a dismal tank of a cubicle, copying letters. Near* Cratchit *is a fire so tiny as to barely cast a light: perhaps it is one pitifully glowing coal?* Cratchit *rubs his hands together, puts on a white comforter[4] and tries to heat his hands around his candle.* Scrooge's Nephew *enters, unseen.*]

2   **Scrooge.** What are you doing, Cratchit? Acting cold, are you? Next, you'll be asking to replenish your coal from my coal-box, won't you? Well, save your breath, Cratchit! Unless you're prepared to find employ elsewhere!

3   **Nephew.** [*Cheerfully; surprising* Scrooge] A merry Christmas to you, Uncle! God save you!

4   **Scrooge.** Bah! Humbug![5]

5   **Nephew.** Christmas a "humbug," Uncle? I'm sure you don't mean that.

6   **Scrooge.** I do! Merry Christmas? What right do you have to be merry? What reason have you to be merry? You're poor enough!

7   **Nephew.** Come, then. What right have you to be dismal? What reason have you to be **morose**? You're rich enough.

8   **Scrooge.** Bah! Humbug!

9   **Nephew.** Don't be cross, Uncle.

10 **Scrooge.** What else can I be? Eh? When I live in a world of fools such as this? Merry Christmas? What's Christmastime to you but a time of paying bills without any money; a time for finding yourself a year older, but not an hour richer. If I could work my will, every idiot who goes about with "Merry Christmas" on his lips, should be boiled with his own pudding, and buried with a stake of holly through his heart. He should!

11 **Nephew.** Uncle!

12 **Scrooge.** Nephew! You keep Christmas in your own way and let me keep it in mine.

13 **Nephew.** Keep it! But you don't keep it, Uncle.

14 **Scrooge.** Let me leave it alone, then. Much good it has ever done you!

4. comforter *n.* long, woolen scarf.

5. Humbug *interj.* nonsense.

morose *adj.* (muh ROHS) gloomy; ill-tempered

CLOSE READ

ANNOTATE: Mark words in paragraph 10 that show Scrooge's attitude toward Christmas.

QUESTION: What does Scrooge think of people, such as his nephew, that celebrate Christmas?

CONCLUDE: What does this attitude reveal about Scrooge's character?

15 **Nephew.** There are many things from which I have derived good, by which I have not profited, I daresay. Christmas among the rest. But l am sure that l always thought of Christmas time, when it has come round—as a good time: the only time I know of, when men and women seem to open their shut-up hearts freely, and to think of people below them as if they really were fellow-passengers to the grave, and not another race of creatures bound on other journeys. And therefore, Uncle, though it has never put a scrap of gold or silver in my pocket, I believe that it *has* done me good, and that it *will* do me good; and I say, God bless it!

16 [*The Clerk in the tank applauds, looks at the furious* Scrooge *and pokes out his tiny fire, as if in exchange for the moment of impropriety.* Scrooge *yells at him.*]

17 **Scrooge.** [*To the clerk*] Let me hear another sound from *you* and you'll keep your Christmas by losing your situation. [*To the nephew*] You're quite a powerful speaker, sir. I wonder you don't go into Parliament.[6]

6. **Parliament** national legislative body of Great Britain, in some ways like the U.S. Congress.

18 **Nephew.** Don't be angry, Uncle. Come! Dine with us tomorrow.

19 **Scrooge.** I'd rather see myself dead than see myself with your family!

20 **Nephew.** But, why? Why?

21 **Scrooge.** Why did you get married?

22 **Nephew.** Because I fell in love.

23 **Scrooge.** That, sir, is the only thing that you have said to me in your entire lifetime which is even more ridiculous than "Merry Christmas!" [*Turns from* Nephew] Good afternoon.

24 **Nephew.** Nay, Uncle, you never came to see me before I married either. Why give it as a reason for not coming now?

25 **Scrooge.** Good afternoon, Nephew!

26 **Nephew.** I want nothing from you; I ask nothing of you; why cannot we be friends?

27 **Scrooge.** Good afternoon!

28 **Nephew.** I am sorry with all my heart, to find you so **resolute**. But I have made the trial in homage to Christmas, and I'll keep my Christmas humor to the last. So A Merry Christmas, Uncle!

resolute (REHZ uh loot) *adj.* determined

29 **Scrooge.** Good afternoon!

30 **Nephew.** And a Happy New Year!

31 **Scrooge.** Good afternoon!

7. Bedlam *n.* hospital in London for the mentally ill.

impossible (ihm POS uh buhl) *adj.* disagreeable; unreasonable

8. liberality *n.* generosity.

32 **Nephew.** [*He stands facing* Scrooge.] Uncle, you are the most . . . [*Pauses*] No, I shan't. My Christmas humor is intact . . . [*Pause*] God bless you, Uncle . . . [Nephew *turns and starts for the door; he stops at* Cratchit's *cage.*] Merry Christmas, Bob Cratchit . . .

33 **Cratchit.** Merry Christmas to you sir, and a very, very happy New Year . . .

34 **Scrooge.** [*Calling across to them*] Oh, fine, a perfection, just fine . . . to see the perfect pair of you; husbands, with wives and children to support . . . my clerk there earning fifteen shillings a week . . . and the perfect pair of you, talking about a Merry Christmas! [*Pauses*] I'll retire to Bedlam![7]

35 **Nephew.** [*To* Cratchit] He's **impossible**!

36 **Cratchit.** Oh, mind him not, sir. He's getting on in years, and he's alone. He's noticed your visit. I'll wager your visit has warmed him.

37 **Nephew.** Him? Uncle Ebenezer Scrooge? *Warmed?* You are a better Christian than I am, sir.

38 **Cratchit.** [*Opening the door for* Nephew; *two* Do-Gooders *will enter, as* Nephew *exits*] Good day to you, sir, and God bless.

39 **Nephew.** God bless . . . [*One man who enters is portly, the other is thin. Both are pleasant.*]

40 **Cratchit.** Can I help you, gentlemen?

41 **Thin Man.** [*Carrying papers and books; looks around* Cratchit *to* Scrooge] Scrooge and Marley's, I believe. Have I the pleasure of addressing Mr. Scrooge, or Mr. Marley?

42 **Scrooge.** Mr. Marley has been dead these seven years. He died seven years ago this very night.

43 **Portly Man.** We have no doubt his liberality[8] is well represented by his surviving partner . . . [*Offers his calling card*]

44 **Scrooge.** [*Handing back the card; unlooked at*] . . . Good afternoon.

45 **Thin Man.** This will take but a moment, sir . . .

46 **Portly Man.** At this festive season of the year, Mr. Scrooge, it is more than usually desirable that we should make some slight provision for the poor and destitute, who suffer greatly at the present time. Many thousands are in want of common necessities; hundreds of thousands are in want of common comforts, sir.

47 **Scrooge.** Are there no prisons?

48 **Portly Man.** Plenty of prisons.

49 **Scrooge.** And aren't the Union workhouses still in operation?

50 **Thin Man.** They are. Still, I wish that I could say that they are not.

51 **Scrooge.** The Treadmill[9] and the Poor Law[10] are in full vigor, then?

52 **Thin Man.** Both very busy, sir.

53 **Scrooge.** Ohhh, I see. I was afraid, from what you said at first, that something had occurred to stop them from their useful course. [*Pauses*] I'm glad to hear it.

54 **Portly Man.** Under the impression that they scarcely furnish Christian cheer of mind or body to the multitude, a few of us are endeavoring to raise a fund to buy the Poor some meat and drink, and means of warmth. We choose this time, because it is a time, of all others, when Want is keenly felt, and Abundance rejoices. [*Pen in hand; as well as notepad*] What shall I put you down for, sir?

55 **Scrooge.** Nothing!

56 **Portly Man.** You wish to be left anonymous?

57 **Scrooge.** I wish to be left alone! [*Pauses; turns away; turns back to them*] Since you ask me what I wish, gentlemen, that is my answer. I help to support the establishments that I have mentioned: they cost enough: and those who are badly off must go there.

58 **Thin Man.** Many can't go there; and many would rather die.

59 **Scrooge.** If they would rather die, they had better do it, and decrease the surplus population. Besides—excuse me—I don't know that.

60 **Thin Man.** But you might know it!

61 **Scrooge.** It's not my business. It's enough for a man to understand his own business, and not to interfere with other people's. Mine occupies me constantly. Good afternoon, gentlemen!

62 [Scrooge *turns his back on the gentlemen and returns to his desk.*]

63 **Portly Man.** But, sir, Mr. Scrooge . . . think of the poor.

64 **Scrooge.** [*Turns suddenly to them. Pauses*] Take your leave of my offices, sirs, while I am still smiling.

65 [*The* Thin Man *looks at the* Portly Man. *They are undone. They shrug. They move to the door.* Cratchit *hops up to open it for them.*]

NOTES

9. **the Treadmill** kind of mill wheel turned by the weight of people treading steps arranged around it, this device is used to punish prisoners.

10. **Poor Law** the original 16th-century Poor Laws called for overseers of the poor in each neighborhood to provide relief for the needy. The New Poor Law of 1834 made the workhouses in which the poor sometimes lived and worked extremely harsh and unattractive places.

CLOSE READ

ANNOTATE: Mark the words in paragraph 54 that describe the Portly Man's reasons for asking for help.

QUESTION: What do these details reveal about the setting?

CONCLUDE: How does this information affect your understanding of the drama?

66 **Thin Man.** Good day, sir . . . [*To* Cratchit] A merry Christmas to you, sir . . .

67 **Cratchit.** Yes. A Merry Christmas to both of you . . .

68 **Portly Man.** Merry Christmas . . .

69 [Cratchit *silently squeezes something into the hand of the* Thin Man.]

70 **Thin Man.** What's this?

71 **Cratchit.** Shhhh . . .

72 [Cratchit *opens the door; wind and snow whistle into the room.*]

73 **Thin Man.** Thank you, sir, thank you.

74 [Cratchit *closes the door and returns to his workplace.* Scrooge *is at his own counting table. He talks to* Cratchit *without looking up.*]

75 **Scrooge.** It's less of a time of year for being merry, and more a time of year for being loony . . . if you ask me.

76 **Cratchit.** Well, I don't know, sir . . . [*The clock's bell strikes six o'clock.*] Well, there it is, eh, six?

77 **Scrooge.** Saved by six bells, are you?

78 **Cratchit.** I must be going home . . . [*He snuffs out his candle and puts on his hat.*] I hope you have a . . . very very lovely day tomorrow, sir . . .

79 **Scrooge.** Hmmm. Oh, you'll be wanting the whole day tomorrow, I suppose?

80 **Cratchit.** If quite convenient, sir.

81 **Scrooge.** It's not convenient, and it's not fair. If I was to stop half-a-crown for it, you'd think yourself ill-used, I'll be bound?

82 [Cratchit *smiles faintly.*]

83 **Cratchit.** I don't know, sir . . .

84 **Scrooge.** And yet, you don't think me ill-used when I pay a day's wages for no work . . .

85 **Cratchit.** It's only but once a year . . .

86 **Scrooge.** A poor excuse for picking a man's pocket every 25th of December! But I suppose you must have the whole day. Be here all the earlier the next morning!

87 **Cratchit.** Oh, I will, sir. I will. I promise you. And, sir . . .

88 **Scrooge.** Don't say it, Cratchit.

89 **Cratchit.** But let me wish you a . . .

90 **Scrooge.** Don't say it, Cratchit. I warn you . . .

91 **Cratchit.** Sir!

CLOSE READ

ANNOTATE: Mark details in paragraphs 78–95 that show Cratchit's attitude toward Scrooge.

QUESTION: Why might the playwright have included this exchange between Cratchit and Scrooge?

CONCLUDE: What does this conversation reveal about Cratchit's character?

92 **Scrooge.** Cratchit!

93 [Cratchit *opens the door*.]

94 **Cratchit.** All right, then, sir . . . well . . . [*Suddenly*] Merry Christmas, Mr. Scrooge!

95 [*And he runs out the door, shutting same behind him. Scrooge moves to his desk; gathering his coat, hat, etc. A* Boy *appears at his window . . . .*]

96 **Boy.** [*Singing*] "Away in a manger . . ."

97 [Scrooge *seizes his ruler and whacks at the image of the* Boy *outside. The* Boy *leaves*.]

98 **Scrooge.** Bah! Humbug! Christmas! Bah! Humbug! [*He shuts out the light*.]

99 *A note on the crossover, following Scene 2:*

100 [Scrooge *will walk alone to his rooms from his offices. As he makes a long slow cross of the stage, the scenery should change. Christmas music will be heard, various people will cross by* Scrooge, *often smiling happily.*

NOTES

11. misanthrope (MIHS uhn throhp) *n.* a person who hates or distrusts everyone.

malcontent (MAL kuhn tehnt) *n.* a person who is always unhappy

miser (MY zuhr) *n.* greedy person who keeps and refuses to spend money, even at the expense of his or her own comfort

12. specter *n.* ghost.

13. deliquesce (dehl ih KWEHS) *v.* melt away.

14. gruel on the hob thin broth warming on a ledge at the back or side of the fireplace.

101 *There will be occasional pleasant greetings tossed at him.*

102 Scrooge, *in contrast to all, will grump and mumble. He will snap at passing boys, as might a horrid old hound.*

103 *In short,* Scrooge's *sounds and movements will define him in contrast from all other people who cross the stage: he is the misanthrope,*[11] *the* **malcontent,** *the* **miser.** *He is* Scrooge.

104 *This statement of* Scrooge's *character, by contrast to all other characters, should seem comical to the audience.*

105 *During* Scrooge's *crossover to his rooms, snow should begin to fall. All passers-by will hold their faces to the sky, smiling, allowing snow to shower them lightly.* Scrooge, *by contrast, will bat at the flakes with his walking-stick, as might an insomniac swat at a sleep-stopping, middle-of-the-night swarm of mosquitoes. He will comment on the blackness of the night, and, finally, reach his rooms and his encounter with the magical specter:*[12] Marley, *his eternal mate.*]

Scene 3

1 **Scrooge.** No light at all . . . no moon . . . *that* is what is at the center of Christmas Eve: dead black: void . . .

2 [Scrooge *puts his key in the door's keyhole. He has reached his rooms now. The door knocker changes and is now* Marley's *face. A musical sound: quickly: ghostly.* Marley's *image is not at all angry, but looks at* Scrooge *as did the old* Marley *look at* Scrooge. *The hair is curiously stirred; eyes wide open, dead: absent of focus.* Scrooge *stares wordlessly here. The face, before his very eyes, does* deliquesce.[13] *It is a knocker again.* Scrooge *opens the door and checks the back of same, probably for* Marley's *pigtail. Seeing nothing but screws and nuts,* Scrooge *refuses the memory.*]

3 Pooh, pooh!

4 [*The sound of the door closing resounds throughout the house as thunder. Every room echoes the sound.* Scrooge *fastens the door and walks across the hall to the stairs, trimming his candle as he goes; and then he goes slowly up the staircase. He checks each room: sitting room, bedrooms, lumber-room. He looks under the sofa, under the table: nobody there. He fixes his evening gruel on the hob,*[14] *changes his jacket.* Scrooge *sits near the tiny low-flamed fire, sipping his gruel. There are various pictures on the walls: all of them now show likenesses of* Marley. Scrooge *blinks his eyes.*]

5 Bah! Humbug!

6 [Scrooge *walks in a circle about the room. The pictures change back into their natural images. He sits down at the table in front of the*

fire. A bell hangs overhead. It begins to ring, of its own accord.
Slowly, surely, begins the ringing of every bell in the house. They
continue ringing for nearly half a minute. Scrooge *is stunned by*
the phenomenon. The bells cease their ringing all at once. Deep
below Scrooge, *in the basement of the house, there is the sound of*
clanking, of some enormous chain being dragged across the floors;
and now up the stairs. We hear doors flying open.]

7   Bah still! Humbug still! This is not happening! I won't
believe it!

8   [Marley's Ghost *enters the room. He is horrible to look at: pigtail,*
vest, suit as usual, but he drags an enormous chain now, to which
is fastened cash-boxes, keys, padlocks, ledgers, deeds, and heavy
purses fashioned of steel. He is transparent. Marley *stands opposite*
the stricken Scrooge.]

9   How now! What do you want of me?

10 **Marley.** Much!

11 **Scrooge.** Who are you?

12 **Marley.** Ask me who I was.

13 **Scrooge** Who were you then?

14 **Marley.** In life, I was your business partner: Jacob Marley.

15 **Scrooge.** I see . . . can you sit down?

16 **Marley.** I can.

17 **Scrooge.** Do it then.

18 **Marley.** I shall. [Marley *sits opposite* Scrooge, *in the chair across*
the table, at the front of the fireplace.] You don't believe in me.

19 **Scrooge.** I don't.

20 **Marley.** Why do you doubt your senses?

21 **Scrooge.** Because every little thing affects them. A slight
disorder of the stomach makes them cheat. You may be an
undigested bit of beef, a blot of mustard, a crumb of cheese, a
fragment of an underdone potato. There's more of gravy than
of grave about you, whatever you are!

22 [*There is a silence between them.* Scrooge *is made nervous by it.*
He picks up a toothpick.]

23 Humbug! I tell you: humbug!

24 [Marley *opens his mouth and screams a ghostly, fearful scream.*
The scream echoes about each room of the house. Bats fly, cats
screech, lightning flashes. Scrooge *stands and walks backwards*
against the wall. Marley *stands and screams again. This time, he*
takes his head and lifts it from his shoulders. His head continues to

15. **apparition** *n.* ghost.

scream. Marley's *face again appears on every picture in the room: all screaming.* Scrooge, *on his knees before* Marley.]

25 Mercy! Dreadful apparition,[15] mercy! Why, O! why do you trouble me so?

26 **Marley.** Man of the worldly mind, do you believe in me, or not?

27 **Scrooge.** I do. I must. But why do spirits such as you walk the earth? And why do they come to me?

28 **Marley.** It is required of every man that the spirit within him should walk abroad among his fellow-men, and travel far and wide; and if that spirit goes not forth in life, it is condemned to do so after death. [Marley *screams again; a tragic scream; from his ghostly bones.*] I wear the chain I forged in life. I made it link by link, and yard by yard. Is its pattern strange to *you*? Or would you know, you, Scrooge, the weight and length of the strong coil you bear yourself? It was full as

heavy and long as this, seven Christmas Eves ago. You have labored on it, since. It is a ponderous chain.

29 [*Terrified that a chain will appear about his body,* Scrooge *spins and waves the unwanted chain away. None, of course, appears. Sees* Marley *watching him dance about the room.* Marley *watches* Scrooge; *silently.*]

NOTES

30 **Scrooge.** Jacob. Old Jacob Marley, tell me more. Speak comfort to me, Jacob . . .

31 **Marley.** I have none to give. Comfort comes from other regions, Ebenezer Scrooge, and is conveyed by other ministers, to other kinds of men. A very little more, is all that is permitted to me. I cannot rest, I cannot stay, I cannot linger anywhere . . . [*He moans again.*] My spirit never walked beyond our counting-house—mark me!—in life my spirit never roved beyond the narrow limits of our money-changing hole; and weary journeys lie before me!

32 **Scrooge.** But you were always a good man of business, Jacob.

33 **Marley.** [*Screams word "business"; a flash-pot explodes with him.*] BUSINESS!!! Mankind was my business. The common welfare was my business; charity, mercy, forbearance, benevolence, were, all, my business. [Scrooge *is quaking.*] Hear me, Ebenezer Scrooge! My time is nearly gone.

34 **Scrooge.** I will, but don't be hard upon me. And don't be flowery, Jacob! Pray!

35 **Marley.** How is it that I appear before you in a shape that you can see, l may not tell. I have sat invisible beside you many and many a day. That is no light part of my penance. I am here tonight to warn you that you have yet a chance and hope of escaping my fate. A chance and hope of my procuring, Ebenezer.

36 **Scrooge.** You were always a good friend to me. Thank'ee!

37 **Marley.** You will be haunted by Three Spirits.

38 **Scrooge.** Would that be the chance and hope you mentioned, Jacob?

39 **Marley.** It is.

40 **Scrooge.** I think I'd rather not.

41 **Marley.** Without their visits, you cannot hope to shun the path I tread. Expect the first one tomorrow, when the bell tolls one.

42 **Scrooge.** Couldn't I take 'em all at once, and get it over, Jacob?

CLOSE READ

ANNOTATE: Mark the words in paragraphs 30–34 that show Scrooge's reaction to Marley.

QUESTION: What do these words reveal about Scrooge at this point in the play?

CONCLUDE: What does Scrooge's reaction in these paragraphs suggest about his character?

43 Marley. Expect the second on the next night at the same hour. The third upon the next night when the last stroke of twelve has ceased to vibrate. Look to see me no more. Others may, but you may not. And look that, for your own sake, you remember what has passed between us!

44 [Marley *places his head back upon his shoulders. He approaches the window and beckons to* Scrooge *to watch. Outside the window, specters fly by, carrying money-boxes and chains. They make a confused sound of lamentation.* Marley, *after listening a moment, joins into their mournful dirge. He leans to the window and floats out into the bleak, dark night. He is gone.*]

45 Scrooge. [*Rushing to the window*] Jacob! No, Jacob! Don't leave me! I'm frightened! [*He sees that* Marley *has gone. He looks outside. He pulls the shutter closed, so that the scene is blocked from his view. All sound stops. After a pause, he re-opens the shutter and all is quiet, as it should be on Christmas Eve. Carolers carol out of doors, in the distance.* Scrooge *closes the shutter and walks down the stairs. He examines the door by which* Marley *first entered.*] No one here at all! Did I imagine all that? Humbug! [*He looks about the room.*] I did imagine it. It only happened in my foulest dream-mind, didn't it? An undigested bit of . . . [*Thunder and lightning in the room; suddenly*] Sorry! Sorry!

46 [*There is silence again. The lights fade out.*]

Scene 4

1 [*Christmas music, choral, "Hark the Herald Angels Sing," sung by an onstage choir of children, spotlighted,* D.C. *Above,* Scrooge *in his bed, dead to the world, asleep, in his darkened room. It should appear that the choir is singing somewhere outside of the house, of course, and a use of scrim*[16] *is thus suggested. When the singing is ended, the choir should fade out of view and* Marley *should fade into view, in their place.*]

2 Marley. [*Directly to audience*] From this point forth . . . I shall be quite visible to you, but invisible to him. [*Smiles*] He will feel my presence, nevertheless, for, unless my senses fail me completely, we are—you and I—witness to the changing of a miser: that one, my partner in life, in business, and in eternity: that one: Scrooge. [*Moves to staircase, below* Scrooge] See him now. He endeavors to pierce the darkness with his ferret eyes.[17] [*To audience*] See him, now. He listens for the hour.

16. **scrim** *n.* see-through fabric backdrop used to create special effects in the theater.

17. **ferret eyes** A ferret is a small, weasel-like animal used for hunting rabbits. This expression means to stare continuously, the way a ferret hunts.

3 [*The bells toll.* Scrooge *is awakened and quakes as the hour approaches one o'clock, but the bells stop their sound at the hour of twelve.*]

4 **Scrooge.** [*Astonished*] Midnight! Why this isn't possible. It was past two when I went to bed. An icicle must have gotten into the clock's works! I couldn't have slept through the whole day and far into another night. It isn't possible that anything has happened to the sun, and this is twelve at noon! [*He runs to window; unshutters same; it is night.*] Night, still. Quiet, normal for the season, cold. It is certainly not noon. I cannot in any way afford to lose my days. Securities come due, promissory notes,[18] interest on investments: these are things that happen in the daylight! [*He returns to his bed.*] Was this a dream?

5 [Marley *appears in his room. He speaks to the audience.*]

6 **Marley.** You see? He does not, with faith, believe in me fully, even still! Whatever will it take to turn the faith of a miser from money to men?

7 **Scrooge.** Another quarter and it'll be one and Marley's ghostly friends will come. [*Pauses; listens*] Where's the chime for one? [*Ding, dong*] A quarter past [*Repeats*] Half-past! [*Repeats*] A quarter to it! But where's the heavy bell of the hour one? This is a game in which I lose my senses! Perhaps, if I allowed myself another short doze . . .

8 **Marley.** . . . Doze, Ebenezer, doze.

9 [*A heavy bell thuds its one ring; dull and definitely one o'clock. There is a flash of light.* Scrooge *sits up, in a sudden. A hand draws back the curtains by his bed. He sees it.*]

10 **Scrooge.** A hand! Who owns it! Hello!

11 [*Ghostly music again, but of a new nature to the play. A strange figure stands before* Scrooge—*like a child, yet at the same time like an old man: white hair, but unwrinkled skin, long, muscular arms, but delicate legs and feet. Wears white tunic; lustrous belt cinches waist. Branch of fresh green holly in its hand, but has its dress trimmed with fresh summer flowers. Clear jets of light spring from the crown of its head. Holds cap in hand. The Spirit is called* Past.]

12 Are you the Spirit, sir, whose coming was foretold to me?

13 **Past.** I am.

14 **Marley.** Does he take this to be a vision of his green grocer?

NOTES

CLOSE READ
ANNOTATE: Mark details in paragraph 4 that describe the setting.

QUESTION: Why might the playwright have included these details?

CONCLUDE: How do these details work together to increase the tension?

18. **promissory notes** *n.* written promises to pay someone a certain sum of money.

15 **Scrooge.** Who, and what are you?

16 **Past.** I am the Ghost of Christmas Past.

17 **Scrooge.** Long past?

18 **Past.** Your past.

19 **Scrooge.** May I ask, please, sir, what business you have here with me?

20 **Past.** Your welfare.

21 **Scrooge.** Not to sound ungrateful, sir, and really, please do understand that I am plenty obliged for your concern, but, really, kind spirit, it would have done all the better for my welfare to have been left alone altogether, to have slept peacefully through this night.

22 **Past.** Your reclamation, then. Take heed!

23 **Scrooge.** My what?

24 **Past.** [*Motioning to* Scrooge *and taking his arm*] Rise! Fly with me! [*He leads* Scrooge *to the window.*]

25 **Scrooge.** [*Panicked*] Fly, but I am a mortal and cannot fly!

26 **Past.** [*Pointing to his heart*] Bear but a touch of my hand here and you shall be upheld in more than this!

27 [Scrooge *touches the spirit's heart and the lights dissolve into sparkly flickers. Lovely crystals of music are heard. The scene dissolves into another. Christmas music again*]

Scene 5

1 [Scrooge *and the* Ghost of Christmas Past *walk together across an open stage. In the background, we see a field that is open; covered by a soft, downy snow: a country road.*]

2 **Scrooge.** Good Heaven! I was bred in this place. I was a boy here!

3 [Scrooge *freezes, staring at the field beyond.* Marley's *ghost appears beside him; takes* Scrooge's *face in his hands, and turns his face to the audience.*]

4 **Marley.** You see this Scrooge: stricken by feeling. Conscious of a thousand odors floating in the air, each one connected with a thousand thoughts, and hopes, and joys, and care long, long forgotten. [*Pause*] This one—this Scrooge—before your very eyes, returns to life, among the living. [*To audience, sternly*] You'd best pay your most careful attention. I would suggest rapt.[19]

19. rapt *adj.* giving complete attention; totally carried away by something.

5   [*There is a small flash and puff of smoke and* Marley *is gone again*.]

6   **Past.** Your lip is trembling, Mr. Scrooge. And what is that upon your cheek?

7   **Scrooge.** Upon my cheek? Nothing . . . a blemish on the skin from the eating of overmuch grease . . . nothing . . . [*Suddenly*] Kind Spirit of Christmas Past, lead me where you will, but quickly! To be stagnant in this place is, for me, unbearable!

8   **Past.** You recollect the way?

9   **Scrooge.** Remember it! I would know it blindfolded! My bridge, my church, my winding river! [*Staggers about, trying to see it all at once. He weeps again*.]

10 **Past.** These are but shadows of things that have been. They have no consciousness of us.

11 [*Four jocund travelers enter, singing a Christmas song in four-part harmony—"God Rest Ye Merry Gentlemen."*]

12 **Scrooge.** Listen! I know these men! I remember the beauty of their song!

13 **Past.** But, why do you remember it so happily? It is Merry Christmas that they say to one another! What is Merry Christmas to you, Mr. Scrooge? Out upon Merry Christmas, right? What good has Merry Christmas ever done you, Mr. Scrooge? . . .

14 **Scrooge.** [*After a long pause*] None. No good. None . . . [*He bows his head.*]

15 **Past.** Look, you, sir, a school ahead. The schoolroom is not quite deserted. A solitary child, neglected by his friends, is left there still.

16 [Scrooge *falls to the ground; sobbing as he sees, and we see, a small boy, the young* Scrooge, *sitting and weeping, bravely, alone at his desk: alone in a vast space, a void.*]

17 **Scrooge.** I cannot look on him!

18 **Past.** You must, Mr. Scrooge, you must.

19 **Scrooge.** It's me. [*Pauses; weeps*] Poor boy. He lived inside his head . . . alone . . . [*Pauses; weeps*] poor boy. [*Pauses; stops his weeping*] I wish . . . [*Dries his eyes on his cuff*] ah! it's too late!

20 **Past.** What is the matter?

21 **Scrooge.** There was a boy singing a Christmas Carol outside my door last night. I should like to have given him something: that's all.

NOTES

CLOSE READ

ANNOTATE: Mark words in paragraphs 15–19 that describe Scrooge's emotions and behavior.

QUESTION: What does the playwright reveal through these words?

CONCLUDE: What can you conclude about the Ghost of Christmas Past's effect on Scrooge based on this description?

22 **Past.** [*Smiles; waves his hand to* Scrooge] Come. Let us see another Christmas.

23 [*Lights out on a little boy. A flash of light. A puff of smoke. Lights up on older boy*]

24 **Scrooge.** Look! Me, again! Older now! [*Realizes*] Oh, yes . . . still alone.

25 [*The boy—a slightly older* Scrooge—*sits alone in a chair, reading. The door to the room opens and a young girl enters. She is much, much younger than this slightly older* Scrooge. *She is, say, six, and he is, say, twelve. Elder* Scrooge *and the* Ghost of Christmas Past *stand watching the scene, unseen.*]

26 **Fan.** Dear, dear brother, I have come to bring you home.

27 **Boy.** Home, little Fan?

28 **Fan.** Yes! Home, for good and all! Father is so much kinder than he ever used to be, and home's like heaven! He spoke so gently to me one dear night when I was going to bed that I was not afraid to ask him once more if you might come home; and he said "yes" . . . you should; and sent me in a coach to bring you. And you're to be a man and are never to come back here, but first, we're to be together all the Christmas long, and have the merriest time in the world.

29 **Boy.** You are quite a woman, little Fan!

30 [*Laughing; she drags at boy, causing him to stumble to the door with her. Suddenly we hear a mean and terrible voice in the hallway. Off. It is the* Schoolmaster.]

31 **Schoolmaster.** Bring down Master Scrooge's travel box at once! He is to travel!

32 **Fan.** Who is that, Ebenezer?

33 **Boy.** O! Quiet, Fan. It is the Schoolmaster, himself!

34 [*The door bursts open and into the room bursts with it the* Schoolmaster.]

35 **Schoolmaster.** Master Scrooge?

36 **Boy.** Oh, Schoolmaster, I'd like you to meet my little sister, Fan, sir . . .

37 [*Two boys struggle on with* Scrooge's *trunk.*]

38 **Fan.** Pleased, sir . . . [*She curtsies.*]

39 **Schoolmaster.** You are to travel, Master Scrooge.

40 **Scrooge.** Yes, sir, I know sir . . .

41 [*All start to exit, but* Fan *grabs the coattail of the mean old* Schoolmaster.]

42 **Boy.** Fan!

43 **Schoolmaster.** What's this?

44 **Fan.** Pardon, sir, but l believe that you've forgotten to say your goodbye to my brother, Ebenezer, who stands still now awaiting it . . . [*She smiles, curtsies, lowers her eyes.*] pardon, sir.

45 **Schoolmaster.** [*Amazed*] I . . . uh . . . harumph . . . uhh . . . well, then . . . [*Outstretches hand*] Goodbye, Scrooge.

46 **Boy.** Uh, well, goodbye, Schoolmaster . . .

47 [*Lights fade out on all but* Boy *looking at* Fan; *and* Scrooge *and* Past *looking at them.*]

48 **Scrooge.** Oh, my dear, dear little sister, Fan . . . how I loved her.

NOTES

49 **Past.** Always a delicate creature, whom a breath might have withered, but she had a large heart . . .

50 **Scrooge.** So she had.

51 **Past.** She died a woman, and had, as I think, children.

52 **Scrooge.** One child.

53 **Past.** True. Your nephew.

54 **Scrooge.** Yes.

55 **Past.** Fine, then. We move on, Mr. Scrooge. That warehouse, there? Do you know it?

56 **Scrooge.** Know it? Wasn't I apprenticed[20] there?

57 **Past.** We'll have a look.

58 [*They enter the warehouse. The lights crossfade with them, coming up on an old man in Welsh wig:* Fezziwig.]

59 **Scrooge.** Why, it's old Fezziwig! Bless his heart; it's Fezziwig, alive again!

60 [Fezziwig *sits behind a large, high desk, counting. He lays down his pen; looks at the clock: seven bells sound.*]

61 Quittin' time . . .

62 **Fezziwig.** Quittin' time . . . [*He takes off his waistcoat and laughs: calls off*] Yo ho, Ebenezer! Dick!

63 [Dick Wilkins *and* Ebenezer Scrooge—*a young man version— enter the room.* Dick *and* Ebenezer *are* Fezziwig's *apprentices.*]

64 **Scrooge.** Dick Wilkins, to be sure! My fellow-'prentice! Bless my soul, yes. There he is. He was very much attached to me, was Dick. Poor Dick! Dear, dear!

65 **Fezziwig.** Yo ho, my boys. No more work tonight. Christmas Eve, Dick. Christmas, Ebenezer!

66 [*They stand at attention in front of* Fezziwig; *laughing*]

67 Hilli-ho! Clear away, and let's have lots of room here! Hilli-ho, Dick! Chirrup, Ebenezer!

68 [*The young men clear the room, sweep the floor, straighten the pictures, trim the lamps, etc. The space is clear now. A fiddler enters, fiddling.*]

69 Hi-ho, Matthew! Fiddle away . . . where are my daughters?

70 [*The fiddler plays. Three young daughters of* Fezziwig *enter followed by six young adult male suitors. They are dancing to the music. All employees come in: workers, clerks, housemaids, cousins, the baker, etc. All dance. Full number wanted here. Throughout the*

20. apprenticed (uh PREHN tihst) *v.* received instruction in a trade as well as food and housing or wages in return for work.

dance, food is brought into the feast. It is "eaten" in dance, by the dancers. Ebenezer dances with all three of the daughters, as does Dick. They compete for the daughters, happily, in the dance. Fezziwig dances with his daughters. Fezziwig dances with Dick and Ebenezer. The music changes: Mrs. Fezziwig *enters. She lovingly scolds her husband. They dance. She dances with Ebenezer, lifting him and throwing him about. She is enormously fat. When the dance is ended, they all dance off, floating away, as does the music.* Scrooge *and the* Ghost of Christmas Past *stand alone now. The music is gone.*]

71 **Past.** It was a small matter, that Fezziwig made those silly folks so full of gratitude.

72 **Scrooge.** Small!

73 **Past.** Shhh!

74 [*Lights up on* Dick *and* Ebenezer]

75 **Dick.** We are blessed, Ebenezer, truly, to have such a master as Mr. Fezziwig!

76 **Young Scrooge.** He is the best, best, the very and absolute best! If ever I own a firm of my own, I shall treat my apprentices with the same dignity and the same grace. We have learned a wonderful lesson from the master, Dick!

77 **Dick.** Ah, that's a fact, Ebenezer. That's a fact!

78 **Past.** Was it not a small matter, really? He spent but a few pounds[21] of his mortal money on your small party. Three or four pounds, perhaps. Is that so much that he deserves such praise as you and Dick so lavish now?

79 **Scrooge.** It isn't that! It isn't that, Spirit. Fezziwig had the power to make us happy or unhappy; to make our service light or burdensome; a pleasure or a toil. The happiness he gave is quite as great as if it cost him a fortune.

80 **Past.** What is the matter?

81 **Scrooge.** Nothing particular.

82 **Past.** Something, I think.

83 **Scrooge.** No, no. I should like to be able to say a word or two to my clerk just now! That's all!

84 [Ebenezer *enters the room and shuts down all the lamps. He stretches and yawns. The* Ghost of Christmas Past *turns to* Scrooge *all of a sudden.*]

85 **Past.** My time grows short! Quick!

86 [*In a flash of light,* Ebenezer *is gone, and in his place stands an* Older Scrooge, *this one a man in the prime of his life. Beside him*

NOTES

CLOSE READ
ANNOTATE: Mark details in paragraphs 70–76 that describe young Scrooge's behavior and personality.

QUESTION: Why might the playwright have included these descriptions?

CONCLUDE: How do these details deepen your understanding of Scrooge?

21. **pounds** *n.* common type of money used in Great Britain.

stands a young woman in a mourning dress. She is crying. She speaks to the man, with hostility.]

87 **Woman.** It matters little . . . to you, very little. Another idol has displaced me.

88 **Man.** What idol has displaced you?

89 **Woman.** A golden one.

90 **Man.** This is an even-handed dealing of the world. There is nothing on which it is so hard as poverty; and there is nothing it professes to condemn with such severity as the pursuit of wealth!

91 **Woman.** You fear the world too much. Have I not seen your nobler aspirations fall off one by one, until the master-passion, Gain, engrosses you? Have I not?

92 **Scrooge.** No!

93 **Man.** What then? Even if I have grown so much wiser, what then? Have I changed towards you?

94 **Woman.** No . . .

95 **Man.** Am I?

96 **Woman.** Our contract is an old one. It was made when we were both poor and content to be so. You are changed. When it was made, you were another man.

97 **Man.** I was not another man: I was a boy.

98 **Woman.** Your own feeling tells you that you were not what you are. I am. That which promised happiness when we were one in heart is fraught with misery now that we are two . . .

99 **Scrooge.** No!

100 **Woman.** How often and how keenly I have thought of this, I will not say. It is enough that I have thought of it, and can release you . . .

101 **Scrooge.** [*Quietly*] Don't release me, madame . . .

102 **Man.** Have I ever sought release?

103 **Woman.** In words. No. Never.

104 **Man.** In what then?

105 **Woman.** In a changed nature: in an altered spirit. In everything that made my love of any worth or value in your sight. If this has never been between us, tell me, would you seek me out and try to win me now? Ah, no!

106 **Scrooge.** Ah, yes!

107 **Man.** You think not?

108 **Woman.** I would gladly think otherwise if I could, heaven knows! But if you were free today, tomorrow, yesterday, can even I believe that you would choose a dowerless girl²²—you who in your very confidence with her weigh everything by Gain; or, choosing her, do I not know that your repentance and regret would surely follow? I do; and I release you. With a full heart, for the love of him you once were.

109 **Scrooge.** Please, I . . . I . . .

110 **Man.** Please, I . . . I . . .

111 **Woman.** Please. You may—the memory of what is past half makes me hope you will—have pain in this. A very, very brief time, and you will dismiss the memory of it, as an unprofitable dream, from which it happened well that you awoke. May you be happy in the life that you have chosen for yourself . . .

112 **Scrooge.** No!

113 **Woman.** Yourself . . . alone . . .

114 **Scrooge.** No!

115 **Woman.** Goodbye, Ebenezer . . .

116 **Scrooge.** Don't let her go!

117 **Man.** Goodbye.

118 **Scrooge.** No!

119 [*She exits*. Scrooge *goes to younger man: himself.*]

120 You fool! Mindless loon! You fool!

121 **Man.** [*To exited woman*] Fool. Mindless loon. Fool . . .

122 **Scrooge.** Don't say that! Spirit, remove me from this place.

123 **Past.** I have told you these were shadows of the things that have been. They are what they are. Do not blame me, Mr. Scrooge.

124 **Scrooge.** Remove me! I cannot bear it!

125 [*The faces of all who appeared in this scene are now projected for a moment around the stage: enormous, flimsy, silent.*]

126 Leave me! Take me back! Haunt me no longer!

127 [*There is a sudden flash of light: a flare. The Ghost of Christmas Past is gone. Scrooge is, for the moment, alone onstage. His bed is turned down, across the stage. A small candle burns now in* Scrooge's *hand. There is a child's cap in his other hand. He slowly crosses the stage to his bed, to sleep.* Marley *appears behind* Scrooge, *who continues his long, elderly cross to bed.* Marley *speaks directly to the audience.*]

NOTES

22. a dowerless girl girl without a dowry, the property or wealth a woman brought to her husband in marriage.

CLOSE READ

ANNOTATE: In paragraphs 111–122, mark Scrooge's words to his younger self.

QUESTION: What do these words reveal about the ways in which Scrooge's feelings have changed?

CONCLUDE: How does this change deepen the reader's understanding of Scrooge's personality?

Copyright © SAVVAS Learning Company LLC. All Rights Reserved.

23. **donned . . . regret** To *don* and *doff* a hat means to put it on and take it off, *askew* means "crooked," and *at a rakish angle* means "having a dashing or jaunty look."

128 **Marley.** Scrooge must sleep now. He must surrender to the irresistible drowsiness caused by the recognition of what was. [*Pauses*] The cap he carries is from ten lives past: his boyhood cap . . . donned atop a hopeful hairy head . . . askew, perhaps, or at a rakish angle. Doffed now in honor of regret.[23] Perhaps even too heavy to carry in his present state of weak remorse . . .

129 [Scrooge *drops the cap. He lies atop his bed. He sleeps. To audience*]

130 He sleeps. For him, there's even more trouble ahead. [*Smiles*] For you? The play house tells me there's hot cider, as should be your anticipation for the specter Christmas Present and Future, for I promise you both. [*Smiles again*] So, I pray you hurry back to your seats refreshed and ready for a miser—to turn his coat of gray into a blazen Christmas holly-red. [*A flash of lightning. A clap of thunder. Bats fly. Ghosty music. Marley is gone.*] ❧

Comprehension Check

Complete the following items after you finish your first read.

1. When Marley was alive, what relationship did he have with Scrooge?

2. In what year and city is the play set?

3. What does Scrooge say to those who wish him a "Merry Christmas"?

4. 📓 **Notebook** Write a brief summary of *A Christmas Carol: Scrooge and Marley,* Act I.

- -

RESEARCH

Research to Clarify Choose at least one unfamiliar detail from the text. Briefly research that detail. In what way does the information you learned shed light on an aspect of the play?

A CHRISTMAS CAROL: SCROOGE AND MARLEY, ACT I

Close Read the Text

1. This model, from Scene 5, paragraph 4, shows two sample annotations, along with questions and conclusions. Close read the passage, and find another detail to annotate. Then, write a question and conclusion.

> **ANNOTATE:** I notice that the playwright has used lots of *s*'s in this dialogue.
>
> **QUESTION:** Why might the writer have made this choice?
>
> **CONCLUDE:** The repeated s sound makes it seem as if Marley were hissing or whispering, creating an eerie mood.

> **ANNOTATE:** After a series of long, hypnotic statements, these are short and formal.
>
> **QUESTION:** What effect does this change in word choice and sentence structure create?
>
> **CONCLUDE:** Marley is unpredictable and used to being obeyed.

> **Marley.** You see this Scrooge: stricken by feeling. Conscious of a thousand odors floating in the air, each one connected with a thousand thoughts, and hopes, and joys, and care long, long forgotten. [*Pause*] This one— this Scrooge—before your very eyes, returns to life, among the living. [*To audience, sternly*] You'd best pay your most careful attention. I would suggest rapt.

🔧 Tool Kit
Close-Read Guide and Model Annotation

2. For more practice, go back into the text and complete the close-read notes.

3. Revisit a section of the text you found important during your first read. Read this section closely and **annotate** what you notice. Ask yourself **questions** such as "Why did the author make this choice?" What can you **conclude**?

- -

Analyze the Text

CITE TEXTUAL EVIDENCE to support your answers.

📓 **Notebook** Respond to these questions.

1. **Connect** Why does Marley's ghost drag a chain fastened to cash-boxes, keys, padlocks, ledgers, deeds, and heavy steel purses?

2. (a) **Deduce** What effects have Scrooge's past experiences had on the person he has become? (b) **Evaluate** Based on Scrooge's past experiences, do you think he should be excused for his current attitudes and behavior? Explain.

3. **Essential Question:** *What can cause a sudden change in someone's life?* What have you learned about what can cause a sudden change in someone's life by reading Act I of this play?

☰ STANDARDS
Reading Literature
• Analyze how particular elements of a story or drama interact.
• Analyze how a drama's or poem's form or structure contributes to its meaning.

Analyze Craft and Structure

Text Structure: Dialogue in Drama **Dialogue** is a conversation between characters. In a play, dialogue serves several key functions.

- When a play is performed, dialogue helps the audience understand what characters feel and think.
- Characters' words and speech patterns give clues to their personalities.
- Dialogue advances the plot and develops the **conflict,** or struggle between opposing forces.
- In a dramatic script, a character's name appears before the lines he or she speaks. For example:

> MRS. PEREZ. Come on, kids! We're leaving.
>
> JEN. Wait for me! *Please* wait for me!

Practice

CITE TEXTUAL EVIDENCE
to support your answers.

Use the chart below to identify and analyze examples of dialogue in Act I of *A Christmas Carol: Scrooge and Marley.*

EXAMPLE OF DIALOGUE	WHAT DOES IT SAY?	WHAT DOES IT MEAN?	WHAT DOES IT SHOW ABOUT THE CHARACTER?
How now! What do you want of me?... Humbug! I tell you: humbug! (Scene 3, paragraphs 9–23)			
MARLEY. [Directly to audience] *From this point . . . for the hour.* (Scene 4, paragraph 2)			

A CHRISTMAS CAROL: SCROOGE AND MARLEY, ACT I

Concept Vocabulary

covetous	resolute	malcontent
morose	impossible	miser

Why These Words? The concept vocabulary words relate to Scrooge's character and personality in Act I of the play. For example, Scrooge shows he is a *miser* by refusing to share his coal with Cratchit, and demonstrates he is a *malcontent* when he walks through the street, unhappy about the Christmas activities going on around him.

1. How does the concept vocabulary sharpen the reader's understanding of Scrooge?

2. What other words in the selection describe Scrooge's character and personality?

Practice

📓 **Notebook** The concept vocabulary words appear in *A Christmas Carol.* Respond to the prompts, using the vocabulary words to show your understanding.

1. What might someone do if he or she were *covetous*?

2. How might a person behave if he or she were *morose*?

3. Describe a situation in which someone might be *resolute*.

4. What character traits might cause a person to be viewed as *impossible?*

5. How would a *malcontent* behave at a party?

6. What actions and behaviors might be expected of a *miser?*

Word Study

Latin Prefix: *mal-* The Latin prefix *mal-* means "bad." As an adjective, the word *malcontent* means "dissatisfied with current conditions or circumstances." As a noun, *malcontent* means "a discontented, or unhappy, person."

1. Write your own sentence that correctly uses the word *malcontent,* either as a noun or an adjective.

2. Using a dictionary or thesaurus, find three other words that have the prefix *mal-*. Record a definition for each word and write a sentence that correctly uses it.

⬡ WORD NETWORK

Add interesting words related to turning points from the text to your Word Network.

☰ STANDARDS

Language

Determine or clarify the meaning of unknown and multiple-meaning words and phrases based on *grade 7 reading and content,* choosing flexibly from a range of strategies.

b. Use common, grade-appropriate Greek or Latin affixes and roots as clues to the meaning of a word.

c. Consult general and specialized reference materials, both print and digital, to find the pronunciation of a word or determine or clarify its precise meaning or its part of speech.

Conventions

Subject-Verb Agreement Writers need to maintain **subject-verb agreement**, which means that subjects and their verbs must agree in number.

- To check subject-verb agreement, determine whether a subject is singular or plural, and then make sure its verb matches.

SUBJECT	EXAMPLE
Singular subject and verb	**Jake writes** a new poem every day.
Plural subject and verb	**Books take** us to new places.

- A **compound subject** consists of two subjects joined by a conjunction such as *and, or,* or *nor.* When the subjects joined are plural, they take a plural verb. When the subjects joined are singular or when they differ in number, refer to the rules in the chart below.

AGREEMENT RULES	EXAMPLE
Two or more singular subjects joined by *and* take a plural verb.	English **and** math **are** my favorite subjects.
Singular subjects joined by *or* or *nor* take a singular verb.	Painting **or** drawing **is** a creative activity. Neither Lucy **nor** Carmen **takes** this class.
When a singular subject and a plural subject are joined by *or* or *nor,* the verb agrees with the closer subject.	Neither the bear nor the **tigers are** happy in that enclosure. Flowers or a **tree is** what this yard needs.

Read It

Underline the subject-verb agreement in these sentences from the selection.

1. These are but shadows of things that have been.

2. The young men clear the room, sweep the floor, straighten the pictures, trim the lamps, etc.

3. He is the best, best, the very and absolute best!

Write It

Respond to these items.

1. Rewrite the following sentences to correct the subject-verb agreement.

    a. Mexico and Canada is part of North America.

    b. Wood or stone are a good material for this house.

    c. A truck or several cars is what we need for this trip.

2. 🔲 **Notebook** Write a four-sentence paragraph in which at least two sentences have compound subjects. Make sure that all the sentences have correct subject-verb agreement.

EVIDENCE LOG

Before moving on to a new selection, go to your Evidence Log and record what you've learned from Act I of *A Christmas Carol: Scrooge and Marley.*

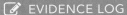
STANDARDS

Language
Demonstrate command of the conventions of standard English grammar and usage when writing or speaking.

Playwright

Israel Horovitz

A Christmas Carol: Scrooge and Marley, Act II

Concept Vocabulary

You will encounter the following words as you read *A Christmas Carol: Scrooge and Marley,* Act II. Before reading, note how familiar you are with each word. Then, rank the words in order from most familiar (1) to least familiar (6).

WORD	YOUR RANKING
parallel	
altered	
strive	
dispelled	
earnest	
infinitely	

After completing the first read, come back to the concept vocabulary and review your rankings. Mark changes to your original rankings as needed.

First Read DRAMA

Apply these strategies as you conduct your first read. You will have an opportunity to complete the close-read notes after your first read.

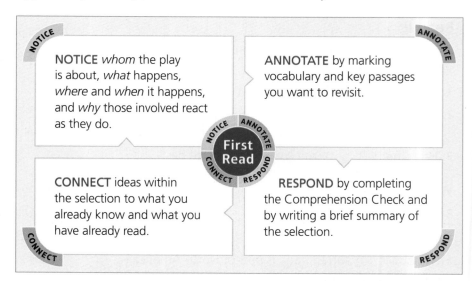

NOTICE *whom* the play is about, *what* happens, *where* and *when* it happens, and *why* those involved react as they do.

ANNOTATE by marking vocabulary and key passages you want to revisit.

CONNECT ideas within the selection to what you already know and what you have already read.

RESPOND by completing the Comprehension Check and by writing a brief summary of the selection.

First Read

⊞ STANDARDS
Reading Literature
By the end of the year, read and comprehend literature, including stories, dramas, and poems, in the grades 6–8 text complexity band proficiently, with scaffolding as needed at the high end of the range.

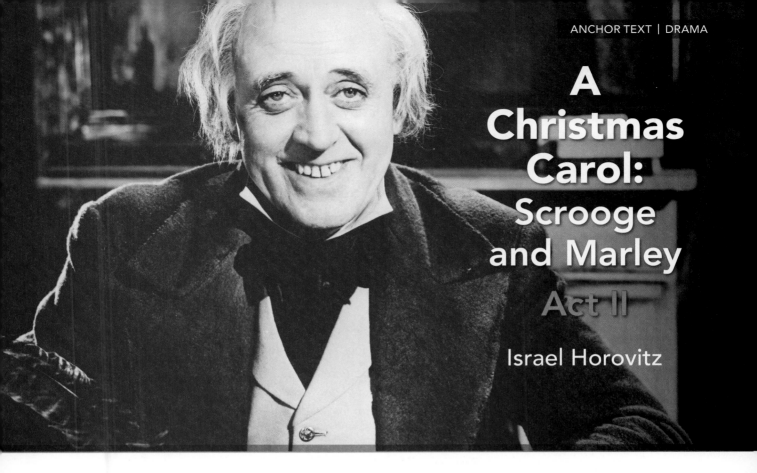

A Christmas Carol: Scrooge and Marley

Act II

Israel Horovitz

SCAN FOR MULTIMEDIA

BACKGROUND

In mid-nineteenth century England, millions of peasants moved to the cities. There, they lived in overcrowded slums. Adults and many children worked up to 12 hours a day, 6 days a week. In contrast, factory owners and professionals lived in grand houses with at least one—and often many—servants. These differences in social conditions play a part in *A Christmas Carol*.

Scene 1

1 [*Lights. Choral music is sung. Curtain.* Scrooge, *in bed, sleeping, in spotlight. We cannot yet see the interior of his room.* Marley, *opposite, in spotlight equal to* Scrooge's. Marley *laughs. He tosses his hand in the air and a flame shoots from it, magically, into the air. There is a thunder clap, and then another; a lightning flash, and then another. Ghostly music plays under. Colors change.* Marley's *spotlight has gone out and now reappears, with* Marley *in it, standing next to the bed and the sleeping* Scrooge. Marley *addresses the audience directly.*]

2 **Marley.** Hear this snoring Scrooge! Sleeping to escape the nightmare that is his waking day. What shall I bring to him now? I'm afraid nothing would astonish old Scrooge now. Not after what he's seen. Not a baby boy, not a rhinoceros, nor anything in between would astonish Ebenezer Scrooge

NOTES

just now. l can think of nothing . . . [*Suddenly*] that's it! Nothing! [*He speaks confidentially.*] I'll have the clock strike one and, when he awakes expecting my second messenger, there will be no one . . . nothing. Then I'll have the bell strike twelve. And then one again . . . and then nothing. Nothing . . . [*Laughs*] nothing will . . . astonish him. I think it will work.

3 [*The bell tolls one.* Scrooge *leaps awake.*]

4 **Scrooge.** One! One! This is it; time! [*Looks about the room*] Nothing!

5 [*The bell tolls midnight.*]

6 Midnight! How can this be? I'm sleeping backwards.

7 [*One again*]

8 Good heavens! One again! I'm sleeping back and forth! [*A pause.* Scrooge *looks about.*] Nothing! Absolutely nothing!

9 [*Suddenly, thunder and lightning.* Marley *laughs and disappears. The room shakes and glows. There is suddenly springlike music.* Scrooge *makes a run for the door.*]

10 **Marley.** Scrooge!

11 **Scrooge.** What?

12 **Marley.** Stay you put!

13 **Scrooge.** Just checking to see if anyone is in here.

14 [*Lights and thunder again: more music.* Marley *is of a sudden gone. In his place sits the* Ghost of Christmas Present—*to be called in the stage directions of the play,* Present—*center of room. Heaped up on the floor, to form a kind of throne, are turkeys, geese, game, poultry, brawn, great joints of meat, suckling pigs, long wreaths of sausages, mince-pies, plum puddings, barrels of oysters, red hot chestnuts, cherry-cheeked apples, juicy oranges, luscious pears, immense twelfth cakes, and seething bowls of punch, that make the chamber dim with their delicious steam. Upon this throne sits* Present, *glorious to see. He bears a torch, shaped as a Horn of Plenty.*[1] Scrooge *hops out of the door, and then peeks back again into his bedroom.* Present *calls to* Scrooge.]

15 **Present.** Ebenezer Scrooge. Come in, come in! Come in and know me better!

16 **Scrooge.** Hello. How should I call you?

17 **Present.** I am the Ghost of Christmas Present. Look upon me.

18 [Present *is wearing a simple green robe. The walls around the room are now covered in greenery, as well. The room seems to be a perfect grove now: leaves of holly, mistletoe and ivy reflect the stage lights.*

1. **Horn of Plenty** horn overflowing with fruits, flowers, and grain, representing wealth and abundance.

Suddenly, there is a mighty roar of flame in the fireplace and now the hearth burns with a lavish, warming fire. There is an ancient scabbard girdling the Ghost's *middle, but without sword. The sheath is gone to rust.*]

19 You have never seen the like of me before?

20 **Scrooge.** Never.

21 **Present.** You have never walked forth with younger members of my family: my elder brothers born on Christmases past.

22 **Scrooge.** I don't think I have. I'm afraid I've not. Have you had many brothers, Spirit?

23 **Present.** More than eighteen hundred.

24 **Scrooge.** A tremendous family to provide for! [*Present stands*] Spirit, conduct me where you will. I went forth last night on compulsion, and learnt a lesson which is working now. Tonight, if you have aught to teach me, let me profit by it.

25 **Present.** Touch my robe.

26 [Scrooge *walks cautiously to* Present *and touches his robe. When he does, lightning flashes, thunder claps, music plays. Blackout*]

Scene 2

1 [*PROLOGUE:* Marley *stands spotlit, L. He speaks directly to the audience.*]

2 **Marley.** My ghostly friend now leads my living partner through the city's streets.

3 [*Lights up on* Scrooge *and* Present]

4 See them there and hear the music people make when the weather is severe, as it is now.

5 [*Winter music. Choral group behind scrim, sings. When the song is done and the stage is re-set, the lights will fade up on a row of shops, behind the singers. The choral group will hum the song they have just completed now and mill about the streets,*[2] *carrying their dinners to the bakers' shops and restaurants. They will, perhaps, sing about being poor at Christmastime, whatever.*]

6 **Present.** These revelers, Mr. Scrooge, carry their own dinners to their jobs, where they will work to bake the meals the rich men and women of this city will eat as their Christmas dinners. Generous people these . . . to care for the others, so . . .

NOTES

CLOSE READ
ANNOTATE: Mark the details in paragraphs 5–6 that describe the setting.

QUESTION: Why might the playwright have chosen to begin the scene with these details?

CONCLUDE: How does this information help you to better understand the play?

2. **mill about the streets** walk around aimlessly.

7 [Present *walks among the choral group and a sparkling incense[3] falls from his torch on to their baskets, as he pulls the covers off of the baskets. Some of the choral group become angry with each other.*]

8 **Man #1.** Hey, you, watch where you're going.

9 **Man #2.** Watch it yourself, mate!

10 [Present *sprinkles them directly, they change.*]

11 **Man #1.** I pray go in ahead of me. It's Christmas. You be first!

12 **Man #2.** No, no. I must insist that YOU be first!

13 **Man #1.** All right, I shall be, and gratefully so.

14 **Man #2.** The pleasure is equally mine, for being able to watch you pass, smiling.

15 **Man #1.** I would find it a shame to quarrel on Christmas Day . . .

16 **Man #2.** As would I.

17 **Man #1.** Merry Christmas then, friend!

18 **Man #2.** And a Merry Christmas straight back to you!

19 [*Church bells toll. The choral group enter the buildings: the shops and restaurants; they exit the stage, shutting their doors closed behind them. All sound stops.* Scrooge *and* Present *are alone again.*]

20 **Scrooge.** What is it you sprinkle from your torch?

21 **Present.** Kindness.

22 **Scrooge.** Do you sprinkle your kindness on any particular people or on all people?

23 **Present.** To any person kindly given. And to the very poor most of all.

24 **Scrooge.** Why to the very poor most?

25 **Present.** Because the very poor need it most. Touch my heart . . . here, Mr. Scrooge. We have another journey.

26 [Scrooge *touches the* Ghost's *heart and music plays, lights change color, lightning flashes, thunder claps. A choral group appears on the street, singing Christmas carols.*]

Scene 3

1 [Marley *stands spotlit in front of a scrim on which is painted the exterior of* Cratchit's *four-roomed house. There is a flash and a clap and* Marley *is gone. The lights shift color again, the scrim flies away, and we are in the interior of the* Cratchit *family home.*

Scrooge *is there, with the spirit* (Present)*, watching*
Mrs. Cratchit *set the table, with the help of* Belinda Cratchit
and Peter Cratchit*, a baby, pokes a fork into the mashed potatoes
on his highchair's tray. He also chews on his shirt collar.*]

2 **Scrooge.** What is this place, Spirit?

3 **Present.** This is the home of your employee, Mr. Scrooge.
Don't you know it?

4 **Scrooge.** Do you mean Cratchit, Spirit? Do you mean this is
Cratchit's home?

5 **Present.** None other.

6 **Scrooge.** These children are his?

7 **Present.** There are more to come presently.

8 **Scrooge.** On his meager earnings! What foolishness!

9 **Present.** Foolishness, is it?

10 **Scrooge.** Wouldn't you say so? Fifteen shillings[4] a week's
what he gets!

11 **Present.** I would say that he gets the pleasure of his family,
fifteen times a week times the number of hours a day! Wait,
Mr. Scrooge. Wait, listen and watch. You might actually learn
something . . .

12 **Mrs. Cratchit.** What has ever got your precious father then?
And your brother, Tiny Tim? And Martha warn't as late last
Christmas by half an hour!

13 [Martha *opens the door, speaking to her mother as she does.*]

14 **Martha.** Here's Martha, now, Mother! [*She laughs. The*
Cratchit Children *squeal with delight.*]

15 **Belinda.** It's Martha, Mother! Here's Martha!

16 **Peter.** Marthmama, Marthmama! Hullo!

17 **Belinda.** Hurrah! Martha! Martha! There's such an enormous
goose for us, Martha!

18 **Mrs. Cratchit.** Why, bless your heart alive, my dear, how late
you are!

19 **Martha.** We'd a great deal of work to finish up last night, and
had to clear away this morning, Mother.

20 **Mrs. Cratchit.** Well, never mind so long as you are come. Sit
ye down before the fire, my dear, and have a warm, Lord
bless ye!

21 **Belinda.** No, no! There's Father coming. Hide, Martha, hide!

22 [Martha *giggles and hides herself.*]

NOTES

4. **fifteen shillings** small amount
of money for a week's work.

A Christmas Carol: Scrooge and Marley, ACT II **269**

Copyright © SAVVAS Learning Company LLC. All Rights Reserved.

23 **Martha.** Where? Here?

24 **Peter.** Hide, hide!

25 **Belinda.** Not there! *THERE!*

26 [Martha *is hidden.* Bob Cratchit *enters, carrying* Tiny Tim *atop his shoulder. He wears a threadbare and fringeless comforter hanging down in front of him.* Tiny Tim *carries small crutches and his small legs are bound in an iron frame brace.*]

27 **Bob and Tiny Tim.** Merry Christmas.

28 **Bob.** Merry Christmas my love, Merry Christmas Peter, Merry Christmas Belinda. Why, where is Martha?

29 **Mrs. Cratchit.** Not coming.

30 **Bob.** Not coming: Not coming upon Christmas Day?

31 **Martha.** [*Pokes head out*] Ohhh, poor Father. Don't be disappointed.

32 **Bob.** What's this?

33 **Martha.** 'Tis I!

34 **Bob.** Martha! [*They embrace.*]

35 **Tiny Tim.** Martha! Martha!

36 **Martha.** Tiny Tim!

37 [Tiny Tim *is placed in* Martha's *arms.* Belinda *and* Peter *rush him offstage.*]

38 **Belinda.** Come, brother! You must come hear the pudding singing in the copper.

39 **Tiny Tim.** The pudding? What flavor have we?

40 **Peter.** Plum! Plum!

41 **Tiny Tim.** Oh, Mother! I love plum!

42 [*The children exit the stage giggling.*]

43 **Mrs. Cratchit.** And how did little Tim behave?

44 **Bob.** As good as gold, and even better. Somehow he gets thoughtful sitting by himself so much, and thinks the strangest things you ever heard. He told me, coming home, that he hoped people saw him in the church, because he was a cripple, and it might be pleasant to them to remember upon Christmas Day, who made lame beggars walk and blind men see. [*Pauses*] He has the oddest ideas sometimes, but he seems all the while to be growing stronger and more hearty . . . one would never know. [*Hears* Tim's *crutch on floor outside door*]

45 **Peter.** The goose has arrived to be eaten!

46 **Belinda.** Oh, mama, mama, it's beautiful.

CLOSE READ

ANNOTATE: Mark the pauses and the sound effect in paragraph 44.

QUESTION: Why might the playwright have included the pauses and sound effects in the dialogue?

CONCLUDE: What can you conclude about Bob Cratchit's state of mind as a result of these details?

47 **Martha.** It's a perfect goose, Mother!

48 **Tiny Tim.** To this Christmas goose, Mother and Father I say
. . . [*Yells*] Hurrah! Hurrah!

49 **Other Children.** [*Copying* Tim] Hurrah! Hurrah!

50 [*The family sits round the table. Bob and Mrs. Cratchit serve the
trimmings, quickly. All sit; all bow heads; all pray.*]

51 **Bob.** Thank you, dear Lord, for your many gifts . . . our dear
children; our wonderful meal; our love for one another; and
the warmth of our small fire—[*Looks up at all*] A merry
Christmas to us, my dear. God bless us!

52 **All.** [*Except* Tim] Merry Christmas! God bless us!

53 **Tiny Tim.** [*In a short silence*] God bless us every one.

54 [*All freeze. Spotlight on* Present *and* Scrooge]

55 **Scrooge.** Spirit, tell me if Tiny Tim will live.

56 **Present.** I see a vacant seat . . . in the poor chimney corner,
and a crutch without an owner, carefully preserved. If these
shadows remain unaltered by the future, the child will die.

57 **Scrooge.** No, no, kind Spirit! Say he will be spared!

58 **Present.** If these shadows remain unaltered by the future, none other of my race will find him here. What then? If he be like to die, he had better do it, and decrease the surplus population.

59 [Scrooge *bows his head. We hear* Bob's *voice speak* Scrooge's *name.*]

60 **Bob.** Mr. Scrooge . . .

61 **Scrooge.** Huh? What's that? Who calls?

62 **Bob.** [*His glass raised in a toast*] I'll give you Mr. Scrooge, the Founder of the Feast!

63 **Scrooge.** Me, Bob? You toast *me*?

64 **Present.** Save your breath, Mr. Scrooge. You can't be seen or heard.

65 **Mrs. Cratchit.** The Founder of the Feast, indeed! I wish I had him here, that miser Scrooge. I'd give him a piece of my mind to feast upon, and I hope he'd have a good appetite for it!

66 **Bob.** My dear! Christmas Day!

67 **Mrs. Cratchit.** It should be Christmas Day, I am sure, on which one drinks the health of such an odious, stingy, unfeeling man as Mr. Scrooge . . .

68 **Scrooge.** Oh. Spirit, must I? . . .

69 **Mrs. Cratchit.** You know he is, Robert! Nobody knows it better than you do, poor fellow!

70 **Bob.** This is Christmas Day, and I should like to drink to the health of the man who employs me and allows me to earn my living and our support and that man is Ebenezer Scrooge . . .

71 **Mrs. Cratchit.** I'll drink to his health for your sake and the day's, but not for his sake . . . a Merry Christmas and a Happy New Year to you, Mr. Scrooge, wherever you may be this day!

72 **Scrooge.** Just here, kind madam . . . out of sight, out of sight . . .

73 **Bob.** Thank you, my dear. Thank you.

74 **Scrooge.** Thank you, Bob . . . and Mrs. Cratchit, too. No one else is toasting me, . . . not now . . . not ever. Of that I am sure . . .

75 **Bob.** Children . . .

76 **All.** Merry Christmas to Mr. Scrooge.

77 **Bob.** I'll pay you sixpence, Tim, for my favorite song.

CLOSE READ

ANNOTATE: In paragraphs 62–71, mark words and phrases that highlight the differences between Mrs. Cratchit's and Bob Cratchit's attitudes toward Scrooge.

QUESTION: Why might the playwright have chosen to show this contrast in their attitudes through their dialogue?

CONCLUDE: What does the contrast reveal about the personality of each character?

78 **Tiny Tim.** Oh, Father, I'd so love to sing it, but not for pay. This Christmas goose—this feast—you and Mother, my brother and sisters close with me: that's my pay—

79 **Bob.** Martha, will you play the notes on the lute, for Tiny Tim's song.

80 **Belinda.** May I sing, too, Father?

81 **Bob.** We'll all sing.

82 [*They sing a song about a tiny child lost in the snow—probably from Wordsworth's poem.* Tim *sings the lead vocal; all chime in for the chorus. Their song fades under, as the* Ghost of Christmas Present *speaks.*]

83 **Present.** Mark my words, Ebenezer Scrooge. I do not present the Cratchits to you because they are a handsome, or brilliant family. They are not handsome. They are not brilliant. They are not well-dressed, or tasteful to the times. Their shoes are not even waterproofed by virtue of money or cleverness spent. So when the pavement is wet, so are the insides of their shoes and the tops of their toes. These are the Cratchits, Mr. Scrooge. They are not highly special. They are happy, grateful, pleased with one another, contented with the time and how it passes. They don't sing very well, do they? But, nonetheless, they do sing . . . [*Pauses*] think of that, Scrooge. Fifteen shillings a week and they do sing . . . hear their song until its end.

84 **Scrooge.** I am listening. [*The chorus sings full volume now, until . . . the song ends here.*] Spirit, it must be time for us to take our leave. I feel in my heart that it is . . . that I must think on that which I have seen here . . .

85 **Present.** Touch my robe again . . .

86 [Scrooge *touches* Present's *robe. The lights fade out on the* Cratchits, *who sit, frozen, at the table.* Scrooge *and* Present *in a spotlight now. Thunder, lightning, smoke. They are gone.*]

Scene 4

1 [Marley *appears* D.L. *in single spotlight. A storm brews. Thunder and lightning.* Scrooge *and* Present *"fly" past,* U. *The storm continues, furiously, and, now and again,* Scrooge *and* Present *will zip past in their travels.* Marley *will speak straight out to the audience.*]

2 **Marley.** The Ghost of Christmas Present, my co-worker in this attempt to turn a miser, flies about now with that very miser, Scrooge, from street to street, and he points out

partygoers on their way to Christmas parties. If one were to judge from the numbers of people on their way to friendly gatherings, one might think that no one was left at home to give anyone welcome . . . but that's not the case, is it? Every home is expecting company and . . . [*He laughs.*] Scrooge is amazed.

3 [Scrooge *and* Present *zip past again. The lights fade up around them. We are in the* Nephew's *home, in the living room.* Present *and* Scrooge *stand watching the* Nephew: Fred *and his wife, fixing the fire.*]

4 **Scrooge.** What is this place? We've moved from the mines!

5 **Present.** You do not recognize them?

6 **Scrooge.** It is my nephew! . . . and the one he married . . .

7 [Marley *waves his hand and there is a lightning flash. He disappears.*]

8 **Fred.** It strikes me as sooooo funny, to think of what he said . . . that Christmas was a humbug, as I live! He believed it!

9 **Wife.** More shame for him, Fred!

10 **Fred.** Well, he's a comical old fellow, that's the truth.

11 **Wife.** I have no patience with him.

12 **Fred.** Oh, I have! I am sorry for him; I couldn't be angry with him if I tried. Who suffers by his ill whims? Himself, always . . .

13 **Scrooge.** It's me they talk of, isn't it, Spirit?

14 **Fred.** Here, wife, consider this. Uncle Scrooge takes it into his head to dislike us, and he won't come and dine with us. What's the consequence?

15 **Wife.** Oh . . . you're sweet to say what I think you're about to say, too, Fred . . .

16 **Fred.** What's the consequence? He don't lose much of a dinner by it, I can tell you that!

17 **Wife.** Ooooooo, Fred! Indeed, I think he loses a very good dinner . . . ask my sisters, or your bachelor friend, Topper . . . ask any of them. They'll tell you what old Scrooge, your uncle, missed: a dandy meal!

18 **Fred.** Well, that's something of a relief, wife. Glad to hear it! [*He hugs his wife. They laugh. They kiss.*] The truth is, he misses much yet. I mean to give him the same chance every year, whether he likes it or not, for I pity him. Nay, he is my only uncle and I feel for the old miser . . . but, I tell you, wife: I see

my dear and perfect mother's face on his own wizened cheeks and brow: brother and sister they were, and I cannot erase that from each view of him I take . . .

19 **Wife.** I understand what you say, Fred, and I am with you in your yearly asking. But he never will accept, you know. He never will.

20 **Fred.** Well, true, wife. Uncle may rail at Christmas till he dies. I think I shook him some with my visit yesterday . . . [*Laughing*] I refused to grow angry . . . no matter how nasty he became . . . [*Whoops*] It was HE who grew angry, wife! [*They both laugh now.*]

21 **Scrooge.** What he says is true, Spirit . . .

22 **Fred and Wife.** Bah, humbug!

23 **Fred.** [*Embracing his wife*] There is much laughter in our marriage, wife. It pleases me. You please me . . .

24 **Wife.** And you please me, Fred. You are a good man . . . [*They embrace.*] Come now. We must have a look at the meal . . . our guests will soon arrive . . . my sisters, Topper . . .

25 **Fred.** A toast first . . . [*He hands her a glass*] A toast to Uncle Scrooge . . . [*Fills their glasses*]

26 **Wife.** A toast to him?

27 **Fred.** Uncle Scrooge has given us plenty of merriment, I am sure, and it would be ungrateful not to drink to his health. And I say . . . *Uncle Scrooge!*

28 **Wife.** [*Laughing*] You're a proper loon,[5] Fred . . . and I'm a proper wife to you . . . [*She raises her glass.*] Uncle Scrooge! [*They drink. They embrace. They kiss.*]

29 **Scrooge.** Spirit, please, make me visible! Make me audible! I want to talk with my nephew and my niece!

30 [*Calls out to them. The lights that light the room and* Fred *and wife fade out.* Scrooge *and* Present *are alone, spotlit.*]

31 **Present.** These shadows are gone to you now, Mr. Scrooge. You may return to them later tonight in your dreams. [*Pauses*] My time grows short, Ebenezer Scrooge. Look you on me! Do you see how I've aged?

32 **Scrooge.** Your hair has gone gray! Your skin, wrinkled! Are spirits' lives so short?

33 **Present.** My stay upon this globe is very brief. It ends tonight.

34 **Scrooge.** Tonight?

35 **Present.** At midnight. The time is drawing near!

5. **a proper loon** silly person.

36 [*Clock strikes 11:45.*]

37 Hear those chimes? In a quarter hour, my life will have been spent! Look, Scrooge, man. Look you here.

38 [*Two gnarled baby dolls are taken from* Present's *skirts.*]

39 **Scrooge.** Who are they?

40 **Present.** They are Man's children, and they cling to me, appealing from their fathers. The boy is Ignorance; the girl is Want. Beware them both, and all of their degree, but most of all beware this boy, for I see that written on his brow which is doom, unless the writing be erased.

41 [*He stretches out his arm. His voice is now amplified: loudly and oddly.*]

42 **Scrooge.** Have they no refuge or resource?

43 **Present.** Are there no prisons? Are there no workhouses? [*Twelve chimes*] Are there no prisons? Are there no workhouses?

44 [*A Phantom,* hooded, *appears in dim light,* D., *opposite.*]

45 Are there no prisons? Are there no workhouses?

46 [Present *begins to deliquesce.* Scrooge *calls after him.*]

47 **Scrooge.** Spirit, I'm frightened! Don't leave me! Spirit!

48 **Present.** Prisons? Workhouses? Prisons? Workhouses . . .

49 [*He is gone.* Scrooge *is alone now with the* Phantom, *who is, of course, the* Ghost of Christmas Future. *The* Phantom *is shrouded in black. Only its outstretched hand is visible from under his ghostly garment.*]

50 **Scrooge.** Who are you, Phantom? Oh, yes. I think I know you! You are, are you not, the Spirit of Christmas Yet to Come? [*No reply*] And you are about to show me the shadows of the things that have not yet happened, but will happen in time before us. Is that not so, Spirit? [*The* Phantom *allows* Scrooge *a look at his face. No other reply wanted here. A nervous giggle here.*] Oh, Ghost of the Future, I fear you more than any Specter I have seen! But, as I know that your purpose is to do me good and as I hope to live to be another man from what I was, I am prepared to bear you company. [Future *does not reply, but for a stiff arm, hand and finger set, pointing forward.*] Lead on, then, lead on. The night is waning fast, and it is precious time to me. Lead on, Spirit!

51 [Future *moves away from* Scrooge *in the same rhythm and motion employed at its arrival.* Scrooge *falls into the same pattern, a considerable space apart from the* Spirit. *In the space between them,* Marley *appears. He looks to* Future *and then to* Scrooge. *He claps his hands. Thunder and lightning. Three* Businessmen *appear, spotlighted singularly: One is D.L.; one is D.R.; one is U.C. Thus, six points of the stage should now be spotted in light.* Marley *will watch this scene from his position,* C. Scrooge *and* Future *are R. and L. of* C.]

52 **First Businessman.** Oh, no, I don't know much about it either way, I only know he's dead.

53 **Second Businessman.** When did he die?

54 **First Businessman.** Last night, I believe.

55 **Second Businessman.** Why, what was the matter with him? I thought he'd never die, really . . .

56 **First Businessman.** [*Yawning*] Goodness knows, goodness knows . . .

57 **Third Businessman.** What has he done with his money?

58 **Second Businessman.** I haven't heard. Have you?

59 **First Businessman.** Left it to his Company, perhaps. Money to money; you know the expression . . .

NOTES

CLOSE READ
ANNOTATE: Mark the words and phrases that the Ghost of Christmas Present repeats in paragraphs 43–48.

QUESTION: Why might the playwright have chosen to have the Ghost of Christmas Present repeat these words and phrases upon departing?

CONCLUDE: What effect does this repetition have on the reader?

60 **Third Businessman.** He hasn't left it to *me*. That's all I know . . .

61 **First Businessman.** [*Laughing*] Nor to me . . . [*Looks at* Second Businessman] You, then? You got his money???

62 **First Businessman.** [*Laughing*] Me, me, his money? Nooooo!

63 [*They all laugh.*]

64 **Third Businessman.** It's likely to be a cheap funeral, for upon my life, I don't know of a living soul who'd care to venture to it. Suppose we make up a party and volunteer?

65 **Second Businessman.** I don't mind going if a lunch is provided, but I must be fed, if I make one.

66 **First Businessman.** Well, I am the most disinterested among you, for I never wear black gloves, and I never eat lunch. But I'll offer to go, if anybody else will. When I come to think of it, I'm not all sure that I wasn't his most particular friend: for we used to stop and speak whenever we met. Well, then . . . bye, bye!

67 **Second Businessman.** Bye, bye . . .

68 **Third Businessman.** Bye, bye . . .

69 [*They glide offstage in three separate directions. Their lights follow them.*]

70 **Scrooge.** Spirit, why did you show me this? Why do you show me businessmen from my streets as they take the death of Jacob Marley? That is a thing past. You are *future!*

71 [Jacob Marley *laughs a long, deep laugh. There is a thunder clap and lightning flash, and he is gone.* Scrooge *faces* Future, *alone on stage now.* Future *wordlessly stretches out his arm-hand-and-finger-set, pointing into the distance, U. There, above them, scoundrels "fly" by, half-dressed and slovenly. When this scene has passed, a woman enters the playing area. She is almost at once followed by a second woman; and then a man in faded black; and then, suddenly, an old man, who smokes a pipe. The old man scares the other three. They laugh, anxious.*]

72 **First Woman.** Look here, old Joe, here's a chance! If we haven't all three met here without meaning it!

73 **Old Joe.** You couldn't have met in a better place. Come into the parlor. You were made free of it long ago, you know; and the other two ain't strangers [*He stands; shuts a door. Shrieking*] We're all suitable to our calling. We're well matched. Come into the parlor. Come into the parlor . . . [*They follow him* D. Scrooge *and* Future *are now in their midst, watching; silent. A truck comes in on which is set a small wall with*

fireplace and a screen of rags, etc. All props for the scene.] Let me just rake this fire over a bit . . .

74 [*He does. He trims his lamp with the stem of his pipe. The* First Woman *throws a large bundle on to the floor. She sits beside it, crosslegged, defiantly.*]

NOTES

75 **First Woman.** What odds then? What odds, Mrs. Dilber? Every person has a right to take care of themselves. HE always did!

76 **Mrs. Dilber.** That's true indeed! No man more so!

77 **First Woman.** Why, then, don't stand staring as if you was afraid, woman! Who's the wiser? We're not going to pick holes in each other's coats, I suppose?

78 **Mrs. Dilber.** No, indeed! We should hope not!

79 **First Woman.** Very well, then! That's enough. Who's the worse for the loss of a few things like these? Not a dead man, I suppose?

80 **Mrs. Dilber.** [*Laughing*] No, indeed!

81 **First Woman.** If he wanted to keep 'em after he was dead, the wicked old screw, why wasn't he natural in his lifetime? If he had been, he'd have had somebody to look after him when he was struck with Death, instead of lying gasping out his last there, alone by himself.

82 **Mrs. Dilber.** It's the truest word that was ever spoke. It's a judgment on him.

83 **First Woman.** I wish it were a heavier one, and it should have been, you may depend on it, if I could have laid my hands on anything else. Open that bundle, old Joe, and let me know the value of it. Speak out plain. I'm not afraid to be the first, nor afraid for them to see it. We knew pretty well that we were helping ourselves, before we met here, I believe. It's no sin. Open the bundle, Joe.

84 **First Man.** No, no, my dear! I won't think of letting you being the first to show what you've . . . earned . . . earned from this. I throw in mine.

85 [*He takes a bundle from his shoulder, turns it upside down, and empties its contents out on to the floor.*]

86 It's not very extensive, see . . . seals . . . a pencil case . . . sleeve buttons . . .

87 **First Woman.** Nice sleeve buttons, though . . .

88 **First Man.** Not bad, not bad . . . a brooch there . . .

89 **Old Joe.** Not really valuable, I'm afraid . . .

CLOSE READ
ANNOTATE: In paragraph 75, mark the word that is emphasized.

QUESTION: Why did the playwright choose to emphasize this word?

CONCLUDE: How does emphasizing this word reveal the First Woman's attitude toward the man of whom she speaks?

90 **First Man.** How much, old Joe?

91 **Old Joe.** [*Writing on the wall with chalk*] A pitiful lot, really. Ten and six and not a sixpence more!

92 **First Man.** You're not serious!

93 **Old Joe.** That's your account and I wouldn't give another sixpence if I was to be boiled for not doing it. Who's next?

94 **Mrs. Dilber.** Me! [*Dumps out contents of her bundle*] Sheets, towels, silver spoons, silver sugar-tongs . . . some boots . . .

95 **Old Joe.** [*Writing on wall*] I always give too much to the ladies. It's a weakness of mine and that's the way I ruin myself. Here's your total comin' up . . . two pounds-ten . . . if you asked me for another penny, and made it an open question, I'd repent of being so liberal and knock off half-a-crown.

96 **First Woman.** And now do MY bundle, Joe.

97 **Old Joe.** [*Kneeling to open knots on her bundle*] So many knots, madam . . . [*He drags out large curtains; dark*] What do you call this? Bed curtains!

98 **First Woman.** [*Laughing*] Ah, yes, bed curtains!

99 **Old Joe.** You don't mean to say you took 'em down, rings and all, with him lying there?

100 **First Woman.** Yes, I did, why not?

101 **Old Joe.** You were born to make your fortune and you'll certainly do it.

102 **First Woman.** I certainly shan't hold my hand, when I can get anything in it by reaching it out, for the sake of such a man as he was. I promise you, Joe. Don't drop that lamp oil on those blankets, now!

103 **Old Joe.** His blankets?

104 **First Woman.** Whose else's do you think? He isn't likely to catch cold without 'em, I daresay.

105 **Old Joe.** I hope that he didn't die of anything catching? Eh?

106 **First Woman.** Don't you be afraid of that. I ain't so fond of his company that I'd loiter about him for such things if he did. Ah! You may look through that shirt till your eyes ache, but you won't find a hole in it, nor a threadbare place. It's the best he had, and a fine one, too. They'd have wasted it, if it hadn't been for me.

107 **Old Joe.** What do you mean "They'd have wasted it"?

108 **First Woman.** Putting it on him to be buried in, to be sure. Somebody was fool enough to do it, but I took it off again . . .

109 [*She laughs, as do they all, nervously.*]

110 If calico[6] ain't good enough for such a purpose, it isn't good enough then for anything. It's quite as becoming to the body. He can't look uglier than he did in that one!

111 **Scrooge.** [*A low-pitched moan emits from his mouth; from the bones.*] OOOOOOOoooooOOOOOooooooOOOOOOO ooooOOOOOOoooooOO!

112 **Old Joe.** One pound six for the lot. [*He produces a small flannel bag filled with money. He divvies it out. He continues to pass around the money as he speaks. All are laughing.*] That's the end of it, you see! He frightened every one away from him when he was alive, to profit us when he was dead! Hah ha ha!

113 **All.** HAHAHAHAhahahahahahah!

114 **Scrooge.** *OOoooOOoooOOOoooOOOoooOOoooOOoooOOOooo!* [*He screams at them.*] Obscene demons! Why not market the corpse itself, as sell its trimming??? [*Suddenly*] Oh, Spirit, I see it, I see it! This unhappy man—this stripped-bare corpse . . . could very well be my own. My life holds **parallel**! My life ends that way now!

115 [Scrooge *backs into something in the dark behind his spotlight.* Scrooge *looks at* Future, *who points to the corpse.* Scrooge *pulls back the blanket. The corpse is, of course,* Scrooge, *who screams. He falls aside the bed; weeping.*]

116 Spirit, this is a fearful place. In leaving it, I shall not leave its lesson, trust me. Let us go!

117 [Future *points to the corpse.*]

118 Spirit, let me see some tenderness connected with a death, or that dark chamber, which we just left now, Spirit, will be forever present to me.

119 [Future *spreads his robes again. Thunder and lightning. Lights up, U., in the* Cratchit *home setting.* Mrs. Cratchit *and her daughters, sewing*]

120 **Tiny Tim's Voice.** [*Off*] And He took a child and set him in the midst of them.

121 **Scrooge.** [*Looking about the room; to* Future] Huh? Who spoke? Who said that?

122 **Mrs. Cratchit.** [*Puts down her sewing*] The color hurts my eyes. [*Rubs her eyes*] That's better. My eyes grow weak sewing by candlelight. I shouldn't want to show your father weak eyes when he comes home . . . not for the world! It must be near his time . . .

NOTES

6. **calico** (KAL ih koh) *n.* coarse and inexpensive cotton cloth.

CLOSE READ

ANNOTATE: Mark the sounds and sound effects in paragraphs 111–114.

QUESTION: Why do you think the author chose to include these details?

CONCLUDE: What effect does this choice have on the reader?

parallel (PAR uh lehl) *adj.* having the same direction or nature; similar

CLOSE READ

ANNOTATE: In paragraphs 123–136, mark the terms the characters use to identify each other in the dialogue.

QUESTION: Why might the playwright have included these terms in the dialogue?

CONCLUDE: How do these terms help the reader to better understand the conversation?

123 **Peter.** [*In corner, reading. Looks up from book*] Past it, rather. But l think he's been walking a bit slower than usual these last few evenings, Mother.

124 **Mrs. Cratchit.** I have known him walk with . . . [*Pauses*] I have known him walk with Tiny Tim upon his shoulder and very fast indeed.

125 **Peter.** So have I, Mother! Often!

126 **Daughter.** So have I.

127 **Mrs. Cratchit.** But he was very light to carry and his father loved him so, that it was not trouble—no trouble. [*Bob, at door*]

128 And there is your father at the door.

129 [*Bob Cratchit enters. He wears a comforter. He is cold, forlorn.*]

130 **Peter.** Father!

131 **Bob.** Hello, wife, children . . .

132 [*The daughter weeps; turns away from* Cratchit.]

133 Children! How good to see you all! And you, wife. And look at this sewing! I've no doubt, with all your industry, we'll have a quilt to set down upon our knees in church on Sunday!

134 **Mrs. Cratchit.** You made the arrangements today, then, Robert, for the . . . service . . . to be on Sunday.

135 **Bob.** The funeral. Oh, well, yes, yes, I did. I wish you could have gone. It would have done you good to see how green a place it is. But you'll see it often. I promised him that I would walk there on Sunday, after the service. [*Suddenly*] My little, little child! My little child!

136 **All Children.** [*Hugging him*] Oh, Father . . .

137 **Bob.** [*He stands*] Forgive me. I saw Mr. Scrooge's nephew, who you know I'd just met once before, and he was so wonderful to me, wife . . . he is the most pleasant-spoken gentleman I've ever met . . . he said "I am heartily sorry for it and heartily sorry for your good wife. If I can be of service to you in any way, here's where I live." And he gave me this card.

138 **Peter.** Let me see it!

139 **Bob.** And he looked me straight in the eye, wife, and said, meaningfully, "I pray you'll come to me, Mr. Cratchit, if you need some help. I pray you do." Now it wasn't for the sake of anything that he might be able to do for us, so much as for his kind way. It seemed as if he had known our Tiny Tim and felt with us.

140 **Mrs. Cratchit.** I'm sure that he's a good soul.

141 **Bob.** You would be surer of it, my dear, if you saw and spoke to him. I shouldn't be at all surprised, if he got Peter a situation.

142 **Mrs. Cratchit.** Only hear that, Peter!

143 **Martha.** And then, Peter will be keeping company with someone and setting up for himself!

144 **Peter.** Get along with you!

145 **Bob.** It's just as likely as not, one of these days, though there's plenty of time for that, my dear. But however and whenever we part from one another, I am sure we shall none of us forget poor Tiny Tim—shall we?—or this first parting that was among us?

146 **All Children.** Never, Father, never!

147 **Bob.** And when we recollect how patient and mild he was, we shall not quarrel easily among ourselves, and forget poor Tiny Tim in doing it.

148 **All Children.** No, Father, never!

149 **Little Bob.** I am very happy, I am. I am. I am very happy.

150 [Bob *kisses his little son, as does* Mrs. Cratchit, *as do the other children. The family is set now in one sculptural embrace. The lighting fades to a gentle pool of light, tight on them.*]

151 **Scrooge.** Specter, something informs me that our parting moment is at hand. I know it, but I know not how I know it.

152 [Future *points to the other side of the stage. Lights out on* Cratchits. Future *moves slowing, gliding.* Scrooge *follows.* Future *points opposite.* Future *leads* Scrooge *to a wall and a tombstone. He points to the stone.*]

153 Am I that man those ghoulish parasites[7] so gloated over? [*Pauses*] Before I draw nearer to that stone to which you point, answer me one question. Are these the shadows of things that will be, or the shadows of things that MAY be, only?

154 [Future *points to the gravestone.* Marley *appears in light well* U. *He points to grave as well. Gravestone turns front and grows to ten feet high. Words upon it:* Ebenezer Scrooge: *Much smoke billows now from the grave. Choral music here.* Scrooge *stands looking up at gravestone.* Future *does not at all reply in mortals' words, but points once more to the gravestone. The stone undulates and glows. Music plays, beckoning* Scrooge. Scrooge *reeling in terror*]

155 Oh, no. Spirit! Oh, no, no!

156 [Future's *finger still pointing*]

NOTES

7. **ghoulish parasites** (GOOL ish PAR uh syts) referring to the men and women who stole and divided Scrooge's goods after he died.

altered (AWL tuhrd) *adj.* changed

strive (STRYV) *v.* make a great effort; try very hard

157 Spirit! Hear me! I am not the man I was. I will not be the man I would have been but for this intercourse. Why show me this, if I am past all hope?

158 [Future *considers* Scrooge's *logic. His hand wavers.*]

159 Oh. Good Spirit, I see by your wavering hand that your good nature intercedes for me and pities me. Assure me that I yet may change these shadows that you have shown me by an **altered** life!

160 [Future's *hand trembles; pointing has stopped.*]

161 I will honor Christmas in my heart and try to keep it all the year. I will live in the Past, the Present, and the Future. The Spirits of all Three shall **strive** within me. I will not shut out the lessons that they teach. Oh, tell me that I may sponge away the writing that is upon this stone!

162 [Scrooge *makes a desperate stab at grabbing* Future's *hand. He holds firm for a moment, but* Future, *stronger than* Scrooge, *pulls away.* Scrooge *is on his knees, praying.*]

163 Spirit, dear Spirit, I am praying before you. Give me a sign that all is possible. Give me a sign that all hope for me is not lost. Oh, Spirit, kind Spirit, I beseech thee: give me a sign . . .

164 [Future *deliquesces, slowly, gently. The* Phantom's *hood and robe drop gracefully to the ground in a small heap. Music in. There is nothing in them. They are mortal cloth. The* Spirit *is elsewhere.* Scrooge *has his sign.* Scrooge *is alone. Tableau. The light fades to black.*]

Scene 5

1 [*The end of it.* Marley, *spotlighted, opposite* Scrooge, *in his bed, spotlighted.* Marley *speaks to audience, directly.*]

2 **Marley.** [*He smiles at* Scrooge.] The firm of Scrooge and Marley is doubly blessed; two misers turned; one, alas, in Death, too late; but the other miser turned in Time's penultimate nick.[8] Look you on my friend, Ebenezer Scrooge . . .

3 **Scrooge.** [*Scrambling out of bed; reeling in delight*] I will live in the Past, in the Present, and in the Future! The Spirits of all Three shall strive within me!

4 **Marley.** [*He points and moves closer to* Scrooge's *bed.*] Yes, Ebenezer, the bedpost is your own. Believe it! Yes, Ebenezer, the room is your own. Believe it!

5 **Scrooge.** Oh, Jacob Marley! Wherever you are, Jacob, know ye that I praise you for this! I praise you . . . and heaven . . . and Christmastime! [*Kneels facing away from* Marley] I say it to you on my knees, old Jacob, on my knees! [*He touches his bed curtains.*] Not torn down. My bed curtains are not at all torn down! Rings and all, here they are! They are here: I am here: the shadows of things that would have been, may now be **dispelled**. They will be, Jacob! I know they will be!

6 [*He chooses clothing for the day. He tries different pieces of clothing and settles, perhaps, on a dress suit, plus a cape of the bed clothing: something of color.*]

7 I am light as a feather, I am happy as an angel. I am as merry as a schoolboy. [*Yells out window and then out to audience*] Merry Christmas to everybody! Merry Christmas to everybody! A Happy New Year to all the world! Hallo here! Whoop! Whoop! Hallo! Hallo! I don't know what day of the month it is! I don't care! I don't know anything! I'm quite a baby! I don't care! I don't care a fig! I'd much rather be a baby

NOTES

8. in Time's penultimate nick just at the last moment.

dispelled (dihs PEHLD) *v.* driven away; scattered

ANNOTATE: In paragraphs 12–22, mark words that show Scrooge's attitude and behavior toward Adam.

QUESTION: What do these word choices reveal about Scrooge?

CONCLUDE: How does Scrooge's attitude and behavior toward Adam reveal a transformation in his character?

9. **poulterer's** (POHL tuhr uhrz) *n.* British term for a person or a store that sells poultry.

earnest (UR nihst) *adj.* serious and heartfelt; not joking

than be an old wreck like me or Marley! (Sorry, Jacob. wherever ye be!) Hallo! Hallo there!

8 [*Church bells chime in Christmas Day. A small boy, named* Adam, *is seen now* D.R., *as a light fades up on him.*] Hey, you boy! What's today? What day of the year is it?

9 **Adam.** Today, sir? Why, it's Christmas Day!

10 **Scrooge.** It's Christmas Day, is it? Whoop! Well, I haven't missed it after all, have I? The Spirits did all they did in one night. They can do anything they like, right? Of course they can! Of course they can!

11 **Adam.** Excuse me, sir?

12 **Scrooge.** Huh? Oh, yes, of course. What's your name, lad?

13 [Scrooge *and* Adam *will play their scene from their own spotlights.*]

14 **Adam.** Adam, sir.

15 **Scrooge.** Adam! What a fine, strong name! Do you know the poulterer's⁹ in the next street but one, at the corner?

16 **Adam.** I certainly should hope I know him, sir!

17 **Scrooge.** A remarkable boy! An intelligent boy! Do you know whether the poulterer's have sold the prize turkey that was hanging up there? I don't mean the little prize turkey, Adam. I mean the big one!

18 **Adam.** What, do you mean the one they've got that's as big as me?

19 **Scrooge.** I mean, the turkey the size of Adam: that's the bird!

20 **Adam.** It's hanging there now, sir.

21 **Scrooge.** It is? Go and buy it! No, no. I am absolutely in **earnest**. Go and buy it and tell 'em to bring it here, so that I may give them the directions to where I want it delivered, as a gift. Come back here with the man, Adam, and I'll give you a shilling. Come back here with him in less than five minutes, and I'll give you half-a-crown!

22 **Adam.** Oh, my sir! Don't let my brother in on this.

23 [Adam *runs offstage.* Marley *smiles.*]

24 **Marley.** An act of kindness is like the first green grape of summer: one leads to another and another and another. It would take a queer man indeed to not follow an act of kindness with an act of kindness. One simply whets the tongue for more . . . the taste of kindness is too too sweet. Gifts—goods—are lifeless. But the gift of goodness one feels in the giving is full of life. It . . . is . . . a . . . wonder.

25 [*Pauses; moves closer to* Scrooge, *who is totally occupied with his dressing and arranging of his room and his day. He is making lists, etc.* Marley *reaches out to* Scrooge.]

26 **Adam.** [Calling, off] I'm here! I'm here!

27 [Adam *runs on with a man, who carries an enormous turkey.*]

28 Here I am, sir. Three minutes flat! A world record! I've got the poultryman and he's got the poultry! [*He pants, out of breath.*] I have earned my prize, sir, if I live . . .

29 [*He holds his heart, playacting.* Scrooge *goes to him and embraces him.*]

30 **Scrooge.** You are truly a champion, Adam . . .

31 **Man.** Here's the bird you ordered, sir . . .

32 **Scrooge.** *Oh, my, MY!!!* Look at the size of that turkey, will you! He never could have stood upon his legs, that bird! He would have snapped them off in a minute, like sticks of

sealingwax! Why you'll never be able to carry that bird to Camden-Town, I'll give you money for a cab . . .

33 **Man.** Camden-Town's where it's goin', sir?

34 **Scrooge.** Oh, I didn't tell you? Yes, I've written the precise address down just here on this . . . [*Hands paper to him*] Bob Cratchit's house. Now he's not to know who sends him this. Do you understand me? Not a word . . . [*Handing out money and chuckling*]

35 **Man.** I understand, sir, not a word.

36 **Scrooge.** Good. There you go then . . . this is for the turkey . . . [*Chuckle*] . . . and this is for the taxi. [*Chuckle*] . . . and this is for your world-record run, Adam . . .

37 **Adam.** But I don't have change for that, sir.

38 **Scrooge.** Then keep it, my lad. It's Christmas!

39 **Adam.** [*He kisses* Scrooge's *cheek, quickly.*] Thank you, sir. Merry, Merry Christmas! [*He runs off.*]

40 **Man.** And you've given me a bit overmuch here, too, sir . . .

41 **Scrooge.** Of course I have, sir. It's Christmas!

42 **Man.** Oh, well, thanking you, sir. I'll have this bird to Mr. Cratchit and his family in no time, sir. Don't you worry none about that. Merry Christmas to you, sir, and a very happy New Year, too . . .

43 [*The man exits.* Scrooge *walks in a large circle about the stage, which is now gently lit. A chorus sings Christmas music far in the distance. Bells chime as well, far in the distance. A gentlewoman enters and passes.* Scrooge *is on the streets now.*]

44 **Scrooge.** Merry Christmas, madam . . .

45 **Woman.** Merry Christmas, sir . . .

46 [*The portly businessman from the first act enters.*]

47 **Scrooge.** Merry Christmas, sir.

48 **Portly Man.** Merry Christmas, sir.

49 **Scrooge.** Oh, you! My dear sir! How do you do? I do hope that you succeeded yesterday! It was very kind of you. A Merry Christmas.

50 **Portly Man.** Mr. Scrooge?

51 **Scrooge.** Yes, Scrooge is my name though I'm afraid you may not find it very pleasant. Allow me to ask your pardon. And will you have the goodness to—[*He whispers into the man's ear.*]

CLOSE READ

ANNOTATE: In paragraphs 49–56, mark words and phrases that indicate the Portly Man's reaction to Scrooge.

QUESTION: Why might the playwright have included these details?

CONCLUDE: What does the Portly Man's reaction show about Scrooge's character at this point in the play?

52 **Portly Man.** Lord bless me! My dear Mr. Scrooge, are you *serious!?!*

NOTES

10. **farthing** (FAHR thihng) *n.* small British coin.

53 **Scrooge.** If you please. Not a farthing[10] less. A great many back payments are included in it, I assure you. Will you do me that favor?

54 **Portly Man.** My dear sir, I don't know what to say to such munifi—

55 **Scrooge.** [*Cutting him off*] Don't say anything, please. Come and see me. Will you?

56 **Portly Man.** I will! I will! Oh I will, Mr. Scrooge! It will be my pleasure!

57 **Scrooge.** Thank'ee, I am much obliged to you. I thank you fifty times. Bless you!

58 [Portly Man *passes offstage, perhaps by moving backwards. Scrooge now comes to the room of his* Nephew *and* Niece. *He stops at the door, begins to knock on it, loses his courage, tries again, loses his courage again, tries again, fails again, and then backs off and runs at the door, causing a tremendous bump against it. The* Nephew *and* Niece *are startled.* Scrooge, *poking head into room*]

59 Fred!

60 **Nephew.** Why, bless my soul! Who's that?

61 **Nephew and Niece.** [*Together*] How now? Who goes?

62 **Scrooge.** It's I. Your Uncle Scrooge.

63 **Niece.** Dear heart alive!

64 **Scrooge.** I have come to dinner. May I come in, Fred?

65 **Nephew.** *May you come in???!!!* With such pleasure for me you may, Uncle!!! What a treat!

66 **Niece.** What a treat, Uncle Scrooge! Come in, come in!

67 [*They embrace a shocked and delighted* Scrooge: Fred *calls into the other room.*]

68 **Nephew.** Come in here, everybody, and meet my Uncle Scrooge! He's come for our Christmas party!

69 [*Music in. Lighting here indicates that day has gone to night and gone to day again. It is early, early morning.* Scrooge *walks alone from the party, exhausted, to his offices, opposite side of the stage. He opens his offices. The offices are as they were at the start of the play.* Scrooge *seats himself with his door wide open so he can see into the tank, as he awaits* Cratchit, *who enters, head down, full of guilt.* Cratchit, *starts writing almost before he sits.*]

Scrooge. What do you mean by coming in here at this time of day, a full eighteen minutes late, Mr. Cratchit? Hallo, sir? Do you hear me?

71 **Bob.** I am very sorry, sir. I *am* behind my time.

72 **Scrooge.** You are? Yes, I certainly think you are. Step this way, sir, if you please . . .

73 **Bob.** It's only but once a year, sir . . . It shall not be repeated. I was making rather merry yesterday and into the night . . .

74 **Scrooge.** Now, I'll tell you what, Cratchit. I am not going to stand this sort of thing any longer. And therefore . . .

75 [*He stands and pokes his finger into* Bob's *chest*.]

76 I am . . . about . . . to . . . raise . . . your salary.

77 **Bob.** Oh, no, sir. I . . . [*Realizes*] what did you say, sir?

78 **Scrooge.** A Merry Christmas, Bob . . . [*He claps* Bob's *back*.] A merrier Christmas, Bob, my good fellow! than I have given you for many a year. I'll raise your salary and endeavor to assist your struggling family and we will discuss your affairs this very afternoon over a bowl of smoking bishop.[11] Bob! Make up the fires and buy another coal scuttle before you dot another i, Bob. It's too cold in this place! We need warmth and cheer, Bob Cratchit! Do you hear me? DO . . . YOU . . . HEAR . . . ME?

79 [Bob Cratchit *stands, smiles at* Scrooge: Bob Cratchit *faints. Blackout. As the main lights black out, a spotlight appears on* Scrooge: C. *Another on* Marley: *He talks directly to the audience*.]

80 **Marley.** Scrooge was better than his word. He did it all and **infinitely** more; and to Tiny Tim, who did NOT die, he was a second father. He became as good a friend, as good a master, as good a man, as the good old city knew, or any other good old city, town, or borough in the good old world. And it was always said of him that he knew how to keep Christmas well, if any man alive possessed the knowledge. [*Pauses*] May that be truly said of us, and all of us. And so, as Tiny Tim observed . . .

81 **Tiny Tim.** [*Atop* Scrooge's *shoulder*] God Bless Us, Every One . . .

82 [*Lights up on chorus, singing final Christmas Song.* Scrooge *and* Marley *and all spirits and other characters of the play join in. When the song is over, the lights fade to black*.] ❧

11. smoking bishop a type of mulled wine or punch that was especially popular in Victorian England at Christmas time.

infinitely (IHN fuh niht lee) *adv.* enormously; remarkably

Comprehension Check

Complete the following items after you finish your first read.

1. Who is the second spirit that Scrooge encounters?

2. What does the Ghost of Christmas Present sprinkle on people in the street?

3. Who is the third spirit that Scrooge encounters?

4. What is the last thing the Ghost of Christmas Future shows Scrooge?

5. ⊟ **Notebook** Write a brief summary of *A Christmas Carol: Scrooge and Marley*, Act II.

RESEARCH

Research to Clarify Choose at least one unfamiliar detail from the text. Briefly research that detail. In what way does the information you learned shed light on an aspect of the play?

A CHRISTMAS CAROL: SCROOGE AND MARLEY, ACT II

Close Read the Text

1. This model, from Scene 1, paragraph 18, shows two sample annotations, along with questions and conclusions. Close read the passage, and find another detail to annotate. Then, write a question and conclusion.

ANNOTATE | QUESTION
Close Read
CONCLUDE

> **ANNOTATE:** The words *flame, fireplace, burns, warming,* and *fire* appear in one sentence.
>
> **QUESTION:** What effect is created with this word choice?
>
> **CONCLUDE:** The Ghost of Christmas Present has brought warmth and comfort into Scrooge's home.

ANNOTATE: The Ghost of Christmas Present wears a rusty scabbard and there is no sword in it.

QUESTION: What idea is being conveyed by these details?

CONCLUDE: The Ghost of Christmas Present represents peace.

> Present is wearing a simple green robe.... Suddenly, there is a mighty roar of flame in the fireplace and now the hearth burns with a lavish, warming fire. There is an ancient scabbard girdling the Ghost's middle, but without sword. The sheath is gone to rust.

🔧 Tool Kit
Close-Read Guide and
Model Annotation

2. For more practice, go back into the text and complete the close read notes.

3. Revisit a section of the text you found important during your first read. Read this section closely and **annotate** what you notice. Ask yourself **questions** such as "Why did the author make this choice?" What can you **conclude**?

- -

Analyze the Text

CITE TEXTUAL EVIDENCE
to support your answers.

📓 Notebook Respond to these questions.

1. (a) Analyze Why is Scrooge happy at the end of the play? **(b) Predict** How well do you think Scrooge will live up to his promise to learn his "lessons"? **(c) Support** What details in Act II support your prediction?

2. Take a Position Do you think Cratchit and Scrooge's nephew do the right thing by forgiving Scrooge immediately? Explain.

3. Essential Question *What can cause a sudden change in someone's life?* What have you learned about what can cause a sudden change in someone's life by reading Act II of this play?

≣ STANDARDS
Reading Literature
• Cite several pieces of textual evidence to support analysis of what the text says explicitly as well as inferences drawn from the text.
• Analyze how particular elements of a story or drama interact.
• Analyze how a drama's or poem's form or structure contributes to its meaning.

Analyze Craft and Structure

Text Structure: Stage Directions The written text of a play is called a **script.** The two main parts of a script are **dialogue,** or conversations between characters, and stage directions. **Stage directions** instruct actors on how to move and speak, or they describe what the stage should look and sound like. If you are reading a play instead of watching a performance, you get certain information *only* from the stage directions. Stage directions are usually written in italic type and set off by brackets or parentheses.

Stage directions are the playwright's instructions to the director and actors to guide them in performing and interpreting the script. Through stage directions, playwrights convey important information about:

- the setting and the context
- the scenery, lighting, and sound effects
- the behavior and actions of the actors
- the ways in which actors should deliver lines

Practice

CITE TEXTUAL EVIDENCE to support your answers.

Use the chart to analyze the playwright's use of stage directions in Act II of *A Christmas Carol: Scrooge and Marley.* In the center column, identify key details that are important to understanding the stage direction; for example, the actors involved or the types of sound effects. In the right column, summarize what you learn from the stage direction; for example, how the characters feel or move.

STAGE DIRECTION	KEY DETAILS	WHAT YOU LEARN FROM IT
[Lights. Choral music is sung….the audience directly.] (Scene 1, paragraph 1)		
[Church bells toll….are alone again.] (Scene 2, paragraph 19)		
[Jacob Marley laughs…They laugh, anxious.] (Scene 4, paragraph 71)		

A CHRISTMAS CAROL:
SCROOGE AND MARLEY, ACT II

Concept Vocabulary

parallel	strive	earnest
altered	dispelled	infinitely

Why These Words? The concept vocabulary words relate to Scrooge's transforming character and personality. For example, after the Spirits' visits he is an *altered* man who is *infinitely* more pleasant and willing to help other people.

1. How does the concept vocabulary sharpen the reader's understanding of how Scrooge changes?

2. What other words in the selection describe Scrooge's change in character and personality?

Practice

📓 **Notebook** Confirm the definitions for the six concept vocabulary words. Consult a dictionary as necessary to verify the meanings. Then, complete the activities.

1. Use each concept vocabulary word in a sentence that demonstrates its meaning.

2. Rewrite each sentence using a **synonym,** or word with a similar meaning, for the concept vocabulary word. How does the replacement change the meaning of the sentence?

Word Study

Greek Prefix: *para-* The Greek prefix *para-* means "beside." In the word *parallel*, the prefix is combined with a Greek root that means "of one another." So, *parallel* means "beside one another." Two lines that are *parallel* extend in the same direction beside one another and are always the same distance apart.

1. Write your own sentence that correctly uses the word *parallel*.

2. Using a dictionary or thesaurus, find two other words or phrases that contain the Greek prefix *para-*. Record a definition for each word or phrase, and write a sentence that correctly uses it.

Conventions

Sentence Structures In English, there are four types of sentence structure.

- A **simple sentence** consists of one independent clause—a group of words that has a subject and a verb and that can stand by itself as a complete thought.

  EXAMPLE: My cousin Tyrone and I are close friends.

- A **compound sentence** consists of two or more independent clauses linked by a conjunction such as *and, but,* or *or.*

  EXAMPLE: I like spending time with Tyrone, **and** we like doing the same things.

- A **complex sentence** contains one **independent clause** and one or more dependent clauses. A dependent clause is a group of words that has a subject and verb but is not a complete thought.

  EXAMPLE **Tyrone lives in my neighborhood,** although his house is not very close to mine.

- A **compound-complex sentence** consists of two or more **independent clauses** and one or more dependent clauses.

  EXAMPLE: **We often go to the park,** and, if we have all afternoon, **we might go to a movie.**

Read It

Reread these sentences from the selection. Identify each sentence structure, and then underline and label the clauses as independent or dependent.

1. He has the oddest ideas sometimes, but he seems all the while to be growing stronger and more hearty.

2. Tonight, if you have aught to teach me, let me profit by it.

3. The lights shift color again, the scrim flies away, and we are in the interior of the Cratchit family home.

4. I'll have the clock strike one and, when he awakes expecting my second messenger, there will be no one.

Write It

📝 Notebook Write an example of each sentence type.

1. simple

2. compound

3. complex

4. compound-complex

⊞ STANDARDS

Language
Choose among simple, compound, complex, and compound-complex sentences to signal differing relationships among ideas.

A Christmas Carol: Scrooge and Marley, Act II **295**

A CHRISTMAS CAROL:
SCROOGE AND MARLEY, ACT II

Writing to Sources

An **explanatory essay** defines, explains, or interprets ideas, events, or processes in an organized, logical way.

Assignment

Write an **explanatory essay** in which you analyze how the stage directions in *A Christmas Carol: Scrooge and Marley* enhance your understanding and enjoyment of the play. Be sure to provide details and specific examples from the play to support your ideas.

- Begin with an introductory paragraph in which you state the central idea of your essay.

- Organize your essay so that each paragraph or section clearly supports your central idea.

- Support your analysis with details, quotations, and examples from the play.

- Maintain a formal style in your writing, and use precise words and phrases that help your audience understand your ideas.

- Provide a conclusion that reinforces the explanation you present in your essay.

Vocabulary and Conventions Connection Consider including several of the concept vocabulary words in your essay. Also, remember to use a variety of sentence structures to make your writing more interesting.

| parallel | strive | earnest |
| altered | dispelled | infinitely |

Reflect on Your Writing

After you have written your essay, answer these questions.

1. Was it easy or difficult to find stage directions that helped you enjoy or understand the play?

2. Have your ideas about stage directions changed after writing this essay? Why, or why not?

3. **Why These Words?** The words you choose make a difference in your writing. Which words did you specifically choose to make your ideas clear?

STANDARDS

Writing
- Write informative/explanatory texts to examine a topic and convey ideas, concepts, and information through the selection, organization, and analysis of relevant content.
  a. Introduce a topic clearly, previewing what is to follow; organize ideas, concepts, and information, using strategies such as definition, classification, comparison/contrast, and cause/ effect; include formatting, graphics, and multimedia when useful to aiding comprehension.
  b. Develop the topic with relevant facts, definitions, concrete details, quotations, or other information and examples.
  d. Use precise language and domain-specific vocabulary to inform about or explain the topic.
  e. Establish and maintain a formal style.
  f. Provide a concluding statement or section that follows from and supports the information or explanation presented.
- Draw evidence from literary or informational texts to support analysis, reflection, and research.
  a. Apply *grade 7 Reading standards* to literature.

Speaking and Listening

Costume plans provide descriptions and sketches or images of the clothing that actors will wear on stage during the performance of a drama. Costume plans should reflect the drama's setting as well as the vision of the playwright who created the characters.

Assignment

Work with a partner to conduct research on the clothing that was worn in Victorian-era England. Then, create and present **costume plans** for two different characters from *A Christmas Carol: Scrooge and Marley*.

---

1. **Analyze the Characters** Work with your partner to review the play and analyze the characters. Select two characters on which to focus. Take notes on the following details:

   - the social positions of the characters

   - how the season would influence the characters' clothing

2. **Conduct Research** Use the Internet and library resources to find information and visuals to accurately develop realistic costume plans for both characters. You will need to know:

   - the types of clothing the characters would have worn based on their social position

   - the types of clothing that were typically popular during the season

   - fabrics and materials that were available during the time period

3. **Develop Your Costume Plans** Use the information from your analysis and your research to create costume plans. In your plans, show and describe the types of clothing, including the colors and fabrics. Include pictures and sketches to illustrate your descriptions.

4. **Deliver Your Presentation**

   - Explain why you chose each costume.

   - Ask classmates for feedback about whether your costumes reflect what they imagined as they read the play.

PRESENTATION EVALUATION GUIDE

Rate each statement on a scale of 1 (not demonstrated) to 5 (demonstrated).

☐ The costume plans were creative and original.

☐ The costume plans accurately reflected both the characters and the time period.

☐ The speakers clearly explained the decisions behind each costume.

☐ The presentation was illustrated with pictures and sketches.

✎ EVIDENCE LOG

Before moving on to a new selection, go to your Evidence Log and record what you've learned from *A Christmas Carol: Scrooge and Marley,* Act II.

☷ STANDARDS

Writing
Conduct short research projects to answer a question, drawing on several sources and generating additional related, focused questions for further research and investigation.

Speaking and Listening
• Present claims and findings, emphasizing salient points in a focused, coherent manner with pertinent descriptions, facts, details, and examples; use appropriate eye contact, adequate volume, and clear pronunciation.
• Include multimedia components and visual displays in presentations to clarify claims and findings and emphasize salient points.

A CHRISTMAS CAROL: SCROOGE AND MARLEY

Comparing Text to Media

In this lesson, you will watch a clip from the film *Scrooge*. You will then compare the film clip to the written dramatic adaptation of *A Christmas Carol: Scrooge and Marley*. While watching the film clip, note the differences in how each medium—text and film—tells the story.

from SCROOGE

from Scrooge

Media Vocabulary

The following words or concepts will be useful to you as you analyze, discuss, and write about media.

screenplay: the written script of a film, including acting instructions and scene directions	All films begin with a screenplay, including those based on other works.
director: the creative artist responsible for interpreting the screenplay	The director is responsible for the film's visual and dramatic effect on an audience.
performance: an actor's portrayal of a character	An actor's performance affects how the audience responds to a character.
editing: how separate shots filmed during production are arranged to tell a story, add suspense, and set pacing	An editor combines, rearranges, and cuts film and adds things, such as music and special effects.

First Review MEDIA: VIDEO

Apply these strategies as you watch the video. Be sure to note time codes so you can revisit specific sections later.

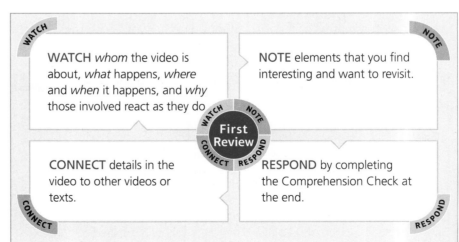

WATCH *whom* the video is about, *what* happens, *where* and *when* it happens, and *why* those involved react as they do

NOTE elements that you find interesting and want to revisit.

CONNECT details in the video to other videos or texts.

RESPOND by completing the Comprehension Check at the end.

First Review

WATCH · NOTE · CONNECT · RESPOND

STANDARDS

Reading Literature
By the end of the year, read and comprehend literature, including stories, dramas, and poems, in the grades 6–8 text complexity band proficiently, with scaffolding as needed at the high end of the range.

Language
Acquire and use accurately grade-appropriate general academic and domain-specific words and phrases; gather vocabulary knowledge when considering a word or phrase important to comprehension or expression.

from Scrooge

Directed by Henry Edwards

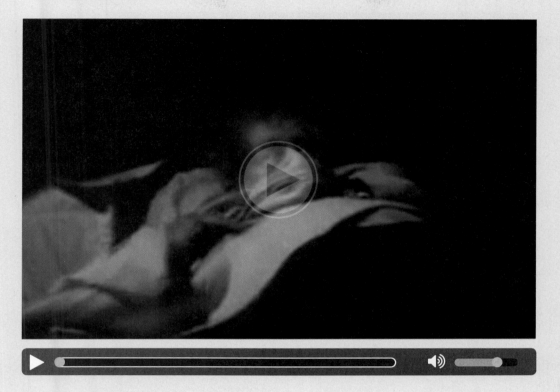

BACKGROUND

Charles Dickens first published *A Christmas Carol* in 1843. The novella was an instant success and has become a holiday classic. *A Christmas Carol* has inspired many television and film adaptations, including this 1935 British film *Scrooge*. The title role of Ebenezer Scrooge is played by Seymour Hicks, a British actor, playwright, and producer.

SCAN FOR MULTIMEDIA

NOTES

Comprehension Check

Complete the following items after you finish your first review.

1. What part of the story does the film clip show?

2. What joke does the Cratchit family play on Bob Cratchit when he returns home?

3. What hopeful statement does Cratchit make about Tiny Tim? Does Mrs. Cratchit agree with him?

4. 📓 **Notebook** Write a few sentences in which you explain which actor you think gives the most engaging performance in the film clip.

RESEARCH

Research to Clarify Choose one element of the film, such as the direction, performance, or editing. Briefly research that element. In what way does the information you learned shed light on the experience of watching the film?

Close Review

Watch the excerpt from *Scrooge* again. Write any new observations that seem important. What **questions** do you have? What can you **conclude**?

from SCROOGE

Analyze the Media

CITE TEXTUAL EVIDENCE
to support your answers.

📓 **Notebook** Complete the activities.

1. (a) **Interpret** What do you think the Ghost of Christmas Present means when he says Scrooge may be "more worthless than millions"?
   (b) **Make Inferences** Based on the details in the clip, do you think Scrooge understands and appreciates the Ghost's meaning? Why or why not?

2. **Essential Question:** *What can cause a sudden change in someone's life?* What have you learned about what can cause a sudden change in someone's life by watching *Scrooge*?

LANGUAGE DEVELOPMENT

Media Vocabulary

screenplay	director
performance	editing

Use the vocabulary words in your responses to the questions.

1. Identify something that a film can allow viewers to see or experience that a text version of the same story would not.

2. How did the film portray the Cratchit family?

3. How did the film clip capture the experience of both Scrooge and the Cratchit family?

4. Do you think the film clip portrayed the story accurately and realistically? Why or why not?

STANDARDS

Reading Literature
Cite several pieces of textual evidence to support analysis of what the text says explicitly as well as inferences drawn from the text.

Language
Acquire and use accurately grade-appropriate general academic and domain-specific words and phrases; gather vocabulary knowledge when considering a word or phrase important to comprehension or expression.

from Scrooge **301**

A CHRISTMAS CAROL:
SCROOGE AND MARLEY

from SCROOGE

Writing to Compare

Both the drama *A Christmas Carol: Scrooge and Marley* and the film *Scrooge* tell the same story, but they reflect the use of different techniques that are unique to each medium. To compare reading the play with watching the film, look for similarities and differences in how the two mediums present the same subject.

Assignment

Write a **comparison-and-contrast essay** in which you analyze the similarities and differences between the two versions of Charles Dickens's famous novel. Describe the techniques unique to each medium, and conclude your essay by explaining which adaptation you think is more effective.

Planning and Prewriting

Compare Play and Film Techniques Discuss the techniques used in the play and in the film to tell the same story. Use the chart below to guide your analysis of the two mediums. Identify the similarities and differences in the ways the play and the film develop characters, setting, and mood.

	PLAY	FILM
Characters	How are characters described and developed?	How do actors' performances develop the characters?
Setting	How do stage directions convey the setting?	What setting details have the greatest impact on the viewer?
Mood	How does the playwright create the mood, or atmosphere, in different scenes?	How do lighting, editing, directing, and sound effects create the mood in different scenes?

Notebook Respond to these questions.

1. Which medium, written drama or film, gives the audience's imagination more room to fill in details? Explain.
2. Which version of this story is more effective? Why?

STANDARDS

Reading Literature
Compare and contrast a written story, drama, or poem to its audio, filmed, staged, or multimedia version, analyzing the effects of techniques unique to each medium.

Writing
• Write informative/explanatory texts to examine a topic and convey ideas, concepts, and information through the selection, organization, and analysis of relevant content.
  b. Develop the topic with relevant facts, definitions, concrete details, quotations, or other information and examples.

• Draw evidence from literary or informational texts to support analysis, reflection, and research.
  a. Apply grade *7 Reading standards* to literature.

Speaking and Listening
Analyze the main ideas and supporting details presented in diverse media and formats and explain how the ideas clarify a topic, text, or issue under study.

Drafting

Create an Outline There are two main ways to organize a comparison-and-contrast essay: the block method and the point-by-point method. If you choose the block method of comparison, you will write about each medium separately. If you choose the point-by-point method, each paragraph will analyze one feature as it is developed in both the play and the film. Create an outline, using one of the following models as a guide.

📝 EVIDENCE LOG

Before moving on to a new selection, go to your Evidence Log and record what you've learned from the film clip from *Scrooge*.

Block Method of Comparison

I. **Introduction** Present the topic and identify the two sources you will compare and contrast.

II. *A Christmas Carol: Scrooge and Marley*
   A. Techniques used in the written play
   B. Strengths of the medium
   C. Limitations of the medium

III. **from *Scrooge***
   A. Techniques used in the film
   B. Strengths of the medium
   C. Limitations of the medium

IV. **Conclusion** Explain which version you think is more effective and why.

Point-by-Point Method of Comparison

I. **Introduction** Present the topic and identify the two sources you will compare and contrast.

II. **Characters**
   A. *A Christmas Carol: Scrooge and Marley*
   B. from *Scrooge*

III. **Setting**
   A. *A Christmas Carol: Scrooge and Marley*
   B. from *Scrooge*

IV. **Mood**
   A. *A Christmas Carol: Scrooge and Marley*
   B. from *Scrooge*

V. **Conclusion** Explain which version you think is more effective and why.

Use Precise Language When comparing a written play and a film, using precise language and technical vocabulary will enable you to accurately discuss your subjects. For example, when discussing the sounds in a film, you might use technical terms such as *soundtrack, dialogue,* and *sound effects.*

Support Your Conclusion In the final paragraph of your essay, present an evaluation in which you explain which medium tells the story more effectively. Support your evaluation with evidence.

Review, Revise, and Edit

Review the assignment to make sure your essay fulfills the requirements. Ask yourself:

- Does my essay have a clear organization that highlights the points of comparison?
- Are my ideas supported by relevant evidence?
- Does my conclusion state and support my evaluation as to which medium is more effective?
- Is my essay free from errors in spelling, punctuation, and grammar?

≡ STANDARDS

Reading Literature
Compare and contrast a written story, drama, or poem to its audio, filmed, staged, or multimedia version, analyzing the effects of techniques unique to each medium.

Writing
• Write informative/explanatory texts to examine a topic and convey ideas, concepts, and information through the selection, organization, and analysis of relevant content.
   d. Use precise language and domain-specific vocabulary to inform about or explain the topic.
   f. Provide a concluding statement or section that follows from and supports the information or explanation presented.

• Produce clear and coherent writing in which the development, organization, and style are appropriate to task, purpose, and audience.

ACADEMIC VOCABULARY

As you craft your essay, consider using some of the academic vocabulary you learned in the beginning of the unit.

contribute
consistent
maintain
observation
sufficient

 Tool Kit

Student Model of an Informative/Explanatory Essay

STANDARDS
Writing
• Write informative/explanatory texts to examine a topic and convey ideas, concepts, and information through the selection, organization, and analysis of relevant content.

• Write routinely over extended time frames and shorter time frames for a range of discipline-specific tasks, purposes, and audiences.

Write an Explanatory Essay

You have just read and watched selections that relate to someone experiencing a turning point in life. In *A Christmas Carol: Scrooge and Marley* and in the clip from the film *Scrooge*, we meet Ebenezer Scrooge, a bitter miser who undergoes a transformation when he is visited by three spirits.

Assignment

Review the selections in this section, and analyze the ways in which specific events and experiences contribute to Scrooge's transformation. Then, write a **cause-and-effect essay** in which you address the following prompt:

> How does Scrooge's character transform over the course of the play?

Elements of a Cause-and-Effect Essay

A **cause-and-effect essay** explains why something happens or what happens as a result of something else. A successful cause-and-effect essay includes the following elements:

• an introduction that grabs readers' interest and a strong, insightful conclusion

• a well-defined central idea that is supported by textual evidence

• detailed analysis and factual explanations of events or experiences and the relationships among them

• a clear, logical organization with effective transitions that show causes and effects

• precise language and specific vocabulary that is appropriate to the topic and audience

• a formal style and an objective tone

Model Essay For a model of a well-crafted cause-and-effect essay, see the Launch Text, "At the Crossroads."

Challenge yourself to find all of the elements of a cause-and-effect essay in the text. You will have an opportunity to review these elements as you prepare to write your own essay.

Prewriting / Planning

Develop Your Ideas To develop ideas for your essay, consider the various causes for and effects of the transformation in Scrooge's character over the course of the play. Review the play, and identify three key events or experiences that you think are most significant in bringing about this transformation. The topic web shown provides an example of causes and effects in the Launch Text. To develop your ideas, create a topic web for each key event and experience you will discuss in your essay.

✐ EVIDENCE LOG

Review your Evidence Log and identify key details you may want to include in your essay.

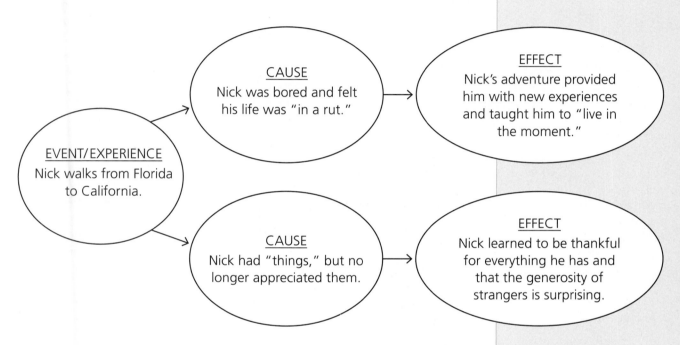

Connect Across Texts In order to effectively support the analysis you present, you will need relevant details, quotations, and examples from the selections. Review the texts that you have read so far in this unit, using your topic webs as a guide, and take notes on passages that strongly support the causes and effects on which you are focusing. Try to vary the ways in which you incorporate support. For example, you can use **direct quotations,** or the playwright's exact words, when these words are important to making your point. Alternatively, you can **paraphrase,** or restate in your own words, a complex idea or a broad example to make its importance clear to your audience.

STANDARDS
Writing
Write informative/explanatory texts to examine a topic and convey ideas, concepts, and information through the selection, organization, and analysis of relevant content.

a. Introduce a topic clearly, previewing what is to follow; organize ideas, concepts, and information, using strategies such as definition, classification, comparison/contrast, and cause/effect; include formatting, graphics, and multimedia when useful to aiding comprehension.

b. Develop the topic with relevant facts, definitions, concrete details, quotations, or other information and examples.

Drafting

Develop Your Introduction To introduce your topic and show why it is interesting, begin your essay with an engaging opening sentence. For example, you might begin with a rhetorical question or an interesting quotation. You should then provide a clear statement of your central idea as well as background information to establish context for your readers.

Organize Logically To help readers follow your explanation for the transformation of Scrooge's character, you must logically organize your ideas and information so that readers can easily follow the causes and effects of key events and experiences. To do so, use one of the following structures:

- **Order of Importance:** In this type of organization, each paragraph or section of your essay should focus on explaining the causes and effects of one key event or experience. You may choose either to begin with the most important event or experience in order to capture your readers' attention, or to arouse their curiosity by beginning with your least important event or experience and building toward your most important one.

- **Chronological Order:** This organizational structure is especially useful if your key events and experiences build on each other as a result of a sequence of causes and effects. First, sequence the events or experiences in the order in which they occurred in the play. In the first paragraph or section of your essay, explain the causes that resulted in the first event as well as the effects the event had—these effects serve as the cause for the event or experience you will discuss next, and so on.

Use Transitions Transition words and phrases will help you to explain the links between causes and effects and clarify the analysis on which your explanation is based. Incorporate transitions, such as the ones shown, to help your audience to follow your train of thought.

TO SHOW A CAUSE	*if, when, because of, since, due to, until, in order to, provided that*
TO SHOW AN EFFECT	*then, as a result, consequently, therefore, after, eventually*

STANDARDS

Writing
Write informative/explanatory texts to examine a topic and convey ideas, concepts, and information through the selection, organization, and analysis of relevant content.

a. Introduce a topic clearly, previewing what is to follow; organize ideas, concepts, and information, using strategies such as definition, classification, comparison/contrast, and cause/effect; include formatting, graphics, and multimedia when useful to aiding comprehension.

c. Use appropriate transitions to create cohesion and clarify the relationships among ideas and concepts.

LANGUAGE DEVELOPMENT: CONVENTIONS

Revise Sentences to Heighten Interest

Playwrights, such as Israel Horovitz, typically use a variety of sentence structures in their writing to create interesting dialogue and effective stage directions. Use the following strategies to revise your sentences to create variety:

- Combine short, choppy sentences.
- Combine sentences that repeat ideas.
- Combine sentences to clarify the connections among ideas.

As you apply these strategies, use a variety of sentence structures.

Read It

These sentences from the Launch Text show how the author revised sentences to create variety by using the strategies listed.

PROBLEM	BEFORE REVISION	SOLUTION AND REVISION
short, choppy sentences	He had a good income. He had a house. He had a new car. He had a new motorcycle.	Combine ideas into one simple sentence by using a conjunction: *He had a good income, a house, a new car, and a new motorcycle.*
two sentences that repeat an idea	By society's standards he should have been happy. He wasn't happy.	Use a compound sentence to combine sentences: *By society's standards he should have been happy—but he wasn't.*
two sentences that lack a clear connection between ideas	In the towns and cities, he slept on the street. He knew people would help him out.	Use a complex sentence to clarify connections: *In the towns and cities, he slept on the street, where he knew that there were people to help him out.*

Write It

As you draft your essay, use a variety of sentence structures to heighten readers' interest. Revise sentences, using the chart as a reference.

TIP

PUNCTUATION

Use dashes to indicate a quick break in thought and a return to that thought. (*I know—and I'm sure I'm right—who the culprit is.*)

▤ **STANDARDS**

Writing
Write informative/explanatory texts to examine a topic and convey ideas, concepts, and information through the selection, organization, and analysis of relevant content.

d. Use precise language and domain-specific vocabulary to inform about or explain the topic.

Language
- Demonstrate command of the conventions of standard English grammar and usage when writing or speaking.

b. Choose among simple, compound, complex, and compound-complex sentences to signal differing relationships among ideas.

- Use knowledge of language and its conventions when writing, speaking, reading, or listening.

a. Choose language that expresses ideas precisely and concisely, recognizing and eliminating wordiness and redundancy.

Revising

Evaluating Your Draft

Use the following checklist to evaluate your first draft. Then, use your evaluation and the instruction on this page to guide your revision.

FOCUS AND ORGANIZATION	EVIDENCE AND ELABORATION	CONVENTIONS
☐ Provides an engaging introduction and an insightful conclusion.	☐ Provides detailed analysis and factual explanations of events and experiences.	☐ Attends to the norms and conventions of the discipline, especially the correct use of a variety of sentence structures.
☐ Contains a clear statement of the central idea as well as the context surrounding it.	☐ Supports analysis and explanations with a variety of evidence.	☐ Establishes and maintains a formal style and objective tone.
☐ Uses a clear organization with effective transitions that show causes and effects.	☐ Uses precise language that is appropriate to audience and purpose.	

🕁 WORD NETWORK

Include interesting words from your Word Network in your essay.

☰ STANDARDS

Writing
Write informative/explanatory texts to examine a topic and convey ideas, concepts, and information through the selection, organization, and analysis of relevant content.

d. Use precise language and domain-specific vocabulary to inform about or explain the topic.

f. Provide a concluding statement or section that follows from and supports the information or explanation presented.

Revising for Focus and Organization

Review Your Conclusion In a cause-and-effect essay, an effective conclusion not only summarizes the central idea, but it also provides new insight into the relationship between the causes and effects. The concluding section should suggest to readers how the ideas in your essay might deepen their understanding of the topic. Review your conclusion to be sure that it addresses the prompt, summarizes your central idea, and provides new insight into the subject matter.

Use Domain-Specific Vocabulary To express your thoughts as precisely as possible in your writing, it is important to choose the right words. You can use signal words and phrases to indicate your certainty of the validity of a particular cause or effect, or to show how important specific causes and effects are in relation to each other. Use signal words, such as the ones shown, to make your explanation clear and precise.

SIGNAL WORDS	
DEGREES OF CERTAINTY	*may, certainly, probably, necessarily, perhaps, definitely, without a doubt, conclusively, possibly, in some way*
LEVELS OF IMPORTANCE	*primarily, most important, equally relevant, fundamentally, of greater concern, meaningless, insignificant, secondary, lesser*

PEER REVIEW

Exchange essays with a classmate. Use the checklist to evaluate your classmate's essay and provide supportive feedback.

1. Is there an engaging introduction and an insightful conclusion?

☐ yes   ☐ no   If no, suggest that the writer add these elements.

2. Is there support from the selections for the writer's analysis and explanation?

☐ yes   ☐ no   If no, point out where the writer should provide support.

3. Is the essay logically organized so that the relationships between causes and effects are clear?

☐ yes   ☐ no   If no, point out where the writer should make these connections clearer.

4. What is the strongest part of your classmate's essay? Why?

_____

_____

Editing and Proofreading

Edit for Conventions Reread your draft for accuracy and consistency. Correct errors in grammar and word usage. Be sure you have maintained a formal style and an objective tone in your writing by identifying and replacing any slang terms, abbreviations, and casual expressions. Your essay should use academic language and vocabulary that conveys knowledge and credibility.

Proofread for Accuracy Read your draft carefully, looking for errors in spelling and punctuation. Pay careful attention to the punctuation, indentation, and capitalization of quotations. Use quotation marks to set off short quotations. Longer quotations of four or more lines should begin on a new line, be indented, and appear without quotation marks.

Publishing and Presenting

Create a final version of your essay and share it with your class by posting it on a class or school Web site. Then, review several classmates' essays, and respond online by leaving comments and suggestions. Remember to be respectful and polite when offering feedback.

Reflecting

Reflect on what you learned as you wrote your essay. How did writing about the events and experiences that caused Scrooge's transformation help to deepen your understanding of what defines a turning point in a person's life?

▤ STANDARDS
Writing
- Write informative/explanatory texts to examine a topic and convey ideas, concepts, and information through the selection, organization, and analysis of relevant content.
  e. Establish and maintain a formal style.
- With some guidance and support from peers and adults, develop and strengthen writing as needed by planning, revising, editing, rewriting, or trying a new approach, focusing on how well purpose and audience have been addressed.
- Use technology, including the Internet, to produce and publish writing and link to and cite sources as well as to interact and collaborate with others, including linking to and citing sources.

ESSENTIAL QUESTION:

What can cause a sudden change in someone's life?

Can someone's life change in the course of a day or even an hour or even a minute? Is it possible to wake up the next day and be a different person? You will read selections that talk about changes, both big and small. You will work in a group to continue your exploration of turning points.

Small-Group Learning Strategies

Throughout your life, in school, in your community, and in your career, you will continue to learn and work with others.

Look at these strategies and the actions you can take to practice them as you work in teams. Add ideas of your own for each step. Use these strategies during Small-Group Learning.

STRATEGY	ACTION PLAN
Prepare	• Complete your assignments so that you are prepared for group work. • Organize your thinking so you can contribute to your group's discussion. •
Participate fully	• Make eye contact to signal that you are listening and taking in what is being said. • Use text evidence when making a point. •
Support others	• Build off ideas from others in your group. • Invite others who have not yet spoken to do so. •
Clarify	• Paraphrase the ideas of others to ensure that your understanding is correct. • Ask follow-up questions. •

SCAN FOR
MULTIMEDIA

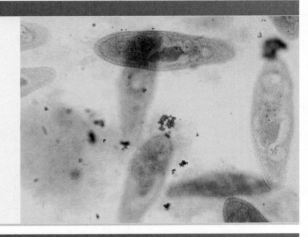

PERFORMANCE TASK

SPEAKING AND LISTENING FOCUS
Present an Explanatory Essay

The Small-Group readings feature different turning points that have caused sudden changes—big and small—in people's thinking and their lives in general. After reading the selections, your group will plan and deliver a multimedia presentation about turning points.

Working as a Team

1. **Take a Position** In your group, discuss the following question:

   Can people truly change?

   As you take turns sharing your positions, be sure to provide reasons for your choice. After all group members have shared, discuss the personality traits that would be necessary to realize such a genuine change.

2. **List Your Rules** As a group, decide on the rules that you will follow as you work together. Two samples are provided. Add two more of your own. You may add or revise rules based on your experience together.

   • Everyone should participate in group discussions.

   • People should not interrupt.

   • _____

     _____

   • _____

     _____

3. **Apply the Rules** Share what you have learned about turning points. Make sure each person in the group contributes. Take notes, and be prepared to share with the class one thing that you heard from another member of your group.

4. **Name Your Group** Choose a name that reflects the unit topic.

   Our group's name: _____

5. **Create a Communication Plan** Decide how you want to communicate with one another. For example, you might use online collaboration tools, email, or instant messaging.

   Our group's decision: _____

   _____

Making a Schedule

First, find out the due dates for the small-group activities. Then, preview the texts and activities with your group, and make a schedule for completing the tasks.

SELECTION	ACTIVITIES	DUE DATE
Thank You, M'am		
from An American Childhood		
Urban Farming Is Growing a Greener Future		

Working on Group Projects

As your group works together, you'll find it more effective if each person has a specific role. Different projects require different roles. Before beginning a project, discuss the necessary roles and choose one for each group member. Here are some possible roles; add your own ideas.

Project Manager: monitors the schedule and keeps everyone on task

Researcher: organizes research activities

Recorder: takes notes during group meetings

_____

_____

_____

_____

_____

SCAN FOR MULTIMEDIA

About the Author

Langston Hughes
(1902–1967) published his
first work just a year after
his high school graduation.
Though he wrote in many
genres, Hughes is best
known for his poetry. He
was one of the main figures
in the Harlem Renaissance,
a creative movement among
African Americans that took
place during the 1920s in
Harlem, an area in New
York City.

Thank You, M'am

Concept Vocabulary

As you perform your first read of "Thank You, M'am," you will encounter
these words.

> permit   release   contact

Context Clues If these words are unfamiliar to you, try using **context
clues** to help you determine their meanings. There are various types of
context clues that you may encounter as you read.

> **Synonyms:** The thieves **purloined** the letter and hid it. The police
> could not find the stolen item for months.
>
> **Restatement of an Idea:** The woman showed **largesse** when she
> donated a large sum of money to the charity.
>
> **Contrast of Ideas:** I did not like the view of the **barren** mountaintop
> because I am used to being surrounded by lush greenery.

Apply your knowledge of context clues and other vocabulary strategies to
determine the meanings of unfamiliar words you encounter during your
first read.

First Read FICTION

Apply these strategies as you conduct your first read. You will have an
opportunity to complete a close read after your first read.

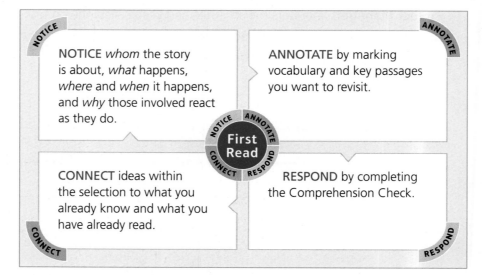

NOTICE *whom* the story is about, *what* happens, *where* and *when* it happens, and *why* those involved react as they do.

ANNOTATE by marking vocabulary and key passages you want to revisit.

CONNECT ideas within the selection to what you already know and what you have already read.

RESPOND by completing the Comprehension Check.

First Read

Copyright © SAVVAS Learning Company LLC. All Rights Reserved.

STANDARDS

Reading Literature
By the end of the year, read and
comprehend literature, including
stories, dramas, and poems, in the
grades 6–8 text complexity band
proficiently, with scaffolding as
needed at the high end of the range.

Language
Use context as a clue to the meaning
of a word or phrase.

Thank You, M'am

Langston Hughes

SCAN FOR MULTIMEDIA

BACKGROUND

In this story, published in 1958, Roger, the protagonist, really wants a pair of blue suede shoes. This particular fashion item became popular after Carl Perkins released his hit song "Blue Suede Shoes" in 1956. Elvis Presley also famously covered the song in the same year.

1 She was a large woman with a large purse that had everything in it but hammer and nails. It had a long strap, and she carried it slung across her shoulder. It was about eleven o'clock at night, dark, and she was walking alone, when a boy ran up behind her and tried to snatch her purse. The strap broke with the sudden single tug the boy gave it from behind. But the boy's weight and the weight of the purse combined caused him to lose his balance. Instead of taking off full blast as he had hoped, the boy fell on his back on the sidewalk and his legs flew up. The large woman simply turned around and kicked him right square in his blue-jeaned sitter. Then she reached down, picked the boy up by his shirt front, and shook him until his teeth rattled.

NOTES

2 After that the woman said, "Pick up my pocketbook, boy, and give it here."

3 She still held him tightly. But she bent down enough to **permit** him to stoop and pick up her purse. Then she said, "Now ain't you ashamed of yourself?"

4 Firmly gripped by his shirt front, the boy said, "Yes'm."

5 The woman said, "What did you want to do it for?"

6 The boy said, "I didn't aim to."

7 She said, "You a lie!"

8 By that time two or three people passed, stopped, turned to look, and some stood watching.

9 "If I turn you loose, will you run?" asked the woman.

10 "Yes'm," said the boy.

11 "Then I won't turn you loose," said the woman. She did not **release** him.

12 "Lady, I'm sorry," whispered the boy.

13 "Um-hum! Your face is dirty. I got a great mind to wash your face for you. Ain't you got nobody home to tell you to wash your face?"

14 "No'm," said the boy.

15 "Then it will get washed this evening," said the large woman starting up the street, dragging the frightened boy behind her.

16 He looked as if he were fourteen or fifteen, frail and willow-wild, in tennis shoes and blue jeans.

17 The woman said, "You ought to be my son. I would teach you right from wrong. Least I can do right now is to wash your face. Are you hungry?"

18 "No'm," said the being-dragged boy. "I just want you to turn me loose."

19 "Was I bothering *you* when I turned that corner?" asked the woman.

20 "No'm."

21 "But you put yourself in **contact** with *me*," said the woman. "If you think that that contact is not going to last awhile, you got another thought coming. When I get through with you, sir, you are going to remember Mrs. Luella Bates Washington Jones."

22 Sweat popped out on the boy's face and he began to struggle. Mrs. Jones stopped, jerked him around in front of her, put a half nelson[1] about his neck, and continued to drag him up the street. When she got to her door, she dragged the boy inside, down a hall, and into a large kitchenette-furnished room at the rear of the house. She switched on the light and left the door open. The boy could hear other roomers laughing and talking in the large house. Some of their doors were open, too, so he knew he and the

---

1. **half nelson** wrestling hold in which an arm is placed under the opponent's armpit from behind with the palm of the hand pressed against the back of the neck.

woman were not alone. The woman still had him by the neck in the middle of her room.

23   She said, "What is your name?"

24   "Roger," answered the boy.

25   "Then, Roger, you go to that sink and wash your face," said the woman, whereupon she turned him loose—at last. Roger looked at the door—looked at the woman—looked at the door—*and went to the sink.*

26   "Let the water run until it gets warm," she said. "Here's a clean towel."

27   "You gonna take me to jail?" asked the boy, bending over the sink.

28   "Not with that face, I would not take you nowhere," said the woman. "Here I am trying to get home to cook me a bite to eat and you snatch my pocketbook! Maybe, you ain't been to your supper either, late as it be. Have you?"

29   "There's nobody home at my house," said the boy.

30   "Then we'll eat," said the woman, "I believe you're hungry—or been hungry—to try to snatch my pocketbook."

31   "I wanted a pair of blue suede shoes," said the boy.

32   "Well, you didn't have to snatch *my* pocketbook to get some suede shoes," said Mrs. Luella Bates Washington Jones. "You could of asked me."

33   "M'am?"

34   The water dripping from his face, the boy looked at her. There was a long pause. A very long pause. After he had dried his face and not knowing what else to do dried it again, the boy turned around, wondering what next. The door was open. He could make a dash for it down the hall. He could run, run, run, *run!*

35   The woman was sitting on the day bed. After a while she said, "I were young once and I wanted things I could not get."

36   There was another long pause. The boy's mouth opened. Then he frowned, not knowing he frowned.

37   The woman said, "Um-hum! You thought I was going to say *but*, didn't you? You thought I was going to say, *but I didn't snatch people's pocketbooks.* Well, I wasn't going to say that." Pause. Silence. "I have done things, too, which I would not tell you, son—neither tell God, if He didn't already know. Everybody's got something in common. So you set down while I fix us something to eat. You might run that comb through your hair so you will look presentable."

38   In another corner of the room behind a screen was a gas plate[2] and an icebox. Mrs. Jones got up and went behind the screen. The woman did not watch the boy to see if he was going to run now, nor did she watch her purse, which she left behind her on the day

---

2. **gas plate** hot plate heated by gas that is used for cooking.

bed. But the boy took care to sit on the far side of the room, away from her purse, where he thought she could easily see him out of the corner of her eye if she wanted to. He did not trust the woman *not* to trust him. And he did not want to be mistrusted now.

39   "Do you need somebody to go to the store," asked the boy, "maybe to get some milk or something?"

40   "Don't believe I do," said the woman, "unless you just want sweet milk yourself. I was going to make cocoa out of this canned milk I got here."

41   "That will be fine," said the boy.

42   She heated some lima beans and ham she had in the icebox, made the cocoa, and set the table. The woman did not ask the boy anything about where he lived, or his folks, or anything else that would embarrass him. Instead, as they ate, she told him about her job in a hotel beauty-shop that stayed open late, what the work was like, and how all kinds of women came in and out, blondes, redheads, and Spanish. Then she cut him a half of her ten-cent cake.

43   "Eat some more, son," she said.

44   When they were finished eating she got up and said, "Now, here, take this ten dollars and buy yourself some blue suede shoes. And next time, do not make the mistake of latching onto *my* pocketbook *nor nobody else's*—because shoes got by devilish ways will burn your feet. I got to get my rest now. But from here on in, son, I hope you will behave yourself."

45   She led him down the hall to the front door and opened it. "Good night! Behave yourself, boy!" she said, looking out into the street.

46   The boy wanted to say something else other than "Thank you, m'am" to Mrs. Luella Bates Washington Jones, but although his lips moved, he couldn't even say that as he turned at the foot of the barren stoop and looked up at the large woman in the door. Then she shut the door. ❧

Comprehension Check

Complete the following items after you finish your first read. Review and clarify details with your group.

1. How do Mrs. Jones and Roger meet?

2. What does Roger expect Mrs. Jones to do?

3. What does Mrs. Jones do instead?

4. 📓 **Notebook** Confirm your understanding of the story by drawing a storyboard of key events.

- -

RESEARCH

Research to Clarify Research a topic that you think will help you better understand this story. For instance, you might want to learn more about its author, Langston Hughes. In what way does the information you learned shed light on the story? Share your findings with your group.

THANK YOU, M'AM

Close Read the Text

With your group, revisit sections of the text you marked during your first read. **Annotate** details that you notice. What **questions** do you have? What can you **conclude**?

Analyze the Text

CITE TEXTUAL EVIDENCE
to support your answers.

Complete the activities.

1. **Review and Clarify** With your group, reread paragraph 38 of the story. Why doesn't Roger want to be mistrusted?

2. **Present and Discuss** Now, work with your group to share the passages from the text that you found especially important. Take turns presenting your passages. Discuss what you noticed in the text, the questions you asked, and the conclusions you reached.

3. **Essential Question: *What can cause a sudden change in someone's life?*** What has this story taught you about the kinds of events, actions, and people that can cause a change in someone's life? Discuss with your group.

LANGUAGE DEVELOPMENT

Concept Vocabulary

permit	release	contact

Why These Words? The concept vocabulary words from the text are related. With your group, determine what the words have in common. Record your ideas, and add another word that fits the category.

Practice

📓 **Notebook** Confirm your understanding of these words by using each word in a sentence. Be sure to use context clues that hint at each word's meaning. Use a dictionary to verify your understanding of each word.

Word Study

Multiple-Meaning Words Many words have more than one meaning. If you are not sure of the meaning of a multiple-meaning word, use context clues to make an educated guess. Then, confirm the word's meaning in a dictionary.

All three concept vocabulary words are multiple-meaning words. First, write the meaning of each word as it is used in the story. Then, use a dictionary to find at least two other meanings for each word.

TIP

GROUP DISCUSSION

When you work in your group to answer the Analyze the Text questions, be sure to direct listeners to specific words, sentences, and paragraphs in the story.

🔧 WORD NETWORK

Add interesting words related to turning points from the text to your Word Network.

☰ STANDARDS

Language
Determine or clarify the meaning of unknown and multiple-meaning words and phrases based on *grade 7 reading and content*, choosing flexibly from a range of strategies.
  c. Consult general and specialized reference materials, both print and digital, to find the pronunciation of a word or determine or clarify its precise meaning or its part of speech.
  d. Verify the preliminary determination of the meaning of a word or phrase.

ESSENTIAL QUESTION: What can cause a change in someone's life?

Thank You, M'am **321**

Analyze Craft and Structure

Elements of a Short Story: Plot Plot is the related sequence of events in a story. Each event in the plot moves the story forward. A plot has the following elements:

- **Exposition:** introduction of the characters, the setting, and the basic situation
- **Rising Action:** events that introduce a **conflict,** or struggle, and increase the tension; may also include events that explain characters' past actions
- **Climax:** the story's high point, or moment of greatest intensity; often a turning point in the story at which the eventual outcome becomes clear
- **Falling Action:** events that follow the climax
- **Resolution:** the story's final outcome and tying up of loose ends

This diagram will help you to visualize the sequence of plot elements.

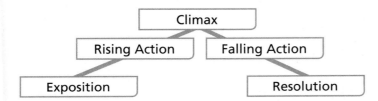

:≡ STANDARDS

Reading Literature
- Cite several pieces of textual evidence to support analysis of what the text says explicitly as well as inferences drawn from the text.
- Analyze how particular elements of a story or drama interact.

Practice

CITE TEXTUAL EVIDENCE to support your answers.

Work with your group to fill in this graphic organizer by identifying the elements of plot in "Thank You, M'am."

PLOT ELEMENT	LOCATION IN "THANK YOU, M'AM"
Exposition	
Rising Action	
Climax	
Falling Action	
Resolution	

📓 **Notebook As a group, respond to the following questions.**

1. **(a)** Identify two plot events that increase the tension between Mrs. Jones and Roger. **(b)** How does this tension contribute to the rising action in the story?

2. What clues in the story enabled you to identify the climax, or turning point?

3. Do you think the story's resolution provides a sense of satisfaction for the reader? Why or why not?

THANK YOU, M'AM

Conventions

Prepositions and Prepositional Phrases A **preposition** relates a noun or a pronoun that follows it to another word in the sentence. Some commonly used prepositions include *at, after, between, for, in, of, on, to, through,* and *with*.

> **EXAMPLE:** The book is <u>on</u> the table.
> The preposition *on* relates the noun *table* to another word in the sentence, *book*.

A **prepositional phrase** begins with a preposition and ends with a noun or pronoun—called the **object of the preposition.**

> **EXAMPLE:** The book is <u>on the table</u>.
> The prepositional phrase *on the table* begins with the preposition *on* and ends with the noun *table,* which is the object of the preposition.

Read It

Work with your group to identify examples of prepositions and prepositional phrases in "Thank You, M'am." Write your examples in the chart. Mark the prepositional phrases, as shown in Example 1.

EXAMPLE 1	*She was a large woman <u>with a large purse</u> that had everything <u>in it</u> but hammer and nails.*
EXAMPLE 2	
EXAMPLE 3	
EXAMPLE 4	

Write It

📓 **Notebook** Write a paragraph in which you describe someone who has had a positive impact on your life. Correctly use at least three prepositional phrases in your paragraph. Mark the object of the preposition in each phrase.

STANDARDS

Language
Demonstrate command of the conventions of standard English grammar and usage when writing or speaking.
  a. Explain the function of phrases and clauses in general and their function in specific sentences.

Writing to Sources

In real life, you can often understand a situation better by putting yourself in someone else's shoes. Similarly, when reading a work of fiction, you can often deepen your understanding of the work by considering the points of view of different characters.

> **Assignment**
>
> Use your imagination and details from "Thank You, M'am" to write a **journal entry** about events in the story from the point of view of one of the characters, either Roger or Mrs. Jones. In your journal entry, focus on one of the following:
>
> ☐ Mrs. Jones's perspective on meeting Roger
>
> ☐ Roger's perspective on meeting Mrs. Jones
>
> Consider the following questions as you write: What feelings would he or she be likely to express in a journal entry about the experience? What words would he or she use? Refer to details in the story to accurately convey the point of view and personality of the character you chose.

Project Plan Before you begin, decide as a group whether you want to write a journal entry from the point of view of Roger or Mrs. Jones. Make a list of the tasks you will need to complete to fulfill the assignment. Decide how you will organize the work. Then, appoint individual group members to each task.

Clarifying Ideas and Evidence Brainstorm your impressions of Mrs. Jones or Roger. What are they thinking? What are their impressions of each other? What sensory details do you want to include? Use your own imagination and evidence from the text to support your ideas.

Use Transitions Use transitions to show shifts in time or setting in your journal entry. Transition words, phrases, and clauses, such as *meanwhile, while Roger waited, afterwards,* and *all of a sudden*, will help to show the connection between the events you describe as well as the differences between your memories of events and your current reflections on them.

Present After you have completed your journal entry, present your finished work to the class. Make sure all group members have a role to play in the presentation.

Discuss and Reflect Pay close attention and take notes as you listen to the presentations of other groups. When all the groups are done presenting, briefly discuss your thoughts with your group. Are there any ideas that were used by multiple groups? Are there any ideas from other groups' presentations that impressed you? Is there anything you would do differently next time?

📝 EVIDENCE LOG

Before moving on to a new selection, go to your Evidence and record what you learned from "Thank You M'am."

STANDARDS

Writing
Write narratives to develop real or imagined experiences or events using effective technique, relevant descriptive details, and well-structured event sequences.
a. Engage and orient the reader by establishing a context and point of view and introducing a narrator and/or characters; organize an event sequence that unfolds naturally and logically.
c. Use a variety of transition words, phrases, and clauses to convey sequence and signal shifts from one time frame or setting to another.
d. Use precise words and phrases, relevant descriptive details, and sensory language to capture the action and convey experiences and events.

Speaking and Listening
Engage effectively in a range of collaborative discussions with diverse partners on *grade 7 topics, texts, and issues,* building on others' ideas and expressing their own clearly.
b. Follow rules for collegial discussions, track progress toward specific goals and deadlines, and define individual roles as needed.
d. Acknowledge new information expressed by others and, when warranted, modify their own views.

About the Author

Annie Dillard (b.1945) published her memoir, *An American Childhood,* in 1987. Dillard's memoir describes her experiences growing up in Pittsburgh, Pennsylvania, during the 1950s. A Pulitzer Prize winner, Dillard received the National Humanities Award from President Barack Obama in 2015.

from An American Childhood

Technical Vocabulary

You will encounter the following words as you read the excerpt from *An American Childhood.*

tissue	enlarged	amoeba

Base Words If these words are unfamiliar to you, analyze each one to see whether it contains a **base word**, or "inside" word, that you know. Then, use your knowledge of the "inside" word, along with context, to determine the meaning of the technical vocabulary word. Here is an example of how to apply the strategy.

> **Unfamiliar Word:** *research*
>
> **Familiar "Inside" Word:** *search*
>
> **Context:** The scientist was celebrated for her *research* in microscopic organisms.
>
> **Conclusion:** Scientists study how things work. Because "search" is in the word *research*, the scientist may have been celebrated for the information she "searched for," or found out, about microscopic organisms.

Apply your knowledge of base words and other vocabulary strategies to determine the meanings of unfamiliar words you encounter during your first read.

First Read NONFICTION

Apply these strategies as you conduct your first read. You will have an opportunity to complete a close read after your first read.

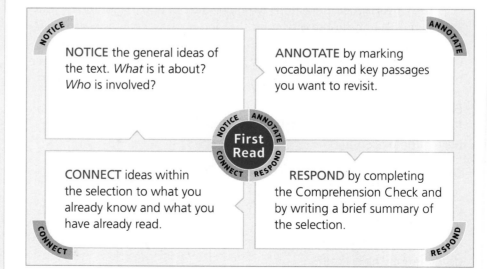

NOTICE the general ideas of the text. *What* is it about? *Who* is involved?

ANNOTATE by marking vocabulary and key passages you want to revisit.

CONNECT ideas within the selection to what you already know and what you have already read.

RESPOND by completing the Comprehension Check and by writing a brief summary of the selection.

STANDARDS

Reading Informational Text
By the end of the year, read and comprehend literary nonfiction in the grades 6–8 text complexity band proficiently, with scaffolding as needed at the high end of the range.

Language
Use the relationship between particular words to better understand each of the words.

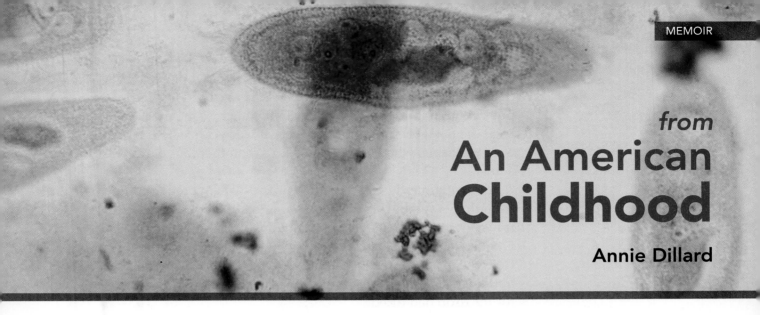

from

An American Childhood

Annie Dillard

BACKGROUND

In the beginning of the excerpt, Annie Dillard mentions *The Field Book of Ponds and Streams*, which sparked her curiosity in microscopes and science. Published in 1930, this text became an important resource for anyone interested in learning about plants and animals in freshwater environments. The book is typically praised for the instructive photographs and drawings it contains, and remains popular today.

SCAN FOR MULTIMEDIA

1   After I read *The Field Book of Ponds and Streams* several times, I longed for a microscope. Everybody needed a microscope. Detectives used microscopes, both for the FBI and at Scotland Yard. Although usually I had to save my tiny allowance for things I wanted, that year for Christmas my parents gave me a microscope kit.

2   In a dark basement corner, on a white enamel table, I set up the microscope kit. I supplied a chair, a lamp, a batch of jars, a candle, and a pile of library books. The microscope kit supplied a blunt black three-speed microscope, a booklet, a scalpel, a dropper, an ingenious device for cutting thin segments of fragile **tissue**, a pile of clean slides and cover slips, and a dandy array of corked test tubes.

3   One of the test tubes contained "hay infusion." Hay infusion was a wee brown chip of grass blade. You added water to it, and after a week it became a jungle in a drop, full of one-celled animals. This did not work for me. All I saw in the microscope after a week was a wet chip of dried grass, much **enlarged**.

4   Another test tube contained "diatomaceous earth." This was, I believed, an actual pinch of the white cliffs of Dover. On my palm it was an airy, friable[1] chalk. The booklet said it was composed of the silicaceous[2] bodies of diatoms—one-celled creatures that lived in, as it were, small glass jewelry boxes with fitted lids. Diatoms, I read, come in a variety of transparent

---

1. **friable** (FRY uh buhl) *adj.* easy to crumble.
2. **silicaceous** (sihl ih KAY shee uhs) *adj.* made of silica, like sand.

NOTES

Mark base words or indicate another strategy you used that helped you determine meaning.

tissue (TIHSH oo) *n.*
MEANING:

enlarged (ehn LAHRJD) *adj.*
MEANING:

geometrical shapes. Broken and dead and dug out of geological deposits, they made chalk, and a fine abrasive used in silver polish and toothpaste. What I saw in the microscope must have been the fine abrasive—grit enlarged. It was years before I saw a recognizable, whole diatom. The kit's diatomaceous earth was a bust.

5   All that winter I played with the microscope. I prepared slides from things at hand, as the books suggested. I looked at the transparent membrane inside an onion's skin and saw the cells. I looked at a section of cork and saw the cells, and at scrapings from the inside of my cheek, ditto. I looked at my blood and saw not much; I looked at my urine and saw long iridescent crystals, for the drop had dried.

6   All this was very well, but I wanted to see the wildlife I had read about. I wanted especially to see the famous amoeba, who had eluded me. He was supposed to live in the hay infusion, but I hadn't found him there. He lived outside in warm ponds and streams, too, but I lived in Pittsburgh, and it had been a cold winter.

7   Finally late that spring I saw an amoeba. The week before, I had gathered puddle water from Frick Park; it had been festering in a jar in the basement. This June night after dinner I figured I had waited long enough. In the basement at my microscope table I spread a scummy drop of Frick Park puddle water on a slide, peeked in, and lo, there was the famous amoeba. He was as blobby and grainy as his picture; I would have known him anywhere.

8   Before I had watched him at all, I ran upstairs. My parents were still at the table, drinking coffee. They, too, could see the famous amoeba. I told them, bursting, that he was all set up, that they should hurry before his water dried. It was the chance of a lifetime.

9   Father had stretched out his long legs and was tilting back in his chair. Mother sat with her knees crossed, in blue slacks, smoking a Chesterfield. The dessert dishes were still on the table. My sisters were nowhere in evidence. It was a warm evening; the big dining-room windows gave onto blooming rhododendrons.

10   Mother regarded me warmly. She gave me to understand that she was glad I had found what I had been looking for, but that she and Father were happy to sit with their coffee, and would not be coming down.

11   She did not say, but I understood at once, that they had their pursuits (coffee?) and I had mine. She did not say, but I began to understand then, that you do what you do out of your private passion for the thing itself.

12   I had essentially been handed my own life. In subsequent years my parents would praise my drawings and poems, and supply

Mark base words or indicate another strategy you used that helped you determine meaning.

amoeba (uh MEE buh) *n.*

MEANING:

me with books, art supplies, and sports equipment, and listen to my troubles and enthusiasms, and supervise my hours, and discuss and inform, but they would not get involved with my detective work, nor hear about my reading, nor inquire about my homework or term papers or exams, nor visit the salamanders I caught, nor listen to me play the piano, nor attend my field hockey games, nor fuss over my insect collection with me, or my poetry collection or stamp collection or rock collection. My days and nights were my own to plan and fill.

13   When I left the dining room that evening and started down the dark basement stairs, I had a life. I sat with my wonderful amoeba, and there he was, rolling his grains more slowly now, extending an arc of his edge for a foot and drawing himself along by that foot, and absorbing it again and rolling on. I gave him some more pond water.

14   I had hit pay dirt. For all I knew, there were paramecia, too, in that pond water, or daphniae, or stentors, or any of the many other creatures I had read about and never seen: volvox, the spherical algal colony; euglena with its one red eye; the elusive, glassy diatom; hydra, rotifers, water bears, worms. Anything was possible. The sky was the limit. ❧

Comprehension Check

Complete the following items after you finish your first read. Review and clarify details with your group.

1. What does Dillard most want to see through her microscope?

2. How do Dillard's parents react when she tells them what she discovered when looking through her microscope?

3. 🖥 **Notebook** Confirm your understanding of the text by writing a summary. Your summary should include Dillard's main points, but it should not include your own opinions of the memoir.

- -

RESEARCH

Research to Clarify Choose at least one unfamiliar scientific detail mentioned in the memoir. Briefly research that detail, and share your findings with your group.

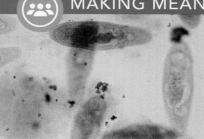

from AN AMERICAN CHILDHOOD

TIP

GROUP DISCUSSION

When you work in your group to answer the Analyze the Text questions, be sure to support your opinions and ideas with evidence from the text.

 WORD NETWORK

Add interesting words related to turning points from the text to your Word Network.

STANDARDS

Language
• Determine or clarify the meaning of unknown and multiple-meaning words and phrases based on *grade 7 reading and content*, choosing flexibly from a range of strategies.
 d. Verify the preliminary determination of the meaning of a word or phrase.
• Demonstrate understanding of figurative language, word relationships, and nuances in word meanings.
 b. Use the relationship between particular words to better understand each of the words.

Close Read the Text

With your group, revisit sections of the text you marked during your first read. What do you **notice**? What **questions** do you have? What can you **conclude**?

Analyze the Text

CITE TEXTUAL EVIDENCE to support your answers.

Complete the activities.

1. **Review and Clarify** With your group, reread paragraphs 7–14 of the excerpt. What happens that leads the narrator to a realization about life? What does she realize? How does this realization affect her?

2. **Present and Discuss** Now, work with your group to share the passages from the text that you found especially important.

3. **Essential Question:** *What can cause a sudden change in someone's life?* What does the memoir reveal about the ways in which a experience can change someone's life? Discuss.

LANGUAGE DEVELOPMENT

Technical Vocabulary

tissue	enlarged	amoeba

Why These Words? The technical vocabulary words from the text are related. With your group, determine what the words have in common. Write your ideas, and add another word that fits the category.

Practice

📓 **Notebook** Confirm your understanding of these words by verifying their meanings in a dictionary. Then, use each word in a sentence. Be sure to include context clues that reveal the words' meanings in your sentences.

Word Study

Prefix: *en-* The prefix *en-* is often used to turn nouns or adjectives into verbs. In the memoir, Annie Dillard writes about how she used her microscope to see small organisms *enlarged*, or "made larger." The word *large* is an adjective used to describe the size of something. Adding the prefix *en-* to the word *large* creates the verb *enlarge*, which means "to make larger or bigger." For each of the following words, determine how the prefix *en-* turns the base word into a verb, and write a definition for each verb based on your understanding of the meaning of the adjective or noun: *enable, enact, endanger.*

Analyze Craft and Structure

Reflective Writing A **reflective essay** is a short work of nonfiction that expresses an author's thoughts and feelings—or reflections—about an experience or idea. The purpose of reflective writing is to spark readers to respond to the author's ideas with thoughts and feelings of their own.

In a reflective essay, an author typically develops his or her **central ideas**, or most important points, through details about individuals, events, and ideas. Although an author may sometimes state his or her central ideas directly, often the reader must **make inferences**, or educated guesses, based on the details in the text. To do so, notice how the author groups details, and look for sentences or passages that pull these details together.

As you read a reflective essay, think about the thoughts and feelings the author shares and analyze interactions among individuals, events, and ideas. Use the details you notice in your analysis to determine the central ideas.

≣ STANDARDS

Reading Informational Text
• Cite several pieces of textual evidence to support analysis of what the text says explicitly as well as inferences drawn from the text.
• Determine two or more central ideas in a text and analyze their development over the course of the text; provide an objective summary of the text.
• Analyze the interactions between individuals, events, and ideas in a text.

Practice

CITE TEXTUAL EVIDENCE
to support your answers.

📝 **Notebook** Reread the excerpt from *An American Childhood*, and work with your group to analyze the memoir. Use a chart, such as the one shown, to guide your analysis and record your ideas. Then, answer the questions that follow.

PARAGRAPHS	INTERACTIONS	DILLARD'S THOUGHTS AND FEELINGS	MY THOUGHTS AND FEELINGS
1–7			
8–11			
12–14			

1. **(a)** Based on your analysis, what is one of the central ideas in the excerpt from *An American Childhood*? **(b)** What might be another central idea Dillard explores in the excerpt? **(c)** What specific details helped you to identify the central ideas?
2. After analyzing the excerpt, do you feel that Dillard achieved her purpose in writing a reflective piece? Why or why not?

from AN AMERICAN
CHILDHOOD

Conventions

Appositives and Appositive Phrases An **appositive** is a noun or pronoun placed next to another noun or pronoun to identify, rename, or explain it.

An **appositive phrase** is an appositive with modifiers, such as adjectives.

APPOSITIVE	APPOSITIVE PHRASE
Our cat, Midnight, likes to sleep on my bed.	Karina—a talented violinist—played a solo.

If the information in an appositive or appositive phrase is essential to understanding the sentence, *do not* set it off with commas or dashes.

EXAMPLE: Have you read the story "Fish Cheeks"?

If the sentence is clear without the information in the appositive or appositive phrase, *do* use commas or dashes to set it off.

EXAMPLE: The author of that story, Amy Tan, is one of my favorites.

Read It

Work with your group to identify examples of appositives and appositive phrases in the selection. Then, discuss Annie Dillard's purpose for including them. Did the appositives and appositive phrases provide useful information to help you understand unfamiliar words or technical terms? Did the information add to your understanding of the excerpt as a whole?

Appositive or Appositive Phrase From the Selection	Noun or Pronoun It Identifies, Renames, or Explains

Write It

📓 **Notebook** Write a paragraph about something in which you are an expert. It could be a type of music, a sport, or a hobby. In your paragraph, use appositives and appositive phrases to help readers understand unfamiliar or technical words, as well as specific references to books or Web sites with which they may be unfamiliar. Use commas or dashes as necessary.

⊞ STANDARDS

Language
• Demonstrate command of the conventions of standard English grammar and usage when writing or speaking.
  a. Explain the function of phrases and clauses in general and their function in specific sentences.
• Demonstrate command of the conventions of standard English capitalization, punctuation, and spelling when writing.

Speaking and Listening

Assignment

With your group, engage in a **collaborative discussion** in response to one of these questions:

- [ ] What are the advantages and disadvantages of pursuing an interest on your own, without supervision?
- [ ] What are the advantages and disadvantages of sharing hobbies and interests with family or friends?

Project Plan Assign a role to each member of your group. Roles can include a group leader, who keeps the discussion on topic; a timekeeper, who makes sure that the discussion stays within the time alloted by your teacher; and a note taker to record the group's ideas.

Gather Support Work with your group to identify evidence from the excerpt as well as examples from your own experience that support your responses to the question your group chose to discuss. Create a T-chart to list the pros and cons, or advantages and disadvantages, for your topic.

Discuss Here are some things to keep in mind as you hold your group discussion.

- Use the information you noted in the T-chart as well as your own experiences to support your ideas during the discussion.
- Consider the strength of each pro and con. Just because one position has more items does not necessarily mean it is better supported.
- During the discussion, be respectful of others' opinions even if they are different from your own. Express disagreement respectfully by offering **constructive criticism**, or well-reasoned opinions that include both the positive and negative aspects of another group member's contributions. This type of criticism is most likely to persuade another person to adopt your viewpoint, or opinion.
- If a group member provides new information or insights, consider whether this new knowledge changes your views and opinions on the topic.
- Ensure every group member has an opportunity to contribute to the discussion. If you don't fully understand the ideas another group member expresses, ask a question that will help that person elaborate on the ideas he or she expressed.

✎ EVIDENCE LOG

Before moving on to a new selection, go to your Evidence Log and record what you learned from the excerpt from *An American Childhood*.

☰ STANDARDS

Speaking and Listening
Engage effectively in a range of collaborative discussions with diverse partners on *grade 7 topics, texts, and issues,* building on others' ideas and expressing their own clearly.

a. Come to discussions prepared, having read or researched material under study; explicitly draw on that preparation by referring to evidence on the topic, text, or issue to probe and reflect on ideas under discussion.
b. Follow rules for collegial discussions, track progress toward specific goals and deadlines, and define individual roles as needed.
c. Pose questions that elicit elaboration and respond to others' questions and comments with relevant observations and ideas that bring the discussion back on topic as needed.
d. Acknowledge new information expressed by others and, when warranted, modify their own views.

About the Author

Hillary Schwei (b. 1980) studied Sustainable Food and Farming at Rutgers University and the University of Montana–Missoula and has worked on various urban gardening and farming programs, both in the United States and abroad. Schwei's belief that sustainable food production reconnects us to our environment and our communities informs her work with urban youth. She strives to educate young people about the benefits that urban, local food production can provide to the communities in which they live.

Urban Farming Is Growing a Greener Future

Concept Vocabulary

These words will be useful to you as you analyze, discuss, and write about the photographs.

rural: characteristic of the country; of or pertaining to agriculture
EXAMPLE: The family moved from a busy city to a quiet **rural** neighborhood surrounded by farms.
agricultural: related to the science and art of farming
EXAMPLE: A lot of the **agricultural** land that used to surround the town has been turned from cornfields into houses and stores.
localizing: gathering, collecting, or concentrating in a particular place
EXAMPLE: **Localizing** food production helps to provide consumers with fresher produce because the produce comes from places near where they live.

First Review MEDIA: ART AND PHOTOGRAPHY

Study the photographs using these strategies.

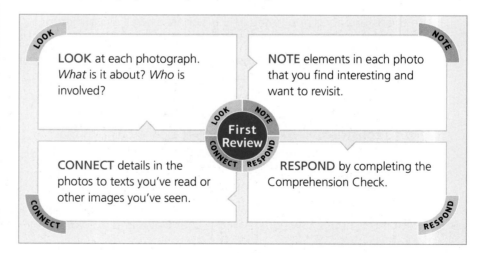

LOOK at each photograph. *What* is it about? *Who* is involved?

NOTE elements in each photo that you find interesting and want to revisit.

CONNECT details in the photos to texts you've read or other images you've seen.

RESPOND by completing the Comprehension Check.

First Review — LOOK — NOTE — CONNECT — RESPOND

STANDARDS

Reading Informational Text
By the end of the year, read and comprehend literary nonfiction in the grades 6–8 text complexity band proficiently, with scaffolding as needed at the high end of the range.

Language
Acquire and use accurately grade-appropriate general academic and domain-specific words and phrases; gather vocabulary knowledge when considering a word or phrase important to comprehension or expression.

Urban Farming Is Growing a Greener Future

Hillary Schwei

BACKGROUND

The year 2008 marked the first time that more people on Earth lived in cities than in **rural** areas. One significant consequence of this turning point is that most people no longer live in the **agricultural** areas that provide them with food.

Some city dwellers are transforming their concrete environments by establishing farms, often in the most unlikely locations. These urban farms create a new landscape that adapts the man-made structures of the city to the purposes of sustainable food production. **Localizing** food production through urban farming provides aesthetic, health, environmental, and economic benefits. Locally grown food not only supplies people with fresh, seasonal produce, but it also strengthens local economies by supporting family farmers and other local businesses. Farming in urban areas reduces the need to transport food over long distances to reach the consumer. The decrease in transportation creates environmental advantages such as lower levels of pollution and decreased fossil fuel use. This photo gallery provides a glimpse at unique and innovative urban farming projects.

PHOTO 1: Urban farms are not a new idea. During both world wars, the government encouraged Americans to plant Victory Gardens where they could grow their own food. Here, in 1943, children work in a garden in New York City.

PHOTO 2: Urban farms can make use of vacant city lots that are often considered **eyesores**, or ugly, unpleasant sights in public places. The farms become not only a source of food and beauty, but provide a location for members of the community to gather. An area of neglected, polluted land next to a railway station in Perth, Australia, has been revived as an organic farm.

NOTES

PHOTO 3: New York City will never completely return to its long-lost agricultural origins, but in 2011, this midtown hotel began growing fruit, vegetables, and herbs on the building's roof to supply the hotel's kitchen. The hotel also keeps honeybees, which roam for miles pollinating city plants.

NOTES

PHOTO 4: Only 12 percent of Japan's land is suitable for agriculture, but in this company's headquarters in Tokyo, office workers can take time to cultivate produce. One-fifth of the nine-story building is devoted to farming.

NOTES

PHOTO 5: Urban farming, like traditional farming, is a year-round operation. The greenhouses at this farm in Chicago have to be maintained regardless of the season. Each acre of the farm produces 20,000 pounds of produce annually.

NOTES

PHOTO 6: This 30-year-old pickup truck is a mobile farm and travels around giving students in city schools a chance to experience how food grows. The farmers who own the truck made a film about their exploits and strive to support others who grow produce in creative ways.

NOTES

NOTES

Comprehension Check

The selection uses both words and photographs to provide information about urban farming. Use the chart below to note specific details about each photo. Then, describe how each photo relates to the text that accompanies it.

PHOTO	WHAT THE PHOTO SHOWS	HOW THE PHOTO RELATES TO THE TEXT
PHOTO 1 		
PHOTO 2 		
PHOTO 3 		
PHOTO 4 		
PHOTO 5 		
PHOTO 6 		

URBAN FARMING IS GROWING A GREENER FUTURE

Close Review

With your group, revisit the selection and your first-review notes. Write any new observations that seem important. What **questions** do you have? What can you **conclude**?

- -

Analyze the Media

CITE TEXTUAL EVIDENCE to support your answers.

📓 **Notebook** Complete the activities.

1. **Present and Discuss** Choose the photo you found most interesting or powerful. Explain what you noticed in the photo, the questions it raised for you, and the conclusions you reached about it.

2. **Review and Synthesize** With your group, review all the photos. In what ways do they increase your understanding of the information communicated in the text?

3. **Essential Question:** *What can cause a sudden change in someone's life?* What has this selection taught you about turning points? Discuss with your group.

🔗 WORD NETWORK

Add interesting words related to turning points from the text to your Word Network.

▤ STANDARDS

Writing
• Use technology, including the Internet, to produce and publish writing and link to and cite sources as well as to interact and collaborate with others, including linking to and citing sources.
• Conduct short research projects to answer a question, drawing on several sources and generating additional related, focused questions for further research and investigation.
• Gather relevant information from multiple print and digital sources, using search terms effectively; assess the credibility and accuracy of each source; and quote or paraphrase the data and conclusions of others while avoiding plagiarism and following a standard format for citation.

Speaking and Listening
• Analyze the main ideas and supporting details presented in diverse media and formats and explain how the ideas clarify a topic, text, or issue under study.
• Include multimedia components and visual displays in presentations to clarify claims and findings and emphasize salient points.

LANGUAGE DEVELOPMENT

Concept Vocabulary

Use the concept vocabulary words in your responses to the following questions.

rural	agricultural	localizing

1. What turning point is described in the background information for this selection?

2. Identify at least one thing that all of the images have in common.

3. Did the photo gallery change your views on what types of changes can be considered "turning points"? Why or why not? Explain the reasons for your response.

Research

Copyright © SAVVAS Learning Company LLC. All Rights Reserved.

Assignment

Work in your group to research and create a **digital multimedia presentation** on one of the following topics:

☐ urban farms and community gardens in your area

☐ how to start an urban farm or community garden

☐ the health and environmental benefits of urban farming

☐ where the food used in your school cafeteria comes from and how many "food miles" it travels ("Food miles" is the distance food travels from where it is grown to where it is consumed.)

Focus Your Research Begin by working with your group to formulate a research question to guide and focus your search for sources. A focused research question will also help you avoid sources that are not useful to your topic. Consider the following example:

topic: turning points in modern American literature

vague research question: What are works of American literature that discuss turning points?

revised research question: What new American short stories explore the theme of turning points?

Plan the Project Use the questions in the chart to prepare your presentation. Record your notes in the right column of the chart.

What relevant, reliable print, digital, and multimedia sources can you use in your research? Take notes on the information you obtain from each source. Your final presentation should include a digital Works-Cited list with electronic links to Internet sources.	
What information will be better conveyed by text?	
What information will be better conveyed by images?	
What information will be better conveyed by spoken word, music, or sound?	

TIP

GROUP DISCUSSION

With your group, consider the relationships among your visuals. Should they have a similar look or can they differ? If you decide they should be uniform, how can you achieve that?

✎ EVIDENCE LOG

Before moving on to a new selection, go to your Evidence Log and record what you learned from "Urban Farming Is Growing a Greener Future."

SOURCES

• THANK YOU, M'AM

• *from* AN AMERICAN CHILDHOOD

• URBAN FARMING IS GROWING A GREENER FUTURE

Present an Explanatory Essay

Assignment

With your group, review the selections you have read in this section, and consider the ways the different turning points are described in the selections. Then, present an **explanatory essay in the form of a multimedia presentation** in response to the following prompt:

> How are the turning points in the selections similar to and different from each other?

Use images and other multimedia to emphasize and clarify key points in your presentation.

Plan With Your Group

Analyze the Text With your group, analyze the ways in which the turning points in the selections are similar to and different from each other. Use this chart to organize your ideas about what each text says about turning points and their significance.

SELECTION	What led to the turning point?	Details that describe the turning point	What was the significance of the turning point?
Thank You, M'am			
from An American Childhood			
Urban Farming Is Growing a Greener Future			

Gather Details and Media Each group member should then choose one selection on which he or she will focus for the presentation. Work individually to gather details and information about the turning point in the selection you chose. Next, organize your ideas and draft a brief explanatory essay for your section of the presentation. Your essay should compare and contrast the turning point in the selection you chose to the turning points in the other selections in this section. Then, conduct research to find relevant multimedia to include in your presentation.

Organize Your Ideas As a group, organize the sections of the presentation and decide how you will transition smoothly from one section to the next and one speaker to the next. How will you tie all the information and ideas back together at the end of your presentation?

≡ STANDARDS

Writing
Write informative/explanatory texts to examine a topic and convey ideas, concepts, and information through the selection, organization, and analysis of relevant content.

Rehearse With Your Group

Practice With Your Group Before you deliver your presentation, rehearse the presentation as a group. Plan the ways in which you will present your multimedia elements: Will you hold up images or prop them against something, or will you present your information digitally? Practice delivering the presentation using a formal tone, appropriate eye contact, adequate volume, and clear pronunciation.

As you deliver your portion of the presentation, use this checklist to evaluate the effectiveness of your group's rehearsal. Then, use your evaluation and the instruction here to guide your revisions to the presentation.

CONTENT	USE OF MEDIA	PRESENTATION TECHNIQUES
☐ The presentation clearly responds to the prompt.	☐ The presentation includes a variety of multimedia.	☐ The speaker uses a formal tone and speaks with adequate volume and clear pronunciation.
☐ The presentation includes relevant details from the text.	☐ The multimedia emphasizes and clarifies key points.	☐ The speaker maintains eye contact with the audience.
☐ The presentation effectively compares and contrasts the turning points in the selections.		

Fine-Tune the Content Put yourself in the position of a person hearing the presentation for the first time. Is there anything he or she might not understand? If so, try restating unclear ideas in several ways to see what way works best.

Improve Your Use of Media Be sure to sequence your multimedia elements in a way that emphasizes your key points. Each piece of multimedia should relate directly to a key point in your presentation and should help your audience to better understand the information.

Brush Up on Your Presentation Techniques Take turns presenting with your group members. Point out places where the speaker may sound flat, be too quiet, or lack clarity.

Present and Evaluate

As you listen to other groups, consider their content, use of media, and presentation techniques. Be ready to ask questions, and discuss the ways in which other groups' presentations helped deepen your understanding of the ways in which turning points impact people's lives.

STANDARDS

Speaking and Listening
• Engage effectively in a range of collaborative discussions with diverse partners on *grade 7 topics, texts, and issues,* building on others' ideas and expressing their own clearly.
• Analyze the main ideas and supporting details presented in diverse media and formats and explain how the ideas clarify a topic, text, or issue under study.
• Present claims and findings, emphasizing salient points in a focused, coherent manner with pertinent descriptions, facts, details, and examples; use appropriate eye contact, adequate volume, and clear pronunciation.
• Include multimedia components and visual displays in presentations to clarify claims and findings and emphasize salient points.
• Adapt speech to a variety of contexts and tasks, demonstrating command of formal English when indicated or appropriate.

ESSENTIAL QUESTION:

What can cause a sudden change in someone's life?

A sudden change in a person's life may come from an inner realization or it may be a result of external forces, such as the actions of others or the environment that surrounds that person. In this section, you will complete your study of turning points by exploring an additional selection related to the topic. You'll then share what you learn with classmates. To choose a text, follow these steps.

Look Back Think about the selections you have already studied. What most interests you about the topic of turning points?

Look Ahead Preview the texts by reading the descriptions. Which one seems most interesting and appealing to you?

Look Inside Take a few minutes to scan through the text you chose. Choose a different one if this text doesn't meet your needs.

Independent Learning Strategies

Throughout your life, in school, in your community, and in your career, you will need to rely on yourself to learn and work on your own. Review these strategies and the actions you can take to practice them during Independent Learning. Add ideas of your own for each category.

STRATEGY	ACTION PLAN
Create a schedule	• Understand your goals and deadlines. • Make a plan for what to do each day. •
Practice what you have learned	• Use first-read and close-read strategies to deepen your understanding. • After you read, evaluate the usefulness of the evidence to help you understand the topic. • Consider the quality and reliability of the source. •
Take notes	• Record important ideas and information. • Review notes before preparing to share with a group. •

SCAN FOR
MULTIMEDIA

CONTENTS

Choose one selection. Selections are available online only.

PERFORMANCE-BASED ASSESSMENT PREP

Review Evidence for an Explanatory Essay
Complete your Evidence Log for the unit by evaluating what you've learned and synthesizing the information you've recorded.

SCAN FOR
MULTIMEDIA

First-Read Guide

Use this page to record your first-read ideas.

Selection Title: _____

🔧 **Tool Kit**
First-Read Guide and
Model Annotation

NOTICE new information or ideas you learn about the unit topic as you first read this text.

ANNOTATE by marking vocabulary and key passages you want to revisit.

First Read

CONNECT ideas within the selection to other knowledge and the selections you have read.

RESPOND by writing a brief summary of the selection.

🔳 STANDARD

Reading Read and comprehend complex literary and informational texts independently and proficiently.

Close-Read Guide

Use this page to record your close-read ideas.

🔧 **Tool Kit**
Close-Read Guide and
Model Annotation

Selection Title: _____

Close Read the Text

Revisit sections of the text you marked during your first read. Read these sections closely and **annotate** what you notice. Ask yourself **questions** about the text. What can you **conclude**? Write down your ideas.

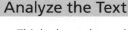

Analyze the Text

Think about the author's choices of patterns, structure, techniques, and ideas included in the text. Select one, and record your thoughts about what this choice conveys.

QuickWrite

Pick a paragraph from the text that grabbed your interest. Explain the power of this passage.

_____
_____
_____
_____
_____
_____
_____
_____
_____
_____

▥ STANDARD

Reading Read and comprehend complex literary and informational texts independently and proficiently.

Share Your Independent Learning

Prepare to Share

What can cause a sudden change in someone's life?

Even when you read or learn something independently, your understanding continues to grow when you share what you've learned with others. Reflect on the text you explored independently, and write notes about its connections to the unit topic and Essential Question. In your notes, explain why this text belongs in this unit.

Learn From Your Classmates

💬 **Discuss It** Share your ideas about the text you explored on your own. As you talk with your classmates, jot down ideas that you learn from them.

Reflect

Review your notes, and underline the most important insight you gained from these writing and discussion activities. Explain how this idea adds to your understanding of the topic of turning points.

Review Evidence for an Explanatory Essay

At the beginning of this unit, you expressed your ideas about the following question:

What can cause a significant change in someone's life?

✏ **EVIDENCE LOG**

Review your Evidence Log and your QuickWrite from the beginning of the unit. Did you learn anything new?

NOTES

Identify three things you learned about that can cause a sudden change in someone's life.

1.

2.

3.

Identify a real-life experience that illustrates one of your ideas about turning points.

_____

Develop your thoughts into a topic sentence for an explanatory essay. Complete this sentence starter:

As details in _____
show, significant changes in someone's life can be caused by

_____

_____

Evaluate Your Evidence Consider your ideas about turning points. How did the texts you read affect your ideas?

▤ STANDARDS

Writing
Write informative/explanatory texts to examine a topic and convey ideas, concepts, and information through the selection, organization, and analysis of relevant content.

a. Introduce a topic clearly, previewing what is to follow; organize ideas, concepts, and information, using strategies such as definition, classification, comparison/contrast, and cause/effect; include formatting, graphics, and multimedia when useful to aiding comprehension.
b. Develop the topic with relevant facts, definitions, concrete details, quotations, or other information and examples.

SOURCES

- WHOLE-CLASS SELECTIONS
- SMALL-GROUP SELECTIONS
- INDEPENDENT-LEARNING SELECTION

⊕ WORD NETWORK

As you write and revise your explanation, use your Word Network to help vary your word choices.

▤ STANDARDS

Writing
- Write informative/explanatory texts to examine a topic and convey ideas, concepts, and information through the selection, organization, and analysis of relevant content.
- Produce clear and coherent writing in which the development, organization, and style are appropriate to task, purpose, and audience.
- Draw evidence from literary or informational texts to support analysis, reflection, and research.
- Write routinely over extended time frames and shorter time frames for a range of discipline-specific tasks, purposes, and audiences.

PART 1
Writing to Sources: Explanatory Essay

In this unit, you read about different examples of turning points. Write an informative essay in which you explain what can cause a significant change in someone's life, how it might have a lasting effect, and what it tells you about someone who has undergone a meaningful change. Develop your topic with relevant facts, details, and information from the texts.

Assignment

Write an **explanatory essay** in response to the following question:

> What can cause a significant change in someone's life?

Develop a clear thesis, or controlling idea, in response to the prompt. Then, use sufficient examples and quotations from the selections that you read in this unit to support your response. Your essay should be logically organized and include transitions to show the relationships between ideas. Be sure to maintain a formal style and tone in your writing.

Reread the Assignment Review the assignment to be sure you fully understand it. The assignment may reference some of the academic words presented at the beginning of the unit. Be sure you understand each of the words given below in order to complete the assignment correctly.

Academic Vocabulary

contribute	consistent	maintain
observation	sufficient	

Review the Elements of an Effective Explanatory Essay Before you begin writing, read the Explanatory Essay Rubric. Once you have completed your first draft, check it against the rubric. If one or more of the elements is missing or not as strong as it could be, revise your essay to add or strengthen that component.

Explanatory Essay Rubric

	Focus and Organization	Evidence and Elaboration	Conventions
4	The introduction is engaging and includes a clear thesis. The thesis is supported by specific details, examples, and quotations from the selections. Ideas are logically organized so that the information is easy to follow. Transitions clearly show the relationships among ideas. The conclusion supports the information in the essay and offers fresh insight into the topic.	Details, examples, and quotations from the selections are specific and relevant. The style and tone are formal and objective. Words are carefully chosen and suited to purpose and audience.	The essay intentionally follows standard English conventions of usage and mechanics.
3	The introduction includes a clear thesis. The thesis is supported by details, examples, and quotations from the selections. Ideas are organized so that the information is easy to follow. Transitions show the relationships among ideas. The conclusion supports the information in the essay.	Details, examples, and quotations are relevant. The style and tone are mostly formal and objective. Words are generally suited to purpose and audience.	The essay follows standard English conventions of usage and mechanics.
2	The introduction states the thesis. The thesis is supported by some details, examples, and quotations from the selections. Ideas are vaguely organized, with a few transitions to orient readers. The conclusion relates to the information in the essay.	Some details and examples are relevant. The style and tone are occasionally formal and objective. Words are somewhat suited to purpose and audience.	The essay sometimes follows standard English conventions of usage and mechanics.
1	The thesis is not clearly stated in the introduction. The thesis is not supported by details, examples, and quotations. Ideas are disorganized and the information is difficult to follow. The conclusion does not include relevant information.	There is little or no relevant support. The style and tone are informal. Words are not appropriate to purpose or audience.	The essay contains many mistakes in standard English conventions of usage and mechanics.

PART 2
Speaking and Listening: Oral Presentation

Assignment

After completing the final draft of your explanatory essay, use it as the foundation for a brief **oral presentation.**

■ STANDARDS
Speaking and Listening
• Present claims and findings, emphasizing salient points in a focused, coherent manner with pertinent descriptions, facts, details, and examples; use appropriate eye contact, adequate volume, and clear pronunciation.

• Include multimedia components and visual displays in presentations to clarify claims and findings and emphasize salient points.

Do not simply read your essay aloud. Take the following steps to make your presentation lively and engaging.

- Review your explanation and annotate the most important ideas and supporting details.
- Choose multimedia elements that add interest to your presentation.

Review the Rubric Before you deliver your presentation, check your plans against this rubric.

	Content	Organization	Presentation Techniques
3	The introduction is engaging and states the thesis in a compelling way. The presentation includes specific examples, quotations, and multimedia elements to support the thesis. The conclusion offers fresh insight into the topic.	The speaker uses time effectively, spending the right amount on each part. Ideas progress logically, with clear transition among ideas so the information is easy for listeners to follow. The timing of the images matches the timing of the explanation.	The speaker maintains effective eye contact and speaks clearly and with adequate volume.
2	The introduction states a thesis. The presentation includes examples, quotations, and multimedia elements to support the thesis. The conclusion offers some insight and restates important information.	The speaker uses time effectively, spending the right amount of time on most parts. Ideas progress logically with some transitions among ideas. Listeners can mostly follow the speaker's information.	The speaker sometimes maintains effective eye contact and speaks somewhat clearly and with adequate volume.
1	The introduction does not clearly state a thesis. The presentation does not include examples, quotations, or multimedia elements. The conclusion does not restate important information.	The speaker does not use time effectively and focuses too much time on some parts and too little on others. Ideas do not progress logically. Listeners have trouble following the information.	The speaker does not maintain effective eye contact or speak clearly with adequate volume.

Reflect on the Unit

Now that you've completed the unit, take a few moments to reflect on your learning.

Reflect on the Unit Goals

Look back at the goals at the beginning of the unit. Use a different colored pen to rate yourself again. Think about readings and activities that contributed the most to the growth of your understanding. Record your thoughts.

Reflect on the Learning Strategies

② Discuss It Write a reflection on whether you were able to improve your learning based on your Action Plans. Think about what worked, what didn't, and what you might do to keep working on these strategies. Record your ideas before a class discussion.

Reflect on the Text

Choose a selection that you found challenging and explain what made it difficult.

Explain something that surprised you about a text in the unit.

Which activity taught you the most about turning points? What did you learn?

SCAN FOR
MULTIMEDIA

People and the Planet

Many people wonder at the beauty of nature, but do they wonder about the future of our planet?

Arctic Ice

💬 **Discuss It** In what way are people and animals dependent on our planet?

Write your response before sharing your ideas.

SCAN FOR
MULTIMEDIA

UNIT 4

UNIT INTRODUCTION

ESSENTIAL QUESTION: ## What effects do people have on the environment?

LAUNCH TEXT
ARGUMENT MODEL
Rethinking the Wild

WHOLE-CLASS LEARNING

ANCHOR TEXT: DESCRIPTIVE NONFICTION

from Silent Spring
Rachel Carson

COMPARE

ANCHOR TEXT: SPEECH

Nobel Speech
Al Gore

MEDIA: VIDEO

Nobel Speech
Al Gore

SMALL-GROUP LEARNING

POETRY COLLECTION

Turtle Watchers
Linda Hogan

"Nature" is what We see—
Emily Dickinson

The Sparrow
Paul Laurence Dunbar

MEDIA: PHOTO GALLERY

Eagle Tracking at Follensby Pond
The Nature Conservancy

SHORT STORY

He—y, Come On Ou—t!
Shinichi Hoshi, translated by Stanleigh Jones

INDEPENDENT LEARNING

NOVEL EXCERPT

from My Side of the Mountain
Jean Craighead George

MYTH

How Grandmother Spider Stole the Sun
Michael J. Caduto and Joseph Bruchac

EXPOSITORY NONFICTION

The Story of Victor d'Aveyron, the Wild Child
Eloise Montalban

ESSAY

from Of Wolves and Men
Barry Lopez

PERFORMANCE TASK

WRITING FOCUS:
Write an Argument

PERFORMANCE TASK

SPEAKING AND LISTENING FOCUS:
Present an Argument

PERFORMANCE-BASED ASSESSMENT PREP

Review Evidence for an Argument

PERFORMANCE-BASED ASSESSMENT

Argument: Essay and Oral Presentation

PROMPT:
Are the needs of people ever more important than the needs of animals and the planet?

Unit Goals

Throughout this unit, you will deepen your perspective about space exploration by reading, writing, speaking, listening, and presenting. These goals will help you succeed on the Unit Performance-Based Assessment.

Rate how well you meet these goals right now. You will revisit your ratings later when you reflect on your growth during this unit.

SCALE	1	2	3	4	5
	NOT AT ALL WELL	NOT VERY WELL	SOMEWHAT WELL	VERY WELL	EXTREMELY WELL

READING GOALS 1 2 3 4 5

- Evaluate written arguments by analyzing how authors state and support their claims. ○─○─○─○─○

- Expand your knowledge and use of academic and concept vocabulary. ○─○─○─○─○

WRITING AND RESEARCH GOALS 1 2 3 4 5

- Write an argumentative essay in which you effectively incorporate the key elements of an argument. ○─○─○─○─○

- Conduct research projects of various lengths to explore a topic and clarify meaning. ○─○─○─○─○

LANGUAGE GOALS 1 2 3 4 5

- Demonstrate command of the use of participles and participial phrases. ○─○─○─○─○

SPEAKING AND LISTENING GOALS 1 2 3 4 5

- Collaborate with your team to build on the ideas of others, develop consensus, and communicate. ○─○─○─○─○

- Integrate audio, visuals, and text in presentations. ○─○─○─○─○

STANDARDS

Language
Acquire and use accurately grade appropriate general academic and domain-specific words and phrases; gather vocabulary knowledge when considering a word or phrase important to comprehension or expression.

SCAN FOR MULTIMEDIA

Academic Vocabulary: Argument

Academic terms appear in all subjects and can help you read, write, and discuss with more precision. Here are five academic words that will be useful to you in this unit as you analyze and write arguments.

Complete the chart.

1. Review each word, its root, and mentor sentences.

2. Use the information and your own knowledge to predict the meaning of each word.

3. For each word, list at least two related words.

4. Refer to the dictionary or other resources if needed.

TIP

FOLLOW THROUGH

Study the words in this chart, and mark them or their forms wherever they appear in the unit.

WORD	MENTOR SENTENCES	PREDICT MEANING	RELATED WORDS
ethical ROOT: **-eth-** "character" or "custom"	1. The company was praised for its *ethical* business practices. 2. The animal-rights activists argued that it is not *ethical* to experiment on chimpanzees.		ethics; unethical
dissent ROOT: **-sent-** "feel"	1. Robin expressed her *dissent* from the opinion that was held by the majority of the class. 2. The king used all of his power to suppress political *dissent* within his country.		
interject ROOT: **-jec-** "throw"	1. Every time I tried to express my opinion, Eric would *interject* with his own ideas. 2. As I explain the directions, please feel free to *interject* a question if anything is unclear.		
discord ROOT: **-cord-** "heart"	1. Jake acted as a mediator to end the *discord* between his two arguing friends. 2. The two countries signed a peace treaty to end their long history of *discord*.		
accuracy ROOT: **-cur-** "care for"	1. He could shoot an arrow with great *accuracy*, almost never missing his target. 2. I was impressed with the *accuracy* of her painting. The portrait looked just like me.		

This text presents an **argument,** a type of writing in which an author states and defends a position on a topic. This is the type of writing you will develop in the Performance-Based Assessment at the end of the unit.

As you read, think about the way the writer presents a position. Notice ways in which the writer weaves together elements of story-telling and informative writing in support of the argument.

Rethinking the Wild

NOTES

1 There are seven billion people on the planet, and each of us has an impact on the animals and plants we share it with. It's a constant give-and-take, and people have strong opinions. Even though the correct course of action isn't always obvious, sometimes the needs of human beings have to take priority.

2 In Jon Mooallem's book *Wild Ones,* he describes the attempt of one organization to save the whooping crane from extinction. It's a story that may challenge what you thought you knew about the sometimes competing interests of people and animals.

3 The North American whooping crane—one of the few living relics of the Pleistocene era—suffered a huge drop in population in the nineteenth and twentieth centuries. In 1860 there were 1,400 whooping cranes. In 1941 there were just 15, and in 1967 the whooping crane was listed as "endangered."

4 Mooallem explains how Operation Migration planned to save the whooping crane by raising a new flock in Wisconsin. The hard part would come next: getting the birds to migrate to Florida. Here's how they did it: they led the birds there themselves. In a disguised aircraft, that looked and flew like a bird, they flew along with the flock. They avoided talking, and even wore all-white costumes, so that the cranes wouldn't get too comfortable with humans and would remain wild.

5 When the cranes reached Florida, they were put into a "release pen" with no top netting, so the birds could fly away themselves when they were ready. The complex was surrounded by houses. In fact, it was practically in the backyard of a couple named Gibbs. And that's where the second part of the story starts.

SCAN FOR MULTIMEDIA

NOTES

6   The Gibbses—an elderly couple who'd lived there for 50 years—loved nothing better than to sit on their back porch, sip tea, and watch the birds as they fed from the two bird feeders they'd set up in the backyard. There were all kinds of birds around—but the Gibbs' favorites were the whooping cranes that had started showing up lately.

7   As far as Operation Migration was concerned, this could destroy their project. Unless something were done about those feeders, the birds would continue to hang around the Gibbs' house. They would no longer be wary of people, and wouldn't be able to survive on their own.

8   After explaining the situation to Mrs. Gibbs, representatives from Operation Migration asked her to remove the feeders from her backyard. She refused! Her husband, it turns out, was dying of Alzheimer's and the only thing that made him happy and brought him into the present was seeing the family of whooping cranes in his own backyard.

9   The scientists were unmoved by Mrs. Gibbs' story. They were thinking of the birds that people had spent 24 hours a day trying to keep wild. They were thinking of all the time and money they had invested in this group of cranes. But in the end they had to back down. How can you ask a woman to choose between her husband and a flock of birds?

10   According to Jon Mooallem, Mrs. Gibbs did what any of us would do. As humans, we're hard-wired to put our particular set of needs above others. We also have a responsibility to be the earth's caretakers, because of the power we have over other species. And sometimes we have to be comfortable balancing our needs with theirs. ✍

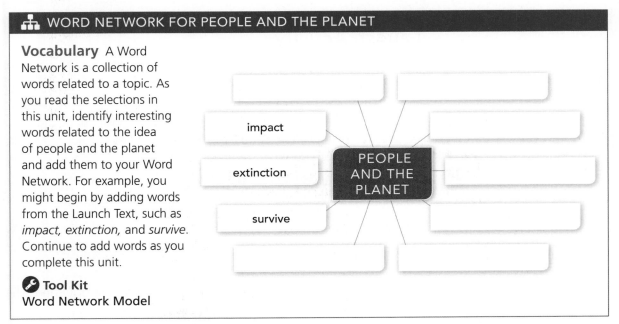

WORD NETWORK FOR PEOPLE AND THE PLANET

Vocabulary A Word Network is a collection of words related to a topic. As you read the selections in this unit, identify interesting words related to the idea of people and the planet and add them to your Word Network. For example, you might begin by adding words from the Launch Text, such as *impact, extinction,* and *survive.* Continue to add words as you complete this unit.

🔧 **Tool Kit**
Word Network Model

impact

extinction

survive

PEOPLE AND THE PLANET

Summary

Write a summary of "Rethinking the Wild." A **summary** is a concise, complete, and accurate overview of a text. It should not include a statement of your opinion or an analysis.

Launch Activity

Let the People Decide Consider this statement: *Mrs. Gibbs was wrong in refusing to remove the bird feeders from her backyard*. Decide your position and explain why you feel this way.

- Prepare a brief statement that expresses your position. Include reasons why you feel as you do. Your statement should be written as a short speech designed to influence people.

- A class discussion will be conducted as if it were a political campaign gathering. When the "campaign" begins, have your statement ready.

- When it's time for you to speak, deliver your statement as if you were giving a political speech. Try to persuade those listening to agree with your position.

- The class will vote on whether Mrs. Gibbs was right or wrong when she refused to remove the bird feeders.

QuickWrite

Consider class discussions, presentations, the video, your own knowledge, and the Launch Text as you think about the prompt. Record your first thoughts here.

PROMPT: **Are the needs of people ever more important than the needs of animals and the planet?**

✐ EVIDENCE LOG FOR PEOPLE AND THE PLANET

Review your QuickWrite. Summarize your point of view in one sentence to record in your Evidence Log. Then, record evidence from "Rethinking the Wild" that supports your point of view.

After each selection, you will continue to use your Evidence Log to record the evidence you gather and the connections you make. This graphic shows what your Evidence Log looks like.

🔧 **Tool Kit**
Evidence Log Model

Title of Text: _____   Date: _____

CONNECTION TO PROMPT	TEXT EVIDENCE/DETAILS	ADDITIONAL NOTES/IDEAS

How does this text change or add to my thinking?   Date: _____

SCAN FOR
MULTIMEDIA

ESSENTIAL QUESTION:

What effects do people have on the environment?

Our environment provides us with the basic necessities we need to survive—air, water, and soil in which to grow food. However, it's not just a one-way relationship. People's actions also have an impact on the environment. In an era of rapid technological change, we have become very aware of the complex inter-relationship between people and their environment. We depend on the Earth and it depends on us: Getting the balance right is the challenge of our age.

Whole-Class Learning Strategies

Review these strategies and the actions you can take to practice them as you work with your whole class. Add ideas of your own for each strategy.

STRATEGY	ACTION PLAN
Listen actively	• Eliminate distractions. For example, put your cellphone away. • Keep your eyes on the speaker. •
Clarify by asking questions	• If you're confused, other people probably are, too. Ask a question to help your whole class. • If you see that you are guessing, ask a question instead. •
Monitor understanding	• Notice what information you already know and be ready to build on it. • Ask for help if you are struggling. •
Interact and share ideas	• Share your ideas and answer questions, even if you are unsure. • Build on the ideas of others by adding details or making a connection. •

SCAN FOR MULTIMEDIA

CONTENTS

PERFORMANCE TASK

WRITING FOCUS

Write an Argument

There are many ways in which people affect the environment, both positively and negatively. The Whole-Class readings and the video address serious problems with our environment. After reading and viewing, you will write an argument on the topic of the environment.

About the Author

Even as a child, **Rachel Carson** (1907–1964) wanted to be a writer. Once in college, she renewed her interest in nature and majored in marine biology. She later earned a master's degree in zoology. Carson had long been worried about the overuse of pesticides and wanted to raise awareness about this problem. Her book *Silent Spring* became one of the most influential environmental texts ever written.

🔧 **Tool Kit**
First-Read Guide and Model Annotation

from Silent Spring

Concept Vocabulary

You will encounter the following words as you read the excerpt from *Silent Spring*. Before reading, note how familiar you are with each word. Then, rank the words in order from most familiar (1) to least familiar (6).

WORD	YOUR RANKING
blight	
maladies	
puzzled	
stricken	
stillness	
deserted	

After completing your first read, come back to the concept vocabulary and review your rankings. Mark changes to your original rankings as needed.

First Read NONFICTION

Apply these strategies as you conduct your first read. You will have an opportunity to complete the close-read notes after your first read.

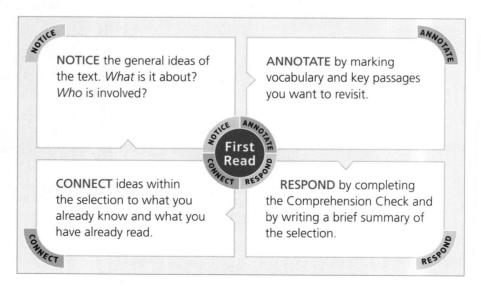

NOTICE the general ideas of the text. *What* is it about? *Who* is involved?

ANNOTATE by marking vocabulary and key passages you want to revisit.

First Read

CONNECT ideas within the selection to what you already know and what you have already read.

RESPOND by completing the Comprehension Check and by writing a brief summary of the selection.

▤ STANDARDS

Reading Informational Text
By the end of the year, read and comprehend literary nonfiction in the grades 6–8 text complexity band proficiently, with scaffolding as needed at the high end of the range.

from
Silent Spring

Rachel Carson

BACKGROUND

Pesticides are chemical compounds designed to destroy crop-eating insects. Pesticides can be deadly to many species—including humans—in addition to the insects and other pests they are intended to kill. In 1962, Rachel Carson published *Silent Spring,* which revealed to the public the dangers of DDT, a pesticide in wide use at the time. The awareness raised by *Silent Spring* eventually led the United States to ban DDT entirely in 1972. This excerpt comes from the opening pages of the book.

SCAN FOR
MULTIMEDIA

1   There was once a town in the heart of America where all life seemed to live in harmony with its surroundings. The town lay in the midst of a checkerboard of prosperous farms, with fields of grain and hillsides of orchards where, in spring, white clouds of bloom drifted above the green fields. In autumn, oak and maple and birch set up a blaze of color that flamed and flickered across a backdrop of pines. Then foxes barked in the hills and deer silently crossed the fields, half hidden in the mists of the fall mornings.

2   Along the roads, laurel, viburnum and alder, great ferns and wildflowers delighted the traveler's eye through much of the year. Even in winter the roadsides were places of beauty, where countless birds came to feed on the berries and on the seed heads of the dried weeds rising above the snow. The countryside was, in fact, famous for the abundance and variety of its bird life, and when the flood of migrants was pouring through in spring and fall people traveled from great distances to observe them. Others came to fish the streams, which flowed clear and cold out of the

NOTES

CLOSE READ

ANNOTATE: In paragraph 2, mark details the author uses to describe the rich environment of the town.

QUESTION: Why might the author have used such vivid, descriptive details to describe the town?

CONCLUDE: What can you conclude about the town from these details?

blight (blyt) *n.* something that spoils, prevents growth, or destroys

maladies (MAL uh deez) *n.* illnesses or diseases

puzzled (PUHZ uhld) *adj.* confused and unable to understand something

stricken (STRIHK uhn) *adj.* very badly affected by trouble or illness

stillness (STIHL nihs) *n.* absence of noise or motion

deserted (dih ZUR tihd) *adj.* abandoned; empty

hills and contained shady pools where trout lay. So it had been from the days many years ago when the first settlers raised their houses, sank their wells, and built their barns.

3   Then a strange **blight** crept over the area and everything began to change. Some evil spell had settled on the community: mysterious **maladies** swept the flocks of chickens; the cattle and sheep sickened and died. Everywhere was a shadow of death. The farmers spoke of much illness among their families. In the town the doctors had become more and more **puzzled** by new kinds of sickness appearing among their patients. There had been several sudden and unexplained deaths, not only among adults but even among children, who would be **stricken** suddenly while at play and die within a few hours.

4   There was a strange **stillness**. The birds, for example—where had they gone? Many people spoke of them, puzzled and disturbed. The feeding stations in the backyards were deserted. The few birds seen anywhere were moribund; they trembled violently and could not fly. It was a spring without voices. On the mornings that had once throbbed with the dawn chorus of robins, catbirds, doves, jays, wrens, and scores of other bird voices, there was now no sound; only silence lay over the fields and woods and marsh.

5   On the farms the hens brooded, but no chicks hatched. The farmers complained that they were unable to raise any pigs—the litters were small and the young survived only a few days. The apple trees were coming into bloom but no bees droned among the blossoms, so there was no pollination and there would be no fruit.

6   The roadsides, once so attractive, were now lined with browned and withered vegetation as though swept by fire. These, too, were silent, **deserted** by all living things. Even the streams were now lifeless. Anglers* no longer visited them, for all the fish had died.

7   In the gutters under the eaves and between the shingles of the roofs, a white granular powder still showed a few patches; some weeks before it had fallen like snow upon the roofs and the lawns, the fields and streams.

8   No witchcraft, no enemy action had silenced the rebirth of new life in this stricken world. The people had done it themselves.

9   This town does not actually exist, but it might easily have a thousand counterparts in America or elsewhere in the world. I know of no community that has experienced all the misfortunes I describe. Yet every one of these disasters has actually happened somewhere, and many real communities have already suffered a substantial number of them. A grim specter has crept upon us almost unnoticed, and this imagined tragedy may easily become a stark reality we all shall know. ❧

* **anglers** (ANG gluhrz) *n.* people who fish with a line and hook.

Comprehension Check

Complete the following items after you finish your first read.

1. What are two animals that attracted visitors to the town?

2. What happened to the animals and the people in the town?

3. What fell on the roofs, lawns, fields, and streams?

4. ⊟ **Notebook** Write a brief summary of the excerpt from *Silent Spring*.

- -

RESEARCH

Research to Clarify Choose at least one unfamiliar detail from the text. Briefly research that detail. In what way does the information you learned shed light on an aspect of the text?

from SILENT SPRING

Close Read the Text

1. This model, from paragraph 3 of the text, shows two sample annotations, along with questions and conclusions. Close read the passage, and find another detail to annotate. Then, write a question and your conclusion.

ANNOTATE: The author uses descriptive details to show the changes in the town.

QUESTION: What kind of mood do these words create?

CONCLUDE: This description creates a sense of destruction and despair.

> Then a strange blight crept over the area and everything began to change. Some evil spell had settled on the community: mysterious maladies swept the flocks of chickens; the cattle and sheep sickened and died. Everywhere was a shadow of death. The farmers spoke of much illness among their families.

ANNOTATE: The author uses the words *everything* and *everywhere*.

QUESTION: Why does the author use two words containing the word *every*?

CONCLUDE: The use of these words shows the widespread impact of the blight.

Close Read
ANNOTATE · QUESTION · CONCLUDE

Tool Kit
Close-Read Guide and Model Annotation

2. For more practice, go back into the text and complete the close-read notes.

3. Revisit a section of the text you found important during your first read. Read this section closely and **annotate** what you notice. Ask yourself **questions** such as "Why did the author make this choice?" What can you **conclude**?

- -

Analyze the Text

CITE TEXTUAL EVIDENCE
to support your answers.

Notebook Respond to these questions.

1. (a) **Interpret** In paragraph 1, what does the phrase "heart of America" suggest? (b) **Speculate** Why does Carson use this phrase in the first paragraph?

2. **Make Inferences** In the book, the excerpt you read is called "A Fable for Tomorrow." Why does Carson use this title for this section of the book?

3. **Essential Question:** *What effects do people have on the environment?* What have you learned about the effects people have on the environment by reading this selection?

STANDARDS

Reading Informational Text
• Cite several pieces of textual evidence to support analysis of what the text says explicitly as well as inferences drawn from the text.
• Determine two or more central ideas in a text and analyze their development over the course of the text; provide an objective summary of the text.
• Determine the meaning of words and phrases as they are used in a text, including figurative, connotative, and technical meanings; analyze the impact of a specific word choice on meaning and tone.

Language
Distinguish among the connotations of words with similar denotations.

Analyze Craft and Structure

Author's Word Choice: Imagery **Imagery** is language that includes **images**—words or phrases that appeal to one or more of the five senses. A writer uses imagery to bring his or her writing to life with vivid descriptions of how the subjects look, sound, feel, taste, or smell. A writer's word choice, or the specific words, phrases, and expressions he or she uses, contributes to memorable imagery. Look at the following examples of imagery, and note the ways in which the individual words help create a realistic image for readers:

- The phrase "sweet, slippery mango slices" appeals to the senses of taste and touch.
- The phrase "glaring lights and wailing sirens" appeals to the senses of sight and hearing.

Writers also create mood through their use of imagery, word choice, and descriptive details. **Mood** is the feeling created in the reader by a piece of writing. The mood of a work may be described with adjectives such as *joyous* or *frightening*. To fully appreciate images and experience the mood of a text, use these strategies:

- determine the specific meanings of unfamiliar words
- consider the **connotations**, or emotional associations, of words, as well as their **figurative**, or nonliteral, **meanings**
- analyze the author's word choice, and make inferences, or educated guesses, as to why the author may have chosen certain words

As you review the excerpt from *Silent Spring,* notice how Carson uses word choice and imagery to create a mood that helps make her central idea more powerful and compelling.

Practice

CITE TEXTUAL EVIDENCE to support your answers.

📓 **Notebook** Respond to these questions.

1. Review the selection. Then, use a chart like this one to list four images in the text and the sense to which each image appeals.

IMAGE	SENSE

2. (a) A *specter* is a source of terror or dread. Why might Carson have chosen to use this word in the last sentence of the excerpt? (b) What mood does this word choice create?
3. How does Carson's use of imagery help to develop the central idea of the excerpt? Cite at least two textual examples to support your response.

from SILENT SPRING

Concept Vocabulary

blight	puzzled	stillness
maladies	stricken	deserted

Why These Words? The concept vocabulary words from the text are related to unwelcome change—in this case, to a town's landscape. For example, after the town is *stricken* with the mysterious *blight*, there is a strange *stillness* everywhere.

1. How does the concept vocabulary sharpen the reader's understanding of what happens to the town and its people?

2. What other words in the selection are related to this concept?

WORD NETWORK

Add interesting words related to people and the planet from the text to your Word Network.

Practice

📓 **Notebook** First, correctly complete each sentence using a concept vocabulary word. Then, identify one **synonym**, or word with a similar meaning, and one **antonym**, or word with an opposite meaning, for each vocabulary word.

1. When she returned home from the music festival, the woman found the _____ of her apartment strange in comparison.

2. When the concert hall was _____, you could hear a pin drop from across the room.

3. After carefully following the recipe, Alfredo was _____ when the cake came out of the oven, hard as a rock.

4. The _____ destroyed the potatoes grown in the county.

5. Common _____, such as colds and flus, affect the most people during the winter.

6. Before the return of their lost pet, the family had been _____ with worry and fear.

Word Study

📓 **Notebook** **Anglo-Saxon Suffix: -ness** The Anglo-Saxon suffix -*ness* means "the condition or quality of being." It usually indicates that the word in which it appears is a noun. In the text, Carson describes the *stillness* that occurs after the blight as "strange." It is strange because the absence of noise and movement is unusual in the town.

1. Write your own sentence that correctly uses the word *stillness*.

2. Find a word in paragraph 3 of the excerpt that ends with the suffix -*ness*, and write a sentence that shows your understanding of it.

STANDARDS

Language
• Demonstrate command of the conventions of standard English grammar and usage when writing or speaking.
• Use knowledge of language and its conventions when writing, speaking, reading, or listening.
• Determine or clarify the meaning of unknown and multiple-meaning words and phrases based on *grade 7 reading and content,* choosing flexibly from a range of strategies.
• Use the relationship between particular words to better understand each of the words.

Conventions

Verb Mood—The Subjunctive Speakers and writers convey their attitudes toward the actions expressed by verbs by using different **moods**. The **indicative mood** is used for statements of fact. By contrast, the **subjunctive mood** expresses one of the following:

- a wish or desire
- a condition that is highly unlikely or contrary to fact
- a request or demand for action

Subjunctive verbs are often found in clauses that begin with *if, as if, as though*, or *that*. This chart shows situations in which a speaker or writer would use the subjunctive mood.

INDICATIVE MOOD	SUBJUNCTIVE MOOD	WHAT SUBJUNCTIVE EXPRESSES
Jill *is coming* with us. She *knows* the answer.	I wish that Jill *were coming* with us. She wishes that she *knew* the answer.	wish
He *will not be* elected.	If he *were* elected, we'd be shocked.	condition that is highly unlikely
I *am* at home. Jake *has* a new car.	If I *were* at home, I'd take a nap. If Jake *had* a new car, he'd be happy.	condition that is contrary to fact
They *are* quiet.	We asked that they *be* quiet.	request
Matt *works* hard.	Kia insisted that Matt *work* hard.	demand or strong suggestion

Avoid using the incorrect verb form to express the subjunctive mood, especially for third-person singular verbs and all forms of the verb *be*.

Incorrect: Blake speaks as if he *was* in charge.

Correct: Blake speaks as if he *were* in charge.

Incorrect: Julia's mother requires that she *gets* home before dinner.

Correct: Julia's mother requires that she *get* home before dinner.

Read It

Identify the mood of each sentence, and tell what it expresses.

1. I wish that the town were filled with birds again.

2. If the town's settlers were present, they would be sad.

Write It

📓 **Notebook** Identify the incorrect verb form in each sentence. Then, rewrite the sentence correctly.

1. Carson wishes that she was wrong about the fate of the town.

2. The situation Carson relates seems to demand that I am more aware of my effects on the environment.

from SILENT SPRING

Writing to Sources

Assignment

In *Silent Spring*, Rachel Carson paints a harsh picture of the future. Write an **argument** in which you answer this question: Does Carson's description inspire readers to take action, or does it discourage action because the problem seems so big?

First, decide on your position. Then, review the selection to find specific details that support your position. As you draft, be sure to do the following:

- State your position clearly in the introduction.
- In the body of your argument, support your position with reasons and evidence, including specific details from *Silent Spring*.
- Address alternate, or opposing, positions, and respond with counterarguments that address these views.
- Use transitional words and phrases to connect your ideas and show the relationships among them.
- Establish and maintain a formal style.

Vocabulary and Conventions Connection Think about including several of the concept vocabulary words in your writing. Also, remember to avoid improper shifts in mood in your writing by using verbs in the indicative and subjunctive moods correctly.

blight	puzzled	stillness
maladies	stricken	deserted

Reflect on Your Writing

After you have written your argument, answer these questions.

1. Was it easy or difficult to determine your position?

2. Have your ideas about our ability to solve environmental problems changed after writing this argument? Why or why not?

3. **Why These Words?** The words you choose make a difference in your writing. Which words did you specifically choose to make your argument stronger?

STANDARDS

Writing
Write arguments to support claims with clear reasons and relevant evidence.
  a. Introduce claim(s), acknowledge alternate or opposing claims, and organize the reasons and evidence logically.
  b. Support claim(s) with logical reasoning and relevant evidence, using accurate, credible sources and demonstrating an understanding of the topic or text.
  c. Use words, phrases, and clauses to create cohesion and clarify the relationships among claim(s), reasons, and evidence.
  d. Establish and maintain a formal style.

Speaking and Listening

Assignment

Choose one of the following topics, conduct research on the topic, and deliver a **multimedia presentation** of your findings to the class.

☐ the importance of *Silent Spring* and the impact it had on the way in which humans view their environment

☐ the struggle to ban DDT and the ban's eventual victory

☐ the parallels between the current threats to bee populations worldwide and the impacts DDT had on wildlife when Carson wrote *Silent Spring*

1. Organize Your Presentation

- Research the topic you have chosen.
- Use credible Internet and library resources to gather information and relevant visual aids.

2. Prepare Your Presentation

- Use the information you find to create your presentation.
- Decide how to sequence textual and visual information so that each emphasizes your main points.

3. Deliver Your Presentation

- Explain why you chose your topic.
- Maintain eye contact with your audience.
- Speak at an appropriate volume and with clear pronunciation so as to be heard by the entire class.

4. Evaluate Presentations
Use a presentation evaluation guide like the one shown to analyze your classmates' presentations.

PRESENTATION EVALUATION GUIDE

Rate each statement on a scale of 1 (Not Demonstrated) to 5 (Demonstrated).

☐ The speaker clearly explained the topic and his or her reasons for choosing the topic.

☐ The presentation included well-sequenced multimedia that emphasized the main points.

☐ The presentation was easy to follow, and the speaker maintained appropriate volume and eye contact.

EVIDENCE LOG

Before moving on to a new selection, go to your log and record what you've learned from *Silent Spring*.

STANDARDS

Writing
- Conduct short research projects to answer a question, drawing on several sources and generating additional related, focused questions for further research and investigation.
- Gather relevant information from multiple print and digital sources, using search terms effectively; assess the credibility and accuracy of each source; and quote or paraphrase the data and conclusions of others while avoiding plagiarism and following a standard format for citation.

Speaking and Listening
- Present claims and findings, emphasizing salient points in a focused, coherent manner with pertinent descriptions, facts, details, and examples; use appropriate eye contact, adequate volume, and clear pronunciation.
- Include multimedia components and visual displays in presentations to clarify claims and findings and emphasize salient points.

NOBEL SPEECH (TEXT)

Comparing Text to Media

In this lesson, you will read Al Gore's Nobel Prize acceptance speech and then watch a video of Gore delivering the speech. First, you will complete the first-read and close-read activities for the text of the speech. These activities will help prepare you to compare the speech and the video.

NOBEL SPEECH (VIDEO)

About the Author

Former United States Vice President **Al Gore** (b.1948) was practically born into politics. His father was a senator, and after Gore served a tour of duty in Vietnam, he went on to serve in both houses of Congress before becoming vice president in 1993. As a congressman, Gore became active in environmental issues. He has written several books about the dangers of climate change, and his campaign to educate the public about climate change is the subject of *An Inconvenient Truth*, which won the Academy Award for Best Documentary Feature in 2007.

🔧 Tool Kit

First-Read Guide and Model Annotation

☰ STANDARDS

Reading Informational Text
By the end of the year, read and comprehend literary nonfiction in the grades 6–8 text complexity band proficiently, with scaffolding as needed at the high end of the range.

Nobel Speech
Concept Vocabulary

You will encounter the following words as you read the speech. Before reading, note how familiar you are with each word. Then, rank the words in order from most familiar (1) to least familiar (6).

WORD	YOUR RANKING
crisis	
pollution	
urgency	
universal	
illusion	
environment	

After completing your first read, come back to the concept vocabulary and review your rankings. Mark any changes to your original rankings.

First Read NONFICTION

Apply these strategies as you conduct your first read. You will have an opportunity to complete the close-read notes after your first read.

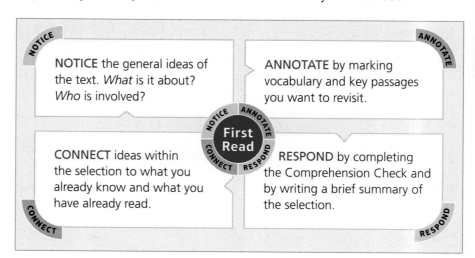

NOTICE the general ideas of the text. *What* is it about? *Who* is involved?

ANNOTATE by marking vocabulary and key passages you want to revisit.

First Read

CONNECT ideas within the selection to what you already know and what you have already read.

RESPOND by completing the Comprehension Check and by writing a brief summary of the selection.

Nobel Speech — Al Gore

BACKGROUND

The Nobel Peace Prize is a prestigious award granted to those who have done outstanding work to promote peace in the world. The Nobel Prize was established by Alfred Nobel, a Swedish chemist and engineer known for inventing dynamite. The 2007 Nobel Peace Prize was awarded to Al Gore for his efforts to educate people about the threats posed by man-made climate change and to urge people to act against the effects of climate change.

SCAN FOR MULTIMEDIA

Nobel Lecture, Oslo, December 10, 2007

NOTES

1   Your Majesties, Your Royal Highnesses, Honorable members of the Norwegian Nobel Committee, Excellencies, Ladies and gentlemen.

2   I have a purpose here today. It is a purpose I have tried to serve for many years. I have prayed that God would show me a way to accomplish it.

3   Sometimes, without warning, the future knocks on our door with a precious and painful vision of what might be. One hundred and nineteen years ago, a wealthy inventor read his own obituary, mistakenly published years before his death. Wrongly believing the inventor had just died, a newspaper printed a harsh judgment of his life's work, unfairly labeling him "The Merchant of Death" because of his invention—dynamite. Shaken by this

CLOSE READ
ANNOTATE: Mark words in the quotation in paragraph 7 that show the two different futures to which Gore refers.

QUESTION: Why might Gore have chosen this quotation to show the two different futures facing society?

CONCLUDE: What effect does the inclusion of this quotation have on readers?

crisis (KRY sihs) *n.* time when a situation is very bad or dangerous; turning point at which a change must be made for better or worse

pollution (puh LOO shuhn) *n.* presence or introduction into a space of a substance or thing that has harmful or poisonous effects

condemnation, the inventor made a fateful choice to serve the cause of peace.

4   Seven years later, Alfred Nobel created this prize and the others that bear his name.

5   Seven years ago tomorrow, I read my own political obituary[1] in a judgment that seemed to me harsh and mistaken—if not premature. But that unwelcome verdict also brought a precious if painful gift: an opportunity to search for fresh new ways to serve my purpose.

6   Unexpectedly, that quest has brought me here. Even though I fear my words cannot match this moment, I pray what I am feeling in my heart will be communicated clearly enough that those who hear me will say, "We must act."

7   The distinguished scientists with whom it is the greatest honor of my life to share this award have laid before us a choice between two different futures—a choice that to my ears echoes the words of an ancient prophet: "Life or death, blessings or curses. Therefore, choose life, that both thou and thy seed may live."

8   We, the human species, are confronting a planetary emergency—a threat to the survival of our civilization that is gathering ominous and destructive potential even as we gather here. But there is hopeful news as well: we have the ability to solve this **crisis** and avoid the worst—though not all—of its consequences, if we act boldly, decisively and quickly.

9   However, despite a growing number of honorable exceptions, too many of the world's leaders are still best described in the words Winston Churchill applied to those who ignored Adolf Hitler's threat:[2] "They go on in strange paradox, decided only to be undecided, resolved to be irresolute, adamant for drift, solid for fluidity, all powerful to be impotent."

10   So today, we dumped another 70 million tons of global-warming **pollution** into the thin shell of atmosphere surrounding our planet, as if it were an open sewer. And tomorrow, we will dump a slightly larger amount, with the cumulative concentrations now trapping more and more heat from the sun.

11   As a result, the earth has a fever. And the fever is rising. The experts have told us it is not a passing affliction that will heal by itself. We asked for a second opinion. And a third. And a fourth. And the consistent conclusion, restated with increasing alarm, is that something basic is wrong.

12   We are what is wrong, and we must make it right.

---

1.   **Seven years ago tomorrow . . . obituary** Gore is referring to the highly contested 2000 presidential election, which he lost to George W. Bush.
2.   **Winston Churchill . . . threat** Churchill, a British statesman at the time, gave a speech to the House of Commons in 1937 to criticize their failure to respond to the threat of Nazi Germany.

13　　Last September 21, as the Northern Hemisphere tilted away from the sun, scientists reported with unprecedented distress that the North Polar ice cap is "falling off a cliff." One study estimated that it could be completely gone during summer in less than 22 years. Another new study, to be presented by U.S. Navy researchers later this week, warns it could happen in as little as 7 years.

14　　Seven years from now.

15　　In the last few months, it has been harder and harder to misinterpret the signs that our world is spinning out of kilter.[3] Major cities in North and South America, Asia and Australia are nearly out of water due to massive droughts and melting glaciers. Desperate farmers are losing their livelihoods. Peoples in the frozen Arctic and on low-lying Pacific islands are planning evacuations of places they have long called home. Unprecedented wildfires have forced a half million people from their homes in one country and caused a national emergency that almost brought down the government in another. Climate refugees have migrated into areas already inhabited by people with different cultures, religions, and traditions, increasing the potential for conflict. Stronger storms in the Pacific and Atlantic have threatened whole cities. Millions have been displaced by massive flooding in South Asia, Mexico, and 18 countries in Africa. As temperature extremes have increased, tens of thousands have lost their lives. We are recklessly burning and clearing our forests and driving more and more species into extinction. The very web of life on which we depend is being ripped and frayed.

16　　We never intended to cause all this destruction, just as Alfred Nobel never intended that dynamite be used for waging war. He had hoped his invention would promote human progress. We shared that same worthy goal when we began burning massive quantities of coal, then oil and methane.

17　　Even in Nobel's time, there were a few warnings of the likely consequences. One of the very first winners of the Prize in chemistry worried that, "We are evaporating our coal mines into the air." After performing 10,000 equations by hand, Svante Arrhenius calculated that the earth's average temperature would increase by many degrees if we doubled the amount of CO_2[4] in the atmosphere.

18　　Seventy years later, my teacher, Roger Revelle, and his colleague, Dave Keeling, began to precisely document the increasing CO_2 levels day by day.

NOTES

CLOSE READ
ANNOTATE: Mark geographic locations in paragraph 15.

QUESTION: Why do you think Gore chooses to include these details?

CONCLUDE: What effect does the inclusion of these locations have on Gore's argument?

---

3. **out of kilter** off balance; not functioning right.
4. **CO₂** carbon dioxide, a naturally occurring gas that is also created through human activities such as burning oil and coal; it is considered a major cause of man-made climate change.

19   But unlike most other forms of pollution CO_2 is invisible, tasteless, and odorless—which has helped keep the truth about what it is doing to our climate out of sight and out of mind. Moreover, the catastrophe now threatening us is unprecedented—and we often confuse the unprecedented with the improbable.

20   We also find it hard to imagine making the massive changes that are now necessary to solve the crisis. And when large truths are genuinely inconvenient, whole societies can, at least for a time, ignore them. Yet as George Orwell reminds us: "Sooner or later a false belief bumps up against solid reality, usually on a battlefield."

21   In the years since this prize was first awarded, the entire relationship between humankind and the earth has been radically transformed. And still, we have remained largely oblivious to the impact of our cumulative actions.

22   Indeed, without realizing it, we have begun to wage war on the earth itself. Now, we and the earth's climate are locked in a relationship familiar to war planners: "Mutually assured destruction."

23   More than two decades ago, scientists calculated that nuclear war could throw so much debris and smoke into the air that it would block life-giving sunlight from our atmosphere, causing a "nuclear winter." Their eloquent warnings here in Oslo helped galvanize the world's resolve to halt the nuclear arms race.

24   Now science is warning us that if we do not quickly reduce the global warming pollution that is trapping so much of the heat our planet normally radiates back out of the atmosphere, we are in danger of creating a permanent "carbon summer."[5]

25   As the American poet Robert Frost wrote, "Some say the world will end in fire; some say in ice." Either, he notes, "would suffice."

26   But neither need be our fate. It is time to make peace with the planet.

urgency (UR juhn see) *n.* state of being very important and needing to be dealt with right away

27   We must quickly mobilize our civilization with the **urgency** and resolve that has previously been seen only when nations mobilized for war. These prior struggles for survival were won when leaders found words at the eleventh hour[6] that released a mighty surge of courage, hope and readiness to sacrifice for a protracted and mortal challenge.

28   These were not comforting and misleading assurances that the threat was not real or imminent; that it would affect others but not ourselves; that ordinary life might be lived even in the presence of extraordinary threat; that Providence[7] could be trusted to do for us what we would not do for ourselves.

---

5. **"carbon summer"** a permanent summer caused by too much heat in the atmosphere.
6. **eleventh hour** latest possible moment before it is too late to make a change.
7. **Providence** (PROV uh duhns) *n.* protective care of nature or God.

29 No, these were calls to come to the defense of the common future. They were calls upon the courage, generosity and strength of entire peoples, citizens of every class and condition who were ready to stand against the threat once asked to do so. Our enemies in those times calculated that free people would not rise to the challenge; they were, of course, catastrophically wrong.

30 Now comes the threat of climate crisis—a threat that is real, rising, imminent, and **universal**. Once again, it is the 11th hour. The penalties for ignoring this challenge are immense and growing, and at some near point would be unsustainable and unrecoverable. For now we still have the power to choose our fate, and the remaining question is only this: Have we the will to act vigorously and in time, or will we remain imprisoned by a dangerous **illusion**?

31 Mahatma Gandhi[8] awakened the largest democracy on earth and forged a shared resolve with what he called "Satyagraha"—or "truth force."

32 In every land, the truth—once known—has the power to set us free.

NOTES

universal (yoo nuh VUR suhl) *adj.* involving everyone in the world or in a particular group; true or appropriate in every situation

illusion (ih LOO zhuhn) *n.* something that appears real but actually is not

---

8. **Mahatma Gandhi** (1869–1948) Indian activist known for leading the movement against British rule of India and for his doctrine of nonviolent protest.

33   Truth also has the power to unite us and bridge the distance between "me" and "we," creating the basis for common effort and shared responsibility.

34   There is an African proverb that says, "If you want to go quickly, go alone. If you want to go far, go together." We need to go far, quickly.

35   We must abandon the conceit that individual, isolated, private actions are the answer. They can and do help. But they will not take us far enough without collective action. At the same time, we must ensure that in mobilizing globally, we do not invite the establishment of ideological conformity and a new lock-step "ism."

36   That means adopting principles, values, laws, and treaties that release creativity and initiative[9] at every level of society in multifold responses originating concurrently and spontaneously.

37   This new consciousness requires expanding the possibilities inherent in all humanity. The innovators who will devise a new way to harness the sun's energy for pennies or invent an engine that's carbon negative may live in Lagos or Mumbai or Montevideo. We must ensure that entrepreneurs and inventors everywhere on the globe have the chance to change the world.

38   When we unite for a moral purpose that is manifestly good and true, the spiritual energy unleashed can transform us. The generation that defeated fascism throughout the world in the 1940s found, in rising to meet their awesome challenge, that they had gained the moral authority and long-term vision to launch the Marshall Plan,[10] the United Nations, and a new level of global cooperation and foresight that unified Europe and facilitated the emergence of democracy and prosperity in Germany, Japan, Italy and much of the world. One of their visionary leaders[11] said, "It is time we steered by the stars and not by the lights of every passing ship."

39   In the last year of that war, you gave the Peace Prize to a man from my hometown of 2,000 people, Carthage, Tennessee. Cordell Hull was described by Franklin Roosevelt as the "Father of the United Nations." He was an inspiration and hero to my own father, who followed Hull in the Congress and the U.S. Senate and in his commitment to world peace and global cooperation.

40   My parents spoke often of Hull, always in tones of reverence and admiration. Eight weeks ago, when you announced this prize, the deepest emotion I felt was when I saw the headline in my hometown paper that simply noted I had won the same prize that

CLOSE READ

ANNOTATE: In paragraph 38, mark the example Gore uses to support his claim.

QUESTION: Why do you think Gore chooses to include this specific example?

CONCLUDE: How does this example help to persuade readers?

---

9. **initiative** (ih NIHSH uh tihv) *n.* ability to act or take the first step without being urged.
10. **Marshall Plan** United States–financed plan to rebuild Europe after World War II.
11. **One . . . leaders** Omar Bradley (1893–1981), a notable field commander in the United States Army.

Cordell Hull had won. In that moment, I knew what my father and mother would have felt were they alive.

41   Just as Hull's generation found moral authority in rising to solve the world crisis caused by fascism, so too can we find our greatest opportunity in rising to solve the climate crisis. In the Kanji characters used in both Chinese and Japanese, "crisis" is written with two symbols, the first meaning "danger," the second "opportunity." By facing and removing the danger of the climate crisis, we have the opportunity to gain the moral authority and vision to vastly increase our own capacity to solve other crises that have been too long ignored.

42   We must understand the connections between the climate crisis and the afflictions of poverty, hunger, HIV-AIDS and other pandemics. As these problems are linked, so too must be their solutions. We must begin by making the common rescue of the global **environment** the central organizing principle of the world community.

43   Fifteen years ago, I made that case at the "Earth Summit" in Rio de Janeiro. Ten years ago, I presented it in Kyoto. This week, I will urge the delegates in Bali to adopt a bold mandate for a treaty that establishes a universal global cap on emissions and uses the market in emissions trading[12] to efficiently allocate resources to the most effective opportunities for speedy reductions.

44   This treaty should be ratified and brought into effect everywhere in the world by the beginning of 2010—two years sooner than presently contemplated. The pace of our response must be accelerated to match the accelerating pace of the crisis itself.

45   Heads of state should meet early next year to review what was accomplished in Bali and take personal responsibility for addressing this crisis. It is not unreasonable to ask, given the gravity of our circumstances, that these heads of state meet every three months until the treaty is completed.

46   We also need a moratorium[13] on the construction of any new generating facility that burns coal without the capacity to safely trap and store carbon dioxide.

47   And most important of all, we need to put a *price* on carbon—with a CO_2 tax that is then rebated back to the people, progressively, according to the laws of each nation, in ways that shift the burden of taxation from employment to pollution. This is by far the most effective and simplest way to accelerate solutions to this crisis.

NOTES

environment (ehn VY uhrn muhnt) *n.* land, air, and water in which people, animals, and plants live, and all the natural features of these places

---

12. **universal global cap on emissions . . . market in emissions trading** type of law that uses the market to limit how much pollution factories can emit.
13. **moratorium** (mawr uh TAWR ee uhm) *n.* law to stop or delay something.

48 The world needs an alliance—especially of those nations that weigh heaviest in the scales where earth is in the balance. I salute Europe and Japan for the steps they've taken in recent years to meet the challenge, and the new government in Australia, which has made solving the climate crisis its first priority.

49 But the outcome will be decisively influenced by two nations that are now failing to do enough: the United States and China. While India is also growing fast in importance, it should be absolutely clear that it is the two largest CO_2 emitters—most of all, my own country—that will need to make the boldest moves, or stand accountable before history for their failure to act.

50 Both countries should stop using the other's behavior as an excuse for stalemate and instead develop an agenda for mutual survival in a shared global environment.

51 These are the last few years of decision, but they can be the first years of a bright and hopeful future if we do what we must. No one should believe a solution will be found without effort, without cost, without change. Let us acknowledge that if we wish to redeem squandered time and speak again with moral authority, then these are the hard truths:

52 The way ahead is difficult. The outer boundary of what we currently believe is feasible is still far short of what we actually must do. Moreover, between here and there, across the unknown, falls the shadow.

53 That is just another way of saying that we have to expand the boundaries of what is possible. In the words of the Spanish poet, Antonio Machado, "Pathwalker, there is no path. You must make the path as you walk."

54 We are standing at the most fateful fork in that path. So I want to end as I began, with a vision of two futures—each a palpable possibility—and with a prayer that we will see with vivid clarity the necessity of choosing between those two futures, and the urgency of making the right choice now.

55 The great Norwegian playwright, Henrik Ibsen, wrote, "One of these days, the younger generation will come knocking at my door."

56 The future is knocking at our door right now. Make no mistake, the next generation *will* ask us one of two questions. Either they will ask: "What were you thinking; why didn't you act?"

57 Or they will ask instead: "How did you find the moral courage to rise and successfully resolve a crisis that so many said was impossible to solve?" We have everything we need to get started, save perhaps political will, but political will is a renewable resource.

58 So let us renew it, and say together: "We have a purpose. We are many. For this purpose we will rise, and we will act." ❧

Comprehension Check

Complete the following items after you finish your first read.

1. Why has Al Gore been asked to give this speech?

2. What is the planetary emergency about which Gore is so concerned?

3. According to Gore, how much global-warming pollution was added to the atmosphere on the day he gave the speech?

4. Which American poet does Gore quote in his speech?

5. 📄 **Notebook** Write a brief summary of paragraphs 7–21 of the speech.

- -

RESEARCH

Research to Clarify Choose at least one unfamiliar detail from the text. Briefly research that detail. For example, you might want to find out more about Alfred Nobel, the United Nations, or "Earth Summit." In what way does the information you learned shed light on an aspect of the speech?

NOBEL SPEECH

Close Read the Text

1. This model, from paragraph 11 of the text, shows two sample annotations, along with questions and conclusions. Close read the passage and find another detail to annotate. Then, write a question and your conclusion.

ANNOTATE: Gore uses the word *fever* twice.

QUESTION: Why does Gore emphasize this word?

CONCLUDE: Gore is personifying the earth as being vulnerable and feverish—due to global warming.

As a result, the earth has a fever. And the fever is rising. The experts have told us it is not a passing affliction that will heal by itself. We asked for a second opinion. And a third. And a fourth. And the consistent conclusion, restated with increasing alarm, is that something basic is wrong.

ANNOTATE: These short bursts of thought are interesting.

QUESTION: What is the purpose behind this passage?

CONCLUDE: Gore creates a metaphor of earth as a patient and scientists as doctors. The shortness of the passages creates a sense of urgency.

2. For more practice, go back into the text and complete the close-read notes.

3. Revisit a section of the text you found important. Read this section closely and **annotate** what you notice. Ask **questions** such as "Why did the author make this choice?" What can you **conclude**?

🔧 **Tool Kit**
Close-Read Guide and Model Annotation

Analyze the Text

CITE TEXTUAL EVIDENCE to support your answers.

📓 **Notebook** Respond to these questions.

1. Compare and Contrast How does Gore compare Alfred Nobel's intentions and goals with those of modern society?

2. (a) Interpret What does Gore mean by "mutually assured destruction"?
(b) **Make a Judgment** Do you think Gore is correct? Explain.

3. Essential Question *What effects do people have on the environment?* What have you learned about the effects people have on the environment by reading this selection?

Copyright © SAVVAS Learning Company LLC. All Rights Reserved.

⚏ STANDARDS
Reading Informational Text
Trace and evaluate the argument and specific claims in a text, assessing whether the reasoning is sound and the evidence is relevant and sufficient to support the claims.

ESSENTIAL QUESTION: What effects do people have on the environment?

Nobel Speech **383**

Analyze Craft and Structure

Argument: Persuasive Speech A **persuasive speech** is a work of nonfiction that presents a series of arguments to convince people to think or act in a certain way. When you read or listen to a persuasive speech, be alert to the use of persuasive techniques. Then, decide whether a particular technique provides reasonable and relevant support that persuades you to accept or act on the author's ideas.

- **Appeals to authority** use the statements of experts and well-known people.
- **Appeals to emotion** use words that convey strong feelings.
- **Appeals to reason** use logical arguments backed by facts.

Most arguments will combine these techniques to appeal to their audience on many levels. As you read Gore's speech, analyze his use of persuasive techniques.

Practice

CITE TEXTUAL EVIDENCE
to support your answers.

Notebook Respond to these questions.

1. Review the speech. Then, use the chart to identify at least one example of each type of persuasive technique.

PERSUASIVE TECHNIQUE	EXAMPLE

2. Analyze the examples of persuasive techniques that you identified in the chart. Determine whether each example is relevant and reasonable support for Gore's argument.

3. **(a)** What "massive changes" does Gore say must be made to solve the climate crisis? **(b)** Has Gore persuaded you that these changes are possible? Why or why not?

4. **(a)** According to Gore, what is "shared responsibility"? **(b)** Is the support he provides to highlight this idea persuasive and convincing? Why or why not?

5. Write a paragraph in which you briefly summarize Gore's overall argument, and evaluate whether his reasons, evidence, and appeals convinced you of his claims.

NOBEL SPEECH

Concept Vocabulary

crisis	urgency	illusion
pollution	universal	environment

Why These Words? The concept vocabulary words describe situations or settings. For example, in paragraph 10 of his speech, Gore states that "we dumped another 70 million tons of global-warming *pollution* into the thin shell of atmosphere surrounding our planet, as if it were an open sewer." The word *pollution* describes a poisonous component of a setting—Earth's atmosphere.

1. Select two concept vocabulary words other than *pollution*. Explain how each word describes a setting or a situation.

2. What other words in the selection might describe a setting or a situation?

Practice

📓 **Notebook** Confirm your understanding of the concept vocabulary words by using them to complete the sentences.

1. Environmental groups work to educate the public and eliminate the _____ that the earth is perfectly healthy.

2. Despite scientific evidence, many world leaders have yet to consider the health of the environment a _____.

3. Water shortages are common across the world, making the problem _____.

4. Leaders such as Gore work with a variety of organizations to create a sense of _____ about environmental issues.

5. Increased instances of wildfires show how the _____ is changing.

6. _____ can affect all parts of our environment, from the water we drink to the air we breathe.

Word Study

Latin Prefix: *uni-* The Latin prefix *uni-* means "one." In his speech, Gore defines the climate crisis as *universal* because it affects everyone in the world similarly, as if all people were one entity.

1. Write your own sentence that correctly uses the word *universal*.

2. Using a dictionary, find three other words with the prefix *uni-*. Record a definition for each word and write a sentence using it.

🔲 WORD NETWORK

Add interesting words related to people and the planet from the text to your Word Network

▤ STANDARDS

Language
• Demonstrate command of the conventions of standard English grammar and usage when writing or speaking.
  a. Explain the function of phrases and clauses in general and their function in specific sentences.
• Determine or clarify the meaning of unknown and multiple-meaning words and phrases based on *grade 7 reading and content,* choosing flexibly from a range of strategies.
  b. Use common, grade-appropriate Greek or Latin affixes and roots as clues to the meaning of a word.

Conventions

Infinitive Phrases and Gerund Phrases Writers and speakers, such as Al Gore, use various types of phrases to add detail to sentences and to clarify the relationships among ideas. Two types of phrases are infinitive phrases and gerund phrases. An **infinitive** is a verb form that acts as a noun, an adjective, or an adverb. An infinitive usually begins with the word *to*. An **infinitive phrase** is an infinitive plus its own modifiers, objects, or complements.

- **Noun** (functioning as a subject): *To speak Spanish fluently* is my goal.
- **Noun** (functioning as an object): I want *to learn other languages*.
- **Adjective** (modifying *one*): She is the one *to see immediately*,
- **Adverb** (modifying *waited*): Everyone waited *to hear the news*.

A **gerund** is a verb form that ends in *-ing* and acts as a noun. It can function as a subject, an object, a predicate noun, or the object of a preposition. A **gerund phrase** is a gerund plus its own modifiers, objects, or complements.

- **Subject:** *Remodeling the building* was a good idea.
- **Direct Object:** Mischa enjoys *painting with watercolors*.
- **Predicate Noun:** Her favorite sport is *cross-country skiing*.
- **Object of a Preposition:** Nina never tires of *singing holiday songs*.

TIP

CLARIFICATION
In each example, the infinitive or gerund is underlined, and the infinitive phrase or gerund phrase is italicized. Refer to the Grammar Handbook to learn more about these terms.

Read It

1. Reread these sentences from the selection. Mark each infinitive or infinitive phrase and each gerund or gerund phrase. Identify the function each performs in the sentence.

   a. It is a purpose I have tried to serve for many years.

   b. This new consciousness requires expanding the possibilities inherent in all humanity.

   c. It is time to make peace with the planet.

   d. Indeed, without realizing it, we have begun to wage war on the earth itself.

Write It

📓 **Notebook** Write an example of each sentence named below.

1. A sentence that uses an infinitive as a noun
2. A sentence that uses a gerund as a subject
3. A sentence that uses an infinitive as an adverb
4. A sentence that uses a gerund as an object

NOBEL SPEECH (TEXT)

Comparing Text to Media

In this lesson, you will watch Al Gore's Nobel Prize acceptance speech. While you watch and listen, think about how the written speech and spoken speech have different effects.

NOBEL SPEECH (VIDEO)

About the Author

Former United States Vice President **Al Gore** (b.1948) continues dedicating his life to environmental issues and is a prominent advocate for solutions to climate change. Since winning a Nobel Prize and donating his portion of the $1.6 million award, Gore has established and runs a nonprofit organization, The Climate Reality Project. He released another book on climate change, *The Future: Six Drivers of Global Change*. Gore also collaborated with NASA, the National Oceanic and Atmospheric Organization (NOAA), and the United States Air Force to launch a satellite into space that would allow anyone to see Earth and track its changes online.

STANDARDS

Reading Informational Text
By the end of the year, read and comprehend literary nonfiction in the grades 6–8 text complexity band proficiently, with scaffolding as needed at the high end of the range.

Nobel Speech
Concept Vocabulary

You will encounter the following words as you listen to the speech.

unprecedented (uhn PREHS uh dehn tihd) *adj.* never having happened before; unheard of
recklessly (REHK lihs lee) *adv.* without regard for consequences; carelessly
imminent (IHM uh nuhnt) *adj.* threatening and likely to occur at any moment
unsustainable (uhn suh STAY nuh buhl) *adj.* unable to continue at the same rate or in the same way
emissions (ih MIHSH uhnz) *n.* gas or other substance sent into the air
efficiently (uh FIHSH uhnt lee) *adv.* with the least amount of effort and waste; effectively

First Review MEDIA: VIDEO

Apply these strategies as you conduct your first review. You will have an opportunity to complete a close review after your first review.

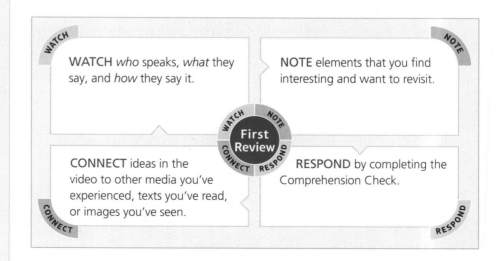

WATCH *who* speaks, *what* they say, and *how* they say it.

NOTE elements that you find interesting and want to revisit.

CONNECT ideas in the video to other media you've experienced, texts you've read, or images you've seen.

RESPOND by completing the Comprehension Check.

First Review

Nobel Speech

Al Gore

BACKGROUND

Human activities, such as the use of power plants and automobiles, produce large amounts of greenhouse gases such as carbon dioxide. Greenhouse gases trap heat in the atmosphere and are the primary cause of global climate change. Temperature changes that result from global climate change could have disastrous consequences, such as the melting of polar ice caps, extreme weather, and the extinction of many species.

SCAN FOR
MULTIMEDIA

NOTES

Comprehension Check

Complete the following items after you finish your first review.

1. Whom is Gore addressing in his speech?

2. What do recent studies say about the North Polar ice cap?

3. Who is Cordell Hull?

4. 📓 **Notebook** Choose an example of powerful language in the speech, and explain why this language is so powerful.

- -

RESEARCH

Research to Clarify Choose at least one unfamiliar detail from the text. Briefly research that detail. In what way does the information you learned shed light on an aspect of the speech?

Close Review

Watch the video of Al Gore's Nobel speech again. Write any new observations that seem important. What **questions** do you have? What can you **conclude**?

NOBEL SPEECH (VIDEO)

Analyze the Media

📓 **Notebook** Complete the activities.

1. Identify a section in the video of Al Gore's speech that you found particularly persuasive. Then, write a short paragraph in which you briefly describe this section, and explain why you chose it.

2. **Essential Question: *What effects do people have on the environment?*** What have you learned about the ways in which people affect the environment from watching the video of Al Gore's speech?

LANGUAGE DEVELOPMENT

Concept Vocabulary

unprecedented	imminent	emissions
recklessly	unsustainable	efficiently

📓 **Notebook** Demonstrate your understanding of these words in your responses to these questions.

1. Why does Gore most likely use the word *unprecedented* to describe scientists' distress about the North Polar ice cap?

2. Why does Gore most likely use the word *recklessly* to describe the burning and clearing of forests?

3. Why is the word *emissions* important to the speech?

4. According to Gore, what threat to humanity is *imminent*?

5. Why does Gore consider our current approach to climate change *unsustainable*?

6. Name one thing we must do *efficiently* if we are to successfully address global warming.

🔗 WORD NETWORK

Add interesting words about people and the planet from the text to your Word Network.

⬛ STANDARDS

Speaking and Listening
Delineate a speaker's argument and specific claims, evaluating the soundness of the reasoning and the relevance and sufficiency of the evidence.

Language
Determine or clarify the meaning of unknown and multiple-meaning words and phrases based on *grade 7 reading and content*, choosing flexibly from a range of strategies.

NOBEL SPEECH (TEXT)

NOBEL SPEECH (VIDEO)

Writing to Compare

You have studied the written version and video of Al Gore's Nobel Prize acceptance speech. Now, analyze both versions and consider how the medium in which the message is provided—written or video—affects how persuaded you are by Gore's message.

Assignment

Both the written and video versions of Gore's Nobel speech contain the same message. However, the different modes of delivery, text and speech, may affect how an audience is persuaded by the message.

Write an **argument** in which you state a claim as to which medium more persuasively conveys Gore's argument. Explain how the elements of the video or the written text either strengthen or weaken the argument.

Prewriting

Gather Evidence Review both the text and video. Use a chart like this to gather your notes. In the left column, record key ideas that are conveyed in both the text and video. Then, take note of how effectively that key idea is portrayed in each medium.

KEY IDEA	EFFECTIVENESS IN TEXT	EFFECTIVENESS IN VIDEO

Notebook Respond to these questions.

1. Does the text reveal aspects of the argument that the video does not? Explain.

2. Does the video communicate the author's tone in a way the text does not? Explain.

Copyright © SAVVAS Learning Company LLC. All Rights Reserved.

STANDARDS

Reading Informational Text
Compare and contrast a text to an audio, video, or multimedia version of the text, analyzing each medium's portrayal of the subject.

Writing
Write arguments to support claims with clear reasons and relevant evidence.
  b. Support claim(s) with logical reasoning and relevant evidence, using accurate, credible sources and demonstrating an understanding of the topic or text.

Speaking and Listening
Delineate a speaker's argument and specific claims, evaluating the soundness of the reasoning and the relevance and sufficiency of the evidence.

Drafting

Craft Your Claim Decide which version of the speech you think is more convincing and write a **claim** in which you state your position. Choose your words carefully so that you state your position in a clear and strong way.

Claim: _____

_____

Use Transitions to Connect Ideas Use your notes from the analysis you did earlier to analyze the similarities and differences in the video and the text. Explain the ways in which these differences made one version more persuasive than the other.

To show similarities and differences, use transitions to connect your ideas.

Transitions that show differences

however, unlike, on the other hand, yet, in contrast, but, although

Transitions that show similarities

also, similarly, likewise, too, in addition

Provide Counterarguments To make your argument stronger and more convincing, you must address opposing viewpoints. To do so, summarize the opposing view without offering your opinion about it. Then, use reasons and evidence to offer a counterargument in which you prove why this position is wrong.

Opposing View: _____

_____

Counterargument: _____

_____

Review, Revise, and Edit

Once you are done drafting, review and revise your essay. Be sure you have provided enough support for your position. Pay close attention to be sure you have used transitions effectively to show the relationships among claims, reasons, and evidence. Identify areas where you can add additional examples to strengthen your argument.

✏ EVIDENCE LOG

Before moving on to a new selection, go to your Evidence Log and record what you've learned from the text and video of Al Gore's Nobel Prize acceptance speech.

≣ STANDARDS

Reading Informational Text
Compare and contrast a text to an audio, video, or multimedia version of the text, analyzing each medium's portrayal of the subject.

Writing
Write arguments to support claims with clear reasons and relevant evidence.
   a. Introduce claim(s), acknowledge alternate or opposing claims, and organize the reasons and evidence logically.
   b. Support claim(s) with logical reasoning and relevant evidence, using accurate, credible sources and demonstrating an understanding of the topic or text.
   c. Use words, phrases, and clauses to create cohesion and clarify the relationships among claim(s), reasons, and evidence.

WRITING TO SOURCES

• *from* SILENT SPRING

• NOBEL SPEECH (text)

• NOBEL SPEECH (video)

🔧 Tool Kit

Student Model of an
Argument

ACADEMIC
VOCABULARY

As you craft your
argument, consider using
some of the academic
vocabulary you learned in
the beginning of the unit.

ethical

dissent

interject

discord

accuracy

 STANDARDS

Writing

• Write arguments to support claims
with clear reasons and relevant
evidence.

• Use technology, including the
Internet, to produce and publish
writing and link to and cite sources
as well as to interact and collaborate
with others, including linking to and
citing sources.

• Write routinely over extended time
frames and shorter time frames for
a range of discipline-specific tasks,
purposes, and audiences.

Write an Argument

You have read and watched selections that relate to the effects people
have on the environment. In *Silent Spring*, Rachel Carson raised
awareness by exposing the negative effects that certain human activities
have on the world around them. Decades after *Silent Spring* was
published, the public is coming to terms with a new challenge due to
the effects of human activity on the environment—climate change. In his
Nobel Prize acceptance speech, Al Gore urges society to take action and
change its behavior before it is too late.

Assignment

Use the knowledge you gained from the selections in this section as
well as from your own experience to write an **argument** in which you
take a position on the following question:

> **What is the most significant effect that people have
> on the environment?**

After you write your argument, turn it into a blog post, and post it to
a school or class website. Be sure to include links to your sources.

Elements of an Argument

In an **argument,** the writer states and supports a claim based on factual
evidence. An effective argument includes the following elements:

• a clear statement of your claim, or position, on an issue that has
  more than one side

• the context surrounding the issue

• persuasive evidence and logical reasoning that supports your claim

• statements that acknowledge **counterclaims,** or opposing views,
  and offer counterarguments to disprove these views

• a clear organizational structure

• words, phrases, and clauses that show the relationships among
  claims, reasons, and evidence

• a formal style that appeals mainly to the audience's sense of reason

Model Argument For a model of an argument,
see the Launch text, "Rethinking the Wild."

Challenge yourself to find the elements of an
effective argument in the text. You will have an
opportunity to review these elements as you
prepare to write your own argument.

Prewriting / Planning

Craft a Claim Review the notes you took on the selections. Craft a one- or two-sentence **thesis statement** that clearly states your claim, or position. Make sure your statement can be supported with several reasons and a variety of relevant evidence.

Address Counterclaims Strong arguments address **counterclaims,** or opposing positions, and explain why these views are flawed. In your argument, address at least one counterclaim and provide a response in which you disprove it, or your counterargument.

Possible counterclaim: _____

Reasons and evidence that support counterclaim: _____

My counterargument: _____

Reasons and evidence that support my counterargument: _____

Gather Evidence Before you begin drafting, gather details that support your claim. Include the strongest and most convincing details to support your claim. In the Launch Text, the writer uses an **anecdote,** a quick story that reinforces a main point, to illustrate how difficult it can be to balance the needs of people and animals.

> *In Jon Mooallem's book,* Wild Ones *he describes the attempt of one organization to save the whooping crane from extinction. It's a story that may challenge what you thought you knew about the sometimes competing interests of people and animals.*

Connect Across Texts To effectively present and support your argument with evidence from the selections, review the texts and note key ideas, examples, and important details. If the exact words are important, use **direct quotations** from the text, or an author's exact words. To simplify a complicated idea and make it easier to understand, **paraphrase** the idea, or restate it in your own words. When using direct quotations, place quotation marks around the exact words of another author. When paraphrasing, be sure your paraphrases correctly reflect the ideas in the original text.

Analyze the ways in which the Launch Text presents and supports an argument. To do so, ask questions such as:

- What important information does the author use to support his or her position? Why might the author have chosen this evidence?
- How does the author's **diction,** or word choice, affect the strength of the argument?

Seeing how an author effectively presents and supports an argument will enable you to better apply these skills to your own writing.

EVIDENCE LOG

Review your Evidence Log and identify key details you may want to include in your argument.

STANDARDS

Writing
- Introduce claim(s), acknowledge alternate or opposing claims, and organize the reasons and evidence logically.
- Support claim(s) with logical reasoning and relevant evidence, using accurate, credible sources and demonstrating an understanding of the topic or text.

Drafting

Organize Your Argument As you draft, present the supporting evidence you have gathered, starting with your least important points and building to your most important ones. Use transitional words and phrases to unify your writing and show the relationships among your ideas. Use the method shown in the pyramid diagram to outline your argument before you write your first draft.

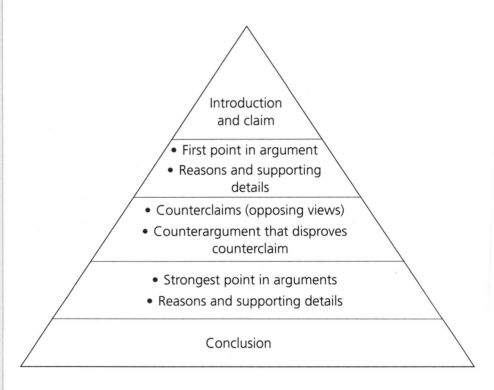

Introduction and claim

- First point in argument
- Reasons and supporting details

- Counterclaims (opposing views)
- Counterargument that disproves counterclaim

- Strongest point in arguments
- Reasons and supporting details

Conclusion

Appeal to Your Audience An **author's style** is the "sound" of his or her writing—it refers to the unique ways an author uses words. Word choice and **tone,** or the author's attitude toward his or her subject, are important elements of style. To keep your audience engaged choose words that add interest. Regardless of your audience, your style should be formal in an argument—never include slang and always maintain standard English.

Address Counterclaims Address counterclaims to your position directly—do not avoid them. To do so, respond to counterclaims with statements that show why these claims are flawed. These statements are your counterargument and should be supported by logical reasons and relevant evidence.

Write a First Draft Review the elements of an effective argument, and write your first draft based on your completed outline and the information you have gathered. Use a variety of sources and different types of evidence for support as you draft your argument.

STANDARDS

Writing
• Write arguments to support claims with clear reasons and relevant evidence.

   d. Establish and maintain a formal style.

LANGUAGE DEVELOPMENT: CONVENTIONS

Sentence Fluency: Revising Sentences Using Participles

To make your writing flow smoothly, combine sentences using participles and participial phrases. A **participle** is a verb form that acts as an adjective, modifying a noun or pronoun. Present participles end in *-ing*. Past participles usually end in *-ed,* but may have an irregular ending, such as the *-en* in *spoken.*

> past participle   noun
>
> She banged her fist against the closed windows.

A **participial phrase** consists of a participle and its modifiers.
A **misplaced modifier** is placed far away from the word it describes.

> **Misplaced modifier:** I heard her voice *listening to the song*.
>
> **Revised:** *Listening to the song,* I heard her voice.

A **dangling modifier** is not logically connected to any word in the sentence.

> **Dangling modifier:** *Raising the flag,* the wind felt strong.
>
> **Revised:** *Raising the flag,* the sailors felt the strong wind.

Fixing Choppy Passages Using Participles To fix a choppy passage, identify sentences that can be combined. Then, rewrite the passage using one or more of the following methods:

- **Combine sentences using a present participle.**
  Example: We arranged a tour. We would walk the grounds.
  We arranged a walking tour of the grounds.

- **Combine sentences using a past participle.**
  Example: The food is cooked. It will not spoil.
  The cooked food will not spoil.

- **Combine sentences using a participial phrase.**
  Example: Marisol ate her food quickly. She was running late.
  Running late, Marisol ate her food quickly.

Read It

Review the Launch Text, and identify two sentences that use participles or participial phrases.

Write It

1. Revise each sentence to correct the misplaced or dangling modifier.

   a. Having arrived late for school, a written explanation was needed.

   b. Running swiftly, the audience watched the track star.

2. Choose three paragraphs in your draft. Read the paragraphs aloud, marking any passages that sound choppy. Using one of the methods described, fix the choppy passages by combining sentences.

▤ STANDARDS

Language
• Demonstrate command of the conventions of standard English grammar and usage when writing or speaking.

c. Place phrases and clauses within a sentence, recognizing and correcting misplaced and dangling modifiers.
• Use knowledge of language and its conventions when writing, speaking, reading, or listening.

a. Choose language that expresses ideas precisely and concisely, recognizing and eliminating wordiness and redundancy.

Revising

Evaluating Your Draft

Use the following checklist to evaluate the effectiveness of your first draft. Then, use your evaluation and the instruction on this page to guide your revision.

FOCUS AND ORGANIZATION	EVIDENCE AND ELABORATION	CONVENTIONS
☐ Provides a clearly stated claim and information about the context surrounding the issue.	☐ Supports claims with logical reasoning and persuasive evidence.	☐ Uses a formal style and tone.
☐ Establishes a clear organizational structure that highlights the main points.	☐ Acknowledges opposing claims and offers counterarguments to these views.	☐ Attends to the norms and conventions of the discipline, especially using participles to make writing flow smoothly while avoiding misplaced and dangling modifiers.
☐ Uses words, phrases, and clauses to create cohesion and clarify the relationships among claims, reasons, and evidence.	☐ Word choice reflects consideration of the intended audience.	
☐ Provides a concluding statement that follows from and supports the argument.		

⬡ WORD NETWORK

Include interesting words from your Word Network in your essay.

☰ STANDARDS

Writing
• Introduce claim(s), acknowledge alternate or opposing claims, and organize the reasons and evidence logically.
• Use words, phrases, and clauses to create cohesion and clarify the relationships among claim(s), reasons, and evidence.
• Provide a concluding statement or section that follows from and supports the argument presented.

Revising for Focus and Organization

Use Transitions To make the connections between ideas in your argument clear to readers, use transition words and phrases such as *however, nevertheless, even so,* and *in addition.* Consider the relationship between ideas you are trying to express. Then, choose transitional words or phrases that show that relationship.

- to show examples: *for instance, also, in addition*
- to contrast ideas: *however, yet, unlike*
- to show causes and effects: *therefore, since, because, as a result*

Write a Memorable Conclusion Bring your argument to a close by restating your thesis statement and synthesizing, or briefly pulling together, the evidence you presented. End with a memorable statement or section that summarizes your argument in a new way and provides a fresh insight into your claim.

Revising for Evidence and Elaboration

Evaluate Your Evidence To make sure your argument is convincing, evaluate your evidence by asking yourself the following questions.

- Does every piece of evidence support my claim?
- Where can I add evidence to make my argument stronger?
- Have I given proper credit to the source of each piece of evidence I used?

PEER REVIEW

Exchange essays with a classmate. Use the checklist to evaluate your classmate's argument and provide supportive feedback.

1. Is there a clearly stated claim?

☐ yes ☐ no   If no, suggest ways in which the writer might clarify it.

2. Is there support for the claim based on logical reasoning and relevant evidence from accurate, credible sources?

☐ yes ☐ no   If no, point out where the writer should provide more support.

3. Are opposing claims acknowledged and effectively addressed with counterarguments?

☐ yes ☐ no   If no, suggest ways in which the writing can acknowledge and address opposing claims.

4. What is the strongest part of your classmate's essay? Explain.

_____

_____

Editing and Proofreading

Edit for Conventions Quotations from persuasive sources can make an argument more powerful and convincing. Pay careful attention to the punctuation, indentation, and capitalization of the quotations you include. Use quotation marks to set off short quotations. Longer quotations of four or more lines should begin on a new line, be indented, and appear without quotation marks. Always remember to follow a standard format for citation when using quotations in your writing.

Proofread for Accuracy The syllables in some words are barely heard. Because of this, letters are often left out in spelling. Proofread your argument to make sure you have spelled words with tricky syllables correctly. Double-check the spellings of words such as *different*, *average*, and *restaurant* in a dictionary. Notice how each word is broken into syllables. Say the word aloud while you look at it, and exaggerate your pronunciation of the sounds and syllables.

Publishing and Presenting

Create a final version of your argument. Then, post it on a class or school website as a blog post. Include links to the sources you used to support your argument.

Reflecting

Reflect on what you learned as you wrote your argument. What was the most challenging part of writing your argument? Did you learn something from transforming your argument into a blog post and posting it on a website?

≔ STANDARDS

Writing
• Use technology, including the Internet, to produce and publish writing and link to and cite sources as well as to interact and collaborate with others, including linking to and citing sources.
• Gather relevant information from multiple print and digital sources, using search terms effectively; assess the credibility and accuracy of each source; and quote or paraphrase the data and conclusions of others while avoiding plagiarism and following a standard format for citation.

Language
• Demonstrate command of the conventions of standard English capitalization, punctuation, and spelling when writing.
  b. Spell correctly.
  c. Consult general and specialized reference materials, both print and digital, to find the pronunciation of a word or determine or clarify its precise meaning or its part of speech.

ESSENTIAL QUESTION:

What effects do people have on the environment?

Our world is filled with amazing natural wonders. Will our children's children be able to enjoy these wonders as we have? In this section, you will read selections that discuss the relationship between humans and our environment. You will work as a group to continue your exploration of the ways in which people affect the environment.

Small-Group Learning Strategies

Throughout your life, in school, in your community, and in your career, you will continue to learn and work with others.

Look at these strategies and the actions you can take to practice them as you work in teams. Add ideas of your own for each step. Use these strategies during Small Group Learning.

STRATEGY	ACTION PLAN
Prepare	• Complete your assignments so that you are prepared for group work. • Organize your thinking so you can contribute to your group's discussions. •
Participate fully	• Make eye contact to signal that you are listening and taking in what is being said. • Use text evidence when making a point. •
Support others	• Build off ideas from others in your group. • Invite others who have not yet spoken to join the discussion. •
Clarify	• Paraphrase the ideas of others to ensure that your understanding is correct. • Ask follow-up questions. •

SCAN FOR MULTIMEDIA

CONTENTS

PERFORMANCE TASK

SPEAKING AND LISTENING FOCUS
Present an Argument
The Small-Group readings present different perspectives on the ways in which humans impact the natural environment. After reading, your group will plan and deliver a multimedia presentation about our relationship to the natural environment.

Working as a Team

1. Take a Position In your group, discuss the following question:

What is our relationship with the natural environment?

As you take turns sharing your positions, be sure to provide examples for your choice. After all group members have shared, discuss the characteristics of this relationship that are suggested by your responses.

2. List Your Rules As a group, decide on the rules that you will follow as you work together. Two samples are provided. Add two more of your own. You may add or revise rules based on your experience together.

- Come prepared for group discussions.
- Acknowledge other people's opinions.

- _____

  _____

- _____

  _____

3. Apply the Rules Practice working as a group. Share what you have learned about survival. Make sure each person in the group contributes. Take notes and be prepared to share with the class one thing that you heard from another member of your group.

4. Name Your Group Choose a name that reflects the unit topic.

Our group's name: _____

5. Create a Communication Plan Decide how you want to communicate with one another. For example, you might use online collaboration tools, email, or instant messaging.

Our group's decision: _____

_____

Making a Schedule

First, find out the due dates for the small-group activities. Then, preview the texts and activities with your group and make a schedule for completing the tasks.

SELECTION	ACTIVITIES	DUE DATE
Turtle Watchers "Nature" is what We see— The Sparrow		
Eagle Tracking at Follensby Pond		
He—y, Come On Ou—t!		

Working on Group Projects

Different projects require different roles. As your group works together, you'll find it more effective if each person has a specific role. Before beginning a project, decide among yourselves on each group member's role. Here are some possible roles; add your own ideas.

Project Manager: monitors the schedule and keeps everyone on task

Researcher: organizes research activities

Recorder: takes notes during group meetings

_____

_____

_____

_____

_____

 SCAN FOR MULTIMEDIA

POETRY COLLECTION

Turtle Watchers
"Nature" is what We see—
The Sparrow

Concept Vocabulary

As you perform your first read, you will encounter these words.

ancestors	wisdom	heed

Using a Dictionary To check the meanings of unfamiliar words, consult a print or online dictionary. Dictionaries provide a word's definition, pronunciation, part of speech, variant forms, and etymology, or word origin.

This box shows an example of a dictionary entry for the word *anthology*. Note that the pronunciation is in parentheses, and the etymology is in square brackets.

> **anthology** (an THOL uh jee) *n., pl.* **-gies** [Gr. *anthologia*, a garland, collection of short poems < *anthologos*, gathering flowers < *anthos*, flower + *legein*, to gather] a collection of poems, stories, songs, excerpts, etc., chosen by the compiler.

Apply your knowledge of using a dictionary and other vocabulary strategies to determine the meanings of unfamiliar words you encounter during your first read.

First Read POETRY

Apply these strategies as you conduct your first read. You will have an opportunity to complete a close read after your first read.

NOTICE *who* or *what* is "speaking" the poem and whether the poem tells a story or describes a single moment.

ANNOTATE by marking vocabulary and key passages you want to revisit.

First Read

CONNECT ideas within the selection to what you already know and what you have already read.

RESPOND by completing the Comprehension Check.

STANDARDS

Reading Literature
By the end of the year, read and comprehend literature, including stories, dramas, and poems, in the grades 6–8 text complexity band proficiently, with scaffolding as needed at the high end of the range.

Language
Determine or clarify the meaning of unknown and multiple-meaning words and phrases based on *grade 7 reading and content,* choosing flexibly from a range of strategies.
  c. Consult general and specialized reference materials, both print and digital, to find the pronunciation of a word or determine or clarify its precise meaning or its part of speech.

About the Poets

Linda Hogan (b. 1947) is an award-winning Chickasaw novelist, essayist, poet, and environmentalist. Her writing often addresses topics such as the environment, ecofeminism, and Native American history. An activist and educator, Hogan has spoken at various global conferences and events including the Environmental Literature Conference in Turkey in 2009. She lives in the Colorado mountains and teaches creative writing.

Emily Dickinson (1830–1886) considered books her "strongest friend." Withdrawn and shy, she spent most of her time at home in Amherst, Massachusetts, reading and writing. Most of her 1,775 poems were discovered after her death, including one that begins, "I'm nobody! Who are you?" Today, Dickinson is considered one of the most important American poets.

Paul Laurence Dunbar (1872–1906) was the son of former slaves. Encouraged by his mother, he began writing poetry at an early age. Dunbar was inspired by Harriet Beecher Stowe's novel *Uncle Tom's Cabin,* and in his own work he honored people who fought for the rights of African Americans. Over the course of his life, Dunbar published more than ten volumes of poetry, four novels, and four volumes of short stories.

Backgrounds

Turtle Watchers

Some sea turtles, such as loggerhead sea turtles, travel thousands of miles to lay their eggs on the same beach where they were born. The turtles dig a small nest in the sand, where they lay their eggs, sometimes over a hundred in a single nest. When the eggs hatch, the baby turtles make the dangerous trek back to the ocean to continue the cycle.

"Nature" is what We see—

From ancient Greeks to English romantics to Japanese haiku masters, poets from every period of time have contemplated the beauty of the natural world. The poet William Wordsworth wrote, "Come forth into the light of things, let Nature be your teacher."

The Sparrow

Sparrows are one of the most common birds in the world. They are often seen in North America, but this was not always the case. In the mid-1800s, a man named Nicholas Pike decided to bring several dozen over from England and release them in New York. Since then, these small brown birds have flourished and spread across the continent.

Turtle Watchers

Linda Hogan

SCAN FOR
MULTIMEDIA

NOTES

Use a dictionary or indicate
another strategy you used that
helped you determine meaning.

ancestors (AN sehs tuhrz) *n.*

MEANING:

Old mother at water's edge
used to bow down to them,
the turtles coming in from the sea,
their many eggs,
5 their eyes streaming water like tears,
and I'd see it all,
old mother as if in prayer,
the turtles called back to where they were born,
the hungry watchers standing at the edge of trees
10 hoping for food when darkness gathers.

Years later, swimming in murky waters
a sea turtle swam beside me
both of us watching as if clasped together
in the lineage of the same world
15 the sweep of the same current,
even rising for a breath of air at the same time
still watching.
My **ancestors** call them
the keepers of doors
20 and the shore a realm to other worlds,
both ways and
water moves the deep shift of life
back to birth and before
as if there is a path where beings truly meet,
25 as if I am rounding the human corners.

"Nature" is what We see—

Emily Dickinson

SCAN FOR
MULTIMEDIA

"Nature" is what We see—
The Hill—the Afternoon—
Squirrel—Eclipse—the Bumble bee—
Nay—Nature is Heaven—

5 "Nature" is what We hear—
The Bobolink[1]—the Sea—
Thunder—the Cricket—
Nay—Nature is Harmony—

"Nature" is what We know—
10 But have no Art to say—
So impotent our **Wisdom** is
To Her Sincerity—

---

1. **Bobolink** *n.* small bird.

NOTES

Use a dictionary or indicate
another strategy you used that
helped you determine meaning.

wisdom (WIHZ duhm) *n.*

MEANING:

The Sparrow

Paul Laurence Dunbar

SCAN FOR
MULTIMEDIA

NOTES

Use a dictionary or indicate
another strategy you used that
helped you determine meaning.

heed (heed) *v.*

MEANING:

A little bird, with plumage brown,
Beside my window flutters down,
A moment chirps its little strain,
Ten taps upon my window-pane,
5 And chirps again, and hops along,
To call my notice to its song;
But I work on, nor **heed** its lay,[1]
Till, in neglect, it flies away.

So birds of peace and hope and love
10 Come fluttering earthward from above,
To settle on life's window-sills,
And ease our load of earthly ills;
But we, in traffic's rush and din
Too deep engaged to let them in,
15 With deadened heart and sense plod on,
Nor know our loss till they are gone

———————————
1. **lay** *n.* song.

Comprehension Check

Complete the following items after you finish your first read. Review and clarify details with your group.

TURTLE WATCHERS

1. What are the "hungry watchers" doing?

2. What happens years later?

"NATURE" IS WHAT WE SEE—

1. What does the first stanza say nature is?

2. What does the second stanza say nature is?

3. What does the third stanza say nature is?

THE SPARROW

1. What does the speaker do in response to the bird beside his or her window?

2. According to the speaker, how do we "plod on"?

- -

RESEARCH

Research to Explore Choose one unfamiliar detail mentioned in one of the poems. Briefly research that detail. For instance, you might research the life cycle of the sea turtle. In what way does the information you learned affect your understanding of the poem? Explain.

Close Read the Text

With your group, revisit sections of the text you marked during your first read. **Annotate** what you notice. What **questions** do you have? What can you **conclude**?

Analyze the Text

CITE TEXTUAL EVIDENCE
to support your answers.

📓 **Notebook** Complete the activities.

1. **Review and Clarify** With your group, reread the poems. Analyze each poem, and determine the theme about nature that each poem suggests.

2. **Present and Discuss** Now, work with your group to share the lines from the poems that you found especially important. Take turns presenting your lines. Discuss what you noticed in the poems, what questions you asked, and what conclusions you reached.

3. **Essential Question: *What effects do people have on the environment?*** What have these poems taught you about the effects people have on the environment? Discuss with your group.

LANGUAGE DEVELOPMENT

Concept Vocabulary

ancestors	wisdom	heed

Why These Words? The concept vocabulary words from the poems are related. With your group, determine what the words have in common. Write your ideas and add another word that fits the category.

Practice

📓 **Notebook** Use each concept vocabulary word in a sentence that demonstrates its meaning. Read aloud your sentences to a partner, and discuss any differences in your understandings.

Word Study

Etymology The etymology, or word origin, of the word *ancestors* can help you understand and remember its meaning. *Ancestors* was formed from the Latin prefix *ante-*, meaning "before," and the Latin verb *cedere,* meaning "go." Thus, *ancestors* literally means "those who have gone before us." With your group, discuss "Turtle Watchers." How does understanding the etymology of the word *ancestors* deepen your understanding of the poem?

🔗 **WORD NETWORK**

Add interesting words related to people and the planet from the text to your Word Network.

STANDARDS

Reading Literature
Analyze how a drama's or poem's form or structure contributes to its meaning.

Language
Determine or clarify the meaning of unknown and multiple-meaning words and phrases based on *grade 7 reading and content,* choosing flexibly from a range of strategies.
  b. Use common, grade-appropriate Greek or Latin affixes and roots as clues to the meaning of a word.

Analyze Craft and Structure

The Speaker in Lyric Poetry When you read a poem you can "hear" a voice speaking to you. That is the voice of the poem's **speaker**. Like the narrator in a story, the speaker in a poem is an imaginary voice created by the poet. The speaker presents a unique view that expresses his or her thoughts, feelings, personality, and attitude toward the subject. Although they sometimes overlap, the speaker's point of view is not necessarily the point of view of the poet.

All three poems in this collection are examples of lyric poetry. A **lyric poem** expresses the thoughts and feelings of a speaker about a setting, a moment, or an idea, such as nature. In this form of poetry, a poet typically uses vivid, musical language to express the speaker's observations, feelings, and insights. As a consequence, the reader's understanding is filtered through and shaped by the speaker's perceptions.

Practice

CITE TEXTUAL EVIDENCE to support your answers.

Work with your group to analyze the poetry in this collection. Answer the questions and use the chart to examine the similarities and differences in approach in each of the poems.

QUESTIONS	Turtle Watchers	"Nature" is what We see—	The Sparrow
What is the poem's subject and the speaker's attitude toward the subject?			
What vivid words and descriptions are used?			
What is the speaker saying about people's relationship to nature?			

POETRY COLLECTION

Author's Style

Diction and Tone An author's word choice, or **diction,** includes not only the specific words but also the phrases and expressions an author uses. In poetry, a poet's word choice plays an important role in creating poetic language, which is specific, imaginative, and rich with emotion. A poet's use of language helps to develop the **tone** of a poem, or the poet's attitude toward his or her subject.

To achieve these effects in a poem, a poet often chooses words not only for their **denotations,** or dictionary definitions, but for the connotations the words evoke in readers. **Connotations** are the ideas and feelings a word brings to mind. Although, two words many have similar denotations, a poet may choose one word over another because of the connotations associated with the word. Consider the following lines of poetry:

- They rolled over the swells until they slid ashore.
- They slammed over the waves until they hit land.

Both examples convey roughly the same information. However, in the first example, the words *rolled, swells,* and *slid* have calming connotations and create a peaceful tone. In the second example, the words *slammed, waves,* and *hit* have harsher connotations and create a dangerous, anxious tone.

A poet's word choice and tone help develop meaning in poem. Analyzing a poet's word choice and tone can help you to **make inferences,** or educated guesses, about the **theme** of a poem, or the insight about life that it suggests.

Read It

Notebook Work with your group to identify specific word choices in each poem, and note how these choices affect meaning and tone. When you have completed the chart, discuss the possible themes your examples suggest.

POEM	WORD OR PHRASE	EFFECT ON MEANING OR TONE
Turtle Watchers		
"Nature" is what We see—		
The Sparrow		

Write It

Notebook Using your notes from the chart and your discussion, work individually to write a brief paragraph about the theme of each poem. In each paragraph, support your ideas about the theme with the specific examples you gathered while working with your group. To ensure you describe your thoughts accurately and concisely, consider the connotations of the words you use.

STANDARDS

Reading Literature
- Cite several pieces of textual evidence to support analysis of what the text says explicitly as well as inferences drawn from the text.
- Determine a theme or central idea of a text and analyze its development over the course of the text; provide an objective summary of the text.
- Determine the meaning of words and phrases as they are used in a text, including figurative and connotative meanings; analyze the impact of rhymes and other repetitions of sounds on a specific verse or stanza of a poem or section of a story or drama.

Speaking and Listening

Assignment

Using the analysis you have done so far, work with your group to create an **oral presentation** that highlights the theme of one of the poems in the collection. Choose from the following options:

☐ a **dramatic reading** in which you use multimedia, such as music, props, and costumes, to convey the meaning and theme of the poem

☐ a **digital multimedia presentation** in which you use videos, images, and other digital media to convey the meaning and theme of the poem

Project Plan Assign roles for each member of your group. For groups who have chosen the dramatic reading, roles can include speakers to recite the poem, a sound person, a costume designer, and a person to identify and organize visuals and music. For groups who have chosen the digital multimedia presentation, roles can include a speaker, a multimedia researcher, and a person to organize the information for the presentation.

Plan and Practice Your Delivery To project confidence and a positive attitude, plan and practice your delivery both individually and as a group. As you practice, use the following strategies to refine your presentation techniques:

- **Check equipment.** If your presentation involves use of audio or video, practice your presentation along with the media. Work on the timing of media and how it relates to the rest of the performance.

- **Use your voice well.** Be energetic, but speak clearly and precisely. Enunciate every word. Vary the pitch and speed of your voice to keep listeners engaged. Make sure you are speaking loudly enough to be heard by the entire class.

- **Make eye contact.** Memorize as much of your part of the presentation as possible. Doing so will enable you to make eye contact with your audience more frequently.

Present and Evaluate Once you have rehearsed, present your work to the class. After the presentation, invite comments and feedback from your classmates. Be prepared to answer their questions.

When other groups present their work, listen attentively. Evaluate their performance, and provide feedback to them in a respectful way.

✎ EVIDENCE LOG

Before moving on to a new selection, go to your log and record what you learned from "Turtle Watchers," "'Nature' is what We see—," and "The Sparrow."

☰ STANDARDS

Speaking and Listening
- Present claims and findings, emphasizing salient points in a focused, coherent manner with pertinent descriptions, facts, details, and examples; use appropriate eye contact, adequate volume, and clear pronunciation.
- Include multimedia components and visual displays in presentations to clarify claims and findings and emphasize salient points.
- Adapt speech to a variety of contexts and tasks, demonstrating command of formal English when indicated or appropriate.

About The Nature Conservancy

The Nature Conservancy is a charitable organization that was founded in Virginia in 1951. Its mission is to "conserve the lands and waters on which all life depends." The organization has over one million members and works in 35 countries, as well as all of the 50 states, protecting habitats ranging from grasslands to coral reefs.

Eagle Tracking at Follensby Pond

Media Vocabulary

These words will be useful to you as you view, analyze, and discuss photography.

documentary photography: photographs taken with the main purpose of recording a place, an event, or a person	• Documentary photography aims to portray subjects objectively, or in a way that is based on facts and not influenced by feelings and opinions. • Documentary photos may evoke feelings in viewers based on the subject matter.
vantage point: place where the photographer positions the camera	• A photographer may use a particular vantage point in order to capture the subject in a particular position or in a certain light. • Different vantage points can cause the same subject to be seen differently by the viewer.
monochrome: photos that are black and white	• In early photography, all photographs were monochrome. • Although color photography has existed for decades, photographers still use monochrome to create specific artistic effects.

First Review MEDIA: ART AND PHOTOGRAPHY

Study each photograph and its caption using these strategies.

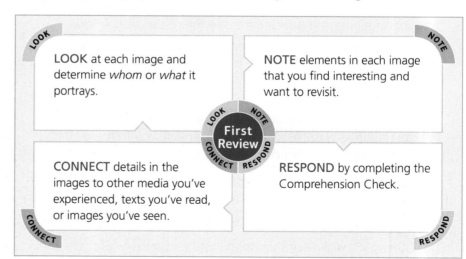

LOOK at each image and determine *whom* or *what* it portrays.

NOTE elements in each image that you find interesting and want to revisit.

CONNECT details in the images to other media you've experienced, texts you've read, or images you've seen.

RESPOND by completing the Comprehension Check.

First Review

STANDARDS

Reading Informational Text
By the end of the year, read and comprehend literary nonfiction in the grades 6–8 text complexity band proficiently, with scaffolding as needed at the high end of the range.

Language
Acquire and use accurately grade-appropriate general academic and domain-specific words and phrases; gather vocabulary knowledge when considering a word or phrase important to comprehension or expression.

Eagle Tracking
at Follensby Pond
The Nature Conservancy

BACKGROUND

The bald eagle has been a national symbol of the United States since 1782. But by the mid-1900s, decades of habitat destruction, hunting, and the use of pesticides, such as DDT, had brought the bald eagle population within danger of extinction. Since then, social awareness and government protections have helped the bald eagle population make great steps toward recovery.

SCAN FOR
MULTIMEDIA

PHOTO 1: Bald eagles had been absent from Adirondack skies for nearly three decades before they were reintroduced at Follensby Pond in the 1980s.

NOTES

PHOTO 2: In 1981, Endangered Species Unit leader Peter Nye of the New York State Department of Environmental Conservation (NYSDEC) traveled to Alaska to collect eaglets to release at Follensby Pond. At the time, Alaska was one of the few states in the nation with a healthy bald eagle population.

NOTES

PHOTO 3: The eaglets traveled by boat across Alaska's open waters to meet an airplane that was waiting to take them to the continental United States.

NOTES

PHOTO 4: NYSDEC's Endangered Species Unit rushed the birds to their new home at Follensby Pond.

NOTES

PHOTO 5: Follensby Pond was chosen as the perfect site for this eagle restoration project because of its habitat, abundant food sources, and isolation.

NOTES

PHOTO 6: Today, bald eagles can be seen near many Adirondack lakes as a result of the efforts of NYSDEC's Endangered Species Unit. In 1975, prior to restoration efforts, only one pair of eagles remained in New York. As of 2008, more than 145 pairs of eagles are thriving.

NOTES

NOTES

Comprehension Check

Complete the following items after you finish your first review. Review and clarify details with your group.

1. According to the information in the captions, how long were bald eagles missing from the Adirondacks?

2. Where did conservationists collect eaglets for eventual release in New York State?

3. How did the eaglets travel?

4. According to the information in the captions, what is the result of the restoration project?

5. ⊟ **Notebook** Confirm your understanding of the selection by writing a brief summary of the eagle restoration project at Follensby Pond.

EAGLE TRACKING AT
FOLLENSBY POND

Close Review

With your group, revisit the selection and your first-review notes. Jot down any new observations that seem important. What **questions** do you have? What can you **conclude**?

Analyze the Media

📓 **Notebook** Complete the activities.

1. **Present and Discuss** Choose the photo and caption that you found most interesting or informative. Share your choice with the group, and discuss why you chose it. Explain what you noticed in the photo and caption, what questions it raised for you, and what conclusions you reached about it.

2. **Review and Synthesize** With your group, review the photo gallery. How do the captions add meaning to the photographs? Would the photographs be less effective without the captions? Why or why not?

3. 📓 **Notebook Essential Question: *What effects do people have on the environment?*** How did this photo gallery contribute to your understanding of the ways in which people affect the environment?

Media Vocabulary

documentary photography	vantage point	monochrome

Confirm your understanding of the vocabulary words by answering these questions.

1. Do you think the photo gallery effectively conveys information about the eagle restoration project at Follensby Pond?

2. Describe the vantage point of each photograph, and explain how the vantage point affects the subject.

3. How do the monochrome photographs differ from the color photographs?

📇 STANDARDS

Speaking and Listening
Analyze the main ideas and supporting details presented in diverse media and formats and explain how the ideas clarify a topic, text, or issue under study.

Language
Acquire and use accurately grade-appropriate general academic and domain-specific words and phrases; gather vocabulary knowledge when considering a word or phrase important to comprehension or expression.

Research

Assignment

Work in your group to research and write a short **research paper** on one of the following topics:

- [ ] eagle restoration and tracking programs in other states
- [ ] restoration and tracking programs for other endangered species
- [ ] the origins and history of the Endangered Species Act

In your paper, highlight the relationship between the topic you chose to research and the photo gallery, "Eagle Tracking at Follensby Pond."

Formulate a Research Question Work with your group to formulate a research question that will guide your research process. An effective research question should be specific and manageable, and the purpose of your paper will be to answer this question. If you do not limit the scope of your research question, you will find it difficult to address the question fully. Consider the following examples:

> **Broad Research Question:** How do people affect the environment?
> **Specific Research Question:** How does coal mining affect rivers and streams?

Organize Your Information Take notes from each research source to answer your research question. Include only information that is meaningfully related to your topic. Use your notes to organize an outline for your research paper. Consider the following methods of organization:

- **chronological order:** sequencing information about events in the order in which they occur

- **comparison and contrast:** analyzing and explaining the similarities and differences between two or more related subjects

- **cause and effect:** analyzing and explaining reasons or results for something that happens

📓 **Notebook** Use a chart such as the one shown to organize information for your research paper.

What is our research question?	
What are at least three relevant, reliable print or digital sources we can use?	
What organizational structure will we use to present the information?	

📝 EVIDENCE LOG

Before moving on to a new selection, go to your Evidence Log and record what you learned from "Eagle Tracking at Follensby Pond."

☰ STANDARDS

Writing

- Write informative/explanatory texts to examine a topic and convey ideas, concepts, and information through the selection, organization, and analysis of relevant content.
  a. Introduce a topic clearly, previewing what is to follow; organize ideas, concepts, and information, using strategies such as definition, classification, comparison/ contrast, and cause/ effect; include formatting, graphics, and multimedia when useful to aiding comprehension.
  b. Develop the topic with relevant facts, definitions, concrete details, quotations, or other information and examples.

- Conduct short research projects to answer a question, drawing on several sources and generating additional related, focused questions for further research and investigation.
- Gather relevant information from multiple print and digital sources, using search terms effectively; assess the credibility and accuracy of each source; and quote or paraphrase the data and conclusions of others while avoiding plagiarism and following a standard format for citation.

About the Author

Shinichi Hoshi
(1926–1997), a Japanese
writer, is best known
for his "short-short
stories," in which he
makes observations about
human nature and society.
Hoshi wrote more than
a thousand short-short
stories, as well as longer
fantasy stories, detective
stories, biographies, and
travel articles. In addition,
he was one of the first
Japanese science-fiction
writers. Hoshi's stories
have been translated into
many languages, and
devoted readers enjoy their
unexpected plot turns.

He—y, Come On Ou—t!

Concept Vocabulary

As you perform your first read of "He—y, Come On Ou—t!" you will
encounter these words.

disposal	consequences	resolved

Context Clues If these words are unfamiliar to you, try using **context
clues**—or words and phrases that appear nearby in the text—to help you
determine their meanings. There are various types of context clues that
you may encounter as you read.

> **Synonyms:** A **throng** gathered around the hole, so the village built
> a fence to keep the crowd from getting too close.
>
> **Restatement of an Idea:** People traveled to the village to see the
> hole, and when they arrived, they were so impressed by its depth
> that they **gawked** at it.
>
> **Contrast of Ideas:** The scientist was able to keep his **composure**
> despite the fact that he was scared of the deep hole.

Apply your knowledge of context clues and other vocabulary strategies to
determine the meanings of unfamiliar words you encounter during your
first read.

First Read FICTION

Apply these strategies as you conduct your first read. You will have an
opportunity to complete a close read after your first read.

NOTICE *whom* the story is about, *what* happens, *where* and *when* it happens, and *why* those involved react as they do.

ANNOTATE by marking vocabulary and key passages you want to revisit.

First Read

CONNECT ideas within the selection to what you already know and what you have already read.

RESPOND by completing the Comprehension Check.

STANDARDS

Reading Literature
By the end of the year, read and
comprehend literature, including
stories, dramas, and poems, in the
grades 6–8 text complexity band
proficiently, with scaffolding as
needed at the high end of the range.

Language
Determine or clarify the meaning
of unknown and multiple-meaning
words and phrases based on *grade 7
reading and content,* choosing
flexibly from a range of strategies.
  a. Use context as a clue to the
  meaning of a word or phrase.

He—y, Come On Ou—t!

Shinichi Hoshi
translated by Stanleigh Jones

BACKGROUND

Each year, the world generates billions of tons of waste. Much of that waste is disposed of in landfills, where heavy metals and toxins can leak into the environment. The oceans have also been polluted with vast amounts of trash because, for many decades, it was common practice to get rid of chemicals, garbage, and even nuclear waste by dumping them directly into the ocean.

SCAN FOR MULTIMEDIA

NOTES

1   The typhoon had passed and the sky was a gorgeous blue. Even a certain village not far from the city had suffered damage. A little distance from the village and near the mountains, a small shrine had been swept away by a landslide.

2   "I wonder how long that shrine's been here."

3   "Well, in any case, it must have been here since an awfully long time ago."

4   "We've got to rebuild it right away."

5   While the villagers exchanged views, several more of their number came over.

6   "It sure was wrecked."

7   "I think it used to be right here."

8   "No, looks like it was a little more over there."

9   Just then one of them raised his voice. "Hey what in the world is this hole?"

10   Where they had all gathered there was a hole about a meter in diameter. They peered in, but it was so dark nothing could be seen. However, it gave one the feeling that it was so deep it went clear through to the center of the earth.

11   There was even one person who said, "I wonder if it's a fox's hole."

12   "He—y, come on ou—t!" shouted a young man into the hole. There was no echo from the bottom. Next he picked up a pebble and was about to throw it in.

13   "You might bring down a curse on us. Lay off," warned an old man, but the younger one energetically threw the pebble in. As before, however, there was no answering response from the bottom. The villagers cut down some trees, tied them with rope and made a fence which they put around the hole. Then they repaired to the village.

14   "What do you suppose we ought to do?"

15   "Shouldn't we build the shrine up just as it was over the hole?"

16   A day passed with no agreement. The news traveled fast, and a car from the newspaper company rushed over. In no time a scientist came out, and with an all-knowing expression on his face he went over to the hole. Next, a bunch of gawking curiosity seekers showed up; one could also pick out here and there men of shifty glances who appeared to be concessionaires.[1] Concerned that someone might fall into the hole, a policeman from the local substation kept a careful watch.

17   One newspaper reporter tied a weight to the end of a long cord and lowered it into the hole. A long way down it went. The cord ran out, however, and he tried to pull it out, but it would not come back up. Two or three people helped out but when they all pulled too hard, the cord parted at the edge of the hole. Another reporter, a camera in hand, who had been watching all of this, quietly untied a stout rope that had been wound around his waist.

18   The scientist contacted people at his laboratory and had them bring out a high-powered bull horn, with which he was going to check out the echo from the hole's bottom. He tried switching through various sounds, but there was no echo. The scientist was puzzled, but he could not very well give up with everyone watching him so intently. He put the bull horn right up to the hole, turned it to its highest volume, and let it sound continuously for a long time. It was a noise that would have carried several dozen kilometers above ground. But the hole just calmly swallowed up the sound.

19   In his own mind the scientist was at a loss, but with a look of apparent composure he cut off the sound and, in a manner

---

1. **concessionaires** (kuhn sehsh uh NAIRZ) *n.* businesspersons.

suggesting that the whole thing had a perfectly plausible explanation, said simply, "Fill it in."

20 Safer to get rid of something one didn't understand.

21 The onlookers, disappointed that this was all that was going to happen, prepared to disperse. Just then one of the concessionaires, having broken through the throng and come forward, made a proposal.

22 "Let me have that hole. I'll fill it in for you."

23 "We'd be grateful to you for filling it in." replied the mayor of the village, "but we can't very well give you the hole. We have to build a shrine there."

24 "If it's a shrine you want, I'll build you a fine one later. Shall I make it with an attached meeting hall?"

25 Before the mayor could answer, the people of the village all shouted out.

26 "Really? Well, in that case, we ought to have it closer to the village."

27 "It's just an old hole. We'll give it to you!"

28 So it was settled. And the mayor, of course, had no objection.

29 The concessionaire was true to his promise. It was small, but closer to the village he did build for them a shrine with an attached meeting hall.

30 About the time the autumn festival was held at the new shrine, the hole-filling company established by the concessionaire hung out its small shingle at a shack near the hole.

31 The concessionaire had his cohorts mount a loud campaign in the city. "We've got a fabulously deep hole! Scientists say it's at least five thousand meters deep! Perfect for the **disposal** of such things as waste from nuclear reactors."

32 Government authorities granted permission. Nuclear power plants fought for contracts. The people of the village were a bit worried about this, but they consented when it was explained that there would be absolutely no above-ground contamination[2] for several thousand years and that they would share in the profits. Into the bargain, very shortly a magnificent road was built from the city to the village.

33 Trucks rolled in over the road, transporting lead boxes. Above the hole the lids were opened, and the wastes from nuclear reactors tumbled away into the hole.

34 From the Foreign Ministry and the Defense Agency boxes of unnecessary classified documents were brought for disposal. Officials who came to supervise the disposal held discussions on golf. The lesser functionaries, as they threw in the papers, chatted about pinball.

Use context clues or indicate another strategy you used that helped you determine meaning.

disposal (dihs POH zuhl) *n.*

MEANING:

---

2. **contamination** (kuhn tam uh NAY shuhn) *n.* pollution by poison or another dangerous substance.

consequences (KON suh kwehns ihz) *n.*

MEANING:

resolved (rih ZOLVD) *v.*

MEANING:

35   The hole showed no signs of filling up. It was awfully deep, thought some; or else it might be very spacious at the bottom. Little by little the hole-filling company expanded its business.

36   Bodies of animals used in contagious disease experiments at the universities were brought out and to these were added the unclaimed corpses of vagrants. Better than dumping all of its garbage in the ocean, went the thinking in the city, and plans were made for a long pipe to carry it to the hole.

37   The hole gave peace of mind to the dwellers of the city. They concentrated solely on producing one thing after another. Everyone disliked thinking about the eventual **consequences**. People wanted only to work for production companies and sales corporations; they had no interest in becoming junk dealers. But, it was thought, these problems too would gradually be **resolved** by the hole.

38   Young girls whose betrothals[3] had been arranged discarded old diaries in the hole. There were also those who were inaugurating new love affairs and threw into the hole old photographs of themselves taken with former sweethearts. The police felt comforted as they used the hole to get rid of accumulations of expertly done counterfeit bills. Criminals breathed easier after throwing material evidence into the hole.

39   Whatever one wished to discard, the hole accepted it all. The hole cleansed the city of its filth; the sea and sky seemed to have become a bit clearer than before.

40   Aiming at the heavens, new buildings went on being constructed one after another.

41   One day, atop the high steel frame of a new building under construction, a workman was taking a break. Above his head he heard a voice shout:

42   "He—y, come on ou—t!"

43   But, in the sky to which he lifted his gaze there was nothing at all. A clear blue sky merely spread over all. He thought it must be his imagination. Then, as he resumed his former position, from the direction where the voice had come, a small pebble skimmed by him and fell on past.

44   The man, however, was gazing in idle reverie[4] at the city's skyline growing ever more beautiful, and he failed to notice. ❧

---

3. **betrothals** (bih TROTH uhlz) *n.* promises of marriage.
4. **idle reverie** (Y duhl REHV uh ree) daydreaming.

Comprehension Check

Complete the following items after you finish your first read. Review and clarify details with your group.

1. What does the young man shout into the hole at the beginning of the story?

2. Why do the villagers tell the young man not to throw the pebble into the hole?

3. How is the hole used?

4. What does the workman hear at the end of the story?

5. 📓 **Notebook** Confirm your understanding of the story by drawing a storyboard of key events.

- -

RESEARCH

Research to Clarify Briefly research an unfamiliar detail in the story. For instance, you might want to learn more about sinkholes or the disposal of waste from nuclear power plants. How does the information you learned deepen your understanding of the story? Share your findings with your small group.

HE—Y, COME ON OU—T

Close Read the Text

With your group, revisit sections of the text you marked during your first read. **Annotate** what you notice. What **questions** do you have? What can you **conclude**?

Analyze the Text

> **CITE TEXTUAL EVIDENCE** to support your answers.

:::notebook-icon::: **Notebook** Complete the activities.

1. **Review and Clarify** Review the short story with your group. Why do you think the author includes so many details about what people put into the hole? What effect do these details have on the reader?

2. **Present and Discuss** Now, work with your group to share the passages from the text that you found especially important. Take turns presenting your passages.

3. **Essential Question: *What effects do people have on the environment?*** What has this story taught you about the effects that people have on the environment? Discuss with your group.

LANGUAGE DEVELOPMENT

Concept Vocabulary

consequences	resolved	disposal

Why These Words? The concept vocabulary words from the text are related. With your group, determine what the words have in common. Write your ideas and add another word that fits the category.

Practice

:::notebook-icon::: **Notebook** Confirm your understanding of these words by using them to write a response to this question: *How should we dispose of the toxic and polluting byproducts of human activity?*

Word Study

Latin Root: *-sequ-* The Latin root *-sequ-* means "to follow." In the story, the author writes that people disliked thinking of the *consequences* of dumping things in the hole because people did not want to think of the things that might *follow* as a result of their actions.

1. Write your own sentence that correctly uses the word *consequences*.

2. Use a dictionary to find three other words that contain the root *-sequ-*. Write each word's definition in your own words and write an example sentence for each.

Analyze Craft and Structure

Literary Elements: Irony **Irony** is a literary element that involves a contradiction or contrast of some kind. In literature, authors often use irony to entertain and to convey a **theme,** or message. There are several types of irony.

TYPE OF IRONY	DEFINITION	EXAMPLE	PURPOSE
DRAMATIC IRONY	a contrast between what the reader knows and what the character knows	an unaware character approaching a door that only the audience can see is actually a trap set by another character	to create excitement, suspense, or tragedy or to keep the readers' interest
SITUATIONAL IRONY	a contrast between what a reader or character expects and what actually happens	expecting a big, strong man to be the hero of a story and finding out that a young girl actually saves the day	to create humor or tragedy
VERBAL IRONY	a contrast between what a narrator or character says and what he or she means	a character saying "I love cleaning up other peoples' messes" when the character actually hates cleaning up after others	to create humor or build suspense

Depending on how an author chooses to use a certain type of irony, all types of irony can help the author to develop the theme of a story.

Practice

CITE TEXTUAL EVIDENCE to support your answers.

📓 **Notebook** Work with your group to respond to these questions.

1. (a) What type of irony is used in the story? (b) What details in the story enabled you to identify this type of irony?

2. (a) What theme is conveyed through Hoshi's use of irony? (b) What details in the story enabled you to identify this theme?

3. (a) What does the irony tell you about the characters? (b) What details from the story support this inference?

4. What comment do you think the author may be making about the relationship between people and the environment?

STANDARDS

Reading Literature
• Cite several pieces of textual evidence to support analysis of what the text says explicitly as well as inferences drawn from the text.
• Determine a theme or central idea of a text and analyze its development over the course of the text; provide an objective summary of the text.
• Analyze how particular elements of a story or drama interact.

Conventions

Punctuation Marks Writers use **punctuation marks** to make their meaning clearer. Each punctuation mark serves a specific purpose, as shown in this chart.

PUNCTUATION/USAGE	EXAMPLE
A **colon (:)** introduces information that defines, explains, or provides a list of what came before the colon.	Huck likes to fetch various things: sticks, balls, toys, and old shoes.
A **semicolon (;)** joins related independent clauses to form compound sentences.	We hiked in the woods in the morning; in the afternoon, we swam in the lake.
A **hyphen (-)** joins two or more separate words into a single word.	Maria was the front-runner in the election.
A **dash (—)** sets off information that interrupts a thought.	I could hear music—what's the name of that song?—floating through the open window.
Brackets ([ ]) add clarifying information within a quotation.	Arjun said, "That was the year [2015] that we won the championship game."
Parentheses (( )) enclose extra information in a sentence without changing its meaning.	Can you explain that term to me (linear equations)?

Read It

Work with your group to identify examples of uses of punctuation marks in "He—y, Come On Ou—t!" Write your examples in the chart, identifying the punctuation marks.

EXAMPLE	PUNCTUATION MARK

Write It

⊖ **Notebook** Write a paragraph describing a place you go to enjoy nature. Your place might be a balcony, park, beach, or garden. Use specific sensory details to help readers see and feel the place you are describing. Practice using punctuation marks by including three of the punctuation marks you learned.

STANDARDS

Language
Demonstrate command of the conventions of standard English capitalization, punctuation, and spelling when writing.

Writing to Sources

You can often understand a situation better by thinking about what might happen next. The same thing is true of a fictional story. By imagining what happens after the story ends, you can deepen your understanding of the story itself.

Assignment

Use your imagination to write an **alternate ending** in which you explore what might happen after the story ends. Write at least three paragraphs that narrate what happens after the pebble skims past the man at the end of "He—y, Come On Ou—t!"

Discuss Purpose Based on what you know from the story, what do you think might happen next? In your group, decide the kind of ending you want to create. Do you want your ending to be funny, sad, ironic, or hopeful?

Brainstorm Consider several ideas for alternative endings. For each idea, list which characters will be involved and jot down what they say and do. Consider the effect the ending will have on the reader. Track ideas in a chart like this one.

IDEA	CHARACTERS	ACTIONS THAT HAPPEN	EFFECT

Capture the Action and Experiences To create a vivid engaging picture for your readers, use narrative techniques, descriptive details, and sensory language to capture the action and convey experiences and events. Consider the following strategies:

- **Develop Characters Through Dialogue:** Bring your characters to life by using dialogue—what the characters say to each other. Do not report everything a character says. Instead, create conversations that vividly show characters' feelings, gestures, and expressions as he or she reacts to events and experiences.

- **Develop Description Through Sensory Language:** When describing the setting, context, characters, and events, use sensory language to enhance your descriptions. Try to incorporate precise and colorful nouns, adjectives, verbs, and adverbs into your writing to engage readers.

Review and Revise After you have completed your alternate ending, each group member should review it individually, and note suggestions for revisions. Then, meet as a group to discuss members' suggestions, and come to a consensus, or agreement, on how to revise the first draft of your narrative.

EVIDENCE LOG

Before moving on to a new selection, go to your log and record what you learned from "He—y, Come On Ou—t!"

STANDARDS

Writing
Write narratives to develop real or imagined experiences or events using effective technique, relevant descriptive details, and well-structured event sequences.

b. Use narrative techniques, such as dialogue, pacing, and description, to develop experiences, events, and/or characters.

d. Use precise words and phrases, relevant descriptive details, and sensory language to capture the action and convey experiences and events.

e. Provide a conclusion that follows from and reflects on the narrated experiences or events.

• With some guidance and support from peers and adults, develop and strengthen writing as needed by planning, revising, editing, rewriting, or trying a new approach, focusing on how well purpose and audience have been addressed.

Present an Argument

Assignment

You have read different perspectives on the relationship between human beings and the natural environment. With your group, develop and deliver a **multimedia presentation** in which you respond to the following question:

> Do people always have a negative impact on the environment?

Plan With Your Group

Analyze the Texts With your group, review the selections you have read in Small-Group Learning. What message does each selection send about the relationship between people and nature? Consider changes in the environment and ways people's actions contribute to the changes. Discuss as a group, and write your ideas in the chart. Then, come to a consensus, or agreement, on the claim you will make in your presentation.

SELECTION	What does the selection suggest about people's impact on the environment?
Turtle Watchers "Nature" is what We see— The Sparrow	
Eagle Tracking at Follensby Pond	
He—y, Come On Ou—t!	

Gather Evidence and Media Examples Determine which group members will work to identify examples from the texts that support your claim, and which members will work on gathering multimedia. Then, brainstorm ideas for your multimedia presentation. Identify photos, illustrations, audio, and video that illustrate the examples you will use to support your claim.

STANDARDS
Speaking and Listening
• Engage effectively in a range of collaborative discussions with diverse partners on *grade 7 topics, texts, and issues,* building on others' ideas and expressing their own clearly.
  a. Come to discussions prepared, having read or researched material under study; explicitly draw on that preparation by referring to evidence on the topic, text, or issue to probe and reflect on ideas under discussion.
  b. Follow rules for collegial discussions, track progress toward specific goals and deadlines, and define individual roles as needed.
• Analyze the main ideas and supporting details presented in diverse media and formats and explain how the ideas clarify a topic, text, or issue under study.

Organize Your Presentation Decide the order of your multimedia presentation and the role each group member will play. Choose your words carefully to make your claim clear. Select multimedia that best illustrate your ideas and will make the most impact on your audience. Then, write a script for your presentation that details what each speaker will say to audience during the presentation. Your script is where you can add important details, and explain the relationship between your multimedia and the point that it highlights.

MULTIMEDIA PRESENTATION SCRIPT		
	Slide	Script
Speaker 1		
Speaker 2		
Speaker 3		

Rehearse With Your Group

Practice With Your Group As you run through rehearsals, use this checklist to evaluate the effectiveness of your multimedia presentation.

CONTENT	USE OF MEDIA	PRESENTATION TECHNIQUES
☐ The presentation includes a clearly stated claim.	☐ Multimedia elements support and elaborate on the claim.	☐ Transitions between speakers' sections are smooth.
☐ The evidence from the texts supports the claim.	☐ Multimedia elements add to and strengthen the presentation.	☐ Each speaker speaks clearly.
☐ The presentation is logically organized.		

Fine-Tune the Content To strengthen your multimedia presentation, review each speaker's section to make sure it clearly expresses and supports the group's claim about whether or not people always negatively impact the environment.

Improve Your Use of Media Review all multimedia in your presentation. Make sure each piece adds something interesting to the presentation and contributes toward your overall claim.

Present and Evaluate

When you present as a group, be sure that each member has taken into account each of the checklist items. As you watch other groups, evaluate how well their presentations meet the checklist requirements.

STANDARDS
Speaking and Listening
• Delineate a speaker's argument and specific claims, evaluating the soundness of the reasoning and the relevance and sufficiency of the evidence.
• Present claims and findings, emphasizing salient points in a focused, coherent manner with pertinent descriptions, facts, details, and examples; use appropriate eye contact, adequate volume, and clear pronunciation.
• Include multimedia components and visual displays in presentations to clarify claims and findings and emphasize salient points.
• Adapt speech to a variety of contexts and tasks, demonstrating command of formal English when indicated or appropriate.

ESSENTIAL QUESTION:

What effects do people have on the environment?

Our natural environment has an impact on everybody and everything on the planet. In this section, you will complete your study of people and the planet by exploring an additional selection related to the topic. You'll then share what you learn with classmates. To choose a text, follow these steps.

Look Back Think about the selections you have already studied. What more do you want to know about the environment?

Look Ahead Preview the texts by reading the descriptions. Which one seems most interesting and appealing to you?

Look Inside Take a few minutes to scan through the text you chose. Choose a different one if this text doesn't meet your needs.

Independent Learning Strategies

Throughout your life, in school, in your community, and in your career, you will need to rely on yourself to learn and work on your own. Review these strategies and the actions you can take to practice them during Independent Learning. Add ideas of your own for each category.

STRATEGY	ACTION PLAN
Create a schedule	• Understand your goals and deadlines. • Make a plan for what to do each day. •
Practice what you have learned	• Use first-read and close-read strategies to deepen your understanding. • After you read, evaluate the usefulness of the evidence to help you understand the topic. • Consider the quality and reliability of the source. •
Take notes	• Record important ideas and information. • Review your notes before preparing to share with a group. •

SCAN FOR MULTIMEDIA

CONTENTS

Choose one selection. Selections are available online only.

PERFORMANCE-BASED ASSESSMENT PREP

Review Evidence for an Argument

Complete your Evidence Log for the unit by evaluating what you've learned and synthesizing the information you have recorded.

SCAN FOR MULTIMEDIA

First-Read Guide

Use this page to record your first-read ideas.

🔧 **Tool Kit**
First-Read Guide and
Model Annotation

Selection Title: _____

NOTICE

NOTICE new information or ideas you learn about the unit topic as you first read this text.

ANNOTATE

ANNOTATE by marking vocabulary and key passages you want to revisit.

First Read
NOTICE ANNOTATE CONNECT RESPOND

CONNECT

CONNECT ideas within the selection to other knowledge and the selections you have read.

RESPOND

RESPOND by writing a brief summary of the selection.

📑 **STANDARD**

Reading Read and comprehend complex literary and informational texts independently and proficiently.

Close-Read Guide

Use this page to record your first-read ideas.

Selection Title: _____

Close Read the Text

Revisit sections of the text you marked during your first read. Read these sections closely and **annotate** what you notice. Ask yourself **questions** about the text. What can you **conclude**? Write down your ideas.

Analyze the Text

Think about the author's choices of patterns, structure, techniques, and ideas included in the text. Select one and record your thoughts about what this choice conveys.

QuickWrite

Pick a paragraph from the text that grabbed your interest. Explain the power of this passage.

▤ STANDARD

Reading Read and comprehend complex literary and informational texts independently and proficiently.

Share Your Independent Learning

Prepare to Share

What effects do people have on the environment?

Even when you read something independently, your understanding continues to grow when you share what you've learned with others. Reflect on the text you explored independently and write notes about its connection to the unit. In your notes, consider why this text belongs in this unit.

Learn From Your Classmates

💬 **Discuss It** Share your ideas about the text you explored on your own. As you talk with your classmates, jot down ideas that you learn from them.

Reflect

Mark the most important insight you gained from these writing and discussion activities. Explain how this idea adds to your understanding of the topic of our environment.

▤ STANDARDS

Speaking and Listening
Engage effectively in a range of collaborative discussions with diverse partners on *grade 7 topics, texts, and issues,* building on others' ideas and expressing their own clearly.

Review Evidence for an Argument

At the beginning of this unit, you took a position on the following question:

> Are the needs of people ever more important than the needs of animals and the planet? Explain your position.

✎ EVIDENCE LOG

Review your Evidence Log and your QuickWrite from the beginning of the unit. Has your position changed?

☐ YES	☐ NO
Identify at least three pieces of evidence that convinced you to change your mind.	Identify at least three pieces of evidence that reinforced your initial position.
1.	1.
2.	2.
3.	3.

State your position: _____

_____

_____

Identify a possible counterclaim: _____

_____

_____

Evaluate the Strength of Your Evidence

Do you have enough evidence to support your argument? Do you have enough evidence to refute a counterclaim? If not, make a plan.

☐ Do more research.　　　　☐ Talk with my classmates.

☐ Reread a selection.　　　　☐ Ask an expert.

☐ Other: _____

⬛ STANDARDS

Writing
Write arguments to support claims with clear reasons and relevant evidence.

　a. Introduce claim(s), acknowledge alternate or opposing claims, and organize the reasons and evidence logically.
　b. Support claim(s) with logical reasoning and relevant evidence, using accurate, credible sources and demonstrating an understanding of the topic or text.

SOURCES

- WHOLE-CLASS SELECTIONS
- SMALL-GROUP SELECTIONS
- INDEPENDENT-LEARNING SELECTION

PART 1
Writing to Sources: Argument

In this unit, you read about the effect that people have on the environment. You read selections, both fiction and nonfiction, that express different perspectives on the relationship between people and the environment.

Write an Argument

Write an **argument** in which you state and defend a claim in response to the following question:

> **Are the needs of people ever more important than the needs of animals and the planet?**

State your claim with accuracy and support it with logical reasoning and specific, relevant evidence from the selections in this unit. Organize your ideas effectively, and use transitions to create cohesion and show the relationships between your claim, reasons, and evidence. Provide a conclusion that supports your argument and offers new insight into the topic. Remember to maintain a formal style and tone in your writing.

Reread the Assignment Review the assignment to be sure you fully understand it. The assignment may reference some of the academic vocabulary words presented at the beginning of the unit. Be sure you understand each of these words in order to complete the assignment correctly.

ethical	dissent	interject
discord	accuracy	

Review the Elements of Effective Argument Before you begin writing, review the Argument Rubric. Once you have completed your first draft, check it against the rubric. If one or more of the elements is missing or not as strong as it could be, revise your essay to add or strengthen that component.

⬡ WORD NETWORK

As you write and revise your argument, use your Word Network to help vary your word choices.

≣ STANDARDS
Writing
• Write arguments to support claims with clear reasons and relevant evidence.

• Produce clear and coherent writing in which the development, organization, and style are appropriate to task, purpose, and audience.

• Write routinely over extended time frames and shorter time frames for a range of discipline-specific tasks, purposes, and audiences.

Argument Rubric

	Focus and Organization	Evidence and Elaboration	Language Conventions
4	The introduction is engaging and states the claim in a persuasive way. The claim is supported by logical reasons and relevant evidence, and opposing claims are addressed. Reasons and evidence are logically organized so that the argument is easy to follow. Transitions clearly show the relationships between the claim, reasons, and evidence. The conclusion supports the argument and offers a new insight into the topic.	Details, examples, and quotations from the selections are specific and relevant. The style and tone of the argument are formal and objective. Words are carefully chosen and suited to purpose and audience.	The argument intentionally follows standard English conventions of usage and mechanics.
3	The introduction is somewhat engaging and states the claim clearly. The claim is supported by reasons and evidence, and opposing claims are acknowledged. Reasons and evidence are organized so that the argument is easy to follow. Transitions show the relationships between the claim, reasons, and evidence. The conclusion supports the argument.	Details, examples, and quotations from the selections are relevant. The style and tone of the argument are mostly formal and objective. Words are generally suited to purpose and audience.	The argument demonstrates accuracy in standard English conventions of usage and mechanics.
2	The introduction states the claim. The claim is supported by some reasons and evidence, and opposing claims may be briefly acknowledged. Reasons and evidence are vaguely organized with a few transitions to orient readers. The conclusion relates to the argument.	Some details and examples from the selections are relevant. The style and tone of the argument are occasionally formal and objective. Words are somewhat suited to purpose and audience.	The argument demonstrates some accuracy in standard English conventions of usage and mechanics.
1	The claim is not clearly stated. The claim is not supported by reasons and evidence, and opposing claims are not acknowledged. Reasons and evidence are disorganized and the argument is difficult to follow. The conclusion does not include relevant information.	There is little or no relevant support. The style and tone are informal. Words are not appropriate to purpose or audience.	The argument contains mistakes in standard English conventions of usage and mechanics.

PART 2
Speaking and Listening: Oral Presentation

STANDARDS
Speaking and Listening
• Present claims and findings, emphasizing salient points in a focused, coherent manner with pertinent descriptions, facts, details, and examples; use appropriate eye contact, adequate volume, and clear pronunciation.
• Include multimedia components and visual displays in presentations to clarify claims and findings and emphasize salient points.
• Adapt speech to a variety of contexts and tasks, demonstrating command of formal English when indicated or appropriate.

Assignment
After completing the final draft of your argument, use it as the foundation for a three- to five-minute **oral presentation.**

Do not simply read your argument aloud. Take these steps to make your presentation engaging.

- Review your argument, and mark reasons and evidence that best support your claim.
- Choose multimedia components to add interest to your presentation.
- Deliver your argument with confidence, and remember to use a formal tone.

Review the Rubric Before you deliver your presentation, rehearse it with a peer and check your plans against this rubric.

	Content	Organization	Presentation Techniques
3	The introduction is engaging and establishes the claim in a persuasive way. The presentation includes strong, valid reasons and evidence to support the claim and answers counterclaims. The conclusion supports the argument and offers fresh insight into the topic.	The speaker uses time effectively, spending the right amount on each part. Ideas progress logically, with clear transitions among ideas. The sequence of the multimedia matches the timing of the speaker.	The speaker maintains eye contact and speaks clearly. The speaker presents the argument with confidence and uses a formal tone.
2	The introduction establishes a claim. The presentation includes valid reasons and evidence to support the claim. The conclusion supports the argument.	The speaker uses time effectively, spending the right amount of time on most parts. Ideas progress logically with some transitions among ideas. The sequence of multimedia sometimes matches the timing of the speaker.	The speaker sometimes maintains eye contact and speaks somewhat clearly. The speaker uses a formal tone when presenting the argument.
1	The introduction does not state a claim. The presentation does not include reasons or evidence to support the claim. The conclusion does not relate to the argument presented.	The speaker does not use time effectively and focuses too much time on some parts. Ideas do not progress logically. Listeners have trouble following the argument. The sequence of multimedia does not match the timing of the speaker.	The speaker does not maintain eye contact or speak clearly. The speaker uses an informal tone and presents the argument in a way that lacks confidence.

Reflect on the Unit

Now that you've completed the unit, take a few moments to reflect on your learning.

Reflect on the Unit Goals

Review the goals at the beginning of the unit. Use a different colored pen to rate yourself again. Think about readings and activities that contributed the most to the growth of your understanding. Record your thoughts.

Reflect on the Learning Strategies

Discuss It Write a reflection on whether you were able to improve your learning based on your Action Plans. Think about what worked, what didn't, and what you might do to keep working on these strategies. Record your ideas before a class discussion.

Reflect on the Text

Choose a selection that you found challenging and explain what made it difficult.

Explain something that surprised you about a text in the unit.

Which activity taught you the most about the environment? What did you learn?

SCAN FOR MULTIMEDIA

Facing Adversity

Sometimes life can feel like an obstacle course, but if we try hard enough we can usually make it over the hurdles.

Exclusive: Bethany Hamilton

💬 Discuss It Are there any obstacles that are too difficult to overcome?

Write your response before sharing your ideas.

SCAN FOR
MULTIMEDIA

UNIT 5

UNIT INTRODUCTION

ESSENTIAL QUESTION:

How do we overcome obstacles?

LAUNCH TEXT
INFORMATIVE
MODEL
Against the Odds

WHOLE-CLASS LEARNING

COMPARE

MEDIA: VIDEO

The Dust Bowl
CriticalPast

ANCHOR TEXT: NOVEL EXCERPT

from **The Grapes of Wrath**
John Steinbeck

ANCHOR TEXT: SHORT STORY

The Circuit
Francisco Jiménez

PERFORMANCE TASK

WRITING FOCUS:
Write an Informative `Essay

SMALL-GROUP LEARNING

PERSONAL NARRATIVE

A Work in Progress
Aimee Mullins

COMPARE

AUTOBIOGRAPHY EXCERPT

from **The Story of My Life**
Helen Keller

MEDIA: INTERVIEW

How Helen Keller Learned to Talk
Helen Keller, with Anne Sullivan

NEWS ARTICLE

A Young Tinkerer Builds a Windmill, Electrifying a Nation
Sarah Childress

PERFORMANCE TASK

SPEAKING AND LISTENING FOCUS:
Present Multimedia Profiles

INDEPENDENT LEARNING

PERSONAL NARRATIVE

The Girl Who Fell from the Sky
Juliane Koepcke

NOVEL EXCERPT

Four Skinny Trees
from The House on Mango Street
Sandra Cisneros

SHORT STORY

Rikki-tikki-tavi
Rudyard Kipling

MEMOIR

from **Facing the Lion: Growing Up Maasai on the African Savanna**
Joseph Lemasolai Lekuton

PERFORMANCE-BASED ASSESSMENT PREP

Review Evidence for an Informative Essay

PERFORMANCE-BASED ASSESSMENT

Informative Text: Essay and Oral Presentation

PROMPT:

How can people overcome adversity in the face of overwhelming obstacles?

Unit Goals

Throughout this unit you will deepen your perspective about facing adversity by reading, writing, speaking, listening, and presenting. These goals will help you succeed on the Unit Performance-Based Assessment.

Rate how well you meet these goals right now. You will revisit your ratings later when you reflect on your growth during this unit.

SCALE	1	2	3	4	5
	NOT AT ALL WELL	NOT VERY WELL	SOMEWHAT WELL	VERY WELL	EXTREMELY WELL

READING GOALS	1	2	3	4	5
• Read and analyze informative texts.	○	○	○	○	○
• Expand your knowledge and use of academic and concept vocabulary.	○	○	○	○	○

WRITING AND RESEARCH GOALS	1	2	3	4	5
• Write an informative essay to examine a topic and convey ideas.	○	○	○	○	○
• Conduct research projects of various lengths to explore a topic and clarify meaning.	○	○	○	○	○

LANGUAGE GOAL	1	2	3	4	5
• Demonstrate command of coordinate adjectives.	○	○	○	○	○

SPEAKING AND LISTENING GOALS	1	2	3	4	5
• Collaborate with your team to build on the ideas of others, develop consensus, and communicate.	○	○	○	○	○
• Integrate audio, visuals, and text in presentations.	○	○	○	○	○

STANDARDS

Language
Acquire and use accurately grade appropriate general academic and domain-specific words and phrases; gather vocabulary knowledge when considering a word or phrase important to comprehension or expression.

SCAN FOR MULTIMEDIA

Academic Vocabulary: Informative Text

Academic terms appear in all subjects and can help you read, write, and discuss with more precision. Informative writing relies on facts to inform or explain. Here are five academic words that will be useful to you in this unit as you analyze and write informative texts.

 TIP

FOLLOW THROUGH
Study the words in this chart, and mark them or their forms wherever they appear in the unit.

Complete the chart.

1. Review each word, its root, and the mentor sentences.

2. Use the information and your own knowledge to predict the meaning of each word.

3. For each word, list at least two related words.

4. Refer to the dictionary or other resources if needed.

WORD	MENTOR SENTENCES	PREDICT MEANING	RELATED WORDS
deviate ROOT: **-via-** "way"	1. Don't *deviate* from the route I gave you or you'll get lost! 2. She was making an important point, but she allowed herself to *deviate* into side issues.		viable; viaduct
persevere ROOT: **-sever-** "strict; serious"	1. Despite the difficulties Claudine had finding time to study, she *persevered* and received a degree. 2. Though the soccer team was losing in the first half, they were able to *persevere* and win the game.		
determination ROOT: **-term-** "end"	1. Because of his *determination* to do well on the test, Robert studied for many hours. 2. Despite the heavy rain, Jenny's *determination* allowed her to complete her first marathon.		
diversity ROOT: **-ver-** "turn"	1. There is cultural *diversity* in the United States because people come from many different places. 2. The oceans are filled with a *diversity* of marine life.		
tradition ROOT: **-tra-/-tran-** "across"	1. My grandfather passed along many family *traditions* that had been practiced for generations. 2. Many people follow *tradition* and serve turkey on Thanksgiving.		

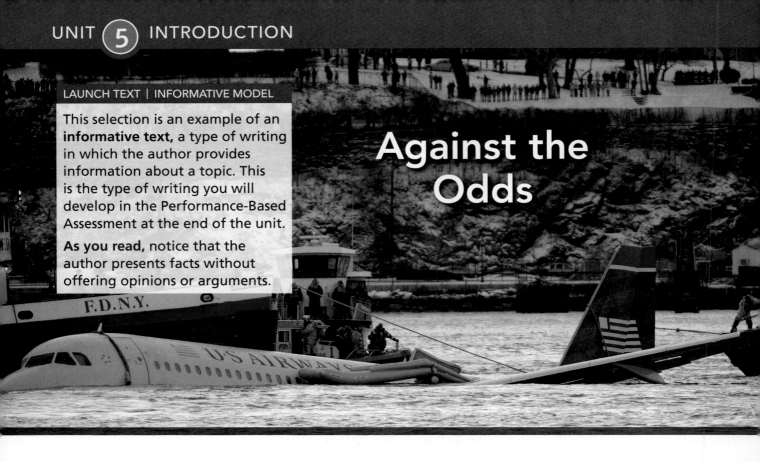

This selection is an example of an **informative text,** a type of writing in which the author provides information about a topic. This is the type of writing you will develop in the Performance-Based Assessment at the end of the unit.

As you read, notice that the author presents facts without offering opinions or arguments.

Against the Odds

NOTES

1   "If you have to ditch a commercial aircraft in the Hudson River," the news anchor joked, "this is the guy you want."

2   The "guy" was US Airways pilot Chesley "Sully" Sullenberger III, a 57-year-old former Air Force fighter pilot and a 29-year veteran of US Airways.

3   On January 15, 2009, Sullenberger was the pilot on US Airways Flight 1549 from New York's LaGuardia Airport to Charlotte, North Carolina.

4   Flight 1549 left the tarmac at 3:25 P.M. Sullenberger thought he was in for an average flight—a routine, everyday trip.

5   The flight was unremarkable for the first 90 seconds. Then something caught the eye of copilot Jeff Skiles. At 3,000 feet, he saw a flock of Canada geese headed toward the plane. Moments later the geese struck the fuselage, wings, and engine.

6   The 150 passengers felt a powerful thud against the airplane, followed by severe vibrations from the engine. One passenger said it sounded like sneakers thumping around in a dryer. There was a loud explosion. The cabin filled up with smoke. There was a horrible smell and then an eerie quiet: both engines were disabled.

7   Sullenberger made a Mayday radio call to air traffic control and calmly explained the situation. They discussed the options: The plane could either return to LaGuardia or land at Teterboro Airport in New Jersey.

8   Sullenberger knew the situation was too dire for the plane to stay in the air long enough for either plan to be successful. He had about 30 seconds to find an alternative. The pilot decided on a

SCAN FOR
MULTIMEDIA

radical move: He'd ditch the plane in the Hudson River—despite the fact that passenger jets are not built to land on water.

9   "Brace for impact!" came the captain's voice over the intercom. A hush fell over the passengers. They thought they were going to die.

10   Sullenberger lowered the plane's nose in a gradual glide toward the river. The plane managed to clear the George Washington Bridge and, against the odds, land safely on the surface of the Hudson. It skidded across the water at 145 mph and finally slowed to a stop.

11   "He was thinking in nanoseconds," said a former airline pilot, speaking of Sullenberger. "He made all the right choices at all the right times. He might have been staring at the instruments, but he was feeling that airplane in his hands. He picked his landing spot and went for it."

12   Now Sullenberger's job was to get the people off the plane, which was quickly filling up with water.

13   Witnesses were convinced that everyone on Flight 1549 was dead. What they couldn't see was that passengers were already exiting the plane. With water seeping into the plane, Sullenberger and Skiles walked the length of the cabin twice, calling "Is anyone there?" The water was so cold they had to walk on top of the seats. But they would not leave the plane until they were sure everyone was out.

14   "He's the man," said one of the rescued passengers. "If you want to talk to a hero, get a hold of him."

15   After all the thanking was over, Sullenberger was humble. "You're welcome," he said simply. Like most heroes, he didn't want the label. According to him, he was just doing his job.

16   But 154 men, women, and children owed their lives to a modest man who faced adversity with cool competence on one of the most remarkable days in aviation history. 🐦

NOTES

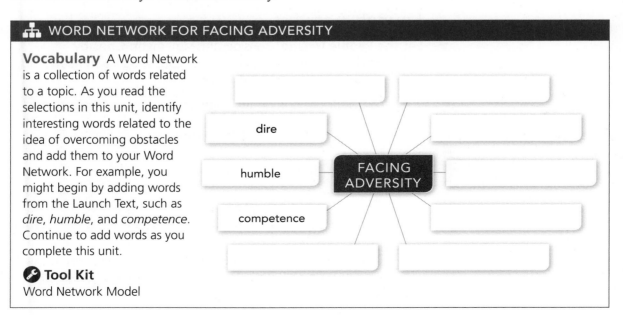

🔠 WORD NETWORK FOR FACING ADVERSITY

Vocabulary A Word Network is a collection of words related to a topic. As you read the selections in this unit, identify interesting words related to the idea of overcoming obstacles and add them to your Word Network. For example, you might begin by adding words from the Launch Text, such as *dire*, *humble*, and *competence*. Continue to add words as you complete this unit.

🔧 **Tool Kit**
Word Network Model

dire

humble

competence

FACING ADVERSITY

Summary

Write a summary of "Against the Odds." A **summary** is a concise, complete, and accurate overview of a text. It should not include a statement of your opinion or an analysis.

Launch Activity

Let the People Decide Consider this statement: Chesley Sullenberger wasn't really a hero because, as he himself said, facing adversity was part of his job.

- Record your position on the statement and explain your thinking.

  ☐ Strongly Agree ☐ Agree ☐ Disagree ☐ Strongly Disagree

  _____

  _____

- As a class, discuss what makes someone a hero.
- After the discussion, determine whether you have changed your mind.
- Those who changed their mind will be given a chance to read a new statement.

QuickWrite

Consider class discussions, presentations, the video, and the Launch Text as you think about the prompt. Record your first thoughts here.

PROMPT: **How can people overcome adversity in the face of overwhelming obstacles?**

📝 EVIDENCE LOG FOR FACING ADVERSITY

Review your QuickWrite and summarize your point of view in one sentence to record in your Evidence Log. Then, record evidence from "Against the Odds" that supports your point of view.

Prepare for the Performance-Based Assessment at the end of the unit by completing the Evidence Log after each selection.

🔧 **Tool Kit**
Evidence Log Model

Title of Text: _____ Date: _____

CONNECTION TO PROMPT	TEXT EVIDENCE/DETAILS	ADDITIONAL NOTES/IDEAS

How does this text change or add to my thinking?   Date: _____

SCAN FOR MULTIMEDIA

ESSENTIAL QUESTION:

How do we overcome obstacles?

Everyone has a bad day now and then. Most of the time we take a deep breath and keep going, but what happens when we meet an obstacle we don't think we can overcome? You will work with your whole class to explore the concept of facing adversity. The selections you are going to read present different examples of obstacles that had to be overcome.

Whole-Class Learning Strategies

Throughout your life, in school, in your community, and in your career, you will continue to learn and work in large-group environments.

Review these strategies and the actions you can take to practice them as you work with your whole class. Add ideas of your own for each step. Get ready to use these strategies during Whole-Class Learning.

STRATEGY	ACTION PLAN
Listen actively	• Eliminate distractions. For example, put your cellphone away. • Keep your eyes on the speaker. •
Clarify by asking questions	• If you're confused, other people probably are, too. Ask a question to help your whole class. • If you see that you are guessing, ask a question instead. •
Monitor understanding	• Notice what information you already know and be ready to build on it. • Ask for help if you are struggling. •
Interact and share ideas	• Share your ideas and answer questions, even if you are unsure. • Build on the ideas of others by adding details or making a connection. •

SCAN FOR MULTIMEDIA

CONTENTS

COMPARE

THE DUST BOWL

Comparing Media to Text

You will now watch a video about the Dust Bowl. First, complete the first-review and close-review activities. In the next lesson, you will read an excerpt from *The Grapes of Wrath* and then compare the depiction of historical events in the video and the novel excerpt.

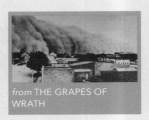

from THE GRAPES OF WRATH

The Dust Bowl

Media Vocabulary

These words will be useful as you analyze, discuss, and write about the video.

panoramic shot: film shot showing a wide, unbroken view	• The panoramic shot of the Grand Canyon was breathtaking. • Directors often use panoramic shots in the beginning of films to establish the setting.
voiceover: voice commenting or narrating off-camera	• The voiceover helps the audience to follow a narrative. • If there is a break in the sequence of events, a voiceover can re-orient the audience.
transition: in media, changes from one scene or shot to another	• One example of a transition is when a scene changes to another location. • Another example of a transition is when a director signals the end of a scene by using a "fade to black."

First Review MEDIA: VIDEO

Study the video and take notes as you watch.

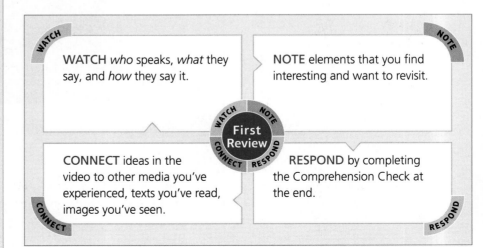

WATCH *who* speaks, *what* they say, and *how* they say it.

NOTE elements that you find interesting and want to revisit.

First Review

CONNECT ideas in the video to other media you've experienced, texts you've read, images you've seen.

RESPOND by completing the Comprehension Check at the end.

STANDARDS
Reading Informational Text
By the end of the year, read and comprehend literary nonfiction in the grades 6–8 text complexity band proficiently, with scaffolding as needed at the high end of the range.

The Dust Bowl

CriticalPast

BACKGROUND

One of the most devastating events in U.S. history was the formation of the Dust Bowl. After a period of over-farming in the 1920s, a severe drought struck the region around the Oklahoma panhandle in the early 1930s. The extended drought caused the topsoil to dry up, and without a strong root system of grasses to hold it in place, the soil was blown by winds. These dust storms blackened the sky and were sometimes referred to as black blizzards.

NOTES

Comprehension Check

Complete the following items after you finish your first review.

1. (a) According to the video, what did the cattlemen do? (b) What group followed the cattlemen to the area, and what did they do?

2. Why did so many people move to the area that eventually became known as the Dust Bowl?

3. (a) When did the climate first start to change? (b) What effects did the change have?

4. 📓 **Notebook** How did human activity contribute to creating the Dust Bowl?

- -

RESEARCH

Research to Clarify Choose at least one unfamiliar detail from the video. Briefly research that detail. In what way does the information you learned shed light on an aspect of the story told in this video?

THE DUST BOWL

Close Review

Watch "The Dust Bowl" again. Write any new observations that seem important. What **questions** do you have? What can you **conclude**?

Analyze the Media

📑 **Notebook** Complete the activities.

1. **Evaluate** What moment, image, or detail in "The Dust Bowl" did you find particularly powerful? Why?

2. **Analyze** (a) What sort of information do you learn from the first-person accounts in the video? (b) What sort of information do you learn from voiceover narration? (c) Do you find these types of information to be of equal value? Explain why or why not.

3. **Essential Question:** *How do we overcome obstacles?* What have you learned about how people deal with obstacles by seeing "The Dust Bowl"? Explain.

LANGUAGE DEVELOPMENT

Media Vocabulary

panoramic shot	voiceover	transition

Use the media vocabulary words in your responses to these questions.

1. How does the *panoramic shot* at the beginning of the video help you understand what follows?

2. How does the *voiceover* contribute to the images in "Surviving the Dust Bowl"?

3. Which *transition* in the video creates the most powerful dramatic effect? Explain.

📝 **EVIDENCE LOG**

Before moving on to a new selection, go to your Evidence Log and record what you've learned from the video "The Dust Bowl."

🏷 **STANDARDS**

Language
Acquire and use accurately grade-appropriate general academic and domain-specific words and phrases; gather vocabulary knowledge when considering a word or phrase important to comprehension or expression.

THE DUST BOWL

Comparing Media to Text

You will now read an excerpt from *The Grapes of Wrath*. Complete the first-read and close-read activities. Then, compare the depiction of historical events in the video with that in the novel excerpt.

from THE GRAPES OF WRATH

About the Author

Few writers portray more vividly than **John Steinbeck** (1902–1968) what it was like to live through the Great Depression of the 1930s. His stories and novels capture the poverty, desperation, and social injustice experienced by many working-class Americans during this bleak period. While many of his characters suffer tragic fates, they almost always exhibit bravery and dignity in their struggles.

🔧 Tool Kit
First-Read Guide and Model Annotation

▥ STANDARDS

Reading Literature
By the end of the year, read and comprehend literature, including stories, dramas, and poems, in the grades 6–8 text complexity band proficiently, with scaffolding as needed at the high end of the range.

from The Grapes of Wrath

Concept Vocabulary

You will encounter the following words as you read an excerpt from *The Grapes of Wrath*. Before reading, note how familiar you are with each word. Then, rank the words in order from most familiar (1) to least familiar (6).

WORD	YOUR RANKING
ruthless	
bitterness	
toil	
sorrow	
doomed	
frantically	

After completing your first read, come back to the concept vocabulary and review your rankings. Mark any changes to your original rankings.

First Read FICTION

Apply these strategies as you conduct your first read. You will have an opportunity to complete the close-read notes after your first read.

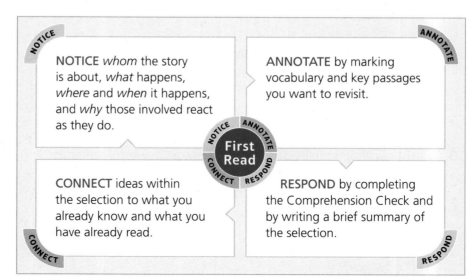

NOTICE *whom* the story is about, *what* happens, *where* and *when* it happens, and *why* those involved react as they do.

ANNOTATE by marking vocabulary and key passages you want to revisit.

First Read

CONNECT ideas within the selection to what you already know and what you have already read.

RESPOND by completing the Comprehension Check and by writing a brief summary of the selection.

from
The Grapes of Wrath

John Steinbeck

BACKGROUND

During the Great Depression, a severe drought in Oklahoma caused massive dust storms that blew away topsoil and destroyed farmland. Devastated farming families had no choice but to sell all their belongings and leave. This is the situation faced by the Joad family in John Steinbeck's novel *The Grapes of Wrath*. In this excerpt, the narrator describes the aftermath of the devastating drought.

SCAN FOR
MULTIMEDIA

1   In the little houses the tenant people sifted their belongings and the belongings of their fathers and of their grandfathers. Picked over their possessions for the journey to the west. The men were **ruthless** because the past had been spoiled, but the women knew how the past would cry to them in the coming days. The men went into the barns and the sheds.

2   That plow, that harrow, remember in the war we planted mustard? Remember a fella wanted us to put in that rubber bush they call guayule?[1] Get rich, he said. Bring out those tools—get a few dollars for them. Eighteen dollars for that plow, plus freight—Sears Roebuck.[2]

NOTES

ruthless (ROOTH lihs) *adj.* having no compassion or pity

---

1. **guayule** (gwy YOO lee) a desert shrub containing rubber, native to Mexico and Texas. During the Great Depression, it was thought that guayule could be profitably processed for rubber.
2. **Sears Roebuck** company that sold clothes, farm equipment, and other goods by mail order, which supplied much of rural America.

bitterness (BIHT uhr nihs) *n.* quality of having a sharp, unpleasant taste; condition causing pain or sorrow

3   Harness, carts, seeders, little bundles of hoes. Bring 'em out. Pile 'em up. Load 'em in the wagon. Take 'em to town. Sell 'em for what you can get. Sell the team and the wagon, too. No more use for anything.

4   Fifty cents isn't enough to get for a good plow. That seeder cost thirty-eight dollars. Two dollars isn't enough. Can't haul it all back—Well, take it, and a **bitterness** with it. Take the well pump and the harness. Take halters, collars, hames, and tugs.[3] Take the little glass brow-band jewels, roses red under glass. Got those for the bay gelding.[4] 'Member how he lifted his feet when he trotted?

5   Junk piled up in a yard.

6   Can't sell a hand plow any more. Fifty cents for the weight of the metal. Disks and tractors, that's the stuff now.

7   Well, take it—all junk—and give me five dollars. You're not buying only junk, you're buying junked lives. And more—you'll see—you're buying bitterness. Buying a plow to plow your own children under, buying the arms and spirits that might have saved you. Five dollars, not four. I can't haul 'em back—Well, take 'em for four. But I warn you, you're buying what will plow your own children under. And you won't see. You can't see. Take 'em for four. Now, what'll you give for the team and wagon? Those fine bays, matched they are, matched in color, matched the way they walk, stride to stride. In the stiff pull-straining hams[5] and buttocks, split-second timed together. And in the morning, the light on them, bay light. They look over the fence sniffing for us, and the stiff ears swivel to hear us, and the black forelocks! I've got a girl. She likes to braid the manes and forelocks, puts little red bows on them. Likes to do it. Not any more. I could tell you a funny story about that girl and that off bay. Would make you laugh. Off horse is eight, near is ten, but might of been twin colts the way they work together. See? The teeth. Sound all over. Deep lungs. Feet fair and clean. How much? Ten dollars? For both? And the wagon—I'd shoot 'em for dog feed first. Oh, take 'em! Take 'em quick, mister. You're buying a little girl plaiting the forelocks, taking off her hair ribbon to make bows, standing back, head cocked, rubbing the soft noses with her cheek. You're buying years of work, **toil** in the sun; you're buying a **sorrow** that can't talk. But watch it, mister. There's a premium goes with this pile of junk and the bay horses—so beautiful—a packet of bitterness to grow in your house and to flower, some day. We could have saved you, but you cut us down, and soon you will be cut down and there'll be none of us to save you.

toil (TOYL) *v.* work hard and with difficulty

sorrow (SOR oh) *n.* great sadness; suffering

---

3. **halters, collars, hames, and tugs** parts of the harnesses used to attach horses to horse-drawn plows.
4. **bay gelding** reddish-brown male horse.
5. **hams** back of a horse's knee.

8   And the tenant men came walking back, hands in their pockets, hats pulled down. Some bought a pint and drank it fast to make the impact hard and stunning. But they didn't laugh and they didn't dance. They didn't sing or pick the guitars. They walked back to the farms, hands in pockets and heads down, shoes kicking the red dust up.

9   Maybe we can start again, in the new rich land—in California, where the fruit grows. We'll start over.

10   But you can't start. Only a baby can start. You and me—why, we're all that's been. The anger of a moment, the thousand pictures, that's us. This land, this red land, is us; and the flood years and the dust years and the drought years are us. We can't start again. The bitterness we sold to the junk man—he got it all right, but we have it still. And when the owner men told us to go, that's us; and when the tractor hit the house, that's us until we're dead. To California or any place—every one a drum major leading a parade of hurts, marching with our bitterness. And some day—the armies of bitterness will all be going the same way. And they'll all walk together, and there'll be a dead terror from it.

11   The tenant men scuffed home to the farms through the red dust.

12   When everything that could be sold was sold, stoves and bedsteads, chairs and tables, little corner cupboards, tubs and tanks, still there were piles of possessions; and the women sat among them, turning them over and looking off beyond and back, pictures, square glasses, and here's a vase.

13   Now you know well what we can take and what we can't take. We'll be camping out—a few pots to cook and wash in, and mattresses and comforts, lantern and buckets, and a piece of canvas. Use that for a tent. This kerosene can. Know what that is? That's the stove. And clothes—take all the clothes. And—the rifle? Wouldn't go out naked of a rifle. When shoes and clothes and food, when even hope is gone, we'll have the rifle. When grampa came—did I tell you?—he had pepper and salt and a rifle. Nothing else. That goes. And a bottle for water. That just about fills us. Right up the sides of the trailer, and the kids can set in the trailer, and granma on a mattress. Tools, a shovel and saw and wrench and pliers. An ax, too. We had that ax forty years. Look how she's wore down. And ropes, of course. The rest? Leave it—or burn it up.

14   And the children came.

15   If Mary takes that doll, that dirty rag doll, I got to take my Indian bow. I got to. An' this roun' stick—big as me. I might need this stick. I had this stick so long—a month, or maybe a year. I got to take it. And what's it like in California?

16   The women sat among the doomed things, turning them over and looking past them and back. This book. My father had it. He

NOTES

CLOSE READ
ANNOTATE: Mark examples of repetition of words and phrases in paragraph 10.

QUESTION: What ideas are being emphasized through repetition? Why does the narrator keep using the pronouns "us" and "we"?

CONCLUDE: What can you conclude about the narrator by the words he uses and ideas he conveys?

doomed (doomd) *adj.* destined to a bad outcome

CLOSE READ

ANNOTATE: Mark the punctuation in paragraphs 17 and 18.

QUESTION: What patterns are created by the questions and statements? What do the dashes indicate?

CONCLUDE: What effect do the patterns and use of dashes create? How do they bring to life this unnamed narrator?

frantically (FRAN tuh klee) *adv.* acting wildly with anger, worry, or pain

liked a book. *Pilgrim's Progress.*[6] Used to read it. Got his name in it. And his pipe—still smells rank. And this picture—an angel. I looked at that before the fust three come—didn't seem to do much good. Think we could get this china dog in? Aunt Sadie brought it from the St. Louis Fair.[7] See? Wrote right on it. No, I guess not. Here's a letter my brother wrote the day before he died. Here's an old-time hat. These feathers—never got to use them. No, there isn't room.

17 How can we live without our lives? How will we know it's us without our past? No. Leave it. Burn it.

18 They sat and looked at it and burned it into their memories. How'll it be not to know what land's outside the door? How if you wake up in the night and know—and *know* the willow tree's not there? Can you live without the willow tree? Well, no, you can't. The willow tree is you. The pain on that mattress there—that dreadful pain—that's you.

19 And the children—if Sam takes his Indian bow an' his long roun' stick, I get to take two things. I choose the fluffy pilla. That's mine.

20 Suddenly they were nervous. Got to get out quick now. Can't wait. We can't wait. And they piled up the goods in the yards and set fire to them. They stood and watched them burning, and then **frantically** they loaded up the cars and drove away, drove in the dust. The dust hung in the air for a long time after the loaded cars had passed. ❧

---

6. ***Pilgrim's Progress*** Christian story by John Bunyan about living virtuously.
7. **St. Louis Fair:** The World's Fair of 1904, celebrating a hundred years of American ownership of lands west of the Mississippi River.

"Chapter 9," from *The Grapes of Wrath* by John Steinbeck, copyright 1939, renewed © 1967 by John Steinbeck. Used by permission of Viking Books, an imprint of Penguin Publishing Group, a division of Penguin Random House LLC.

Comprehension Check

Complete the following items after you finish your first read.

1. What big change is taking place in the lives of these characters?

2. What are the men doing in paragraph 7?

3. What happens after the people burn their belongings?

4. 🗐 **Notebook** Write a brief summary of this excerpt from *The Grapes of Wrath*.

- -

RESEARCH

Research to Clarify Choose at least one unfamiliar detail from the text. Briefly research that detail. In what way does the information you learned shed light on an aspect of the story?

from THE GRAPES OF WRATH

⚙ Tool Kit
Close-Read Guide and
Model Annotation

Close Read the Text

1. This model, from paragraph 1, shows two sample annotations, along with questions and conclusions. Close read the passage, and find another detail to annotate. Then, write a question and your conclusion.

ANNOTATE: There is repetition here, of words and ideas.

QUESTION: What ideas are being emphasized through repetition?

CONCLUDE: The tenants are sorting through generations of memories and belongings.

> In the little houses the tenant people sifted their belongings and the belongings of their fathers and of their grandfathers. Picked over their possessions for the journey to the west. The men were ruthless because the past had been spoiled, but the women knew how the past would cry to them in the coming days.

ANNOTATE: The author personifies the past by saying it "would cry to them in the coming days."

QUESTION: Why did the author make this choice?

CONCLUDE: The women understand how much they will miss the past.

Close Read
ANNOTATE · QUESTION · CONCLUDE

2. For more practice, go back into the text and complete the close-read notes.

3. Revisit a section of the text you found important during your first read. Read this section closely and **annotate** what you notice. Ask yourself **questions** such as "Why did the author make this choice?" What can you **conclude**?

- -

Analyze the Text

CITE TEXTUAL EVIDENCE to support your answers.

⊜ Notebook Respond to these questions.

1. Classify What story details reveal that these characters are farm people?

2. Interpret What is the general attitude of the characters? How can you tell?

3. Analyze Why do the characters burn their belongings at the end of the excerpt?

4. Essential Question: *How do we overcome obstacles?* What have you learned about how people deal with obstacles by reading this selection?

⬛ STANDARDS
Reading Literature
• Determine a theme or central idea of a text and analyze its development over the course of the text; provide an objective summary of the text.
• Analyze how particular elements of a story or drama interact.

Analyze Craft and Structure

Theme Every successful literary work develops at least one **theme**, or central message. Themes can be expressed as general truths about people or life. Writers develop themes through careful selection of significant story details, including the following elements:

- **Setting** is the time and place in which a story occurs.

- **Cultural and historical context** is the social, cultural, and historical environment of the characters, including major events that affect them.

- Characters' actions and reactions to situations can reveal **themes**, or insights about human nature.

In *The Grapes of Wrath*, Steinbeck uses the setting of Oklahoma during the Great Depression to develop themes about how people respond to great hardships, such as drought. The cultural and historical context of the novel includes the ongoing drought and the disappearance of usable farmland, the resulting conditions of poverty, and the different roles that men and women traditionally follow in that time and place.

Practice

CITE TEXTUAL EVIDENCE to support your answers.

📓 **Notebook** Complete the following activity, and then respond to the questions.

1. Complete the chart to analyze how story elements determine theme.

Identifying Theme

SETTING	THEME
What are the most important details about the setting of this excerpt?	What general truth is developed by these story elements?
CULTURAL AND HISTORICAL CONTEXT	
What parts of the characters' environment have the greatest impact on their choices?	
CHARACTERS' ACTIONS	
How do men and women in the excerpt respond differently to their situation?	

2. Repeated words and ideas can highlight key themes. What theme about human nature is suggested by the narrator's repetition of the noun *bitterness*?

3. Would the themes suggested by this passage of *The Grapes of Wrath* be much different if the story were adapted and set in modern-day Oklahoma? Why or why not?

from THE GRAPES OF WRATH

Concept Vocabulary

ruthless	toil	doomed
bitterness	sorrow	frantically

Why These Words? The concept vocabulary words describe extreme emotions or conditions that people experience. For example, the men feel much *bitterness* as they sell their belongings, the women feel great *sorrow* as they say good-bye to their homes, and the characters *frantically* load their cars and leave their homes behind.

1. How does the concept vocabulary sharpen the reader's understanding of the story's characters and setting?

2. What other words in the selection describe or relate to the difficult conditions these characters face?

Practice

📝 **Notebook** The concept vocabulary words appear in the excerpt from *The Grapes of Wrath*. Use each word in a sentence that demonstrates your understanding of the word's meaning.

Word Study

Old English Suffix: -*less* The Old English suffix -*less* means "not having" or "unable to be acted on or to act." It usually indicates that the word in which it appears is an adjective. For example, the word *ruthless* means "having no pity," "merciless," or "cruel." In the story, the men are described as *ruthless* as they pick through belongings with no outward show of emotion or feeling.

1. Write your own sentence that correctly uses the word *ruthless*.

2. Write definitions for these words, consulting a dictionary if you need help: *heartless, pitiless, purposeless*.

3. Think of two other words that have the suffix -*less*. Record a definition for each word, and write a sentence that correctly uses it.

WORD NETWORK

Add interesting words from the text about facing adversity to your Word Network.

STANDARDS

Language
• Determine or clarify the meaning of unknown and multiple-meaning words and phrases based on *grade 7 reading and content,* choosing flexibly from a range of strategies.
  b. Use common, grade-appropriate Greek or Latin affixes and roots as clues to the meaning of a word.

• Acquire and use accurately grade-appropriate general academic and domain-specific words and phrases; gather vocabulary knowledge when considering a word or phrase important to comprehension or expression.

Author's Style

Description Descriptions of people, places, and things are shaped by **word choice**, the specific language an author uses to create a strong impression.

Word choice also helps a writer create **imagery** —descriptive language that appeals to one or more of the five senses.

	EXAMPLES FROM THE TEXT	NOTES
Precise words	That <u>plow</u>, that <u>harrow</u>, remember in the war we planted <u>mustard</u>?	Plow, harrow, mustard are all simple, precise words.
	The tenant men <u>scuffed</u> home to the farms through the red dust.	The verb *scuffed* is much more precise than a verb such as *walked* or *went*.
Imagery	Take the <u>little glass brow-band jewels, roses red under glass</u>.	These words appeal to the sense of sight.
	And his pipe—<u>still smells rank</u>.	These words appeal to the sense of smell.
	I choose the <u>fluffy pilla</u>.	These words appeal to the sense of touch.

Practice

CITE TEXTUAL EVIDENCE to support your answers.

Complete the activity, and then respond to the questions.

1. Reread paragraph 7 of "*The Grapes of Wrath*." Use the chart below to show three examples of Steinbeck's word choice to describe the horses.

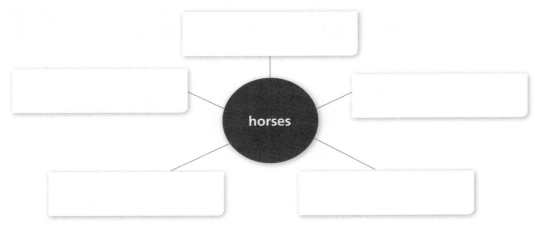

horses

2. **Evaluate** (a) Which words from the graphic organizer enable you to imagine the horses most clearly? Explain your choices. (b) To which senses do the words you chose appeal?

3. **Interpret** (a) To what sense do the images in paragraph 13 mostly appeal? (b) What mood or atmosphere does the use of these images create?

THE DUST BOWL

from THE GRAPES OF WRATH

Writing to Compare

The documentary video you watched provides in-depth information about the Dust Bowl, the historical event that is an essential part of the setting of John Steinbeck's novel *The Grapes of Wrath*. Now, deepen your understanding of the topic by analyzing what you have learned and expressing your ideas in writing.

Assignment

The video "The Dust Bowl" and the novel *The Grapes of Wrath* present very different perspectives, or points of view, about the role of farmers in the 1930s drought and its aftermath. Were farmers innocent victims of a natural disaster, or were they guilty of creating the disaster due to poor land management?

Write an **argumentative essay** in which you state and support an argument about the role of farmers in the Dust Bowl. Use details from Steinbeck's novel and the documentary video as evidence to support your claim. Strengthen your support by addressing one counterclaim.

Prewriting

Analyze Perspectives Review both sources to understand how the video and the novel present different perspectives on farmers during the Dust Bowl. Complete the chart to summarize how each source depicts the role of farmers. Then, include details from each source that produce a strong impression or impact.

	HISTORICAL VIDEO: "THE DUST BOWL"	LITERARY TEXT: from *THE GRAPES OF WRATH*
Role of Farmers in the Dust Bowl		
Strong Impressions		

Notebook Respond to these questions.

1. How do the video and the novel use different techniques to influence an audience's response?

2. Which perspective on the role of farmers in the Dust Bowl is more persuasive? Why?

STANDARDS

Reading Literature
Compare and contrast a fictional portrayal of a time, place, or character and a historical account of the same period as a means of understanding how authors of fiction use or alter history.

Writing
• Write arguments to support claims with clear reasons and relevant evidence.
  a. Introduce claim(s), acknowledge alternate or opposing claims, and organize the reasons and evidence logically.
  b. Support claim(s) with logical reasoning and relevant evidence, using accurate, credible sources and demonstrating an understanding of the topic or text.

Drafting

Outline Your Essay Complete the outline to plan and draft your argumentative essay. Adjust the outline as needed.

I. Introduction Begin with a strong opening that clearly states the claim you are making about how much responsibility farmers should bear for the Dust Bowl.

Opening Claim: _____

_____

_____

II. Body

   A. Provide Evidence from Sources Choose evidence from the sources that supports your argument. Consider whether you will begin with your strongest evidence, or present your strongest evidence last.

   Evidence: _____

   _____

   Evidence: _____

   _____

   Evidence: _____

   _____

   B. Address a Counterclaim Introduce the counterclaim, or opposite position, presented in the video or novel. Then, explain why you think this argument is weak or incomplete.

   Counterclaim: _____

   _____

   Your Response: _____

   _____

III. Conclusion End your essay by summarizing your claim and leaving your readers with an important idea or perspective on the subject.

Closing Idea: _____

_____

_____

Reviewing, Revising, and Editing

Once you have written a complete draft, revise it for clarity and effectiveness. Is your claim clear and strong? Do you provide enough evidence to support your argument? Do you describe the counterclaim fairly and explain why you think your claim is stronger?

Swap drafts with a partner to review and proofread one another's work. Make changes and correct errors to prepare a final draft.

✐ EVIDENCE LOG

Before moving on to a new selection, go to your Evidence Log and record what you've learned from this excerpt from *The Grapes of Wrath*.

☰ STANDARDS

Reading Literature
Compare and contrast a fictional portrayal of a time, place, or character and a historical account of the same period as a means of understanding how authors of fiction use or alter history.

Writing
Write arguments to support claims with clear reasons and relevant evidence.

  a. Support claim(s) with logical reasoning and relevant evidence, using accurate, credible sources and demonstrating an understanding of the topic or text.
  c. Use words, phrases, and clauses to create cohesion and clarify the relationships among claim(s), reasons, and evidence.

  • Draw evidence from literary or informational texts to support analysis, reflection, and research.
  a. Apply grade 7 Reading standards to literature.

About the Author

Francisco Jiménez
(b. 1943) was born in
Mexico and came to the
United States with his
family when he was four
years old. The family
settled in California and
became migrant workers.
Although he could not go
to school before the harvest
ended, Jiménez studied in
the fields. His hard work
paid off as he went on to
become an outstanding
teacher and award-winning
writer.

🔧 **Tool Kit**
First-Read Guide and Model
Annotation

The Circuit

Concept Vocabulary

You will encounter the following words as you read "The Circuit."
Before reading, note how familiar you are with each word. Then, rank
the words in order from most familiar (1) to least familiar (6).

WORD	YOUR RANKING
thoroughly	
wearily	
instinctively	
enthusiastically	
hesitantly	
understandingly	

After completing your first read, come back to the concept vocabulary
and review your rankings. Mark any changes to your original rankings.

First Read FICTION

Apply these strategies as you conduct your first read. You will have an
opportunity to complete the close-read notes after your first read.

NOTICE *whom* the story is about, *what* happens, *where* and *when* it happens, and *why* those involved react as they do.

ANNOTATE by marking vocabulary and key passages you want to revisit.

CONNECT ideas within the selection to what you already know and what you have already read.

RESPOND by completing the Comprehension Check and by writing a brief summary of the selection.

First Read
NOTICE · ANNOTATE · CONNECT · RESPOND

STANDARDS
Reading Literature
By the end of the year, read and
comprehend literature, including
stories, dramas, and poems, in the
grades 6–8 text complexity band
proficiently, with scaffolding as
needed at the high end of the range.

The Circuit

Francisco Jiménez

SCAN FOR
MULTIMEDIA

BACKGROUND

This selection is from *The Circuit: Stories from the Life of a Migrant Child,* a collection of autobiographical short stories by Francisco Jiménez. In this story, the narrator, Panchito, tells of his difficult early years as part of a family of migrant farm workers. To him, life consisted of constant moving and work, with school wedged in around harvesting jobs. The "circuit" in the title refers to the path migrant workers take every year to find jobs.

NOTES

1 It was that time of year again. Ito, the strawberry sharecropper,[1] did not smile. It was natural. The peak of the strawberry season was over and the last few days the workers, most of them braceros,[2] were not picking as many boxes as they had during the months of June and July.

2 As the last days of August disappeared, so did the number of braceros. Sunday, only one—the best picker—came to work. I liked him. Sometimes we talked during our half-hour lunch break. That is how I found out he was from Jalisco, the same state in Mexico my family was from. That Sunday was the last time I saw him.

3 When the sun had tired and sunk behind the mountains, Ito signaled us that it was time to go home. "*Ya esora,*"[3] he yelled in his broken Spanish. Those were the words I waited for twelve hours a day, every day, seven days a week, week after week. And the thought of not hearing them again saddened me.

1. **sharecropper** (SHAIR krop uhr) *n.* one who works for a share of a crop; tenant farmer.
2. **braceros** (bruh SAIR ohs) *n.* migrant Mexican farm laborers who harvest crops.
3. *Ya esora* (yah ehs AW rah) Spanish for "It's time." (*Ya es hora.*)

4   As we drove home Papá did not say a word. With both hands on the wheel, he stared at the dirt road. My older brother, Roberto, was also silent. He leaned his head back and closed his eyes. Once in a while he cleared from his throat the dust that blew in from outside.

5   Yes, it was that time of year. When I opened the front door to the shack, I stopped. Everything we owned was neatly packed in cardboard boxes. Suddenly I felt even more the weight of hours, days, weeks, and months of work. I sat down on a box. The thought of having to move to Fresno[4] and knowing what was in store for me there brought tears to my eyes.

6   That night I could not sleep. I lay in bed thinking about how much I hated this move.

7   A little before five o'clock in the morning, Papá woke everyone up. A few minutes later, the yelling and screaming of my little brothers and sisters, for whom the move was a great adventure, broke the silence of dawn. Shortly, the barking of the dogs accompanied them.

8   While we packed the breakfast dishes, Papá went outside to start the "Carcanchita."[5] That was the name Papá gave his old '38 black Plymouth. He bought it in a used-car lot in Santa Rosa in the Winter of 1949. Papá was very proud of his little jalopy. He had a right to be proud of it. He spent a lot of time looking at other cars before buying this one. When he finally chose the Carcanchita, he checked it **thoroughly** before driving it out of the car lot. He examined every inch of the car. He listened to the motor, tilting his head from side to side like a parrot, trying to detect any noises that spelled car trouble. After being satisfied with the looks and sounds of the car, Papá then insisted on knowing who the original owner was. He never did find out from the car salesman, but he bought the car anyway. Papá figured the original owner must have been an important man because behind the rear seat of the car he found a blue necktie.

thoroughly (THUR oh lee) *adv.* completely; entirely

9   Papá parked the car out in front and left the motor running. "*Listo*,"[6] he yelled. Without saying a word Roberto and I began to carry the boxes out to the car. Roberto carried the two big boxes and I carried the two smaller ones. Papá then threw the mattress on top of the car roof and tied it with ropes to the front and rear bumpers.

10   Everything was packed except Mamá's pot. It was an old large galvanized[7] pot she had picked up at an army surplus store in Santa Maria. The pot had many dents and nicks, and the

---

4. **Fresno** (FREHZ noh) *n.* city in central California.
5. **Carcanchita** (kahr kahn CHEE tah) affectionate name for the car.
6. *Listo* (LEES toh) Spanish for "Ready."
7. **galvanized** (GAL vuh nyzd) *adj.* coated with zinc to prevent rusting.

more dents and nicks it acquired the more Mamá liked it. "*Mi olla*,"[8] she used to say proudly.

11   I held the front door open as Mamá carefully carried out her pot by both handles, making sure not to spill the cooked beans. When she got to the car, Papá reached out to help her with it. Roberto opened the rear car door and Papá gently placed it on the floor behind the front seat. All of us then climbed in. Papá sighed, wiped the sweat from his forehead with his sleeve, and said **wearily**: "*Es todo.*"[9]

12   As we drove away, I felt a lump in my throat. I turned around and looked at our little shack for the last time.

13   At sunset we drove into a labor camp near Fresno. Since Papá did not speak English, Mamá asked the camp foreman if he needed any more workers. "We don't need no more," said the foreman, scratching his head. "Check with Sullivan down the road. Can't miss him. He lives in a big white house with a fence around it."

14   When we got there, Mamá walked up to the house. She went through a white gate, past a row of rose bushes, up the stairs to the front door. She rang the doorbell. The porch light went on and a tall husky man came out. They exchanged a few words. After the man went in, Mamá clasped her hands and hurried back to the car. "We have work! Mr. Sullivan said we can stay there the whole season," she said, gasping and pointing to an old garage near the stables.

15   The garage was worn out by the years. It had no windows. The walls, eaten by termites, strained to support the roof full of holes. The dirt floor, populated by earth worms, looked like a gray road map.

16   That night, by the light of a kerosene lamp, we unpacked and cleaned our new home. Roberto swept away the loose dirt, leaving the hard ground. Papá plugged the holes in the walls with old newspapers and tin can tops. Mamá fed my little brothers and sisters. Papá and Roberto then brought in the mattress and placed it on the far corner of the garage. "Mamá, you and the little ones sleep on the mattress. Roberto, Panchito, and I will sleep outside under the trees," Papá said.

17   Early next morning Mr. Sullivan showed us where his crop was, and after breakfast, Papá, Roberto, and I headed for the vineyard to pick.

18   Around nine o'clock the temperature had risen to almost one hundred degrees. I was completely soaked in sweat and my mouth felt as if I had been chewing on a handkerchief. I walked over to the end of the row, picked up the jug of water we had

---

8. ***Mi olla*** (mee OH yah) Spanish for "My pot."
9. ***Es todo*** (ehs TOH thoh) Spanish for "That's everything."

NOTES

wearily (WIHR uh lee) *adv.* in a tired manner

CLOSE READ
ANNOTATE: Mark the words and phrases in paragraph 15 that the describe the garage.

QUESTION: What effect do these words create?

CONCLUDE: What can you conclude about the lives of migrant workers from this passage?

brought, and began drinking. "Don't drink too much; you'll get sick," Roberto shouted. No sooner had he said that than I felt sick to my stomach. I dropped to my knees and let the jug roll off my hands. I remained motionless with my eyes glued on the hot sandy ground. All I could hear was the drone of insects. Slowly I began to recover. I poured water over my face and neck and watched the dirty water run down my arms to the ground.

19   I still felt dizzy when we took a break to eat lunch. It was past two o'clock and we sat underneath a large walnut tree that was on the side of the road. While we ate, Papá jotted down the number of boxes we had picked. Roberto drew designs on the ground with a stick. Suddenly I noticed Papá's face turn pale as he looked down the road. "Here comes the school bus," he whispered loudly in alarm. **Instinctively**, Roberto and I ran and hid in the vineyards. We did not want to get in trouble for not going to school. The neatly dressed boys about my age got off. They carried books under their arms. After they crossed the street, the bus drove away. Roberto and I came out from hiding and joined Papá. "*Tienen que tener cuidado,*"[10] he warned us.

20   After lunch we went back to work. The sun kept beating down. The buzzing insects, the wet sweat, and the hot dry dust made the afternoon seem to last forever. Finally the mountains around the valley reached out and swallowed the sun. Within an hour it was too dark to continue picking. The vines blanketed the grapes, making it difficult to see the bunches. "*Vamonos,*"[11] said Papá, signaling to us that it was time to quit work. Papá then took out a pencil and began to figure out how much we had earned our first day. He wrote down numbers, crossed some out, wrote down some more. "*Quince,*"[12] he murmured.

21   When we arrived home, we took a cold shower underneath a water hose. We then sat down to eat dinner around some wooden crates that served as a table. Mamá had cooked a special meal for us. We had rice and tortillas with "*carne con chile,*"[13] my favorite dish.

22   The next morning I could hardly move. My body ached all over. I felt little control over my arms and legs. This feeling went on every morning for days until my muscles finally got used to the work.

23   It was Monday, the first week of November. The grape season was over and I could now go to school. I woke up early that morning and lay in bed, looking at the stars and savoring the

instinctively (ihn STIHNGK tihv lee) *adv.* done automatically, without thinking

CLOSE READ

ANNOTATE: Mark the verbs in paragraph 20 that describe the actions of the sun, mountains and valley, and vines.

QUESTION: Why has the author chosen verbs that make nonhuman things seem human?

CONCLUDE: Would the text be as effective if the author had made different choices?

---

10. *Tienen que tener cuidado* (tee EHN ehn kay tehn EHR kwee THAH thoh) Spanish for "You have to be careful."
11. *Vámonos* (VAH moh nohs) Spanish for "Let's go."
12. *Quince* (KEEN say) Spanish for "Fifteen."
13. **"carne con chile"** (KAHR nay kuhn CHIHL ay) dish of ground meat, hot peppers, beans, and tomatoes.

thought of not going to work and of starting sixth grade for the first time that year. Since I could not sleep, I decided to get up and join Papá and Roberto at breakfast. I sat at the table across from Roberto, but I kept my head down. I did not want to look up and face him. I knew he was sad. He was not going to school today. He was not going tomorrow, or next week, or next month. He would not go until the cotton season was over, and that was sometime in February. I rubbed my hands together and watched the dry, acid stained skin fall to the floor in little rolls.

24   When Papá and Roberto left for work, I felt relief. I walked to the top of a small grade next to the shack and watched the Carcanchita disappear in the distance in a cloud of dust. Two hours later, around eight o'clock, I stood by the side of the road waiting for school bus number twenty. When it arrived I climbed in. Everyone was busy either talking or yelling. I sat in an empty seat in the back.

25   When the bus stopped in front of the school, I felt very nervous. I looked out the bus window and saw boys and girls carrying books under their arms. I put my hands in my pant pockets and walked to the principal's office. When I entered I heard a woman's voice say: "May I help you?" I was startled. I had not heard English for months. For a few seconds I remained speechless. I looked at the lady who waited for an answer. My first instinct was to answer her in Spanish, but I held back. Finally, after struggling for English words, I managed to tell her that I wanted to enroll in the sixth grade. After answering many questions, I was led to the classroom.

> "**F**inally, after struggling for English words, I managed to tell her that I wanted to enroll in the sixth grade."

26   Mr. Lema, the sixth grade teacher, greeted me and assigned me a desk. He then introduced me to the class. I was so nervous and scared at that moment when everyone's eyes were on me that I wished I were with Papá and Roberto picking cotton. After taking roll, Mr. Lema gave the class the assignment for the first hour. "The first thing we have to do this morning is finish reading the story we began yesterday," he said **enthusiastically**. He walked up to me, handed me an English book, and asked me to read. "We are on page 125," he said politely. When I heard this, I felt my blood rush to my head; I felt dizzy. "Would you like to read?" he asked **hesitantly**. I opened the book to page 125. My mouth was dry. My eyes began to water. I could not begin. "You can read later," Mr. Lema said **understandingly**.

27   For the rest of the reading period I kept getting angrier and angrier at myself. I should have read, I thought to myself.

enthusiastically (ehn thoo zee AS tihk lee) *adv.* with eager interest

hesitantly (HEHZ uh tuhnt lee) *adv.* in an unsure or cautious way

understandingly (uhn duhr STAN dihng lee) *adv.* in a knowing way; kindly

28   During recess I went into the rest room and opened my English book to page 125. I began to read in a low voice, pretending I was in class. There were many words I did not know. I closed the book and headed back to the classroom.

29   Mr. Lema was sitting at his desk correcting papers. When I entered he looked up at me and smiled. I felt better. I walked up to him and asked if he could help me with the new words. "Gladly," he said.

30   The rest of the month I spent my lunch hours working on English with Mr. Lema, my best friend at school.

31   One Friday during lunch hour Mr. Lema asked me to take a walk with him to the music room. "Do you like music?" he asked me as we entered the building. "Yes, I like *corridos*,"[14] I answered. He then picked up a trumpet, blew on it, and handed it to me. The sound gave me goose bumps. I knew that sound. I had heard it in many corridos. "How would you like to learn how to play it?" he asked. He must have read my face because before I could answer, he added: "I'll teach you how to play it during our lunch hours."

32   That day I could hardly wait to tell Papá and Mamá the great news. As I got off the bus, my little brothers and sisters ran up to meet me. They were yelling and screaming. I thought they were happy to see me, but when I opened the door to our shack, I saw that everything we owned was neatly packed in cardboard boxes. ❧

---

14. ***corridos*** (koh REE thohs) *n.* ballads.

Comprehension Check

Complete the following items after you finish your first read.

1. What kind of work does Panchito's family do?

2. Why does the family move at the beginning of the story?

3. Why does Papá warn his sons that the school bus is coming when they are picking grapes?

4. Who befriends Panchito at school?

5. 📓 **Notebook** Write a brief summary of "The Circuit" to confirm your understanding of the story.

- -

RESEARCH

Research to Clarify Choose at least one unfamiliar detail from the text. Briefly research that detail. In what way does the information you learned shed light on an aspect of the story?

THE CIRCUIT

Close Read the Text

1. This model, from paragraph 3, shows two sample annotations, along with questions and conclusions. Close read the passage, and find another detail to annotate. Then, write a question and your conclusion.

Close Read
ANNOTATE · QUESTION · CONCLUDE

ANNOTATE: The author describes the sun as being "tired."

QUESTION: Why did the author choose to describe the sun in this way?

CONCLUDE: The author personifies the sun as "tired" to suggest the fatigue of the workers.

ANNOTATE: This sentence has a repetitive structure.

QUESTION: What effect is created by the repetition?

CONCLUDE: The structure of this sentence mirrors the long, repetitive working days in the fields.

> When the sun had tired and sunk behind the mountains, Ito signaled us that it was time to go home. "*Ya esora,*" he yelled in his broken Spanish. Those were the words I waited for twelve hours a day, every day, seven days a week, week after week. And the thought of not hearing them again saddened me.

Tool Kit
Close-Read Guide and Model Annotation

2. For more practice, go back into the text and complete the close-read notes.

3. Revisit a section of the text you found important during your first read. Read this section closely and **annotate** what you notice. Ask yourself **questions** such as "Why did the author make this choice?" What can you **conclude**?

Analyze the Text

CITE TEXTUAL EVIDENCE to support your answers.

Notebook Respond to these questions.

1. (a) Interpret How does Panchito feel as his family drives away from the "little shack"? **(b) Make Inferences** What does this detail suggest about him?

2. (a) What is the best thing that happens to Panchito on the last day of school? **(b) Make Inferences** What is the worst thing?

3. Draw Conclusions How does Panchito most likely feel when he sees the packed boxes at the end of the story? Why?

4. Essential Question *How do we overcome obstacles?* What have you learned about facing adversity by reading this selection?

STANDARDS

Reading Literature
• Cite several pieces of textual evidence to support analysis of what the text says explicitly as well as inferences drawn from the text.
• Determine a theme or central idea of a text and analyze its development over the course of the text; provide an objective summary of the text.

Analyze Craft and Structure

Theme The **theme**, or central idea of a story, is an insight about life that the story conveys. Although the themes of a work are sometimes directly stated, more often they are hinted at or suggested.

- **Stated themes** are expressed directly within a text. Classic fables, like *The Fox and the Grapes*, have stated themes provided at the story's end.

- **Implied themes** are suggested by the author by story details and are not directly expressed. Most narratives, like "The Circuit," have implied themes. It's important to note that there is no single "correct" theme for a work: You must infer, or make educated guesses, about themes based on story clues.

To infer a theme—

- Identify the main conflict of the story and its outcome.
- Examine characters' responses to conflicts, and identify any lessons learned.
- Look for repeated ideas expressed by story characters.
- Analyze the story's title to see if it hints at or reveals an important aspect of the story.

Practice

> **CITE TEXTUAL EVIDENCE** to support your answers.

📓 **Notebook** Complete the activity, and then respond to the questions.

1. To begin inferring theme, complete this chart with clues from the text. Then, in the final row of the chart, write your ideas about theme, based on your analysis of the clues you gathered.

MAIN CONFLICT	CHARACTERS' RESPONSES	REPEATED IDEAS	STORY'S TITLE
Theme(s)			

2. **(a)** Why do you think Francisco Jiménez titled this story "The Circuit"? **(b)** What clues to theme might the title reveal?

3. If you were to adapt this story and provide a stated theme, what would be the theme, how would it be revealed, and by whom?

THE CIRCUIT

Concept Vocabulary

thoroughly	instinctively	hesitantly
wearily	enthusiastically	understandingly

Why These Words? The concept vocabulary words from the text describe ways in which characters act or respond. For example, after Papá works hard to load the car, he wipes his forehead *wearily*; when the narrator and his brother are told the school bus is coming, they run away *instinctively* (done automatically without thinking).

1. How does the concept vocabulary sharpen the reader's understanding of characters in "The Circuit"?

2. What other words in the selection are used to describe feelings or actions?

Practice

📓 **Notebook** The concept vocabulary words appear in "The Circuit." Respond to these questions, based on your knowledge of each word.

1. What is a task that should be done *thoroughly*?

2. When might someone behave *wearily*?

3. How might someone *instinctively* react to danger?

4. How might people behave if they were responding *enthusiastically*?

5. How might someone sound when asking a question *hesitantly*?

6. What might someone do when listening to a friend *understandingly*?

Word Study

Old English Suffix: -ly When added to the ends of adjectives, the Old English suffix *-ly* creates an adverb that describes how something was done. For example, when *-ly* is added to the adjective *thorough*, it creates an adverb, *thoroughly*, which means "in a thorough way or manner."

1. Write your own sentence that correctly uses the word *instinctively*.

2. Think of three other words that contain the suffix *-ly*. Record a definition and write a context sentence for each word.

⬣ WORD NETWORK

Add interesting words from the text about facing adversity to your Word Network.

▤ STANDARDS

Language
Determine or clarify the meaning of unknown and multiple-meaning words and phrases based on *grade 7 reading and content*, choosing flexibly from a range of strategies.

  a. Use context as a clue to the meaning of a word or phrase.
  b. Use common, grade-appropriate Greek or Latin affixes and roots as clues to the meaning of a word.

Conventions

Commas Commas are essential tools for writers. **Commas (,)** signal a brief pause; they enable readers to absorb information in meaningful, accurate chunks.

Use the chart to review the functions of commas.

USING COMMAS	EXAMPLE
Use a comma before a conjunction that joins independent clauses—groups of words that can stand on their own in sentences.	Julia started laughing, and she could not stop.
Use a comma after an introductory word, phrase, or clause.	If it rains, will you still be able to start the project?
Use commas to separate three or more words, phrases, or clauses in a series.	The salad consisted of lettuce, carrots, cucumber, and olives.
Use a comma to separate coordinate adjectives. These are consecutive adjectives that modify the same noun and whose order can be reversed. Coordinate adjectives can be linked together smoothly with the word *and*.	John wrote a funny, insightful play. John wrote an insightful, funny play. [John wrote a funny *and* insightful play.]

Read It

1. Reread these sentences from "The Circuit." Identify the function of the comma or commas in each sentence.

   a. As the last days of August disappeared, so did the number of braceros.

   b. Suddenly I felt even more the weight of hours, days, weeks, and months of work.

   c. I sat at the table across from Roberto, but I kept my head down.

   d. After the man went in, Mamá clasped her hands and hurried back to the car.

Write It

⊟ Notebook

1. Write a sentence using two coordinate adjectives to describe a house.
2. Write a sentence using three coordinate adjectives to describe a person.
3. Write a sentence correctly using commas to separate three or more words in a series.
4. Write a compound sentence correctly using a comma to separate independent clauses.

▤ STANDARDS

Language
• Demonstrate command of the conventions of standard English capitalization, punctuation, and spelling when writing.
• Use a comma to separate coordinate adjectives..

Writing to Sources

Assignment

In "The Circuit," the narrator's life follows a pattern as his family moves from workplace to workplace. Write a short **explanation** of additional patterns you find in the story (related to characters' behavior, actions, seasons, and so on). Conclude your explanation with observations about how these patterns give meaning to the story.

When you write your explanation:

- Analyze evidence from the text to determine the main idea you want to convey.
- Include details from the text to support your ideas.
- Organize your explanation in a clear, logical way.
- Conclude by restating your main idea and providing an additional thought or idea.

Vocabulary and Conventions Connection Think about including several of the concept vocabulary words in your writing. Also, remember to correctly use commas in your sentences.

thoroughly	instinctively	hesitantly
wearily	enthusiastically	understandingly

- -

Reflect on Your Writing

After you have written your explanation, answer these questions.

1. Was it easy or difficult to identify and analyze patterns in the story? Why?

2. (a) What decisions did you make about organizing your ideas?
(b) What did you end up liking or disliking about those decisions?

3. Why These Words? The words you choose make a difference in your writing. Which words did you choose to describe the effect of patterns on the story's meaning?

☷ STANDARDS

Reading Literature
Determine a theme or central idea of a text and analyze its development over the course of the text; provide an objective summary of the text.

Writing
• Write informative/explanatory texts to examine a topic and convey ideas, concepts, and information through the selection, organization, and analysis of relevant content.
 b. Develop the topic with relevant facts, definitions, concrete details, quotations, or other information and examples.
• Draw evidence from literary or informational texts to support analysis, reflection, and research.
 a. Apply *grade 7 Reading standards* to literature.

Speaking and Listening

Assignment

Work with a partner to research what life was like for migrant farm workers and their families in the time period of "The Circuit" (from about the 1940s to the 1960s, mainly in California—but also in other parts of the United States). Come up with questions such as:

- Where did families travel to harvest grapes, strawberries, and cotton?
- How did the children of migrant farm workers attend school?

Then, work with your partner to answer the questions, drawing on information from the story and research. Then, **role-play** an interview between a reporter and a farm worker to present your information.

1. Plan Your Presentation

- Research and discuss the topic and questions.
- Use the Internet and library resources to gather information.

2. Rehearse Your Presentation

- Decide who will role-play the reporter and who will role-play the farm worker.
- Practice what each of you will say during your role-play.

3. Deliver Your Presentation

- Once you begin, stay in character until the role-play is finished.
- Speak as if you were the person you are role-playing.
- Maintain appropriate eye contact with each other.

4. Evaluate Presentations
Use a presentation evaluation guide like the one shown to analyze your own as well as your classmates' presentations.

PRESENTATION EVALUATION GUIDE

Rate each statement on a scale of 1 (not demonstrated) to 5 (demonstrated).

☐ The role-play presented important, relevant information.

☐ The role-play was realistic.

☐ The people role-playing stayed in character.

☐ The role-players maintained eye contact with each other.

☐ The role-players spoke loudly enough to hear them.

EVIDENCE LOG

Before moving on to a new selection, go to your Evidence Log and record what you've learned from "The Circuit."

STANDARDS

Speaking and Listening
- Engage effectively in a range of collaborative discussions (one-on-one, in groups, and teacher-led) with diverse partners on *grade 7 topics, texts, and issues,* building on others' ideas and expressing their own clearly.
  a. Come to discussions prepared, having read or researched material under study; explicitly draw on that preparation by referring to evidence on the topic, text, or issue to probe and reflect on ideas under discussion.
  c. Pose questions that elicit elaboration and respond to others' questions and comments with relevant observations and ideas that bring the discussion back on topic as needed.

- Present claims and findings, emphasizing salient points in a focused, coherent manner with pertinent descriptions, facts, details, and examples; use appropriate eye contact, adequate volume, and clear pronunciation.

Writing
- Conduct short research projects to answer a question, drawing on several sources and generating additional related, focused questions for further research and investigation.

WRITING TO SOURCES

- THE DUST BOWL

- *from* THE GRAPES OF WRATH

- THE CIRCUIT

Write an Informative Essay

You have just read and watched selections that relate to how people deal with obstacles. "The Dust Bowl" shows the devastating effects of a drought. The excerpt from *The Grapes of Wrath* depicts farmers who lost their land and had to leave their homes. "The Circuit" portrays farm workers who don't have permanent homes.

Assignment

Write an **informative essay** in which you answer this question:

> How did the individuals in the selections cope with the obstacles they faced?

Describe the hardships faced by the people or characters in the selections, and inform the reader about how they dealt with those obstacles. Use details from the selections to support your ideas.

ACADEMIC VOCABULARY

As you craft your essay, consider using some of the academic vocabulary you learned in the beginning of the unit.

deviate
persevere
determination
diversity
tradition

 Tool Kit
Student Model of an Informative Essay

Elements of a Informative Essay

A **informative essay** presents information about a topic. Ideas are supported with precise, factual details.

An effective informative essay contains these elements:

- an introduction in which the topic and thesis are revealed
- supporting factual details that support the writer's ideas
- clear, consistent organization
- a conclusion in which the writer's thesis is restated and additional insights are provided
- a formal, objective tone

Model Informative Essay For a model of an informative essay, see the Launch text, "Against the Odds."

Challenge yourself to find all of the elements of an informative essay in the text. You will have an opportunity to review these elements as you prepare to write your own essay.

■ STANDARDS

Writing
• Write informative/explanatory texts to examine a topic and convey ideas, concepts, and information through the selection, organization, and analysis of relevant content.
• Write routinely over extended time frames and shorter time frames for a range of discipline-specific tasks, purposes, and audiences.

Prewriting / Planning

Gather Details Revisit the selections to gather specific details that provide information you will share in your essay. Complete this chart as you identify obstacles and coping strategies, or methods of handling or overcoming challenges. In some sources, different people may exhibit methods of dealing with problems.

	OBSTACLE	COPING STRATEGIES
The Grapes of Wrath		
"The Dust Bowl"		
"The Circuit"		

Formulate a Thesis A strong thesis statement will give your essay a sharp focus, indicating both your subject and the central message you want to share with readers. An effective thesis statement should:

- State one key idea clearly and directly.
- Use precise, formal language.
- Avoid overgeneralizations and vague or unnecessary words.

Notice how one of the following statements would be a much stronger stronger thesis statement for an informative essay.

> **Overgeneralization and informal language:** Everybody's afraid of something, and that's just how it is no matter who you are.

> **Sharply focused thesis:** Many literary works show that facing one's greatest fear is a difficult but worthwhile challenge that can build character and solve problems.

Review the details you gathered and look for a single idea about obstacles and coping strategies that connects them. Use your analysis to formulate a thesis statement below.

My thesis about how individuals cope with obstacles: _____

_____

✍ EVIDENCE LOG

Review your Evidence Log and identify key details you may want to include in your essay.

⊞ STANDARDS

Writing
- Write informative/explanatory texts to examine a topic and convey ideas, concepts, and information through the selection, organization, and analysis of relevant content.

a. Introduce a topic clearly, previewing what is to follow; organize ideas, concepts, and information, using strategies such as definition, classification, comparison/contrast, and cause/effect; include formatting, graphics, and multimedia when useful to aiding comprehension.
b. Develop the topic with relevant facts, definitions, concrete details, quotations, or other information and examples.
c. Use appropriate transitions to create cohesion and clarify the relationships among ideas and concepts.

Organize Details Your informative essay will explain specific coping strategies presented in three selections. Before you draft, decide the order in which you will discuss the works. For example, you might begin by discussing the work that contains the strongest support for your thesis statement. On the other hand, you might decide to build up to your strongest ideas.

Complete this outline to plan the details and ideas you will include in the body of your essay.

> **First Selection:**
> **Details and Analysis:**

> **Second Selection:**
> **Details and Analysis:**

> **Third Selection:**
> **Details and Analysis:**

Copyright © SAVVAS Learning Company LLC. All Rights Reserved.

Drafting

Write a First Draft As you draft, focus on writing down your ideas without worrying about word choice and grammar. You will have a chance to revise and edit your work once your draft is finished.

Follow these steps to create your draft:

- Begin with a strong introduction that presents your thesis statement and clearly identifies the selections you will discuss.
- Follow the organization you planned in the body of your essay, using transitions, such as *similarly, in contrast,* or *however,* to make comparisons, move from one topic to another, or emphasize key ideas.
- End your draft with a conclusion that connects ideas from the body to your thesis statement and leaves readers with a single, powerful message.

STANDARDS

Writing

Write informative/explanatory texts to examine a topic and convey ideas, concepts, and information through the selection, organization, and analysis of relevant content.

a. Introduce a topic clearly, previewing what is to follow; organize ideas, concepts, and information, using strategies such as definition, classification, comparison/contrast, and cause/effect; include formatting, graphics, and multimedia when useful to aiding comprehension.

b. Develop the topic with relevant facts, definitions, concrete details, quotations, or other information and examples.

f. Provide a concluding statement or section that follows from and supports the information or explanation presented.

LANGUAGE DEVELOPMENT: CONVENTIONS

The Use of Commas

Revise Incorrect Use of Commas The correct use of commas will help to ensure that your informative essay is clear to readers. Knowing when not to use commas is just as important as knowing when to use them. Here are some guidelines and examples taken from the Launch Text:

	INCORRECTLY PUNCTUATED SENTENCE	CORRECTLY PUNCTUATED SENTENCE
Separate **coordinate adjectives** with a comma, but do not separate the adjectives from the noun they modify.	Sullenberger thought he was in for an average flight—a routine, everyday, trip.	Sullenberger thought he was in for an average flight—a routine, everyday trip.
Do not separate **compound subjects** with a comma.	With water seeping into the plane, Sullenberger, and Skiles, walked the length of the cabin twice, calling "Is anyone there?"	With water seeping into the plane, Sullenberger and Skiles walked the length of the cabin twice, calling "Is anyone there?"
Do not separate **compound verbs** with a comma.	Sullenberger made a Mayday radio call to air traffic control, and calmly explained the situation.	Sullenberger made a Mayday radio call to air traffic control and calmly explained the situation.

TIP

COORDINATE ADJECTIVES
You can recognize coordinate adjectives because they can be separated by the word *and*. (He was a rich, famous writer = He was a rich <u>and</u> famous writer.)

Read It

Read this paragraph and identify the coordinate adjectives, compound subjects, and compound verbs.

Commas and other punctuation marks are critical to clear writing. Be sure to review and revise any incorrect uses of commas and punctuation in your writing. Strive to create clear, understandable sentences.

Write It

As you draft your essay, remember to use commas properly. Copy the faulty sentences and re-punctuate them, either adding or removing commas.

FAULTY SENTENCE	MY REVISION
We inched across the rickety, swaying, bridge.	
Studying together, Glenda, and Jasmine, helped each other earn better grades.	
At summer camp we learned archery, and knots.	
The actor bowed, and smiled.	

≡ STANDARDS

Language
• Demonstrate command of the conventions of standard English capitalization, punctuation, and spelling when writing.
  a. Use a comma to separate coordinate adjectives.

Revising

Evaluating Your Draft

Use the checklist to evaluate the effectiveness of your draft. Then, use your evaluation and instruction on this page to guide your revision.

FOCUS AND ORGANIZATION	EVIDENCE AND ELABORATION	CONVENTIONS
☐ Provides an introduction that reveals the topic and thesis.	☐ Clearly shows relationships among ideas.	☐ Uses words, phrases, and clauses that create cohesion and clarify the relationships among ideas.
☐ Is organized clearly and logically.	☐ Supports ideas with relevant evidence and details from the selections.	
☐ Provides a concluding statement that brings the essay to a satisfying close.	☐ Maintains a formal tone.	☐ Attends to the norms and conventions of the discipline, especially correct use of commas.

Revising for Focus and Organization

Provide a Clear Conclusion Review the conclusion you have drafted, and check to be sure that it follows logically from your thesis and body paragraphs. Strive to keep your conclusion brief but engaging. You might consider ending your conclusion with a question or with a powerful quotation from a text you read.

Revising for Evidence and Elaboration

Support Ideas With Relevant Evidence Evaluate with a critical eye the details you have used to support ideas. First mark the ideas or claims you make. Then, mark support you have given. Add details as needed, and delete unneeded or irrelevant information.

Maintain a Formal Tone A writer's tone is his or her attitude toward the audience or subject. Apply the following steps to revise for a formal tone in your essay:

- Identify any informal language or any slang expressions in your essay. Change them to formal, academic language appropriate for an essay.

- Underline any **clichés** (overused expressions, such as "what goes around comes around") or **idioms** (figurative expressions, such as "a chip on your shoulder"). Replace clichés and slang with fresh, original language that better suits your audience.

⬡ WORD NETWORK

Include interesting words from your Word Network in your essay.

▤ STANDARDS

Writing
- Write informative/explanatory texts to examine a topic and convey ideas, concepts, and information through the selection, organization, and analysis of relevant content.
  a. Introduce a topic clearly, previewing what is to follow; organize ideas, concepts, and information, using strategies such as definition, classification, comparison/contrast, and cause/effect; include formatting (e.g., headings), graphics (e.g., charts, tables), and multimedia when useful to aiding comprehension.
  b. Develop the topic with relevant facts, definitions, concrete details, quotations, or other information and examples.
  d. Use precise language and domain-specific vocabulary to inform about or explain the topic.
  e. Establish and maintain a formal style.

PEER REVIEW

Exchange essays with a classmate. Use the checklist to evaluate your classmate's essay and provide supportive feedback.

1. Is there an effective introduction?

☐ yes ☐ no   If no, suggest a better way the writer could introduce the topic.

2. Are the writer's ideas supported by details and support from the selections?

☐ yes ☐ no   If no, point out where the writer should provide support.

3. Are there clear connections among ideas?

☐ yes ☐ no   If no, point out where the writer should use transitions to make these connections clearer.

4. What is the strongest part of your classmate's essay?

Editing and Proofreading

Edit for Conventions Reread your draft for accuracy and consistency. Correct errors in grammar and word usage. Review your use of commas to ensure that you have followed punctuation rules.

Proofread for Accuracy Read your draft carefully, looking for errors in spelling and punctuation. Also, check your spelling of homonyms—words that sound the same but are spelled differently and have different meanings: for example, *their, they're,* and *there.*

Publishing and Presenting

Create a final version of your essay. Share it with your class or with a small group of classmates, so you can get constructive feedback. In turn, review and comment on your classmates' work. As a group, discuss what your essays have in common and the ways in which they are different.

Reflecting

Reflect on what you learned as you wrote your essay. How did writing the essay heighten your understanding of how people deal with obstacles? What did you learn from peer review that might help you with future writing assignments?

▤ STANDARDS

Language
Demonstrate command of the conventions of standard English capitalization, punctuation, and spelling when writing.
   a. Use a comma to separate coordinate adjectives.
   b. Spell correctly.

ESSENTIAL QUESTION:

How do we overcome obstacles?

You've hit a bump in the road. Now what should you do? You will read selections that describe obstacles that people have faced and how they were able to overcome them. You will work in a group to continue your exploration of the topic of facing adversity.

Small-Group Learning Strategies

Throughout your life, in school, in your community, and in your career, you will continue to learn and work with others.

Look at these strategies and the actions you can take to practice them as you work in teams. Add ideas of your own for each step. Use these strategies during Small-Group Learning.

STRATEGY	ACTION PLAN
Prepare	• Complete your assignments so that you are prepared for group work. • Organize your thinking so you can contribute to your group's discussions. •
Participate fully	• Make eye contact to signal that you are listening and taking in what is being said. • Use text evidence when making a point. •
Support others	• Build off ideas from others in your group. • Invite others who have not yet spoken to do so. •
Clarify	• Paraphrase the ideas of others to ensure that your understanding is correct. • Ask follow-up questions. •

SCAN FOR
MULTIMEDIA

CONTENTS

Working as a Team

1. Take a Position In your group, discuss the following question:

Are any challenges impossible to overcome?

As you take turns sharing your ideas, be sure to provide examples to make your response clear. After all group members have shared, discuss your responses. Were other group members' responses similar to yours? Did other group members share challenges that you had not thought of, but could relate to?

2. List Your Rules As a group, decide on the rules that you will follow as you work together. Samples are provided; add two more of your own. You may add or revise rules based on your experience together.

- Everyone should participate in group discussions.
- People should not interrupt.

- _____
  _____

- _____
  _____

3. Apply the Rules Practice working as a group. Share what you have learned about overcoming obstacles. Make sure each person in the group contributes. Take notes and be prepared to share with the class one thing that you heard from another member of your group.

4. Name Your Group Choose a name that reflects the unit topic.

Our group's name: _____

5. Create a Communication Plan Decide how you want to communicate with one another. For example, you might use online collaboration tools, email, or instant messaging.

Our group's decision: _____
_____

Making a Schedule

First, find out the due dates for the Small-Group activities. Then, preview the texts and activities with your group, and make a schedule for completing the tasks.

SELECTION	ACTIVITIES	DUE DATE
A Work in Progress		
from The Story of My Life		
How Helen Keller Learned to Talk		
A Young Tinkerer Builds a Windmill, Electrifying a Nation		

Working on Group Projects

As your group works together, you'll find it more effective if each person has a specific role. Different projects require different roles. Before beginning a project, discuss the necessary roles and choose one for each group member. Here are some possible roles; add your own ideas.

Project Manager: monitors the schedule and keeps everyone on task

Researcher: organizes research activities

Recorder: takes notes during group meetings

_____

_____

_____

_____

_____

 SCAN FOR MULTIMEDIA

About the Author

Aimee Mullins (b. 1976) is an athlete, model, and actor. At the age of one, she needed to have both of her legs amputated below the knee. Mullins learned how to walk and run with prosthetics, enabling her to participate in the 1996 Paralympic Games, where she set three world records in running and jumping events.

A Work in Progress

Concept Vocabulary

As you perform your first read of "A Work in Progress," you will encounter these words.

accomplishments	extraordinary	celebrate

Context Clues If these words are unfamiliar to you, try using **context clues** to help you determine their meanings. To do so, look for clues given by other words in the text that surround the unfamiliar words. There are various types of context clues that you may encounter as you read.

Synonyms: His **aberrant** behavior was unexpected. It is strange for him to be impolite.

Restatement of an idea: Because of a rare bone disease, her bones are **delicate** and more likely to break.

Contrast of ideas and topics: James will not eat foods made with **artificial** ingredients; he shops only at organic food stores.

Apply your knowledge of context clues and other vocabulary strategies to determine the meanings of other unfamiliar words you encounter during your first read.

First Read NONFICTION

Apply these strategies as you conduct your first read. You will have an opportunity to complete a close read after your first read.

NOTICE the general ideas of the text. *What* is it about? *Who* is involved?

ANNOTATE by marking vocabulary and key passages you want to revisit.

First Read

NOTICE ANNOTATE
CONNECT RESPOND

CONNECT ideas within the selection to what you already know and what you have already read.

RESPOND by completing the Comprehension Check and by writing a brief summary of the selection.

STANDARDS

Reading Informational Text
By the end of the year, read and comprehend literary nonfiction in the grades 6–8 text complexity band proficiently, with scaffolding as needed at the high end of the range.

Language
Determine or clarify the meaning of unknown and multiple–meaning words and phrases based on *grade 7 reading and content,* choosing flexibly from a range of strategies.
  a. Use context as a clue to the meaning of a word or phrase.

A Work in Progress

Aimee Mullins

BACKGROUND

A prosthetic is an artificial substitute for a missing body part. Over the past few decades, prosthetic technology has advanced greatly. Modern prosthetics can often fully replace the function of a missing limb due to the invention of lighter materials and more sophisticated designs.

SCAN FOR MULTIMEDIA

1   So two weeks ago I was a bridesmaid, and the reception was actually here at the New York Public Library, and I will never forget this wedding. Yes, it was very beautiful. But more importantly, I survived the slick marble floors that are all over this building. Tile and marble floors are public enemy number one to a stiletto-loving girl like me. And I had five-inch heels on that night.

2   Most people learn to walk in very high heels. They bend their ankle so that the ball of the foot touches the ground first; you have more stability.

NOTES

3   I don't have ankles, so I hit each step on the stiletto, which makes the possibility of the banana peel wipeout very likely. But given the choice between practicality and theatricality, I say, "Go big or go home, man. Go down in flames if you're gonna go."

4   I guess I'm a bit of a daredevil. I think that the nurses at DuPont Institute would agree. I spent a lot of time there as a child. Doctors amputated[1] both of my legs below the knee when I was an infant, and then when I was five, I had a major surgery to correct the wonky direction in which my tibia was growing. So I had two metal pins to hold that—full plaster casts on both legs. I had to use a wheelchair because I couldn't wear prosthetics.

5   One of the best things about getting out of the hospital is the anticipation of the day you return to school—I had missed so much class, I just couldn't wait to get back and see all my friends. But my teacher had a different idea about that. She tried to prevent me from returning to class, because she said that in the condition I was in, I was "inappropriate," and that I would be a distraction to the other students (which of course I was, but not because of the casts and the wheelchair).

6   Clearly she needed to make my difference invisible because she wanted to control her environment and make it fit into her idea of what "normal" looked like.

7   And it would've been a lot easier for me to fit into what "normal" looked like. I know I wanted that back then. But instead I had these wooden legs with a rubber foot that the toes broke off of, and they were held on with a big bolt that rusted out because I swam in the wooden legs.

8   You're not supposed to swim in the wooden legs, because, you know, the wood rots out.

9   So there I was in second grade music class, doing the twist, and mid-twist I hear this [*makes loud cracking sound*]. And I'm on the floor, and the lower half of my left leg is in splinters across the room. The teacher faints on the piano, and the kids are screaming. And all I'm thinking is, *My parents are gonna kill me. I broke my leg!*

10   It's a mess.

11   But then a few years later, my prosthetist[2] tells me, "Aimee, we got waterproof legs for you. No more rusty bolts!"

12   This is a revelation, right? This is gonna change my life. I was so excited to get these legs . . . until I saw them.

1. **amputated** (AM pyoo tayt ihd) *v.* removed surgically.
2. **prosthetist** (PROS thuh tihst) *n.* professional who fits and designs prosthetic limbs.

13   They were made of polypropylene, which is that white plastic "milk jug" material. And when I say "white," I'm not talking about skin color; I'm talking about *the color white*. The "skin color" was the rubber foam foot painted "Caucasian," which is the nastiest shade of nuclear peach that you've ever seen in your life. It has nothing to do with any human skin tone on the planet. And these legs were so good at being waterproof that they were *buoyant*. So when I'd go off the high dive, I'd go down and come straight back up feet first. They were the bane of my existence.

14   But then we're at the Jersey Shore one summer. By the time we get there, there's three hundred yards of towels between me and the sea. And I know this is where I first honed my ability to run really fast. I was the white flash. I didn't wanna feel hundreds of pairs of eyes staring at me. And so I'd get myself into the ocean, and I was a good swimmer, but no amount of swimming technique can control buoyant legs.

15   So at some point I get caught in a rip current, and I'm migrating from my vantage point of where I could see my parents' towel. And I'm taking in water, and I'm fighting, fighting, fighting. And all I could think to do was pop off these legs and put one under each armpit, with the peach feet sticking up, and just bob, thinking, *Someone's gotta find me*.

16   And a lifeguard did. And I'm sure he will collect for therapy bills. You know? Like, they don't show that on *Baywatch*.[3]

17   But they saved my life, those legs.

18   And then when I was fourteen it was Easter Sunday, and I was gonna be wearing a dress that I had purchased with my own money—the first thing I ever bought that wasn't on sale.

19   Momentous event; you never forget it. I'd had a paper route since I was twelve, and I went to The Limited, and I bought this dress that I thought was the height of sophistication—sleeveless safari dress, belted, hits at the knee.

20   Coming downstairs into the living room, I see my father waiting to take us to church. He takes one look at me, and he says, "That doesn't look right. Go upstairs and change."

21   I was like, "What? My super-classy dress? What are you talking about? It's the best thing I own."

---

3. **Baywatch** popular television show from the late 1990s about the lives of fictional lifeguards.

22　He said, "No, you can see the knee joint when you walk. It doesn't look right. It's inappropriate to go out like that. Go change."

23　And I think something snapped in me. I refused to change. And it was the first time I defied my father. I refused to hide something about myself that was true, and I refused to be embarrassed about something so that other people could feel more comfortable.

24　I was grounded for that defiance.

25　So after church the extended family convenes at my grandmother's house, and everybody's complimenting me on how nice I look in this dress, and I'm like, "Really? You think I look nice? Because my parents think I look inappropriate."

26　I outed them (kinda mean, really).

27　But I think the public utterance of this idea that I should somehow hide myself was so shocking to hear that it changed their mind about why they were doing it.

28　And I had always managed to get through life with somewhat of a positive attitude, but I think this was the start of me being able to accept myself. You know, okay, I'm not normal. I have strengths. I've got weaknesses. It is what it is.

29　And I had always been athletic, but it wasn't until college that I started this adventure in Track and Field. I had gone through a lifetime of being given legs that just barely got me by. And I thought, *Well, maybe I'm just having the wrong conversations with the wrong people. Maybe I need to go find people who say, "Yes, we can create* anything *for you in the space between where your leg ends and the ground."*

30　And so I started working with engineers, fashion designers, sculptors, Hollywood prosthetic makeup artists, wax museum designers to build legs for me.

31　I decided I wanted to be the fastest woman in the world on artificial legs, and I was lucky enough to arrive in track at just the right time to be the first person to get these radical sprinting legs modeled after the hind leg of a cheetah, the fastest thing that runs—woven carbon fiber.[4] I was able to set three world records with those legs. And they made no attempt at approximating humanness.

32　Then I get these incredibly lifelike silicon legs—hand-painted, capillaries, veins. And, hey, I can be as tall as I wanna be, so I get different legs for different heights. I don't have to shave. I can wear open-toed shoes in the winter. And most importantly,

---

4. **carbon fiber** (KAHR buhn FY buhr) *n.* very strong, lightweight material.

I can opt out of the cankles[5] I most certainly would've inherited genetically.

33   And then I get these legs made for me by the late, great Alexander McQueen, and they were hand-carved of solid ash with grapevines and magnolias all over them and a six-inch heel. And I was able to walk the runways of the world with supermodels. I was suddenly in this whirlwind of adventure and excitement. I was being invited to go around the world and speak about these adventures, and how I had legs that looked like glass, legs covered in feathers, porcelain legs, jellyfish legs—all wearable sculpture.

34   And I get this call from a guy who had seen me speak years ago, when I was at the beginning of my track career, and he says, "We loved it. We want you to come back." And it was clear to me he didn't know all these amazing things that had happened to me since my sports career.

35   So as I'm telling him, he says, "Whoa, whoa, whoa. Hold on, Aimee. The reason everybody liked you all those years ago was because you were this sweet, vulnerable, naïve girl, and if you walk onstage today, and you are this polished young woman with too many **accomplishments**, I'm afraid they won't like you."

36   For real, he said that. Wow.

37   He apparently didn't think I was vulnerable enough now. He was asking me to be *less than*, a little more downtrodden. He was asking me to disable myself for him and his audience.

38   And what was so shocking to me about that was that I realized I had moved past mere acceptance of my difference. I was having *fun* with my difference. Thank *God* I'm not normal. I get to be *extraordinary*. And I'll decide what is a weakness and what is a strength.

39   And so I refused his request.

40   And a few days later, I'm walking in downtown Manhattan at a street fair, and I get this tug on my shirt, and I look down. It's this little girl I met a year earlier when she was at a pivotal moment in her life. She had been born with a brittle bone disease that resulted in her left leg being seven centimeters shorter than her right. She wore a brace and orthopedic[6] shoes and they got her by, but she wanted to do more.

---

5. **cankles** (KANG kuhlz) *n.* informal term for thick ankles.
6. **orthopedic** (awr thuh PEE dihk) *adj.* designed to treat a muscular or skeletal problem.

NOTES

Mark context clues or indicate another strategy you used that helped you determine meaning.

accomplishments (uh KOM plihsh muhnts) *n.*

MEANING:

extraordinary (ehk STRAWR duh nehr ee) *adj.*

MEANING:

A Work in Progress **497**

41   And like all Internet-savvy kindergarteners, she gets on the computer and Googles "new leg," and she comes up with dozens of images of prosthetics, many of them mine. And she prints them out, goes to school, does show-and-tell on it, comes home, and makes a startling pronouncement to her parents:

42   "I wanna get rid of my bad leg," she says. "When can I get a new leg?"

43   And ultimately that was the decision her parents and doctors made for her. So here she was, six months after the amputation, and right there in the middle of the street fair she hikes up her jeans leg to show me her cool new leg. And it's pink, and it's tattooed with the characters of *High School Musical 3*, replete with red, sequined Mary Janes on her feet.

44   And she was proud of it. She was proud of herself. And the marvelous thing was that this six-year-old understood something that it took me twenty-something years to get, but that we both did discover—that when we can **celebrate** and truly own what it is that makes us different, we're able to find the source of our greatest creative power. ❧

Mark context clues or indicate another strategy you used that helped you determine meaning.

celebrate (SEHL uh brayt) *v.*

MEANING:

Comprehension Check

Complete the following items after you finish your first read. Review and clarify details with your group.

1. Why does the author, Aimee Mullins, have difficulty walking across the marble floor of the library?

2. What happened between Mullins and her father that caused her to be grounded?

3. What does Mullins do to become more involved with the quality of her limbs?

4. According to the author, what is the source of the "greatest creative power"?

5. 🗒 **Notebook** Confirm your understanding of the selection by briefly summarizing key events.

- -

RESEARCH

Research to Clarify Choose at least one unfamiliar detail from the text. Briefly research that detail. In what way does the information you learned shed light on the selection? Share your findings with your small group.

Research to Explore Choose something from the text that interested you. For instance, you might want to learn more about the newest kinds of prosthetic limbs. How does this information deepen your understanding of the personal narrative? Share your findings with your small group.

A WORK IN PROGRESS

Close Read the Text

With your group, revisit sections of the text you marked during your first read. What do you **notice**? What **questions** do you have? What can you **conclude**?

Analyze the Text

> **CITE TEXTUAL EVIDENCE**
> to support your answers.

🖾 **Notebook** Complete the activities.

1. **Review and Clarify** With your group, reread paragraphs 5–6. What reason did the narrator's teacher give for not wanting her to return to class? What do you think might have been the real reason?

2. **Present and Discuss** Now, work with your group to share the passages from the text that you found especially important. Take turns presenting your passages. Discuss what you noticed in the text, the questions you asked, and the conclusions you reached.

3. **Essential Question:** *How do we overcome obstacles?* What has this selection taught you about facing adversity? Discuss with your group.

TIP

GROUP DISCUSSION

When you work with your group, be sure to cite textual details to support your ideas.

🔠 **WORD NETWORK**

Add interesting words related to facing adversity from the text to your Word Network.

LANGUAGE DEVELOPMENT

Concept Vocabulary

| accomplishments | extraordinary | celebrate |

Why These Words? The concept vocabulary words from the text are related. With your group, determine what the words have in common. Write down your ideas, and add another word that fits the category.

Practice

Confirm your understanding of the concept vocabulary words by using them in a discussion with your group in which you address the following question: *What makes a person extraordinary?*

Word Study

Latin Prefix extra- The Latin prefix *extra-* means "beyond the scope of" or "in addition to what is usual or expected." At the end of the selection, the author realizes that what makes her different also makes her *extraordinary*, or beyond what is ordinary or expected. With your group, identify and define two other words you know that include this prefix.

STANDARDS

Reading Informational Text
• Analyze the interactions between individuals, events, and ideas in a text.
• Determine the meaning of words and phrases as they are used in a text, including figurative, connotative, and technical meanings; analyze the impact of a specific word choice on meaning and tone.
• Determine an author's point of view or purpose in a text and analyze how the author distinguishes his or her position from that of others.

Language
Determine or clarify the meaning of unknown and multiple-meaning words and phrases based on *grade 7 reading and content*, choosing flexibly from a range of strategies.
  b. Use common, grade-appropriate Greek or Latin affixes and roots as clues to the meaning of a word.

Analyze Craft and Structure

Author's Purpose: Word Choice and Humor The main purpose of humorous writing is to entertain readers. Authors may incorporate elements of humorous writing into more serious writing in order to express the lighter, human side of otherwise difficult situations. Some literary techniques that authors use to create humor are:

LITERARY TECHNIQUE	DEFINITION	EXAMPLE
HYPERBOLE	intentional, sometimes outrageous, exaggeration for effect	describing a small patch of ice as a "vast, frozen lake"
COMIC DICTION	words chosen to make the reader laugh; these word choices often include slang and other informal language	"Letting the cat out of the bag is a lot easier than putting it back in."
INCONGRUITY	when something is out of place or inappropriate for a situation or setting	wearing bunny ears instead of a veil with a bridal outfit

Practice

CITE TEXTUAL EVIDENCE to support your answers.

Reread "A Work in Progress." Then, work with your group to analyze the narrative. Use the chart to record your ideas. The first two rows have identified humorous passages for you to analyze. In the last two rows, identify the humorous passages on your own.

PARAGRAPHS	HUMOROUS ELEMENT	PURPOSE AND EFFECT
1: "But more importantly, I survived the slick marble floors that are all over this building."		
3: "I don't have ankles, so I hit each step on the stiletto, which makes the possibility of a banana peel wipeout very likely."		
4–21		
22–44		

A WORK IN PROGRESS

Copyright © SAVVAS Learning Company LLC. All Rights Reserved.

Conventions

Informal Grammar "A Work in Progress" is transcribed, or copied, from a speech that Aimee Mullins gave at the New York Public Library. While speaking, Mullins chose **informal grammar,** or casual language rules, to connect with her audience. Some features of her spoken language include:

- **Colloquial Contractions** Words such as *gonna* (going to), *wanna* (want to) and *kinda* (kind of) combine two words in a way that imitates casual conversation.

- **Informal Transitions** People often add casual words and phrases such as *man, I'm like, so there I was,* and *you know* when they speak to link ideas or create emphasis.

- **Introductory Conjunctions** Starting sentences with the conjunctions *and, but,* or *so* can smooth the transition from one sentence into another in informal speech, even though they are discouraged in more formal writing.

Read It

1. Work with your group to find two more examples of informal grammar in "A Work in Progress." Then, rewrite each example of informal grammar to follow standard English grammar rules.

INFORMAL GRAMMAR FROM TEXT	STANDARD GRAMMAR
And all I'm thinking is, *My parents are gonna kill me.*	
This is a revelation, right? This is gonna change my life.	
And a lifeguard did. And I'm sure he will collect for therapy bills. You know? Like, they don't show that on *Baywatch.*	
For real, he said that. Wow.	

2. Compare the impact of Mullins's original words and the versions that follow standard grammar rules. What are the advantages of Mullins's original language choices?

Write It

📓 **Notebook** Write a paragraph that uses informal language to tell about a funny incident that happened to you or someone you know. Imagine that you are sharing this story aloud with an audience, and writing down what you say as you are speaking. Use colloquial contractions, informal transitions, and introductory conjunctions to create a feeling of lively, spoken language.

STANDARDS

Speaking and Listening
Engage effectively in a range of collaborative discussions with diverse partners on *grade 7 topics, texts, and issues,* building on others' ideas and expressing their own clearly.
 a. Come to discussions prepared, having read or researched material under study; explicitly draw on that preparation by referring to evidence on the topic, text, or issue to probe and reflect on ideas under discussion.
 b. Follow rules for collegial discussions, track progress toward specific goals and deadlines, and define individual roles as needed.
 c. Pose questions that elicit elaboration and respond to others' questions and comments with relevant observations and ideas that bring the discussion back on topic as needed.

Language
• Demonstrate command of the conventions of standard English grammar and usage when writing or speaking.
• Demonstrate command of the conventions of standard English capitalization, punctuation, and spelling when writing.

Speaking and Listening

Assignment

With your group, conduct a **discussion** in which you analyze one of the following quotations from the selection.

☐ "And I had always been athletic, but it wasn't until college that I started this adventure in Track and Field. I had gone through a lifetime of being given legs that just barely got me by. And I thought, *Well, maybe I'm just having the wrong conversations with the wrong people. Maybe I need to go find people who say, 'Yes, we can create* anything *for you in the space between where your leg ends and the ground.'"* (paragraph 29)

☐ "And the marvelous thing was that this six-year-old understood something that it took me twenty-something years to get, but that we both did discover—that when we can celebrate and truly own what it is that makes us different, we're able to find the source of our greatest creative power." (paragraph 44)

Organize Your Discussion Assign roles for each member of your group. Roles can include a group leader, who keeps the discussion on topic; a timekeeper, who makes sure that the discussion takes no longer than 15 minutes; and a note-taker to record the group's ideas. Once you have chosen a quotation, use these questions to guide your group's discussion. Use a chart like this one to record ideas from your discussion.

Here are some things to keep in mind as you hold your group discussion.

- Draw on the selection to explore and support ideas. Support viewpoints with examples and details from the selection.

- Take turns speaking. Listen to other students' ideas, and respond with relevant observations and questions that prompt them to elaborate on their thoughts.

📝 EVIDENCE LOG

Before moving on to a new selection, go to your Evidence Log and record what you learned from "A Work in Progress."

DISCUSSION QUESTIONS	RESPONSES
1. What does the quotation mean? How could you paraphrase it, or restate the ideas in your own words?	
2. What happens that causes the author to express these ideas? What caused her to reach this understanding?	
3. Do you think it would help society if more people felt as this author feels? Why or why not?	

from THE STORY OF MY LIFE

HOW HELEN KELLER LEARNED TO TALK

Comparing Text to Media

In this lesson, you will compare a passage from Helen Keller's autobiography with a scene from "How Helen Keller Learned to Talk." First, complete the first-read and close-read activities for the excerpt from *The Story of My Life*. The work you do with your group will help prepare you to compare the excerpt and the video.

About the Author

A serious illness left **Helen Keller** (1880–1968) blind and deaf before she was two years old. When Keller was nearly seven, her family hired Anne Sullivan, a teacher from the Perkins School for the Blind, to help her learn to communicate. Keller and Sullivan developed a remarkable teacher-student relationship as well as a unique friendship.

⠿ STANDARDS

Reading Informational Text
By the end of the year, read and comprehend literary nonfiction in the grades 6–8 text complexity band proficiently, with scaffolding as needed at the high end of the range.
Language
Determine or clarify the meaning of unknown and multiple–meaning words and phrases based on *grade 7 reading and content*, choosing flexibly from a range of strategies.
  a. Use context as a clue to the meaning of a word or phrase.

from The Story of My Life

Concept Vocabulary

As you perform your first read of the excerpt from *The Story of My Life*, you will encounter these words.

imitate	mystery	barriers

Context Clues If these words are unfamiliar to you, try using **context clues** to help you determine their meanings. There are various types of context clues that you may encounter as you read.

> **Synonyms:** With the help of her teacher, she was able to **comprehend** or <u>understand</u> new ideas.
>
> **Restatement of an idea:** There were many **obstacles** on her path, but she would not let them <u>block</u> her progress.

Apply your knowledge of context clues and other vocabulary strategies to determine the meanings of other unfamiliar words you encounter during your first read.

First Read NONFICTION

Apply these strategies as you conduct your first read. You will have an opportunity to complete a close read after your first read.

NOTICE the general ideas of the text. *What* is it about? *Who* is involved?

ANNOTATE by marking vocabulary and key passages you want to revisit.

First Read

CONNECT ideas within the selection to what you already know and what you have already read.

RESPOND by completing the Comprehension Check and by writing a brief summary of the selection.

from **The Story of My Life**

Helen Keller

BACKGROUND

In this excerpt from her autobiography, Helen Keller describes her first experience with language at the age of six. *The Story of My Life* was published in 1903, when Keller was 23 years old.

SCAN FOR MULTIMEDIA

1   The morning after my teacher came she led me into her room and gave me a doll. The little blind children at the Perkins Institution[1] had sent it and Laura Bridgman had dressed it; but I did not know this until afterward.

2   When I had played with it a little while, Miss Sullivan slowly spelled into my hand the word "d-o-l-l." I was at once interested in this finger play and tried to **imitate** it. When I finally succeeded in making the letters correctly I was flushed with childish pleasure

NOTES

Mark context clues or indicate another strategy you used that helped you determine meaning.

imitate (IHM uh tayt) *v.*

MEANING:

1. **Perkins Institution** The Perkins School for the Blind, founded in 1829 in Boston.

and pride. Running downstairs to my mother I held up my hand and made the letters for *doll*. I did not know that I was spelling a word or even that words existed; I was simply making my fingers go in monkey-like imitation. In the days that followed I learned to spell in this uncomprehending way a great many words, among them *pin, hat, cup,* and a few verbs like *sit, stand,* and *walk*. But my teacher had been with me several weeks before I understood that everything has a name.

3   One day, while I was playing with my new doll, Miss Sullivan put my big rag doll into my lap also, spelled "d-o-l-l" and tried to make me understand that "d-o-l-l" applied to both. Earlier in the day we had had a tussle over the words "m-u-g" and "w-a-t-e-r." Miss Sullivan had tried to impress it upon me that "m-u-g" is *mug* and that "w-a-t-e-r" is *water*, but I persisted in confounding the two. In despair she had dropped the subject for the time, only to renew it at the first opportunity. I became impatient at her repeated attempts and, seizing the new doll, I dashed it upon the floor. I was keenly delighted when I felt the fragments of the broken doll at my feet. Neither sorrow nor regret followed my passionate outburst. I had not loved the doll. In the still, dark world in which I lived there was no strong sentiment or tenderness. I felt my teacher sweep the fragments to one side of the hearth, and I had a sense of satisfaction that the cause of my discomfort was removed. She brought me my hat, and I knew I was going out into the warm sunshine. This thought, if a wordless sensation may be called a thought, made me hop and skip with pleasure.

4   We walked down the path to the well-house,[2] attracted by the fragrance of the honeysuckle with which it was covered. Someone was drawing water and my teacher placed my hand under the spout. As the cool stream gushed over one hand she spelled into the other the word *water*, first slowly, then rapidly. I stood still, my whole attention fixed upon the motions of her fingers. Suddenly I felt a misty consciousness as of something forgotten—a thrill of returning thought; and somehow the **mystery** of language was revealed to me. I knew then that "w-a-t-e-r" meant the wonderful cool something that was flowing over my hand. That living word awakened my soul, gave it light, hope, joy, set it free! There were **barriers** still, it is true, but barriers that could in time be swept away.

5   I left the well-house eager to learn. Everything had a name, and each name gave birth to a new thought. As we returned to the house every object which I touched seemed to quiver with life.

---

2. **well-house** small building containing a well.

Mark context clues or indicate another strategy you used that helped you determine meaning.

mystery (MIHS tuh ree) *n.*

MEANING:

barriers (BAR ee uhrz) *n.*

MEANING:

That was because I saw everything with the strange, new sight that had come to me. On entering the door I remembered the doll I had broken. I felt my way to the hearth and picked up the pieces. I tried vainly to put them together. Then my eyes filled with tears; for I realized what I had done, and for the first time I felt repentance and sorrow.

6   I learned a great many new words that day. I do not remember what they all were; but I do know that *mother, father, sister, teacher* were among them—words that were to make the world blossom for me, "like Aaron's rod, with flowers."[3] It would have been difficult to find a happier child than I was as I lay in my crib at the close of that eventful day and lived over the joys it had brought me, and for the first time longed for a new day to come. ❧

---

3. **"like Aaron's rod, with flowers"** in the Old Testament of the Bible, the staff of Aaron miraculously gives forth buds and flowers.

NOTES

Comprehension Check

Complete the following items after you finish your first read. Review and clarify details with your group.

1. What attracts Keller and her teacher toward the well-house?

2. Through which sense does Keller experience the water?

3. Once Helen Keller learns the word for water, what is she eager to do next?

4. 🗐 **Notebook** Confirm your understanding of the excerpt by writing a brief summary of it.

- -

RESEARCH

Research to Clarify Research an unfamiliar detail in the excerpt. For example, you might want to learn more about Helen Keller's teacher, Anne Sullivan. In what way does the information you learned shed light on the excerpt? Share your findings with your group.

Research to Explore Choose something from the text that interested you. For example, you might want to learn more about how blind people learn to read. How does this information deepen your understanding of the text? Share your findings with your group.

Close Read the Text

With your group, revisit sections of the text you marked during your first read. **Annotate** details that you notice. What **questions** do you have? What can you **conclude**?

from THE STORY OF MY LIFE

Analyze the Text

> **CITE TEXTUAL EVIDENCE**
> to support your answers.

Notebook Complete the activities.

1. **Review and Clarify** With your group, reread the excerpt. How does the author use **imagery,** or words and phrases that appeal to the five senses? How does her use of imagery affect the reader?

2. **Present and Discuss** Now work with your group to share the passages from the text that you found especially important. Take turns presenting your passages. Discuss what you noticed in the text, the questions you asked, and the conclusions you reached.

3. **Essential Question: *How do we overcome obstacles?*** What has this excerpt taught you about how people overcome obstacles? Discuss with your group.

> **TIP**
>
> **GROUP DISCUSSION**
> When you work in your group to answer the Analyze the Text questions, be sure to direct listeners to specific words, sentences, and paragraphs in the selection.

LANGUAGE DEVELOPMENT

Concept Vocabulary

> imitate   mystery   barriers

Why These Words? The concept vocabulary words from the text are related. With your group, determine what the words have in common. Write your ideas and add another word that fits the category.

Practice

Notebook Confirm your understanding of these words from the text by using them in sentences. Be sure to use context clues that demonstrate your understand of the meaning of each word.

Word Study

Greek Root: *-myst-* The Greek root *-myst-* means "secret." In the selection, Helen Keller describes how the *mystery*, or "secret," of language was revealed to her through her experience with water at the well-house. Identify another word you know with the Greek root *-myst-*, and use it in a sentence that shows your understanding of the word's meaning.

WORD NETWORK

Add interesting words related to facing adversity from the text to your Word Network.

STANDARDS

Reading Informational Text
Determine the meaning of words and phrases as they are used in a text, including figurative, connotative, and technical meanings; analyze the impact of a specific word choice on meaning and tone.

Language
Determine or clarify the meaning of unknown and multiple-meaning words and phrases based on *grade 7 reading and content*, choosing flexibly from a range of strategies.
  b. Use common, grade-appropriate Greek or Latin affixes and roots as clues to the meaning of a word.

from THE STORY OF MY LIFE

☰ STANDARDS

Reading Informational Text
• Determine the meaning of words and phrases as they are used in a text, including figurative, connotative, and technical meanings; analyze the impact of a specific word choice on meaning and tone.
• Determine an author's point of view or purpose in a text and analyze how the author distinguishes his or her position from that of others.

Analyze Craft and Structure

Author's Purpose: Autobiographical Writing Autobiographical writing is a form of nonfiction narrative writing in which the author provides true accounts of events which he or she directly experienced. Autobiographical writing relates the author's thoughts, feelings, and reflections on the events he or she describes in the narrative. In autobiographical writing, the author is the narrator and uses the **first-person point of view** because he or she takes part in the events described.

In an autobiographical work, an author may have many purposes, or reasons for writing. For example, a comedian might write an autobiography to both entertain readers with humor and to inform them about the events surrounding his or her experiences. You can determine an author's purpose by analyzing the author's word choice and the author's **tone,** or his or her attitude toward the subject and audience.

Practice

CITE TEXTUAL EVIDENCE
to support your answers.

Reread the excerpt from *The Story of My Life.*

⊟ **Notebook** Use the chart to identify specific sentences or passages from the selection that contribute to the author's purpose. Make inferences, or educated guesses, about the ways in which the author's tone and word choice in these sections suggest her purpose for writing.

SELECTION DETAIL	POSSIBLE PURPOSE

When you have finished, share your ideas with your small group. Work together to determine Helen Keller's purpose or purposes for writing. List several details from the excerpt that support your inferences about Keller's purpose. Then, answer the following question: *How does Helen Keller use autobiographical writing to effectively express her purpose and unique point of view?*

Conventions

Types of Dependent Clauses Good writers use a variety of clauses to enliven their writing and to provide detail.

A **clause** is a group of words with its own subject and verb. An **independent clause,** or **main clause,** can stand alone as a complete sentence. A **dependent**, or **subordinate, clause** also has a subject and a verb, but it cannot stand alone as a complete sentence.

Dependent clauses are classified according to how they function in a sentence.

- An **adverb clause** acts as an adverb in a sentence. It begins with a subordinating conjunction, such as *although, if, when,* or *because.*
- A **relative**, or **adjective**, **clause** acts as an adjective. It usually begins with a relative pronoun, such as *who, whom, whose, which,* or *that.*
- A **noun clause** acts as a noun. It begins with a word such as *what, whatever, when, where, how,* or *why.*

In the examples in this chart, each type of dependent clause is underlined.

TYPE OF CLAUSE	EXAMPLE
Adverb Clause	<u>Because Keller could not see or hear</u>, she struggled to understand language. (acts as an adverb, modifying the verb *struggled*)
Relative Clause	Anne Sullivan, <u>who was her teacher</u>, helped Keller break through the barriers that challenged her. (acts as an adjective, modifying *Anne Sullivan*)
Noun Clause	Keller made the connection between the feel of the water and <u>what Sullivan was writing on her hand.</u> (acts as a noun, the object of the preposition *between*)

Read It

Work with your group to identify examples of dependent clauses in the excerpt. Write your examples in the chart, and label the type of dependent clause shown in each example.

EXAMPLE FROM THE TEXT	TYPE OF DEPENDENT CLAUSE

Write It

📓 **Notebook** Write a paragraph describing a time you overcame a barrier to learning. Use specific sensory details to help readers see, hear, smell, and feel the experience. In your paragraph, correctly use at least one adverb clause, one relative clause, and one noun clause.

from THE STORY OF MY LIFE

Comparing Text to Media

You will now watch "How Helen Keller Learned to Talk," an interview that shows Keller with her teacher, Anne Sullivan. As you watch the video, consider the differences in how Helen Keller's experience is portrayed in her autobiography and in the interview.

HOW HELEN KELLER LEARNED TO TALK

About Anne Sullivan
This video shows Helen Keller with her teacher, **Anne Sullivan** (1866–1936). Sullivan herself was visually impaired, and in her early years she lived in a home for the poor following the death of her mother. She rose from these conditions to become a legendary teacher. Her first step was finding an opening as a student at the Perkins School for the Blind when she was 14. At age 21, she became Helen Keller's teacher.

How Helen Keller Learned to Talk

Media Vocabulary

These words will be useful to you as you analyze, discuss, and write about the video.

long shot: camera shot in which the entire subject is visible as well as some of the background around the subject	• Long shots are often used to show something happening in the background behind the subject. • Filmmakers will sometimes use a long shot to establish the setting of a scene.
medium shot: camera shot in which the subject is seen from a medium distance, usually from the waist up	• A medium shot is useful for showing two characters engaging in dialogue. • Medium shots are often used in the transition between a long shot and close-up shot.
close-up shot: camera shot in which the subject is shown at close range; typically the subject's head and shoulders are shown, with no background visible	• A close-up shot is often used to show the facial expression of a character. • Close-up shots can also be used to show a detail on a prop or what characters are doing with their hands.

First Review MEDIA: VIDEO

Study the video and take notes as you watch.

WATCH *who* speaks, *what* they say, and *how* they say it.

NOTE elements that you find interesting and want to revisit.

First Review

WATCH · NOTE · CONNECT · RESPOND

CONNECT ideas in the video to other media you've experienced, texts you've read, or images you've seen.

RESPOND by completing the Comprehension Check at the end.

≡ STANDARDS

Reading Informational Texts
By the end of the year, read and comprehend literary nonfiction in the grades 6–8 text complexity band proficiently, with scaffolding as needed at the high end of the range.

Language
Acquire and use accurately grade-appropriate general academic and domain-specific words and phrases; gather vocabulary knowledge when considering a word or phrase important to comprehension or expression.

How Helen Keller Learned to Talk

Helen Keller, with Anne Sullivan

BACKGROUND

This video interview with Helen Keller and Anne Sullivan was made in 1928. In the interview, Sullivan demonstrates and explains how Keller learned to talk by feeling the vibrations that are made in a person's mouth and throat when he or she is speaking.

NOTES

Comprehension Check

Complete the following items after you finish your first review.

1. How old was Helen Keller when Anne Sullivan first met her?

2. In what position on her teacher's face did Keller have to place her hand in order to feel the vibrations of the spoken word?

3. What does Keller say at the end of the interview?

Close Review

Watch the film clip again. Record any new observations that seem important. What **questions** do you have? What can you **conclude**?

HOW HELEN KELLER LEARNED TO TALK

Analyze the Media

Notebook Complete the activities.

1. **Present and Discuss** Choose the section of the video you find most interesting or powerful. Share your choice with the group, and discuss why you chose it. Explain what you noticed in the section, the questions it raised for you, and the conclusions you reached about it.

2. **Review and Synthesize** With your group, review the video interview. How does the video deepen your understanding of the challenges Helen Keller faced? How does it highlight her triumphs? Explain.

3. **Notebook** Essential Question: *How do we overcome obstacles?* What have you learned about overcoming obstacles and facing adversity from the interview?

Media Vocabulary

Use the vocabulary words in your responses to the items.

long shot	medium shot	close-up shot

1. What type of shot is used at the very beginning of the video? Why do you think the director used that shot?

2. What type of shot is used as Anne Sullivan is introducing Helen Keller at the beginning of the video?

3. What type of shot is used when Sullivan is demonstrating how Keller placed her hand on Sullivan's face? What does the shot enable the director of the video to show?

STANDARDS

Language
Acquire and use accurately grade-appropriate general academic and domain-specific words and phrases; gather vocabulary knowledge when considering a word or phrase important to comprehension or expression.

from THE STORY OF MY LIFE

HOW HELEN KELLER LEARNED
TO TALK

Writing to Compare

Both the *The Story of My Life* and "How Helen Keller Learned to Talk" show the sense of triumph that Keller experiences from overcoming challenges with language through the help of her teacher, Anne Sullivan.

Assignment

Create a **multimedia presentation** about Keller's life and education in which you compare and contrast the text and the video. In your presentation, explain how the written account and the video portray the subject, Helen Keller, in different ways. Choose from these options:

☐ an **instructional booklet** illustrating Sullivan's lessons to Keller

☐ an **informational Web site** about Keller and her education

☐ a **museum guide** for an exhibit about Keller and her education

Planning and Prewriting

Compare the Text and Video Using a chart, such as the one shown, work with your group to analyze the ways in which the text and video portray the subjects of Keller and Sullivan as well as Keller's educational process.

PORTRAYAL	AUTOBIOGRAPHY EXCERPT	VIDEO INTERVIEW	SIMILARITIES AND DIFFERENCES
Keller			
Sullivan			
Educational Process			

🗨 **Notebook** Respond to the following items.

1. What details in the text help readers to understand Keller's thoughts and experiences? Does the video enable viewers to gain the same understanding of Keller's personality?

2. How does the portrayal of Sullivan and Keller in the video expand your understanding of them from the text?

3. Briefly summarize the strengths and weaknesses of each medium's portrayal of Keller.

STANDARDS

Reading Informational Text
Compare and contrast a text to an audio, video, or multimedia version of the text, analyzing each medium's portrayal of the subject.

Assign Tasks Make a list of tasks you will have to accomplish in order to finish your presentation. Assign the tasks to individual group members. Adapt this list to suit the needs of your group.

TASK LIST

Research the Topic: Decide whether you need more background information on Keller and Sullivan. If you do, research and gather the information.

Assigned To: _____

Locate Media: Find multimedia elements—audio, video, and images—that will highlight the information in your presentation and engage your audience.

Assigned To: _____

Gather Quotes and Details: Identify details from both selections that support and clarify your central ideas. Note direct quotations that will strengthen the support for your main points.

Assigned To: _____

Make a Rough Outline: Organize a sequence for your content so that the text and multimedia elements complement each other. You can change the sequence as you develop your presentation.

Assigned To: _____

Drafting

Determine Your Central Idea Write a one-sentence thesis in which you state your central idea.

Thesis: _____

Work with your group to incorporate the media so that it supports your central idea.

Include Comparisons of Text to Video Use your notes from the analysis you did earlier to create a script that explains how the text and the video contribute in different ways to your understanding of Helen Keller and her education.

Reviewing, Revising, and Editing

Before presenting your finished work to the class, check to be sure that all the media and text you have chosen to include add value to the presentation. If necessary, revise the arrangement of content so that the text and multimedia elements transition more smoothly.

EVIDENCE LOG

Before moving on to a new selection, go to your Evidence Log and record what you've learned from the text excerpt from *The Story of My Life* and the video "How Helen Keller Learned to Talk."

STANDARDS
Writing
• Write informative/explanatory texts to examine a topic and convey ideas, concepts, and information through the selection, organization, and analysis of relevant content.
  a. Introduce a topic clearly, previewing what is to follow; organize ideas, concepts, and information, using strategies such as definition, classification, comparison/ contrast, and cause/ effect; include formatting, graphics, and multimedia when useful to aiding comprehension.
  b. Develop the topic with relevant facts, definitions, concrete details, quotations, or other information and examples.
• Draw evidence from literary or informational texts to support analysis, reflection, and research.
  b. Apply *grade 7 Reading standards* to literary nonfiction.
Speaking and Listening
• Engage effectively in a range of collaborative discussions with diverse partners on *grade 7 topics, texts, and issues,* building on others' ideas and expressing their own clearly.
  b. Follow rules for collegial discussions, track progress toward specific goals and deadlines, and define individual roles as needed.
• Analyze the main ideas and supporting details presented in diverse media and formats and explain how the ideas clarify a topic, text, or issue under study.
• Include multimedia components and visual displays in presentations to clarify claims and findings and emphasize salient points.

About the Author
Sarah Childress (b. 1980) is a Senior Reporter at *Frontline,* PBS's investigative journalism series. Childress has also written articles for *Newsweek* and *The Wall Street Journal*.

A Young Tinkerer Builds a Windmill, Electrifying a Nation

Concept Vocabulary

As you perform your first read of "A Young Tinkerer Builds a Windmill, Electrifying a Nation," you will encounter these words.

| scarcity | desire | attempts |

Context Clues If these words are unfamiliar to you, try using **context clues** to help you determine their meanings. There are various types of context clues that you may encounter as you read.

Synonyms: Due to the **insufficiency**, or lack, of electricity, he was inspired to come up with a solution to power his home.

Restatement of an Idea: More power supplies are needed for the expansion of the electrical grid, which will lead to the **proliferation** of the home use of electric appliances.

Contrast of Ideas and Topics: He **strived** to make his invention work, but he eventually had to quit.

Apply your knowledge of context clues and other vocabulary strategies to determine the meaning of other unfamiliar words you encounter during your first read.

First Read NONFICTION

Apply these strategies as you conduct your first read. You will have an opportunity to complete a close read after your first read.

NOTICE the general ideas of the text. *What* is it about? *Who* is involved?

ANNOTATE by marking vocabulary and key passages you want to revisit.

CONNECT ideas within the selection to what you already know and what you have already read.

RESPOND by completing the Comprehension Check and by writing a brief summary of the selection.

STANDARDS

Reading Informational Text
By the end of the year, read and comprehend literary nonfiction in the grades 6–8 text complexity band proficiently, with scaffolding as needed at the high end of the range.

Language
Determine or clarify the meaning of unknown and multiple-meaning words and phrases based on *grade 7 reading and content,* choosing flexibly from a range of strategies.
　a. Use context as a clue to the meaning of a word or phrase.

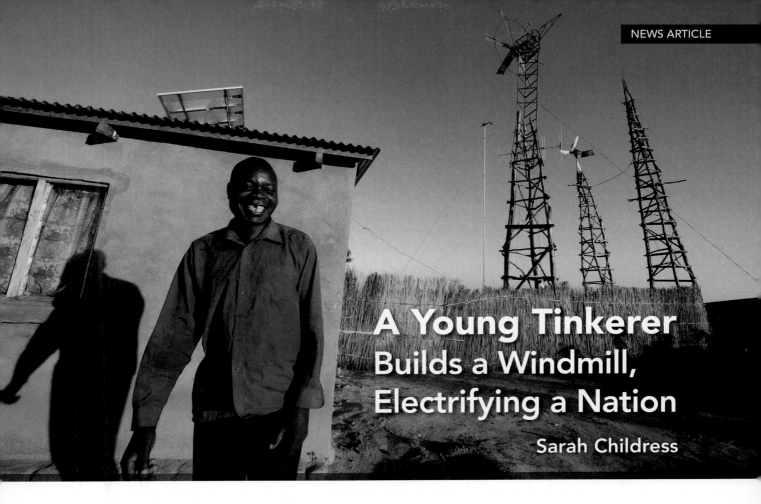

A Young Tinkerer
Builds a Windmill, Electrifying a Nation

Sarah Childress

BACKGROUND

Malawi is a landlocked country in southeastern Africa, one-fifth of which is taken up by the enormous Lake Malawi. Malawi's economy is mostly farming-based, and most of its citizens live in rural areas. Only a small number of the almost seventeen million Malawians have access to electricity, which is typically limited to large cities.

SCAN FOR MULTIMEDIA

1   Masitala, Malawi—On a continent woefully short of electricity, 20-year-old William Kamkwamba has a dream: to power up his country one windmill at a time.

2   So far, he has built three windmills in his yard here, using blue-gum trees and bicycle parts. His tallest, at 39 feet, towers over this windswept village, clattering away as it powers his family's few electrical appliances: 10 six-watt light bulbs, a TV set, and a radio. The machine draws in visitors from miles around.

3   Self-taught, Mr. Kamkwamba took up windmill building after seeing a picture of one in an old textbook. He's currently working on a design for a windmill powerful enough to pump water from wells and provide lighting for Masitala, a cluster of buildings where about 60 families live.

4   Then, he wants to build more windmills for other villages across the country. Betting he can do it, a group of investors are putting him through school.

NOTES

Mark context clues or indicate another strategy you used that helped you determine meaning.

scarcity (SKAYR suh tee) *n.*

MEANING:

5   "I was thinking about electricity," says Mr. Kamkwamba, explaining how he got hooked on wind. "I was thinking about what I'd like to have at home, and I was thinking, 'What can I do?'"

6   To meet his family's growing power needs, he recently hammered in a shiny store-bought windmill next to the big one at his home and installed solar panels. He has another windmill still in its box that he'll put up at a house 70 miles away in the capital, Lilongwe, where he now goes to school.

7   A few years ago, he built a windmill for the primary school in Masitala. He used it to teach an informal windmill-building course. Lately, he has offered to help the village handyman down the road build his own machine.

8   "Energy poverty"—the scarcity of modern fuels and electrical supplies in poor parts of the world—is a subject of great interest to development economists. The windmill at the Kamkwamba family compound, a few brick buildings perched on a hill overlooking the village, has turned it into a stop for the curious: People trekking across Malawi's arid plains drop by. Villagers now regularly make the dusty walk up the hill to charge their cellphones.

9   The contraption causing all the fuss is a tower made from lashed-together blue-gum tree trunks. From a distance, it resembles an old oil derrick.[1] For blades, Mr. Kamkwamba used flattened plastic pipes. He built a turbine from spare bicycle parts. When the wind kicks up, the blades spin so fast they rock the tower violently back and forth.

10   Mr. Kamkwamba's wind obsession started six years ago. He wasn't going to school anymore because his family couldn't afford the $80-a-year tuition.

11   When he wasn't helping his family farm groundnuts and soybeans, he was reading. He stumbled onto a photograph of a windmill in a text donated to the local library and started to build one himself. The project seemed a waste of time to his parents and the rest of Masitala.

12   "At first, we were laughing at him," says Agnes Kamkwamba, his mother. "We thought he was doing something useless."

13   The laughter ended when he hooked up his windmill to a thin copper wire, a car battery, and a light bulb for each room of the family's main house.

14   The family soon started enjoying the trappings of modern life: a radio and, more recently, a TV. They no longer have to buy paraffin for lantern light. Two of Mr. Kamkwamba's six sisters stay up late studying for school.

---

1. **derrick** (DER ik) *n.* metal framework used in oil drilling.

15   "Our lives are much happier now," Mrs. Kamkwamba says.

16   The new power also attracted a swarm of admirers. Last November, Hartford Mchazime, a Malawian educator, heard about the windmill and drove out to the Kamkwamba house with some reporters. After the news hit the blogosphere, a group of entrepreneurs scouting for ideas in Africa located Mr. Kamkwamba. Called TED, the group, which invites the likes of Al Gore and Bono to share ideas at conferences, invited him to a brainstorming session earlier this year.

17   In June, Mr. Kamkwamba was onstage at a TED conference in Tanzania. (TED stands for Technology Entertainment Design.) "I got information about a windmill, and I try and I made it," he said in halting English to a big ovation. After the conference, a group of entrepreneurs, African bloggers, and venture capitalists[2]—some teary-eyed at the speech—pledged to finance his education.

18   His backers have also showered him with new gadgets, including a cellphone with a hip-hop ringtone, a laptop, and an iPod. (Kelly Clarkson's "Breakaway" is his current favorite tune.) They rewired his family's house, replacing the homemade switches he made out of flip-flop parts.

19   They're paying for him to attend an expensive international academy in the capital, Lilongwe, for children of expatriate missionaries and aid workers. But his teacher, Lorilee MacLean, sometimes worries about his one-track mind and about all the attention he's getting.

20   "I don't want him to be seen as William the windmill maker," said Mrs. MacLean one day recently. While Mr. Kamkwamba quietly plowed through homework, his classmates were busy gossiping and checking their Facebook profiles.

21   Mr. Kamkwamba has taught his family to maintain the windmill when he's away at school. His sister Dolice and cousin Geoffrey can quickly scamper up the tower, as it sways and clatters in the wind, to make repairs.

22   A steady stream of curiosity seekers make the trip to the Kamkwamba compound—mostly unannounced. The visits are unsettling for the reserved family.

23   One afternoon, a pair of Malawian health workers came by to get a closer look and meet Mr. Kamkwamba. The family scattered, leaving the pair—dressed in shirts and ties for the occasion—standing awkwardly in the yard.

24   "We have heard about this windmill, and so we wanted to see it for ourselves," one finally spoke up. Mr. Kamkwamba

---

2. **venture capitalists** *n.* people who provide money to small companies in exchange for partial ownership of those companies. If the companies grow, venture capitalists make money.

Mark context clues or indicate another strategy you used that helped you determine meaning.

desire (dih ZY uhr) *v.*

MEANING:

attempts (uh TEMPTS) *n.*

MEANING:

came around to shake hands, then quickly moved away to show another visitor around.

25   Jealousy is a social taboo in these parts, but Fred Mwale, an educator who works in Wimbe, the area that includes Masitala, says the family's new prosperity is causing some tensions.

26   "People do **desire** what is happening here. They come, and admire," he says. "They think that they might get the same support if they build a windmill."

27   Down the hill, the village handyman started building his own windmill after secretly studying Mr. Kamkwamba's. A gust of wind blew the blades off the man's first few **attempts**. Mr. Kamkwamba offered to help him rebuild, but got no reply.

28   "I'm waiting to see if he's serious," Mr. Kamkwamba says. ❧

Comprehension Check

Complete the following items after you finish your first read. Review and clarify details with your group.

1. What inspired William Kamkwamba to build a windmill?

2. What materials did Kamkwamba use to build his first windmill?

3. What is "energy poverty"?

4. ⊟ **Notebook** Confirm your understanding of the article by writing a brief summary of it.

- -

RESEARCH

Research to Clarify Research an unfamiliar detail in the article. In what way does the information you learned shed light on the article? Share your findings with your small group.

Research to Explore Research other ways that energy poverty is being addressed in poor parts of the world. Share your findings with your group.

A YOUNG TINKERER BUILDS
A WINDMILL, ELECTRIFYING
A NATION

TIP

GROUP DISCUSSION

When you work in your group to answer the Analyze the Text questions, be sure to direct listeners to specific words, sentences, and paragraphs in the story.

⬥ WORD NETWORK

Add interesting words related to facing adversity from the text to your Word Network.

☰ STANDARDS

Reading Informational Text
• Cite several pieces of textual evidence to support analysis of what the text says explicitly as well as inferences drawn from the text.
• Analyze the interactions between individuals, events, and ideas in a text.
• Analyze the structure an author uses to organize a text, including how the major sections contribute to the whole and to the development of the ideas.

Language
Determine or clarify the meaning of unknown and multiple-meaning words and phrases based on *grade 7 reading and content*, choosing flexibly from a range of strategies.
  b. Use common, grade-appropriate Greek or Latin affixes and roots as clues to the meaning of a word.

Close Read the Text

With your group, revisit sections of the text you marked during your first read. What do you **notice**? What **questions** do you have? What can you **conclude**?

Analyze the Text

CITE TEXTUAL EVIDENCE
to support your answers.

⊟ **Notebook** Complete the activities.

1. **Review and Clarify** Review the selection with your group. How did the lack of modern conveniences inspire William Kamkwamba to be innovative? What were the results of his innovations?

2. **Present and Discuss** Now, work with your group to share the passages from the text that you found especially important. Take turns presenting your passages. Discuss what you noticed in the text, the questions you asked, and the conclusions you reached.

3. **Essential Question: *How do we overcome obstacles?*** What has this selection taught you about how people overcome obstacles?

LANGUAGE DEVELOPMENT

Concept Vocabulary

scarcity	desire	attempts

Why These Words? The concept vocabulary words from the text are related. With your group, determine what the words have in common. Record your ideas, and add another word that fits the category.

Practice

⊟ **Notebook** Confirm your understanding of these words by using them in sentences containing context clues.

Word Study

Etymology The **etymology** of a word is its origin. Etymologies show how words enter the English language and how they change over time. Check a dictionary for a guide to the symbols and abbreviations used in etymologies. *Desire* comes from Middle English *desiren* < Old French *desirer* < Latin *desiderare*, which means "from the stars." Knowing this, you can gain a better understanding of the meaning of *desire* ("to wish for").

With your group, look up the etymology of at least three other words in the selection. Describe how knowing each etymology helps you better understand the words.

Analyze Craft and Structure

Text Structure: Biographical Writing When a nonfiction text tells a story, it is a work of **narrative nonfiction**. **Biographical writing** is a type of narrative nonfiction in which the author tells about events in another person's life. The elements of biographical writing include:

- a real-life person who is the subject of the biography
- factual information about the setting and context
- details and descriptions that help develop the subject's character
- **direct quotations**, a person's exact words, from the subject and other people that have a relationship with or significant knowledge of the subject, such as a close friend or a historian
- the use of **narrative pacing**, which is the way an author shapes the flow of information in a text—how much information readers receive in a given section of text and the order in which they receive it

Practice

Work with your group to analyze the elements of biographical writing in the article and the ways the author structures information to effectively develop her ideas. Model your analysis on the example in the chart, using the blank rows to capture the information you find.

PARAGRAPH	ELEMENTS OF BIOGRAPHICAL WRITING	CONTRIBUTION TO DEVELOPMENT OF IDEAS
8	• relevant facts • information about the setting • descriptive details	• The definition of "energy poverty" and the facts about the setting show why the windmill is important. • The descriptive details enable the reader to picture the setting.

A YOUNG TINKERER BUILDS
A WINDMILL, ELECTRIFYING
A NATION

Conventions

Capitalization Capital letters signal the beginning of a sentence or quotation and identify proper nouns and proper adjectives. Learning to use correct capitalization will ensure that your writing looks professional and authoritative.

Proper nouns include the names of people, geographic locations, specific events and time periods, organizations, languages, historical events and documents, and religions. **Proper adjectives** are derived from proper nouns, as in *French* (from *France*) and *Canadian* (from *Canada*). Here are some examples taken from the selection you have just read:

> **Sentence beginning:** The contraption causing all the fuss . . .
>
> **Quotation:** ". . . I was thinking, 'What can I do?'"
>
> **Proper nouns:** His sister Dolice and cousin Geoffrey . . .
>
> **Proper adjectives:** One afternoon, a pair of Malawian health workers . . .

Read It

Work with your group to identify examples of correct capitalization in the selection. Find two examples in the selection for each of the following items.

1. a sentence beginning

2. a proper adjective

3. a person's name

4. a quotation

Write It

Identify the errors in capitalization in each sentence, and note the reason each word should or should not begin with a capital letter. Then, revise each sentence to correct the capitalization.

1. William kamkwamba is only Twenty Years Old, but he has built a Windmill to provide electricity to his family in malawi.

2. william's Windmill has brought a lot of attention to the Small Village of Masitala, where his kamkwamba Family lives.

🔲 **Notebook** Finally, write a biographical paragraph in which you briefly describe a person you admire. In your paragraph, use at least three proper nouns, one proper adjective, and a quotation. Reread your paragraph to confirm that you have used correct capitalization.

:≣ STANDARDS

Language
Demonstrate command of the conventions of standard English capitalization, punctuation, and spelling when writing.

Writing to Sources

A **how-to essay** is a written, step-by-step explanation of how to make or do something.

Assignment

Work with your group to write a **how-to essay** in which you address one of the following topics:

- [ ] How to make a windmill. What do you need to make a windmill? What steps should you take? How can it be designed and connected to make it a source of electric power?

- [ ] Where is Masitala, Malawi? Is it close to the capital of Malawi? What directions would you give someone who wants to travel from Malawi's capital to Masitala?

Conduct Research Work with your group to find the information you will need to write your essay. Consult multiple print and digital sources, and evaluate the credibility of each source you use. Take notes on each source so that you can cite your sources accurately in a **Works-Cited list,** or **bibliography,** at the end of your essay.

Organize Your Essay Use **chronological organization**, or step-by-step organization, when you write your how-to essay. A reader needs clear, well-organized directions in order to complete a task successfully. If the steps are out of order, or if they are unclear, he or she will have a difficult time following your directions.

Use Clarifying Transitions Be sure to use transitions that indicate time and sequence as you write your essay. Transitions, such as *first, next, until,* and *meanwhile* will help you to organize and clarify the steps in your essay.

Format Your Essay To help readers follow your directions include headings, illustrations, and graphics in your essay. Place headings before each section of your essay, and place graphics and illustrations in the section of your essay that describes the step the image shows.

✎ EVIDENCE LOG

Before moving on to a new selection, go to your Evidence Log and record what you learned from "A Young Tinkerer Builds a Windmill, Electrifying a Nation."

▤ STANDARDS

Writing

- Introduce a topic clearly, previewing what is to follow; organize ideas, concepts, and information, using strategies such as definition, classification, comparison/contrast, and cause/ effect; include formatting, graphics, and multimedia when useful to aiding comprehension.
- Develop the topic with relevant facts, definitions, concrete details, quotations, or other information and examples.
- Conduct short research projects to answer a question, drawing on several sources and generating additional related, focused questions for further research and investigation.
- Gather relevant information from multiple print and digital sources, using search terms effectively; assess the credibility and accuracy of each source; and quote or paraphrase the data and conclusions of others while avoiding plagiarism and following a standard format for citation.

SOURCES

• A WORK IN PROGRESS

• *from* THE STORY OF MY LIFE

• HOW HELEN KELLER LEARNED TO TALK

• A YOUNG TINKERER BUILDS A WINDMILL, ELECTRIFYING A NATION

Present Multimedia Profiles

Assignment

Review the selections you have just read and viewed. Work in your small group to present a series of multimedia profiles, in which you address this question:

How do people overcome enormous challenges?

Plan with Your Group

Analyze the Text With your group, review the selections you have read in this section. Discuss the people, the challenges they faced, and the strengths and qualities that enabled them to overcome these obstacles. Use this chart to organize your ideas.

SELECTION	PERSON	CHALLENGE(S) FACED	STRENGTHS OR QUALITIES POSSESSED BY THE PERSON	OUTCOME
A Work in Progress				
from The Story of My Life				
How Helen Keller Learned to Talk				
A Young Tinkerer Builds a Windmill, Electrifying a Nation				

Gather Details and Media Each member should draft a brief informative profile about one of the people described in one of the selections. The profile should be able to stand alone as a section of the group presentation. Then, find relevant multimedia to include in your report. Be sure to sequence the multimedia elements so that they clarify and emphasize your important points.

Organize Your Ideas As a group, decide how you will transition from one section to the next and from one speaker to the next.

STANDARDS
Writing
• Write informative/explanatory texts to examine a topic and convey ideas, concepts, and information through the selection, organization, and analysis of relevant content.
• Draw evidence from literary or informational texts to support analysis, reflection, and research.

Rehearse with Your Group

Practice with Your Group Before your presentation, rehearse as a group. Plan the ways in which you will present your multimedia elements, and prepare to begin any necessary equipment. Ensure that each member uses a formal tone, appropriate eye contact, adequate volume, and clear pronunciation.

As you deliver your portion of the presentation, use this checklist to evaluate the effectiveness of your group's rehearsal. Then, use your evaluation and the instruction that follows to guide your revisions to the presentation.

CONTENT	USE OF MEDIA	PRESENTATION TECHNIQUES
☐ The presentation clearly responds to the prompt.	☐ The presentation includes a variety of multimedia.	☐ Presenters speak loudly and clearly.
☐ The presentation includes relevant details from the texts.	☐ The multimedia emphasizes and clarifies key points.	☐ Presenters maintain eye contact.
☐ The sections of the presentation are logically organized.	☐ Equipment functions properly.	

Fine-Tune the Content To make your presentation stronger, you may need to go back into the texts to find more details to support your main ideas. Work with your group to identify key points that are not clear to listeners. Find another way to word these ideas.

Improve Your Use of Media Be sure to sequence your multimedia so that each piece relates directly to a key point in your presentation and helps your audience to better understand the information.

Brush Up on Your Presentation Techniques Practice delivering your presentation several times as a group so you are comfortable. Give one another feedback and encouragement to improve and polish your presentation.

Present and Evaluate

Remember that you must work as a team to make your presentation effective. Give all classmates your full attention when they are presenting. As you listen to other groups, consider their content, use of media, and presentation techniques. Ask questions to clarify your understanding of the information presented in other classmates' presentations.

STANDARDS

Speaking and Listening
Engage effectively in a range of collaborative discussions with diverse partners on *grade 7 topics, texts, and issues,* building on others' ideas and expressing their own clearly.

a. Come to discussions prepared, having read or researched material under study; explicitly draw on that preparation by referring to evidence on the topic, text, or issue to probe and reflect on ideas under discussion.

• Present claims and findings, emphasizing salient points in a focused, coherent manner with pertinent descriptions, facts, details, and examples; use appropriate eye contact, adequate volume, and clear pronunciation.

• Include multimedia components and visual displays in presentations to clarify claims and findings and emphasize salient points.

ESSENTIAL QUESTION:

How do we overcome obstacles?

Sometimes people feel overwhelmed by life's problems. The selections you read are about people who faced big problems and managed to overcome them. In this section, you will complete your study of facing adversity by exploring an additional selection related to the topic. You'll then share what you learn with classmates. To choose a text, follow these steps.

Look Back Think about the selections you have already studied. What more do you want to know about facing adversity?

Look Ahead Preview the selections by reading the descriptions. Which one seems the most interesting and appealing to you?

Look Inside Take a few minutes to scan through the text you chose. Choose a different one if this text doesn't meet your needs.

Independent Learning Strategies

Throughout your life, in school, in your community, and in your career, you will need to rely on yourself to learn and work on your own. Review these strategies and the actions you can take to practice them during Independent Learning. Add ideas of your own for each category.

STRATEGY	ACTION PLAN
Create a schedule	• Understand your goals and deadlines. • Make a plan for what to do each day. •
Practice what you have learned	• Use first-read and close-read strategies to deepen your understanding. • After you read, evaluate the usefulness of the evidence to help you understand the topic. • Consider the quality and reliability of the source. •
Take notes	• Record important ideas and information. • Review your notes before preparing to share with a group. •

SCAN FOR
MULTIMEDIA

CONTENTS

Choose one selection. Selections are available online only.

PERFORMANCE-BASED ASSESSMENT PREP

Review Evidence for an Informative Essay
Complete your Evidence Log for the unit by evaluating what you have learned and synthesizing the information you have recorded.

SCAN FOR MULTIMEDIA

First-Read Guide

Use this page to record your first-read ideas.

Selection Title: _____

Tool Kit
First-Read Guide and
Model Annotation

NOTICE new information or ideas you learn about the unit topic as you first read this text.

ANNOTATE by marking vocabulary and key passages you want to revisit.

First Read

NOTICE ANNOTATE
CONNECT RESPOND

CONNECT ideas within the selection to other knowledge and the selections you have read.

RESPOND by writing a brief summary of the selection.

▤ STANDARD

Reading Read and comprehend complex literary and informational texts independently and proficiently.

Close-Read Guide

Use this page to record your close-read ideas.

Selection Title: _____

Tool Kit
Close-Read Guide and
Model Annotation

Close Read the Text

Revisit sections of the text you marked during your first read. Read these sections closely and **annotate** what you notice. Ask yourself **questions** about the text. What can you **conclude?** Write down your ideas.

Close Read
ANNOTATE · QUESTION · CONCLUDE

Analyze the Text

Think about the author's choices of patterns, structure, techniques, and ideas included in the text. Select one, and record your thoughts about what this choice conveys.

QuickWrite

Pick a paragraph from the text that grabbed your interest. Explain the power of this passage.

STANDARD
Reading Read and comprehend complex literary and informational texts independently and proficiently.

Share Your Independent Learning

Prepare to Share

How do we overcome obstacles?

Even when you read something independently, your understanding continues to grow when you share what you have learned with others. Reflect on the text you explored independently and write notes about its connection to the unit. In your notes, consider why this text belongs in this unit.

Learn From Your Classmates

💬 **Discuss It** Share your ideas about the text you explored on your own. As you talk with your classmates, jot down ideas that you learn from them.

Reflect

Review your notes, and mark the most important insight you gained from these writing and discussion activities. Explain how this idea adds to your understanding of the topic of facing adversity.

🏳 STANDARDS

Speaking and Listening
Engage effectively in a range of collaborative discussions with diverse partners on *grade 7 topics, texts, and issues*, building on others' ideas and expressing their own clearly.

Review Evidence for an Informative Essay

At the beginning of this unit, you expressed your ideas about the following question:

> ## How can people overcome adversity in the face of overwhelming obstacles?

✒ EVIDENCE LOG

Review your Evidence Log and your QuickWrite from the beginning of the unit. Did you learn anything new?

NOTES

Identify at least three things that you learned about how we overcome obstacles.

1.

2.

3.

Identify a real-life experience that illustrates one of your ideas about how we overcome obstacles. _____

_____

_____

Develop your thoughts into a topic sentence for an informative essay. Complete this sentence starter:

As events and details in _____

show, people can overcome obstacles by _____

_____

Evaluate the Strength of Your Evidence Consider your ideas about overcoming obstacles. How did the texts you read affect your ideas? Identify relevant details in the texts that deepened your understanding of the ways in which people overcome obstacles. Also, note specific passages in the texts that gave you key insights or changed your ideas about facing adversity.

☷ STANDARDS

Writing
Write informative/explanatory texts to examine a topic and convey ideas, concepts, and information through the selection, organization, and analysis of relevant content.

a. Introduce a topic clearly, previewing what is to follow; organize ideas, concepts, and information, using strategies such as definition, classification, comparison/contrast, and cause/effect; include formatting, graphics, and multimedia when useful to aiding comprehension.

b. Develop the topic with relevant facts, definitions, concrete details, quotations, or other information and examples.

SOURCES

- WHOLE-CLASS SELECTIONS
- SMALL-GROUP SELECTIONS
- INDEPENDENT-LEARNING SELECTION

🔗 WORD NETWORK

As you write and revise your essay, use your Word Network to help vary your word choices.

PART 1

Writing to Sources: Informative Essay

In this unit, you read about people who overcame various obstacles. You will now write an informative essay in which you explore the topic of facing adversity as illustrated by the selections in this unit.

Assignment

Write an **informative essay** in response to the following question:

> How can people overcome adversity in the face of overwhelming obstacles?

Develop a clear thesis in response to the prompt. Your thesis for this informative essay should make a generalization about ways in which people persevere as they struggle to overcome adversity.

Then, use specific examples and quotations from the selections to support your response. Your ideas should be logically organized, and your essay should include transitions to show the relationships between ideas. Use precise vocabulary and a formal tone in your writing. Be sure to include a conclusion that follows from and supports the information in your essay.

Reread the Assignment Review the assignment to be sure you fully understand it. The assignment may reference some of the academic words presented at the beginning of the unit. Be sure you understand each of the words given below in order to complete the assignment correctly.

Academic Vocabulary

deviate	determination	tradition
persevere	diversity	

STANDARDS

Writing
• Write informative/explanatory texts to examine a topic and convey ideas, concepts, and information through the selection, organization, and analysis of relevant content.
• Produce clear and coherent writing in which the development, organization, and style are appropriate to task, purpose, and audience.
• Draw evidence from literary or informational texts to support analysis, reflection, and research.
• Write routinely over extended time frames and shorter time frames for a range of discipline-specific tasks, purposes, and audiences.

Review the Elements of an Effective Informative Essay Before you begin writing, read the Informative Essay Rubric. Once you have completed your first draft, check it against the rubric. If one or more of the elements is missing or not as strong as it could be, revise your essay to add or strengthen that component.

Informative Essay Rubric

	Focus and Organization	Evidence and Elaboration	Conventions
4	The introduction is engaging and includes a clear thesis. The thesis is supported by specific details, examples, and quotations from the selections. Ideas are logically organized so that the explanation is easy to follow. Transitions clearly show the relationships among ideas. The conclusion supports the information in the essay and offers fresh insight into the topic.	Details, examples, and quotations from the selections are specific and relevant. The style and tone is formal and objective. Words are carefully chosen and suited to purpose and audience.	The essay consistently adheres to standard English conventions of usage and mechanics.
3	The introduction includes a clear thesis. The thesis is supported by details, examples, and quotations from the selections. Ideas are organized so that the information is easy to follow. Transitions show the relationships among ideas. The conclusion supports the information in the essay.	Details, examples, and quotations from the selections are relevant. The style and tone is mostly formal and objective. Words are generally suited to purpose and audience.	The essay mostly adheres to standard English conventions of usage and mechanics.
2	The introduction states the thesis. The thesis is supported by some details, examples, and quotations from the selections. Ideas are vaguely organized, with a few transitions to orient readers. The conclusion relates to the information in the essay.	Some details and examples from the selection are relevant. The style and tone is occasionally formal and objective. Words are somewhat suited to purpose and audience.	The essay contains some mistakes in standard English conventions of usage and mechanics.
1	The thesis is not clearly stated. The thesis is not supported by details, examples, and quotations from the selections. Ideas are disorganized and the explanation is difficult to follow. The conclusion does not include relevant information.	There is little or no relevant support. The style and tone is informal. Words are not appropriate to purpose or audience.	The essay contains many mistakes in standard English conventions of usage and mechanics.

PART 2
Speaking and Listening: Oral Presentation

Assignment
After completing your informative essay, use it as the foundation for a brief **multimedia presentation.** Record your presentation and post it on a class or school Web site so you can watch the presentations outside of class and respond and interact digitally.

Use these tips to make your presentation engaging:

- Review your essay, and mark the most important ideas and supporting details from your introduction, body paragraphs, and conclusion.
- Use appropriate eye contact, and speak with clear pronunciation and adequate volume.
- Include well-sequenced multimedia that emphasizes key points.

Review the Oral Presentation Rubric Before you deliver your presentation, check your plans against this rubric.

	Content	Organization	Presentation Techniques
3	The introduction states the thesis in a compelling way. The presentation includes specific examples, quotations, and multimedia elements. The conclusion offers fresh insight into the topic.	The speaker uses time effectively. Ideas progress logically, with clear transition among ideas. The timing of the images matches the timing of the explanation.	The speaker maintains effective eye contact and speaks clearly and with adequate volume.
2	The introduction states a thesis. The presentation includes examples, quotations, and multimedia elements. The conclusion offers some insight into the topic.	The speaker uses time effectively, spending the right amount of time on most parts. Ideas progress logically with some transitions among ideas. Listeners can mostly follow the speaker's explanation.	The speaker sometimes maintains effective eye contact and speaks somewhat clearly and with adequate volume.
1	The introduction does not clearly state a thesis. The presentation does not include examples, quotations, or multimedia elements. The conclusion does not restate important information.	The speaker does not use time effectively. Ideas do not progress logically.	The speaker does not maintain effective eye contact or speak clearly with adequate volume.

Reflect on the Unit

Now that you've completed the unit, take a few moments to reflect on your learning.

Reflect on the Unit Goals

Look back at the goals at the beginning of the unit. Use a different colored pen to rate yourself again. Think about readings and activities that contributed the most to the growth of your understanding. Record your thoughts.

Reflect on the Learning Strategies

Discuss It Write a reflection on whether you were able to improve your learning based on your Action Plans. Think about what worked, what didn't, and what you might do to keep working on these strategies. Record your ideas before a class discussion.

Reflect on the Text

Choose a selection that you found challenging and explain what made it difficult.

Describe something that surprised you about a text in the unit.

Which activity taught you the most about facing adversity and overcoming obstacles? What did you learn?

SCAN FOR
MULTIMEDIA

RESOURCES

CONTENTS

Marking the Text: Strategies and Tips for Annotation

When you close read a text, you read for comprehension and then reread to unlock layers of meaning and to analyze a writer's style and techniques. Marking a text as you read it enables you to participate more fully in the close-reading process.

Following are some strategies for text mark-ups, along with samples of how the strategies can be applied. These mark-ups are suggestions; you and your teacher may want to use other mark-up strategies.

✱	Key Idea
!	I love it!
?	I have questions
◯	Unfamiliar or important word
- - - -	Context Clues

Suggested Mark-Up Notations

WHAT I NOTICE	HOW TO MARK UP	QUESTIONS TO ASK
Key Ideas and Details	• Highlight key ideas or claims. • Underline supporting details or evidence.	• What does the text say? What does it leave unsaid? • What inferences do you need to make? • What details lead you to make your inferences?
Word Choice	• Circle unfamiliar words. • Put a dotted line under context clues, if any exist. • Put an exclamation point beside especially rich or poetic passages.	• What inferences about word meaning can you make? • What tone and mood are created by word choice? • What alternate word choices might the author have made?
Text Structure	• Highlight passages that show key details supporting the main idea. • Use arrows to indicate how sentences and paragraphs work together to build ideas. • Use a right-facing arrow to indicate foreshadowing. • Use a left-facing arrow to indicate flashback.	• Is the text logically structured? • What emotional impact do the structural choices create?
Author's Craft	• Circle or highlight instances of repetition, either of words, phrases, consonants, or vowel sounds. • Mark rhythmic beats in poetry using checkmarks and slashes. • Underline instances of symbolism or figurative language.	• Does the author's style enrich or detract from the reading experience? • What levels of meaning are created by the author's techniques?

CLOSE READING

First Read

* **Key Idea**
! **I love it!**
? **I have questions**
◯ **Unfamiliar or important word**
---- **Context Clues**

In a first read, work to get a sense of the main idea of a text. Look for key details and ideas that help you understand what the author conveys to you. Mark passages which prompt a strong response from you.

Here is how one reader marked up this text.

NOTES

MODEL

INFORMATIONAL TEXT

from **Classifying the Stars**

Cecilia H. Payne

1   Sunlight and starlight are composed of waves of various lengths, which the eye, even aided by a telescope, is unable to separate. We must use more than a telescope. In order to sort out the component colors, the light must be dispersed by a prism, or split up by some other means. For instance, sunbeams passing through rain drops are transformed into the myriad-tinted rainbow. The familiar rainbow spanning the sky is Nature's most glorious demonstration that light is composed of many colors.

2   The very beginning of our knowledge of the nature of a star dates back to 1672, when Isaac Newton gave to the world the results of his experiments on passing sunlight through a prism. To describe the beautiful band of rainbow tints, produced when sunlight was dispersed by his three-cornered piece of glass, he took from the Latin the word *spectrum*, meaning an appearance. The rainbow is the spectrum of the Sun. . . .

3   In 1814, more than a century after Newton, the spectrum of the Sun was obtained in such purity that an amazing detail was seen and studied by the German optician, Fraunhofer. He saw that the multiple spectral tints, ranging from delicate violet to deep red, were crossed by hundreds of fine dark lines. In other words, there were narrow gaps in the spectrum where certain shades were wholly blotted out. We must remember that the word spectrum is applied not only to sunlight, but also to the light of any glowing substance when its rays are sorted out by a prism or a grating.

First-Read Guide

Use this page to record your first-read ideas.

You may want to use a guide like this to organize your thoughts after you read. Here is how a reader completed a First-Read Guide.

Selection Title: _____ Classifying the Stars _____

NOTICE

NOTICE new information or ideas you learned about the unit topic as you first read this text.

Light = different waves of colors. (Spectrum)

Newton - the first person to observe these waves using a prism.

Faunhofer saw gaps in the spectrum.

ANNOTATE

ANNOTATE by marking vocabulary and key passages you want to revisit.

Vocabulary
    myriad
    grating
    component colors

Different light types = different lengths

Isaac Newton also worked theories of gravity.

Multiple spectral tints? "colors of various appearance"

Key Passage:
Paragraph 3 shows that Fraunhofer discovered more about the nature of light spectrums: he saw the spaces in between the tints.

First Read

CONNECT

CONNECT ideas within the selection to other knowledge and the selections you have read.

I remember learning about prisms in science class.

Double rainbows! My favorite. How are they made?

RESPOND

RESPOND by writing a brief summary of the selection.

Science allows us to see things not visible to the naked eye. What we see as sunlight is really a spectrum of colors. By using tools, such as prisms, we can see the components of sunlight and other light. They appear as single colors or as multiple colors separated by gaps of no color. White light contains a rainbow of colors.

CLOSE READING

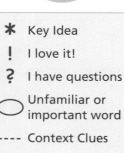

* **Key Idea**

! **I love it!**

? **I have questions**

◯ **Unfamiliar or important word**

---- **Context Clues**

In a close read, go back into the text to study it in greater detail. Take the time to analyze not only the author's ideas but the way that those ideas are conveyed. Consider the genre of the text, the author's word choice, the writer's unique style, and the message of the text.

Here is how one reader close read this text.

MODEL

INFORMATIONAL TEXT

from Classifying the Stars
Cecilia H. Payne

NOTES

explanation of sunlight and starlight

What is light and where do the colors come from?

This paragraph is about Newton and the prism.

What discoveries helped us understand light?

Fraunhofer and gaps in spectrum

1　Sunlight and starlight are composed of waves of various lengths, which the eye, even aided by a telescope, is unable to separate. We must use more than a telescope. In order to sort out the component colors, the light must be dispersed by a prism, or split up by some other means. For instance, sunbeams passing through rain drops are transformed into the myriad-tinted rainbow. The familiar rainbow spanning the sky is Nature's most glorious demonstration that light is composed of many colors.

2　The very beginning of our knowledge of the nature of a star dates back to 1672, when Isaac Newton gave to the world the results of his experiments on passing sunlight through a prism. To describe the beautiful band of rainbow tints, produced when sunlight was dispersed by his three-cornered piece of glass, he took from the Latin the word *spectrum*, meaning an appearance. The rainbow is the spectrum of the Sun. . . .

3　In 1814, more than a century after Newton, the spectrum of the Sun was obtained in such purity that an amazing detail was seen and studied by the German optician, Fraunhofer. He saw that the multiple spectral tints, ranging from delicate violet to deep red, were crossed by hundreds of fine dark lines. In other words, there were narrow gaps in the spectrum where certain shades were wholly blotted out. We must remember that the word spectrum is applied not only to sunlight, but also to the light of any glowing substance when its rays are sorted out by a prism or a grating.

Close-Read Guide

Use this page to record your close-read ideas.

Selection Title: _Classifying the Stars_

You can use the Close-Read Guide to help you dig deeper into the text. Here is how a reader completed a Close-Read Guide.

Close Read the Text

Revisit sections of the text you marked during your first read. Read these sections closely and **annotate** what you notice. Ask yourself **questions** about the text. What can you **conclude?** Write down your ideas.

Paragraph 3: Light is composed of waves of various lengths. Prisms let us see different colors in light. This is called the spectrum. Fraunhofer proved that there are gaps in the spectrum, where certain shades are blotted out.

More than one researcher studied this and each built off the ideas that were already discovered.

Analyze the Text

Think about the author's choices of patterns, structure, techniques, and ideas included in the text. Select one, and record your thoughts about what this choice conveys.

The author showed the development of human knowledge of the spectrum chronologically. Helped me see how ideas were built upon earlier understandings. Used dates and "more than a century after Newton" to show time.

QuickWrite

Pick a paragraph from the text that grabbed your interest. Explain the power of this passage.

The first paragraph grabbed my attention, specifically the sentence "The familiar rainbow spanning the sky is Nature's most glorious demonstration that light is composed of many colors." The paragraph began as a straightforward scientific explanation. When I read the word "glorious," I had to stop and deeply consider what was being said. It is a word loaded with personal feelings. With that one word, the author let the reader know what was important to her.

Argument

When you think of the word *argument,* you might think of a disagreement between two people, but the word has another meaning, too. An argument is a logical way of presenting a belief, conclusion, or stance. A good argument is supported with reasoning and evidence.

Argument writing can be used for many purposes, such as changing a reader's opinion or bringing about an action or a response from a reader.

Elements of an Argumentative Text

An **argument** sets forth a belief or stand on an issue. A well-written argument may convince the reader, change the reader's mind, or motivate the reader to take a certain action.

An effective argument contains these elements:

- a precise claim
- consideration of alternate claims, or opposing positions, and a discussion of their strengths and weaknesses
- logical organization that makes clear connections among claim, reasons, and evidence
- valid reasoning and evidence
- a concluding statement or section that follows from and supports the argument
- formal and objective language and tone
- error-free grammar, including accurate use of transitions

ARGUMENT: SCORE 1

Celebrities Should Try to Be Better Role Models

A lot of Celebrities are singers or actors or actresses or athletes. Kids spend tons of time watching Celebrities on TV. They listen to their songs. They read about them. They watch them play and perform. No matter weather the Celebrities are good people or bad people. Kids still spend time watching them. The kids will try to imitate what they do. Some of them have parents or brothers and sisters who are famous also.

Celebrities don't seem to watch out what they do and how they live. Some say, *"Why do I care? It's none of you're business"*! Well, that's true. But it's bad on them if they do all kinds of stupid things. Because this is bad for the kids who look up to them.

Sometimes celebrity's say they wish they are not role models. *"I'm just an actor!" "I'm just a singer"*! they say. But the choice is not really up to them. If their on TV all the time, then kids' will look up to them, no matter what. It's stupid when Celebrities mess up and then nothing bad happens to them. That gives kids a bad lesson. Kids will think that you can do stupid things and be fine. That is not being a good role model.

Some Celebrities give money to charity. That's a good way to be a good role model. But sometimes it seems like Celebrities are just totally messed up. It's hard always being in the spotlight. That can drive Celebrities kind of crazy. Then they act out.

It is a good idea to support charities when you are rich and famous. You can do a lot of good. For a lot of people. Some Celebrities give out cars or houses or free scholarships. You can even give away your dresses and people can have an auction to see who will pay the most money for them. This can help for example the Humane Society. Or whatever charity or cause the celebrity wants to support.

Celebrities are fun to watch and follow, even when they mess up. I think they don't realize that when they do bad things, they give teens wrong ideas about how to live. They should try to keep that under control. So many teens look up to them and copy them, no matter what.

The claim is not clearly stated in the introduction or elsewhere.

Some of the ideas in the essay do not relate to the stated position or focus on the issue.

The word choice in the essay is not effective and lends it an informal tone.

The progression of ideas is not logical or well-controlled.

Errors in spelling, capitalization, punctuation, grammar, usage, and sentence boundaries are frequent. The fluency of the writing and effectiveness of the essay are affected by these errors.

The conclusion does not clearly restate the claim.

TOOL KIT: WRITING

MODEL

ARGUMENT: SCORE 2

Celebrities Should Try to Be Better Role Models

Most kids spend tons of time watching celebrities on TV, listening to their songs, and reading about them. No matter how celebrities behave—whether they do good things or bad—they are role models for kids. They often do really dumb things, and that is not good considering they are role models.

Sometimes celebrity's say they wish they were not role models. *"I'm just an actor!"* or, *"I'm just a singer!"* they say. But the choice is not really up to them. If they are on TV all the time, then kids' will look up to them. No matter what. It's really bad when celebrities mess up and then nothing bad happens to them. That gives kids a false lesson because in reality there are bad things when you mess up. That's why celebrities should think more about what they are doing and what lessons they are giving to kids.

Some celebrities might say, *"Why do I care? Why should I be bothered?"* Well, they don't have to. But it's bad on them if they do all kinds of stupid things and don't think about how this affects the kids who look up to them. Plus, they get tons of money, much more even than inventors or scientists or other important people. Being a good role model should be part of what they have to do to get so much money.

When you are famous it is a good idea to support charities. Some celebrities give out cars, or houses, or free scholarships. They even sometimes give away their dresses and people have an auction to see who will pay the most money for them. This can help for example the Humane Society, or whatever charity or cause the celebrity wants to support.

Sometimes it seems like celebrities are more messed up than anyone else. That's in their personal lives. Imagine if people wanted to take pictures of you wherever you went, and you could never get away. That can drive celebrities kind of crazy, and then they act out.

Celebrities can do good things and they can do bad things. They don't realize that when they do bad things, they give teens wrong ideas about how to live. So many teens look up to them and copy them, no matter what. They should make an effort to be better role models.

The introduction does not state the argument claim clearly enough.

Errors in spelling, grammar, and sentence boundaries decrease the effectiveness of the essay.

The word choice in the essay contributes to an informal tone.

The writer does not make use of transitions and sentence connections.

Some of the ideas in the essay do not relate to the stated position or focus on the issue.

The essay has a clear conclusion.

Celebrities Should Try to Be Better Role Models

Kids look up to the celebrities they see on TV and want to be like them. Parents may not *want* celebrities to be role models for their children, but they are anyway. Therefore, celebrities should think about what they say and do and live lives that are worth copying. Celebrities should think about how they act because they are role models.

"I'm just an actor!" or, *"I'm just a singer!"* celebrities sometimes say. *"Their parents and teachers are the ones who should be the role models!"* But it would be foolish to misjudge the impact that celebrities have on youth. Kids spend hours every day digitally hanging with their favorite stars. Children learn by imitation, so, for better or worse, celebrities are role models. That's why celebrities should start modeling good decision-making and good citizenship.

With all that they are given by society, celebrities owe a lot back to their communities and the world. Celebrities get a lot of attention, time, and money. Often they get all that for doing not very much: acting, singing, or playing a sport. It's true; some of them work very hard. But even if they work very hard, do they deserve to be in the news all the time and earn 100 or even 1000 times more than equally hard-working teachers, scientists, or nurses? I don't think so. After receiving all that, it seems only fair that celebrities take on the important job of being good role models for the young people who look up to them.

Celebrities can serve as good role models is by giving back. Quite a few use their fame and fortune to do just that. They give scholarships, or even build and run schools; they help veterans; they visit hospitals; they support important causes such as conservation, and women's rights. They donate not just money but their time and talents too. This is a great way to be a role model.

Celebrities should recognize that as role models, they have a responsibility to try to make good decisions and be honest. Celebrities should step up so they can be a force for good in people's lives and in the world.

The writer's word choice is good but could be better.

The introduction mostly states the claim.

The ideas relate to the stated position and focus on the issue.

The sentences are varied and well controlled and enhance the effectiveness of the essay.

The progression of ideas is logical, but there could be better transitions and sentence connections to show how ideas are related.

The conclusion mostly follows from the claim.

TOOL KIT: WRITING

MODEL

ARGUMENT: SCORE 4

Celebrities Should Try to Be Better Role Models

Like it or not, kids look up to the celebrities they see on TV and want to be like them. Parents may not *want* celebrities to be role models for their children, but the fact is that they are. With such an oversized influence on young people, celebrities have a responsibility to think about what they say and do and to live lives that are worth emulating. In short, they should make an effort to be better role models.

Sometimes celebrities say they don't want to be role models. "I'm just an actor!" or "I'm just a singer!" they protest. "Their parents and teachers are the ones who should be guiding them and showing them the right way to live!" That is all very well, but it would be foolish to underestimate the impact that celebrities have on children. Kids spend hours every day digitally hanging out with their favorite stars. Children learn by imitation, so for better or worse, celebrities act as role models.

Celebrities are given a lot of attention, time, and money. They get all that for doing very little: acting, singing, or playing a sport very well. It's true some of them work very hard. But even if they work hard, do they deserve to be in the news all the time and earn 100 or even 1,000 times more than equally hardworking teachers, scientists, or nurses? I don't think so.

With all that they are given, celebrities owe a lot to their communities and the world. One way they can serve as good role models is by giving back, and quite a few celebrities use their fame and fortune to do just that. They give scholarships or even build and run schools; they help veterans; they entertain kids who are sick; they support important causes such as conservation and women's rights. They donate not just money but their time and talents too.

Celebrities don't have to be perfect. They are people too and make mistakes. But they should recognize that as role models for youth, they have a responsibility to try to make good decisions and be honest about their struggles. Celebrities should step up so they can be a force for good in people's lives.

The writer has chosen words that contribute to the clarity of the essay.

The writer clearly states the claim of the argument in the introduction.

The essay is engaging and varied.

There are no errors to distract the reader from the fluency of the writing and effectiveness of the essay.

The writer uses transitions and sentence connections to show how ideas are related.

The writer clearly restates the claim and the most powerful idea presented in the essay.

Argument Rubric

	Focus and Organization	Evidence and Elaboration	Conventions
4	The introduction is engaging and states the claim in a compelling way. The claim is supported by clear reasons and relevant evidence. Reasons and evidence are logically organized so that the argument is easy to follow. The conclusion clearly restates the claim and the most powerful idea.	Sources are effectively credible and accurate. The argument demonstrates an understanding of the thesis by providing strong examples. The tone of the argument is formal and objective.	The argument intentionally uses standard English conventions of usage and mechanics. The argument effectively uses words, phrases, and clauses to clarify the relationships among claim(s) and reasons.
3	The introduction is mostly engaging and states the claim. The claim is mostly supported by logical reasons and evidence. Reasons and evidence are organized so that the argument is mostly easy to follow. The conclusion mostly restates the claim.	Sources are mostly credible and accurate. The argument mostly demonstrates an understanding of the thesis by providing adequate examples. The tone of the argument is mostly formal and objective.	The argument mostly demonstrates accuracy in standard English conventions of usage and mechanics. The argument mostly uses words, phrases, and clauses to clarify the relationships among claim(s) and reasons.
2	The introduction somewhat states the claim. The claim is supported by some reasons and evidence. Reasons and evidence are organized somewhat logically with a few transitions to orient readers. The conclusion somewhat relates to the claim.	Some sources are relevant. The argument somewhat demonstrates an understanding of the thesis by providing some examples. The tone of the argument is occasionally formal and objective.	The argument demonstrates some accuracy in standard English conventions of usage and mechanics. The argument somewhat uses words, phrases, and clauses to clarify the relationships among claim(s) and reasons.
1	The claim is not clearly stated. The claim is not supported by reasons and evidence. Reasons and evidence are disorganized and the argument is difficult to follow. The conclusion does not include relevant information.	There is little or no reliable, relevant evidence The argument does not demonstrate an understanding of the thesis and does not provide examples. The tone of the argument is informal.	The argument contains mistakes in standard English conventions of usage and mechanics. The argument does not use words, phrases, and clauses to clarify the relationships among claim(s) and reasons.

Information/Explanatory Texts

Informative and explanatory writing should rely on facts to inform or explain. Informative writing serves several purposes: to increase readers' knowledge of a subject, to help readers better understand a procedure or process, or to provide readers with an enhanced comprehension of a concept. It should also feature a clear introduction, body, and conclusion.

Information/explanatory texts present facts, details, data, and other kinds of evidence to give information about a topic. Readers turn to informational and explanatory texts when they wish to learn about a specific idea, concept, or subject area, or if they want to learn how to do something.

An effective informational/explanatory text contains these elements:

- a topic sentence or thesis statement that introduces the concept or subject
- relevant facts, examples, and details that expand upon a topic
- definitions, quotations, and/or graphics that support the information given
- headings (if desired) to separate sections of the essay
- a structure that presents information in a direct, clear manner
- clear transitions that link sections of the essay
- precise words and technical vocabulary where appropriate
- formal and objective language and tone
- a conclusion that supports the information given and provides fresh insights

INFORMATIVE: SCORE 1

Kids, School, and Exercise: Problems and Solutions

In the past, children ran around and even did hard physical labor. Today most kid's just sit most of the time. They don't know the old Outdoor Games. Like tether ball. and they don't have hard chores to do. Like milking the cows. But children should be Physically Active quite a bit every day. That doesn't happen very much any more. Not as much as it should anyway.

Even at home when kid's have a chance to run around, they choose to sit and play video games, for example. Some schools understand that it's a problem when students don't get enough exercise. Even though they have had to cut Physical Education classes. Some also had to make recess shorter.

But lots of schools are working hard to find ways to get kid's moving around again. Like they used to long ago.

Schools use volunteers to teach kid's old-fashioned games. Old-fashioned games are an awesome way to get kid's moving around like crazy people.

Some schools have before school activities. Such as games in the gym. Other schools have after school activities. Such as bike riding or outdoor games. They can't count on kid's to be active. Not even on their own or at home. So they do the activities all together. Kids enjoy doing stuff with their friends. So that works out really well.

If you don't exercise you get overweight. You can end up with high blood pressure and too much colesterol. Of course its also a problem if you eat too much junk food all the time. But not getting enough exercise is part of the problem too. That's why schools need to try to be part of the solution.

A break during class to move around helps. Good teachers know how to use exercise during classes. There are all kinds of ways to move in the classroom that don't mean you have to change your clothes. Classes don't have to be just about math and science.

Schools are doing what they can to get kids moving, doing exercise, being active. Getting enough exercise also helps kid's do better in school. Being active also helps kids get strong.

There are extensive errors in spelling, capitalization, punctuation, grammar, usage, and sentence boundaries.

Many of the ideas in the essay do not focus on the topic.

The word choice shows the writer's lack of awareness of the essay's purpose and tone.

The essay's sentences are not purposeful, varied, or well-controlled. The writer's sentences decrease the effectiveness of the essay.

The essay is not well organized. Its structure does not support its purpose or respond well to the demands of the prompt.

The essay is not particularly thoughtful or engaging.

MODEL

INFORMATIVE: SCORE 2

Kids, School, and Exercise: Problems and Solutions

In the past, children ran around a lot and did chores and other physical work. Today most kid's sit by a TV or computer screen or play with their phones. But children should be active for at least 60 minutes a day. Sadly, most don't get nearly that much exercise. And that's a big problem.

Some schools understand that it's a problem when students don't get enough exercise. Even though they have had to cut Physical Education classes due to budget cuts. Some also had to make recess shorter because there isn't enough time in the schedule. But they are working hard to find creative ways that don't cost too much or take up too much time to get kid's moving. Because there's only so much money in the budget, and only so much time in the day, and preparing to take tests takes lots of time.

Schools can use parent volunteers to teach kid's old-fashioned games such as kick-the-can, hopscotch, foursquare, tetherball, or jump rope. Kid's nowadays often don't know these games! Old-fashioned games are a great way to get kid's moving. Some schools have before school activities, such as games in the gym. Other schools have after school activities, such as bike riding or outdoor games. They can't count on kid's to be active on their own or at home.

A break during class can help students concentrate when they go back to work. There are all kinds of ways to move in the classroom. And you don't have to change your clothes or anything. Wiggling, stretching, and playing a short active game are all good ideas. Good teachers know how to squeeze in time during academic classes like math and language arts.

Not getting enough exercise is linked to many problems. For example, unhealthy wait, and high blood pressure and colesterol. When students don't' get enough exercise, they end up overweight.

Physical activity also helps kid's do better in school. Kids who exercise have better attendance rates. They have increased attention span. They act out less. They have less stress and learn more. Being active also helps muscles and bones. It increases strength and stamina.

Schools today are doing what they can to find a solution by being creative and making time for physical activity before, during, and after school. They understand that it is a problem when kid's don't get enough exercise.

Not all the ideas in the essay focus on the topic.

The writer uses some transitions and sentence connections.

Some of the ideas in the essay are reasonably well developed. Some details and examples add substance to the essay.

Some ideas are well developed. Some examples and details are well chosen and specific and add substance to the essay.

Some details are specific and well chosen.

There are errors in spelling, punctuation, grammar, usage, and sentence boundaries that decrease the effectiveness of the essay.

The essay is not well organized. Its organizing structure does not support its purpose well or respond well to the demands of the prompt.

Kids, School, and Exercise: Problems and Solutions

A 2008 report said school-age children should be physically active for at least 60 minutes a day. Sadly, most children don't get nearly that much exercise. Lots of schools have cut Physical Education classes because of money and time pressures. And there's less recess than there used to be. Even at home when kids have a chance to run around, many choose screen time instead. No wonder so many of us are turning into chubby couch potatoes!

Not getting exercise is linked to many problems, for example unhealthy weight, and high blood pressure and cholesterol. Studies show physical activity also helps students do better in school: it means better attendance rates, increased attention span, fewer behavioral problems, less stress, and more learning. Being active helps develop strong muscles and bones. It increases strength and stamina.

Many schools around the country get that there are problems when students are inactive. They are working hard to find creative solutions that don't cost too much or take up precious time in the school schedule.

Some schools are using parent volunteers to teach kids active games such as kick-the-can, hopscotch, foursquare, tetherball, or jump rope. These games are more likely to get kids moving than just sitting gossiping with your friends or staring at your phone. Some schools have before school activities such as run-around games in the gym. Other schools have after school activities such as bike riding or outdoor games. They can't count on kids to be active on their own.

There are all kinds of fun and healthy ways to move in the classroom, without changing clothes. An active break during class can help students concentrate when they go back to work. Creative teachers know how to squeeze in active time even during academic classes. Wiggling, stretching, and playing a short active game are all good ideas.

Schools today understand that it is a problem when kids don't get enough exercise. They are doing what they can to find a solution by being creative and making time for physical activity before, during, and after school.

The essay is fairly thoughtful and engaging.

Almost all the ideas focus on the topic.

The ideas in the essay are well developed, with well-chosen and specific details and examples.

The writer uses transitions and connections, such as
"Not getting exercise is linked…"
"Many schools …"
"Some schools…"
"Other schools…"

Ideas in the essay are mostly well developed.

Words are chosen carefully and contribute to the clarity of the essay.

TOOL KIT: WRITING

WRITING

INFORMATIVE: SCORE 4

Kids, School, and Exercise: Problems and Solutions

In 2008, the U.S. Department of Health and Human Services published a report stating that all school-age children need to be physically active for at least 60 minutes a day. Sadly, most children don't get nearly the recommended amount of exercise. Due to budget cuts and time pressure, many schools have cut Physical Education classes. Even recess is being squeezed to make room for more tests and test preparation.

Lack of exercise can lead to many problems, such as unhealthy weight, high blood pressure, and high cholesterol. Physical activity helps develop strong muscles and bones, and it increases strength and stamina. Studies show physical activity leads to better attendance rates, increased attention span, fewer behavioral problems, less stress, and more learning. When kids don't get enough physical activity, a lot is at stake!

Many schools around the country are stepping up to find innovative solutions—even when they don't have time or money to spare. Some have started before-school activities such as active games in the gym. Others have after-school activities such as bike riding or outdoor games. Just a few extra minutes a day can make a big difference!

Some schools try to make the most of recess by using parent volunteers to teach kids active games such as kick-the-can, hopscotch, foursquare, tetherball, or jump rope. Volunteers can also organize races or tournaments—anything to get the kids going! At the end of recess, everyone should be a little bit out of breath.

Creative educators squeeze in active time even during academic classes. It could be a quick "brain break" to stretch in the middle of class, imaginary jump rope, or a game of rock-paper-scissors with legs instead of fingers. There are all kinds of imaginative ways to move in the classroom, without moving furniture or changing clothes. And research shows that an active break during class can help students focus when they go back to work.

Schools today understand the problems that can arise when kids don't have enough physical activity in their lives. They are meeting the challenge by finding opportunities for exercise before, during, and after school. After all, if students do well on tests but end up unhealthy and unhappy, what is the point?

The writer explains the problem and its causes.

The writer clearly lays out the effects of the problem.

The writer turns to the solution. The essay's organizing structure supports its purpose and responds to the demands of the prompt.

The writer includes specific examples and well-chosen details.

The progression of ideas is logical and well controlled.

Details and examples add substance to the essay.

The essay is thoughtful and engaging.

Informative Rubric

	Focus and Organization	Evidence and Elaboration	Conventions
4	The introduction is engaging and sets forth the topic in a compelling way. The ideas progress logically. A variety of transitions are included to show the relationship among ideas. The conclusion follows from the rest of the essay.	The topic is developed with relevant facts, definitions, details, quotations, and examples. The tone of the essay is formal. The vocabulary is precise and relevant to the topic, audience, and purpose.	The essay uses standard English conventions of usage and mechanics. The essay uses correct pronoun case.
3	The introduction is somewhat engaging and sets forth the topic in a way that grabs readers' attention. The ideas progress somewhat logically. Some transitions are included to show the relationship among ideas. The conclusion mostly follows from the rest of the essay.	The topic is developed with some relevant facts, definitions, details, quotations, and other examples. The tone of the essay is mostly formal. The vocabulary is generally appropriate for the topic, audience, and purpose.	The essay demonstrates general accuracy in standard English conventions of usage and mechanics. The essay generally uses correct pronoun case.
2	The introduction sets forth the topic. More than one idea is presented. A few transitions are included that show the relationship among ideas. The conclusion does not completely follow from the rest of the essay.	The topic is developed with a few relevant facts, definitions, details, quotations, or other examples. The tone of the essay is occasionally formal. The vocabulary is somewhat appropriate for the topic, audience, and purpose.	The essay demonstrates some accuracy in standard English conventions of usage and mechanics. The essay somewhat uses correct pronoun case.
1	The topic is not clearly stated. Ideas do not follow a logical progression. Transitions are not included. The conclusion does not follow from the rest of the essay.	The topic is not developed with reliable or relevant evidence. The tone is informal. The vocabulary is limited or ineffective.	The essay contains mistakes in standard English conventions of usage and mechanics. The essay does not use correct pronoun case.

TOOL KIT: WRITING

Narrative

Narrative writing conveys an experience, either real or imaginary, and uses time order to provide structure. Usually its purpose is to entertain, but it can also instruct, persuade, or inform. Whenever writers tell a story, they are using narrative writing. Most types of narrative writing share certain elements, such as characters, setting, a sequence of events, and, often, a theme.

Elements of a Narrative Text

A **narrative** is any type of writing that tells a story, whether it is fiction, nonfiction, poetry, or drama.

An effective nonfiction narrative contains these elements:

- an engaging beginning in which characters and setting are established
- characters who participate in the story events
- a well-structured, logical sequence of events
- details that show time and place
- effective story elements such as dialogue, description, and reflection
- a narrator who relates the events from a particular point of view
- use of language that brings the characters and setting to life

An effective fictional narrative usually contains these elements:

- an engaging beginning in which characters, setting, or a main conflict is introduced
- a main character and supporting characters who participate in the story events
- a narrator who relates the events of the plot from a particular point of view
- details that show time and place
- narrative techniques such as dialogue, description, and suspense
- use of language that vividly brings to life characters and events

NARRATIVE: SCORE 1

Mind Scissors

There's a bike race. Right away people start losing. But me and Thad were winning. Thad is the kid who always wins is who is also popular. I don't like Thad. I pumped pumping hard at my pedals, I knew the end was coming. I looked ahead and all I could see was Thad, and the woods.

I pedaled harder and then I was up to Thad. That was swinging at me, I swerved, I kept looking at him, I was worried!

That's stick had untied my shoelace and it was wrapped around my pedal! But I didn't know it yet.

We were out of the woods. I still wanted to win, I pedaled even faster. than my pedals stopped!

I saw with my mind the shoelace was caught in my pedal. No worries, I have the superpower of mind scissors. That's when my mind looked down and I used my mind scissors. I used the mind scissors to cut the shoelace my right foot was free.

That's how I became a superhero. I save people with my mind scissors now.

The story's beginning is not clear or engaging.

The narrative does not include sensory language and precise words to convey experiences and to develop characters.

Events do not progress logically. The ideas seem disconnected, and the sentences do not include transitions.

The narrative contains mistakes in standard English conventions of usage and mechanics.

The conclusion does not connect to the narrative.

TOOL KIT: WRITING

MODEL

NARRATIVE: SCORE 2

Mind-Scissors

When I was a baby I wound up with a tiny pair of scissors in my head. What the doctors couldn't have predicted is the uncanny ability they would give me. This past summer that was when I discovered what I could do with my mind-scissors.

Every summer there's a bike race. The kid who always wins is Thad who is popular.

The race starts. Right away racers start losing. After a long time pumping hard at my pedals, I knew the end was coming. I looked ahead and all I could see was Thad, and the woods.

I pedaled harder than ever. I was up to Thad. I turned my head to look at him. He was swinging a stick at me, I swerved, I kept looking at him, boy was I worried.

We were now out of the woods. Still hopeful I could win, I pedaled even faster. Suddenly, my pedals stopped!

Oh no! Thad's stick had untied my shoelace and it was wrapped around my pedal!

I was going to crash my bike. That's when my mind looked down. That's when I knew I could use my mind-scissors. I used the mind scissors to cut the shoelace my right foot was free.

That's how I won the race.

The story's beginning introduces the main character.

Events in the narrative progress somewhat logically, and the writer use some transition words.

The writer uses some description in the narrative.

The narrative demonstrates some accuracy in standard English conventions of usage and mechanics.

The words vary between vague and precise. The writer uses some sensory language.

The conclusion is weak and adds very little to the narrative.

NARRATIVE: SCORE 3

Mind-Scissors

When I was a baby I wound up with a tiny pair of scissors in my head. Lots of people live with pieces of metal in their heads. We just have to be careful. What the doctors couldn't have predicted is the uncanny ability they would give me.

> The story's beginning is engaging and clearly introduces the main character and situation.

Every summer there's a bike race that ends at the lake. The kid who always wins is Thad Thomas the Third, who is popular. This past summer that was about to change. It's also when I discovered what I could do with my mind-scissors.

> Events in the narrative progress logically, and the writer uses transition words frequently.

The race starts. Right away racers start falling behind. After what seemed an eternity pumping hard at my pedals, I knew the end had to be in sight. I looked ahead and all I could see was Thad, and the opening to the woods—the last leg of the race.

I felt like steam was coming off my legs. I could see Thad's helmet. I turned my head to flash him a look. Only, Thad was the one who was gloating! And then I saw it—he was holding a stick he had pulled off a low-hanging branch.

> The writer uses precise words and some sensory language to convey the experiences in the narrative and to describe the characters and scenes.

He jabbed it toward me. I swerved out of the way. I kept pedaling, shifting my eyes to the right, to see what he was going to do.

But I waited too long. Then Thad made a slashing motion. Then he tossed the stick aside, yelled, "Yes!" and zoomed forward.

> The writer uses some description and dialogue to add interest to the narrative and develop experiences and events.

What happened? I felt nothing. We were now out of the woods and into the clearing before the finish line. Still hopeful I could win, I pedaled even faster. Suddenly, there was a jerk. My pedals had stopped!

I looked down. Oh no! My shoelace was wrapped around my pedal! Thad's stick had untied it!

> The narrative demonstrates accuracy in standard English conventions of usage and mechanics.

I looked for a place to crash. That's when my head started tingling. I looked down at the shoelace. I concentrated really hard. I could see the scissors in my mind, floating just beside the pedal. Snip! The shoelace broke and my foot was free.

Thad was too busy listening to his fans cheer him on as I rode past him. Thanks to the mind-scissors, I won.

> The conclusion follows from the rest of the narrative.

TOOL KIT: WRITING

WRITING

NARRATIVE: SCORE 4

Mind-Scissors

As long as I wear my bike helmet, they say I'll be okay. Lots of people live with pieces of metal in their heads. We just have to be careful. When I was a baby I wound up with a tiny pair of scissors in mine. What the doctors couldn't have predicted is the uncanny ability they would give me.

Every summer there's a bike race that ends at the lake. The kid who always wins is Thad Thomas the Third, who is popular, but if you ask me, it's because he knows how to sweet-talk everyone. This past summer that was about to change. It's also when I discovered what I could do with my mind-scissors.

The race starts. Right away, racers start falling behind. After what seemed an eternity pumping hard at my pedals, I knew the end had to be in sight. I looked ahead and all I could see was Thad and the opening to the woods—the last leg of the race.

I put my stamina to the test—pedaling harder than ever, I felt like steam was coming off my legs. Thad's red helmet came into view. As I could sense I was going to overtake him any second, I turned my head to flash him a look. Only, to my befuddlement, Thad was the one who was gloating! And then I saw it—he was holding a stick he had pulled off a low-hanging branch.

He jabbed it toward me. I swerved out of the way. Was he trying to poke me with it? I kept pedaling, shifting my eyes to the right, to see what he was going to do.

But I waited too long. Thad made a slashing motion. Then he tossed the stick aside, yelled, "Yes!" and zoomed forward.

What happened? I felt nothing. We were now out of the woods and into the clearing before the finish line. Still hopeful I could win, I pedaled even faster. Suddenly, there was a jerk. My pedals had stopped!

I looked down. Oh no! My shoelace was wrapped around my pedal! Thad's stick had untied the shoelace!

I coasted as I looked for a place to crash. That's when my head started tingling. I got this funny notion to try something. I looked down. I had the tangled shoelace in my sights. I concentrated really hard. I could see the scissors in my mind, floating just beside the pedal. Snip! The shoelace broke and my right foot was free.

Thad was busy motioning his fans to cheer him on as I made my greatest effort to pedal back up to speed. Guess who made it to the finish line first?

The story's beginning is engaging and introduces the main character and situation in a way that appeals to a reader.

The writer uses techniques such as dialogue and description to add interest to the narrative and to develop the characters and events.

Events in the narrative progress in logical order and are linked by clear transitions.

Writer uses vivid description and sensory language to convey the experiences in the narrative and to help the reader imagine the characters and scenes.

The writer uses standard English conventions of usage and mechanics.

Writer's conclusion follows from the events in the narrative.

Copyright © SAVVAS Learning Company LLC. All Rights Reserved.

R22 RESOURCES: TOOL KIT

Narrative Rubric

	Focus and Organization	Development of Ideas/Elaboration	Conventions
4	The introduction is engaging and introduces the characters and situation in a way that appeals to readers. Events in the narrative progress in logical order and are linked by clear transitions. The conclusion effectively follows from and reflects on the narrated experiences or events.	The narrative effectively includes techniques such as dialogue and description to add interest and to develop the characters and events. The narrative effectively includes precise words and phrases, relevant descriptive details, and sensory language to convey experiences and events. The narrative effectively establishes voice through word choice, sentence structure, and tone.	The narrative intentionally uses standard English conventions of usage and mechanics. The narrative effectively varies sentence patterns for meaning, reader interest, and style.
3	The introduction is somewhat engaging and clearly introduces the characters and situation. Events in the narrative progress logically and are often linked by transition words. The conclusion mostly follows from and reflects on the narrated experiences or events.	The narrative mostly includes dialogue and description to add interest and develop experiences and events. The narrative mostly includes precise words and sensory language to convey experiences and events. The narrative mostly establishes voice through word choice, sentence structure, and tone.	The narrative mostly demonstrates accuracy in standard English conventions of usage and mechanics. The narrative mostly varies sentence patterns for meaning, reader interest, and style.
2	The introduction occasionally introduces characters. Events in the narrative progress somewhat logically and are sometimes linked by transition words. The conclusion adds very little to the narrated experiences or events.	The narrative includes some dialogue and descriptions. The words in the narrative vary between vague and precise, and some sensory language is included. The narrative occasionally establishes voice through word choice, sentence structure, and tone.	The narrative demonstrates some accuracy in standard English conventions of usage and mechanics. The narrative occasionally varies sentence patterns for meaning, reader interest, and style.
1	The introduction does not introduce characters and an experience or there is no clear introduction. The events in the narrative do not progress logically. The ideas seem disconnected and the sentences are not linked by transitions. The conclusion does not connect to the narrative or there is no conclusion.	Dialogue and descriptions are not included in the narrative. The narrative does not incorporate sensory language or precise words to convey experiences and to develop characters. The narrative does not establish voice through word choice, sentence structure, and tone.	The narrative contains mistakes in standard English conventions of usage and mechanics. The narrative does not vary sentence patterns for meaning, reader interest, and style.

Conducting Research

You can conduct research to gain more knowledge about a topic. Sources such as articles, books, interviews, or the Internet have the facts and explanations that you need. Not all of the information that you find, however, will be useful—or reliable. Strong research skills will help you find accurate information about your topic.

Narrowing or Broadening a Topic

The first step in any research is finding your topic. Choose a topic that is narrow enough to cover completely. If you can name your topic in just one or two words, it is probably too broad. Topics such as mythology, hip hop music, or Italy are too broad to cover in a single report. Narrow a broad topic into smaller subcategories.

When you begin to research, pay attention to the amount of information available. If there is way too much information on your topic, you may need to narrow your topic further.

You might also need to broaden a topic if there is not enough information for your purpose. A topic is too narrow when it can be thoroughly presented in less space than the required size of your assignment. It might also be too narrow if you can find little or no information in library and media sources. Broaden your topic by including other related ideas.

Generating Research Questions

Use research questions to focus your research. Specific questions can help you avoid wasting time. For example, instead of simply hunting for information about Peter Pan, you might ask, "What inspired J. M. Barrie to write the story of Peter Pan?" or "How have different artists shown Peter Pan?"

A research question may also lead you to find your topic sentence. The question can also help you focus your research plan. Write your question down and keep it in mind while you hunt for facts. Your question can prevent you from gathering unnecessary details. As you learn more about your topic, you can always rewrite your original question.

Consulting Print and Digital Sources

An effective research project combines information from multiple sources. It is important not to rely too heavily on a single source. The creativity and originality of your research depends on how you combine ideas from many places. Plan to include a variety of these resources:

- **Primary and Secondary Sources:** Use both primary sources (firsthand or original accounts, such as interview transcripts and newspaper articles) and secondary sources (accounts that are not created at the time of an event, such as encyclopedia entries).
- **Print and Digital Resources:** The Internet allows fast access to data, but print resources are often edited more carefully. Plan to include both print and digital resources in order to guarantee that your work is accurate.
- **Media Resources:** You can find valuable information in media resources such as documentaries, television programs, podcasts, and museum exhibitions.
- **Original Research:** Depending on your topic, you may wish to conduct original research to include among your sources. For example, you might interview experts or eyewitnesses or conduct a survey of people in your community.

Evaluating Sources It is important to evaluate the credibility and accuracy of any information you find. Ask yourself questions such as these to evaluate other sources:

- **Authority:** Is the author well known? What are the author's credentials? Does the source include references to other reliable sources? Does the author's tone win your confidence? Why or why not?
- **Bias:** Does the author have any obvious biases? What is the author's purpose for writing? Who is the target audience?
- **Currency:** When was the work created? Has it been revised? Is there more current information available?

Using Online Encyclopedias

Online encyclopedias are often written by anonymous contributors who are not required to fact-check information. These sites can be very useful as a launching point for research, but should not be considered accurate. Look for footnotes, endnotes, or hyperlinks that support facts with reliable sources that have been carefully checked by editors.

TOOL KIT: RESEARCH

RESEARCH

Using Search Terms

Finding information on the Internet is easy, but it can be a challenge to find facts that are useful and trustworthy. If you type a word or phrase into a search engine, you will probably get hundreds—or thousands—of results. However, those results are not guaranteed to be relevant or accurate.

These strategies can help you find information from the Internet:

- Create a list of topic keywords before you begin using a search engine. Use a thesaurus to expand your list.
- Enter six to eight keywords.
- Choose unique nouns. Most search engines ignore articles and prepositions. Verbs may lead to sources that are not useful. Use modifiers, such as adjectives, when necessary to specify a category. For example, you might enter "ancient Rome" instead of "Rome."
- Use quotation marks to focus a search. Place a phrase in quotation marks to find pages that include exactly that phrase. Add several phrases in quotation marks to narrow your results.
- Spell carefully. Many search engines correct spelling automatically, but they cannot catch every spelling error.
- Scan search results before you click them. The first result isn't always the most useful. Read the text and notice the domain before make a choice.
- Consult more than one search engine.

Evaluating Internet Domains

Not everything you read on the Internet is true, so you have to evaluate sources carefully. The last three letters of an Internet URL identify the site's domain, which can help you evaluate the information of the site.

- **.gov**—Government sites are sponsored by a branch of the United States federal government and are considered reliable.
- **.edu**—Information from an educational research center or department is likely to be carefully checked, but may include student pages that are not edited or monitored.
- **.org**—Organizations are nonprofit groups and usually maintain a high level of credibility but may still reflect strong biases.
- **.com** and **.net**—Commercial sites exist to make a profit. Information might be biased to show a product or service in a good light.

Taking Notes

Use different strategies to take notes:

- Use index cards to create notecards and source cards. On each source card, record information about each source you use—author, title, publisher, date of publication, and relevant page numbers. On each notecard, record information to use in your writing. Use quotation marks when you copy exact words, and indicate the page number(s) on which the information appears.
- Photocopy articles and copyright pages. Then, highlight relevant information. Remember to include the Web addresses of printouts from online sources.
- Print articles from the Internet or copy them directly into a "notes" folder.

You will use these notes to help you write original text.

Source Card

```
                                    [A]
Papp, Joseph,
and Elizabeth Kirkland

Shakespeare Alive!

Bantam Books, 1988
```

Notecard

```
Only the upper classes could read.

Most of the common people in
Shakespeare's time could not read.
Source Card: A, p. 5.
```

Quote Accurately Responsible research begins with the first note you take. Be sure to quote and paraphrase your sources accurately so you can identify these sources later. In your notes, circle all quotations and paraphrases to distinguish them from your own comments. When photocopying from a source, include the copyright information. Include the Web addresses of printouts from online sources.

Reviewing Research Findings

You will need to review your findings to be sure that you have collected enough accurate and appropriate information.

Considering Audience and Purpose

Always keep your audience in mind as you gather information. Different audiences may have very different needs. For example, if you are writing a report for your class about a topic you have studied together, you will not need to provide background information in your writing. However, if you are writing about the topic for a national student magazine, you cannot assume that all of your readers have the same information. You will need to provide background facts from reliable sources to help inform those readers about your subject. When thinking about your research and your audience, ask yourself:

- Who am I writing for?
- Have I collected enough information to explain my topic to this audience?
- Do I need to conduct more research to explain my topic clearly?
- Are there details in my research that I can leave out because they are already familiar to my audience?

Your purpose for writing will also affect your research review. If you are researching to satisfy your own curiosity, you can stop researching when you feel you understand the answer completely. If you are writing a research report that will be graded, you need to think about your assignment. When thinking about whether or not you have enough information, ask yourself:

- What is my purpose for writing?
- Will the information I have gathered be enough to achieve my purpose?
- If I need more information, where might I find it?

Synthesizing Sources

Effective research writing is more than just a list of facts and details. Good research synthesizes—gathers, orders, and interprets—those elements. These strategies will help you synthesize effectively:

- Review your notes. Look for connections and patterns among the details you have collected.
- Organize notes or notecards to help you plan how you will combine details.
- Pay close attention to details that emphasize the same main idea.
- Also look for details that challenge each other. For many topics, there is no single correct opinion. You might decide to conduct additional research to help you decide which side of the issue has more support.

Types of Evidence

When reviewing your research, also think about the kinds of evidence you have collected. The strongest writing combines a variety of evidence. This chart describes three of the most common types of evidence.

TYPE OF EVIDENCE	DESCRIPTION	EXAMPLE
Statistical evidence includes facts and other numerical data used to support a claim or explain a topic.	Statistical evidence are facts about a topic, such as historical dates, descriptions about size and number, and poll results.	Jane Goodall began to study chimpanzees when she was 26 years old.
Testimonial evidence includes any ideas or opinions presented by others. Testimonies might be from experts or people with special knowledge about a topic.	Firsthand testimonies present ideas from eyewitnesses to events or subjects being discussed.	Goodall's view of chimps has changed: "When I first started at Gombe, I thought the chimps were nicer than we are. But time has revealed that they are not. They can be just as awful."
	Secondary testimonies include commentaries on events by people who were not directly involved.	Science writer David Quammen points out that Goodall "set a new standard, a very high standard, for behavioral study of apes in the wild."
Anecdotal evidence presents one person's view of the world, often by describing specific events or incidents.	An anecdote is a story about something that happened. Personal stories can be part of effective research, but they should not be the only kind of evidence presented. Anecdotes are particularly useful for proving that broad generalizations are not accurate.	It is not fair to say that it is impossible for dogs to use tools. One researcher reports the story of a dog that learned to use a large bone as a back scratcher.

Incorporating Research into Writing

Avoiding Plagiarism

Whether you are presenting a formal research paper or an opinion paper on a current event, you must be careful to give credit for any ideas or opinions that are not your own. Presenting someone else's ideas, research, or opinion as your own—even if you have phrased it in different words—is *plagiarism*, the equivalent of academic stealing, or fraud.

Do not use the ideas or research of others in place of your own. Read from several sources to draw your own conclusions and form your own opinions. Incorporate the ideas and research of others to support your points. Credit the source of the following types of support:

- Statistics
- Direct quotations
- Indirectly quoted statements of opinions
- Conclusions presented by an expert
- Facts available in only one or two sources

When you are drafting and revising, circle any words or ideas that are not your own. Follow the instructions on pages R32 and R33 to correctly cite those passages.

Reviewing for Plagiarism Take time to review your writing for accidental plagiarism. Read what you have written and take note of any ideas that do not have your personal writing voice. Compare those passages with your resource materials. You might have copied them without remembering the exact source. Add a correct citation to give credit to the original author. If you cannot find the questionable phrase in your notes, think about revising your word choices. You want to be sure that your final writing reflects your own thinking and not someone else's work.

Quoting and Paraphrasing

When including ideas from research into your writing, you will decide to quote directly or paraphrase.

Direct Quotation Use the author's exact words when they are interesting or persuasive. You might decide to include direct quotations in these situations:

- to share a strong statement
- to reference a historically significant passage
- to show that an expert agrees with your position
- to present an argument to which you will respond

Include complete quotations, without deleting or changing words. If you need to leave out words for space or clarity, use ellipsis points to show where you removed words. Enclose direct quotations in quotation marks.

Paraphrase A paraphrase restates an author's ideas in your own words. Be careful to paraphrase accurately. Beware of making sweeping generalizations in a paraphrase that were not made by the original author. You may use some words from the original source, but a good paraphrase does more than simply rearrange an author's phrases, or replace a few words with synonyms.

Original Text	"Some teens doing homework while listening to music and juggling tweets and texts may actually work better that way, according to an intriguing new study performed by two high-school seniors." *Sumathi Reddy, "Teen Researchers Defend Media Multitasking"*
Patchwork Plagiarism phrases from the original are rearranged, but they too closely follow the original text.	An intriguing new study conducted by two high-school seniors suggests that teens work better when they are listening to music and juggling texts and tweets.
Good Paraphrase	Two high-school students studied homework habits. They concluded that some people do better work while multitasking, such as studying and listening to music or checking text messages at the same time.

Maintaining the Flow of Ideas

Effective research writing is much more that just a list of facts. Maintain the flow of ideas by connecting research information to your own ideas. Instead of simply stating a piece of evidence, use transitions to connect information you found from outside resources and your own thinking. The transitions in the box on the page can be used to introduce, compare, contrast, and clarify.

Choosing an effective organizational strategy for your writing will help you create a logical flow of ideas. Once you have chosen a clear organization, add research in appropriate places to provide evidence and support.

Useful Transitions

When providing examples:

for example   for instance   to illustrate   in [name of resource], [author]

When comparing and contrasting ideas or information:

in the same way   similarly   however   on the other hand

When clarifying ideas or opinions:

in other words   that is   to explain   to put it another way

ORGANIZATIONAL STRUCTURE	USES
Chronological order presents information in the sequence in which it happens.	historical topics; science experiments; analysis of narratives
Part-to-whole order examines how several categories affect a larger subject.	analysis of social issues; historical topics
Order of importance presents information in order of increasing or decreasing importance.	persuasive arguments; supporting a bold or challenging thesis
Comparison-and-contrast organization presents similarities and differences.	addressing two or more subjects

Formats for Citing Sources

When you cite a source, you acknowledge where you found your information and you give your readers the details necessary for locating the source themselves. Within the body of a paper, you provide a short citation, a footnote number linked to a footnote, or an endnote number linked to an endnote reference. These brief references show the page numbers on which you found the information. Prepare a reference list at the end of a research report to provide full bibliographic information on your sources. These are two common types of reference lists:

- A bibliography provides a listing of all the resources you consulted during your research.
- A works-cited list indicates the works your have referenced in your writing.

The chart on the next page shows the Modern Language Association format for crediting sources. This is the most common format for papers written in the content areas in middle school and high school. Unless instructed otherwise by your teacher, use this format for crediting sources.

Focus on Citations When you revise your writing, check that you cite the sources for quotations, factual information, and ideas that are not your own. Most word-processing programs have features that allow you to create footnotes and endnotes.

Identifying Missing Citations These strategies can help you find facts and details that should be cited in your writing:

- Look for facts that are not general knowledge. If a fact was unique to one source, it needs a citation.
- Read your report aloud. Listen for words and phrases that do not sound like your writing style. You might have picked them up from a source. If so, use you notes to find the source, place the words in quotation marks, and give credit.
- Review your notes. Look for ideas that you used in your writing but did not cite.

MLA (8th Edition) Style for Listing Sources

Book with one author	Pyles, Thomas. *The Origins and Development of the English Language.* 2nd ed., Harcourt Brace Jovanovich, 1971. [Indicate the edition or version number when relevant.]
Book with two authors	Pyles, Thomas, and John Algeo. *The Origins and Development of the English Language.* 5th ed., Cengage Learning, 2004.
Book with three or more authors	Donald, Robert B., et al. *Writing Clear Essays.* Prentice Hall, 1983.
Book with an editor	Truth, Sojourner. *Narrative of Sojourner Truth.* Edited by Margaret Washington, Vintage Books, 1993.
Introduction to a work in a published edition	Washington, Margaret. Introduction. *Narrative of Sojourner Truth,* by Sojourner Truth, edited by Washington, Vintage Books, 1993, pp. v–xi.
Single work in an anthology	Hawthorne, Nathaniel. "Young Goodman Brown." *Literature: An Introduction to Reading and Writing,* edited by Edgar V. Roberts and Henry E. Jacobs, 5th ed., Prentice Hall, 1998, pp. 376–385. [Indicate pages for the entire selection.]
Signed article from an encyclopedia	Askeland, Donald R. "Welding." *World Book Encyclopedia,* vol. 21, World Book, 1991, p. 58.
Signed article in a weekly magazine	Wallace, Charles. "A Vodacious Deal." *Time,* 14 Feb. 2000, p. 63.
Signed article in a monthly magazine	Gustaitis, Joseph. "The Sticky History of Chewing Gum." *American History,* Oct. 1998, pp. 30–38.
Newspaper article	Thurow, Roger. "South Africans Who Fought for Sanctions Now Scrap for Investors." *Wall Street Journal,* 11 Feb. 2000, pp. A1+. [For a multipage article that does not appear on consecutive pages, write only the first page number on which it appears, followed by the plus sign.]
Unsigned editorial or story	"Selective Silence." Editorial. *Wall Street Journal,* 11 Feb. 2000, p. A14. [If the editorial or story is signed, begin with the author's name.]
Signed pamphlet or brochure	[Treat the pamphlet as though it were a book.]
Work from a library subscription service	Ertman, Earl L. "Nefertiti's Eyes." *Archaeology,* Mar.–Apr. 2008, pp. 28–32. *Kids Search,* EBSCO, New York Public Library. Accessed 7 Jan. 2017. [Indicating the date you accessed the information is optional but recommended.]
Filmstrips, slide programs, videocassettes, DVDs, and other audiovisual media	*The Diary of Anne Frank.* 1959. Directed by George Stevens, performances by Millie Perkins, Shelley Winters, Joseph Schildkraut, Lou Jacobi, and Richard Beymer, Twentieth Century Fox, 2004. [Indicating the original release date after the title is optional but recommended.]
CD-ROM (with multiple publishers)	Simms, James, editor. *Romeo and Juliet.* By William Shakespeare, Attica Cybernetics / BBC Education / Harper, 1995.
Radio or television program transcript	"Washington's Crossing of the Delaware." *Weekend Edition Sunday,* National Public Radio, 23 Dec. 2013. Transcript.
Web page	"Fun Facts About Gum." ICGA, 2005–2017, www.gumassociation.org/index.cfm/facts-figures/fun-facts-about-gum. Accessed 19 Feb. 2017. [Indicating the date you accessed the information is optional but recommended.]
Personal interview	Smith, Jane. Personal interview, 10 Feb. 2017.

All examples follow the style given in the MLA Handbook, 8th edition, published in 2016.

MODEL

Evidence Log

Unit Title: __Discovery__

Perfomance-Based Assessment Prompt:
Do all discoveries benefit humanity?

My initial thoughts:
Yes - all knowledge moves us forward.

As you read multiple texts about a topic, your thinking may change. Use an Evidence Log like this one to record your thoughts, to track details you might use in later writing or discussion, and to make further connections.

Here is a sample to show how one reader's ideas deepened as she read two texts.

Title of Text: __Classifying the Stars__   Date: __Sept. 17__

CONNECTION TO THE PROMPT	TEXT EVIDENCE/DETAILS	ADDITIONAL NOTES/IDEAS
Newton shared his discoveries and then other scientists built on his discoveries.	Paragraph 2: "Isaac Newton gave to the world the results of his experiments on passing sunlight through a prism." Paragraph 3: "In 1814 . . . the German optician, Fraunhofer . . . saw that the multiple spectral tints . . . were crossed by hundreds of fine dark lines."	It's not always clear how a discovery might benefit humanity in the future.

How does this text change or add to my thinking? This confirms what I think.   Date: __Sept. 20__

Title of Text: __Cell Phone Mania__   Date: __Sept. 21__

CONNECTION TO THE PROMPT	TEXT EVIDENCE/DETAILS	ADDITIONAL NOTES/IDEAS
Cell phones have made some forms of communication easier, but people don't talk to each other as much as they did in the past.	Paragraph 7: "Over 80% of young adults state that texting is their primary method of communicating with friends. This contrasts with older adults who state that they prefer a phone call."	Is it good that we don't talk to each other as much? Look for article about social media to learn more about this question.

How does this text change or add to my thinking?
Maybe there are some downsides to discoveries. I still think that knowledge moves us forward, but sometimes there are negative effects.   Date: __Sept. 25__

Word Network

A word network is a collection of words related to a topic. As you read the selections in a unit, identify interesting theme-related words and build your vocabulary by adding them to your Word Network.

Use your Word Network as a resource for your discussions and writings. Here is an example:

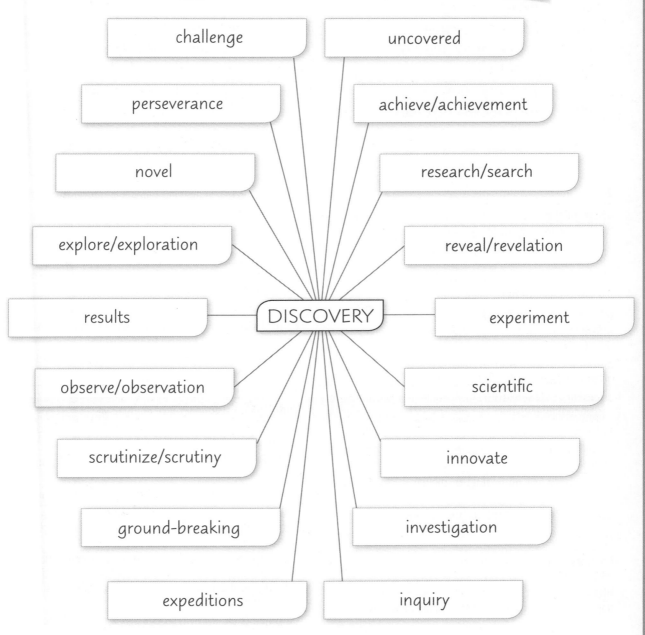

ACADEMIC / CONCEPT VOCABULARY

Academic vocabulary appears in **blue type**.

Pronunciation Key

Symbol	Sample Words	Symbol	Sample Words
a	*at, catapult, Alabama*	oo	*boot, soup, crucial*
ah	*father, charms, argue*	ow	*now, stout, flounder*
ai	*care, various, hair*	oy	*boy, toil, oyster*
aw	*law, maraud, caution*	s	*say, nice, press*
awr	*pour, organism, forewarn*	sh	*she, abolition, motion*
ay	*ape, sails, implication*	u	*full, put, book*
ee	*even, teeth, really*	uh	*ago, focus, contemplation*
eh	*ten, repel, elephant*	ur	*bird, urgent, perforation*
ehr	*merry, verify, terribly*	y	*by, delight, identify*
ih	*it, pin, hymn*	yoo	*music, confuse, few*
o	*shot, hopscotch, condo*	zh	*pleasure, treasure, vision*
oh	*own, parole, rowboat*		

A

accomplishments (uh KOM plihsh muhnts) *n.* goals reached; achievements; tasks done skillfully

accuracy (AK yuhr uh see) *n.* being without errors; correctness

agricultural (ag ruh KUHL chuhr uhl) *adj.* related to the science and art of farming

altered (AWL tuhrd) *adj.* changed

alternative (awl TUR nuh tihv) *adj.* representing a different option

amoeba (uh MEE buh) *n.* microscopic, single-celled animal

ancestors (AN sehs tuhrz) *n.* people from whom one is descended; forefathers

aptitude (AP tuh tood) *n.* natural ability or talent

assumption (uh SUHMP shuhn) *n.* something taken for granted

atmosphere (AT muhs fihr) *n.* the gas surrounding the earth; the air

attempts (uh TEHMPTS) *n.* tries; attacks

B

barriers (BAR ee uhrz) *n.* obstructions; things that block passage

bitterness (BIHT uhr nihs) *n.* quality of having a sharp, unpleasant taste; condition causing pain or sorrow

blight (blyt) *n.* something that spoils, prevents growth, or destroys

bond (bond) *n.* uniting connection; link

C

calculus (KAL kyuh luhs) *n.* math used to study change

canals (kuh NALZ) *n.* artificial waterways for transportation or irrigation

capitalistic (kap uh tuh LIHS tihk) *adj.* characteristic of an economic system that is privately owned

catapulted (KA tuh puhl tihd) *v.* launched forward with machine-like force

catastrophic (kat uh STROF ihk) *adj.* disastrous

cede (seed) *v.* formally give up rights

celebrate (SEHL uh brayt) *v.* mark a happy occasion by engaging in a pleasurable activity

certainty (SUR tuhn tee) *n.* sure fact; freedom from doubt

charitable (CHAR ih tuh buhl) *adj.* kind and forgiving; lenient

chronic (KRON ihk) *adj.* lasting a long time or recurring often

close-up shot (KLOHS uhp) (shot) *n.* camera shot in which the subject is shown at close range; typically, the subject's head and shoulders are shown, with no visible background

colonize (KOL uh nyz) *v.* establish a new home far away

composition (kom puh ZIHSH uhn) *n.* arrangement of elements in a drawing

connects (kuh NEHKTS) *v.* joins together

consequence (KON suh kwehns) *n.* result; outcome; effect

consequences (KON suh kwehns ihz) *n.* results of an action or actions

consistent (kuhn SIHS tuhnt) *n.* keeping to the same principles; reliable

contact (KON takt) *n.* connection; communication; *v.* get in touch with; communicate with

contradict (kon truh DIHKT) *v.* dispute or disagree with

contribute (kuhn TRIHB yoot) *v.* give to a cause, event, project, etc.

covetous (KUHV uh tuhs) *adj.* greedy and jealous

crisis (KRY sihs) *n.* time when a situation is very bad or dangerous; turning point at which a change must be made for better or worse

D

deserted (dih ZUR tihd) *adj.* abandoned; empty

desire (dih ZYR) *v.* want; long for

determination (dih tuhr muh NAY shuhn) *n.* conclusion; firm decision

devastated (DEH vuh stay tihd) *v.* destroyed; completely upset

deviate (DEE vee ayt) *v.* depart from an established plan

dialogue (DY uh log) *n.* conversation; words spoken by characters in a story, drama, etc.

director (duh REHK tuhr) *n.* creative artist responsible for interpreting a screenplay

discord (DIHS kawrd) *n.* disagreement; lack of harmony

discordant (dihs KAWRD uhnt) *adj.* lacking harmony

discredit (dihs KREHD iht) *v.* disbelieve; cast doubt on *n.* loss of trust or faith; disbelief

dispelled (dihs PEHLD) *v.* driven away; scattered

disposal (dihs POH zuhl) *n.* act of getting rid of somehting

dissent (dih SEHNT) *v.* disagree; *n.* disagreement

diversity (dy VUR suh tee) *n.* variety; differences within a group

documentary photography (dok yuh MEHN tuhr ee) (fuh TOG ruh fee) *n.* photographs taken with the main purpose of recording a place, an event, or a person

doomed (doomd) *adj.* destined to a bad outcome

E

earnest (UR nihst) *adj.* serious and heartfelt; not joking

editing (EHD ih tihng) *n.* how separate shots filmed during production are arranged to tell a story, add suspense, and set pacing

efficiently (ih FIHSH uhnt lee) *adv.* with the least amount of effort and waste; effectively

emissions (ih MIHSH uhnz) *n.* gas or other substance sent into the air

encouraged (ehn KUR ihjd) *v.* inspired; offered support to

enlarged (ehn LAHRJD) *v.* made bigger; increased in size

enterprise (EHN tuhr pryz) *n.* business venture or company

enthusiastically (ehn thoo zee AS tuh klee) *adv.* with eager interest

environment (ehn VY ruhn muhnt) *n.* land, air, and water in which people, animals, and plants live, and all the natural features of these places

ethical (EHTH uh kuhl) *adj.* conforming to moral standards

excruciatingly (ehk SKROO shee ay tihng lee) *adv.* painfully; miserably

extinct (ehk STIHNGKT) *adj.* no longer in existence

extraordinary (ehk STRAWR duh nehr ee) *adj.* better than ordinary; exceptional

F

flung (fluhng) *v.* threw with force

forlorn (fawr LAWRN) *adj.* abandoned or deserted

frantically (FRAN tuh klee) *adv.* acting wildly with anger, worry, or pain

frustrated (FRUHS trayt ihd) *adj.* prevented from accomplishing

G

generosity (jehn uhr OS uh tee) *n.* willingness to give or share

H

heed (heed) *v.* pay close attention to

hesitantly (HEHZ uh tuhnt lee) *adv.* in an unsure or cautious way

human voice (HYOO muhn) (voys) *n.* central conveyer of events and interactions in a radio play

I

illusion (ih LOO zhuhn) *n.* something that appears real but actually is not

imitate (IHM uh tayt) *v.* act the same as; copy

immense (ih MEHNS) *adj.* very large

imminent (IHM uh nuhnt) *adj.* threatening and likely to occur at any moment

impairments (ihm PAIR muhnts) *n.* injury; damage

impossible (ihm POS uh buhl) *adj.* disagreeable; unreasonable

indignity (ihn DIHG nuh tee) *n.* feeling that one has been disrespected

infinitely (IHN fuh niht lee) *adv.* enormously; remarkably

influence (IHN floo uhns) *v.* affect someone in an important way

instinctively (ihn STIHNGK tihv lee) *adv.* done automatically, without thinking

interject (ihn tuhr JEHKT) *v.* throw in between; interrupt

interstellar (ihn tuhr STEHL uhr) *adj.* between or among stars in space

J

justify (JUHS tuh fy) *v.* give good reason for an action

L

lamented (luh MEHNT ihd) *v.* expressed regret

light/shadow (lyt) / (SHAD oh) *n.* techniques that add depth to a drawing and make it more realistic

localizing (LOH kuh lyz ihng) *v.* gathering, collecting, or concentrating in a particular place

long shot (lawng) (shot) *n.* camera shot in which the entire subject is visible as well as some of the background around the subject

lurched (lurcht) *v.* staggered; moved unsteadily

M

maintain (mayn TAYN) *v.* keep up; declare to be true

maladies (MAL uh deez) *n.* illnesses or diseases

malcontent (MAL kuhn tehnt) *n.* person who is always unhappy

medium shot (MEE dee uhm) (shot) *n.* camera shot in which the subject is seen from a medium distance, usually from the waist up

miser (MY zuhr) *n.* greedy person who keeps and refuses to spend money, even at the expense of his or her own comfort

mission control (MIHSH uhn) (kuhn TROHL) *n.* command center for the control, monitoring, and support of activities connected with manned space flight

monochrome (MON uh krohm) *n.* photos that are black and white

monotony (muh NOT uh nee) *n.* sameness; boredom

morose (muh ROHS) *adj.* gloomy; ill-tempered

mosaic (moh ZAY ihk) *adj.* made of many small pieces of colored glass or stone

mutation (myoo TAY shuhn) *n.* change in form, nature, or qualities

mystery (MIHS tuh ree) *n.* quality of being unexplained or kept secret

N

notable (NOH tuh buhl) *adj.* important; remarkable

O

observation (ob zuhr VAY shuhn) *n.* act of watching or noticing; something observed

P

panoramic shot (pan uh RAM ihk) (shot) *n.* film shot showing a wide, unbroken view

parallel (PAR uh lehl) *adj.* having the same direction or nature; similar

performance (puhr FAWR muhns) *n.* actor's portrayal of a character

permit (puhr MIHT) *v.* allow

perseverance (puhr suh VIHR uhns) *n.* continued, patient effort

persevere (puhr suh VIHR) *v.* continue despite difficulty

perspective (puhr SPEHK tihv) *n.* particular way of looking at something; point of view

perspective (puhr SPEHK tihv) *n.* technique used to create the illusion of a three-dimensional world on a two-dimensional surface, such as a piece of paper

philanthropist (fih LAN thruh pihst) *n.* wealthy person who donates to charities

planetary (PLAN uh tehr ee) *adj.* having to do with planets

pollution (puh LOO shuhn) *n.* presence or introduction into a space of a substance or thing that has harmful or poisonous effects

puzzled (PUHZ uhld) *adj.* confused and unable to understand something

Q

questions (KWEHS chuhnz) *n.* what the interviewer chooses to ask an interviewee to elicit specific information

R

recklessly (REHK lihs lee) *adv.* without regard for consequences; carelessly

release (rih LEES) *n.* act of letting go; *v.* let go; set free

reproach (rih PROHCH) *n.* criticism or disapproval

resilience (rih ZIHL yuhns) *n.* ability to recover quickly

resolute (REHZ uh loot) *adj.* determined

resolved (rih ZOLVD) *v.* offered a solution for; solved

rural (RUR uhl) *adj.* characteristic of the country; of or pertaining to agriculture

ruthless (ROOTH lihs) *adj.* having no compassion or pity

S

scarcity (SKAIR suh tee) *n.* quality of being hard to find; rarity

screenplay (SKREEN play) *n.* written script of a film, including acting instructions and scene directions

set (seht) *n.* where the interview takes place

silence (SY luhns) *n.* absence of sound

sorrow (SAWR oh) *n.* great sadness; suffering

sound effects (sownd) (uh FEHKTS) *n.* sounds produced artificially for a radio production

squabbling (SKWOB lihng) *v.* fighting noisily over small matters

stillness (STIHL nihs) *n.* absence of noise or motion

stimulus (STIHM yuh luhs) *n.* something that causes action or reaction

stricken (STRIHK uhn) *adj.* very badly affected by trouble or illness

strive (stryv) *v.* make a great effort; try very hard

struggling (STRUHG lihng) *v.* trying to do with difficulty

subconciously (suhb KON shuhs lee) *adv.* occuring in the mind without one's full awareness

submerged (suhb MURJD) *adj.* completely covered with a liquid

sufficient (suh FIHSH uhnt) *adj.* enough; the right amount as needed

supervision (soo puhr VIH zhuhn) *n.* act of watching over someone

T

thoroughly (THUR oh lee) *adv.* completely; entirely

threatening (THREHT uhn ihng) *adj.* dangerous

tissue (TIHSH oo) *n.* masses of cells forming parts of animals or plants

toil (toyl) *v.* work hard and with difficulty

tone (tohn) *n.* attitude of an interviewer or interviewee toward the subject matter or audience

tradition (truh DIHSH uhn) *n.* long-established custom or practice

transition (tran ZIHSH uhn) *n.* in media, change from one scene or shot to another

U

understandingly (uhn duhr STAN dihng lee) *adv.* in a knowing way; kindly

universal (yoo nuh VUR suhl) *adj.* involving everyone in the world or in a particular group; true or appropriate in every situation

unprecedented (uhn PREHS uh dehn tihd) *adj.* never having happened before; unheard of

unsustainable (uhn suh STAY nuh buhl) *adj.* unable to continue at the same rate or in the same way

urgency (UR juhn see) *n.* state of being very important and needing to be dealt with right away

V

vantage point (VAN tihj) (poynt) *n.* place where the photographer positions the camera

voiceover (VOYS oh vuhr) *n.* voice commenting or narrating off-camera

W

wearily (WIHR uh lee) *adv.* in a tired manner

wisdom (WIHZ duhm) *n.* knowledge; the quality of being wise

VOCABULARIO ACADÉMICO/ VOCABULARIO DE CONCEPTOS

El vocabulario académico está en **letra azul**.

A

accomplishments / logros *s.* objetivos alcanzados; hazañas; tareas realizadas hábilmente

accuracy / exactitud *s.* sin errores; corrección

agricultural / agrícola *adj.* relativo a la ciencia o al arte del cultivo y la labranza de la tierra

altered / alteró *v.* cambió

alternate / alterno *adj.* cada dos, uno sí y otro no; *s.* suplente

alternative / alternativa *s.* una opción entre dos o más cosas

amoeba / ameba *s.* / animal microscópico unicelular

ancestors / ancestros *s.* personas de las cuales alguien desciende; antepasados

animation / animación *s.* técnica cinematográfica por medio de la cual se crea la ilusión de movimiento

aptitude / aptitud *s.* habilidad natural o talento

assumption / suposición *s.* algo que se da por hecho

atmosphere / atmósfera *s.* el gas que envuelve la Tierra; el aire

attempts / intentos / atentados *s.* tentativas; ataques

B

barriers / barreras *s.* obstáculos; cosas que bloquean el paso

bitterness / amargura *s.* cualidad de sabor intenso y desagradable; condición que causa dolor o tristeza

blight / plaga *s.* algo que se echa a perder, impide el crecimiento o destruye

bond / vínculo *s.* una conexión que une; lazo

C

calculus / cálculo *s.* cuenta que se usa en matemáticas para estudiar el cambio

canals / canales *s.* cauces de agua artificial para el transporte o el riego

capitalistic / capitalista *adj.* relativo a un sistema económico basado en la propiedad privada

catapulted / catapultó *v.* lanzó con la fuerza de una máquina

catastrophic / catastrófico *adj.* con una consecuencia desastrosa

cede / ceder *v.* dar derechos formalmente a otros

celebrate / celebrar *v.* ensalzar una ocasión especial realizando una actividad placentera

certainty / certeza *s.* conocimiento de que algo es cierto; libre de toda duda

charitable / comprensivo *adj.* benévolo y flexible; indulgente

chronic / crónico *adj.* que dura mucho tiempo o se repite con frecuencia

climate / clima *s.* condiciones atmosféricas de un lugar durante un período de tiempo

close-up shot / primer plano *s.* toma de cámara en la que se muestra al muy de cerca

colonize / colonizar *v.* establecerse en otro territorio lejos de casa

composition / composición *s.* distribución o arreglo de las partes de un cuadro o una escultura

connects / conecta *v.* junta dos cosas

consequence / consecuencia *s.* la relación del efecto a la causa

consequences / consecuencias *s.* resultados de una acción o acciones

consistent / congruente *adj.* que mantiene los mismos principios; coherente

contact / contacto *s.* trato, comunicación; *v.* to get in touch with / contactar, comunicarse

context / contexto *s.* entorno más próximo; entorno de una palabra que influye en su significado

contradict / contradecir *v.* discutir o estar en desacuerdo con alguien o algo

contribute / contribuir *v.* participar en una causa, un evento, un proyecto, etc.

cookies / cookies *s.* pequeños archivos de datos que los sitios webs guardan en las computadoras

covetous / codicioso *adj.* envidioso, avaricioso

crisis / crisis *s.* momento en el que una situación es mala o peligrosa; punto de inflexión en el cual se debe cambiar para bien o para mal

D

deserted / abandonado *adj.* que está desatendido; vacío

desire / deseo *s.* anhelo por algo; petición

determination / determinación *s.* conclusión; decisión firme

devastated / devastó *v.* destruyó; apenó profundamente

development / desarrollo *s.* etapa o aspecto en crecimiento

dialogue / diálogo *s.* conversación

dilemma / dilema *s.* situación en la que se tiene que tomar una decisión difícil

direction / dirección *s.* el plan que tiene el director para una producción o sus instrucciones a los actores y al resto del equipo

discord / discordia *s.* desacuerdo: falta de armonía

discordant / discordante *adj.* sin armonía

discredit / no creer *v.* descreer; *s.* descrédito; pérdida o falta de fe, desprestigio

dispelled / disipó *v.* desvaneció; esparció

disposal / desecho *s.* acción de deshacerse de algo

dissent / disentir *v.* estar en desacuerdo; *s.* disconformidad

diversity / diversidad *s.* variedad; diferencias dentro de un grupo

documentary photography / fotografía documental *s.* fotografías que documentan y retratan un evento

doomed / estaba condenado *v.* estaba destinado a un final desgraciado

E

earnest / serio *adj.* que no bromea

editing / editar *v.* organizar las distintas tomas que se hicieron en la filmación para contar una historia, añadir suspenso y marcar el ritmo de la película

efficiently / eficientemente *adv.* con la mínima cantidad de esfuerzo y gasto; eficazmente

emissions / emisiones *s.* gases y otras sustancias expulsadas en el aire

encouraged / animó *v.* inspiró; ofreció respaldo o apoyo

enlarged / se amplió *v.* se hizo más grande; aumentó de tamaño

enterprise / empresa *s.* iniciativa de negocio o compañía

enthusiastically / con estusiasmo *adv.* con interés y ganas

environment / medio ambiente *s.* la tierra, aire y agua en los que las personas, animales y plantas habitan, así como los rasgos distintivos de esos lugares

ethical / ético *adj.* conforme a unos estándares morales

excruciatingly / terriblemente *adv.* penosamente; miserablemente

extinct / extinto *adj.* que ya no existe

F

flung / lanzado *v.* arrojado con fuerza

forlorn / abandonado *adj.* que lo han dejado o está desierto

fragment / fragmentar *v.* romper o dividir en partes pequeñas; *s.* fragmento; parte pequeña dividida o rota

frantically / frenéticamente *adv.* actuar atacadamente, con enojo, preocupación o dolor

frustrated / frustró *v.* impidió lograr algo

G

generosity / generosidad *s.* voluntad de dar o de compartir

H

heed / prestar atención *v.* mantener plena concentración en algo o alguien

hesitantly / con vacilación *adv.* de manera reacia

I

icon / icono *s.* imagen o símbolo en una computadora

illusion / ilusión *s.* algo que parece real pero no lo es

imitate / imitar *v.* actuar igual a como lo hace alguien; copiar

immense / inmenso *adj.* enorme

imminent / inminente *adj.* amenazador, que puede ocurrir en cualquier momento

impairments / discapacidades *s.* lesiones; daños

impossible / imposible *adj.* incapaz de existir u ocurrir

indignity / indignidad *s.* cualidad de no sentirse digno o respetado

infinitely / infinitamente *adv.* que no se puede; sin límites

influence / influencia *s.* acción de influir en alguien considerablemente

instinctively / instintivamente *adv.* hecho de manera automática, sin pensar

interject / interrumpir *v.* interponer; cortar la continuidad de algo

interstellar / interestelar *adj.* que está en una zona del espacio entre dos o más estrellas

J

justify / justificar *v.* dar buenas razones para llevar a cabo una acción

L

lamented / lamentó *v.* expresó arrepentimiento

light / shadow / claroscuro *s.* técnica que se usa para dar volumen a una imagen

localizing / localizar *v.* juntar, reunir o concentrar en un lugar particular

long shot / plano general *s.* toma de cámara en la que se ve todo el sujeto y parte del fondo

lurched / se tambaleó *v.* dio tumbos, se movió a trompicones

M

maintain / sostener *v.* mantener; afirmar que algo es verdad

maladies / enfermedades *s.* dolencias

malcontent / insatisfecho *s.* persona que está siempre descontenta

manual / manual *s.* instrucciones o información en forma de libro

medium shot / plano medio *s.* toma de cámara en la que se ve al sujeto desde una distancia media

miser / avaro *adj.* avaricioso, tacaño

Mission control / centro de control *s.* centro de mando para vuelos al espacio tripulados

monochrome / monocromático *adj.* fotografías en blanco y negro

monotony / monotonía *s.* falta de variedad; aburrimiento

morose / hosco / taciturno *adj.* malhumorado; melancólico

mosaic / mosaico *s.* obra hecha con muchas piezas pequeñas de vidrio o piedras de colores

mutation / mutación *s.* cambio de forma, naturaleza o atributos

mystery / misterio *s.* cualidad de ser inexplicable o un secreto

N

narration / narración *s.* acción de contar una historia

notable / notable *adj.* extraordinario; destacado

O

observation / observación *s.* acción de contemplar; algo que se observa

P

panoramic shot / plano panorámico *s.* plano cinematográfico que muestra una vista completa y amplia

parallel / paralelo *adj.* que va en la misma dirección o tiene la misma naturaleza; similar

performance / representación *s.* actuación o presentación formal delante de una audiencia; espectáculo

permit / permitir *v.* dar permiso, autorizar

perseverance / perseverancia *s.* esfuerzo constante y paciente

persevere / perseverar *v.* seguir pese a las dificultades

perspective / perspectiva *s.* ilusión de profundidad en el arte

philanthropist / filantrópo *s.* persona rica que hace donativos a causas benéficas

planetary / planetario *adj.* relativo a los planetas

pollution / contaminación *s.* la presencia o introducción a un espacio de sustancias perjudiciales o de cosas que tienen efectos dañinos o venenosos

proportion / proporción *s.* relación del tamaño de los elementos en el arte

puzzled / perplejo *adj.* confundido y sin poder entender algo

Q

questioning / interrogatorio *s.* lo que el entrevistador ha elegido como preguntas

R

recklessly / imprudentemente *adv.* sin dar importancia a las consecuencias; descuidadamente

release / liberar *v.* acción de dejar ir; soltar

reproach / reproche *s.* desaprobación; crítica

resilience / resiliencia *s.* capacidad de recuperarse rápidamente

resolute / resuelto *adj.* firme y con un propósito claro

retain / contratar *v.* emplear; fichar

retain / retener *v.* conservar o recordar

rural / rural *adj.* relativo al campo; perteneciente a la agricultura

ruthless / despiadado *adj.* sin compasión piedad

S

scarcity / escasez *s.* cualidad de ser difícil de encontrar; rareza

screenplay / guión *s.* el texto que se usa en la producción de una película

setting / set *s.* donde tiene lugar la entrevista

solid drawing / dibujo sólido *s.* técnica para hacer que una imagen parezca tridimensional

sorrow / pena *s.* tristeza profunda; sufrimiento

sound effect / efecto de sonido *s.* sonidos producidos artificialmente para acompañar al guión radiofónico y cinematográfico, una obra teatral o una producción

squabbling / reñir *v.* pelearse en voz muy alta sobre asuntos de poca importancia

staging / puesta en escena *s.* la representación de una idea para que quede clara

stillness / quietud *s.* ausencia de ruido o movimiento

stimulus / estímulo *s.* algo que lleva a la acción o la reacción

stricken / afligido *adj.* muy afectado por problemas o por una enfermedad

strive / esforzarse *v.* hacer un gran esfuerzo; luchar

struggling / en apuros *adj.* en aprietos; intentando salir adelante con dificultad

subconciously / subconscientemente *adv.* que ocurre en la mente sin ser consciente de ello

submerged / sumergido *adj.* cubierto completamente

sufficient / suficiente *adj.* bastante; que tiene la cantidad exacta que se necesita

supervision / supervisión *s.* acción de vigilar a alguien

T

thesis / tesis *s.* trabajo formal de investigación; opinión apoyada con argumentos

throroughly / completamente *adv.* totalmente, plenamente

threatening / amenazador *adj.* peligroso

timing / duración *s.* número de fotogramas que se usan para una acción

tissue / tejido *s.* estructuras de células que forman partes de animales o plantas

together / juntos *s.* el uno con el otro

toil / esforzarse *v.* trabajar arduamente

tone / tono *s.* la actitud que adopta el hablante hacia un tema o su audiencia

tradition / tradición *s.* costumbre o práctica establecida desde hace mucho tiempo

transition / transición *s.* cambio de una condición, un lugar o una actividad a otros diferentes

U

understandingly / con comprensión *adv.* compasivamente

universal / universal *adj.* que incluye a todo el mundo o a todo un grupo; certero y adecuado en todas las situaciones

unprecedented / sin precedentes *adj.* que nunca ha pasado antes; inaudito

unsustainable / insostenible *adj.* que no puede continuar con el mismo ritmo o de la misma manera

urgency / urgencia *s.* estado o situación que necesita atención inmediata por su importancia

V

vantage point / punto de vista *s.* posición de la cámara

voiceover / voz en off *s.* voz que comenta o narra detrás de la cámara

W

wearily / con cansancio *adv.* con poca energía

wisdom / sabiduría *s.* conocimiento; cualidad de ser sabio

LITERARY TERMS HANDBOOK

ANALOGY An *analogy* makes a comparison between two or more things that are similar in some ways but otherwise unalike.

ANECDOTE An *anecdote* is a brief nonfiction story about an interesting, amusing, or strange event. Writers tell anecdotes to entertain or to make a point.

ARGUMENT In an *argument*, the writer states and supports a claim, or opinion, based on factual evidence and logical reasoning. Most arguments are composed of an *introduction*, in which a claim is stated; the *body*, in which the claim is supported by evidence; and the *conclusion*, in which the claim is summarized or restated.

AUTHOR'S POINT OF VIEW The attitude toward a topic an author reveals in a piece of nonfiction writing shows the *author's point of view*.

AUTHOR'S PURPOSE An *author's purpose* is his or her main reason for writing. For example, an author may want to entertain, inform, or persuade the reader. Sometimes an author is trying to teach a moral lesson or reflect on an experience. An author may have more than one purpose for writing.

AUTOBIOGRAPHY An *autobiography* is the story of the writer's own life, told by the writer. Autobiographical writing may tell about the person's whole life or only a part of it.

Because autobiographies are about real people and events, they are a form of nonfiction. Most autobiographies are written in the *first-person point of view*.

BIOGRAPHY A *biography* is a form of nonfiction in which a writer tells the life story of another person. Most biographies are written about famous or admirable people. Although biographies are nonfiction, the most effective ones share the qualities of good narrative writing.

BLOG A *blog post* is a piece of online writing added to an online journal, called a *blog*. Writers of blogs provide information or express thoughts on various subjects.

CAUSE AND EFFECT A *cause-and effect essay* examines the relationship between events. Effective essays contain clearly stated events and outcomes, using examples, evidence and logic.

CHARACTER A *character* is a person or an animal that takes part in the action of a literary work. The main, or *major,* character is the most important character in a story, poem, or play. A *minor* character is one who takes part in the action but is not the focus of attention.

Characters are sometimes classified as flat or round. A *flat character* is one-sided and often stereotypical. A *round character,* on the other hand, is fully developed and exhibits many traits—often both faults and virtues. Characters can also be classified as dynamic or static.

A *dynamic character* is one who changes or grows during the course of the work. A *static character* is one who does not change.

CHARACTER TRAITS *Character traits* are the individual qualities that make each character unique.

CHARACTERIZATION *Characterization* is the act of creating and developing a character. Authors use two major methods of characterization—*direct* and *indirect.* When using direct characterization, a writer states the *characters' traits,* or characteristics.

When describing a character indirectly, a writer depends on the reader to draw conclusions about the character's traits. Sometimes the writer tells what other participants in the story say and think about the character.

CHRONOLOGICAL ORDER Writers often sequence events in narratives using *chronological order*, so that one event proceeds to the next in the order in which they actually happened.

CLIMAX The *climax,* also called the turning point, is the high point in the action of the plot. It is the moment of greatest tension, when the outcome of the plot hangs in the balance. See *Plot.*

COLLABORATIVE DISCUSSION The exploration of a topic in a group setting in which all individuals participate is called a *collaborative discussion.*

COMEDY A *comedy* is a literary work, especially a play, which is light, often humorous or satirical, and ends happily. Comedies frequently depict ordinary characters faced with temporary difficulties and conflicts. Types of comedy include *romantic comedy,* which involves problems between lovers, and the *comedy of manners,* which satirically challenges social customs of a society.

COMPARISON-AND-CONTRAST ESSAY An essay in which an author lays out the differences and similarities between two subjects is called a *comparison-and-contrast essay*.

Comparison-and-contrast essays can be organized using *point-by-point organization* in which one aspect of both subjects is discussed, then another aspect, and so on. *Block method organization* presents all the details of one subject, then all details about the next subject.

CONFLICT A *conflict* is a struggle between opposing forces. Conflict is one of the most important elements of stories, novels, and plays because it causes the action. There are two kinds of conflict: external and internal. An *external conflict* is one in which a character struggles against some outside force, such as another person. Another kind of external conflict may occur between a character and some force in nature.

An *internal conflict* takes place within the mind of a character. The character struggles to make a decision, take an action, or overcome a feeling.

CONNOTATIONS The *connotation* of a word is the set of ideas associated with it in addition to its explicit meaning. The connotation of a word can be personal, based on individual experiences. More often, cultural connotations—those recognizable by most people in a group—determine a writer's word choices.

COUNTERCLAIM Opposing views to the main claim of an argument are called *counterclaims*.

CONSTRUCTIVE CRITCISM Respectful disagreements and critiques, meant to improve an outcome, are referred to as *constructive criticism*.

CULTURAL CONTEXT The *cultural context* of a literary work is the economic, social, and historical environment of the characters. This includes the attitudes and customs of that culture and historical period.

DENOTATION The *denotation* of a word is its dictionary meaning, independent of other associations, that the word may have. The denotation of the word *lake,* for example, is "an inland body of water." "Vacation spot" and "place where the fishing is good" are connotations of the word *lake.*

DESCRIPTION A *description* is a portrait, in words, of a person, place, or object. Descriptive writing uses images that appeal to the five senses—sight, hearing, touch, taste, and smell.

DIALECT *Dialect* is the form of a language spoken by people in a particular region or group. Dialects differ in pronunciation, grammar, and word choice. The English language is divided into many dialects. British English differs from American English.

DIALOGUE A *dialogue* is a conversation between characters. In poems, novels, and short stories, dialogue is usually set off by quotation marks to indicate a speaker's exact words.

In a play, dialogue follows the names of the characters, and no quotation marks are used.

DICTION *Diction* is a writer's word choice and the way the writer puts those words together. Diction is part of a writer's style and may be described as formal or informal, plain or fancy, ordinary or technical, sophisticated or down-to-earth, old-fashioned or modern.

DIRECT QUOTATIONS Quotations that show a person's exact words in quotation marks are *direct quotations.* *Personal interviews* are a research method often used by authors as a source of direct quotations.

DRAMA A *drama* is a story written to be performed by actors. Although a drama is meant to be performed, one can also read the script, or written version, and imagine the action. The *script* of a drama is made up of dialogue and stage directions. The *dialogue* is the words spoken by the actors. The *stage directions,* usually printed in italics, tell how the actors should look, move, and speak. They also describe the setting, sound effects, and lighting.

Dramas are often divided into parts called *acts.* The acts are often divided into smaller parts called *scenes.*

EDITORIAL An *editorial* is a type of argument that typically appears in a newspaper and takes a position on a specific topic.

ESSAY An *essay* is a short nonfiction work about a particular subject. Most essays have a single major focus and a clear introduction, body, and conclusion.

There are many types of essays. An *informal essay* uses casual, conversational language. A *historical essay* gives facts, explanations, and insights about historical events. An *expository essay* explains an idea by breaking it down. A *narrative essay* tells a story about a real-life experience. An *informational essay* explains a process. A *persuasive essay* offers an opinion and supports it. A *humorous essay* uses humor to achieve the author's purpose. A *descriptive essay* creates an engaging picture of a subject, by using vivid, sensory details. A *how-to essay* is a step-by-step explanation of how to make or do something. An *explanatory essay* is a short piece of nonfiction in which the author explains, defines, or interprets ideas, events, or processes. A *reflective essay* is a brief prose work in which an author presents his or her thoughts or feelings—or reflections—about an experience or an idea.

EXAMPLE An *example* is a fact, idea or event that supports an idea or insight.

EXPOSITION In the plot of a story or a drama, the *exposition,* or introduction, is the part of the work that introduces the characters, setting, and basic situation.

EXPOSITORY WRITING *Expository writing* is writing that explains or informs.

FANTASY A *fantasy* is highly imaginative writing that contains elements not found in real life. Examples of fantasy include stories that involve supernatural elements, stories that resemble fairy tales, stories that deal with imaginary places and creatures, and science-fiction stories.

FICTION *Fiction* is prose writing that tells about imaginary characters and events. Short stories and novels are works of fiction. Some writers base their fiction on actual events and people, adding invented characters, dialogue, settings, and plots. Other writers rely on imagination alone.

FIGURATIVE LANGUAGE *Figurative language* is writing or speech that is not meant to be taken literally. The many types of figurative language are known as *figures of speech.* Common figures of speech include metaphor, personification, and simile. Writers use figurative language to state ideas in vivid and imaginative ways.

FRAME STORY A *frame story* is a story that brackets—or frames—another story or group of stories. This framing device creates a story-within-a-story narrative structure.

FREE VERSE *Free verse* is poetry not written with a *formal structure*, or in a regular, rhythmical pattern, or meter. The poet is free to write lines of any length or with any number of stresses, or beats. Free verse is therefore less constraining than *metrical verse,* in which every line must have a certain length and a certain number of stresses.

GENRE A *genre* is a division or type of literature. Literature is commonly divided into three major genres: poetry, prose, and drama. Each major genre is, in turn, divided into lesser genres, as follows:

1. *Poetry:* lyric poetry, concrete poetry, dramatic poetry, narrative poetry, epic poetry
2. *Prose:* fiction (novels and short stories) and nonfiction (biography, autobiography, letters, essays, and reports)
3. *Drama:* serious drama and tragedy, comic drama, melodrama, and farce

HISTORICAL CONTEXT The *historical context* of a literary work includes the actual political and social events and trends of the time. When a work takes place in the past, knowledge about that historical time period can help the reader understand its setting, background, culture, and message, as well as the attitudes and actions of its characters. A reader must also take into account the historical context in which the writer was creating the work, which may be different from the time period of the work's setting.

HUMOR *Humor* is writing intended to evoke laughter. While most humorists try to entertain, humor can also be used to convey a serious theme.

HYPERBOLE *Hyperbole* is a form of figurative language that uses exaggeration for effect.

IDIOM An *idiom* is an expression that has a meaning particular to a language or region.

IMAGERY *Imagery* is a technique of writing with images.

IMAGES *Images* are words or phrases that appeal to one or more of the five senses. Writers use images to describe how their subjects look, sound, feel, taste, and smell. Poets often paint images, or word pictures, that appeal to the senses. These pictures help you to experience the poem fully.

INFERENCES An *inference* is a guess based on clues. Very often in literature, authors leave some details unstated; it is up to readers to "fill in the blanks" and infer details about characters, events, and setting.

IRONY *Irony* is a contradiction between what happens and what is expected. There are three main types of irony. *Situational irony* occurs when something happens that directly contradicts the expectations of the characters or the audience. *Verbal irony* is created when words are used to suggest the opposite of their meaning. In *dramatic irony,* the audience is aware of something that the character or speaker is not aware of. The result is suspense or humor.

JOURNAL A *journal* is a daily or periodic account of events and the writer's thoughts and feelings about those events. Personal journals are not normally written for publication, but sometimes they do get published later with permission from the author or the author's family.

LETTERS A *letter* is a written communication from one person to another. In personal letters, the writer shares information and his or her thoughts and feelings with one other person or group. Although letters are not normally written for publication, they sometimes do get published later with the permission of the author or the author's family.

LYRIC POEM A *lyric poem* is a highly musical verse that expresses the observations and feelings of a single speaker. It creates a single, unified impression.

MAIN IDEA The *main idea* is the *central idea* or most important point in a text.

MEDIA Stories and information are shared using different forms of *media*. Books and magazines are a type of media. Film, video, and digital are other forms of media. A *multimedia presentation* is created from combination of words, images, sounds, and video.

MEDIA ACCOUNTS *Media accounts* are reports, explanations, opinions, or descriptions written for television, radio, newspapers, and magazines. While some media accounts report only facts, others include the writer's thoughts and reflections.

METAPHOR A *metaphor* is a figure of speech in which something is described as though it were something else. A metaphor, like a simile, works by pointing out a similarity between two unlike things.

MONOLOGUE A *monologue* is a dramatic speech presented by a single character in a play. The character speaks from the first-person point of view and relates his or her thoughts and feelings.

MOOD The *mood* is the feeling created in a reader by a piece of writing. Writers create mood by using imagery, word choice and descriptive details.

MOTIVE A *motive* is a reason that explains or partially explains a character's thoughts, feelings, actions, or speech. Writers try to make their characters' motives, or motivations, as clear as possible. If the motives of a main character are not clear, then the character will not be believable.

Characters are often motivated by needs, such as food and shelter. They are also motivated by feelings, such as fear, love, and pride. Motives may be obvious or hidden.

NARRATION *Narration* is writing that tells a story. The act of telling a story is also called narration. Any story told in fiction, nonfiction, poetry, or even drama is called a narrative.

Writers of narratives employ many techniques to bring their stories to life. For example, most narratives contain a plot, setting, characters, and theme. The readers' experience can be enhanced by varied **narrative pacing**, in which the writer speeds up or slows down the plot events to create effects such as suspense.

NARRATIVE A *narrative* is a story. Novels and short stories are types of fictional narratives. Biographies and autobiographies are nonfiction narratives.

NARRATIVE POEM A *narrative poem* is a story told in verse. Narrative poems often have all the elements of short stories, including characters, conflict, and plot.

NARRATOR A *narrator* is a speaker or a character who tells a story. The narrator's perspective is the way he or she sees things. A *third-person narrator* is one who stands outside the action and speaks about it. A *first-person narrator* is one who tells a story and participates in its action.

NONFICTION *Nonfiction* is prose writing that presents and explains ideas or that tells about real people, places, objects, or events. Autobiographies, biographies, essays, reports, letters, memos, and newspaper articles are all types of nonfiction.

NOVEL A *novel* is a long work of fiction. Novels contain such elements as characters, plot, conflict, and setting. The writer of novels, or novelist, develops these elements. In addition to its main plot, a novel may contain one or more subplots, or independent, related stories. A novel may also have several themes.

See *Fiction* and *Short Story.*

ONOMATOPOEIA *Onomatopoeia* is the use of words that imitate sounds. *Crash, buzz, screech, hiss, neigh, jingle,* and *cluck* are examples of onomatopoeia. *Chickadee, towhee,* and *whippoorwill* are onomatopoeic names of birds.

ORGANIZATION The structure of a text or media presentation is referred to as its **organization**. Common organizational structures are cause-and-effect, comparison-and-contrast, order of importance, and chronological order. Writers choose organizational structures that best suit their topic and purpose.

OXYMORON An *oxymoron* (pl. *oxymora*) is a figure of speech that links two opposite or contradictory words in order to point out an idea or situation that seems contradictory or inconsistent but on closer inspection turns out to be somehow true.

PARAPHRASE When you *paraphrase*, you restate a text using your own words.

PERSONIFICATION *Personification* is a type of figurative language in which a nonhuman subject is given human characteristics.

PERSUASION *Persuasion* is used in writing or speech that attempts to convince the reader or listener to adopt a particular opinion or course of action. Newspaper editorials and letters to the editor use persuasion. So do advertisements and campaign speeches given by political candidates.

Writers use a combination of persuasive techniques to argue their point of view. **Appeals to authority** use the statements of experts. **Appeals to emotion** use words that convey strong feelings. **Appeals to reason** use logical arguments backed by facts.

PLAYWRIGHT A *playwright* is a person who writes plays. William Shakespeare is regarded as the greatest playwright in English literature.

PLOT *Plot* is the sequence of events in which each event results from a previous one and causes the next. In most novels, dramas, short stories, and narrative poems, the plot involves both characters and a central conflict. The plot usually begins with an *exposition* that introduces the setting, the characters, and the basic situation. This is followed by the *inciting incident,* which introduces the central conflict. The conflict then increases during the *development* until it reaches a high point of interest or suspense, the *climax.* The climax is followed by the *falling action,* or end, of the central conflict. Any events that occur during the *falling action* make up the *resolution* or *denouement.*

Some plots do not have all of these parts. Some stories begin with the inciting incident and end with the resolution. See *Conflict.*

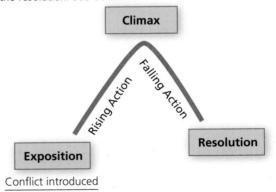

Conflict introduced

POETRY *Poetry* is one of the three major types of literature, the others being prose and drama. Most poems make use of highly concise, musical, and emotionally charged language. Many also make use of imagery, figurative language, and special devices of sound such as rhyme. Major types of poetry include *lyric poetry, narrative poetry,* and *concrete poetry.*

POINT OF VIEW *Point of view* is the perspective, or vantage point, from which a story is told. It is either a narrator outside the story or a character in the story. **First-person point of view** is told by a character who uses the first-person pronoun "I."

The two kinds of **third-person point of view,** limited and omniscient, are called "third person" because the narrator uses third-person pronouns such as he and she to refer to the characters. There is no "I" telling the story.

In stories told from the **omniscient third-person point of view,** the narrator knows and tells about what each character feels and thinks.

In stories told from the **limited third-person point of view,** the narrator relates the inner thoughts and feelings of only one character, and everything is viewed from this character's perspective.

PRESENTATION A presentation is the act of showing or demonstrating something to an audience. **Oral presentations**, spoken aloud to a live audience, may include other **visual presentation** forms, such as charts, diagrams, illustrations, and photos. Video clips and slide shows often are key parts of **digital presentations**, which are created partly or entirely on a computer.

PROSE **Prose** is the ordinary form of written language. Most writing that is not poetry, drama, or song is considered prose. Prose is one of the major genres of literature and occurs in fiction and nonfiction.

QUOTATION **Quotations** are groups of words that are taken from a text, a speech, or from an interview and are used or repeated by someone other than the original author or speaker. Quotations must be attributed to the original writer or speaker.

READ CLOSELY To **read closely** involves careful analysis of a text, its ideas, and the ways in which the author chooses to express those ideas.

REPETITION **Repetition** is the use, more than once, of any element of language—a sound, word, phrase, clause, or sentence. Repetition is used in both prose and poetry.

RESEARCH PAPER A **research paper** provides detailed information on a topic or thesis. Effective research papers are built on information from a variety of credible sources, which are credited.

RESOLUTION The **resolution** is the outcome of the conflict in a plot.

RETELLING A **retelling** of a story can be either written or oral and should include a clear sequence of events and narrative techniques such as dialogue and description.

RHYME **Rhyme** is the repetition of sounds at the ends of words. Poets use rhyme to lend a songlike quality to their verses and to emphasize certain words and ideas. Many traditional poems contain **end rhymes,** or rhyming words at the ends of lines.

Another common device is the use of **internal rhymes,** or rhyming words within lines. Internal rhyme also emphasizes the flowing nature of a poem.

RHYTHM **Rhythm** is the pattern of stressed and unstressed syllables in spoken or written language.

SCAN To **scan** is to run your eyes over the text to find answers to questions, to clarify, or to find supporting details.

SCENE A **scene** is a section of uninterrupted action in the act of a drama.

SCIENCE FICTION **Science fiction** combines elements of fiction and fantasy with scientific fact. Many science-fiction stories are set in the future.

SCRIPT A **script** is the written version of a play or film. It includes **dialogue** and **stage directions**.

SENSORY LANGUAGE **Sensory language** is writing or speech that appeals to one or more of the five senses.

SETTING The **setting** of a literary work is the time and place of the action. The setting includes all the details of a place and time—the year, the time of day, even the weather. The place may be a specific country, state, region, community, neighborhood, building, institution, or home. Details such as dialects, clothing, customs, and modes of transportation are often used to establish setting. In most stories, the setting serves as a backdrop—a context in which the characters interact. Setting can also help to create a feeling, or atmosphere.

SHORT STORY A **short story** is a brief work of fiction. Like a novel, a short story presents a sequence of events, or plot. The plot usually deals with a central conflict faced by a main character, or protagonist. The events in a short story usually communicate a message about life or human nature. This message, or central idea, is the story's theme.

SIMILE A **simile** is a figure of speech that uses **like** or **as** to make a direct comparison between two unlike ideas. Everyday speech often contains similes, such as "pale as a ghost," "good as gold," "spread like wildfire," and "clever as a fox."

SKIM To **skim** is to look over the text quickly, to get a sense of important ideas before reading.

SOUND DEVICES **Sound devices** are techniques used by writers to give musical effects to their writing. Some of these include **onomatopoeia, alliteration, rhyme, meter,** and **repetition.**

SPEAKER The **speaker** is the imaginary voice a poet uses when writing a poem. The speaker is the character who tells the poem. This character, or voice, often is not identified by name. There can be important differences between the poet and the poem's speaker.

SPEECH A *speech* is a work that is delivered orally to an audience. There are many kinds of speeches suiting almost every kind of public gathering. Types of speeches include *dramatic, persuasive,* and *informative.*

STAGE DIRECTIONS *Stage directions* are notes included in a drama to describe how the work is to be performed or staged. Stage directions are usually printed in italics and enclosed within parentheses or brackets. Some stage directions describe the movements, costumes, emotional states, and ways of speaking of the characters.

STAGING *Staging* includes the setting, lighting, costumes, special effects, and music that go into a stage performance of a drama.

SUMMARY A *summary* is a short, clear description of the main ideas of something, such as a text, a film, or a presentation. Effective summaries are objective—free from bias or evaluation.

SYMBOL A *symbol* is anything that stands for or represents something else. Symbols are common in everyday life. A dove with an olive branch in its beak is a symbol of peace. A blindfolded woman holding a balanced scale is a symbol of justice. A crown is a symbol of a king's status and authority.

SYMBOLISM *Symbolism* is the use of symbols. Symbolism plays an important role in many different types of literature. It can highlight certain elements the author wishes to emphasize and also add levels of meaning.

THEME A *theme* is a central message in a literary work that can usually be expressed in a general statement about human beings or about life. The theme of a work is not a summary of its plot.

Although a theme may be stated directly in the text, it is more often presented indirectly. When the theme is stated indirectly, or implied, the reader must figure out what the theme is by looking at what the work reveals about people or life.

TONE The *tone* of a literary work is the writer's attitude toward his or her audience and subject. The tone can often be described by a single adjective, such as *formal* or *informal, serious* or *playful, bitter* or *ironic.* Factors that contribute to the tone are word choice, sentence structure, line length, rhyme, rhythm, and repetition.

UNIVERSAL THEME A *universal theme* is a message about life that is expressed regularly in many different cultures and time periods. Folk tales, epics, and romances often address universal themes like the importance of courage, the power of love, or the danger of greed.

WEIGHTED WORDS Words that have strong emotional associations beyond their basic meanings are *weighted words.*

WORD CHOICE A writer's *word choice* is the way the writer puts those words together. Diction is part of a writer's style and may be described as formal or informal, plain or fancy, ordinary or technical, sophisticated or down-to-earth, old-fashioned or modern.

MANUAL DE TÉRMINOS LITERARIOS

ANALOGY / ANALOGÍA Una *analogía* establece una comparación entre dos o varias cosas que comparten similitudes, pero son distintas en todo lo demás.

ANECDOTE / ANÉCDOTA Una *anécdota* es un relato corto de no ficción sobre un acontecimiento extraño, interesante o divertido. Los escritores cuentan anécdotas para entretener o explicar algo importante.

ARGUMENT / ARGUMENTO En un *argumento* los escritores exponen y defienden una afirmación o una opinión, para lo cual se basan en hechos probados o razonamientos lógicos. Casi todos los argumentos tienen una *introducción*, en la que se expone una afirmación; un *desarrollo*, en el que se respalda la afirmación con evidencia; y una *conclusión*, en la que se resume o replantea la afirmación.

AUTHOR'S POINT OF VIEW / PUNTO DE VISTA DEL AUTOR La postura hacia el tema que revela el autor de un texto de no ficción muestra el *punto de vista del autor*.

AUTHOR'S PURPOSE / PROPÓSITO DEL AUTOR El *propósito del autor* es la razón principal por la que este autor o autora escribe. Por ejemplo, un autor puede buscar entretener, informar o persuadir al lector. En ocasiones un autor intenta enseñarnos una lección moral o reflexionar sobre una experiencia. Un autor puede tener más de un propósito por los que escribir.

AUTOBIOGRAPHY / AUTOBIOGRAFÍA Una *autobiografía* es la historia de la vida del propio autor. Los textos autobiográficos pueden hablar de la vida completa del autor o solo de una parte.

Como las autobiografías tratan sobre gente y acontecimientos reales, son consideradas como no ficción. La mayoría de las autobiografías están escritas en narrador en primera persona.

BIOGRAPHY / BIOGRAFÍA Una *biografía* es un tipo de texto de no ficción donde el escritor explica la historia de la vida de otra persona. La mayoría de las biografías son sobre gente famosa y admirable. Aunque las biografías están consideradas libros de no ficción, las de mayor calidad suelen compartir cualidades con los buenos textos narrativos.

BLOG / BLOG Una *entrada de blog* es un texto en línea que se aporta a un diario en línea llamado *blog*. Los autores de blogs ofrecen información o expresan su opinión sobre distintos temas.

CAUSE AND EFFECT / CAUSA Y EFECTO Un *ensayo de causa y efecto* estudia la relación que hay entre los sucesos. Los ensayos eficaces exponen claramente los sucesos y sus resultados. Para ello utilizan ejemplos, evidencia y lógica.

CHARACTER / PERSONAJE Un *personaje* es una persona o un animal que participa en la acción de una obra literaria. El personaje *principal* o protagonista es el más importante de una historia, poema u obra teatral. El personaje *secundario* participa también en la acción pero no es el centro de atención.

A menudo se clasifican los personajes como planos o redondos.

Un *personaje plano* es unilateral y a menudo estereotipado.

Un *personaje redondo*, por el contrario, está desarrollado completamente y presenta muchos rasgos (a menudo tanto defectos como virtudes). También se pueden clasificar a los personajes como dinámicos o estáticos. Un *personaje dinámico* es aquel que cambia o evoluciona a lo largo de la obra. Un *personaje estático* es aquel que no cambia.

RASGOS DEL PERSONAJE Los *rasgos del personaje* son las características particulares que hacen que cada personaje sea único.

CHARACTERIZATION / CARACTERIZACIÓN La *caracterización* es la acción de crear y desarrollar un personaje. Los autores utilizan dos métodos principales de caracterización: *directa* e *indirecta*. Cuando se utiliza la caracterización directa, el escritor describe los *rasgos del personaje* o sus características.

En cambio, cuando se describe a un personaje indirectamente, el escritor depende del lector para que pueda extraer conclusiones sobre los rasgos del personaje. A veces el escritor cuenta lo que otros personajes que participan en la historia dicen o piensan sobre el personaje en cuestión.

CHRONOLOGICAL ORDER / ORDEN CRONOLÓGICO Los escritores suelen enumerar los sucesos de la narración en *orden cronológico*, de manera que un suceso lleva al siguiente en el orden en el que tuvieron lugar.

CLIMAX / CLÍMAX El *clímax,* también llamado momento culminante, es el punto más elevado de la acción de una trama. Es el momento de mayor tensión, es decir, cuando el desenlace de la trama pende de un hilo. Ver *Trama.*

COLLABORATIVE DISCUSSION / DISCUSIÓN COLABORATIVA Se conoce como *discusión colaborativa* a la exploración de un tema en grupo, con la participación de todos los miembros del grupo.

COMEDY / COMEDIA Una *comedia* es una obra literaria, especialmente una obra de teatro, que es ligera, a menudo cómica o satírica y tiene un final feliz. Las comedias describen a personajes normales que se enfrentan a dificultades y conflictos temporales. Algunos tipos de comedia incluyen la **comedia romántica**, que contiene problemas entre amantes, y la **comedia de costumbres,** que cuestiona satíricamente las costumbres sociales de un sector de la sociedad.

COMPARISON-AND-CONTRAST ESSAY / ENSAYO DE COMPARACIÓN Y CONTRASTE Se conoce como **ensayo de comparación y contraste** al ensayo en el que el autor expone las diferencias y similitudes entre dos asuntos.

Los ensayos de comparación y contraste pueden utilizar una **organización de punto por punto** en la que primero se trata un aspecto de los dos asuntos, después otro y así sucesivamente. También se puede emplear una **organización de método de bloques** en la que primero se presentan todos los detalles de uno de los asuntos, seguidos por los detalles del otro asunto.

CONFLICT / CONFLICTO Un **conflicto** es una lucha entre fuerzas opuestas. El conflicto es uno de los elementos más importantes de los cuentos, novelas y obras de teatro porque provoca la acción. Hay dos tipos de conflictos: externos e internos.

Un **conflicto externo** se da cuando un personaje lucha contra una fuerza ajena a él, como por ejemplo otra persona. Otro tipo de conflicto externo puedo ocurrir entre un personaje y una fuerza de la naturaleza.

Un **conflicto interno** tiene lugar en la mente de un personaje. El personaje lucha por tomar una decisión, llevar a cabo una acción o frenar un sentimiento.

CONNOTATIONS / CONNOTACIONES La **connotación** de una palabra es el conjunto de ideas que se asocian con esta, más allá de su significado explícito. La connotación de una palabra puede ser personal, basada en una experiencia individual. Con frecuencia son las connotaciones culturales, aquellas que son reconocibles por la mayoría de las personas de un grupo, las que determinan la elección de un autor.

COUNTERCLAIM / CONTRAARGUMENTO Se conoce como **contraargumento** a la opinión contraria a la expresada en un argumento anterior.

CONSTRUCTIVE CRITICISM / CRÍTICA CONSTRUCTIVA Se conoce como **crítica constructiva** a las diferencias de opinión que se exponen de manera respetuosa y que tienen como fin mejorar un resultado.

CULTURAL CONTEXT / CONTEXTO CULTURAL El **contexto cultural** de una obra literaria es el entorno económico, social e histórico de los personajes. Este incluye los comportamientos y costumbres de dicho período cultural e histórico.

DENOTATION / DENOTACIÓN La **denotación** de una palabra es su significado del diccionario, independientemente de otras asociaciones que se le puedan otorgar. La denotación de la palabra *lago* sería "una masa de agua que se acumula en un terreno". "Un

lugar de vacaciones" o "un lugar adonde se puede ir de pesca" son connotaciones de la palabra *lago*.

DESCRIPTION / DESCRIPCIÓN Una **descripción** es un retrato en palabras de una persona, lugar u objeto. Los textos descriptivos utilizan imágenes que se relacionan con los cinco sentidos: vista, oído, tacto, gusto y olfato.

DIALECT / DIALECTO Un **dialecto** es la variedad de una lengua que habla un grupo o una región particular. Los dialectos se diferencian en la pronunciación, gramática y elección de las palabras utilizadas. La lengua inglesa está dividida en muchos dialectos. Por ejemplo, el inglés británico es distinto del inglés americano.

DIALOGUE / DIÁLOGO Un **diálogo** es una conversación entre personajes. En los poemas, novelas y cuentos en inglés, los diálogos se indican normalmente entre comillas para señalar que estas son las palabras exactas que dice un personaje.

En una obra de teatro, los diálogos se colocan detrás de los nombres de los personajes y no se utilizan comillas.

DICTION / DICCIÓN La **dicción** es tanto la elección de las palabras que hace un escritor como la manera de combinarlas. La dicción forma parte del estilo de un escritor y puede ser descrita como formal o informal, sencilla o elegante, corriente o técnica, sofisticada o sobria, anticuada o moderna.

DIRECT QUOTATIONS / CITAS DIRECTAS Las **citas directas** presentan las palabras exactas que dijo alguien y se ponen entre comillas. Las **entrevistas personales** son uno de los métodos de investigación que utilizan los autores como fuente de citas directas.

DRAMA / DRAMA Un **drama** es una historia escrita para ser representada por actores. Aunque está destinada a ser representada, también se puede, únicamente, leer su texto e imaginar la acción. El **texto dramático**, o guión, está compuesto de diálogos y acotaciones. Los **diálogos** son palabras que dicen los personajes. Las **acotaciones** aparecen normalmente en cursiva e indican cómo deben verse, moverse o hablar los personajes. También describen el decorado, los efectos de sonido y la iluminación.

Los dramas suelen estar divididos en distintas partes denominadas **actos.** Los actos aparecen a menudo divididos en partes más pequeñas denominadas **escenas.**

EDITORIAL / EDITORIAL Un **editorial** es un tipo de argumento que suele aparecer en los periódicos y que adopta una postura en un asunto determinado.

ESSAY / ENSAYO Un **ensayo** es un texto de no ficción corto sobre un tema particular. La mayoría de los ensayos se concentran en un único aspeco fundamental y tienen una introducción clara, un desarrollo y una conclusión.

Hay muchos tipos de ensayos. Un **ensayo informal** emplea lenguaje coloquial y conversacional. Un **ensayo histórico** nos presenta hechos, explicaciones y conocimientos sobre acontecimientos históricos.

Un *ensayo expositivo* expone una idea desglosándola. Un *ensayo narrativo* cuenta una historia sobre una experiencia real. Un *ensayo informativo* explica un proceso. Un *ensayo argumentativo* ofrece una opinión y la argumenta. Un *ensayo humorístico* utiliza el humor para lograr el propósito del autor. Un *ensayo explicativo* aclara, define e interpreta ideas, acontecimientos o procesos. En un *ensayo reflexivo* el autor presenta sus pensamientos y sentimientos o reflexiones sobre una experiencia o idea.

EXAMPLE / EJEMPLO Un *ejemplo* es un dato, idea o suceso que respalda un concepto o una visión de las cosas.

EXPOSITION / PLANTEAMIENTO En el argumento de una historia o drama, el *planteamiento* o introducción es la parte de la obra que presenta a los personajes, escenarios y situación básica.

EXPOSITORY WRITING / TEXTO EXPOSITIVO Un *texto expositivo* es un texto que explica e informa.

FANTASY / LITERATURA FANTÁSTICA La *literatura fantástica* son textos con elementos muy imaginativos que no pueden encontrarse en la vida real. Algunos ejemplos de literatura fantástica incluyen historias que contienen elementos supernaturales, historias que recuerdan a los cuentos de hadas, historias que tratan de lugares y criaturas imaginarias e historias de ciencia ficción.

FICTION / FICCIÓN La *ficción* son obras en prosa que hablan de sucesos y personajes imaginarios. Los relatos y las novelas son obras de ficción. Algunos escritores se inspiran para sus obras de ficción en sucesos y personas reales, a los que añaden también personajes, diálogos, escenarios y tramas inventados. Otros escritores se sirven únicamente de la imaginación.

FIGURATIVE LANGUAGE / LENGUAJE FIGURADO El *lenguaje figurado* es un texto o diálogo que no se debe interpretar literalmente. A los numerosos tipos de lenguaje figurado se los llama *figuras retóricas.* Algunas de las más comunes son las metáforas, las personificaciones y los símiles. Los escritores utilizan el lenguaje figurado para expresar ideas de una manera imaginativa y vívida.

FRAME STORY / NARRACIÓN ENMARCADA Una *narración enmarcada* es una historia que pone entre paréntesis o enmarca otra historia o grupo de historias. Este recurso literario crea la estructura narrativa de una historia dentro de otra historia.

FREE VERSE / VERSO LIBRE El *verso libre* es poesía que no tiene una *estructura formal*; es decir, que no sigue un patrón rítmico ni métrico normal. El poeta es libre de escribir versos de la extensión que prefiera y con un número libre de acentos. Por consiguiente, el verso libre es menos restrictivo que el *verso métrico*, en el que cada verso debe contener acentos y un número concreto de sílabas.

GENRE / GÉNERO Un *género* es una clase o tipo de literatura. La literatura se divide normalmente en tres géneros principales: poesía, prosa y drama. Cada uno de estos géneros está, a su vez, dividido en otros géneros menores:

    1. *Poesía:* poesía lírica, poesía concreta, poesía dramática, poesía narrativa, poesía épica

    2. *Prosa:* ficción (novelas y cuentos cortos) y no ficción (biografías, autobiografías, cartas, ensayos y reportajes)

    3. *Drama:* drama serio y tragedia, comedia, melodrama y farsa

HISTORICAL CONTEXT / CONTEXTO HISTÓRICO El *contexto histórico* de una obra literaria lo constituyen los verdaderos acontecimientos y tendencias político-sociales de la época. Cuando una obra tiene lugar en el pasado, el conocimiento previo sobre ese período histórico puede ayudar al lector a comprender la ambientación, trasfondo, cultura y mensaje, así como las actitudes y acciones de sus personajes. Un lector también debe tener en cuenta el contexto histórico en el que el escritor creó su obra, ya que puede ser distinto del contexto real en el que se desarrolla la obra.

HUMOR / HUMOR El *humor* es una forma de escribir que incita a la risa. Si bien es cierto que la mayoría de los humoristas tratan de entretener, también se puede utilizar el humor para transmitir un tema serio.

HYPERBOLE / HIPÉRBOLE La *hipérbole* es un tipo de figura retórica que utiliza la exageración para provocar un efecto en el lector.

IDIOM / MODISMOS Los *modismos* son expresiones idiomáticas que tienen un significado particular en una lengua o región.

IMAGERY / IMAGINERÍA La *imaginería* es la técnica de escribir con imágenes.

IMAGES / IMÁGENES La *imágenes* son palabras o frases que se relacionan con uno o varios de los cinco sentidos. Los escritores utilizan imágenes para describir qué apariencia tienen, cómo suenan, sienten, saben y huelen las personas u objetos descritos. Los poetas suelen dibujar imágenes o hacer una descripción visual que se vincula con los sentidos. Estas descripciones visuales nos ayudan a experimentar el poema en su totalidad.

INFERENCES / INFERENCIAS Una inferencia es una suposición que se basa en pistas. Es frecuente en la literatura que los autores no lo expliquen todo; les corresponde a los lectores "llenar los espacios en blanco" e inferir detalles sobre los personajes, sucesos y ambiente.

IRONY / IRONÍA Una *ironía* es una contradicción entre lo que ocurre realmente y lo que se espera que pase. Hay tres tipos principales de ironía. La *ironía situacional* que se da cuando ocurre algo que se contradice directamente con aquello que los personajes o la audiencia espera. La *ironía verbal* que se crea cuando se usan las palabras para insinuar algo distinto a su significado literal. La *ironía dramática,* en la que audiencia conoce algo que el personaje o la persona que habla no sabe. El resultado es el suspenso o el humor.

JOURNAL / DIARIO Un *diario* es un relato periódico o diario de acontecimientos y reflexiones u opiniones que el escritor tiene sobre esos acontecimientos. Los diarios personales no se escriben normalmente para ser publicados, pero en ocasiones se publican más tarde con el permiso del autor o de la familia del autor.

LETTERS / CARTAS Una *carta* es una comunicación escrita de una persona a otra. En las cartas personales, los escritores comparten información, así como sus opiniones y sentimientos sobre otra persona o grupo. Aunque las cartas no se escriben normalmente para ser publicadas, a veces se publican más tarde con el permiso del autor o de la familia del autor.

LYRIC POEM / POEMA LÍRICO Un *poema lírico* es un verso con mucha musicalidad que expresa las observaciones y sentimientos de una sola persona. Crea una impresión única y unificada.

MAIN IDEA / IDEA PRINCIPAL La *idea principal* es la *idea central* o lo más importante de un texto.

MEDIA ACCOUNTS / REPORTAJES PERIODÍSTICOS Los *reportajes periodísticos* son relatos, explicaciones, opiniones o descripciones escritas para televisión, radio, periódicos o revistas. Si bien algunos reportajes periodísticos solo relatan hechos, otros incluyen también las opiniones y reflexiones del autor.

METAPHOR / METÁFORA Una *metáfora* es una figura retórica que se utiliza para identificar una cosa con algo distinto. Una metáfora, al igual que un símil, se obtiene analizando las similitudes que comparten dos cosas distintas.

MONOLOGUE / MONÓLOGO Un *monólogo* en una obra de teatro es un parlamento por parte de un personaje. El personaje habla desde el punto de vista de primera persona y comparte sus pensamientos y sentimientos.

MOOD / ATMÓSFERA La *atmósfera* es la sensación que un texto produce en el lector. Los escritores crean la atmósfera mediante el uso de imaginería, su elección de palabras y los detalles descriptivos.

MOTIVE / MOTIVACIÓN Una *motivación* es una razón que explica total o parcialmente las opiniones, sentimientos, acciones o diálogos de los personajes. El escritor intenta exponer las motivaciones o motivos de la manera más clara posible. Si las motivaciones de un personaje principal no están claras, el personaje no será creíble.

Las motivaciones que mueven con frecuencia a los personajes son necesidades tales como encontrar comida o un refugio. Además les pueden motivar también sentimientos como el miedo, el amor y el orgullo. Las motivaciones pueden ser claras u ocultas.

NARRATION / NARRACIÓN Una *narración* es un texto que cuenta una historia. También se denomina narración a la acción de contar una historia. Una historia contada en ficción, no ficción, poesía o incluso en drama es conocida como narración.

Los escritores emplean distintas técnicas para darles vida a sus historias. Por ejemplo, las narraciones suelen tener una trama, un escenario, varios personajes y un tema. La experiencia de los lectores se enriquece con el uso de distintos *ritmos narrativos*, mediante los que el escritor acelera o desacelera los sucesos de la narración para crear una variedad de efectos como el suspenso.

NARRATIVE / TEXTO NARRATIVO Un *texto narrativo* es una historia. Las novelas y los cuentos son tipos de textos narrativos de ficción. Las biografías y las autobiografías son textos narrativos de no ficción.

NARRATIVE POEM / POEMA NARRATIVO Un *poema narrativo* es una historia contada en verso. Un poema narrativo cuenta a menudo con todos los elementos de los cuentos; incluye personajes, conflicto y trama.

NARRATOR / NARRADOR Un *narrador* es la persona o personaje que cuenta una historia. El punto de vista del narrador es la manera en la que él o ella ve las cosas. Un *narrador en tercera persona* es aquel que solo habla de la acción sin implicarse en ella. Un *narrador en primera persona* es aquel que cuenta una historia y además participa en su acción.

NONFICTION / NO FICCIÓN Una *no ficción* es un texto en prosa que presenta y explica ideas, o que trata de personas, lugares, objetos o acontecimientos de la vida real. Las autobiografías, biografías, ensayos, reportajes, cartas, memorandos y artículos periodísticos son todos diferentes tipos de no ficción.

NOVEL / NOVELA Una *novela* es una obra larga de ficción. Las novelas contienen elementos tales como los personajes, la trama, el conflicto y los escenarios. Los escritores de novelas o novelistas desarrollan estos elementos. Aparte de tu trama principal, una novela puede contener una o varias subtramas, o narraciones independientes o relacionadas con la trama principal. Una novela puede contener también diversos temas. Ver *Ficción* y *Cuento.*

ONOMATOPOEIA / ONOMATOPEYA Una *onomatopeya* es el uso de las palabras que imitan sonidos. *Cataplam, zzzzzz, zas, din don, glu glu glu, achís* y *crag* son ejemplos de onomatopeyas El *cuco,* la *urraca* y el *pitirre* son nombres onomatopéyicos de aves.

ORGANIZATION / ORGANIZACIÓN La estructura de un texto o de una presentación audiovisual es lo que se conoce como su *organización*. Algunas estructuras organizativas comunes son: causa y efecto, comparación y contraste, orden de importancia y orden cronológico. Los escritores eligen la organización que mejor se adapte al tema y propósito de su texto.

OXYMORON / OXÍMORON Un *oxímoron* (pl. *oxímoron*) es una figura retórica que vincula dos palabras contrarias u opuestas con el fin de indicar que una idea o situación, que parece contradictoria o incoherente a simple vista, encierra algo de verdad cuando la analizamos detenidamente.

PARAPHRASE / PARÁFRASIS Una *paráfrasis* es cuando explicamos un texto con nuestras propias palabras.

PERSONIFICATION / PERSONIFICACIÓN La *personificación* es una figura retórica con la que se atribuyen características humanas a un animal o una cosa.

PERSUASION / PERSUASIÓN La *persuasión* se utiliza cuando escribimos o hablamos para convencer a nuestro lector o interlocutor de que debe adoptar una opinión concreta o tomar un rumbo en sus decisiones. Los editoriales periodísticos y las cartas del editor emplean la persuasión. Asimismo, la publicidad y los discursos electorales que los políticos pronuncian en campaña también la utilizan.

Los escritores emplean distintas técnicas persuasivas para defender sus opiniones. Las *apelaciones a la autoridad* usan lo que han dicho diversos expertos. Las *apelaciones a las emociones* usan palabras que transmiten sentimientos profundos. Las *apelaciones a la razón* utilizan argumentos lógicos fundamentados con datos.

PLAYWRIGHT / DRAMATURGO Un *dramaturgo* es una persona que escribe obras de teatro. A William Shakespeare se le considera el mejor dramaturgo de la literatura inglesa.

PLOT / TRAMA Una *trama* es la secuencia de acontecimientos en la cual cada uno de estos acontecimientos es el resultado de otro acontecimiento anterior y la causa de uno nuevo que lo sigue. En la mayoría de novelas, dramas, relatos y poemas narrativos, la trama contiene personajes y un conflicto central. La trama suele comenzar con un *planteamiento* o introducción que presenta el escenario, los personajes y la situación básica. A esto le sigue el *suceso desencadenante*, que presenta el conflicto central. El conflico va aumentando durante el *desarrollo* hasta que alcanza el punto más elevado de interés o suspenso, el *clímax.* El clímax va seguido de una *acción descendente* del conflicto central. Todos los acontecimientos que ocurren durante la *acción descendente* forman el *desenlace.*

Algunas tramas no tienen todas estas partes. Algunas historias comienzan con el suceso desencadenante y acaban con un desenlace. Ver *Conflicto.*

Presentación del conflicto

POETRY / POESÍA La *poesía* es uno de los tres géneros más importantes de la literatura junto con la prosa y el drama. La mayoría de los poemas utilizan lenguaje muy conciso, musical y cargado de emoción. Muchos también emplean imágenes, lenguaje figurado y recursos sonoros especiales como la rima. Los tipos de poesía más importante son: la *poesía lírica,* la *poesía narrativa* y la *poesía concreta.*

POINT OF VIEW / PUNTO DE VISTA El *punto de vista* es la perspectiva, o el punto de observación, desde la que se cuenta una historia. Puede tratarse de un narrador situado fuera de la historia o un personaje dentro de ella. El *punto de vista en primera persona* corresponde a un personaje que utiliza el pronombre "yo" o la conjugación de los verbos en primera persona de singular. Los dos tipos de *punto de vista en tercera persona*, limitado y omnisciente, son conocidos como "tercera persona" porque el narrador utiliza los pronombres de tercera persona como "él" y "ella" y la conjugación de los verbos en tercera persona para referirse a los personajes. Por el contrario, no se utiliza el pronombre "yo".

En las historias contadas desde el *punto de vista en tercera persona omnisciente*, el narrador sabe y cuenta todo lo que sienten y piensan los personajes.

En las historia contadas desde el *punto de vista en tercera pesona limitado*, el narrador relata los pensamientos y sentimientos de solo un personaje, y se cuenta todo desde la perspectiva de ese personaje.

PRESENTATION / PRESENTACIÓN Una *presentación* es el acto de mostrar o enseñar algo a una audiencia. Las *presentaciones orales*, que se comunican a una audiencia en vivo, pueden incluir *presentaciones visuales* como tablas, diagramas, ilustraciones y fotografías. Los videoclips y las diapositivas suelen ser parte de las *presentaciones digitales*, que se crean parcial o totalmente en computadora.

PROSE / PROSA La *prosa* es la forma más corriente del lenguaje escrito. La mayoría de los textos escritos que no se consideran poesía, drama o canción son textos en prosa.

La prosa es uno de los géneros más importantes de la literatura y puede ser de ficción o de no ficción.

QUOTATION / CITA Las *citas* son grupos de palabras que se toman de un texto, de un discurso o de una entrevista y que alguien distinto al autor original las usa o repite. Siempre se debe informar quién es el autor original de la cita.

READ CLOSELY / LEER CON ATENCIÓN *Leer con atención* conlleva un análisis cuidadoso del texto, sus ideas y la manera en la que el autor expresa esas ideas.

REPETITION / REPETICIÓN La *repetición* se da cuando se utiliza más de una vez cualquier elemento del lenguaje (un sonido, una palabra, una expresión, un sintagma o una oración). La repetición se emplea tanto en prosa como en poesía.

RETELLING / TRABAJO DE INVESTIGACIÓN Un *trabajo de investigación* ofrece información detallada sobre un tema. Los trabajos de investigación eficaces se fundamentan en una variedad de fuentes fiables que se citan.

RESOLUTION / DESENLACE El *desenlace* es la resolución del conflicto en una trama.

RETELLING / VOLVER A CONTAR Las historias se pueden *volver a contar* de manera escrita u oral. Al volverse a contar una historia, se debe seguir una secuencia clara de los sucesos y utilizar técnicas narrativas como el diálogo y la descripción.

RHYME / RIMA La *rima* es la repetición de los sonidos finales de las palabras. Los poetas emplean la rima para revestir de musicalidad sus versos y resaltar ciertas palabras e ideas. Muchos poemas tradicionales contienen *rimas finales* o palabras rimadas al final de los versos.

Otro recurso muy común es el uso de *rimas internas* o palabras que riman entre ellas en un mismo verso. La rima interna también resalta la fluidez propia de un poema.

RHYTHM / RITMO El *ritmo* es el patrón de sílabas acentuadas y no acentuadas en el lenguaje hablado o escrito.

SCAN / OJEAR *Ojear* es mirar por encima un texto para buscar la respuesta a una pregunta, clarificar algo o buscar detalles de apoyo.

SCENE / ESCENA Una *escena* es una sección de acción ininterrumpida dentro de alguno de los actos de un drama.

SCIENCE FICTION / CIENCIA FICCIÓN La *ciencia ficción* combina elementos de ficción y fantásticos con hechos científicos. Muchas historias de cienca ficción están situadas en el futuro.

SCRIPT / GUIÓN Un *guión* es la versión escrita de una obra de teatro o de una película. Los guiones se componen de *diálogos* y *acotaciones*.

SENSORY LANGUAGE / LENGUAJE SENSORIAL El *lenguaje sensorial* es texto o diálogo que tiene relación con uno o varios de los cinco sentidos.

SETTING / ESCENARIO El *escenario* de una obra literaria es el tiempo y lugar en los que ocurre la acción. El escenario incluye todos los detalles sobre el tiempo y el lugar: el año, el momento del día o incluso el tiempo atmosférico. El lugar puede ser un país concreto, un estado, una región, una comunidad, un barrio, un edificio, una institución o el propio hogar. Los detalles como los dialectos, ropa, costumbres y medios de trasporte se emplean con frecuencia para componer el escenario. En la mayoría de historias, los escenarios sirven de telón de fondo, es decir, de contexto en el que los personajes interactúan. El escenario también puede contribuir a crear una determinada sensación o un ambiente.

SHORT STORY / CUENTO Un *cuento* es una obra corta de ficción. Al igual que sucede en una novela, los cuentos presentan una secuencia de acontecimientos o trama. La trama suele contener un conflico central al que se enfrenta un personaje principal o protagonista. Los acontecimientos en un cuento normalmente comunican un mensaje sobre la vida o la naturaleza humana. Este mensaje o idea central es el tema de la historia.

SIMILE / SÍMIL Un *símil* es una figura retórica que utiliza *como* o *igual que* para establecer una comparación entre dos ideas distintas. Las conversaciones que mantenemos a diario también contienen símiles como, por ejemplo, "pálido como un muerto", "se propaga igual que un incendio" y "listo como un zorro".

SKIM / ECHAR UN VISTAZO *Echar un vistazo* a un texto es mirarlo rápidamente para tener una idea de lo más importante antes de comenzar a leerlo.

SOUND DEVICES / RECURSOS SONOROS Los *recursos sonoros* o fónicos son técnicas utilizadas por los escritores para dotar de musicalidad a sus textos. Entre ellos se incluyen la **onomatopeya**, la **aliteración**, la **rima**, la **métrica** y la **repetición**.

SPEAKER / YO POÉTICO El *yo poético* es la voz imaginaria que emplea un poeta cuando escribe un poema. El yo poético es el personaje que cuenta el poema. Este personaje o voz no suele identificarse con un nombre. Pueden existir notables diferencias entre el poeta y el yo poético.

SPEECH / DISCURSO Un *discurso* es una creación que se pronuncia de manera oral ante una audiencia. Hay muchas clases de discursos que se ajustan a diversos tipos de reuniones y actos públicos. Algunos tipos de discursos son el **dramático**, el **persuasivo** y el **informativo**.

STAGE DIRECTIONS / ACOTACIONES Las *acotaciones* son las notas de un texto dramático y en las que se describe como se debe interpretar o escenificar la obra. Las acotaciones suelen aparecer en cursiva y encerradas entre paréntesis o corchetes. Algunas acotaciones describen los movimientos, el vestuario, los estados de ánimo y el modo en el que deben hablar los personajes.

STAGING / ESCENOGRAFÍA La *escenografía* engloba la ambientación, iluminación, vestuario, efectos especiales y música que debe aparecer en el escenario donde se representa un drama.

SUMMARY / RESUMEN Un *resumen* es una descripción corta y clara de las ideas principales de algo como un texto, una película o una presentación. Los resúmenes eficaces son objetivos; es decir, son imparciales y no ofrecen valoraciones.

SYMBOL / SÍMBOLO Un *símbolo* es algo que representa una cosa diferente. Los símbolos son muy comunes en nuestra vida diaria. Una paloma con una rama de olivo en el pico es un símbolo de la paz. Una mujer con los ojos vendados sujetando una balanza es un símbolo de la justicia. Una corona es un símbolo del poder y la autoridad de un rey.

SYMBOLISM / SIMBOLISMO El *simbolismo* es el uso de los símbolos. El simbolismo juega un papel importante en muchos tipos de literatura. Puede ayudar a destacar algunos elementos que el autor quiere subrayar y añadir otros niveles de significado.

THEME / TEMA El *tema* es el mensaje central de una obra literaria. Se puede entender como una generalización sobre los seres humanos o la vida. El tema de una obra no es el resumen de su trama.

Aunque el tema puede exponerse directamente en el texto, se suele presentar indirectamente. Cuando se expone el tema indirecta o implícitamente, el lector lo podrá deducir al observar lo que se muestra en la obra sobre la vida y las personas.

TONE / TONO El *tono* de una obra literaria es la actitud del escritor hacia sus lectores o hacia aquello sobre lo que escribe. El tono se puede describir con un único adjetivo como, por ejemplo, *formal* o *informal*, *serio* o *jocoso*, *amargo* o *irónico*. Los factores que contribuyen a crear el tono son la elección de las palabras, la estructura de la oración, el tamaño de un verso, la rima, el ritmo y la repetición.

UNIVERSAL THEME / TEMA UNIVERSAL Un *tema universal* es un mensaje sobre la vida que se expresa habitualmente en muchas culturas y períodos históricos diferentes. Los cuentos populares, las epopeyas y los romances suelen abordar temas universales como la importancia de la valentía, el poder del amor o el peligro de la avaricia.

WEIGHTED WORDS / PALABRAS EMOCIONALMENTE CARGADAS Las palabras que producen fuertes asociaciones emocionales son *palabras emocionalmente cargadas.*

WORD CHOICE / ELECCIÓN DE PALABRAS La *elección de palabras* es la forma que tiene un escritor de escoger su lenguaje. La dicción es parte del estilo de un escritor y se describe como formal o informal, llana o elaborada, común o técnica, sofisticada o popular, anticuada o moderna.

PARTS OF SPEECH

Every English word, depending on its meaning and its use in a sentence, can be identified as one of the eight parts of speech. These are nouns, pronouns, verbs, adjectives, adverbs, prepositions, conjunctions, and interjections. Understanding the parts of speech will help you learn the rules of English grammar and usage.

Nouns A **noun** names a person, place, or thing. A **common noun** names any one of a class of persons, places, or things. A **proper noun** names a specific person, place, or thing.

Common Noun	Proper Noun
writer, country, novel	Charles Dickens, Great Britain, *Hard Times*

Pronouns A **pronoun** is a word that stands for one or more nouns. The word to which a pronoun refers (whose place it takes) is the **antecedent** of the pronoun.

A **personal pronoun** refers to the person speaking (first person); the person spoken to (second person); or the person, place, or thing spoken about (third person).

	Singular	Plural
First Person	I, me, my, mine	we, us, our, ours
Second Person	you, your, yours	you, your, yours
Third Person	he, him, his, she, her, hers, it, its	they, them, their, theirs

A **reflexive pronoun** reflects the action of a verb back on its subject. It indicates that the person or thing performing the action also is receiving the action.

I keep *myself* fit by taking a walk every day.

An **intensive pronoun** adds emphasis to a noun or pronoun.

It took the work of the president *himself* to pass the law.

A **demonstrative** pronoun points out a specific person(s), place(s), or thing(s).

this, that, these, those

A **relative pronoun** begins a subordinate clause and connects it to another idea in the sentence.

that, which, who, whom, whose

An **interrogative pronoun** begins a question.

what, which, who, whom, whose

An **indefinite pronoun** refers to a person, place, or thing that may or may not be specifically named.

all, another, any, both, each, everyone, few, most, none, no one, somebody

Verbs A **verb** expresses action or the existence of a state or condition.

An **action verb** tells what action someone or something is performing.

gather, read, work, jump, imagine, analyze, conclude

A **linking verb** connects the subject with another word that identifies or describes the subject. The most common linking verb is *be*.

appear, be, become, feel, look, remain, seem, smell, sound, stay, taste

A **helping verb,** or **auxiliary verb,** is added to a main verb to make a verb phrase.

be, do, have, should, can, could, may, might, must, will, would

Adjectives An **adjective** modifies a noun or pronoun by describing it or giving it a more specific meaning. An adjective answers the questions:

What kind?	*purple* hat, *happy* face, *loud* sound
Which one?	*this* bowl
How many?	*three* cars
How much?	*enough* food

The articles *the, a,* and *an* are adjectives.

A **proper adjective** is an adjective derived from a proper noun.

French, Shakespearean

Adverbs An **adverb** modifies a verb, an adjective, or another adverb by telling *where, when, how,* or *to what extent*.

will answer *soon, extremely* sad, calls *more* often

Prepositions A **preposition** relates a noun or pronoun that appears with it to another word in the sentence.

Dad made a meal *for* us. We talked *till* dusk. Bo missed school *because of* his illness.

Conjunctions A **conjunction** connects words or groups of words. A **coordinating conjunction** joins words or groups of words of equal rank.

bread *and* cheese, brief *but* powerful

Correlative conjunctions are used in pairs to connect words or groups of words of equal importance.

both Luis *and* Rosa, *neither* you *nor* I

Subordinating conjunctions indicate the connection between two ideas by placing one below the other in rank or importance. A subordinating conjunction introduces a subordinate, or dependent, clause.

We will miss her *if* she leaves. Hank shrieked *when* he slipped on the ice.

Interjections An **interjection** expresses feeling or emotion. It is not related to other words in the sentence.

ah, hey, ouch, well, yippee

PHRASES AND CLAUSES

Phrases A **phrase** is a group of words that does not have both a subject and a verb and that functions as one part of speech. A phrase expresses an idea but cannot stand alone.

Prepositional Phrases A **prepositional phrase** is a group of words that begins with a preposition and ends with a noun or pronoun that is the **object of the preposition.**

before dawn   as a result of the rain

An **adjective phrase** is a prepositional phrase that modifies a noun or pronoun.

Eliza appreciates the beauty **of a well-crafted poem.**

An **adverb phrase** is a prepositional phrase that modifies a verb, an adjective, or an adverb.

She reads Spenser's sonnets **with great pleasure.**

Appositive Phrases An **appositive** is a noun or pronoun placed next to another noun or pronoun to add information about it. An **appositive phrase** consists of an appositive and its modifiers.

Mr. Roth, **my music teacher,** is sick.

Verbal Phrases A **verbal** is a verb form that functions as a different part of speech (not as a verb) in a sentence. **Participles, gerunds,** and **infinitives** are verbals.

A **verbal phrase** includes a verbal and any modifiers or complements it may have. Verbal phrases may function as nouns, as adjectives, or as adverbs.

A **participle** is a verb form that can act as an adjective. Present participles end in *-ing;* past participles of regular verbs end in *-ed.*

A **participial phrase** consists of a participle and its modifiers or complements. The entire phrase acts as an adjective.

Jenna's backpack, **loaded with equipment,** was heavy.

Barking incessantly, the dogs chased the squirrels out of sight.

A **gerund** is a verb form that ends in *-ing* and is used as a noun.

A **gerund phrase** consists of a gerund with any modifiers or complements, all acting together as a noun.

Taking photographs of wildlife is her main hobby. [acts as subject]

We always enjoy **listening to live music.** [acts as object]

An **infinitive** is a verb form, usually preceded by *to,* that can act as a noun, an adjective, or an adverb.

An **infinitive phrase** consists of an infinitive and its modifiers or complements, and sometimes its subject, all acting together as a single part of speech.

She tries **to get out into the wilderness often.** [acts as a noun; direct object of *tries*]

The Tigers are the team **to beat.** [acts as an adjective; describes *team*]

I drove twenty miles **to witness the event.** [acts as an adverb; tells why I drove]

Clauses A **clause** is a group of words with its own subject and verb.

Independent Clauses An independent clause can stand by itself as a complete sentence.

George Orwell wrote with extraordinary insight.

Subordinate Clauses A subordinate clause cannot stand by itself as a complete sentence. Subordinate clauses always appear connected in some way with one or more independent clauses.

George Orwell, **who wrote with extraordinary insight,** produced many politically relevant works.

An **adjective clause** is a subordinate clause that acts as an adjective. It modifies a noun or a pronoun by telling *what kind* or *which one.* Also called relative clauses, adjective clauses usually begin with a **relative pronoun:** *who, which, that, whom,* or *whose.*

"The Lamb" is the poem **that I memorized for class.**

An **adverb clause** is a subordinate clause that, like an adverb, modifies a verb, an adjective, or an adverb. An adverb clause tells *where, when, in what way, to what extent, under what condition,* or *why.*

The students will read another poetry collection **if their schedule allows.**
When I recited the poem, Mr. Lopez was impressed.

A **noun clause** is a subordinate clause that acts as a noun.

William Blake survived on **whatever he made as an engraver.**

SENTENCE STRUCTURE

Subject and Predicate A **sentence** is a group of words that expresses a complete thought. A sentence has two main parts: a *subject* and a *predicate*.

A **fragment** is a group of words that does not express a complete thought. It lacks an independent clause.

The **subject** tells *whom* or *what* the sentence is about. The **predicate** tells what the subject of the sentence does or is.

A subject or a predicate can consist of a single word or of many words. All the words in the subject make up the **complete subject.** All the words in the predicate make up the **complete predicate.**

Complete Subject	Complete Predicate
Both of those girls	have already read *Macbeth*.

The **simple subject** is the essential noun, pronoun, or group of words acting as a noun that cannot be left out of the complete subject. The **simple predicate** is the essential verb or verb phrase that cannot be left out of the complete predicate.

Both of those girls | **have** already **read** *Macbeth*.
[Simple subject: *Both;* simple predicate: *have read*]

A **compound subject** is two or more subjects that have the same verb and are joined by a conjunction.

Neither the horse nor the driver looked tired.

A **compound predicate** is two or more verbs that have the same subject and are joined by a conjunction.

She **sneezed and coughed** throughout the trip.

Complements A **complement** is a word or word group that completes the meaning of the subject or verb in a sentence. There are four kinds of complements: *direct objects, indirect objects, objective complements,* and *subject complements.*

A **direct object** is a noun, a pronoun, or a group of words acting as a noun that receives the action of a transitive verb.

We watched the **liftoff.**
She drove **Zach** to the launch site.

An **indirect object** is a noun or pronoun that appears with a direct object and names the person or thing to which or for which something is done.

He sold the **family** a mirror. [The direct object is *mirror.*]

An **objective complement** is an adjective or noun that appears with a direct object and describes or renames it.

The decision made her **unhappy.**
[The direct object is *her.*]
Many consider Shakespeare the greatest **playwright.** [The direct object is *Shakespeare.*]

A **subject complement** follows a linking verb and tells something about the subject. There are two kinds: *predicate nominatives* and *predicate adjectives.*

A **predicate nominative** is a noun or pronoun that follows a linking verb and identifies or renames the subject.

"A Modest Proposal" is a **pamphlet.**

A **predicate adjective** is an adjective that follows a linking verb and describes the subject of the sentence.

"A Modest Proposal" is **satirical.**

Classifying Sentences by Structure

Sentences can be classified according to the kind and number of clauses they contain. The four basic sentence structures are *simple, compound, complex,* and *compound-complex.*

A **simple sentence** consists of one independent clause.

Terrence enjoys modern British literature.

A **compound sentence** consists of two or more independent clauses. The clauses are joined by a conjunction or a semicolon.

Terrence enjoys modern British literature, but his brother prefers the classics.

A **complex sentence** consists of one independent clause and one or more subordinate clauses.

Terrence, who reads voraciously, enjoys modern British literature.

A **compound-complex sentence** consists of two or more independent clauses and one or more subordinate clauses.

Terrence, who reads voraciously, enjoys modern British literature, but his brother prefers the classics.

Classifying Sentences by Function

Sentences can be classified according to their function or purpose. The four types are *declarative, interrogative, imperative,* and *exclamatory.*

A **declarative sentence** states an idea and ends with a period.

An **interrogative sentence** asks a question and ends with a question mark.

An **imperative sentence** gives an order or a direction and ends with either a period or an exclamation mark.

An **exclamatory sentence** conveys a strong emotion and ends with an exclamation mark.

PARAGRAPH STRUCTURE

An effective paragraph is organized around one **main idea,** which is often stated in a **topic sentence.** The other sentences support the main idea. To give the paragraph **unity,** make sure the connection between each sentence and the main idea is clear.

Unnecessary Shift in Person

Do not change needlessly from one grammatical person to another. Keep the person consistent in your sentences.

Max went to the bakery, but **you** can't buy mints there. [shift from third person to second person]

Max went to the bakery, but **he** can't buy mints there. [consistent]

Unnecessary Shift in Voice

Do not change needlessly from active voice to passive voice in your use of verbs.

Elena and I **searched** the trail for evidence, but no clues **were found.** [shift from active voice to passive voice]

Elena and I **searched** the trail for evidence, but we **found** no clues. [consistent]

AGREEMENT

Subject and Verb Agreement

A singular subject must have a singular verb. A plural subject must have a plural verb.

Dr. Boone uses a telescope to view the night sky.

The **students use** a telescope to view the night sky.

A verb always agrees with its subject, not its object.

Incorrect: The best part of the show were the jugglers.

Correct: The best part of the show was the jugglers.

A phrase or clause that comes between a subject and verb does not affect subject-verb agreement.

His **theory,** as well as his claims, **lacks** support.

Two subjects joined by *and* usually take a plural verb.

The **dog** and the **cat are** healthy.

Two singular subjects joined by *or* or *nor* take a singular verb.

The **dog** or the **cat is** hiding.

Two plural subjects joined by *or* or *nor* take a plural verb.

The **dogs** or the **cats are** coming home with us.

When a singular and a plural subject are joined by *or* or *nor,* the verb agrees with the closer subject.

Either the **dogs** or the **cat is** behind the door.

Either the **cat** or the **dogs are** behind the door.

Pronoun and Antecedent Agreement

Pronouns must agree with their antecedents in number and gender. Use singular pronouns with singular antecedents and plural pronouns with plural antecedents.

Doris Lessing uses **her** writing to challenge ideas about women's roles.

Writers often use **their** skills to promote social change.

Use a singular pronoun when the antecedent is a singular indefinite pronoun such as *anybody, each, either, everybody, neither, no one, one,* or *someone.*

Judge **each** of the articles on **its** merits.

Use a plural pronoun when the antecedent is a plural indefinite pronoun such as *both, few, many,* or *several.*

Both of the articles have **their** flaws.

The indefinite pronouns *all, any, more, most, none,* and *some* can be singular or plural depending on the number of the word to which they refer.

Most of the *books* are in **their** proper places.

Most of the *book* has been torn from **its** binding.

USING VERBS

Principal Parts of Regular and Irregular Verbs

A verb has four principal parts:

Present	Present Participle	Past	Past Participle
learn	learning	learned	learned
discuss	discussing	discussed	discussed
stand	standing	stood	stood
begin	beginning	began	begun

Regular verbs such as *learn* and *discuss* form the past and past participle by adding *-ed* to the present form. **Irregular verbs** such as *stand* and *begin* form the past and past participle in other ways. If you are in doubt about the principal parts of an irregular verb, check a dictionary.

The Tenses of Verbs

The different tenses of verbs indicate the time an action or condition occurs.

The **present tense** expresses an action that happens regularly or states a current condition or general truth.
   Tourists **flock** to the site yearly.

Daily exercise **is** good for your heallth.

The **past tense** expresses a completed action or a condition that is no longer true.
   The squirrel **dropped** the nut and **ran** up the tree.
   I **was** very tired last night by 9:00.

The **future tense** indicates an action that will happen in the future or a condition that will be true.
   The Glazers **will visit** us tomorrow.
   They **will be** glad to arrive from their long journey.

The **present perfect tense** expresses an action that happened at an indefinite time in the past or an action that began in the past and continues into the present.
   Someone **has cleaned** the trash from the park.
   The puppy **has been** under the bed all day.

The **past perfect tense** shows an action that was completed before another action in the past.
   Gerard **had revised** his essay before he turned it in.

The **future perfect tense** indicates an action that will have been completed before another action takes place.
   Mimi **will have painted** the kitchen by the time we finish the shutters.

USING MODIFIERS

Degrees of Comparison

Adjectives and adverbs take different forms to show the three degrees of comparison: the *positive*, the *comparative*, and the *superlative*.

Positive	Comparative	Superlative
fast	faster	fastest
crafty	craftier	craftiest
abruptly	more abruptly	most abruptly
badly	worse	worst

Using Comparative and Superlative Adjectives and Adverbs

Use comparative adjectives and adverbs to compare two things. Use superlative adjectives and adverbs to compare three or more things.
   This season's weather was **drier** than last year's.
   This season has been one of the **driest** on record.
   Jake practices **more often** than Jamal.
   Of everyone in the band, Jake practices **most often.**

USING PRONOUNS

Pronoun Case

The **case** of a pronoun is the form it takes to show its function in a sentence. There are three pronoun cases: *nominative, objective,* and *possessive.*

Nominative	Objective	Possessive
I, you, he, she, it, we, you, they	me, you, him, her, it, us, you, them	my, your, yours, his, her, hers, its, our, ours, their, theirs

Use the **nominative case** when a pronoun functions as a *subject* or as a *predicate nominative.*
   They are going to the movies. [subject]

The biggest movie fan is **she.** [predicate nominative]

Use the **objective case** for a pronoun acting as a *direct object,* an *indirect object,* or the *object of a preposition.*
   The ending of the play surprised **me.** [direct object]
   Mary gave **us** two tickets to the play. [indirect object]
   The audience cheered for **him.** [object of preposition]

Use the **possessive case** to show ownership.
   The red suitcase is **hers.**

Diction The words you choose contribute to the overall effectiveness of your writing. **Diction** refers to word choice and to the clearness and correctness of those words. You can improve one aspect of your diction by choosing carefully between commonly confused words, such as the pairs listed below.

accept, except

Accept is a verb that means "to receive" or "to agree to." *Except* is a preposition that means "other than" or "leaving out."

> Please **accept** my offer to buy you lunch this weekend.

> He is busy every day **except** the weekends.

affect, effect

Affect is normally a verb meaning "to influence" or "to bring about a change in." *Effect* is usually a noun meaning "result."

> The distractions outside **affect** Steven's ability to concentrate.

> The teacher's remedies had a positive **effect** on Steven's ability to concentrate.

among, between

Among is usually used with three or more items, and it emphasizes collective relationships or indicates distribution. *Between* is generally used with only two items, but it can be used with more than two if the emphasis is on individual (one-to-one) relationships within the group.

> I had to choose a snack **among** the various vegetables.

> He handed out the booklets **among** the conference participants.

> Our school is **between** a park and an old barn.

> The tournament included matches **between** France, Spain, Mexico, and the United States.

amount, number

Amount refers to overall quantity and is mainly used with mass nouns (those that can't be counted). *Number* refers to individual items that can be counted.

> The **amount** of attention that great writers have paid to Shakespeare is remarkable.

> A **number** of important English writers have been fascinated by the legend of King Arthur.

assure, ensure, insure

Assure means "to convince [someone of something]; to guarantee." *Ensure* means "to make certain [that something happens]." *Insure* means "to arrange for payment in case of loss."

> The attorney **assured** us we'd win the case.

> The rules **ensure** that no one gets treated unfairly.

> Many professional musicians **insure** their valuable instruments.

bad, badly

Use the adjective *bad* before a noun or after linking verbs such as *feel, look,* and *seem.* Use *badly* whenever an adverb is required.

> The situation may seem **bad**, but it will improve over time.

> Though our team played **badly** today, we will focus on practicing for the next match.

beside, besides

Beside means "at the side of" or "close to." *Besides* means "in addition to."

> The stapler sits **beside** the pencil sharpener in our classroom.

> **Besides** being very clean, the classroom is also very organized.

can, may

The helping verb *can* generally refers to the ability to do something. The helping verb *may* generally refers to permission to do something.

> I **can** run one mile in six minutes.

> **May** we have a race during recess?

complement, compliment

The verb *complement* means "to enhance"; the verb *compliment* means "to praise."

> Online exercises **complement** the textbook lessons.

> Ms. Lewis **complimented** our team on our excellent debate.

compose, comprise

Compose means "to make up; constitute." *Comprise* means "to include or contain." Remember that the whole comprises its parts or is composed of its parts, and the parts compose the whole.

> The assignment **comprises** three different tasks.

> The assignment is **composed** of three different tasks.

> Three different tasks **compose** the assignment.

different from, different than

Different from is generally preferred over *different than,* but *different than* can be used before a clause. Always use *different from* before a noun or pronoun.

> Your point of view is so **different from** mine.

> His idea was so **different from** [or **different than**] what we had expected.

farther, further

Use *farther* to refer to distance. Use *further* to mean "to a greater degree or extent" or "additional."

> Chiang has traveled **farther** than anybody else in the class.

> If I want **further** details about his travels, I can read his blog.

fewer, less

Use *fewer* for things that can be counted. Use *less* for amounts or quantities that cannot be counted. *Fewer* must be followed by a plural noun.

> **Fewer** students drive to school since the weather improved.
> There is **less** noise outside in the mornings.

good, well

Use the adjective *good* before a noun or after a linking verb. Use *well* whenever an adverb is required, such as when modifying a verb.

> I feel **good** after sleeping for eight hours.
> I did **well** on my test, and my soccer team played **well** in that afternoon's game. It was a **good** day!

its, it's

The word *its* with no apostrophe is a possessive pronoun. The word *it's* is a contraction of "it is."

> Angelica will try to fix the computer and **its** keyboard.
> **It's** a difficult job, but she can do it.

lay, lie

Lay is a transitive verb meaning "to set or put something down." Its principal parts are *lay, laying, laid, laid. Lie* is an intransitive verb meaning "to recline" or "to exist in a certain place." Its principal parts are *lie, lying, lay, lain.*

> Please **lay** that box down and help me with the sofa.
> When we are done moving, I am going to **lie** down.
> My hometown **lies** sixty miles north of here.

like, as

Like is a preposition that usually means "similar to" and precedes a noun or pronoun. The conjunction *as* means "in the way that" and usually precedes a clause.

> **Like** the other students, I was prepared for a quiz.
> **As** I said yesterday, we expect to finish before noon.

Use **such as,** not **like,** before a series of examples.

> Foods **such as** apples, nuts, and pretzels make good snacks.

of, have

Do not use *of* in place of *have* after auxiliary verbs such as *would, could, should, may, might,* or *must.* The contraction of *have* is formed by adding -*ve* after these verbs.

> I **would have** stayed after school today, but I had to help cook at home.
> Mom **must've** called while I was still in the gym.

principal, principle

Principal can be an adjective meaning "main; most important." It can also be a noun meaning "chief officer of a school." *Principle* is a noun meaning "moral rule" or "fundamental truth."

> His strange behavior was the **principal** reason for our concern.
> Democratic **principles** form the basis of our country's laws.

raise, rise

Raise is a transitive verb that usually takes a direct object. *Rise* is intransitive and never takes a direct object.

> Iliana and Josef **raise** the flag every morning.
> They **rise** from their seats and volunteer immediately whenever help is needed.

than, then

The conjunction *than* is used to connect the two parts of a comparison. The adverb *then* usually refers to time.

> My backpack is heavier **than** hers.
> I will finish my homework and **then** meet my friends at the park.

that, which, who

Use the relative pronoun *that* to refer to things or people. Use *which* only for things and *who* only for people.

That introduces a restrictive phrase or clause, that is, one that is essential to the meaning of the sentence. *Which* introduces a nonrestrictive phrase or clause—one that adds information but could be deleted from the sentence—and is preceded by a comma.

> Ben ran to the park **that** just reopened.
> The park, **which** just reopened, has many attractions.
> The man **who** built the park loves to see people smiling.

when, where, why

Do not use *when, where,* or *why* directly after a linking verb, such as *is.* Reword the sentence.

> *Incorrect:* The morning is when he left for the beach.
> *Correct:* He left for the beach in the morning.

who, whom

In formal writing, use *who* only as a subject in clauses and sentences. Use *whom* only as the object of a verb or of a preposition.

> **Who** paid for the tickets?
> **Whom** should I pay for the tickets?
> I can't recall to **whom** I gave the money for the tickets.

your, you're

Your is a possessive pronoun expressing ownership. *You're* is the contraction of "you are."

> Have you finished writing **your** informative essay?
> **You're** supposed to turn it in tomorrow. If **you're** late, **your** grade will be affected.

GLOSSARY: GRAMMAR HANDBOOK

Capitalization

First Words

Capitalize the first word of a sentence.

Stories about knights and their deeds interest me.

Capitalize the first word of direct speech.

Sharon asked, "Do you like stories about knights?"

Capitalize the first word of a quotation that is a complete sentence.

Einstein said, "Anyone who has never made a mistake has never tried anything new."

Proper Nouns and Proper Adjectives

Capitalize all proper nouns, including geographical names, historical events and periods, and names of organizations.

Thames River   John Keats   the Renaissance

United Nations   World War II   Sierra Nevada

Capitalize all proper adjectives.

Shakespearean play   British invaision

American citizen   Latin American literature

Academic Course Names

Capitalize course names only if they are language courses, are followed by a number, or are preceded by a proper noun or adjective.

Spanish   Honors Chemistry   History 101

geology   algebra   social studies

Titles

Capitalize personal titles when followed by the person's name.

Ms. Hughes   Dr. Perez   King George

Capitalize titles showing family relationships when they are followed by a specific person's name, unless they are preceded by a possessive noun or pronoun.

Uncle Oscar   Mangan's sister   his aunt Tessa

Capitalize the first word and all other key words in the titles of books, stories, songs, and other works of art.

Frankenstein   "Shooting an Elephant"

Punctuation

End Marks

Use a **period** to end a declarative sentence or an imperative sentence.

We are studying the structure of sonnets.
Read the biography of Mary Shelley.

Use periods with initials and abbreviations.

D. H. Lawrence   Mrs. Browning
Mt. Everest   Maple St.

Use a **question mark** to end an interrogative sentence.

What is Macbeth's fatal flaw?

Use an **exclamation mark** after an exclamatory sentence or a forceful imperative sentence.

That's a beautiful painting!   Let me go now!

Commas

Use a **comma** before a coordinating conjunction to separate two independent clauses in a compound sentence.

The game was very close, but we were victorious.

Use commas to separate three or more words, phrases, or clauses in a series.

William Blake was a writer, artist, and printer.

Use commas to separate coordinate adjectives.

It was a witty, amusing novel.

Use a comma after an introductory word, phrase, or clause.

When the novelist finished his book, he celebrated with his family.

Use commas to set off nonessential expressions.

Old English, of course, requires translation.

Use commas with places and dates.

Coventry, England   September 1, 1939

Semicolons

Use a **semicolon** to join closely related independent clauses that are not already joined by a conjunction.

Tanya likes to write poetry; Heather prefers prose.

Use semicolons to avoid confusion when items in a series contain commas.

They traveled to London, England; Madrid, Spain; and Rome, Italy.

Colons

Use a **colon** before a list of items following an independent clause.

Notable Victorian poets include the following: Tennyson, Arnold, Housman, and Hopkins.

Use a colon to introduce information that summarizes or explains the independent clause before it.

She just wanted to do one thing: rest.
Malcolm loves volunteering: He reads to sick children every Saturday afternoon.

Quotation Marks

Use **quotation marks** to enclose a direct quotation.

"Short stories," Ms. Hildebrand said, "should have rich, well-developed characters."

An **indirect quotation** does not require quotation marks.

Ms. Hildebrand said that short stories should have well-developed characters.

Use quotation marks around the titles of short written works, episodes in a series, songs, and works mentioned as parts of collections.

"The Lagoon"   "Boswell Meets Johnson"

Italics

Italicize the titles of long written works, movies, television and radio shows, lengthy works of music, paintings, and sculptures.

Howards End   *60 Minutes*   *Guernica*

For handwritten material, you can use underlining instead of italics.

<u>The Princess Bride</u>   <u>Mona Lisa</u>

Dashes

Use **dashes** to indicate an abrupt change of thought, a dramatic interrupting idea, or a summary statement.

I read the entire first act of *Macbeth*—you won't believe what happens next.

The director—what's her name again?—attended the movie premiere.

Hyphens

Use a **hyphen** with certain numbers, after certain prefixes, with two or more words used as one word, and with a compound modifier that comes before a noun.

seventy-two

self-esteem

president-elect

five-year contract

Parentheses

Use **parentheses** to set off asides and explanations when the material is not essential or when it consists of one or more sentences. When the sentence in parentheses interrupts the larger sentence, it does not have a capital letter or a period.

He listened intently (it was too dark to see who was speaking) to try to identify the voices.

When a sentence in parentheses falls between two other complete sentences, it should start with a capital letter and end with a period.

The quarterback threw three touchdown passes. (We knew he could do it.) Our team won the game by two points.

Apostrophes

Add an **apostrophe** and an *s* to show the possessive case of most singular nouns and of plural nouns that do not end in *-s* or *-es*.

Blake's poems   the mice's whiskers

Names ending in *s* form their possessives in the same way, except for classical and biblical names, which add only an apostrophe to form the possessive.

Dickens's   Hercules'

Add an apostrophe to show the possessive case of plural nouns ending in *-s* and *-es*.

the girls' songs   the Ortizes' car

Use an apostrophe in a contraction to indicate the position of the missing letter or letters.

She's never read a Coleridge poem she didn't like.

Brackets

Use **brackets** to enclose clarifying information inserted within a quotation.

Columbus's journal entry from October 21, 1492, begins as follows: "At 10 o'clock, we arrived at a cape of the island [San Salvador], and anchored, the other vessels in company."

Ellipses

Use three ellipsis points, also known as an **ellipsis,** to indicate where you have omitted words from quoted material.

Wollestonecraft wrote, "The education of women has of late been more attended to than formerly; yet they are still . . . ridiculed or pitied. . . ."

In the example above, the four dots at the end of the sentence are the three ellipsis points plus the period from the original sentence.

Use an ellipsis to indicate a pause or interruption in speech.

"When he told me the news," said the coach, "I was . . . I was shocked . . . completely shocked."

Spelling

Spelling Rules

Learning the rules of English spelling will help you make **generalizations** about how to spell words.

Word Parts

The three word parts that can combine to form a word are roots, prefixes, and suffixes. Many of these word parts come from the Greek, Latin, and Anglo-Saxon languages.

The **root word** carries a word's basic meaning.

Root and Origin	Meaning	Examples
-leg- (-log-) [Gr.]	to say, speak	*legal, logic*
-pon- (-pos-) [L.]	to put, place	*postpone, deposit*

A **prefix** is one or more syllables added to the beginning of a word that alter the meaning of the root.

Prefix and Origin	Meaning	Example
anti- [Gr.]	against	*antipathy*
inter- [L.]	between	*international*
mis- [A.S.]	wrong	*misplace*

A **suffix** is a letter or group of letters added to the end of a root word that changes the word's meaning or part of speech.

Suffix and Origin	Meaning and Example	Part of Speech
-ful [A.S.]	full of: *scornful*	adjective
-ity [L.]	state of being: *adversity*	noun
-ize (-ise) [Gr.]	to make: *idolize*	verb
-ly [A.S.]	in a manner: *calmly*	adverb

Rules for Adding Suffixes to Root Words

When adding a suffix to a root word ending in *y* preceded by a consonant, change *y* to *i* unless the suffix begins with *i*.

   ply + -able = pliable   happy + -ness = happiness
   defy + -ing = defying   cry + -ing = crying

For a root word ending in *e*, drop the *e* when adding a suffix beginning with a vowel.

   drive + -ing = driving   move + -able = movable
   SOME EXCEPTIONS: traceable, seeing, dyeing

For root words ending with a consonant + vowel + consonant in a stressed syllable, double the final consonant when adding a suffix that begins with a vowel.

   mud + -y = muddy   submit + -ed = submitted
   SOME EXCEPTIONS: mixing, fixed

Rules for Adding Prefixes to Root Words

When a prefix is added to a root word, the spelling of the root remains the same.

   un- + certain = uncertain   mis- + spell = misspell

With some prefixes, the spelling of the prefix changes when joined to the root to make the pronunciation easier.

   in- + mortal = immortal   ad- + vert = avert

Orthographic Patterns

Certain letter combinations in English make certain sounds. For instance, *ph* sounds like *f*, *eigh* usually makes a long *a* sound, and the *k* before an *n* is often silent.

   pharmacy   **n**e**igh**bor   **k**nowledge

Understanding **orthographic patterns** such as these can help you improve your spelling.

Forming Plurals

The plural form of most nouns is formed by adding -*s* to the singular.

   computer**s**   gadget**s**   Washington**s**

For words ending in *s, ss, x, z, sh,* or *ch,* add -*es*.

   circus**es**   tax**es**   wish**es**   bench**es**

For words ending in *y* or *o* preceded by a vowel, add -*s*.

   key**s**   patio**s**

For words ending in *y* preceded by a consonant, change the *y* to an *i* and add -*es*.

   cit**ies**   enem**ies**   troph**ies**

For most words ending in *o* preceded by a consonant, add -*es*.

   echo**es**   tomato**es**

Some words form the plural in irregular ways.

   women   oxen   children   teeth   deer

Foreign Words Used in English

Some words used in English are actually foreign words that have been adopted. Learning to spell these words requires memorization. When in doubt, check a dictionary.

   sushi   enchilada   au pair   fiancé
   laissez faire   croissant

GLOSSARY: GRAMMAR HANDBOOK

Writing

INDEX OF AUTHORS AND TITLES

The following authors and titles appear in the print and online versions of *my*Perspectives.

ADDITIONAL SELECTIONS: AUTHOR AND TITLE INDEX

The following authors and titles appear in the Online Literature Library.

ACKNOWLEDGMENTS AND CREDITS

Acknowledgments

The following selections appear in Grade 7 of *my*Perspectives. Some selections appear online only.

ABC News—Permissions Dept. Bethany Hamilton video ©ABC News.

Abner Stein. "Two Kinds" from *The Joy Luck Club* by Amy Tan. Used with permission of Abner Stein.

BBC News Online. Profile: Malala Yousafzai ©BBC, December 10, 2014.

BBC Worldwide Americas, Inc. Maya Angelou: Learning to love my mother ©BBC Worldwide Learning.

Best Part Productions. Cyber-Seniors Documentary—Official Trailer ©Best Part Productions.

Bloomsbury Publishing Plc. "Four Skinny Trees" from *The House on Mango Street* by Sandra Cisneros. Copyright ©Sandra Cisneros. Used with permission of Bloomsbury Publishing Plc.

Brilliance Audio. "Packing for Mars" from *Packing for Mars: The Curious Science of Life in the Void* by Mary Roach. Copyright ©2010 by Mary Roach. Used with permission of Brilliance Audio.

C.S. Lewis Company. *Science-Fiction Cradlesong* by C. S. Lewis copyright ©C.S. Lewis Pte. Ltd. Reprinted by permission.

Chicago Review Press. "Noor Inayat Khan," excerpted from *Women Heroes of WWII* by Kathryn J. Atwood. Copyright ©2011 by Kathryn J. Atwood. Reprinted by permission of Chicago Review Press.

Coffee House Press. Linda Hogan, "Turtle Watchers" from *Dark. Sweet.: New & Selected Poems*. Copyright ©2008 by Linda Hogan. Reprinted with the permission of The Permissions Company, Inc., on behalf of Coffee House Press, www.coffeehousepress.org.

Critical Past LLC. "The Dust Bowl" courtesy of CriticalPast.

Curtis Brown, Ltd. (UK). "Chapter 9," from *The Grapes of Wrath* by John Steinbeck, copyright 1939, renewed ©1967 by John Steinbeck.

Don Congdon Associates, Inc. "Dark They Were and Golden-Eyed" by Ray Bradbury, reprinted by permission of Don Congdon Associates, Inc. ©1949 by Standard Magazines, renewed 1976 by Ray Bradbury.

Elaine Markson Literary Agency. "Family" from *Begin Again: Collected Poems* by Grace Paley. Used with permission of Elaine Markson Literary Agency.

Farrar, Straus and Giroux. "Family" from *Begin Again: Collected Poems* by Grace Paley. Copyright ©2000 by Grace Paley. Reprinted by permission Farrar, Straus and Giroux, LLC.; "Thank You, M'am" from *Short Stories* by Langston Hughes. Copyright ©1996 by Ramona Bass and Arnold Rampersad. Reprinted by permission of Hill and Wang, a division of Farrar, Straus and Giroux, LLC. CAUTION: Users are warned that this work is protected under copyright laws and downloading is strictly prohibited. The right to reproduce or transfer the work via any medium must be secured with Farrar, Straus and Giroux, LLC.

Fulcrum Publishing, Inc. "How Grandmother Spider Stole the Sun" from *Keepers of the Earth* by Michael Caduto and Joseph Bruchac. Reprinted by permission of Fulcrum Publishing.

Hachette Book Group USA. "Work in Progress" from *The Moth*, edited by Catherine Burns. Copyright ©2013 by The Moth. Copyright ©2013 by Aimee Mullins. Reprinted by permission of Hachette Books.

Harold Ober Associates. "Thank You, M'am" and "Mother to Son" reprinted by permission of Harold Ober Associates Incorporated. Copyright ©1994 by The Estate of Langston Hughes; "One Friday Morning" and "Thank You, M'am" from *Short Stories* by Langston Hughes. Copyright ©1996 by Ramona Bass and Arnold Rampersad. Reprinted by permission of Harold Ober Associates.

HarperCollins Publishers. Excerpt from pp. 147-9 from *An American Childhood* by Annie Dillard. Copyright ©1987 by Annie Dillard. Reprinted by permission of HarperCollins Publishers.

Houghton Mifflin Harcourt Publishing Co. "Science-Fiction Cradlesong" from *Poems* by C.S. Lewis. Copyright ©1964 by the Executors of the Estate of C.S. Lewis and renewed 1992 by C.S. Lewis Pte Ltd. Reprinted by permission of Houghton Mifflin Harcourt Publishing Company. All rights reserved; "A Fable for Tomorrow" from *Silent Spring* by Rachel Carson. Copyright ©1962 by Rachel L. Carson, renewed 1990 by Roger Christie. Reprinted by permission of Houghton Mifflin Harcourt Publishing Company. All rights reserved.

International Publishers. Adapted from "Little Things Are Big" from *A Puerto Rican in New York and Other Sketches* by Jesus Colon. Copyright ©1982. Used with permission of International Publishers.

Jemison, Mae Carol. Mae Jemison "Starship" courtesy of Dorothy Jemison Foundation for Excellence.

Johnson, Sophie. "'Gotcha Day' Isn't a Cause for Celebration" by Sophie Johnson, from *Huffington Post*, November 3, 2014. Used with permission of the author.

Jones, Stanleigh. "He—y, Come On Ou—t!" from *The Best Japanese Science Fiction Stories* by Shinichi Hoshi, translated by Stanleigh Jones. Reprinted by permission of the translator.

Lerner Publications Company. "Robin Hood: Outlaw of Sherwood Forest" by Paul D. Storrie. Copyright ©2007 by Millbrook Press, Inc. Reprinted with the permission of Graphic Universe, a division of Lerner Publishing group, Inc. All rights reserved. No part of this excerpt may be used or reproduced in any manner whatsoever without the prior written permission of Lerner Publishing Group, Inc.

Little, Brown and Co. (UK). *From Mom & Me & Mom* by Maya Angelou. Copyright ©Maya Angelou. Used with permission of Little, Brown Book Group Ltd.

Malala Fund. "Malala Yousafzai United Nations Speech" reproduced with permission of Curtis Brown Group Ltd, London, on behalf of Malala Yousafzai. Copyright ©Malala Yousafzai, 2013.

McCormick, John. "Bridging the Generational Divide between a Football Father and a Soccer Son" by John McCormick, originally appeared in *Huffington Post*, September 30, 1014. Used with permission of the author. John McCormick has been a contributing blogger to the *Huffington Post* since 2012, writing a month column for the *Post's* Parents page. He is also the author of *Dad, Tell Me a Story: How to Revive the Tradition of Storytelling with Your Children* (Nicasio Press 2013). The book contains 25 stories he created with his own two sons, and provides guidance to parents on how to create a storytelling tradition in their own families.

Minna Murra, Inc. *The Last Dog* by Katherine Paterson. Copyright ©1999 by Minna Murra, Inc. Used by permission of PearlCo Literary Agency, LLC.

Moth. "A Work in Progress" from *The Moth*, edited by Catherine Burns. Copyright ©2013 by The Moth. Copyright ©2013 by Aimee Mullins. Reprinted by permission of the Moth.

NASA. Earth Views ©Johnson Space Center/NASA.

National Geographic Books. "Grizzly Moms Teacher Cubs" excerpt from *Facing the Lion* published by National Geographic Society. Copyright ©2003 by Joseph Lemasolai Lekuton wither Herman Viola.

National Geographic Creative. "Grizzly Mom Teaching Cubs" ©National Geographic Creative.

National Public Radio. ©2011 National Public Radio, Inc. News report titled "Tutors Teach Seniors New High-Tech Tricks" by Jennifer Ludden was originally published on NPR.org on December 27, 2011, and is used with the permission of NPR. Any unauthorized duplication is strictly prohibited.

New York Public Library. "To James" ©Schomburg Center for Research in Black Culture, The New York Public Library.

Nobel Media AB. Nobel Lecture, December 10, 2007 by Al Gore. Reprinted by permission of Nobel Media AB; Nobel Lecture by Al Gore ©Nobel Media AB 2007.

OneWorld Publications. "Packing for Mars" from *Packing for Mars: The Curious Science of Life in the Void* by Mary Roach. Copyright ©2010 by Mary Roach. Used with permission of Oneworld Publications.

Paramount Pictures. *A Christmas Carol*, 1935 ©Twickenham Film Studios/Paramount Pictures.

PARS International Corporation. "Danger! This Mission to Mars Could Bore You to Death" from *The New York Times*, July 21, 2013 © 2013 The New York Times. All rights reserved. Used by permission and protected by the Copyright Laws of the United States. The printing, copying, redistribution, or retransmission of this Content without express written permission is prohibited.

Penguin Books, Ltd. (UK) "Chapter 9", from *The Grapes of Wrath* by John Steinbeck, copyright 1939, renewed ©1967 by John Steinbeck. Used by permission of Penguin Books, Ltd.

Penguin Publishing Group. "Two Kinds," from *The Joy Luck Club* by Amy Tan, copyright ©1989 by Amy Tan. Used by permission of G. P. Putnam's Sons, an imprint of Penguin Publishing Group, a division of Penguin Random House LLC; "The Old, Old Tree," from *My Side of the Mountain* by Jean Craighead George, copyright ©1959, renewed ©1987 by Jean Craighead George. Used by permission of Dutton Children's Books, an imprint of Penguin Young Readers Group, a division of Penguin Random House LLC; "Chapter 9", from *The Grapes of Wrath* by John Steinbeck, copyright 1939, renewed ©1967 by John Steinbeck. Used by permission of Viking Books, an imprint of Penguin Publishing Group, a division of Penguin Random House LLC.

Pollinger Limited. Extract from *Silent Spring* by Rachel Carson reprinted by permission of Pollinger Limited (www.pollingerltd.com) on behalf of the Estate of Rachel Carson.

Profile Books. "A Work in Progress" from *The Moth*, edited by Catherine Burns. Copyright ©2013 by The Moth. Copyright ©2013 by Aimee Mullins. Reprinted by permission of Authentic Talent + Literary Management.

Purch. "UFO Sightings and News," from Space.com by Richard Radford. Used with permission.

Random House, Inc. "Mother to Son," "Dream Variation," "I, Too," "The Negro Speaks of Rivers," and "Refugee in America" from *The Collected Poems of Langston Hughes* by Langston Hughes, edited by Arnold Rampersad with David Roessel, Associate Editor, copyright ©1994 by the Estate of Langston Hughes. Used by permission of Alfred A. Knopf, an imprint of the Knopf Doubleday Publishing Group, a division of Penguin Random House LLC. All rights reserved. Any third party use of this material, outside of this publication, is prohibited. Interested parties must apply directly to Penguin Random House LLC for permission; "Chapter 3" and "Chapter 4" from *Mom & Me & Mom* by Maya Angelou, copyright ©2013 by Maya Angelou. Used by permission of Random House, an imprint and division of Penguin Random House LLC. All rights reserved. Any third party use of this material, outside of this publication, is prohibited. Interested parties must apply directly to Penguin Random House LLC for permission.

Robertson, Sarah. Polar Bears - The Quest for Sea Ice ©Arctic Bear Productions.

Russell & Volkening, Inc. Excerpt from *An American Childhood* reprinted by permission of Russell & Volkening as agents for the author. Copyright ©1987 by Annie Dillard.

Sandra Dijkstra Literary Agency. "Two Kinds," from *The Joy Luck Club* by Amy Tan, copyright ©1989 by Amy Tan. Permission granted by the author and the Sandra Dijkstra Literary Agency.

Scholastic, Inc. "An Hour With Abuelo" from *An Island Like You* by Judith Ortiz Cofer. Copyright ©1995 by Judith Ortiz Cofer. Reprinted by permission of Orchard Books, an imprint of Scholastic Inc.

Schroff, Laura. AN INVISIBLE THREAD: Maurice's Toast ©Laura Schroff/Mark Merrett.

Simon & Schuster, Inc. Excerpt from *An Invisible Thread* reprinted with the permission of Howard Books, a Division of Simon & Schuster, Inc. from *An Invisible Thread* by Laura Schroff and Alex Tresniowski. Copyright ©2011 Laura Schroff and Alex Tresniowski; "The Grandfather and His Little Grandson" reprinted with the permission of Little Simon, an imprint of Simon & Schuster Children's Publishing Division from *Twenty-Two Russian Tales for Young Children* by Leo Tolstoy, Selected, Translated, and with an Afterword by Miriam Morton. Translation copyright 1969 Miriam Morton; copyright renewed ©1998 Miriam Morton.

Society for Science & the Public. "Trip to Mars Could Damage Astronauts" by Laura Sanders, *Society for Science and the Public*, May 10, 2015. Reprinted with Permission of Science New for Students.

Sterling Lord Literistic, Inc. Introduction from *Of Wolves and Men* reprinted by permission of SLL/Sterling Lord Literistic, Inc. Copyright by Barry Holstun Lopez.

Susan Bergholz Literary Services. "Four Skinny Trees" from *The House on Mango Street*. Copyright ©1984 by Sandra Cisneros. Published by Vintage Books, a division of Penguin Random House, and in hardcover by Alfred A. Knopf in 1994. By permission of Susan Bergholz Literary Services, New York, NY, and Lamy, NM. All rights reserved.

TallMountain Circle. "The Last Wolf" ©1984 TallMountain Estate.

Time-Life Syndication. "Neil deGrasse Tyson on the Future of U.S. Space Exploration After *Curiosity*" from the pages of TIME ©2012 Time Inc.

Title Town Publishing. "The Girl Who Fell from the Sky" from *When I Fell from the Sky* by Juliane Koepcke. Courtesy of TitleTown Publishing LLC.

University of Georgia Press. "Lineage" from *This Is My Century: New and Collected Poems* by Margaret Walker. Copyright ©1989. Used with permission of University of Georgia Press.

University of New Mexico Press (Rights). "The Circuit" from *The Circuit* by Francisco Jiménez. Copyright ©1997 University of New Mexico Press, 1997.

W. W. Norton & Co. "Water Names" from *Hunger* by Lan Samantha Chang. Copyright ©1998 by Lan Samantha Change. Used by permission of W.W. Norton & Company, Inc.; "Packing for Mars" from *Packing for Mars: The Curious Science of Life in the Void* by Mary Roach. Copyright ©2010 by Mary Roach. Used by permission of W.W. Norton & Company, Inc.

Wall Street Journal. Republished with permission of Dow Jones, Inc., from "A Young Tinkerer Builds a Windmill, Electrifying a Nation" by Sarah Childress, *Wall Street Journal*, December 12, 2007; permission conveyed through Copyright Clearance Center, Inc.

WGBH Stock Sales. Mae Jemison "Starship" ©WGBH.

William Morris Endeavor. *A Christmas Carol: Scrooge and Marley* (Acts I and II) Copyright ©1979 by Fountain Pen, LLC All rights reserved CAUTION: Professionals and amateurs are hereby warned that "A CHRISTMAS CAROL: SCROOGE AND MARLEY" is subject to a royalty. It is fully protected under the copyright laws of the United States of America and of all countries covered by the International Copyright Union (including the Dominion of Canada and the rest of the British Commonwealth), the Berne Convention, the Pan-American Copyright Convention, and the Universal Copyright Convention as well as all countries with which the United States has reciprocal copyright relations. All rights, including professional/amateur stage rights, motion picture, recitation, lecturing, public reading, radio broadcasting, television, video or sound recording, all other forms of mechanical or electronic reproduction, such as CD-ROM, CD-I, information storage and retrieval systems and photocopying, and the rights of translation into foreign languages, are strictly reserved. Particular emphasis is laid upon the matter of readings, permission for which must be secured from the Author's agent in writing. Inquiries concerning rights should be addressed to: William Morris Endeavor Entertainment, LLC 11 Madison Avenue, New York, New York 10010 Attn: Emily Dooley.

Wright's Media. "Future of Space Exploration Could See Humans on Mars, Alien Plants" by Nola Taylor Redd, May 27, 2014, from Space.com. Used with permission of Wright's Media.

Wylie Agency. "Water Names" from *Hunger* by Lan Samantha Chang. Copyright ©1998 by Lan Samantha Chang, used by permission of The Wylie Agency LLC.

Credits

Photo locators denoted as follows Top (T), Center (C), Bottom (B), Left (L), Right (R), Background (Bkgd)

Cover: Evikka/Shutterstock

iv Sergey Novikov/Shutterstock; **viii** Mehau Kulyk/Science Photo Library/Getty Images; **viii** Ollyy/Shutterstock; **x** Romolo Tavani/Shutterstock; **xii** Stephan Kaps/EyeEm/Getty Images; **3** Sergey Novikov/Shutterstock, (B) Ronnie Kaufman/Larry/Blend Images/AGE Fotostock, (CL) ©Mica Hendricks, (BCR) Dan Dalton/Caiaimage/Getty Images, (BL) Aditya Gujaran/EyeEm/Getty Images, (BR) Dean Conger/Corbis, (C) Everett Collection Historical/Alamy, (CL) ©Alex Tresniowski, (CR) Dave Lawrence/Flickr Flash/Getty Images, (T) Keith Bell/123RF, (TCL) Courtesy Laura Schroff, (TCR) ©Alyson Aliano, (TL) Weimin Liu/Flickr RF/Getty Images, (TR) Everett Collection Inc/Alamy; **6** Keith Bell/123RF; **11** (B) ©Alex Tresniowski, (C) Courtesy Laura Schroff, (T) Weimin Liu/Flickr RF/Getty Images; **12** J.J.Guillen/EPA/Newscom; **13** Weimin Liu/Flickr RF/Getty Images; **16** Curt Teich Postcard Archives/Lake County Museum/Getty Images; **23** Dmitrimaruta/123RF; **26, 28, 30** Weimin Liu/Flickr RF/Getty Images; **32** (TL), **33, 38, 40, 42** (TL), **50** (T) Courtesy Laura Schroff; **32** (TR), **42** (TR), **43, 46, 48, 50** (B) ©Alex Tresniowski; (BL) https://intercall.webex.com/join/pr3639298; **52** Keith Bell/123RF; **59** (TC) Everett Collection Historical/Alamy, (BC) ©Mica Hendricks, (B) Aditya Gujaran/EyeEm/Getty Images; **62** John Poole/NPR; **63** Paul Maguire/Alamy; **70** (BL) Ken Charnock/Getty Images; **70** (TL), **71, 77, 80** (TL), **84** (T) Everett Collection Historical/Alamy; **74** Sam Shere/The LIFE Picture Collection/Getty Images; **80** (BL) BBC Worldwide Learning; **87–92** ©Mica Hendricks; **94** Aditya Gujaran/EyeEm/Getty Images; **95** (B) Schomburg Center for Research in Black Culture, (TL) Everett Collection Inc/Alamy; **96** Aditya Gujaran/EyeEm/Getty Images; **97** Cardinal/Corbis; **107** (T) Everett Collection Inc/Alamy, (CR) ©Alyson Aliano, (C) Dave Lawrence/Flickr Flash/Getty Images, (CB) Dan Dalton/Caiaimage/Getty Images, (BC) Dean Conger/Corbis, (B) Ronnie Kaufman/Larry/Blend Images/AGE Fotostock; **116** Mehau Kulyk/Science Photo Library/Getty Images; **117** (BC) NASA/ZUMA Press/Newscom, (BCL) Michael Lewis/Corbis, (BCR) Armando Arorizo/ZUMA Press/Newscom, (BR) Bjorn Meyer/Vetta/Getty Images, (CL) Patrick Koslo/Stockbyte/Getty Images, (CR) Carlos Amarillo/Shutterstock, (T) Everett Historical/Shutterstock, (TC) NG Images/Alamy, (TL) Martin Lovatt/iStock/Getty Images, (TR) Susan Dykstra/Design Pics/Perspectives/Getty Images; **120** Everett Historical/Shutterstock; **125** (B) Michael Lewis/Corbis, (C) Patrick Koslo/Stockbyte/Getty Images, (T) Martin Lovatt/iStock/Getty Images; **126** (BL) Everett Collection Inc/Alamy, (R) Patrick Koslo/Stockbyte/Getty Images; **126** (TL), **127, 142, 144, 146** (TL) Martin Lovatt/iStock/Getty Images; **131** Lonia/Shutterstock; **135** Altanaka/Shutterstock; **146** (BL) ©Michael McDonough, **146** (TR), **147, 149, 150** (B) Patrick Koslo/Stockbyte/Getty Images; **150** (T) Martin Lovatt/iStock/Getty Images; **152** Leah Shaffer; **153–160** Michael Lewis/Corbis; **171** (B) NASA/ZUMA Press/Newscom, (T) NG Images/Alamy; **174** Wenn Ltd/Alamy; **175, 178, 180** NG Images/Alamy; **182** Byron Purvis/AdMedia/Newscom; **200** NASA; **205, 208, 210** NASA/ZUMA Press/Newscom; **215** (BC) Armando Arorizo/ZUMA Press/Newscom, (T) Susan Dykstra/Design Pics/Perspectives/Getty Images, (TC) Carlos Amarillo/Shutterstock, (B) Bjorn Meyer/Vetta/Getty Images; **224** Ollyy/Shutterstock; **225** (B) Vladimir Salman/123RF, (BC) C.P. Cushing/ClassicStock/Corbis, (BR) Noor Inayat Khan (1914–1944) aka "Madeleine" during ww2 she was a british secret agent of Special Operations Executive (SOE) and 1st woman to be sent in France as radio operator/Photo ©PVDE/Bridgeman Art Library, (C) Artem Povarov/123RF, (CL) C.M.Pennington Richards/Everett Collection, (CR) European Pressphoto Agency b.v./Alamy, (T) Wesley Martinez Da Costa/EyeEm/Getty Images, (TC) akg-images/Newscom; (TL) C.M.Pennington Richards/Everett Collection, (TR) Chad McDermott/Fotolia; **228** Wesley Martinez Da Costa/EyeEm/Getty Images; **233** (B) Twickenham Film Studios/Paramount Pictures; **223** (C), **233** (T), **235, 243, 253, 260, 262, 265, 271, 292, 294, 296, 302** (T) C.M.Pennington-Richards/Everett Collection; **234, 264** Jeff Vespa/WireImage/Getty Images; **276, 287** John Springer Collection/Corbis; **284** Hulton Archive/Moviepix/Getty Images; **298** (L) C.M.Pennington-Richards/Everett Collection, (R) Twickenham Film Studios/Paramount Pictures; **299, 301, 302** (B) Twickenham Film Studios/Paramount Pictures; **311** (B) C.P. Cushing/ClassicStock/Corbis, (C) Artem Povarov/123RF, (T) akg images/Newscom; **314** Fred Stein Archive/Archive Photos/Getty Images; **315**-akg

images/Newscom; **320, 322**-akg images/Newscom; **324** Richard Howard/The LIFE Images Collection/Getty Images; **325, 328, 330** Artem Povarov/123RF; **332** hillary schwei; **333** C.P. Cushing/ClassicStock/Corbis; **334** (B) Anthony Behar/Sipa/AP Images, (T) Chris Martin Bahr/REX/Newscom; **335** (B) Scott Olson/Getty Images, (T) Tomohiro Ohsumi/Bloomberg/Getty Images; **336, 337** (B) New York Daily News Archive/Getty Images; **337** (BC) Tomohiro Ohsumi/Bloomberg/Getty Images, (BCL) Scott Olson/Getty Images, (C) Anthony Behar/Sipa/AP Images, (T) C.P. Cushing/ClassicStock/Corbis, (TCL) Chris Martin Bahr/REX/Newscom; **338** C.P. Cushing/ClassicStock/Corbis; **343** (BC) Vladimir Salman/123RF, (C) Noor Inayat Khan (1914–1944) aka "Madeleine": during ww2 she was a british secret agent of Special Operations Executive (SOE) and 1st woman to be sent in France as radio operator/Photo©PVDE/Bridgeman Art Library, (T) Chad McDermott/Fotolia, (TC) European Pressphoto Agency b.v./Alamy; **352** Romolo Tavani/Shutterstock; **353** (BC) Loree Johnson/Shutterstock, (BCR) AF Archive/Alamy, (BR) Carlos Violda/Shutterstock, (C) Copyright ©2015 The Nature Conservancy, (CL) Photos 12/Alamy, (CR) Budimir Jevtic/Shutterstock, (T) Christina N. Elbers/AP Images, (TC) Idreamphoto/Shutterstock, (TL) Christopher Meder/Shutterstock, (TR) Happetr/Shutterstock; **356** Christina N. Elbers/AP Images; **361** (B) ©Nobel Media AB, (C) Photos 12/Alamy, (T) Christopher Meder/Shutterstock; **362** Alfred Eisenstaedt/The Life Picture Collection/Getty Images; **363, 366, 368, 370** Christopher Meder/Shutterstock; **372** (B) LAN/Corbis, (TL) Photos 12/Alamy, (TR) ©Nobel Media AB; **373, 382, 384, 386** (TL), **390** (T) Photos 12/Alamy; **377** Nickolay Khoroshkov/Shutterstock; **386** (B) LAN/Corbis; **386** (TR), **387, 389, 390** (B) ©Nobel Media AB; **392** Christina N. Elbers/AP Images; **399** (B) Loree Johnson/Shutterstock, (C) Copyright ©2015 The Nature Conservancy, (T) Idreamphoto/Shutterstock; **402** Idreamphoto/Shutterstock; **403** (B) Anthony Barboza/Getty Images, (T) Chris Felver/Archive Photos/Getty Images; **404** Idreamphoto/Shutterstock; **405** Aspen Rock/Shutterstock; **406** Erik Karits/Shutterstock; **413, 414** (B), (T), **416, 418** Copyright ©2015 The Nature Conservancy; **420** Koichi Saito/AFLO/Nippon News/Corbis; **421, 426** Loree Johnson/Shutterstock; **433** (T) Happetr/Shutterstock, (TC) Budimir Jevtic/Shutterstock, (BC) AF Archive/Alamy, (B) Carlos Violda/Shutterstock; **442** Stephan Kaps/EyeEm/Getty Images; **443** (BCL) Library of Congress; (BCR) Oleg Senkov/Shutterstock, (BL) Lucas Oleniuk/ZUMApress/Newscom, (BR) Images of Africa Photobank/Alamy, (C) AKG-images, (CL) Everett Collection Inc/Alamy, (CR) Triff/Shutterstock; (T) Justin Lane/EPA/Corbis, (TC) Lynn Johnson/National Geographic Creative/Corbis, (TR) Johan Swanepoel/Shutterstock; **446** Justin Lane/EPA/Corbis; **451** (B) Library of Congress, (T) Everett Collection Inc/Alamy; **452** Everett Collection Inc/Alamy; **456** (L) Heritage Image Partnership Ltd/Alamy, (R) Everett Collection Inc/Alamy; **457, 462, 464, 466** Everett Collection Inc/Alamy; **468** Francisco Jimenez; **469, 476, 478, 480** Library of Congress; **482** Justin Lane/EPA/Corbis; **489** (B) Lucas Oleniuk/ZUMApress/Newscom, (T) Lynn Johnson/National Geographic Creative/Corbis, (TC) AKG-images; **492** Adam Hunger/Reuters/Corbis; **493** Lynn Johnson/National Geographic Creative/Corbis; **500, 502** Lynn Johnson/National Geographic Creative/Corbis; **504** (B) Time Life Pictures/The LIFE Picture Collection/Getty Images, (TL) AKG-images; **505, 509, 510, 512, 516** AKG-images; **519, 524, 526** Lucas Oleniuk/ZUMApress/Newscom; **531** (B) Images of Africa Photobank/Alamy, (BC) Oleg Senkov/Shutterstock, (T) Johan Swanepoel/Shutterstock, (TC) Triff/Shutterstock.

Credits for Images in Interactive Student Edition Only

Unit 1

Eddie Ledesma/Contra Costa Times/ZUMAPRESS/Newscom; Everett Collection/Alamy; John McCormick; Nancy Kaszerman/ZUMA/Corbis; RIA Novosti/Alamy; Courtesy Everett Collection/AGE Fotostock; Photo by Tanya Cofer; ©Alyson Aliano; ©Rue des Archives/Mary Evans;

Unit 2

AF Archive/Alamy; Courtesy of Society for Science & the Public; ©Benjamin Radford;

Unit 3

Centro de Estudios Puertorriquenos; Culture Club/Hulton Archive/Getty Images; PNHF Collection/Alamy; ©John Atwood;

Unit 4

Anthony Barboza/Getty Images; ©Eric Jenks, Awasos Entertainment;

Unit 5

David Livingston/Getty Images; Evgeniya Uvarova/Shutterstock; Franziska Krug/German Select/Getty Images; Heiko Kiera/Shutterstock;

Lovely Bird/Shutterstock; Margaret Thomas/The Washington Post/ Getty Images; Paolo Koch/Science Source; Ullstein bild/Getty Images; Margaret Thomas/The Washington Post/Getty Images.